Beshara and Ibn 'Arabi

Beshara and Ibn 'Arabi

A Movement of Sufi Spirituality
in the Modern World

SUHA TAJI-FAROUKI

ANQA PUBLISHING · OXFORD

Published by Anqa Publishing
PO Box 1178
Oxford OX2 8YS, UK
www.ibn-arabi.com

First published 2007
First US paperback edition, 2010

British Library Cataloguing in Publication Data
A CIP catalogue record for this book is available from the British Library

ISBN   978 1 905937 26 4

Cover design: www.doppelpunkt.com

Printed in the USA by Quad/Graphics, Leominster, Massachusetts

These times now are not like times gone by. This is because today is closer to the Hereafter. Hence people today experience abundant unveilings, and flashes of light have begun to appear and become manifest. The people of our time enjoy more rapid unveiling, more frequent witnessing, a richer gnosis and a more perfect knowledge of divine realities, but they practise fewer works of devotion than in previous times ...

Such practice predominated in the past, but in our times knowledge has gained ascendancy, and this situation will continue to expand and intensify until the descent of Jesus, upon whom be peace, such that our performance of a single prayer-cycle today is equivalent to a whole lifetime of worship by someone of an earlier time ...

Knowledge is one and spread wide, and calls for those who can carry it. When these grow in number by virtue of their righteousness – for it is the knowledge of the righteous – it is apportioned among them ... Knowledge, opening and unveiling are abundant among men of later times. When someone has a portion of this, it becomes manifest in him, because today knowledge predominates ... Glory be to the One who gives freely to all!

Ibn 'Arabi, *Kitab al-Isfar*, pp. 9–11

Our happiness and completion lies in facing Unity with the totality of ourselves, in standing for the truth of humanity, its singularity and largeness, and by denying any limited or diseased identity.

Peter Young, 'Ibn 'Arabi: Towards a Universal Point of View', p. 94

The future of the entire human race may depend on whether large numbers ... can now take the *Direct* Path into claiming humbly their divine humanity and acting from it in order to preserve the environment and see that justice is done to the poor and starving and depressed. What is needed on a large scale ... is ... an army of ... active mystics who work in every field and in every arena to transform the world.

Andrew Harvey, *The Direct Path*, p. 26

Note on spelling and transliteration

The subject of this study intersects with two major languages of the Islamic world, Arabic and Turkish. We adopt the Arabic spelling for all names of people and places and all Islamic and sufi terms, except where a Turkish spelling appears more natural or more immediately recognisable, in the case of Ottoman or modern Turkish contexts. In contrast (and reflecting its close association with the Turkish milieu), materials deriving from Beshara tend to spell many of these names and terms in a form that approximates to the Turkish (for example, *dhikr* is denoted by *zikr* in Beshara materials, and Qunawi is spelled Konevi). We retain the Turkish spelling of the names of certain *tariqa*s or spiritual ways when discussing the Ottoman/Turkish context, viz. Mevlevi/Mevleviyye (for Mawlawi/Mawlawiyya), Halveti/Halvetiyye (for Khalwati/Khalwatiyya, spelled Helveti in some Beshara materials), Celveti/Celvetiyye (for Jilwati/Jilwatiyya, spelled Jelveti in Beshara materials), Bayrami/Bayramiyye (for Bayramiyya), Shabaniyye (for Sha'baniyya) and Melami/Melamiyye/Melamet (for Malami [also Malamati]/Malamatiyya [also Malamiyya]/Malama [also Malamism]). In contrast, we use Naqshbandi, Qadiri, Rifa'i and Bektashi. In modern Turkish spellings, we include the letters ğ, ç, ö, ü and ş, but for the sake of simplicity leave out the distinction between i and ı. For the same reason, we also leave out diacritical marks throughout our transliteration of Arabic and Ottoman Turkish. Finally, although the correct form of his name in Arabic is Ibn al-'Arabi, we adopt the simplified form Ibn 'Arabi, widely used by authors writing in English.

Contents

Acknowledgements

Sincere thanks are due to all those in the UK and Istanbul who gave their time for interviews or to respond to questions; The Institute of Ismaili Studies (London) for generously supporting this work; the Beshara School and the Muhyiddin Ibn 'Arabi Society for their hospitality and help; Michel Chodkiewicz, Paul Heelas and Victoria Rowe Holbrook for their helpful comments; and last but not least, Stephen Hirtenstein and Michael Tiernan.

Chapter 1

Setting the scene

Across Britain today and in various other parts of the non-Muslim world, small groups of committed individuals meet regularly to study in devotion the challenging writings of Muhyi al-Din Ibn 'Arabi (1165–1240), an Andalusian sufi (mystic) widely recognised as the most influential thinker of the second half of Islamic history. This book is the story of their encounter with him. For many, this began during the 'sixties' (often projected as the years 1963–73), when Ibn 'Arabi was discovered by counterculture youth in Britain searching for new spiritual ways. He had arrived there in the company of a descendant of the Ottoman elite, and their joint legacy is the movement that calls itself Beshara. Since the mid-1970s, Beshara has offered substantial courses in 'esoteric education' drawing on Ibn 'Arabi's teaching, through a dedicated school. Those who have studied there make up an extensive international network of individuals personally committed to this teaching and to the actualisation of the Beshara vision.

Through the story of Beshara many other stories can be told, and some of them are unfolded in this book. There is the broad canvas of transformations in the religious–spiritual landscape of the advanced societies of the post-war West: these changes first appeared prominently during the sixties, and have grown significantly since. There is the specific story of sufism in the West: associated with love, beauty and an inclusive humanism, this has long been popular among Westerners (in contrast with suspicions of Islam as dogmatic, rigidly legalistic and exclusivist). And finally there is the particular encounter between sufism (and Ibn 'Arabi) and the New Age.

The story of Beshara and Ibn 'Arabi also raises many questions concerning the future, at a time of tension between 'Islam' and the 'West', and of heightened global interaction and exchange. What does it suggest concerning trends in attitudes towards sufism and Islam in Western contexts? Given that its story includes a successful encounter with a majority Muslim setting, might it also shed light on possible future trends in Muslim attitudes? What does it reveal concerning the current state of sufism and its possible future? This book offers some answers to such questions.

Two fields of study are bridged here: religion and spirituality in the modern West, and historical and modern Islamic and sufi traditions. We have endeavoured to avoid the assumption of detailed specialist knowledge of either, and provide a basic introduction to key studies of recent religious change in the West (including New Age studies), as well as sufism and the life and thought of Ibn 'Arabi. The hope is that readers of diverse backgrounds will find adequate guidance and something of interest in the full notes, where references range from introductory surveys to specialist works.

In the first part of this chapter we briefly outline the historical context out of which Beshara emerged. We profile sixties Britain, discuss the counterculture associated with the period, and introduce the phenomena of New Religious Movements (NRMs) and the New Age. Here and in the subsequent introduction to sufism and sufi spirituality in the modern West, we introduce working definitions of terms and concepts used in the volume.[1] We should point out here that NRMs, the New Age and the sufi presence in the West all predated and outlived the sixties. We draw on analyses of these phenomena as they appeared later in the twentieth century whenever this lends greater clarity (with the necessary qualifications). We also draw on some discussions of the USA/Western Europe where this illuminates the British case.

Having thus set the scene, we introduce Beshara as a movement of sufi spirituality that emerged in sixties Britain, and pose specific questions to map out the agenda for study. We then introduce Ibn 'Arabi as the movement's major inspiration, and clarify the notion of the Oneness of Being attributed to him. (This brief treatment is supplemented with suggested further readings on his life and thought in Appendix 2.) Finally, we discuss methodological orientations and the methods of data collection adopted, addressing questions raised by the use of certain types of sources and data.

Sixties Britain as historical context

Hey, Mr. Tambourine Man, play a song for me.
I'm not sleepy and there is no place I'm going to ...
Take me on a trip upon your magic swirling ship,
My senses have been stripped, my hands can't feel to grip,
My toes too numb to step, wait only for my boot heels to be wanderin'.
I'm ready to go anywhere, I'm ready for to fade
Into my own parade, cast your dancing spell my way,
I promise to go under it.
                                        Bob Dylan, *Mr. Tambourine Man*

The counter culture ... insists that we are men, not things ... It defines the proper (human) categories which make us holy. It is unique in its promise that humanity can finally be human.
                                        Frank Musgrove, p. 19

When the Moon is in the Seventh House and Jupiter aligns with Mars
Then peace will guide the planets and love will steer the stars
This is the dawning of the Age of Aquarius ...
Harmony and understanding, sympathy and trust abounding
No more falsehoods or derisions, golden living dreams of visions
Mystic crystal revelation and the mind's true liberation.
                                        The Fifth Dimension, *Aquarius*

For people of a certain age, memories of the 1967 Summer of Love in San Francisco, Woodstock in 1969 or the Glastonbury Festivals of the early 1970s will never fade. The significance of the social and cultural developments symbolised by such events reached far beyond the lives of those directly involved, however, and scholars, the media and cultural commentators on both sides of the Atlantic have periodically revisited them. In Britain in the summer of 2004, for example, cultural events were organised to debate the achievements and merits of the landmark decade of the 1960s, and to evaluate the legacy for posterity of this moment in history. It was a time that brought substantial and long-lasting change to the country's identity, thanks to certain significant social and cultural transformations. One social–cultural historian of twentieth-century Britain has construed the period c.1958– c.1973 as a 'cultural revolution', in which the dominant features were 'self-expression, participation, joy and release from the social controls which had held British society in thrall since Victorian times.'[2] Dislocations took place in spheres of class, race, relations between the sexes, and relations between the youthful and middle-aged. The youthful emerged as the vanguard in the significant and influential minority comprising what has been widely dubbed the 'counterculture' of the time.[3] It stood for human, egalitarian values against the premises of a society built on economic growth, and was marked by a distrust of authority and suspicion of leadership.[4] Some sociologists have suggested that counterculture youth threw into stark relief the constitutive developments of modernity. They thus embodied a social and existential 'homelessness', generated by the impact of modernisation and its institutions on consciousness and social life in modern societies.[5]

The counterculture evinced certain major orientations, reflecting for those involved the outcome of the individual encounter with the structures of the modern technological–bureaucratic world. There was a bid for liberation from the controls and limitations of primary institutions experienced as coercive and repressive, and radical disillusionment with the 'mainstream' meanings and values they provided. This encompassed traditional religion, its plausibility having in any case been thrown into crisis by the undermining effects of pluralisation, itself a product of the processes of modernisation. In their homelessness, counterculture youth undertook of necessity a turn to the self as the only remaining source of meaning and significance.[6] One major counterculture orientation thus found expression in a search for ways of life that nurture 'the authentic self.'[7] The idea of pursuing this by taking the 'journey to the East' indeed became so popular that the countercultural interest in Eastern traditions (religions of the 'Orient') was one of the most striking features of the sixties.

As hinted at above, changes in patterns of religious belief were not confined to counterculture youth: they were more broadly evident in the industrialised societies of the post-war West. In Britain traditional patterns associated with institutional religion declined significantly, especially from 1960 (measured as ritual participation and institutional attachment). This suggested a future based on an 'empty church' scenario.[8] It also encouraged a confident mood among sociologists convinced that the death-bell had begun to toll for religion in the advanced societies of the West (as it would, eventually, in other societies).[9] At the same time, however, new forms of religious expression began to proliferate, leading to a new level of religious diversity in British society. Such developments added to the mounting evidence that was eventually to confound those who had predicted the inevitable demise of religious belief and life, based on their confidence in the secularisation thesis.[10] The new forms of religious expression in Britain included groups which sociologists describe as NRMs.[11] NRMs are groups that are religious (insofar as they offer an answer to some of the ultimate questions traditionally addressed by religions), and that have been founded in their present form and cultural environment since 1945.[12] The counterculture served as a significant catalyst in the emergence of NRMs, and furnished an important recruitment base: thus many came to prominence during the sixties. Dubbed 'neo-Oriental' NRMs,[13] a good number of them specifically answered to the countercultural 'turn East'.[14]

In the wider society, interest in the phenomenon of NRMs was mostly framed at first in terms of social deviance, when some groups emerged as a social problem.[15] Sociologists have largely driven the academic study of NRMs since: combined with psychologists and scholars of religious studies, they have mapped the field through a voluminous literature.[16] This literature elucidates the profiles and motives of NRM-joiners from the baby-boomer generation (born just after the end of World War II and forming the young adults of the counterculture), and later generations. A typical joiner has been young (often in their twenties), white, better educated, from a middle- to upper middle-class household, and equally likely to be female as male.[17] A major attraction for joiners has been the emphasis in many NRMs of a specifically experiential religiosity, striking a chord with a search for 'an intense experience of the self' and a direct, personal encounter with the transformative sacred.[18] It has typically taken the form of a mystical monism based on the notion that the divine can be found within, a principle found in the mystical traditions of all major religions (but often conflated with Indian traditions). This emphasis is coupled with practices that lead to an experience of union with the sacred/ultimate reality, during which the 'ordinary' self is transcended. It should be clear from this that many NRMs offered joiners 'spirituality' as opposed to 'religion'. The distinction between the spheres denoted by these terms had been long in the making, but it came into particularly sharp focus during the sixties (and has gained further prominence since).[19] Alongside these spiritual offerings, the leader/teacher/guru institution proved an important pull factor for many joiners. It not only responded to their search for leaders with authentic charisma,[20] but also to their implicit yearning for representations of authority in a culture marked by growing uncertainty.[21] The fellowship and supportive community provided by NRMs also had evident appeal for the 'homeless minds' generated by modernity.[22]

Sociologists of religion disagree on the cultural significance of NRMs for Western societies. Their interpretations tend to coincide with the broad lines of the debate on the secularisation thesis. Based on a projection of secularisation as 'a self-limiting process that gives rise to religious revivals,'[23] some see these groups as 'the vanguard of a revival of the sacred in the modern world', pushing back the frontiers of secularisation. Others see them as 'epiphenomenal symptoms' of a further stage in the ongoing secularisation/privatisation of religion in the societies of Western Europe and the USA, positing them as evidence of the continuing decline in religious vitality and influence there.[24] Yet others see them as symptomatic of significant shifts in religious sensibilities and orientations in the West.[25] Taking the case of the USA since the 1960s, Wuthnow has demonstrated that Americans increasingly turned from a religious life marked by a spirituality of 'dwelling' (based on identification with a geographically fixed community), to one of 'seeking', liberated from many traditional constraints and reflecting a new understanding of freedom partly shaped by the civil rights movement.[26] A new religious environment was taking shape at this time, marked by a historically unique emphasis on freedom of choice, which fuelled the spiritual quest and encouraged seekers to make up their own minds in the marketplace of ideas and lifestyles, paying attention to their inner feelings. The upsurge of interest in spirituality among Americans during the late 1960s was further informed by a positive regard for diversity and personal exploration, such that people could move freely among different lifestyles and worldviews. The success of NRMs in the USA at this time, beneficiaries of these changes in the country's religious culture, served as an important indicator of underlying trends that would gain in scope as the twentieth century progressed.[27]

The emergence of the sixties' counterculture in the USA and Western Europe not only fuelled the development of NRMs, but also saw the expansion of the New Age. Those who have studied it have pointed to the difficulty in identifying, describing and delimiting this phenomenon, which seems to elude any universally accepted definition.[28] For the purposes of our historical discussion, it is necessary first to distinguish between the sixties, or counterculture, New Age, and what has been described as the New Age Movement (NAM). The latter term designates specifically a recognisable 'movement' into which the counterculture New Age (and its antecedents) crystallised during the 1980s.[29] Recent analyses of this movement from the 1980s onwards (better informed by virtue of their vantage point) can illuminate the sixties New Age, given important continuities in content and orientation (notwithstanding certain differences that emerged during the 1970s).[30] There are in fact still relatively few scholarly studies of the NAM from a detached viewpoint.[31] At the same time, the eclectic diversity that comprises it presents a challenge to discerning a single worldview or underlying vision.[32] Heelas' 1996 study advances one understanding of this vision, and the characteristic themes and attitudes that flow from it. The basic working concept of the New Age adopted in the present volume, whether in the context of the sixties or beyond, has been influenced by this.[33] It is important to bear in mind that not all the emphases identified by Heelas (and others who have studied the New Age) are necessarily present, or manifest to the same degree, in every New

Ager/New Age group. Where present, they are also subject to considerable variation. Defining New Age themes are set out in what follows, using italics to highlight key concepts.

The most pervasive and significant motif of the New Age, according to Heelas,[34] is the notion that the person is, in essence, spiritual, based on the monistic assumption that 'the Self is sacred' and producing a characteristic *'Self-spirituality'*, the capital S indicating the true, 'higher' self. Positing inner spirituality as the key to moving from everything that is wrong with life to all that is right, New Agers consider it essential for the individual to move beyond the socialised self (the 'ego', 'lower self', 'intellect' or 'mind'). This enables a shift to a new realm of being which constitutes the authentic self and human nature, and represents perfection (as well as helping to change the world into a better place). New Age spiritual disciplines and practices furnish paths to the ultimate within, and by applying these New Agers become aware of what they are (the essential), and what they are not (that part of them which belongs to the artifices of society and culture).[35]

Flowing from this 'Self-spirituality', there is a strong tendency for New Agers to be 'epistemological individualists'[36] who insist that, first and foremost, truths come by way of personal experience.[37] Accordingly, all voices of authority other than the self must ultimately be mediated by way of inner experience. The New Age is thus in large part quite radically *detraditionalised* or in other ways *anti-authoritarian*.[38] Voices of authority rejected include those associated with established traditions and orders: this extends even to a rejection of 'beliefs' as such. Significant consequences arise for attitudes towards religion. In the New Age, it is effectively replaced by teachers 'whose primary job is to set up "contexts" to enable participants to experience their [own] spirituality and authority.'[39] Religion is associated for New Agers with 'the traditional; the dead; the misleading, the exclusivistic'.[40]

The *radical, unmediated individualism* of the New Age manifests in the notion that the individual serves as his or her own guide, in place of tradition and beliefs. The self thus represents an internalised locus of authority, producing a characteristic New Age 'Self-ethic'.[41] This emphasis goes hand in hand with the fact that freedom is a cardinal New Age value, involving liberation from the past, the traditional and the 'ego', but also freedom to live a life expressing all that it is to be 'truly human'.[42] By linking the self directly with the cosmos (and thus tending to bypass society and history), its acute individualism leads the New Age ultimately to employ the cosmic scenario, as Campbell puts it, 'purely as a backcloth or setting for the personal drama of the self'.[43] The individual self thus emerges as 'the very centre and hub of the New Age world-view'.[44]

New Agers are *perennialists*. As the external realm of traditional belief instils little or no faith in them, they can dismiss apparently significant differences between religious traditions as the result of ego-operations and historical–cultural contingencies. What matters instead is the inner reality at the heart of the religious domain as a whole. New Agers go beyond traditions as normally conceived 'to find – by way of experience – the inner, esoteric core'. Hence they can and do draw on traditions, discerning their gnosis or experiential knowledge in detraditionalised fashion, while 'bypassing their explicit authoritative doctrines, dogmas and moral codes'.[45]

A fundamental *holism* and the interconnectedness of all things is a central New Age theme,[46] flowing from the assumption that *reality is monistic in nature*.[47] Accordingly, the divine, humankind, nature, spirit, mind and body are held to be ultimately and in their deepest essence one (hence the notion of the 'sacred Self'). Ultimate reality is itself spiritual: there is a single universal immanent divine presence, often envisaged as a form of consciousness, energy or intellect, and the ubiquitous spiritual is believed to have a controlling function within all life. Such holistic concepts are presented as alternatives to the dualism and reductionism that are perceived to dominate modern Western society,[48] illustrating the basis of the New Age, as Hanegraaff suggests, as cultural criticism directed against the dominant values of the modern West.[49] Holism leads to a general prevalence of unity over diversity in the New Age perspective. Perceptions of the essential unity of humanity are especially common, often expressed in contempt for nationally and ethnically differentiated modes of being.[50]

Two final characteristics must be mentioned. First, New Agers believe that their alternative spiritual worldview is supported, even confirmed, by *the newest results of scientific research*.[51] Second, they presume *the reality of spiritual evolution* (this presumption lay behind the original proclamation of a New Age), issuing in a highly optimistic worldview based on perceptions of the present age as a time of cosmic spiritual awakening and advancing enlightenment.[52]

To return to the sixties, it has been suggested that this period witnessed 'the most significant turn to inner spirituality to have taken place during modernity',[53] bound up with the basic assumption of the developing counterculture that people should be free to express their 'authentic nature'. The youth often used ad hoc resources in their pursuit of Self-spirituality at this time,[54] but their search also found growing expression in newly emerging communities, centres and neo-Oriental NRMs.[55] Fascination with Eastern spirituality came to the fore in Britain with accounts of The Beatles and some of The Rolling Stones visiting the Mahareshi Mahesh Yogi of Transcendental Meditation fame in India in 1968.[56] Meanwhile, through its theme song *Aquarius*, the most well-known lines of which are cited above, the hit London musical *Hair* famously proclaimed that the New Age was dawning.[57] Here as elsewhere, the New Age was widely conceptualised in terms of the Age of Aquarius, destined to supplant the Age of Pisces.[58] Perceiving the particular qualities of the zodiacal Aquarius gradually emerging around them, many counterculture New Agers felt vindicated in their convictions.[59] A general sense of inexorable change predominated with a feeling that, though the outcome was yet unclear, a better way of life was dawning, reflecting a fundamental reorientation of human self-understanding and values.[60]

Sufism and sufi spirituality in the modern West

[For pre-modern Muslim societies] the multifarious activities that we subsume under the terms *Sufism* and *Islam* were not spheres of existence separate or separable from religious life in general. It would not have been possible to formulate the statement 'Sufism has nothing to do with Islam' prior to the nineteenth century.

Carl Ernst, *The Shambhala Guide to Sufism*, p. xv

[T]he lecture hall was almost empty. A few loyal souls had shown up … But the vast majority of the seats were unclaimed. Esfandi had for some reason entitled his lecture 'Fire and Surrender in the Islamic Way', as if not remembering, or even caring, that Islam was hardly a popular subject around here [Santa Barbara, CA]. If he'd substituted the word 'Sufi', there'd have been blondes in the back row.

Pico Iyer, p. 218

Defining sufism is not easy.[61] The term and the concept it is used to designate are highly contested, and insiders and outsiders disagree among themselves and with each other as to what it is.[62] It is a reasonable claim that most of those involved in sufism today (and those who study it) understand it as an intrinsic part of the Islamic religious tradition, reflecting continuity with historical realities. Many Western scholars have narrowly equated it with the 'esoteric' or 'mystical' core of Islam, existing parallel with its 'exoteric' aspect, which is upheld through observance of the revealed law (sharia).[63] However, it can legitimately be projected more simply as 'the interiorization and intensification of Islamic faith and practice'.[64] As such, and as it has been projected by the great historical sufi theoreticians themselves, it is the beating heart of traditional Islamic religion and piety, from which it cannot be separated.[65] Nonetheless, many Muslims today consider sufism the chief internal threat to Islam, and their polemics aim precisely to separate it from the religion. These efforts represent a recapitulation of attempts by its opponents at different points in Islamic history to denounce certain sufi forms, teachings and practices as illegitimate, and extrinsic to the tradition.[66]

The same insistence that it had 'no intrinsic' relation to Islam (or only the most tangential one) was a central characteristic of sufism as 'discovered' two hundred years ago by orientalists. They presented it as an abstract mystical philosophy of possibly external origin, disconnected from Islamic scripture, law and ritual and detached from its profoundly important social context.[67] Many of the assumptions underlying this orientalist image of sufism survive in the West today. This is the case in scholarship and popular perceptions, and among those who have adopted sufi resources as the matrix of their spiritual quest, or a source of inspiration in this. At the same time, other scholars and practitioners of sufism in the contemporary West underline its Islamic context in doctrinal, legal, ritual and sociohistorical terms.

Alongside Indian traditions of Hinduism and Buddhism,[68] from the late nineteenth century the tradition of sufism attracted the attention of Western intellectuals interested in Eastern spirituality. During the twentieth century it gained appeal, and established a presence in the Western arena of alternative religions and spirituality. In recent years, sufism has increasingly caught the popular Western imagination, as suggested by the observation, cited above, made by a character in a novel by Pico Iyer.[69] Expressions of sufism in the West have received relatively little scholarly attention, when compared with other dimensions of the Islamic experience.[70] There have been some recent attempts to bring coherence to study of the field by tracing the history of sufism in the West and developing ways of understanding its great diversity there.[71] Studies tend to converge upon a twofold typology differentiating between expressions that consider sufism an integral part of the Islamic religion and those that do not.[72] Those in the first category may make concessions to the Western context, perhaps through a gradualist approach to their followers' practice of the Islamic ritual prescriptions. They may also focus more on their specifically sufi identity and teaching, rather than the associated Islamic ones. Nevertheless, they can be located squarely within the sphere of mainstream Islamic belief and practice.[73] In contrast, elements of the second type de-emphasise the Islamic source and content of their sufi identity and teaching. They tend to favour a perennialist outlook based on the belief that there is a universal, eternal truth underlying all religions, located in their mystical core, which ultimately renders the external shell unimportant. Accordingly, they do not stress (or even require) the embrace and practice of Islam by their followers.[74]

In order to reflect their respective emphases and for the sake of simplicity, these two types of sufism in the West are described in this volume as 'Islamic' and 'universal',[75] while keeping in mind that the boundaries between them can be blurred. Some Islamic sufi groups have thus evinced a context-driven elasticity that can appear to propel them into the other category, while questions remain as to whether some universal sufi groups harbour the embrace of Islam by their followers as a long-term goal.[76] Mutual perceptions and relations among practitioners of these two forms of sufism are often problematic. Some Islamic sufis denounce universal sufis for practising 'pseudo-sufism', denying that a wholesome spiritual path is possible in the absence of Islam.[77] For their part, the implicit claim of universal sufis to return to the 'essence' of sufism suggests that other forms (read 'Islamic') entail effort wasted on inessentials.[78]

Building on a dichotomy thus evident on the ground, a straightforward typology of Islamic and universal sufi figures in the West that also takes into account their religious and cultural provenance is provided in Appendix 1, as a basis for the proper situating of our subject. With regard to Islamic sufism, recent scholarship has developed more nuanced approaches to understanding the differences that mark its various expressions from each other.[79] Described by one scholar as an area that is 'something of a backwater',[80] universal sufism has generally not attracted the same scholarly attention.[81] As its prominence in the West is increasingly recognised, it is gradually becoming established as a serious subject of study.

It remains to point out that the term 'sufism/sufi' is used in this volume to designate all figures and trends that self-describe thus, be these universal, Islamic, contemporary or historical.[82] This is irrespective of whether other sufis, non-sufi Muslims, opponents of sufism and scholars would agree with this self-description. The term is also applied to those figures and trends that draw substantially on sufi resources without self-describing in terms of sufism. In such cases, and in discussing different forms of sufism in diverse cultural contexts, it seems more appropriate at times to use the term 'sufi spirituality', hinting at a distancing from traditional Muslim forms of sufism in doctrinal and organisational spheres.

Beshara as a movement of sufi spirituality

Introducing the Beshara movement

The physical focus of Beshara is its School of Intensive Esoteric Education located near Hawick in the Scottish Borders. Buried in the grounds is its guiding figure, Bulent Rauf (1911–87). Rauf's lasting contribution was to recruit the legacy of Ibn 'Arabi by way of response to the spiritual search of counterculture youth he encountered in England from the late 1960s. Since 1975, the School has offered extended residential courses centring on study, work, meditation and spiritual practice. The teaching of Ibn 'Arabi forms the heart of the study curriculum, and spiritual practices prescribed derive from the Islamic–sufi tradition. The aim is to enable students to realise their potential for perfectibility through existential self-knowledge based on the notion of the 'Oneness of Being'. Individual self-realisation is situated within a vision of the global unfolding of a new era reflecting a fundamental reorientation of perspective based on universality and unity.

Most of those who have studied at the School establish a relationship with it and join the network of others who have studied there. Returning to society, they nurture and apply the awareness awakened at the School, endeavouring at the same time to serve the ultimate aim of global reorientation through their individual contexts. The wider community that surrounds the School enjoys a distinct internal culture, evincing features that create insider cohesion and support. For example, those who participate in it use internally designated names among themselves. They meet regularly to study together and again on specific dates to join in collective spiritual practice. Many return to the School for intensive 'refresher' study. They give financial donations to the School according to their means, and some have bequeathed funds to it by will. Where possible, they publicise its work and introduce interested individuals to it. They have a common worldview, creating shared responses, values and priorities, in spite of different life circumstances. The perspective that underpins Beshara shapes their self-perception and understanding of the world, and they often pass this on to their children, who as young adults might also attend the School, producing a degree of intergenerational continuity of involvement.

While the School is effectively its pivot, a distinct movement thus emanates from and supports this central institution. We designate it the 'Beshara movement'. For reasons that will become clear later, we eschew the term 'membership/member' in favour of the looser term 'association/associate' to describe participation in it. As used here, the term associate designates an individual who has typically (but not always) completed a Beshara course and remains active in the movement, in the sense of continuing to believe in and support its worldview and goals. They may spend spells at the School, serve full-time as staff for specific periods there, attend study groups at home, or participate in the coordination of relevant activities.[83]

Key questions; scope of this volume

Beshara has not been subjected to significant independent analysis,[84] although both the movement and Rauf have been referred to in passing in some of the literature on sufism in the West.[85] Rauf is typically introduced in the context of discussions of an early associate of his by the name of Tim (Reshad) Feild, as the latter's 'teacher', and most treatments highlight the perceived Mevlevi connections of Feild, Rauf and Beshara.[86] Some mention the Muhyiddin Ibn 'Arabi Society (MIAS), established under the auspices of Beshara, as an example of organisations in the West that disseminate information relating to sufism, but they do not always register the connection between it and Beshara.[87] Literature on NRMs in the West generally fails to mention the movement, or mentions it only in passing.[88]

This volume provides a detailed description of Beshara. It adds an original case study to the relatively limited literature on sufism/sufi spirituality in the modern West, and to the few studies of NRMs there that draw on the Islamic–sufi tradition. Given the insatiable interest in anything to do with the contemporary Islamic–Western encounter, it is a timely contribution. However, its relevance extends beyond the specific fields of Islamic and sufi studies, and relations between Islam and the West. The emergence and continued existence of the subject of this volume thus point to broad religious, cultural and sociological issues in contemporary Western societies that continue to provoke lively debate. At the same time, it throws into sharp relief the interface between religion and modern cultural transformations in a global perspective. For example, Beshara's success in one majority Muslim arena exposes the impact of changes brought by modernisation and globalisation on religious life in these contexts. Such wider themes form the large backdrop to the volume.

By studying Beshara, it is possible to reflect on approaches to the study of sufism in the modern West more generally. For example, a recent conference asked: 'Are insights on "NRM"s/"New Age" movements relevant to an understanding of contemporary Sufism? Or is there a significant difference between both types of movement?'[89] It concluded that no strict boundary operates between sufi groups and 'New Age-type movements', pointing to 'questions of conceptualisation as well as sociological explanation'.[90] By way of contribution to this debate we ask whether, as a NRM, Beshara can be seen as a part of the New Age. Quantities of literature on sufism and translations of sufi texts stocked by New Age booksellers point to a substantial interest among their customers. At the same time, certain sufis in the West have been willing to cooperate and join in activities with New Agers.[91] Some scholars assume the existence of a relationship between certain expressions of sufism in the West and the New Age, but this has not been investigated systematically or in detail.[92] We explore this sufi–New Age nexus through a case study spanning over three and a half decades. We examine conceptual and operational affinities, and investigate the approach that shapes New Age appropriations of sufi resources.[93] We also explore the potential implications of this nexus for contemporary Western attitudes towards sufism and Islam as its tradition of origin.

The primary interest of this volume is in the realm of tradition and its cultural transmission, adaptation and application in modern contexts. In specific terms, it is in the recruitment of teachings, texts and practices associated with the pre-modern Islamic sufi tradition by elements of the counter-culture in sixties Britain, through the intervention of a Muslim descendant of the Ottoman elite. Investigation of this theme through Beshara is certainly sustainable intellectually. Nonetheless, some associates may take issue with the assumption that the 'Islamic–sufi' dimension is sufficiently defining of their movement's character/worldview to justify this focus. We anticipate and acknowledge their potential objections to this primary aspect in our framing of the subject, which we partly reflect in the volume title. Building on it, we consider how Beshara illuminates the trend of Western sufism it reflects, and explore its possible future prospects.

The internally contested Islamic–sufi dimension of Beshara yields various more detailed research questions.[94] How do its teachings and approach to spirituality relate to those of traditional sufi thought, and of Ibn 'Arabi, whose school the movement implicitly claims as its spiritual lineage? Which aspects of doctrine and practice associated with Ibn 'Arabi does Beshara perpetuate? How does the movement relate to the defining tradition of Ibn 'Arabi's world-view? In what ways does it perpetuate this tradition, and how does it utilise its major textual sources? To what extent does it depart from the characteristic values and sociocultural attitudes of this tradition? How (if at all) did Rauf's function in Beshara reflect the role of the traditional sufi teacher/guide? How have the various aspects of his function been undertaken since his death? How does the adopted approach compare with traditional sufi approaches to achieving continuity? Through what imagery, style and language is the Beshara vision conveyed? How does this reflect Rauf's own historical–cultural background, and to what extent does it represent a response to the contemporary Western milieu? What, then, is the matrix of cultural forms through which spiritual teaching and practice take place in Beshara? To what extent and in what ways does Beshara practice reflect traditional elements of Islamic and sufi practice? How do the genres of discourse and methods of communication used by Rauf and Beshara relate to those of traditional sufi spirituality? Are traditional Islamic and sufi understandings of sacred space and its use evident in Beshara? Are the arts and aesthetics used to convey or nurture a sense of the sacred in Beshara, and if so, how does their use relate to traditional Islamic and sufi approaches?

The following chapters reflect on some of these specific lines of investigation. The volume as a whole responds to the key question concerning Beshara and the New Age by elaborating the movement's main features in terms of the context of its formation. Chapter 2 traces its emergence and history, closely following the movement's internal collective memory. Beshara arose out of a syncretic multi-faith centre directed by an English sufi who had encountered Rauf. We map the confluence of trends that led to the centre's formation, exposing the spiritual genealogy of the major figures involved and tracing the gradual crystallisation and preponderance within it of the approach that would characterise Beshara. We examine the consolidation and institutionalisation of the emergent movement, achieved especially through the creation of dedicated schools and an academic society. The distinctive Beshara approach to spiritual education forms the subject of Chapter 3. Here, we examine major study texts prepared for internal use based on Ibn 'Arabi's teaching. We describe residential courses as an integrated framework for spiritual education and explore the School as a purpose-designed facilitating environment. The focus of Chapter 4 is Beshara's guiding figure. We explore Rauf's origins, his family background, formative and possible later influences on him, and his spiritual associations. We characterise his approach as adviser and guide, and evaluate his legacy for the movement.

Chapter 5 sets out the Beshara perspective, and elaborates Rauf's distinctive application of Ibn 'Arabi's teaching in its construction. We consider the movement's perception of the present times, its understanding of its own role in preparing for a new era and its vision of that era. In Chapter 6, we examine the Beshara conceptualisation and practice of the spiritual life, emphasising its perception of the religions and its distinctive spiritual culture, including the relation of the latter to the Islamic–sufi resources on which Rauf drew. Chapter 7 explores the Beshara projection of Ibn 'Arabi. We consider the channels through which the movement brings his teaching (as appropriated by it) to a broader audience, exploring among others the case of the MIAS. We interrogate the characteristic emphases of the image of Ibn 'Arabi projected by Beshara in light of competing projections.

In Chapter 8, we situate Beshara in relation to key themes and questions. We then use the specific case study to explore the possible future of sufism in Western and Muslim arenas. Possible trajectories of universal and Islamic sufism in contemporary Western societies experiencing significant shifts in religiosity are mapped. We turn then to the fate of sufism among certain sectors of Muslim populations, considering the impacts of modernisation and globalisation in shaping constituencies for a reconstituted sufi spirituality that evinces affinities with motifs and approaches widespread in contemporary Western arenas. Finally, we reflect in an Epilogue on some of the volume's findings and methodological implications.

Introducing Ibn 'Arabi and the Oneness of Being

Life and works

Ibn 'Arabi was born in Murcia in the southeast of Muslim Spain in 1165, and spent the first thirty-five years of his life in the western lands of Islam. His father served as a professional soldier in the army of the Almohad sultan in the provincial capital Seville, to where the family had relocated in 1172. Their circumstances were good and the young Ibn 'Arabi acquired a broad education. The seminal experience of his youth took place when he was still an adolescent. It was a sudden mystical 'unveiling' in the form of a dream vision of Jesus, Moses and Muhammad, during a spontaneous retreat outside Seville. By 1184 he had entered upon the sufi path and dedicated himself to the spiritual life, turning his back on a potential career in the military and entrusting all his possessions to his father. He began to frequent spiritual masters in al-Andalus, Tunis and Fez. By 1194 he had composed his first major work, the first of nearly three hundred, all of which he claimed had resulted from divine inspiration.

In 1200 Ibn 'Arabi decided to leave for good the land of his birth, and he began to journey towards Mecca to perform the pilgrimage. This opened the 'eastern' chapter of his career, spent in Anatolia and the Levant, to which his best-known works belong. He passed through Marrakesh, Tunis, Cairo and Palestine, finally arriving in Mecca in 1202. While circumambulating the Ka'ba there, he experienced momentous visions that sparked the beginning of his magnum opus, *al-Futuhat al-Makkiyya*. They ultimately issued also in his famous collection of poems, the *Tarjuman al-ashwaq*, and several other works. More travels in the east followed: for example, he accompanied the father of Sadr al-Din Qunawi, who was to be his chief disciple and transmitter of his teachings, on a diplomatic mission. During this period he edited existing works, continued with the *Futuhat*, added further works to his corpus, and married and had a family. After 1223, he settled finally in Ayyubid Damascus under the patronage of one of its powerful families. His celebrated *Fusus al-hikam* appeared in 1229 received, by his own account, from the hand of the Prophet in a dream. He died in Damascus in 1240 and was buried in his adopted city.

Ibn 'Arabi's self-understanding pivots on an early vision, in which he was shown his destined role as the Seal of Muhammadan Sainthood. He was to become thereby the supreme heir of the Prophet, charged with being the unique, plenary manifestation of the Prophet's implicit sainthood and exerting spiritual authority over the Muslim saints. However, his conception of the reach of his role went beyond both saintly and Muslim communities, for he also highlighted his nature as 'an absolutely merciful being', a messenger of divine mercy who promised to intercede on the Day of Judgement on behalf of everyone he sees.[95]

Many subjects and fields of knowledge are addressed in Ibn 'Arabi's writings, which combine poetry, exegesis, speculative theology, jurisprudence and mythology. His discursive method involves a degree of elusiveness and the use of symbolic images and paradoxes. The latter reflected his conviction that the syllogistic methods of the philosophers and the imitative approach of earlier scholars were inadequate for conveying the complex dynamic of the relationship between God, man[96] and the cosmos. This relationship pivoted on the underlying oneness and common origin of all aspects of the universe. For Ibn 'Arabi, the universe was the product of God's desire to see Himself manifested, as in a mirror. Hence, although the Divine Reality is transcendent, at the same time everything that exists is a manifestation of that Reality. Everything that exists is God, but is simultaneously a veil between the seeker and God. Man and God unite in a contemplative process in which man sees his own reality in the mirror of God's existence, and God knows His Essence in the mirror that is man completed. This is the quintessence of Ibn 'Arabi's metaphysics.[97]

The entire oeuvre of Ibn 'Arabi is ultimately and intimately concerned with the bedrock of Islam, *tawhid* (the unity of God), and its implications for a proper appreciation of the ultimate nature and purpose of humankind in creation. His elaboration of this theme has been perceived by some as contravening the essential Islamic doctrine of divine transcendence, leading to a designation of his thought as a blatant expression of existential monism. In this view, he is the founder of the 'heretical' doctrine of the Oneness of Being.

The Oneness of Being

The doctrine of the Oneness of Being (in Arabic *wahdat al-wujud*)[98] and the existential monism it assumes do appear to capture an important facet of Ibn 'Arabi's thought, for at one level he upholds the identity of God with His creation, and hence with man. Yet this understanding and its potentially antinomian implications must be evaluated in light of the fact that, at the same time, his thought remains deeply rooted in and faithful to the theistic worldview of the Islamic revelation, with its conception of God's utter transcendence and His creation's dependence on Him.[99] Ibn 'Arabi's vision was multifaceted, fluid and open-ended, his discourse shaped by 'the tensions and paradoxes that arise from the attempt to articulate the ineffable nature of a transcendent divine' (and 'the dynamic between the ineffable and the intermediate').[100] It is then only natural that this should have been articulated via a language consciously unfettered by 'fixed' or definitive (and thus

falsifying, reifying or reductionist) propositions and terminology.[101] By way of
illustration, as he used it, the term *wujud* itself combined a number of interrelated meanings, which Ibn 'Arabi constantly kept in play, such as 'being',
'existence', to 'be found' and, by his own explicit definition, 'finding the Real
in ecstasy'.[102] As Chittick puts it, the 'ambiguity' inherent in his understanding
of the cosmic situation can better be suggested with paradox (Ibn 'Arabi's
own *huwa la huwa*, 'He/not He', for example)[103] than in a straightforward
phrase such as *wahdat al-wujud*, which, moreover, he never used himself.
Furthermore, the perceived centrality of *wahdat al-wujud* to his teaching
must itself be questioned, for his major spiritual heir Qunawi makes it clear
that the central point of this is neither *wujud* nor *wahdat al-wujud*, but the
achievement of human perfection.[104]

   Nonetheless, historically the term *wahdat al-wujud* has been the one most
widely applied to designate the cornerstone of Ibn 'Arabi's doctrine, whether
by his advocates or his adversaries.[105] Application of the term reflecting a
particular usage among his advocators first appeared in the late fifteenth
century, when one of the greatest propagators of his teaching ('Abd al-Rahman
Jami [d.1492]) described Ibn 'Arabi and his followers as 'spokesmen for the
doctrine of *wahdat al-wujud*'.[106] For Jami, the doctrine signified '*tawhid* in
philosophical language'.[107] The role of Qunawi in shaping the perception of
Ibn 'Arabi's work vis-à-vis the notion of *wahdat al-wujud* is pivotal.[108] He was
much more inclined than Ibn 'Arabi to engage in debate with the philosophical tradition, having studied the writings of Ibn Sina, who had placed discussion of *wujud* (the term used in this case to render the Greek idea of 'being' or
'existence') at the heart of Islamic philosophy.[109] However, although Qunawi
himself used the term *wahdat al-wujud* in two or three places,[110] this was not
yet as a technical term, and it continued to denote its literal sense of *tawhid*.
Qunawi employed it simply as a phrase appropriate to explaining the nature
of divine unity in philosophical vocabulary. Before the fifteenth century, Ibn
'Arabi's adversaries had applied the term to characterise his doctrine. Indeed
Ibn Taymiyya (d.1328) probably made the greatest single contribution to
'turning *wahdat al-wujud* into the designation for a doctrine'.[111] He labelled
as believers in *wahdat al-wujud* Ibn 'Arabi, Qunawi and others who tended
to use philosophical vocabulary to talk about God. For him, *wahdat al-wujud*
was nothing other than unificationism (*ittihad*) and incarnationism (*hulul*).
It was equivalent to heresy (*ilhad*), atheism (*zandaqa*) and unbelief (*kufr*).[112]

   Notwithstanding the difficulties surrounding it, *wahdat al-wujud* remains
convenient shorthand for Ibn 'Arabi's thought as an adequate definition of
its fundamental theme.[113] Like all shorthand, however, it has a potentially
reductionist character that threatens to distort understanding of the thought
system it purportedly describes.[114] This tendency is compounded in Western
literature by the challenges of translation, given the difficulty of capturing
the shades of meaning conveyed by the term *wujud* as Ibn 'Arabi uses it,
noted above.[115] It is important to keep such concerns in mind whenever
application of the term to Ibn 'Arabi's thought system is encountered. In the

modern period, it has remained virtually synonymous with his name, both in the Islamic world and in Western literature. Muslim authors in particular often assume the doctrinal content signified by it: by citing certain historical authorities to the exclusion of others, they implicitly select one 'content' over another. This is then judged either positively or negatively, and Ibn 'Arabi is either absolved of it or denounced for it, but there is little attempt to define the expression in such a way that it actually accords with the teaching it ostensibly designates.[116]

Impact and legacy

Ibn 'Arabi's teaching pivots upon an appeal to the individual to experience directly God's Self-disclosure in the self and the world. Starting and ending with the Islamic revelation, it maps the individual journey of 'return' to the origin. In this respect, it effectively reinstates at the centre of Islamic belief a realisation of the intrinsic relation of self and the world to Absolute Being, pointing to the means by which this realisation can reach its fullest potential in the individual. Like al-Ghazali (d.1111) before him (who like him was honoured with the title 'revivifier of the faith', *muhyi al-din*), Ibn 'Arabi's emphasis of the interior thus complements or completes the exterior, rather than contradicting it.[117] The concern of such mystics is not to transcend or depart from Islam, but to repudiate a conception of it in which its defining and animating mystical kernel is absent. In presenting an approach that is rooted in the revelation while giving its due to this central concern, Ibn 'Arabi developed an intellectually satisfying resolution to the apparent contradictions between such significant binary oppositions as transcendence and immanence, unity and multiplicity, similarity and incomparability, and even belief and unbelief.

Ibn 'Arabi can reasonably be claimed as the most influential thinker of the second half of Islamic history.[118] Credited with the systematic intellectualisation of the earlier sufi tradition, his contribution has been a point of reference for most doctrinal sufi discourse since. However, his influence has also radiated beyond the sufis to thinkers more typically regarded as philosophers and theologians. Indeed, from the thirteenth century onward, most prominent Muslim thinkers have felt it necessary to define their position vis-à-vis him.[119] Question marks concerning his orthodoxy have fuelled polemics for and against him from the time of his death to the present day.[120] At the same time, some sufis who revere him as a saint remain against the general circulation of his works, lest they sow confusion among those unqualified to read them.[121]

Like other great mystics, Ibn 'Arabi had spiritual disciples and appears to have passed on a *khirqa* (sufi cloak of investiture), symbolising the transmission of his spiritual blessing (*baraka*). Historically, the transmission of his *baraka* has proceeded parallel to the transmission of his teaching.[122] His initiatic lineage continues up to the present,[123] albeit with such discretion that it often remains hidden (those who participate in its transmission are at the same time affiliated to diverse *tariqas*.)[124] His legacy belongs to the common heritage of the *tariqas*, while his practical directives and *baraka* have permeated sufism.[125] Whether acknowledged or denied, the stamp of his teaching can thus be found throughout the sufi universe.[126] The selective study of his corpus remains alive in certain sufi circles, while writings that popularise his teachings circulate among a wider readership.[127] The constant stream of visitors who journey to his shrine complex in Damascus bears witness to the place he occupies in the hearts of Muslims worldwide, while for his immediate neighbours, he is a generous local saint whose blessing brings livelihood, companionship and solace.[128]

Western visitors sometimes appear at Ibn 'Arabi's shrine. Indeed, since the second half of the nineteenth century, his teaching has exerted a particular pull among Westerners attracted to sufism.[129] The last few decades have witnessed a growth of interest in Ibn 'Arabi's thought in the West, evidenced by a steady flow of translations, studies, and, recently, an exploration of the broad spiritual guidance embedded in his teaching. Enthusiasts identify an irenic and ecumenical potential in his thought, much needed in an age of inter-civilisational tension. Some seek within his writings a foil to the theoretical assumptions of the Islamist experiment, and the accompanying cultural impasse in the Muslim arena, out of concern for the Muslim and global future. Others find personal guidance for practical spirituality in his teaching. As in the case of our present subject, they increasingly include non-Muslims, especially as his writings become more widely accessible through translations.

Concerning methodology, data collection and sources

Approaching Beshara

The overarching framework of this volume is built upon a historical–contextual approach, emphasising the historical matrix of the movement's formation and its associated sociocultural forces. This significantly illuminates aspects of its emergence, ethos and worldview. We do not intend any reductionism in prioritising it, however, and give due consideration to the subject in its capacity as a 'manifestation of the sacred' (as it is viewed by those involved in it), recognising the irreducibly sacred character of religion/spirituality as a category in its own right. We adopt the open, empathetic approach characteristic of phenomenological scholarship as far as matters of belief specifically are concerned,[130] aiming to bracket out our own assumptions/prejudices in order to let the subject speak for itself, and in its own terms.[131] At the same time, and in line with the principle of remaining neutral with regard to matters of ultimate truth,[132] we suspend normative judgement. Our aim is to do justice to the integrity of the believer's worldview and to present an accurate picture of the beliefs studied as expressed by those who hold them. While 'objective' knowledge is thus the aspiration, we maintain a constant awareness of the hermeneutical setting in which the collection and interpretation of data necessarily operate (linked to our own subjectivities).[133] We also take particular care to make clear if an opinion or analysis presented is our own, or belongs to the subject under study.

This volume is multidisciplinary in spirit and makes use of social science research methods in addition to historical–contextual and textual analysis. We do not claim to combine all these approaches in equal measure. We make no attempt to provide precise sociological data for a representative sample of associates and do not attempt a focused recruitment of sociological theories to understand the movement's fortunes and joiners' motives, for example.[134] The same goes for psychological theories of conversion and assessment of psychological benefits/(psycho-)therapeutic effects of joining.[135] A systematic exploration of these and related areas is deferred to further research on the movement.[136] Nonetheless, the driving concerns of sociological and psychological studies of conversion have informed the selection of associates interviewed, and relevant themes are illustrated particularly in associates' life stories (Appendix 5). In broader terms, themes, analyses and debates drawn from the sociology of religion inform the large backdrop to the volume and its framing. Finally, most of the statistics we present originate from the movement itself (apart from our own first-hand observations), and it has not been possible to verify these. Evaluations of its extent and impact based on such statistics thus remain tentative.

Internal sources and their use

Given the paucity of external sources, we have relied extensively (and in some places exclusively) on internal sources in significant parts of this volume. These encompass associates' oral narratives,[137] documentation put out by Beshara (for internal or public consumption, including course documentation, newsletters, web pages, etc.) and publications produced by its publishing company (Beshara Publications), under its auspices,[138] or by individual associates.[139] Internal sources inform the treatment of both of the broad areas we address, viz., historical reconstruction, and the transmission and understanding of ideas.

In the area of historical reconstruction (encompassing the movement's emergence and history, and the biography of its guiding figure), we selected as sources associates involved from the movement's inception specifically ('first-generation' associates). Naturally, there are problems associated with recollections of events that may go back more than three decades. Variations in accounts of the same episodes narrated by different internal sources are also inevitable. Use of recollections of specific episodes or narratives constructed many years after the events concerned (be these oral or published) calls for considerable care.[140] Although there is little external material on which to base substantial verification or comparison, whenever possible we have endeavoured to critically assess internal narratives. To do so, however, we invariably had to fall back on the oral recollections of external sources,[141] which are subject to similar problems. In assessing internal narratives we paid particular attention to possible selectivity and the colouring of significant biographies and accounts of pivotal events by a teleological perspective. We must mention finally specific challenges posed by the attempt to reconstruct the movement's genesis, given that it emerged out of a broader trend, abandoning elements within this as the distinctive Beshara identity and approach crystallised. As some associates downplay or dismiss this prelude, the (rather scant) documentation relating to it was particularly important to the construction of our narrative.

Rauf's discourses are pivotal to the Beshara perspective and specific ideas and understandings within it. As there are relatively few written records of these, we relied heavily in reconstructing his views on associates' accounts and observations. In selecting sources to that end, we focused on those associates perceived internally to have been close to him. Our aim was to access his views as conveyed directly to them, avoiding possible distortions and misunderstandings arising in their transmission to third parties. There is little written record of certain themes in the Beshara perspective. This sometimes reflects a deliberate policy, as in the case of especially subtle themes that may be misunderstood or misconstrued by unprepared or unsympathetic readers. To compensate, and to illuminate central themes in the absence of any systematic elaboration of these, we sought out associates' verbal explanations. As in the area of historical reconstruction, here, too, we selected as sources long-standing and particularly first-generation associates.[142] In general, differences of understanding and nuance arise in associates' presentations of the Beshara perspective. As with any system of ideas, individuals gravitate towards certain aspects or interpretations, reflecting their personal histories, inclinations and abilities. While the salient features of the Beshara perspective are more or less in evidence in the understanding of all associates encountered, a degree of diversity is thus also discernible in this. Associates also point out that Rauf shared insights with them in accordance with their receptivity. Some assumed he was conveying something he had also conveyed to all others, but later discovered that a certain insight had been shared with them alone, or with only very few others.

We are hinting here at an apparently intractable problem, summed up in the following question: To what extent do individual associates' understandings and perceptions represent those of the movement 'as a whole'? (This becomes especially pertinent in light of the implications of certain of the movement's characteristics for the operative nature of its belief systems, as will become clear later.) For example, some associates are more informed than others of Muslim culture and Islamic belief, and more knowledgeable of Ibn 'Arabi's writings beyond the texts designated for study within Beshara.[143] Some present systematically ordered and nuanced understandings, while the thoughts of others are more vague. We cannot claim that every opinion or understanding expressed by every associate is, as articulated by that associate, entirely representative of the movement as a whole.[144] However, in the plentiful views, perceptions and opinions cited in this volume, we can be confident of reflecting the movement's main emphases and convictions, without suggesting that it is monolithic. Given certain characteristics of Beshara *qua* movement, we must indeed ask whether we can speak meaningfully of an authoritative or 'official' position concerning any matter. Practically, this issue is settled in terms of Rauf's teaching (enshrined in his few writings and the movement's collective memory), and in the positions elaborated by the Principal of the Beshara School (appointed by Rauf) based on his own understanding and application of this teaching. While we do not attempt a systematic diachronic analysis of all aspects of the movement's perspective, we do probe the possible chronological evolution of this whenever evidence arises of shifts in emphasis and approach across its history as a whole, and during the fifteen years of Rauf's guidance. There is no assumption that the movement is or has been static in its perspective or approach.

Virtual boundaries and methods of data collection

The points we made above relate to the operation of our own selectivity in identifying associates as sources, defined in terms of the focal themes and aims of our study. Selectivity also operates at other levels in the context of the collection of data. For example, some associates (explicitly or implicitly, deliberately or unconsciously) draw virtual boundaries around certain areas and bar the researcher from these.[145] Associates differed significantly in the extents to which they were willing to consider objectively (even critically) the movement's history, or its present approach. A few were surprisingly frank. In general, their reactions to our research were diverse. Some deemed it important, and appreciated the perceived opportunity for the movement's history to be carefully documented. Others were initially suspicious.[146] One associate projected his own understandings on the research, insinuating that our pursuit of it was itself evidence that 'an instruction' to that effect had been received.[147]

We carried out data collection in the context of formal interviews and discussions.[148] Associates typically treated these as solemn occasions appropriate to the perceived gravity of the subject.[149] Alongside formal settings, informal discussions yielded significant insights, as did settings furnishing opportunities to observe and listen to associates more generally.[150] Participant-observation formed another significant fieldwork method.[151] This encompassed spells at Chisholme House, where we could observe and join in the daily schedule, and attendance of Beshara activities elsewhere. In some cases our participation was welcomed and integrated. In others it was not encouraged (we were asked to sit aside and observe), and on one occasion we were refused access. In this case, those concerned argued that it would be much better for us to write from 'our own taste (experience)', by undertaking a (six-month) Beshara course.[152]

Encompassing Ibn 'Arabi

In studying Beshara it is necessary to evaluate its perspective against that of Ibn 'Arabi, its major source of inspiration. Ibn 'Arabi's corpus is both vast and complex. Given the confines of time and the nature of our subject, we have accessed this for the most part through English translations and scholarly secondary sources. These materials raise some questions. Considering first the translations, even when taken together, they represent only (an inevitably selective) fraction of Ibn 'Arabi's writings. Some scholars would argue that it is impossible to have utter confidence in them, while others (particularly, but not exclusively, those unqualified to access the original texts)[153] reject such claims. To compensate, where possible we have supplemented translations used with a general sense of the original texts.

The steadily expanding secondary scholarship offers an increasingly helpful resource. However, the fact that its findings remain subject to ongoing reassessment complicates its use as a frame of reference against which to evaluate appropriations of Ibn 'Arabi's teaching. As Chittick remarked a little over a decade ago, given that most of his works remain unedited, unpublished, and/ or unstudied, 'all scholars who have attempted to explain Ibn 'Arabi's thought have pointed out the tentative nature of their endeavours.'[154] Some dimensions of his thought remain unexplored, and the contours of others exhibit considerable slippage from one treatment to another.[155] Many scholars have underlined the difficulties that arise in the attempt to understand him.[156] To offset the fact that authors' widely divergent interpretations and expectations are reflected in many secondary works,[157] we have made an effort to survey and refer to as a wide a range as possible of these. In the final analysis, however, we accept responsibility for any selectivity of presentation or emphasis (explicit or otherwise) in the characterisation of Ibn 'Arabi's teaching (against which the Beshara perspective is evaluated) in what follows.

One evening during the early days of Beshara at Swyre Farm in the Cotswolds, Rauf told an associate before retiring to bed: 'I will tell you what Beshara is really like. If we wake up and find that this property has been moved from valley to valley that should not surprise us, for this is the grandeur and capability of what Beshara is.' We now begin the story of Beshara, tracing first the emergence and history of the movement.

Chapter 2

Emergence and history

The history of every spiritual movement is multilayered. The outsider observes specific origins, episodes and events. Then there are experiences of these, captured in intimate memories. These are the preserve of those who participated, protagonists in the unfolding drama. Alongside this is an interior history. This is accessible only to those with the vision of the committed, and an understanding shaped by the movement's worldview. Our historical narrative takes the exterior as its basic frame. Within this, we incorporate the experiences, perceptions and understandings of various protagonists. We acknowledge the qualifications that might be brought to bear from the internal perspective on a narrative thus setting weight by 'visible' facets, but defer to a later chapter the interior projection of Beshara as the unfolding of an ancient, ineffable impulse.[1]

Rauf in London: a chance meeting?

It was to England that Bulent Rauf ... was directed in the mid-1960s. He did not know why he had come to England, but soon he came to understand that it was with those who were declaring that 'all you need is Love' that he must begin.

Peter Young, 'United by Oneness', Beshara website

The 'visible' origins of the Beshara movement lie in a timely coincidence between Rauf settling in London and the spiritual search of some counterculture youth. Some associates suggest he decided to settle in London in 1966 on the advice of a relative.[2] The commoner, teleological perception attributes his decision to a conviction that British society offered a hospitable arena for the working out of his ultimate vocation. By this account, he saw Britain as a place of real tolerance with respect to individual belief, and felt the seeds he would plant there might grow unobstructed. One associate holds that Ibn 'Arabi appeared to Rauf in a dream vision, and suggested that he 'go to England'.[3]

Finding himself in London with neither income nor home at the age of fifty-seven, Rauf rented accommodation and took a job at an exclusive jeweller's shop, arranged through contacts made earlier in Egypt.[4] In November 1968 he met Angela Culme-Seymour, who would become his second wife.[5] As his close companion she shared with him financial difficulties and frequent changes of accommodation. When his first job was terminated, he worked for a spell in an antique shop on the corner of Pimlico Road.[6] He completed a book on Turkish cuisine during early 1970.[7] During the winter of that year he took a job at Christopher Gibbs' antique shop in Elystan Street.[8]

In August 1969, Rauf and Culme-Seymour spent a vacation in Istanbul.

While they were staying with Rauf's cousin,[9] a wandering dervish who occasionally visited her appeared. According to Culme-Seymour, 'He used to walk from village to village talking to people, and in Istanbul he used to frequent the cafes and restaurants where students gathered, and tell them to renounce violence, drugs and gambling.'[10] When Rauf told him he was now living in England, 'the dervish cried excitedly: "But you must go back there! Go at once! We have been watching England for the last thirty years".'[11] Associates would later interpret his words as foretelling and confirming Rauf's spiritual role in England. Whether before this episode or not long after it, when he returned to London that autumn, a chance meeting with a young man called Tim Feild prepared the way for the unfolding of what would become his new vocation.

Feild's significance for the fruition of this vocation, and hence for the emergence of Beshara, was twofold. As an individual, he was well connected, energetic and charismatic. More importantly, he was also a significant link in an emerging network of spiritual seekers among counterculture youth disenchanted with institutionalised religion, and the various figures attracting them at this time. By introducing Rauf to this network, Feild would effectively provide the human and resource base for the emergence of Beshara.

Who was Feild? Educated at Eton, he came from a privileged English aristocratic background. By the time he met Rauf at the age of thirty-four, he had already led a colourful life, and had acquired the 'Islamic' name Reshad.[12] He had been involved in pop music as the third member of Dusty Springfield's group The Springfields (alongside Dusty and her brother Ian), which disbanded in the wake of The Beatles' soaring popularity.[13] He had also worked as a sailor (by some accounts a Royal Navy officer), antique dealer and jewellery salesman.[14] Yet there was more to him than this for, by his own account, he had given much attention to his 'inner studies' during the few years before he met Rauf, and had spent considerable time at a Tibetan Centre in Scotland.[15] According to a leaflet from 1970 or 1971 setting out his credentials, he had moreover been trained 'for over seventeen years' in 'many of the Esoteric Schools, including those of Gurdjieff and Ouspensky,'[16] and had received personal training from 'various teachers in both the East and West' during his extensive travels. He had also 'spent time in Buddhist monasteries'. He was especially interested in healing, and practised psychic or esoteric healing himself. Indeed, he led a group that met on a weekly basis at his Chelsea flat in London at this time: most of its members were also engaged in healing, and they met to discuss healing theory and practice.

How did Feild first encounter sufism? He claims that this was at a lecture in London by Pir Vilayat Khan, then leader of the Sufi Order.[17] Vilayat Khan made such an impact on Feild that the latter followed him to Paris the next day, launching 'a totally new cycle' in his spiritual journey.[18] On his return, he decided to introduce his 'healing' group to the teachings of the Sufi Order, and effectively integrated it into the latter.[19] He would deliver talks on the sufi path and read out fragments from writings by the founder of the Sufi Order,

Hazrat Inayat Khan. The group would meditate together, always beginning with the Islamic *basmala*, then proceeding freestyle. Sometimes during meditation Feild employed the Zen Buddhist technique of striking the back with a stick to stimulate/simulate 'awakening'. The group was very eclectic in its practice. There was singing, chanting, and 'sufi dancing',[20] for example, and individuals were given stones on at least one occasion to hold and converse with. Members of the group were assigned Islamic *wazifa*s or litanies derived from those used in the Chishti Order to perform in private.[21] They were also given Islamic names. True to the stance of the Sufi Order, however, they were neither required nor encouraged to embrace Islam. Members saw themselves as part of Vilayat Khan's organisation. Reflecting this, they sought out and read Inayat Khan's books, but no organised study took place during the weekly meetings. For its participants, Feild's role and status within the group was that of a typical shaykh or guru. He was also seen as very close to Vilayat Khan.[22]

How did Feild meet Rauf? According to Culme-Seymour, he walked into the antique shop where Rauf was working, seeking to publicise a forthcoming talk by Vilayat Khan. She describes him as having become by then 'an aspiring Sufi, a Man of God'.[23] Feild dates this first encounter to a few years after his initial meeting with Vilayat Khan.[24] In his account of it he makes no mention of the latter's talk, and writes that he was making the rounds of London antique stores in his capacity as an antique dealer.[25] On encountering Rauf, he immediately knew 'with all his heart' that he was ready to commit fully to the spiritual path, and any lingering doubts about this vanished.[26] He tells of an 'instinctive' conviction that Rauf knew something about 'the dervishes of the Middle East, those extraordinary men who had given their lives totally to God and ... were reputed to have many miraculous powers'.[27] He had come across this subject through his research into healing systems, and it had fascinated him since. Study of their way had indeed become 'almost an obsession' for him, he recalls, but he had yet to meet anyone with personal knowledge of their healing methods and spiritual practices.[28] He asked Rauf if he had such knowledge. Rauf's willingness to talk, he claims, was to 'change the whole course' of his life. According to Culme-Seymour, Feild soon became determined 'to glean all the knowledge he could out of this exciting mysterious Turk', and tried to persuade Rauf to become his teacher. The latter, however, 'refused to become anyone's teacher'.[29] Feild himself claims he became Rauf's 'pupil', and spent as much time as possible with him as their relationship deepened during the following year.[30] For his part, associates maintain, Rauf recognised from the first that Feild would be important to future developments.

A particularly important episode in this relationship appears to have taken place towards the end of 1969 and into early 1970. In November 1969, Rauf left London for Istanbul. Feild claims he told him he could find him in Side (Anatolia) in January 1970, if he wished to 'follow the Way'.[31] Feild sold up and made plans to leave England indefinitely. Rauf equipped him with a list of visits to make in Istanbul and Ankara before proceeding to Side (these included a sufi shaykh and the tomb of a well-known saint).[32] When Feild arrived at Side, Rauf set about imparting to him 'knowledge of the Way'. Feild depicts their relationship during this spell, which he felt was qualitatively different from before, as that between a master and a disciple. Through his experiential knowledge, Rauf was the repository of divine truths. For his part, Feild was required to relinquish all expectations formed by the mind, as well as assumptions and habitual thought patterns. This was a prerequisite for developing complete trust in God, which was indispensable for initiation into the inner path. Feild tells how Rauf taught him the breath,[33] the prayer of the heart which is 'beyond form',[34] the importance of remembering God through invocation or *dhikr*,[35] and metaphysical realities concerning the oneness of God and the true nature of man. He took him to the House of Mary at Ephesus and sent him to visit the tombs of sufi saints in Konya. Feild writes that he failed in many of the tests Rauf set him to gauge his commitment and willingness to abandon false concepts, demonstrating repeatedly that he remained attached to 'the world of attraction'. This reportedly incurred Rauf's anger. He tells frankly of this and of his moments of despair and doubt, when he wondered whether Rauf was manipulating him, or whether he even knew what he was doing.[36] After some hardship, the Konyan Mevlevi shaykh Suleyman Loras Dede (d.1985) embraced him,[37] and his efforts to follow Rauf's guidance thereafter bore fruit.

Probably well before this episode, and possibly quite soon after first meeting Rauf, Feild eventually persuaded him to attend the group meetings he organised in his Chelsea flat,[38] and his lectures on healing and the 'subtle body'.[39] At that time, Feild recently reflected, 'the world was waking up to the possibility of a new way of life, and discussions of [such] subjects drew large crowds, particularly young people'.[40] His weekly group was reportedly fifty or so in number at this time. It had a strong Sufi Order association, as we have noted, but Feild has suggested that it was dedicated to studying 'various forms of meditation from the East and the West that could be used in psychotherapy'.[41] While he agreed to attend the group's meetings, Feild claims Rauf insisted that his presence remain unobtrusive; he also asked him not to reveal their relationship.[42] It seems that things changed at some point, however, for Culme-Seymour recalls that, at these meetings, Rauf was 'placed in an armchair, like a sort of throne, while a crowd of eager, admiring, fascinated young people gazed at him while he answered their questions'.[43] One member of the group who became a Beshara associate remembers Feild preparing the group before he formally introduced Rauf to it. He told the assembled members that he had met someone unlike anyone he had met before. Referring to him as 'the Bey', which caused some confusion, he explained that Rauf had accepted an invitation to talk to them. News of the event had spread, and many additional people came along. Feild was concerned that there would not be enough space in his small flat, and greeted Rauf anxiously when he arrived. Rauf assured him that it was unnecessary to worry for, 'If

He wishes, walls expand.' He said very little on this first occasion, but when he did speak, according to our source, 'it cut through, without excesses or trimmings, and one could see that there was something very special. It could be tasted.' Some members of the group, at least, thus reportedly discerned a clear qualitative difference between the two men, in terms of their style of communication and their presence.

A few members of the group were later invited to meet Rauf and Culme-Seymour, and relationships gradually developed among them. They began to visit Rauf in his flat, and meetings were increasingly held there. Culme-Seymour was given to referring tongue-in-cheek to the eager young people who would come to see Rauf as his 'disciples'. She recalls that they would bring gifts such as flowers or bread, 'as offerings'.[44] The meetings were very informal, and some of those who attended have strong recollections of Rauf's insistence that he did not want to be made into some kind of guru, or put on a pedestal.

In addition to his growing relations with Feild's associates, Rauf also established relationships with young spiritual seekers in London who were not associated with Feild's group.[45] These included the manager of The Kinks pop group, for example, who was to become a key Beshara associate.[46] Having found all the spiritual teachers he had sought out in the USA to be 'charlatans', he had been put in touch with Rauf by an acquaintance sympathetic to his spiritual quest. On first meeting him, he instinctively knew that Rauf was 'the right person' for him. The two men began to meet for lunch weekly while Rauf was working in the antique shop. They discussed metaphysical and spiritual matters, and Rauf assigned *wazifa*s for him to practise. Rauf offered such guidance and *wazifa*s only to those seekers he met who were outside of Feild's group, and apparently did not become involved in this way with those already affiliated to Feild/the Sufi Order. In the words of one early associate, he was 'on the lookout for young people of heart who were prepared to move with whatever was placed within them. He was particularly keen to find people with leadership potential, as he recognised the magnitude of the task ahead of him.'

Rauf had apparently recognised such qualities in Field from the outset. The latter thus attributes to him an explicit intention to prepare him to assume the role of spiritual teacher in England. Towards the end of the few weeks they spent together in Turkey, Rauf reportedly told him: 'Go back to England, assimilate all the knowledge that you have been given. Then, when you are quite sure that you are ready, it will be your turn to pass on what you have learned, to help spread the knowledge of Unity to the world.'[47] Feild would indeed play a role in putting in place a framework in England for such teaching under Rauf's guidance. We turn now to the unfolding of the first steps in that direction.[48]

Coalescence: the establishment of a spiritual centre

During the autumn of 1969 a theology student at Oxford, Peter Dewey, was attending a London 'sufi' group associated with Idries Shah. He was at the time preparing to enter the priesthood.[49] In the group, he met a couple involved with Feild and Vilayat Khan, and eventually accompanied them to a Sufi Order conference held in an Eastbourne hotel. There was no dedicated Sufi Order centre in the UK, and Vilayat Khan's associates would book hotels or conference halls for the organisation's events. Before long, Dewey agreed to pool his energies with this couple in the effort to find a venue for such a centre in England.[50] Focusing on the Cotswolds, they hit upon Swyre Farm just outside the village of Aldsworth. Feild went to investigate and found it suitable. It was agreed that he would run the centre. For his part, Dewey would pursue its establishment as a registered charity pivoting on a Trust with a Board of Trustees, himself assuming the position of its first Chairman.[51] Feild's relationship with Vilayat Khan had been going from strength to strength, and he had just been designated his representative[52] (and thus official head of the Sufi Order) in the UK.[53]

The £14,000 required for the purchase of Swyre Farm was mainly acquired through Feild's London contacts, made during his association with the pop music industry. Dewey (who put up a sum towards the project himself) travelled frequently to London on fundraising missions. He asked each contact to put in £3,000, to function as an interest-free loan for a five-year period. If the project had not developed successfully by then ('in the spiritual sense', Dewey explains), their funds would be returned to them. Those who invested were invited to serve as Trustees. They were all familiar with and sympathetic to Vilayat Khan's work. They all knew Feild personally, and supported him in his capacity as a Sufi Order leader. Dewey's contribution to defining the proposed centre's orientation took the form of an insistence on openness to 'the mystical element in all religious traditions', and to 'all spiritual teachings'.[54] He believed such openness reflected and reinforced the ethos of the Sufi Order's reformulated sufism for the West, with its perennialist orientation. As Chairman of the Board, he claims to have succeeded in securing the support of all Trustees for this principle of openness at the outset.

The setting up of a charitable Trust and the purchase of Swyre Farm were completed by 1971.[55] At some point, the Trust and centre acquired the name 'Beshara'.[56] Feild, insistent that the project should have a name, had reportedly turned to Rauf for this, and Rauf had suggested Beshara.[57] Once this had been agreed, the Swyre Farm centre became known as the 'Beshara centre' (also 'the first major Beshara centre', reflecting an intention to establish additional centres like it, or the later emergence of other, more modest, centres). Sometimes it was referred to simply as 'Beshara' or, in the abstract, as 'a Beshara'.[58] As set out in the registration documentation, the centre's explicit agenda was loosely conceived in terms of spiritual training, meditation and retreat. Writing much later, Feild claimed that the intention had been to dedicate it, in true perennialist fashion, to 'the understanding of Universal Love, which is beyond all concepts of religion and all concepts of form'.[59]

Following the farm's purchase, Feild assumed responsibility for overseeing renovation of the property. He brought members of his London group to help in the building work. Other volunteers arrived independently. Dewey recalls that there were sometimes over a hundred young people at Swyre Farm at this time, and more at weekends. He describes them as belonging to the hippy movement epitomised by the Glastonbury Festival,[60] and associated with liberal use of mind-altering drugs like LSD.[61] Many who had experimented with LSD had experienced, in Dewey's words, 'an opening of the mind to a more visionary, spiritual perspective, induced by the drug'. This generated in them a predisposition towards meditation, and Swyre Farm responded to it.[62] Most who came at this time had either come off LSD or were in the process of doing so, and drug use was strictly forbidden on the premises. In a sense, Swyre Farm thus served as 'a de facto rehabilitation centre for ex-LSD users'.[63] Some young people who had travelled to India, suffered due to over-practice of certain techniques there, and then turned to Feild to help them recover, were also in evidence for a while.

As this suggests, the atmosphere at Swyre Farm during these early days was, in the words of one associate, 'conventionally countercultural'.[64] It was open to anyone, and people could stay for as short or as long a period as they wished. A variety came, ranging from full-time hippies to Oxbridge graduates, some noticeably upper-class. An associate who spent time there in mid-1972 recalls that there were equal numbers of young people with Christian and Jewish backgrounds,[65] more men than women, and several Americans. As Feild recently wrote, in time 'thousands of seekers came from all over the world to spend weeks or even months living in the community'.[66]

The meditation sessions Feild organised and led formed the foundation of the community's spiritual work.[67] He emphasised the plurality of ways to the goal of the mystical path ('Unity'), but explained that, as a teacher, he adopted specifically the sufi way of meditation:

So how do we proceed towards this Unity? This is obviously what we are wanting to know, and why we are assembled here at all. Meditation is undoubtedly one of the ways in which we can approach Unity, and as it is the way in which I am most personally involved I would like if I may to bring forward a few ideas on the subject. It is not for me to give techniques. Even if I could there are ... as many techniques as there are human beings in the world. There are many paths to the top of the mountain and we must choose the one that best suits us in our own particular state of evolution, and naturally some teachers are better for one person than another. However as I am involved with the Sufis I will approach the problem from a Sufi point of view.[68]

A daily programme revolving around three sessions of meditation eventually emerged (early morning, before lunch and early evening). Early memories of this suggest that Feild sometimes used mental imagery to guide it. Otherwise, it appears to have been down to the individual to find a way.

Feild assigned *wazifas*, reportedly adapted from Chishti practice, to each newcomer to Swyre Farm. He also taught them a form of invocation or *dhikr*.[69] Both were performed in private and the invocation additionally during practical work. He taught some form of the Mevlevi turn to at least some early arrivals.[70] A collective *dhikr* was instituted on Thursday evenings. It encompassed several forms in terms of movement and breathing techniques, and was at least for a time accompanied by drumbeats. A few would perform the Mevlevi turn at certain points during it. Across the months the form of the collective *dhikr* was modified and developed, and earlier forms were later abandoned. Ablution was instituted before meditation, *dhikr* and performance of *wazifas*: although the procedure for this was spelled out, the emphasis was on the importance of right intention in it. During weekdays residents were allocated practical work to do, possibly helping in the renovations, in the kitchen or looking after participants' children.

The final element in activities at Swyre Farm comprised regular lectures delivered by Field, and 'conversations' he would lead. At weekends these also supplanted work. He sometimes spoke on subjects related to healing practices,[71] but he generally focused on meditation and the mystical path. In his expositions on this path he introduced Inayat Khan's teaching as a point of reference, justifying this in the following terms:

> There are as many paths as human beings in the world, for each person has his own, and the only purpose of the teacher and the school should be to help guide the pupil toward the reality of the Truth within himself. In the final analysis, all paths lead to the same end, so it must be stressed again that no one school is better, smaller or greater than any other school. However, for the purpose of this school [the Beshara centre, Swyre Farm] we will be using terms which are based on the teaching of Hazrat Inayat Khan.[72]

Yet his illumination of the goals, stages and techniques of the mystical path roved freely among a broad spectrum of figures and sources, including Zen masters, Jesus, St John of the Cross, Ibn 'Arabi,[73] Krishnamurti,[74] Wilhelm,[75] Jung[76] and contemporary literature popular with the counterculture.[77]

Gradually, guest speakers were invited to contribute. They included J. G. Bennett (see below) and later Dom Sylvester Houédard.[78] Feild purchased and settled in the cottage at the entrance to the site, a convenient base from which to run the centre. In just over a year all properties were gradually renovated, and could ultimately provide accommodation for up to sixty people. A library and large study rooms were established in the main building. An onsite pottery and dairy were added, livestock were introduced, and an orchard, vegetable and landscaped gardens created.[79]

In May 1973, on a day chosen to coincide with Khidr's Day, Feild held a 'dedication ceremony'. With this in mind, he had had a wooden dome erected in the interior of the barn, which from the outset had been designated a meditation room. He had dubbed this dome the 'Mihrab'[80] and had had all visitors to the centre contribute to its construction, 'as a form of living meditation'. He invited to the ceremony 'representatives of the major religions'. He recalls that 'They all came – two rabbis, several Christian priests, Tibetan Buddhists, Druids, a Taoist or two'.[81] In all, over 200 people reportedly attended. A resident Zoroastrian[82] made a fire. From it, he lit a candle on an altar 'to symbolise the Light'. 'We had come together', Feild later wrote, 'to pray and turn towards the One Source'. At the end of the ceremony, those gathered 'were all holding hands and loving the Creator unconditionally'.[83] The 'Message of Dedication'[84] conveys something of the flavour of the occasion. Rauf's hand is clearly discernible behind some of its motifs, expressions and emphases, as will become clear later:

> The world is turning. A new generation is born! Once more man is turning towards his Source, and once more he stands on the threshold of the dawning of a new age. All over the world revolution – for revolution means turning – is in the hearts and minds of men and women who care as the narrow boundaries of form and bigotry are being broken down in our time. We are waking up to our destiny; to the mission that we have been given on this planet. The impossible dream is becoming a reality and we ourselves are the dream that, like a seed, has remained waiting, hidden in the hearts of men over hundreds of years, waiting to be watered, waiting to grow and flower. The dream becomes a reality when man turns once again and says 'I will!' to an unconditional life of service to God's Work on earth. Today we celebrate the coming to birth of this great dome, the symbol of the Heaven coming on earth, and of earth sacrificing itself for the world-to-come. In our work we are preparing now for the world-to-come, for the second cycle of mankind,[85] the Golden Age, about which men have dreamed for so long as they descended into the darkness. The Phoenix will rise again! Out of the ashes of the old world a spark has remained which will be kindled into a fire that nothing can stop. Our work here, now, and in the many places of the world where men and women stand firm in their yearning for the Absolute Truth, is the kindling of that spark. During these moments that we share together let us become conscious links with all men who wish to know the Truth so that they, too, may share in all that will become from the word 'Kun' – BE![86] The world is turning. A new generation is born.

Textual extracts tagged on to this message were read out during the ceremony. These represented a dizzying synthesis of religious scriptures with New Age authorities and heroes of the counterculture. They encompassed (in order) a text from the *Baghavad Gita*, a saying attributed to Lord Buddha, a Zoroastrian reading, and extracts from the *Jewish Prayer Book*, the Gospel according to John, and the Qur'an. An account relating to Uways al-Qarani[87] was followed by readings from Rumi and the Acts of St John (from the Apocryphal New Testament). Finally, there were quotations from Alice Bailey's *Esoteric Psychology*,[88] Ibn 'Arabi's *al-Futuhat al-Makkiyya*, Huey Newton,[89] Sri Aurobindo,[90] Thomas Traherne,[91] Rumi again, Martin Luther King, Rabi'a al-'Adawiyya,[92] Rabindranath Tagore,[93] 'Abd al-Qadir al-Jilani[94] and, finally, Bulent Rauf.[95]

The ceremony showcased the perennialist character of the Swyre Farm project at this time, through its assumption of the common core of the religions and their joint participation. It was indeed evocative of the Sufi Order's 'Universal Worship', established by Inayat Khan.[96] The absence of specific reference to Inayat Khan during the ceremony and in the Message is perhaps not significant in itself. Taking into account the explicit reference to Rauf, however, it may have reflected changes behind the scenes at Swyre Farm. These had been afoot for a considerable time before the ceremony. They would ultimately lead to Feild's demise and a reorientation of the Swyre Farm project in such a way that a distinct movement would emerge from it.

Reorientations

If a guru is a natural force, perhaps the most sensible thing is to get out of his way?

Peter Washington, p. 358

Rauf's contribution to the initiative behind Swyre Farm, if any, is unclear. In all likelihood, it was mediated through his relationship with Feild.[97] Once the Beshara Trust was established, he neither became a Trustee of it nor had any 'official' role in the life of Swyre Farm. He was, indeed, in Turkey for long periods during Feild's spell as director, and remained in London when in England.[98] His influence was nonetheless evident at Swyre Farm through his relationship with Feild and other associates, who would visit him in Turkey. From the early days he had sent 'adequately prepared' individuals to Feild at Swyre Farm, and they had naturally maintained direct contact with him without any apparent tension.[99] The stage was set for things to become complicated only when Feild, following one of his visits to Rauf in Turkey, announced that he had accepted Rauf as his teacher (in Dewey's words, 'in the sense of a sufi shaykh'). While it is not possible to date it, this development sowed the seeds of various problems and triggered a series of changes.

As we have intimated, Rauf's reluctance to assume the role of Feild's teacher had been evident from the beginning of their relationship. Dewey recalls that Rauf never agreed to this, and instead reminded Feild that his teacher was Vilayat Khan. Unperturbed, Feild told the Swyre Farm community that it must now listen to Rauf's teachings (which he would convey on Rauf's behalf), and added that the centre's programme would henceforth be based on these. When Rauf returned to London, Feild arranged for the Trustees to meet him formally. Dewey relates that Feild eventually persuaded them and most people involved with the centre to accept Rauf as its primary guide.

Feild had either forgotten or chosen to overlook the fact that Swyre Farm had been purchased and set up as a Sufi Order centre. Dewey, who had led the fundraising effort to that end, found himself, for one, in an awkward position as a result of this reorientation. Although Vilayat Khan never visited Swyre Farm, he was reportedly in no doubt that it was dedicated to the work of the Sufi Order, and formed an integral part of the organisation. As one associate puts it, 'he felt he owned both Feild and the Beshara centre'.[100] Feild's proclamation of his close relationship with Rauf now worsened an already strained relationship with Vilayat Khan.[101]

Having adopted Rauf as his primary reference, Feild at the same time failed to disassociate himself from Vilayat Khan. The centre's identity and focus became subject to some confusion in what unfolded, as Feild continued to 'ride on two horses', in the words of one associate. The experience of an associate who had attended Feild's London meetings and arrived at Swyre Farm during 1972 is illustrative. During his first spell there he found that he disliked many of 'the Sufi Order activities', and went open with his opinions. Dewey called him in for an interview and eventually asked him to leave. When he wanted to return shortly thereafter he contacted Feild, who allowed him back. Soon after he arrived, Feild put his hand on his head and uttered something. He had thereby 'initiated him into the Sufi Order'. At the same time, he told the new initiate that he must meet Rauf.

Feild eventually alienated Vilayat Khan, and problems also surfaced in his relationship with Rauf. An associate who was visiting Rauf in Istanbul in the summer of 1972 recalls telegrams passing between the two men which revealed that things were not well. When Feild came to Istanbul, the tension between the two was palpable.[102] Gradually, it became clear that Rauf did not sanction Feild's approach to spiritual training at Swyre Farm. Feild found himself in a difficult situation, for the very person whose influence he had brought to bear at Swyre Farm could no longer provide him with the endorsement his role there demanded. Rauf had become increasingly important for the Swyre Farm community as its members were exposed to his proposals. As the appeal of Rauf's approach grew, Feild's credibility began to suffer.

How did this process unfold? Initially, Rauf would suggest changes to Feild, perhaps in relation to the schedule or spiritual practices in place at the centre, and Feild would implement these.[103] No problems appear to have arisen out of this arrangement (aside, perhaps, from the confusion we have just described). However, a specific instruction from Rauf in late 1972 was to have significant consequences. Rauf asked Feild to introduce formal study of a summary of the metaphysical teaching of Ibn 'Arabi he had prepared, which became known as *The Twenty-nine Pages*.[104] Feild instituted hour-long study sessions for reading and discussing this text on two mornings a week. While he was reportedly unenthusiastic, the community took well to the new activity. Once study of this text became central to the Swyre Farm project (reflecting Rauf's wish), Feild's days there were 'effectively numbered', as one associate puts it.

Later loyalties invariably colour associates' projections of this time retrospectively. Many depict the ensuing events in terms of a clash between two conflicting approaches to the enterprise of spiritual education and training at Swyre Farm. Under Feild, they suggest, participants 'were not given time to settle'. He would present them with whatever idea he had just encountered, perhaps at a conference, which might have brought him a mystical or ecstatic experience. He would instruct them to 'work' on this for a month or so. Without warning, he would then move them on to something new, leaving them somewhat breathless. One associate tellingly describes the Swyre Farm experience under Feild as 'rushing headlong towards the Absolute'. While there was 'real energy' under his direction, there was an utter lack of focus. The emphasis was squarely on ephemeral feelings, rather then building a genuine understanding. In a sense, everything revolved around Feild person-ally. The situation was carried by his charisma and compelling charm,[105] and he seems to have revelled in his status as director. At the same time, his perception of spiritual education possibly reflected his earlier fascination with 'dervishes'. For him, one associate suggests, the entire project was about 'being a sufi shaykh'.[106]

Rauf's proposals for Swyre Farm targeted these very areas, for they were characterised by a depersonalised approach (allowing no place for the cult of the teacher),[107] and sought to instate disciplined study focusing on a specific text and metaphysical system. The experience of organised study proved overwhelmingly positive for most of the community, but associates recall Rauf's repeated complaint that Feild himself 'just would not study enough'. Even though it was perhaps implemented half-heartedly by Feild, Rauf's approach to spiritual education gradually gained sway, and its contrast with his own approach became increasingly stark. A degree of turmoil followed. At some point, a small number of associates communicated to Rauf that they no longer felt able to accept Feild's authority.

Field's problems did not stop there, however, for Rauf was also concerned about aspects of his personal conduct, which worried the Trustees. Matters came to a head in May 1973 (the month of the dedication), and Rauf urged Dewey as Chairman of the Board of Trustees to bring Feild into line by issuing him with an ultimatum regarding his conduct. As this did not yield the desired results, Dewey reports, the following month Feild was asked to leave. In contrast with this 'eviction' narrative, at least one associate suggests that Feild in fact 'resigned' as a direct result of the reorientation we have just described. ('I cannot go on', he reportedly confided, 'I no longer believe what I am telling these young people.') Feild himself has claimed that he left with Rauf's blessing, based on a 'farewell letter' from the latter suggesting that he move on, and continue his spiritual work in Vancouver.[108] 'Beshara would have to be passed on to others', he wrote some years later. He went, though reluctant to leave the place he loved, for 'Bulent needed someone to pass on the teachings'.[109] Some associates felt they had to choose between accompa-nying Feild and staying on. Of those who left with him, some soon returned to a changing Swyre Farm.

Retrospectively, associates emphasise the catalytic, rather than funda-mental, nature of Feild's contribution. Indeed it was only in the aftermath of his departure from Swyre Farm that the stage was set for the emergence of the Beshara movement.

Emergence, consolidation and expansion of the Beshara movement

With Feild gone, a struggle broke out among the Trustees. This has been characterised by one associate as 'a tussle between two visions of Swyre Farm'. Ibn 'Arabi's teaching, which Rauf had emphasised, had struck a chord with much of the Swyre Farm community, and this prompted a 'popular' move, apparently endorsed by Rauf, to establish it as the focus of spiritual education. In response, the founding Trustees upheld the original concept behind the centre's establishment, and insisted that all mystical teachings should find an equal place there. They stood for perpetuation of the status quo, and projected Swyre Farm as 'an open centre' with an eclectic programme, where residents could 'choose their own way (Christian, sufi, Jewish, etc.)'. Unanimously, they rejected its proposed transformation into what they perceived as 'an Ibn 'Arabi centre'.[110]

The balance was set to change, however, as new Trustees committed to Rauf's perspective were co-opted, with his active encouragement. These were apparently from among students he had acquired independently. Having persuaded some of the founding Trustees of their case, they led a move to outvote the 'opposition'. The ensuing struggle was bitter. Those who resisted the proposed change sought legal advice to ascertain whether the Trust could sustain such a substantial reorientation given that, as a registered charity, its parameters were defined by constitution. Eventually, Dewey and three other founding Trustees threw in the towel and resigned, leaving their like-minded colleagues in the minority. They were then outvoted. A reconstituted Board committed to Rauf's proposals for Beshara was eventually in place under a new Chairman. Rauf's contribution to the Swyre Farm project was acknowledged and his future role secured through his formal designation as Consultant to the Trust.

Meanwhile changes were being made at Swyre Farm. A new director had been appointed to replace Field,[111] and residents were assigned specific responsibilities to ensure the centre's smooth running. The programme was gradually reordered to accommodate the prioritisation of formal study. While meditation, *dhikr* and work continued as before, two and sometimes three daily study sessions of an hour and a half each were introduced. In addition to *The Twenty-nine Pages*, from September 1973 the community also studied a selection of poems by Rumi.[112] Added to this were short essays by Rauf, setting out defining aspects of his spiritual vision.[113] Photocopied excerpts of Culme-Seymour's English translation-in-progress of a French rendering of Ibn 'Arabi's *Fusus al-hikam* were introduced as these became available, from late 1973 or early 1974.

During this time, a closer relationship developed with J. G. Bennett (d.1974), a teacher of the ideas of G. I. Gurdjieff[114] and P. D. Ouspensky[115] for 'the transformation of man'. Bennett had set up his short-lived International Academy for Continuous Education at neighbouring Sherborne House in

Gloucestershire during 1970–71.[116] He had visited Swyre Farm before, but this interaction became more frequent following Feild's departure.[117] An associate characterises Bennett's perception of Beshara in the preface to a collection of talks Bennett delivered at Swyre Farm between 1972 and 1974, which were later published under Beshara's auspices.[118] He reportedly considered it providential that the centre was only a few miles from his Academy: he saw its work as complementary to his own, and was willing to help in its development. This associate suggests that the two projects shared an understanding both of the changes required by the times, and of how these should be implemented. They agreed it was imperative to establish 'small self-sufficient centres'. These should be places to which people could come 'not to join a sect or to listen to any particular guru or teacher, but where the motivation should be for each person to pursue their personal development and find what the responsibility of being human entails.'[119]

An outside visitor described the atmosphere at Swyre Farm at this time as 'very relaxed', and noted an effort to maintain 'an open, un-dogmatic environment.'[120] Reflecting this relaxed ethos, residents drifted in and out at will, and were not required to complete specific periods of residence or, by extension, study. Before long, it became evident that a clear and sustained spiritual education could not be achieved under such free circumstances.[121] The idea gradually emerged that only a dedicated school could provide an effective framework for such an education, and Rauf endorsed this. It should offer formal courses of specific length based on a clear curriculum of study, requiring a serious and sustained commitment on the part of potential students.

In late 1973, the proposal to establish such a school sparked an initiative to locate a suitable venue for it. When Chisholme House near the small town of Hawick in the Scottish Borders was discovered,[122] the Trust set about purchasing it. The imposing house on this large estate (112 acres, encompassing several other properties) had been without a resident owner since 1950. It was in 'an advanced state of dereliction.'[123] The purchase promised to be a lengthy process, given the legal complexities arising out of multiple ownership of the land. Some associates took up residence in the house to stake the Trust's claim to it. A mortgage was raised and 100 acres of the estate were sold to provide repair funds.[124] Many associates and aspiring students came to help.

This major development would eventually put in place the defining institution of Beshara in the form of its first (and, as time would tell, only enduring) school, dedicated to what Rauf termed 'intensive esoteric education.'[125] Its importance must be underlined, for this institution provided the organisational focus, coherence and continuity necessary for the emergence of a distinct Beshara movement. This would share with the Swyre Farm project its perennialist orientation, but would be set apart from it (and from other movements employing sufi resources) in the centrality it afforded to disciplined, intensive study (particularly of Ibn 'Arabi), and to organised, sustained spiritual practice.

There was evidence of considerable momentum and expansion on other fronts, too, at this time. By the mid-1970s, for example, members of the Swyre Farm community had established Beshara centres in several English towns and cities.[126] A particularly important centre was also set up in busy central London, in a property that the Trust rented for this purpose. Many of these centres were little more than study groups, but the more substantial ones offered 'a wide range of activities, including study, discussion, *zikr*, meditation, and even yoga and pottery classes, acupuncture and theatre workshops'. Visitors were welcomed and invited to participate in study sessions and *dhikr*.[127] The reach of activities began to extend beyond Britain, with the establishment of centres by ex-Swyre Farmers or new associates in France, the Netherlands, Canada, the USA and Australia.[128]

Gradually, structured courses were put in place. The first were held in Wales during late 1974, for ten days each. Building on the cycle of activities already tested at Swyre Farm, they encompassed meditation, *dhikr* and study, specifically of *The Twenty-nine Pages* and poetry by Rumi. In Turkey at the time, Rauf sent a letter detailing the course schedule and allocating slots for specific activities. He had meanwhile been engaged in clarifying the ethos of the school at Chisholme, and designing a detailed programme for residential courses there that would be much longer. The first was held over six months from autumn 1975 to spring 1976. Thirty-six students attended. The house itself was not ready and they had to make do with difficult circumstances in the harsh Scottish winter ('frontier conditions', as one of them puts it). They were accommodated in the steading, where the renovation was most advanced, and course activities were held in renovated parts of the house. There may have been an initial aspiration towards self-sufficiency at this time, but practical necessities appear to have dictated otherwise.[129]

During this first long residential course it became clear that it would be impractical to convene the next one, in which there was already substantial interest, at Chisholme. The Trust found a solution by acquiring Sherborne House in Gloucestershire, previously home to Bennett's Academy.[130] This became the venue for four successive long residential courses, the first of six months' duration and the next three each of eight months. The first (from autumn 1976 to spring 1977) attracted fifty-six students. In 1978 a second long course was introduced at Chisholme. Designed for students who had completed the first one, it was designated the 'further intensive course', and Rauf handpicked those who attended it. In subsequent years this course (which we refer to hereafter as the further course) was run parallel with the other long courses, convened from October to April.

Eventually, all long courses became confined to Chisholme. The first course reverted to six months' duration and was henceforth designated the 'six-month intensive course' (we refer to it hereafter as the intensive course). 'Beshara Sherborne' served as a preparatory channel for the Chisholme intake, and specialised in introductory ten-day and weekend residential courses. In 1986, an annual cycle of nine-day introductory courses was also launched at Chisholme. Soon after, a month-long reading retreat and a cycle of reading weeks devoted to the *Fusus al-hikam* were also in place. During the late 1980s, ten-day and weekend introductory courses and introductory study groups were also introduced at Frilford Grange in Oxfordshire, a property that had just been purchased.

As the magnitude of the Chisholme project became clear, Rauf emphasised the need for a body distinct from the Trust to assume responsibility for its administration. His initiative issued in creation of the Chisholme Institute (Ltd) in 1978. This is an educational charitable foundation, more precisely in Scottish law 'a company limited by guarantee with charitable status'. It operates through a board of directors.[131] Its remit is to shoulder responsibility for overseeing infrastructure provision at Chisholme, encompassing legal and financial aspects, buildings and core infrastructure systems.

A series of changes took place in relation to Trust properties during the 1980s. Swyre Farm had been sold, possibly in 1978.[132] The sale aimed to release funds to cover debts arising from the Sherborne House mortgage, renovation at Chisholme and the costs of residential courses (a fee was stipulated for these, but some students had been unable to meet it). At this point (or possibly earlier), the founding Beshara Trustees were repaid the sums they had invested. Sherborne House was also sold in 1981, but the Trust took out a lease on part of the converted stable block until 1988. As its expiry approached, the idea of establishing a permanent centre in the south of England was floated. This would be achieved through group purchase of a large property, which would be developed into private homes.[133] The scheme failed to materialise, however. Activities at the Sherborne centre and later Frilford Grange, which was also sold, were eventually relocated to Chisholme or terminated. In addition to its role as a 'prep school', Sherborne served as a venue for weekly open days and provided a base (along with Frilford Grange) for the Trust's publication company, Beshara Publications.[134] In autumn 1987, Canonach Farm, located near the town of Yackandandah in Victoria (Australia), was purchased by 'Beshara Australia Inc.', a registered body with charitable status. The opening there of a school aspiring to run ten-day, weekend and ultimately long residential courses was announced in 1989.[135]

From 1985, Rauf began to speak of a 'new phase of expansiveness' in Beshara. During 1987 the Trust announced an important development in its conception of the unfolding of the Beshara project as a whole. Hitherto, Beshara had 'necessarily concentrated on the educational aspects of its work'. Yet, 'the need for expression in this world' had naturally led to its extension 'into areas of today's incentive'. This announcement provided post-facto justification and a rationale for a growing diversification of activities beyond the sphere of individual spiritual education, as the true scope of Beshara's concerns became clear. The Trust now explicitly acknowledged both the magnitude of work entailed by the objectives of Beshara, and the urgency surrounding the need for those objectives to gain 'full expression'.[136] Several new activities appeared, mainly during 1987, which reflected this fresh grasp of what was required of Beshara,[137] and the natural evolution 'from the understanding of a principle to its expression'.[138]

The launch of *Beshara Magazine* (in spring 1987) was one such initiative.[139] Its purpose was to serve as a forum where current ideas could be explored 'from a perspective based on unity'. The claim was made in editorials that in recent years this perspective (which had permeated 'traditional views of reality') had begun to emerge 'in a new way' in Western thought.[140] The magazine brought together articles, book reviews and interviews that addressed contemporary unifying perspectives and integrative trends in the sciences, ecology and conservation, the arts and architecture, economics and economic/development theory, in issues relating to globalisation and international organisations, and in the spiritual traditions.

Special coverage was given in the magazine to a new series of seminars convened at Sherborne (and Frilford Grange) at this time. Delivered by eminent speakers, these were designed to stimulate 'a genuine exploration ... of the meaning of Unity in expression'. They would serve as a forum in which Beshara could engage in dialogue with other approaches and various disciplines, and would ultimately facilitate the emergence of 'a unifying and universal vision'.[141] Reflecting a conviction that 'science and finance' were foremost among contemporary 'areas of incentive', scientists and economists featured prominently among speakers. The Trust indeed emphasised these areas as the context of significant changes. Enabling the development of 'a balance and a new understanding of reality', they could provide 'a secure foundation for future expansion'.[142]

The Trust also moved to modify its constitution. In projecting its aim, this now emphasised the broader context:

> the advancement of education in the consideration of the basic unity of all religions, in particular by the provision of courses to provide an understanding of the relationship of man to the universes, the earth, the environment and the society he lives in, to Reality and to God.[143]

Schematisation of activities proceeding under the Trust's auspices was attempted in order to clarify the interrelatedness of its expanding concerns.[144] Major areas were identified and some new strategies announced in relation to them. These areas focused on education,[145] expansion,[146] science,[147] finance[148] and communications. Regarding communications, steps were taken to 'prepare the ground for a large-scale communications exercise involving the press, television and radio'. This was in response to the need for Beshara to 'go out and express and show itself'. The Trust also expressed an intention to train a small number of associates to communicate effectively through the media.

Parallel with these developments, a new one-off course was announced at Chisholme, scheduled from April to September 1987. This adopted the theme of 'reaffirmation' as its focus,[149] and was aimed at associates who had completed both long courses. They were invited to 'join a converse' to reaffirm their intention, resolve and motivation, and to re-establish their potential. An associate who had been designated Director of Courses, then Principal, at Chisholme, projected the course as a direct response to the changes that marked the new phase in Beshara's work:

> Beshara is reaching towards a far greater number of people. Those of us who are its potential representatives must also evolve similarly. There must be a body of people ready, highly tuned, and capable of coping with a surge of interest resulting from these initiatives, or talking to the media, supervising and correlating courses and fulfilling a host of other needs.[150]

It is possible that such expectations concerning the 'new phase' in Beshara reflected the growing vitality, consolidation and expansion of the NAM during the 1980s, and the new opportunities this brought for greater levels of networking and collaboration. *Beshara Magazine* and the Sherborne–Frilford seminar series indeed provided a forum for prominent New Age figures and trends in various fields of thought. Further evidence for such a possibility arises in the fact that, twice during the decade, Beshara sent representatives to the Mind-Body-Spirit Festival in London, a major New Age forum. (Its booth in fact inspired very little interest among the large attendance on either occasion, especially as it was competing with more flamboyant outfits.) There was continuing success internationally at this time. In addition to Australia and the USA, by the second half of the 1980s, study circles were being held regularly in the Netherlands and Israel, for example. Reflecting this overseas expansion and the growing international interest in courses, in 1988 the Trust co-opted new Trustees for Australia and the USA.[151]

The initiatives we have just described were introduced only a few months before Rauf's death on 5 September 1987.[152] This came at a critical point in the expansion of Beshara, marked by anticipation of growing opportunities to deliver its message globally. The Chairman of the Trust addressed the challenges posed by this loss in a speech marking the fortieth day after Rauf's death.[153] He emphasised the importance of cohesion, focus and commitment for associates and the movement as a whole:[154]

> When a great leader dies, the inspiration often dies with him and what he started collapses. In the case of Beshara this is a possibility, but one which can be avoided ... Let us not for a moment be under the illusion that Beshara was Bulent's.[155] The establishment of Beshara was Bulent's life work. All that went before in his life he saw as being to this end – to provide the framework for the complete development of the potential in each human being. Those who worked closely with him will bear witness to the fact that never once did he ever take credit for anything connected with Beshara ... it would be foolish to consider that all that has happened is the product of one person's will and vision ... Beshara belongs now and always to that within each person which loves to be known. The great quality which enabled Bulent to do so much was his love ... it is our obligation that this love be nurtured, for it is both the cause and the effect of Beshara. That which we received we must now ... give back, if we want others to benefit. There is here an immense body of

knowledge, and the vehicle which conveys that knowledge is love. We must be sure to safeguard the aim of Beshara, which begins with Union ... This safeguarding is not by any means the sole responsibility of the Trustees ... Each person who has completed the course is a trustee of what they know, and should treat that knowledge with great respect. In the past it was invariably Bulent who had to coax us back from ... diversions ... to that one point of spiritual reality. We can no longer indulge in such distractions. Each person's responsibility within Beshara has changed, and there must be no vacuum. There will not be another Bulent, and the load he carried must be shared by many, each according to their measure. One of the great strengths of Beshara is the people who are involved, and that strength is all the greater collectively. If one person decides that he or she now wishes to go their own way, we are all the poorer for it, and they will have missed the point of Bulent's time with us if they think anything has changed now he has gone. There is an immense work ahead of each one of us ... the only touchstone of success is if one person who was ignorant of himself comes to know himself ... There is so much growth, and a certain freedom is now necessary so that each place is established in accordance with its own requirements ...[156] There are bound to be problems ... it is by the art of persuasion that problems should be solved, not by an autocratic enforcement of the Trust's wishes.

A period of confusion naturally followed Rauf's death. Some associates reacted by withdrawing. Others stepped forward to assume responsibility. A stable group of staff became established at Chisholme to consolidate affairs there: its members were gradually refreshed from the mid-1990s. Difficulties notwithstanding, the continuing expansion of Beshara and the diversification of its activities to date testify to the movement's successful management of this transitional period.

The continued growth of the MIAS has been one of the most prominent of these activities. Originating from within Beshara, this academic society aims 'to promote a greater understanding of the work of Ibn 'Arabi and his followers'.[157] We introduce its activities and map its evolution here, but defer a detailed consideration of its orientation to a later discussion. The initiative to establish the MIAS emerged with two associates in 1976. The idea quickly met with Rauf's agreement, and the Society was formally launched with his support in 1977.[158] Rauf served as Honorary President until his death. Culme-Seymour was thereafter appointed Life President,[159] and then designated Honorary Life President some time after the mid-1990s.[160] The Society encourages translation of Ibn 'Arabi's works into Western languages with the aim of countering their linguistic inaccessibility. It also promotes publication of new Arabic editions of these, and seeks to stimulate the general expansion of Ibn 'Arabi studies. It enjoys an international presence, with branches in the UK (Oxford, where its headquarters and main office are located) and the USA (Berkeley, CA). For a few years, there were also branches in Turkey (Istanbul)[161] and Spain (Seville).[162] The Society is best known for its publication of a scholarly journal twice yearly (*Journal of the Muhyiddin Ibn 'Arabi Society: JMIAS*); it produces specific additional publications.[163] It convenes annual symposia in the UK[164] and USA (on the West Coast),[165] and administers a significant library collection in Oxford.[166] The Society also publishes articles and translations online on its website, and issues a regular *Newsletter*.[167] Society notices stress that it is 'not affiliated to any particular organisation or institution'. Its finances derive entirely from individual membership subscriptions.[168]

Most of the MIAS membership and the overwhelming part of regular attendance at its events were made up of associates during its first thirteen years. According to a founding officer, in 1990 a conscious attempt was made to achieve a broader and more varied membership and attendance, and to consolidate the Society as an open body promoting no particular perspective. From the outset the Society's officers have all been associates, and associates have taken responsibility for organising its symposia.[169] In contrast, the vast majority of Honorary Fellows have been external scholars, mainly in the field of Islamic mysticism.[170] Few professional scholars of Ibn 'Arabi familiar with the MIAS today choose to remain aloof from the sphere of activities it has carved out,[171] and senior scholars and students alike draw on its resources and contacts. While the Society originally grew out of Beshara, it is thus no longer convincing to conflate its membership and participant pool with those of Beshara. As many scholars of Ibn 'Arabi approach their subject from a position of personal sympathy and engagement, it is not difficult to understand the spirit of mutual acceptance and collaboration that obtains between them and associates who represent or are active in the Society.

Long-standing associates who have served as Society officers set up a small publishing company, Anqa Publishing, during the late 1990s. Dedicated to works associated with Ibn 'Arabi,[172] it has added to the Society's own publishing efforts.[173] A few associates have committed themselves to translating works of Ibn 'Arabi, and more to writing about his teaching. They typically publish in the *JMIAS* or with Anqa. Often, their efforts represent the culmination of years of private (and occasionally some formal) study. In general, commitment of time and resources among associates has been consistently high. In 2000, for example, the Society launched an initiative to catalogue and secure copies of all manuscripts associated with Ibn 'Arabi and his school held in Turkish libraries. This was undertaken on a voluntary basis over a period of years by officers who are long-standing associates, and funded entirely through Society member donations.[174]

Recent years have witnessed further expansion of activities led by Chisholme. Over and above its existing international connections, nine-day courses in Jakarta (Indonesia), held at the invitation of interested individuals there since 1999, have been construed as the beginning of a potentially global reach for Beshara's work. By 2004, discussions were indeed underway to establish 'Beshara Southeast Asia', centred on Jakarta.[175] The Principal spelled out his vision for overseas operations in June 2000. He commented that, while the School continues to be centred at Chisholme, where long courses are held, what is required is that it has an extension in each country which is able to offer Introductory and Intermediate Courses of two and nine days' duration. These courses will be run from each place and with people from the centre coming out periodically to assist in this work.[176]

We can glean an idea of the numbers involved in Beshara from the School's mailing lists. Up to late 2004, about 400 people had completed long courses (this figure encompasses those held both at Sherborne House and Chisholme). Current finances associated with Chisholme provide further evidence of numbers presently involved, and indicate the general consolidation of Beshara to date. For example, the mortgage has been vastly reduced (the property had been remortgaged at some point to release funds for repairs and other work), and as of 2006 only two years of the loan remained to be paid. The Chisholme Institute manages the School's finances. Household costs (oil, food, etc.) are met by the income from course fees and guests' donations,[177] held in a dedicated account. Costs associated with buildings, infrastructure provision and systems (and the mortgage) are met from a second account. Income for this is generated by monthly covenants (tax-free 'gift aid') taken out by associates in the UK,[178] depending on individual circumstances (typically excluding younger associates and students in higher education). At the end of 2004, just over 100 such covenants were in place. Based on internal estimates that about one-third of those who have completed long courses take out covenants, it seems that some 300 people in the UK are seriously committed to Beshara today.

The board of directors of the Chisholme Institute has UK-wide membership. It meets quarterly to address issues in legal and financial spheres, aiming to ensure that the School can operate without constraints or practical problems. Its current chairman recently relocated to Hawick to be close to Chisholme. During 2003, the board expanded to eleven members, in order to 'bring in the next generation' as one director puts it. Five new younger directors were co-opted, including one child of a first-generation associate. The matter of publicity, or, in one director's words, 'the issue of [the] announcement [of Beshara], of how this can be done with the right balance, and where'[179] was the main concern of the board during 2004.

Following a period of inactivity, the Trust began to reassess its role in 2004. To explain its inaction, the current chairman cites its long preoccupation with the problems that arose, shortly after Rauf's death, from an investment scheme that went wrong. In addition to the Trust, many associates had also invested in this through covenants. It appeared to be a success to begin with (the Trust had acquired Frilford Grange thanks to it), but the managing accountant proceeded to embezzle the funds. He was eventually brought to trial and handed a prison sentence, but funds could not be retrieved. Not finally closed until the mid-1990s, this episode had brought anxiety and distraction to all involved. Matters did not pick up for the Trust following its resolution, however, even though the board met regularly two or three times a year. There was a lack of clarity concerning its role and focus, and a tendency to confine attention to Chisholme as the primary point of reference. The chairman believes the Trust is now emerging from its 'quiet' phase. As the legal body constituted to be the 'foot of Beshara in the world', it appreciates the magnitude of its responsibility. This has been described as 'announcing the matter of Beshara' with a potentially global remit. Its six members (all of them long-standing associates) recognise that 'they must apply themselves to [this responsibility] carefully and assiduously'. They have resolved to meet more frequently, and look set to take the Trust into a more active role, perhaps creating broader publicity for Beshara through a newsletter or involvement in the website. The Chisholme Institute focuses on the School specifically, and the Trust's responsibility is conceived in broader terms as being 'for the name Beshara'. The two bodies thus represent complementary aspects of the single endeavour, and continue to work together.

Collective reflection on the position and future priorities of Beshara was organised in August 2003, when all associates were encouraged to meet at Chisholme House for two days' discussion. Pointing to the level of commitment within the community, some 200 attended. The event has become an annual one: in August 2004, it drew an international attendance of 170.[180] In the assessment of a Chisholme Institute director, Beshara can be confident of the future. 'We are currently in a period of stability and expansion, God willing', he suggests. Recent School figures do point to a sustained interest in courses from diverse quarters. From 1998 to 2003, for example, the School received some 550 enquiries about short courses alone. For the last few years, there have consistently been students in double figures on the intensive course, and half a dozen on the further one. Attendance has been drawn from around the world. For example, the intensive course that began in October 2002 brought together Australian, South African, Tanzanian and Israeli students. The one that began the following October was relatively small: there were only four students on this (and no simultaneous further course). In contrast, the October 2004 intake comprised ten on the intensive course (German, British, Irish, Spanish and Indonesian, their ages ranging from seventeen to sixty-eight), and nine on the further one (including Israeli, Belgian and British students). Most students have come to the School by word of mouth, but some do arrive 'cold', as a result of their having discovered the Beshara website. This pattern is consistent with the fact that the children of first-generation associates are noticeable among students.[181]

The evidence suggests that Beshara can indeed be confident of a highly committed community of associates. A sustained level of international interest in the School also promises to provide an ongoing pool of future associates. Some thirty-five years since Rauf's first encounter with counterculture spiritual seekers of sixties London, Beshara is established as a focused and motivated actor on the British and international spiritual landscapes, set apart by its distinctive approach to spiritual education.

Chapter 3

Spiritual education: texts and contexts

Esoteric education ... begins with the most simple yet fundamental questions that are asked by every child: 'Who am I?', 'Where did I come from?' ... In short, it is to do with the mystery of being alive ... It is fuelled by a certainty that there is a purpose in being here, and that the movement of mankind's spiritual evolution is intelligent and has an aim.

'What is Esoteric Education?', Beshara leaflet, April 2003

Education in Beshara is the awakening of the heart: through clarification and magnification, one sees clearly for oneself.

Beshara associate

There are two facets to the distinctive Beshara approach to spiritual education. These are a carefully constructed curriculum that privileges the thought of Ibn 'Arabi, and the use of a dedicated school. We begin our overview of these two areas by exploring Beshara study texts through three major examples. We then examine the School as an environment designed to facilitate spiritual education, reviewing the structure and activities of the courses offered there. Throughout, we combine a mapping of historical developments (such as the preparation of study texts and the evolution of course activities) with a consideration of contemporary emphases and practice.

In 1968, Idries Shah had advised aspiring students of sufism in the West to seek out 'authoritative ... materials and activities designed by Sufis to operate in the student's own culture, time and other circumstances'. He argued that 'the bulk of translations available are unsuitable', and attributed this to the fact that the originals 'were intended for specific communities and cultures'.[1] Tailored to the culture, time and circumstances of non-Muslim youth in sixties Britain, the materials and activities Bulent Rauf developed for Beshara formed a timely contribution to the developing spiritual scene.

Study texts in English

Recognising the importance of these for its work, Beshara has set great store by the production of study texts in English. Reflecting this, individuals involved have been careful to record (or at least keep in memory) the process by which key texts emerged.[2] This process is itself perceived as part of the unfolding of Beshara and, as such, reflects a guiding force. In this section we document this process for three major study texts. We briefly introduce the source texts and the study texts, describe internal perceptions of these, and indicate the use of the study texts in the movement.

An introduction to Ibn 'Arabi's metaphysics in *The Twenty-nine Pages*

The (then) manager of The Kinks, who we met earlier, recalls how the first Beshara study text materialised. Rauf had spoken to him about Ibn 'Arabi's teaching in the context of a relationship they had struck up independently of Feild. When he asked whether there were any English studies on the subject he could consult, he found Rauf was unable to help.[3] He took himself to Probsthains Booksellers, where he found a copy of A. E. Affifi's *The Mystical Philosophy of Muhyid Din-Ibnul 'Arabi*,[4] and S. A. Q. Husaini's *The Pantheistic Monism of Ibn al-'Arabi*.[5] Put off by the title of Husaini's work, he bought Affifi's. He gave this to Rauf, who asked if he might cross out parts that were incorrect. During their next meeting, over lunch, Rauf explained that he had decided to underline what was 'true' in it instead.[6] A few weeks later, he asked him to arrange for the edited highlights to be typed. The typing progressed slowly, but finally the work was ready for copying. It was not easy to find a photocopier in London at the time. When an office containing several was at last located, all the copiers there suddenly broke down at once. Rauf reportedly projected this episode as an indication of the spiritual importance of the task upon which they had embarked, which thus had met with 'obstructive' forces.[7] Eventually twenty copies were made of what was henceforth known as *The Twenty-nine Pages* (after the length of the original edited text).

Who was the author whose work formed the starting point for this first Beshara study text? A graduate in philosophy from the University of Alexandria (Egypt), Affifi proceeded to study for a PhD at Cambridge University. His supervisor was Reynold A. Nicholson (d.1945),[8] who had reportedly suggested his research subject to Affifi. The result was the 'first thesis devoted to Ibn 'Arabi's mystical system',[9] eventually published in 1939 as *The Mystical Philosophy of Muhyid Din-Ibnul 'Arabi*. This pioneering work, the first monograph on the subject to be published in English, presents a comprehensive summary of Ibn 'Arabi's thought.[10] It has been greatly influential among later scholars. From Cambridge, Affifi joined the Department of Philosophy at Alexandria University as a professor, where he trained a generation of scholars and continued to publish on Ibn 'Arabi and sufism.[11]

How did Affifi approach his subject? Reflecting his own training and interests, he effectively reduced Ibn 'Arabi's mysticism to a philosophical system. He projected Ibn 'Arabi first and foremost as a philosopher.[12] He was, moreover, a philosopher struggling to express his philosophical ideas successfully, and exposing himself to philosophical criticism because of the fundamental errors he committed in the process.[13] Equating his 'mystical philosophy' with pantheism (the view that God is identical with the material universe), Affifi credited Ibn 'Arabi with the founding of a 'new religion of Pantheistic Philosophy' in the Muslim world.[14] Based on this, he questioned Ibn 'Arabi's commitment to Islam, and implicitly situated him beyond its recognisable borders.[15] This approach informed an ultimately dismissive attitude on Affifi's part towards the traditional Islamic elements in Ibn 'Arabi's thought:[16]

Ibnul 'Arabi ... has a definite philosophical doctrine of pantheism ... There is also a formal dialectic which dominates the whole of his thought. So, in substance as well as form, Ibnul 'Arabi has the qualifications of the typical mystical *philosopher* ... He was certainly conscious of a complete pantheistic philosophy, but, lacking philosophical training, he did not know how to express it. He also may be said to be a consistent thinker, provided we do not attach too much importance to his *verbal* paradoxes and the way he often tries to reconcile Islamic dogmas with philosophical principles. There is no possible means of reconciling his philosophy with Islam. The orthodox garb with which he so persistently drapes his pantheistic ideas is a sham appearance purposely put there.[17] ... There are at least two possible ways of understanding him on any given point; the orthodox way and the pantheistic way, although in reality there is only one way in which he means to express himself, and this is the latter. Whenever Ibnul 'Arabi feels that he has aroused the suspicion of his reader about his orthodoxy, he tries to defend himself against an imaginary person who is challenging him, by giving his style such a turn as to appear orthodox.[18] ... He interprets the Qur'an in such a way as to fit in with his pantheistic doctrine even at the cost of violating its language and grammar ... Ibnul 'Arabi finds in the Qur'an whatever he wants, but he could have derived the same conclusions from any other text if he had adopted the same method of interpretation.[19] ... realising the glaring inconsistency between Orthodox Islam and his Pantheistic philosophy, he felt it his duty to explain away the former in order to save the latter.[20]

What was Rauf's perception of the work from which he extracted *The Twenty-nine Pages*? The (anonymous) Preface to the first published version of the latter[21] suggests that Affifi had done 'a great service' by 'providing the raw material' in *The Mystical Philosophy*. Though in some respects this work was 'not favourable to Ibn 'Arabi's point of view', the author had 'understood well enough what he was disagreeing with'.[22] We can conclude that Rauf considered Affifi's presentation of Ibn 'Arabi's thought reliably accurate, even if he felt him to be mistaken in his interpretation of this.[23] A comparison of *The Twenty-nine Pages* and *The Mystical Philosophy* indicates that Rauf edited out of the latter anything that might obscure his own projection of Ibn 'Arabi and his teaching. This included first and foremost Affifi's insistence that Ibn 'Arabi was a philosopher[24] and his conflation of Ibn 'Arabi's doctrine with pantheism.[25] (In the latter regard it is significant that, in contrast, *The Twenty-nine Pages* eschews the application of any overarching, pre-defining label to describe this doctrine.)[26] We defer to a later discussion a consideration of Rauf's implicit stance concerning Affifi's projection of Ibn 'Arabi's relation to Islam.

The Twenty-nine Pages encompasses material from throughout *The Mystical Philosophy*, but focuses selectively on certain subsections.[27] It omits the source text Appendix, and all annotations and references. Where an argument by Affifi adduces direct quotations from (or a précis of) Ibn 'Arabi's writings, this is dismantled in *The Twenty-nine Pages* and the quotations/précis are run together as a continuous narrative. Compared with Affifi's scholarly approach, the style of presentation has been simplified in Rauf's text.

Brief interpolations have been added for clarity of meaning.[28] The difficult paragraphs with which Affifi opens his work have been replaced by a simple introduction, thus: 'Ibn 'Arabi's premise is the bird's-eye view – looking down upon a pyramid from above its apex, rather than viewing the pyramid from its base and looking up towards its apex. The apex of Ibn 'Arabi's thought is the point which is the "Absolute Being".'[29] Finally, selected statements are given prominence, indicating where the reader's attention should dwell.[30]

Rauf's intention in *The Twenty-nine Pages* was to provide 'a complete introductory guide to the language and thought of Ibn 'Arabi, particularly those aspects of his doctrine which refer to the Unity of Being and the Perfectibility of Man'.[31] Beshara claims the text as 'perhaps the most lucid and thorough introduction to Ibn 'Arabi's metaphysics of perfection'.[32] Nonetheless, it appears dense and challenging, at least for readers unfamiliar with philosophy, metaphysics and the Islamic tradition (this is over and above the inherent complexity of some of Ibn 'Arabi's ideas). Affifi's explanatory comparisons with Spinoza, Plotinus and Philo of Alexandria have been retained.[33] Several sufi figures are mentioned,[34] but there are few introductions to them. There are references without elaboration to the Islamic philosopher Ibn Rushd and the Mu'tazili and Ash'ari theological schools. An index lists over 100 Arabic terms, many of them specialist and technical. A quotation from Rauf on the opening page explains the importance of grasping this terminology to spiritual education as conceived in Beshara: 'For the study and an understanding of esoteric knowledge as expressed most completely by Ibn 'Arabi, it is necessary to become acquainted with some of the terminology which he uses in his exposition of the way of the mystic in his esoteric advance.'

As its Preface indicates, *The Twenty-nine Pages* is always studied in groups at the School. In these it forms 'the focus for intensive discussion', and acts 'as a mirror for the students' questions concerning their relationship with Reality'.[35] The group setting undoubtedly provides an opportunity for the helpful exchange of knowledge and understanding. Given their backgrounds, it is perhaps unsurprising that some associates underline the difficulties of understanding they encountered when they first studied *The Twenty-nine Pages* at Swyre Farm, towards the end of 1972.[36] During the last three decades an increased ease has reportedly emerged in this regard among students new to the text. As we will discuss later, this greater facility is attributed to the general growth of receptivity for Truth.

Ibn 'Arabi's *Fusus al-hikam*

Of Ibn 'Arabi's vast corpus, the *Fusus al-hikam* is the central study text in Beshara. As an associate puts it, in Beshara Ibn 'Arabi's thought is taught 'with a focus primarily on the *Fusus*'. Through Rauf's initiative, Beshara Publications published the first English translation of the text during the early 1970s. Later, Rauf translated a major commentary on it, which was published by the MIAS. Before exploring the processes by which these texts materialised, we must briefly introduce the *Fusus* itself.

The *Fusus* is widely regarded as Ibn 'Arabi's *chef d'oeuvre*. It provides a résumé of his main ideas.[37] Ibn 'Arabi claimed that he had received it in a vision directly from the Prophet, accompanied by the instruction to reveal it to people, who would benefit by it. This set the text apart from his other works.[38] Its main theme can be characterised as the stations of human perfection, described in terms of particular prophets and specific Divine Attributes.[39] The title of each of its twenty-seven chapters relates to a particular prophet, and Ibn 'Arabi presents aspects of the Divine Wisdom within the context of their lives and persons. Each of these prophets thus becomes 'the human setting in which the gemstone of each kind of wisdom is set, thus making of each prophet the signet or sign, by selection, of a particular aspect of God's wisdom.'[40] Some have suggested that the work is predominantly one of mystical Qur'anic exegesis, for Ibn 'Arabi draws heavily on Qur'anic material to illustrate his main points.[41]

In the *Fusus* Ibn 'Arabi sometimes expresses his ideas in ways unacceptable to the guardians of orthodoxy. Moreover, the implications of some aspects of his teaching elaborated in the work are in danger of leading the (common) reader, as one of his translators puts it, 'far beyond the familiar borders of traditional Islam.'[42] As a result, it is open to potential misinterpretation and misunderstanding. Reflecting this, the work has had a major impact historically in fuelling critical perceptions of its author.[43] Yet at the same time it became the text of choice for study within the school of Ibn 'Arabi, and his other works (the *Futuhat al-Makkiyya*, for example) were recruited to illuminate difficult passages in it. The *Fusus* has indeed been the subject of more commentaries than any other of Ibn 'Arabi's works.[44] The help of these commentaries (or of a teacher conversant with them) soon became indispensable to study of the text.[45]

The Wisdom of the Prophets: translated selections from the Fusus

Preparation of the second major Beshara study text began during a stay in Turkey in spring 1973, when Rauf asked Culme-Seymour to translate into English *La Sagesse des prophètes*, Titus Burckhardt's French translation of selected chapters from the *Fusus*.[46] She had only recently encountered Burckhardt's work, and had indeed just been introduced to Ibn 'Arabi through Rauf.[47] She read a copy of *La Sagesse des prophètes* belonging to Rauf's brother 'two or perhaps three' times during that stay in Turkey, initially without understanding all of it. Shortly after, she acquired her own copy in Paris ('the last one in the shop'), and set about working.[48] Feeling she had had no real choice in the matter, Culme-Seymour explained why she considered it important in the following terms:

> The influence of Muhyi-d-din Ibn 'Arabi was and is immense. This, in addition to the beauty, the knowledge imparted, and the unique quality of his writings are

the reasons why I feel, with the growing interest in the west in mysticism and Sufi doctrines, that his work should be more widely and readily available in English.[49]

When it appeared in autumn 1975, *The Wisdom of the Prophets* (referred to within Beshara as the *Blue Fusus*)[50] was the first English translation of the text to be published.[51]

Burckhardt's work encompasses a brief introduction,[52] translations of nine complete chapters from the *Fusus*, and extracts from three others. He had focused on chapters he deemed most important based on their doctrinal content. Chapters and part-chapters with a more specific content, or which contained exegesis he considered too difficult to render into a European language (given its organic connection to the Arabic original) were omitted.[53] Burckhardt drew on commentaries in preparing his translation,[54] but had chosen not to translate these given their perceived unsuitability for the European reader. Nonetheless, he 'completed the translation by some notes and sometimes interpolations – given in brackets – where it has seemed ... indispensable', for he appreciated that 'all modern translation from an Arabic text written in an elliptical language of the XII century necessitates a certain amount of exigent [sic] work.'[55]

The concentrated and condensed style of the *Fusus* undoubtedly makes it, in the words of another of its translators, 'a peculiarly difficult work to translate ... in a way which makes some sort of sense to the non-Arabic speaking and non-Muslim reader'.[56] To achieve such sense, a detailed commentary would appear to be necessary.[57] *The Wisdom of the Prophets* offers Burckhardt's exegetical additions as an aid to understanding, based on the commentaries he used and his own grasp of the text. There have invariably been further exegetical interventions, however, if only implicitly, through language selection in the course of Culme-Seymour's rendering of Burckhardt's work from French into English.[58] According to a review from 1988, the result is a work that is 'often a bit ponderous for the reader who lacks a solid background in Western philosophy'.[59] An earlier critic attacked its incompleteness, the fact that it is 'distorted by the use of the masonic vocabulary', and for its having 'added parts of al-Qashani's commentary as if it were part of the original text.'[60]

First introduced at Swyre Farm as photocopied extracts from Culme-Seymour's work in progress, *The Wisdom of the Prophets* has since become indispensable to the programme of study in Beshara, and has not been supplanted by other, more recent translations of the *Fusus*. On long courses it is always studied after *The Twenty-nine Pages*. Such study has gradually become integrated with that of parts of a third major study text, a translated commentary on the *Fusus*.

Abdullah Bosnevi's Commentary on the Fusus
Rauf first came upon a copy of this Ottoman Turkish commentary on the *Fusus* (which encompasses an Ottoman Turkish translation of the *Fusus* text)

in 1974, in a shop in an Istanbul book bazaar he frequented.[61] Associates suggest he had thus been 'led to' this particular one among the many commentaries on the *Fusus*. Appreciating the importance of the work he had found, Rauf devoted the summer months, spent in Turkey, to translating parts of it into English. He began with selected passages, then set about translating from the commentary the fifteen chapters of the *Fusus* excluded by Burckhardt and thus missing from *The Wisdom of the Prophets*. The aim was to make these available for study. First, he produced a synopsis of Bosnevi's long introduction to his commentary, together with a translation of the commentary on chapters on Jacob, Hud, David, John (Yahya), Zakariah and Elijah (Elias).[62] Put together in a booklet, these were introduced to the six-month intensive course curriculum (1975–76). Translations of more chapters followed in three further booklets.[63] These were integrated into study at the School as soon as they were available.

Rauf indicates that an associate (the very one who had facilitated preparation of *The Twenty-nine Pages*) later approached him and asked him to prepare the entire work in English translation, with a view to publishing it. He offered to take responsibility for funding the publication himself,[64] and suggested that Rauf aim to complete the task in three years. Rauf acquiesced without knowing the reason for his acceptance or 'His reason' behind all this.[65] This commissioning and Rauf's agreement to it took place in 1980.[66] It resulted in a twofold task. First, Rauf had to prepare the existing translations for publication. He had edited these to varying degrees in the booklets developed for study use, and their revision was necessary. The text of the *Fusus* had to be distinguished from the commentary text, and explanatory notes he had added removed.[67] Second, Rauf had to translate *ab initio* Bosnevi's commentary on the twelve chapters encompassed in *The Wisdom of the Prophets*, which he had not yet addressed at all.

Although he appreciated the benefit for all concerned in making this commentary available in English, Rauf was aware of the enormity of the task he had undertaken. In the Foreword to the first volume of the published work he wrote that he was 'one of the most ignorant' of God's servants, and certainly 'the most inept to translate anything of wisdom, gnosis, or meaning, leave alone from two languages into a third.' 'Why such a person was chosen to undertake such a task is His mystery', he reflected. Only God knew the reason for this, and it would not be good form for him to query it. In retrospect, he insisted that the task had been made possible for him only because 'the Mercy and Compassion of God' had descended within him to accomplish it. The undertaking of the task had itself taught him all that was necessary for its own accomplishment. Thus, 'where it is He who is the Helper, anything, but anything is possible.'[68]

He had approached the task with great rigour, countenancing no interruptions and carrying out the work scrupulously. Associates who had assisted him recall how the work had induced a 'change of level' in him. He acted, they suggest, in accordance with the dictates of complete servanthood, which requires full surrender to the task in hand, 'without questioning or attempting to rearrange things at that level.' On completing a day's work he would spend some silent time in mundane activity, perhaps preparing food, assuming a different mode of operation as part of a process associates describe as 'earthing'.[69] Throughout the work of translation the Celveti saint Ismail Hakki Bursevi (d.1725)[70] had been 'a very strong presence', and Rauf had been helped in the work by him. The associate who had commissioned the work had indeed asked for Bursevi's help specifically in this endeavour, during visits to his tomb in Bursa.

In 1986, the first of four volumes was published under the auspices of the MIAS. Together, these volumes (soon referred to internally as the *White Fusus*) encompass the entire *Fusus* text and commentary.[71] The value of this publication has been acknowledged in its capacity as 'the sole treatment in a modern language' of this major work.[72] The commentary was attributed in all four volumes to Bursevi, although it was established in the course of their publication as the work of Abdullah Bosnevi (d.1644).[73] Throughout much of it, the *Fusus* text appears in bold to distinguish it from the commentary.[74]

This work has been described as 'the major Ottoman commentary' on the *Fusus*,[75] encompassing the three major, preceding Arabic commentaries[76] and making frequent reference to the *Futuhat al-Makkiyya*.[77] Bosnevi's long introduction provides an insight into his motives in writing it,[78] defends at length Ibn 'Arabi's claim concerning the origins of the *Fusus*,[79] and explains in technical detail the principles underlying his exposition.[80] The commentary proper sustains a high level of detail throughout.[81] The knowledge encompassed by the work (even the introduction alone) has been described as 'almost encyclopaedic'. Indeed as its fame spread, the title 'Commentator on the *Fusus*' became attached to Bosnevi's name.[82]

What was Rauf's perception of this commentary and its author? He reportedly deemed it 'the most important contribution to esoteric literature, mapping as it does so comprehensively the Spiritual landscape'.[83] It was, moreover, 'of inestimable value if one were to attempt an understanding of the Meaning [Ibn 'Arabi].[84] The *White Fusus* describes it as 'surely the best of the many commentaries which [the *Fusus*] has inspired, being aligned perfectly and completely to the spirit of the original.' This was attributable to the fact that its author (assumed to be Bursevi) was a great saint, capable of perfect servanthood.[85]

In general, erroneous attributions 'can easily occur for many reasons, and may indicate a tradition of deliberate concealment'.[86] In the present case, there is the simple fact that the volume Rauf purchased in Istanbul had no title page. As it turned out, the commentary was the work not of a Celveti shaykh, but of one emanating from the Melami intellectual tradition, indeed one credited with 'spreading the Melami supra-order to the Arab provinces of the [Ottoman] empire.'[87] Bosnevi became a pupil of Hasan Kabadoz, a shaykh of the Melami branch of the Bayramiyye:[88] he also received spiritual benefit from Halveti shaykhs. At the same time, he was virtually 'brought up' by Ibn

'Arabi.[89] The characteristic approach of the Melami tradition, as manifest in Bosnevi's commentary, had thus implicitly attracted Rauf's profound appreciation well before its correct attribution was uncovered.[90]

How did this uncovering transpire? An associate discovered chronological inconsistencies when setting Bursevi's lifetime against internal evidence concerning the commentary's author.[91] Rauf did not assign any importance to this matter for, in the words of one associate, 'it is not the issue'. He also advised against comparing the two saints to each other in the matter of attribution. While acknowledging that questions of attribution may be important to academics, associates are clear that these are not significant in their own relationship with the text.[92]

Much more important for them is the perceived line of continuity between the *Fusus*, the commentary, and Rauf's translation of it. In the words of one associate, the 'dominant strand which links the original, through [the] commentary, to Bulent Rauf's ... translation' is 'the emphasis on and subservience to Meaning'. Hence, 'Both [the author of the commentary] and Bulent Rauf ... remain true to this principle, that in as much as there is any interpretation it is according to the Meaning of Ibn 'Arabi'.[93] Culme-Seymour expressed this in her own way:

> I know of no other than Bulent who is more adapted to achieve the translation of this tremendous work. Of course others have translated Ibn 'Arabi; and indeed there are scholarly treatises and books on the subject of him and his works; and there are others who know both Turkish and English and can read Ottoman Turkish script. But I do not believe there is another who comes so close to being on the same wavelength, so to speak, as 'Arabi [sic], who grasps instinctively Bursevi's exact meaning, who expresses himself with an originality so similar to 'Arabi [sic] ... And far more than that.[94]

Associates initially found the *White Fusus* much more demanding than *The Wisdom of the Prophets*. Study of this text has become central to the long courses. It has also been the focus of a cycle of retreat and reading weeks, and is read in private study groups outside of the School. Long-term associates are now intimately familiar with it. While it shapes their understandings of Ibn 'Arabi's thought, their articulations of aspects of this draw heavily on its motifs and phraseology.[95]

Other texts

Rauf and Culme-Seymour prepared additional texts for study in Beshara. Early on, Rauf compiled a selection from Nicholson's translation of Ibn 'Arabi's *Tarjuman al-ashwaq*, encompassing an abridged translation of Ibn 'Arabi's commentary on this. He added his own notes to the latter.[96] This booklet was used during special month-long 'retreat' courses, which we describe below. He translated from French into English a work by Burckhardt on Ibn 'Arabi's mystical astrology, which was published in 1977.[97] This was followed by a translation into English of Bursevi's Ottoman Turkish translation of and commentary on Ibn 'Arabi's *Lubb al-lubb*, published in 1981 as *Kernel of the Kernel*.[98] An English translation by Culme-Seymour of Burckhardt's French translation of extracts of *al-Insan al-kamil* (with commentary), by 'Abd al-Karim Jili (d.1482), appeared next. Published in 1983 as *Universal Man*,[99] it represents the most influential and widely known work of this important follower of Ibn 'Arabi. All these texts are used in study.

Beshara and the MIAS have also supported the reprinting of works already published in English, for study use.[100] These are Austin's *Sufis of Andalusia*,[101] a translation of Ibn 'Arabi's own account of his teachers during the early part of his life, and *Whoso Knoweth Himself*, a translation of extracts from a text attributed to Ibn 'Arabi.[102]

Inside the School of Intensive Esoteric Education

Something has been passed around since the Prophet. This is a jewel, a clean, clear perspective. It has been safeguarded across the centuries and passed on. It is here [at Chisholme] now. This is the basis of the School and this is why Bulent came here.

Peter Young

To become a student of the Beshara School is possibly the most significant step one could take in one's lifetime.

Beshara website

In the past, such schools have flowered within different religious traditions – *Cabbalah* in Judaism, for example, the School of Chartres and the *tarikat* in the Sufi tradition. In contradistinction, the Beshara School is not tied to any one form or tradition, but rather to the essence, the real meaning and purpose of them all.

Beshara brochure

From the time of its introduction at Swyre Farm, formal study became the central activity in Beshara in an integrated approach to spiritual education involving three other elements: meditation, practice (*dhikr* and *wazifas*) and work or 'service'. Described as 'disciplines', these four activities provide the framework of the intensive course, which lays the foundations of self-knowledge and spiritual practice.

In what follows, we reflect on the character of the School as an environment tailored to the pursuit of spiritual education as conceived by Beshara, introducing its general features. We then explore the overall ethos of the intensive course and describe its daily schedule and constitutive elements, focusing on its contemporary form. Finally, we characterise the further course, which consolidates and refines spiritual understanding, in comparison with the intensive one, and trace its evolution across the years.

The School and its courses ultimately reflect Rauf's approach to spiritual education and his emphases. We confine ourselves here to describing the materialisation of this in specific forms, methods and activities, deferring a detailed consideration and analysis of his thinking to a later discussion.

Introducing the School

A context for self-knowledge

Young acknowledges that 'the possibility of coming to ... self-knowledge ... alone is always present for everyone'. In practice, however, 'it is the rarest of the rare who come to certain knowledge in this way,' for 'we delude ourselves constantly'. The School provides much-needed help in this respect, for the students are 'mirrors to one another', and the setting itself functions as 'a total mirror'. Consequently, people's illusions are quickly revealed to them.[103]

Citing the saying of Jesus 'When two or three are gathered together in My name', Young remarks that 'there is a reality to that situation, and a help from it, which is not necessarily available when you are sitting at home [reading Ibn 'Arabi].' At Chisholme there are more people involved in common spiritual pursuit, the conditions are right, and 'the rightness of a certain intention' in the individual 'is encouraged and allowed to blossom'.[104] In sum, the School provides 'a context for self-knowledge', while the courses furnish 'the proper understanding of the possibility of self-knowledge.'[105]

Stipulated approach and implications for potential students

Beshara publicity materials announce that 'Each person is in potential the place in which the Essence of existence views Itself as if looking at Itself in a mirror'. The School declares itself and its courses to be for all those 'who aspire to know themselves and to become the mirror that reflects the Reality perfectly'. Accordingly, anyone who has this aim is 'eligible to become a student'. The only stipulation is 'that he or she is ... able and prepared to step beyond his or her own limits, particularities and conditioning.'[106] What is the significance of this stipulation?

The concern with conditioning reflects a classic New Age preoccupation. This is because it is seen as a major vehicle for the construction and entrenchment of the illusory self (which belongs to the artifices of society and culture), from which liberation must be won for the true Self to emerge. The application form for the intensive course probes potential students in relation to this theme, asking them to consider the most significant aspect of their conditioning, its possible impact on their future development, and how it might be overcome.[107] A reluctance to confront one's conditioning might present insurmountable obstacles to education in a School that describes itself in the following terms:

> Consider the possibility of a school of self-knowledge, set aside for the exclusive understanding ... of the Reality; not by means of a religion, nor by a particular way among ways, nor through a teacher, nor by means of any particular faculty, such as the intellect or imagination – without any of these, nor by the denial of any of

these, but only through the knowing, loving and affirmation of what is, by Itself and for Itself alone. This possibility is the Beshara School.[108]

As for particularities, the form requests information concerning the religious affiliation of applicants' parents, their own religious upbringing, and any past or present involvement in 'a spiritual way or group'. Clinging to particularity in these spheres may pose problems in the self-consciously perennialist milieu of the School. Here, the disparate student body is united only by 'a desire for Truth without the limits of dogma or precept'.[109]

Finally, publicity materials hint at students' own responsibility in the course, in terms of their transcending their limits and remaining receptive. For example, '[The] effect [of the course] is profound, and reaches as far as each person allows ... The possibilities implied in the course ... are limited only by what each will allow him or herself to receive'.[110]

The internal 'order' and its requirements

The School upholds a special 'order', conceived as a mirror of 'the order of Being'. Its purpose is to help students differentiate between the essential freedom to comply with 'Reality's own order', and their natural tendencies towards an unwillingness or objection to this.[111] The implications of this internal order for students are explained thus:

> It is impossible for one to know the Being except through Its own order and arrangement; this order is reflected in that of the School. Therefore, the most important prerequisite for the course is an acceptance to come under its order and to total participation on every level. This will include participation in the day to day work of the place ... as well as in study and following the practices given.[112]

Students are asked to comply unhesitatingly with certain rules and regulations. These apply to all at the School, as part of this order. They include abstaining from pork and garlic,[113] and refraining from 'the natural impulses of primitive expression' (encompassing anger, avarice, sloth, pride, and passing judgement).[114] As 'an integral part of esoteric training and practice', complete silence is required in corridors, passages and 'ablution areas'.[115] Small notices are placed throughout the premises to remind students of what is required. In the Nursery the importance of the service they undertake is underlined to parents and carers, for the child is 'an individuation of God'.[116] Next to ablution areas in student accommodation the importance of cleanliness is stressed.[117] Reflecting this, communal spaces are maintained at a very high level of cleanliness (indoor shoes are worn throughout and boot halls provide space for outside shoes), and residents are required to clean their rooms at least weekly.

The staff forms an integral part of the order of the School for, as Young observes, 'to provide an education, one has to be part of what one seeks to convey, and to put oneself under that order, otherwise nothing can be achieved'. All staff members have completed long courses. This is the training which prepares them to provide what is required in directly overseeing the training of others. Whatever the specific nature of their role in the School, however, they remain first and foremost continuing students of esoteric education. Not only course supervisors and 'correlators' (see below) but also the secretary, housekeeper, gardener, maintenance manager, kitchen manager *et al.*[118] are themselves students in the broader sense, while at the same time contributing to the education of those on courses, each in their own particular sphere. For example, the kitchen manager's responsibility does not end with preparing appropriate meals on time. It also extends to educating students whose allocated work is to serve in the kitchen. In this context students must thus acquire an understanding of the best way to do things, and of the impact of the food they prepare on the (spiritual) state as well as the physical condition of those who consume it.[119]

Staff members oversee all course activities. Consequently, serving as a staff member is a way of repeating a course 'from a different perspective', as Young puts it. Staff members can participate in meditation and *dhikr* sessions scheduled for students (and in the open Thursday evening *dhikr*). If an individual feels a strong need, occasional attendance of students' study sessions can also be arranged. In addition, all staff come together regularly for meditation/discussion meetings.[120]

Beauty and the aesthetics of the sacred

Rauf's aim was to make the School a place of stunning beauty inside and out. Outside, he developed a landscape design for the grounds.[121] Indoors, he involved himself in the intimate details of furnishing and presenting the main house, and would go in search of beautiful items like fine china, which he would purchase from auctions on a shoestring. Antiques have been used to harmonise with the Georgian character of the building. The walls are liberally decorated with paintings[122] and framed Islamic calligraphies. There are displays of china and ornaments, and fresh flowers are arranged in every room. Rauf believed that exposure to this beautiful environment could help cultivate in students an appreciation of the 'aesthetics of the sacred'. He hoped it would nurture in them a 'taste for beauty' and 'beauty of taste' (*dhawq*), and that this would ultimately deepen their discernment, a key element in their spiritual understanding. While we will return to these themes later, we would point out here that, as a place of beauty and good taste, the School has a strong impact on those who have newly arrived.[123]

Creating sacred space

Given physical limitations, most spaces in the house are put to more than one use. A space is marked at a particular time by the activity for which it is designated, and is prepared and treated accordingly. Ablution of space is practised in preparation for meditation or *dhikr* (such that it reflects the same degree of preparedness as the physical bodies of those who participate, as will become clear later). It entails cleaning with awareness of purpose and with prayers.[124] Every Thursday before the open *dhikr*, the Principal or a designated person carries a censer, burning frankincense, throughout the house, swinging it three times into the corner of each room while reciting the *basmala*.[125]

The kitchen and food

Special attention is given to the content, preparation and presentation of food, to the regular provision and consumption of meals, and the institution of morning coffee and afternoon tea.[126] A standing grace before main meals marks the importance and appreciation of nourishment. This is simply the utterance aloud and in unison of the *basmala* in English: 'In the Name of God, the All-Compassionate, the Most Merciful'. The kitchen, a room on a grand scale, is a very important space in the house. It is adorned with blue Iznik tiles from Turkey, incorporating an imposing *basmala*. Spacious cooking pots and serving dishes brought from Turkey are on display. The considerable energy he applied to this sphere resulted from Rauf's understanding of the role of food in spiritual education, and the esoteric symbolism of cooking. The emphasis he placed on these themes, to which we return later, is clear from his 'Notice to Cooks', which is given a prominent place in the kitchen. Translating his understanding and emphasis, the application form for the long courses makes the point that no provision will be made at the School for special diets except in the case of proven medical requirements. Instead, there is the promise of a 'nutritious and well-balanced diet' for all.

The intensive course

Beshara materials describe this course as a highly coordinated whole 'in which no aspect of existence is omitted and no real question left unanswerable'.[127] Through the combination of four indispensable disciplines it presents 'all that is necessary for the student to reach his aim and to continue to evolve throughout his life'.[128] Study serves 'to give direction to aspiration'. Meditation helps 'to establish a continuous relationship with one's interior'. *Dhikr* provides a reminder that 'there is only One Existence from which arise all the different qualities and attributes which comprise the world of our perception'. Finally, service helps the student 'to take responsibility'.[129] If study sets in motion the process that brings one to self-knowledge, this process is reinforced through the three other activities, which help to ensure its sustained fruition.

The daily schedule

The day begins early, with a meditation session at 7 a.m. As it must be preceded by an ablution, students are encouraged to rise at 6.30 a.m. Time is divided precisely, with half-hour slots allocated for morning coffee and afternoon tea, and specific periods designated for study and work. There are two types of day, depending on the place accorded to study. 'Study' days incorporate three study periods, each of an hour and a half, two in the morning and one in the afternoon, and two work periods. 'Work' days have no formal study periods. Instead, one and a quarter hours are set aside for private study, providing an opportunity for students to look again at texts studied as a group. Two study days alternate with two work days throughout the course. Every day is punctuated by three thirty-minute meditation sessions (in addition to 7 a.m., there is one at 12.15 p.m. and another at 6 p.m.). Before each of the two later sessions, a slot of fifteen minutes is allocated for ablution. The day ends with a *dhikr* session (beginning at 9.30 p.m.), preceded by a half-hour slot for ablution after dinner. This session incorporates collective performance of a *wazifa*. In addition to the three meal times (an hour and a quarter or an hour and a half each), a quarter hour is specifically allocated for setting the table for lunch.

The course ethos

Ibn 'Arabi relates that his wife had a vision in which five qualities were described to her as the means to the path of unity. These were trust, certainty, patience, resolution and veracity.[130] When he welcomes students at the beginning of the intensive course, the Principal explains that their immediate aim must be to understand and establish within themselves these five qualities. In conjunction with these qualities, the four course disciplines will lead them to 'a truly integrated spiritual vision.'[131] The course as a whole is thus designed to bring students 'to the recognition of ... Reality in all its expressions and dimensions'. Their ultimate aspiration (whether during the course or thereafter) must be to achieve 'constancy of awareness of Reality.'[132]

The first day is marked with a fast from sunrise to sunset. Its purpose is to help students to 'arrive' and clarify their intention. From that day on, they are effectively in retreat. They are expected to remain on the premises for the six months of the course, and leave only for an organised trip to Turkey (and in case of medical emergency). So that maximum benefit can be gained from the course as an opportunity for 'intensive and total involvement, free of all concerns and distractions', contact with the outside world is kept to the necessary minimum. Radios and televisions are not permitted in student rooms. The secluded location, over seven miles from the nearest town and surrounded by farmlands, reinforces the atmosphere of retreat and the sense of withdrawal from regular life. The highly structured routine is indeed designed to help students 'make a complete break with all that has gone before' in the way of their lifestyles and habits, so that they might become 'totally devoted to a single aim.'[133] There is deliberately 'very little respite', and their attention and energies are consumed to the full. Time is in fact so restricted that they spend the entire six months without reaching further into the extensive estate than the distance of a ten- or fifteen-minute walk. The intensity of the situation is such that, as one student has put it, 'There is no escape. It forces you to confront things.'

Taking this into account, the course application form stipulates that students must be in good health and capable of undertaking a rigorous and exacting programme. The School is careful to assess applicants' 'mental robustness' (as one associate puts it), and the application form requests details of 'psychological or mental' conditions. For many students, the demanding schedule is no surprise, for they have already completed nine-day introductory courses. As the latter constitute a 'mini'-version of the intensive course, potential students can use them to test whether they wish to proceed to the long one.[134] Where possible, applicants are interviewed before the course begins or, failing that, on arrival.

Based on long years of observation, Young relates that most students do adjust as they become accustomed to the course rhythm, and their needs (for sleep and rest, for example) gradually change. He suggests that once a student is fully engaged the activities themselves 'generate energy'. During weekly interviews set up for each student individually with Young (or a designated staff member), they can air feelings and communicate concerns, and their situation can be assessed and changes introduced as necessary.

The course is conceived throughout as a time of education and study, whether in the context of formal sessions, work, or at any other times. In Young's words, it is 'study oriented ... by study we don't simply mean poring over books, but study in every aspect of the day. We have days when we study and days when we work, but study is expected to be continuous.'[135] Even at a superficial level, education is 'the keynote', including, for example, in work 'in the garden and estate, workshops and kitchen, where the development of new skills is encouraged.'[136]

The discipline of study and the process of esoteric education

Publicity materials state that the 'simple focus' of the School is 'the Unity of Being and Consciousness'. The 'perspective that unfolds through study' is described as 'single-pointed'. To elaborate on this perspective (which both drives and forms the ultimate goal of study), the analogy of a pyramid (which we met above in *The Twenty-nine Pages*) is introduced:

> there is a point of view from just above the apex from where the entirety of the pyramid may be seen, looking down from the top. From this position, it is possible to make sense of the entire creation ... to perceive that the purpose of the structure is really to ... uphold the apex, the transitional point at which non-dimension overflows to dimension. Thus education at the ... School is founded upon the true situation that even while standing apparently at the base of the pyramid ... there is already present in us the possibility of the view from the top. It is the arrival at this point in consciousness that is the perfection of Man ... The ... School prepares the ground and paves the way for the arrival of ... its students to the perfection of Man.[137]

Study begins with *The Twenty-nine Pages* and *Whoso Knoweth Himself.* When these have been completed and students have grasped the concept of essential unity, each writes a paper (discussing a quotation from *The Twenty-nine Pages*, for example) and delivers a five-minute presentation to an audience of all present at the School.[138] They then focus intensively on the *Fusus*. Study follows the chapter order of the original. *The Wisdom of the Prophets* is supplemented with Rauf's early translations of Bosnevi's translation/commentary in booklet form. By the end of the course students will thus have read the major part of the *Fusus* (having omitted only those sections that do not appear in *The Wisdom of the Prophets* in the case of excerpted chapters), and a substantial part of the Bosnevi commentary. This takes up the lion's share of the time allocated to study, for *The Twenty-nine Pages* and *Whoso Knoweth Himself* are completed during the first month or so. These texts are ultimately seen as preparation for studying the *Fusus*, by providing familiarity with fundamental concepts and terms. As Rauf explained, the *Fusus* should thus be read 'with a pre-understanding of the point of view and reference and the ensuing perspective, for which Ibn 'Arabi is unmatched ... the "theory" of *wahdat-i-wujud*'.[139]

Parallel with the *Fusus*, students also read from *Sufis of Andalusia, Mystical Astrology According to Ibn 'Arabi*, extracts from Rumi's *Mathnawi*,[140] Rauf's *Addresses*,[141] and al-Niffari's *Mawaqif*.[142] Texts are also sampled from spiritual traditions other than sufism. These include the *Baghavad Gita*, the *Tao Te Ching* and writings of Meister Eckhart. Invited speakers provide further introductions to these traditions,[143] while visits to the nearby Samye Ling Tibetan Buddhist Centre enable students to sit in on teaching there. Lectures are also arranged during the course 'on subjects as widely ranging as art and poetry, physics, economics and archaeology'.[144] The aim behind all this is that students should experience 'the reflection of truth in several different modes', as one associate puts it. According to Young, 'The idea is that they ... hear the same thing; because truth is one, however it appears and whatever clothes it wears'.[145] Through exposure to its diverse expressions, students have an opportunity to correlate what they learn with 'its appearance in all other aspects of study and life'.[146]

Study of a language is always incorporated into the course, Turkish during the first three months, and then Hebrew or Arabic depending upon the resources available.[147] According to a staff member who has taught Arabic, the idea is not to equip students with linguistic skills as such, but 'to introduce aspects of the language relevant to the focus of their study'. These might include 'the way the letters relate to each other, how they come together to form words and what this brings in the way of meaning'. Added to this is 'the basics of grammar', so that students can 'recognise words or attempt to read calligraphy'. Young explains the purpose behind the study of language thus: 'so that we see that each language has its own strengths and specialities in communicating realities, and so that we also see that our thought forms are influenced by our mother tongue'.

At the end of this volume we include a detailed description of a study session during the intensive course, by way of illustration (Appendix 3). Sessions take place in a dedicated room with participants seated around a table. Two designated supervisors (staff members) are always present. In turn, individual students read aloud passages from the text, stopping at a natural pause. If a student has a question or comment this is expressed and forms the basis of discussion. Otherwise, reading continues. The supervisor's role is not to answer questions or serve as a reference point, but to ensure that discussion does not stray from the central themes, and to draw it back if necessary. It is thus not to lead the discussion but to 'facilitate' it.[148] In principle there is no imparting of information or a specific understanding. Instead, 'whatever the participant finds in the text is allowed to present itself to them,'[149] as one associate puts it. It is a matter of principle that 'There are no teachers at the School': students are rather urged to rely on 'Reality alone', as 'the best Teacher'.[150]

This principle and the approach to study we have just described reflect Rauf's distinctive understanding of 'esoteric education'. Rather than the acquisition of data or an intellectual grasp of propositions, this signifies the 'retrieval' by students from within themselves of fundamental truths concerning their own essential nature. It is education 'from within', which issues in self-knowledge. Thus:

> Esoteric education is a 'drawing out' of a kind of knowledge that is inseparable from one's own being. It is not knowledge about something, although it might appear so, rather it is a kind of knowledge that is the inherent property of the thing in question. For instance, it is like the knowledge that water has of how to flow – its knowledge is identical to its own aqueous nature ... Following this example, self-knowledge is to know ourselves in the same way, not through received information, or by the intellect, but through our very being ... To know oneself in this way is to know the Unity ... Thus when it is known that the One Real Being is one's very essence ... there follows the realisation that all existence is an intrinsic unity ... This knowledge is the hidden treasure that awaits within oneself, the mystery of existence and the Real Beloved.[151]

As 'the One and Unique Essence cannot be confined to any conceptual understanding and can only be known through direct experience,'[152] study is ultimately experiential in its thrust and aim.[153] It is fundamentally not a cerebral or intellectual activity, even if the intellect must be engaged.[154] Rather it aims to produce in the student (in Young's words) 'the experience of an interior vision'.

Disciplines of meditation and spiritual practice; ablution as preparation

Group meditation takes place in a dedicated room and students are accompanied by a staff member. Participants sit in a circle facing an empty centre point. Some use small kneeling stools or chairs. The meditation begins with the *basmala* and ends with the utterance of *Hu*. There is no other set formula and no training in specific techniques. Students are free to meditate in whatever way feels natural to them, drawing on innate styles. Rauf's projection of the purpose and importance of meditation underpins this discipline; we return to it in a later discussion.

A staff member also accompanies students in nightly collective *dhikr*. This practice encompasses a simple pattern of collective recitation accompanied by movements. Every Thursday evening an open collective *dhikr* is substituted: in this, students join staff, visitors and associates who live locally. (We describe this open *dhikr*, which is held a little later than the routine nightly *dhikr*, in Appendix 4, and analyse its form in a later discussion.) Following the nightly *dhikr* students also perform a second practice, referred to as a *wazifa* (daily/nightly office). This has three formats. There is a private practice, carried out individually just before bed. Alongside this are two collective practices. One proceeds throughout the course, the other only for a six-week period finishing two weeks before the end of the course. Each is supervised by a staff member. We provide details of these *wazifa* practices in a later discussion. Suffice it to note here that the time required for performing the two collective *wazifa*s can reach three hours. This means that students go to bed in the small hours (but continue to rise at 6.30 a.m.).

Students are required to perform an ablution prior to meditation and *dhikr*.[155] A full ablution is required before *dhikr*, and on waking from sleep in the morning before meditation. Adapted from Islamic practice, this is achieved by taking a shower (some associates emphasise that it must extend to the head and hair, while others suggest that symbolic wetting of these is adequate).[156] Before meditation at other times during the day, a regular (partial) ablution is stipulated. A recent School document describes it simply as washing the 'face, hands and feet'.[157] In contrast, according to a longstanding associate (and as recommended at Swyre Farm under Feild), the regular ablution consists in washing the hands, arms (to the wrist and preferably the elbow), face (including nose and mouth), ears, and feet (to the ankle). Its adaptation from Islamic practice is particularly clear here.[158]

Personal cleanliness is emphasised in the School, and it is assumed that everyone within its walls will pay due attention to this. The purpose of ablution is not to achieve bodily cleanliness, but a state of preparedness for encountering the transcendent. In the words of one associate, it is 'washing with intention, focusing on the One you are preparing to meet (in *dhikr* or meditation)'. The most important part of it is thus the intention with which it is carried out. In an Islamic context the practice of ablution is accompanied by certain technical requirements. In contrast, as practised in Beshara today, it deliberately avoids any potential complication, and students are encouraged simply to follow what feels for them to be a state of complete preparedness.

The discipline of work or 'service'

As a distinct activity or discipline, work reflects the broader concept of service. During the early days of Beshara an associate underlined its importance as 'the only step we can take to change our situation and go beyond the laws that govern our "ordinary life"'. It is 'the principle of aligning ourselves to the will of God'.[159] Young elaborates on the relationship between work and service, and on the true nature of service, thus:

Service ... is not simply to do with doing work, although through doing work, we can come to a proper understanding of how it is to serve. If we were to take the example of serving food at the table; a good servant does the job perfectly, with perfect balance; he should serve in such a way that he is not noticed, and so that he does not intrude too much of himself into the situation ... But neither does he hang back; he knows what is needed. At the moment that the request is made, he knows and does, and that is how one should be in a state of perfect awareness, whatever one is doing ... Action is at the right moment in the right quantity, and this is serving reality, because we say: all service is to God, whatever the appearance. Whether you think that you are serving a human being or looking after chickens, all service is to reality.[160]

Allocated work may be in the kitchen or the garden, in caring for the poultry and waterfowl or general cleaning. Staff members allocate and post up specific tasks on a daily basis. Study days incorporate two work periods, one in the afternoon (an hour and a quarter) and one in the evening (an hour). Their purpose is to counterbalance the intensity of organised study. They also provide students with an opportunity to assimilate what they have studied, to focus and to strengthen their intention. The two work days are conceived in terms of enabling students to put what they have studied into practice.[161]

The trip to Turkey

The course breaks in December for a twelve-day visit to Turkey.[162] It is 'both a tour and a pilgrimage', a journey 'for the purpose of intensifying and expanding the sentiment and insights already intimated to the student in the course of their studies.'[163] Rauf prepared a document for students embarking on the trip ('A Trip to Turkey'). Here he elaborated further on its aim, and on the conduct appropriate to it:

The trip to Turkey ... is ... a time for direction and devotion and pleading for the beneficence and *himmah* [spiritual will or 'power'] from the Source of all *Himmah*,[164] so that the intensive course can find its proper function and focus: that of advance towards, and approach to a state of non-being in Union ... Consequently, it is necessary that all persons ... going on this journey take great heed and care to comport themselves first of all in *adab* (good form), and more, in good taste, avoiding to give, even unwittingly, an impression of laxity to those among whom they will pass.[165]

'A Trip to Turkey' provides an overview of the region from ancient times and through Byzantine and Ottoman periods, giving information on archaeological sites, monuments and sultans. The itinerary encompasses visits in and around Istanbul, Ankara, Bursa, Ephesus and Konya, taking in sites, museums, mosques and the tombs of saints.[166] The ultimate focus of the trip, however, is to pay respects 'at the resting-places of those whose teachings concerning the Unity of Being and the perfectibility of man inform the tenor and direction of ... studies at the ... School.'[167] The document indeed dedicates a section to 'Visits to the Saints', providing biographies of saints to whom visits are arranged and brief introductions to others, and reminding students of relevant aspects of their study.[168] We will return to the role and place of the saints in the Beshara perspective later.

The trip is always scheduled to encompass the date of Rumi's death or 'nuptial' night, and includes attendance at the Mevlevi *sama'* (*sema*) in Konya arranged to mark this occasion. 'A Trip to Turkey' describes the stages and significance of the *sama'*, reminding students that it is neither a performance, dance or trance, but a form of *dhikr*:

> It is *Zikr* and therefore it absolutely behoves every one of you to comply with the essential decency and the attitude necessary and suitable for assisting at a *Sema*, even only as a spectator ... Now, knowing that during *Zikr* every part of one and one's surrounding takes part in that *Zikr*, it is understandably unavoidable that the 'spectators' at the *Sema* ... also take part in the *Zikr*, even if they do not know that they do. For you, then, who are necessarily more awake ... this taking part is more immediate and definite ... The first step for being prepared to assist at a *Sema* is ... to be in complete intentional and devotional ablution and then the necessary deferential attitude like proper comportment and suitable behaviour must follow.[169]

The return to society

Completion of the course is marked with a generous buffet, after which students are free to leave.[170] One or two might stay on and assume a specific responsibility for a defined period. They are not encouraged to remain indefinitely, however, for, as one associate puts it, 'the School is not a community where one can live. You go to receive an education and you leave to apply this in your own life'. Young acknowledges that, while the course furnishes a source of constant growth and its impact is felt 'at every moment of ... life to follow', students can find it difficult to reintegrate:

> For six months, the point of reference has been one being, one existence. While it may have begun as a premise, it ends in a degree of certainty, and to find that people in general do not live their lives in awareness of this can be a shock. And things stand out as not conforming to this point of view; the way decisions are made, the way people think and so on. At the same time, this awareness of non-conformity is an endorsement of what [students] have studied.[171]

On leaving, the individual chooses how to maintain their relationship with Beshara. For the majority this means returning to Chisholme to undertake the further course when the opportunity arises.

The further course

The general aim of the further course is to strengthen and refine the five qualities that have become established in students through the intensive course, and to achieve a correlation between what they studied then and their immediate experiences in the present. Rauf identified two specific objectives. The first was to deepen certainty (*yaqin*), in particular, of these qualities, through 'the untying of knots'. The second was to 'cultivate beauty of taste and taste for beauty'.

The course ethos

This course differs markedly in ethos from the intensive one. Young describes it as 'direct involvement in a love affair with the divine, and learning first hand the ways of how to be a lover'. Reflecting this, the order to which students are required to submit is not as explicit as it is in the intensive course:

> The external requirement (with regard to meditation, *dhikr*, etc.) is removed because of the necessities of love. The emphasis is on the supererogatory instead: things are done from a desire to approach the Being and not from a perceived obligation. Students are encouraged to find their interior, essential motivation and to be moved by it, rather than by the secondary pressures. On the first course, they submit to an order. On the second, they respond to something from within. Bulent's way of putting it was that a guest *wants* to lend his help: a student is here in God's House as God's guest.[172]

Capturing this, attendance is by invitation from Young as Principal.[173] If an associate responds positively and accepts this invitation, they effectively come as a guest. The ethos and objectives of this course render students' experiences of it highly personal and individual. Consequently, we describe it here only in general terms, and not at great length. For a detailed narrative of one associate's experience of it, we refer the reader to Story 5 in Appendix 5.

The framework

The 'conversation' session, held every morning and every afternoon, forms the main course element.[174] Historically, some time was given over in it to reading the *White Fusus*, but conversation was the primary and distinctive element by design. It typically centred on a textual fragment (from the *White Fusus* or another text), or endeavoured to relate what students had studied to their individual experiences. Two 'correlators' were assigned to the course. They would sit in on sessions and participate in conversation. The setting was deliberately relaxed, with students on comfortable armchairs in the Mead Hall.

Physical comfort is still projected as a precondition for conversation, and due attention is given to this dimension. Today, however, sessions are dedicated to spontaneous conversation, and there is no textual focus or set agenda. Even if the assumption is that everyone is familiar with these, in practice considerable clarification of ideas and revisiting of materials studied during the intensive course becomes necessary as specific points are brought up.

A work period is scheduled each afternoon. In addition, students may choose to attend meditation and *dhikr* sessions held for students on the intensive course: the two courses typically run parallel. Young frequently suggests to further course students that they do 'whatever is needed'. This poses a challenge for, as guests, they must sense what needs to be done without being asked, balancing this with their own needs for rest, fresh air and the like without feelings of guilt.

The 'untying of knots'

This course provides an opportunity to address any distortions in foundations laid during the intensive course that may have appeared since its completion. It is thus designed to open a space in which to uncover 'knots in our being; un-stated elements that limit how we are', as Young puts it. These may take the form of attitudes, psychological issues or emotional problems. They are described by associates as 'hidden factors within that obscure our vision. They may be things that have become coloured by life since the first course.' The existence of such knots demands a process of 'unlearning'. One associate suggests that Rauf referred specifically to the knots 'which bind one to the illusion of separation'.[175] Once they have been removed through resolution of the underlying issues and problems, greater clarity and certainty become possible.

Free conversation with each participant fully present 'in the moment' (and secure 'in the knowledge of Reality as One')[176] sets the stage for the surfacing of knots. Their untying can then begin to unfold. Sensitive to its intensely private and delicate nature, Young urges correlators to bear in mind two principles in conversation sessions. First, they must respond positively to 'whatever is offered'. Instead of dismissing or negating it, they might turn a miscomprehension into a starting point, for example. Second, they must be constantly aware that, in reality, 'it is never "like this and only like this"'. If a subtle knot comes to the surface and a student wishes to explore it, this must be in a positive and supportive atmosphere, for in this situation students are 'totally naked', as one associate puts it.[177] Beyond such guidance, Young recognises that he cannot prescribe to correlators how to conduct conversation. Its direction is unpredictable, and they must ultimately feel their way in it. In the individual student's experience of conversation, the group chemistry is evidently an important factor. For example, one student may dominate the group or there may be clashes of personality.[178] Young explains that the group must deal with such issues itself. Eventually, it will find its own internal balance.

Cultivating beauty of taste (dhawq)

Much in evidence historically, emphasis of this second objective of the course has receded. Early students who had attended an intensive course at Sherborne House and arrived at Chisholme for the further one encountered a striking contrast in setting. Rauf had prepared the house at Chisholme specifically for the further course, having had in mind the cultivation of 'beauty of taste' and 'taste for beauty' as one of its objectives.

During the early further courses, students were constantly reminded of the 'metaphysical' principles that inform the attention to beauty at the School, and were encouraged to deepen their understanding of these. There was an expectation that their developing 'beauty of taste' and 'taste for beauty' would find practical expression in whatever they did, manifest in a striving for perfection. This might be in flower arranging, decorating, gardening, cooking, presenting food, or setting the table, for example. As they gradually discerned the theophanic aspect in all things, they would come to appreciate that even the most mundane objects should be put to use in the best possible way, and to the end of beauty. Associates recall how even a tea break served as 'an education in taste' during early further courses. Tea would be brought in to them in fine china on a beautifully arranged tray. Careful attention would be paid to details of etiquette in serving it, making sure that a cup was offered with its handle pointing to the person who was to receive it, for example. In the early years the leap in quality of life from the intensive to the further course was great, reflected in the fact that students would dress for dinner on the further course. As both long courses became confined to Chisholme, this sharp contrast disappeared.

A week of retreat

The further course encompasses a week of individual retreat centred on a single activity in the form of a particular *wazifa*. The origins of this practice were in a special one-month course that Rauf had introduced in summer 1977 (or 1978). Designated a 'retreat' course, this was attended by most students who had completed the intensive course and wished to proceed to the further one. The month was divided by weeks. The first week was devoted to studying *Kernel of the Kernel* and the chapter on Jacob in Bosnevi's commentary on the *Fusus*,[179] the second to Jami's *Lawa'ih*[180] and Jili's *al-Insan al-kamil*, and the third to parts of Ibn 'Arabi's *Tarjuman al-ashwaq*. The fourth was a retreat. Each student was assigned a room. They were instructed not to leave it except to wash (they were expected to be in a state of full ablution at all times), and for a brief daily walk undertaken without social interaction. They were brought three meals each day. Two designated associates would take turns to visit students in retreat daily, to check on them. Providing a focus and structure to the days, the only specified activity was the *wazifa*. At the end of the retreat, students reconvened to re-read parts of the *Tarjuman* for a few days. This served as a buffer: were they to proceed 'directly from retreat into the world', it was felt that students would be 'too exposed'. When the month-long retreat course was later terminated, the retreat week and its *wazifa* practice were integrated into the further course.

The School and its distinctive approach to spiritual education owe a great debt to the vision of one man, who had emerged as the guiding figure of Beshara. The bases of this approach can best be illuminated by considering his origins, life and spiritual formation.

Chapter 4

Bulent Rauf as guiding figure

> In reality ... I do nothing, for there is only God. We are His players on the stage that He set so that He might see Himself.
> Bulent Rauf, cited in Reshad Feild, *The Last Barrier*, p.74

Origins

Bulent Rauf's origins and the formative period of his life must be set against the milieu of the late Ottoman and early Republican periods in Turkey. In light of this milieu, which we characterise below, we explore his family background and map out his life up to his arrival in London, paying particular attention to the uncovering of specific spiritual associations. There are few external narratives and autobiographical accounts on which to draw.[1] Generations that might have served as repositories for relevant memories have mostly passed away, so it is difficult to find informative oral sources in Istanbul. Given this, we make extensive use of internal narratives in reconstructing Rauf's family background and life story, evaluating these through internal comparison and, where possible, comparison with external sources. In some cases internal narratives converge, reflecting information conveyed by Rauf. In others there is no consensus and accounts have become confused. We settle on narratives we consider most likely to be authentic, confining to the notes alternative perceptions that have some degree of credibility.

The issue of interpretation in what follows must be acknowledged. A prominent theme is the implicit legitimisation of Rauf's authority as founder–guide in associates' perceptions, based on the establishment of apt credentials and genealogies. We by no means impute to him any explicit intention in this regard: associates would vigorously reject such a motive, and it is not borne out by the profile of the man that unfolds below.

The late Ottoman and Republican milieu: sufism and the *tariqas*

The importance of sufism as a fundamental element of Ottoman Islamic society and the omnipresence of the *tariqa*s in town and rural settings across the Ottoman Empire is universally recognised.[2] Widely accepted also is an involvement with the thought of Ibn 'Arabi among the elite, literate circles, and beyond, through oral teaching.[3] The visibility of Ibn 'Arabi's legacy fluctuated, and there were periodic polemics against it. Yet its influence remained profound and pervasive, and the sultans in particular were concerned to protect and perpetuate it.[4] The result was that mainstream Ottoman discourse did not consider Ibn 'Arabi heretical, while for their part Ottoman sufis widely supported his doctrine.[5]

The *tariqa*s withstood the modernising thrust of the nineteenth-century *Tanzimat* reforms and the impact of European thought.[6] This is attested to by the urgency with which the Kemalist campaign against them was engaged. Like the ulama and the Şeyhülislam (whose authority encompassed them), the *tariqa*s had been part of the Ottoman state. Given this, their centrality to Ottoman social organisation and their significance as the most powerful competing network and focus of loyalty, Republican decree 677 of 30 November 1925 officially banned them.[7] It came in the wake of Ataturk's famous *Nutuk* ('Speech') in August of that year, in the course of which he attacked their shrines, *tekke*s and spiritual figures.[8] *Tekke*s and mausoleums associated with the *tariqa*s were immediately closed down, but it was soon recognised that these were not the core element in their existence. Consequently, during the first Republican reform period further measures were implemented against them.

Many sufis rejected the Kemalist reforms. Among these opponents, four categories have been identified.[9] The first group consisted of original supporters of the National Struggle who then changed their attitude towards the government when the reforms were introduced, as they felt unable to comply with them. A second group engaged in silent opposition (by refusing to accept official positions, for example), while a third openly opposed both the reforms and the regime. The fourth group comprised those who fled Turkey to continue their religious–political activities abroad.

In contrast, some leading figures within the *tariqa*s suggested that their abolition might have a positive impact on their affiliates' spiritual life. This opinion reflected a general sense, captured by Schimmel, that 'much mismanagement and many non-Islamic practices had tinged [the] external life [of the *tariqa*s] ... and the ... *tekke*s, once source for spiritual education and purification, had often lost this lofty meaning.'[10] Two orientations have been discerned among sufis who supported and/or legitimised the reforms. The first group (which encompassed the majority of all sufis) accepted or pretended to accept them. They frequently assumed official positions, and pursued their sufi activities in secret.[11] The second group explicitly supported the reforms. In the face of the relentless pressure of Kemalism, both groups advanced justifications for repudiating the *tariqa*s. Rauf's arguments, conveyed to associates much later in the century, reflect something of the tenor of these earlier justifications. A few examples will illustrate their general thrust.

The Halveti shaykh Mehmed Şemseddin Efendi (d.1936) and the Bektashi shaykh Rahmi Baba (d.1935/6) both gave the reforms their silent assent. After 1925, Mehmed Şemseddin argued that people do not need a *tekke* for *dhikr*, given that the Qur'an urges them 'to remember God wherever they are.'[12] Rahmi Baba originally opposed the reforms. During the 1930s, he arranged for a sufi gathering to place a curse on Ataturk. On the eve of the designated day he had a dream in which the Prophet appeared before a map of the world.

He was assigning parts of it to specific people. Turkey appeared in green surrounded by wide, low, black walls, and Ataturk stood on Thrace with his back to the Prophet. When it came to the turn of Turkey, the Prophet said 'Give this to him [Ataturk]!' The next day Rahmi Baba explained his dream to the gathering. He concluded that, in spite of everything, the Prophet had given his approval (if unwillingly) to Ataturk as leader of Turkey. The green colour of Turkey on the map (associated with Islam) was deemed a good sign, while the negative one indicated by the black of the walls (the colour of unbelief) was mitigated by the fact that the walls were low. Based on this dream, the gathering abandoned the intention to curse Ataturk, and Rahmi Baba and the invited shaykhs ended their opposition to him.[13]

Unlike these figures, Shaykh Kenan Rifai (d.1950) explicitly supported the Kemalist reforms from the outset. He conveyed his approval of the closure of the *tekkes* to the press, arguing that, out of the 300 or so in Istanbul, only a few were 'in the service of knowledge': furthermore, their part in history was over.[14] He maintained that the *tariqas* as a whole had completed their roles, and now had nothing to give the community. In an exchange with a Mevlevi shaykh, he spelled out his views: 'We are now, what we were earlier. Earlier we were in visible *tekkes*, now in an inner, heart, *tekke*. Allah wished so, and made it so. Everything from Him is fine.'[15]

It has been suggested that, in their capacity as 'a cardinal element in traditional Turkish religious life', the *tariqas*' 'survival' of their proscription had been inevitable.[16] Yet the termination of Ottoman government had deconstructed their entire frame of reference, both organisational and symbolic, which had indeed been intrinsic to them. Faced with an uncompromising new context and the threat of their own demise, during the early Republican period some *tariqas* resorted to radical and comprehensive self-reinvention. The resulting changes were compounded by the sharp break with the past instituted by the new regime, and the difficulty in securing continuity of knowledge within such reinvented or reconstituted forms in the new context.

The picture of *tariqa* life and activities in Republican Turkey is far from clear and studies of this remain limited, especially in Western languages.[17] As Ayata notes, a sociological account of their underground history is yet to be attempted.[18] Individuals have continued to represent themselves as shaykhs and to accept followers on this basis,[19] and traditions of transmitting texts and practices have remained vital. At the same time, the associated values and spirit, long internalised, have radiated across Turkish society. Thus sufism, as Kafadar argues, 'has always been much more than the sum of the fortunes of various orders', for the limits of its reach are defined neither by location nor organisation. As a cultural tradition, it 'continues to run as a deep current in modern, including secular, Turkish life.'[20] This deep current forms a prominent aspect of Rauf's origins and family background.

Family background

Rauf was the great-grandson of Ismail Pasha (1830–95), khedive of Egypt from 1863 until his deposition by Sultan Abdülhamid in 1879.[21] Ismail's daughter was Princess Fatma Hanim (b.1850), who died some time after World War I.[22] Rauf writes of her in an autobiographical fragment, describing himself as her favourite grandson.[23] Concerning her genealogy, he relates, 'On my mother's side, my great-grandmother was Georgian, my great-grandfather was of a mixture of Turkish, Circassian and probably Albanian descent. Their second daughter was my grandmother.'[24] Fatma Hanim married twice. She outlived her first husband, 'a Prince who died in his early twenties'.[25] Her second husband was 'a Circassian come over from the Caucasus to study at the Islamic University of Al-Azhar.'[26] This was Mahmut Sirri, 'a pauper and stateless since the Russian persecution'. A clan relative of the wife of the Egyptian Pasha, he was looking after the affairs of the widowed Princess. A romantic affair resulted in their marriage,[27] and he reportedly 'tripled her income'.[28]

The daughter of this marriage was Emire Hanim.[29] She had no claim to the title of Princess, because her father was a commoner in origin (although Mahmut Sirri had been granted the status of Pasha on marrying into the khedival family).[30] Like her mother, Emire Hanim also had two marriages. Her second husband, Abdul Rauf Bey, was the son of Field-Marshal (Mushir) Rauf Pasha. An army officer who had been educated at a Military College in France,[31] Abdul Rauf Bey was the father of Emire Hanim's two sons. The elder was Mahmut, and the younger, the focus of our interest, Mehmet Ali Bulent Rauf. Abdul Rauf Bey is barely mentioned by associates in accounts of Rauf's family background, perhaps because the marriage did not last long.[32]

Rauf's maternal grandfather Mahmut Sirri Pasha had fallen ill and died in 1911 at the staging post of Tebuk, as he was travelling home from Mecca following the hajj.[33] His body was carried to Damascus and interred in the mausoleum of Ibn 'Arabi, in accordance with a wish he had expressed on leaving Istanbul. Rauf related that, when he had conveyed this wish, his grandfather had been told there was no room to accommodate him in the mausoleum. His response had been that, somehow, 'space would be found'. A popular memory in the neighbourhood today relates that, when he was buried, gold coins were distributed for his soul.[34] Embellished with 'the light verse' (Qur'an 24: 35), his fine white marble tomb is one of six within the mausoleum.[35] It is the innermost of three tombs situated in the space presently designated for women to pray in.[36] A framed calligraphy on the adjacent wall marks it: 'This is the tomb of the late Sayyid Pasha Sirri al-Khunaji, brother-in-law of his majesty Fu'ad I, king of Egypt: died 1329.' Ibn 'Arabi's tomb draws countless visitors, bringing attention also to the tombs of his neighbours. Some women have attempted to avail themselves of the *baraka* (blessing) associated with this sacred space by writing their prayers directly onto the tombs where possible. The smooth surface of Mahmut Sirri Pasha's tomb in particular, which is not draped in cloth, has been covered with layer upon layer of penned prayers, submitted by women for their families.[37] In general, visitors hold all those buried alongside Ibn 'Arabi in high regard, assuming that their physical closeness to the great saint in death reflects a close spiritual affinity in life.

Rauf did not indicate the specific nature of his grandfather's association with Ibn 'Arabi, but his wish to be buried alongside him can be seen as evidence of his great esteem for the saint, and of a special bond with him. We do have some indication of Mahmut Sirri Pasha's *tariqa* affiliation, for Rauf wrote to a close associate: 'My grandfather, buried in Damascus, was a *murid* of one of the shaykhs of Shaban Veli (the Shabaniyye) in Kastamonu, and had the area restored and three houses bought and left in trust to the mosque and tomb. Until very recently, they were still in our possession, but not anymore'.[38]

For their part, Fatma Hanim and Emire Hanim appear to have had a special connection with the Celvetiyye, for they undertook to restore the shrine–mosque complex of the prominent Celveti saint Aziz Mahmud Hüdayi (d.1628) in Üsküdar, Istanbul, after this was damaged during a thunderstorm.[39] Recent Turkish studies of the saint and his complex describe the circumstances of this restoration, but introduce an element of confusion concerning the identity of the benefactor who made it possible. In 1910, a thunderbolt had struck the minaret. This fell onto the middle hall, where the well was situated. 'For several years', the author of a recent study of the complex writes, 'the keepers of the mausoleum stood guard at the base of the marble columns. Later ... Rauf Pasha's daughter, Princess Fatma Hanim, who lived in Beylerbeyi, had the present middle hall and conservatory made, and also donated a single-piece carpet to the mausoleum.'[40] According to this account, Princess Fatma also met the cost of publishing a second edition of Hüdayi's collected works in the Ottoman script.[41] These acts of dedication to Hüdayi were most likely the work of mother and daughter together.[42] Rauf had indeed explicitly affirmed to close associates that his mother was a direct descendant of Hüdayi, through one of the saint's daughters. This claim is difficult to investigate,[43] but it may point to Emire Hanim's maternal ancestry and thus explain Fatma Hanim's special interest in the Hüdayi complex.

Emire Hanim also had a close association with the Qadiri shaykh Hz. Mehmet Ali Özkardeş (1895–1980), and with his shaykh Hz. Ahmet Süreyya Emin (1848–1923), who was also a Qadiri.[44] Özkardeş' daughter describes Emire Hanim as 'a spiritual daughter' of Süreyya, and recalls her frequent visits to Özkardeş, with the young Rauf in tow.[45] This does not necessarily indicate a Qadiri *tariqa* affiliation, however, for Arim, herself a close associate of Özkardeş, relates that he admitted members of all *tariqas* to his meetings. Perhaps reflecting her father Mahmut Sirri Pasha's affiliation, at the same time Emire Hanim reportedly had a connection to the Shabaniyye.[46] There are also accounts among associates of her having attended the *sama'* at the Mevlevi *tekke* in Istanbul, accompanied by the young Rauf. Such accounts may be seen in light of the established connection with the Mevlevis enjoyed by the family of her second husband, Abdul Rauf Bey.[47]

Rauf's second cousin, Münevver Ayaşli (d.1999),[48] and her immediate family feature prominently in associates' accounts of his broader family background.[49] Arim suggests that Ayaşli's father Caferi Tayyar, a colonel in the Turkish army, had a close association with Ibn 'Arabi. He always kept a copy of the *Fusus* with the Qur'an by his bed, and would see Ibn 'Arabi in dreams and waking visions. Arim relates an account of one such episode.

The colonel's first child, a daughter,[50] had been born in Thessalonica, where his wife was based while he served during the Greek war. Three years later, he was walking in the market when his name was called out. He turned and saw Ibn 'Arabi before him. The saint asked him for a silver coin and gave him a gold sovereign in its place.[51] Tayyar was then sent to Damascus, where his wife and daughter joined him. Soon afterwards, the little girl died of typhoid. Tayyar buried her 'in the courtyard of Ibn 'Arabi's tomb'.[52] His wife later gave birth to a son, materialising Ibn 'Arabi's 'exchange of gold for silver' in Tayyar's vision.

Tayyar's second daughter, Münevver, was also born in Thessalonica. The family finally joined their father in Istanbul in 1911, but relocated frequently as Tayyar's military career advanced. Münevver travelled in Arab countries and Europe and had a varied, multilingual education. At the age of ten or eleven, her father reportedly introduced her to Ibn 'Arabi. Her marriage later to Nusret Sadullah Ayaşli, an ex-ambassador, brought family connections to the Turkish world of saints and *tariqa*s. Her husband was thus related to Ayaş-i Bünyamin Veli of the Melami-Bayrami *tariqa*.[53] Münevver herself developed relations with many shaykhs in Turkey. During a visit to her brother in Paris, she enrolled at the Sorbonne and reportedly studied Ibn 'Arabi with Louis Massignon, for whom she developed a great sympathy.[54]

In 1947, following her husband's death and in the face of financial difficulties, she began a writing career, translating articles from French for publication in a religious newspaper.[55] Eventually, she became a well-known novelist.[56] In 1969, the newspaper for which she worked sent her on the hajj to record her experiences. When she returned to Istanbul, she opened her doors to anyone who wished to visit. Qadiris, Jerrahis, Rifa'is, Mevlevis and Bektashis reportedly flocked to her, while many young people attached themselves to her.[57] Portrayed by some associates as a 'traditionalist' who insisted on 'external' Islamic practice, it appears she emerged as a self-styled spiritual leader.[58]

The three generations of Rauf's family we have just explored displayed both concrete associations with *tariqa*s, shaykhs and specific spiritual lineages, and connections in the unseen world through the appearance of saintly figures in dreams and waking visions. Rauf's spiritual heritage encompassed both dimensions, but it was through the imaginal realm in particular that his spiritual awakening would find its moment and its direction.[59]

Life-story, formative influences and spiritual associations

Impacted by the Ottoman demise of the 1920s and the Free Officers' revolution in mid-century Egypt, Rauf's life prior to his arrival in London reflected some of the major upheavals and prominent trends of the Muslim twentieth century. He was born in Beylerbeyi, Istanbul on 17 July 1911, in the year his grandfather had been interred in Ibn 'Arabi's mausoleum. He acquired his early education in the opulent family home.[60] Later he attended Robert College, an American secondary school favoured by the late Ottoman elite in Istanbul. Exposed to several languages, he eventually developed competence in French, English, Arabic and Ottoman Turkish.

At the age of seventeen, four years after the Kemalist revolution, Rauf travelled to the USA to complete his studies, in English literature at Cornell and Hittite archaeology at Yale. He then travelled to Switzerland, where he enjoyed the life of a wealthy aristocrat in exile. In 1945 (at the age of thirty-four) he married his second cousin Princess Faize (1923–94).[61] Faize was the younger sister of King Farouk of Egypt (r.1936–52) and daughter of the first king, Fu'ad (r.1922–36). It was a marriage arranged through family relations. They settled into a privileged life together in Egypt.[62]

In the wake of the 1952 revolution and the demise of the Egyptian royal court, the wealth of the royal family was largely confiscated and many of its members went into exile. Rauf and his wife left for Spain and then France, living from the sale of valuables. A decade later, they divorced. Finding work as a landscape garden designer, Rauf remained in Paris. His life had changed. He had lost his home and wife, his money was running out, and poverty threatened, as he could no longer take any source of income for granted. An associate sums up the profound changes that had been visited upon him: 'Once he was a prince, now he was heading towards being a pauper.'[63]

A significant turning point came in the aftermath of a car accident, which left him with a broken leg.[64] Lying in a hospital bed in great discomfort and thinking of all that he had lost, he decided to commit suicide by hurling himself out of a window. The appearance of a nurse at a critical moment arrested his train of thought. She told him that an old lady nursing a broken leg in the neighbouring ward had confessed that she kept going in the knowledge that he too was suffering like her, and with such forbearance. He immediately abandoned the idea of suicide.[65]

One internal narrative frames this episode as a 'conversion' experience, suggesting that Rauf then 'turned to God'. Specifically, he was converted to 'the essential meaning of the spiritual life as elucidated by Ibn 'Arabi.'[66] By this account Rauf's decision to abandon suicide had been the fruit 'of innate compassion', and his 'return' would henceforth be a manifestation of divine mercy. Some time after this episode, Ibn 'Arabi reportedly appeared to Rauf and 'told him to go to England.'[67]

Based on his grandfather's association with the saint, Rauf would later describe his relationship to Ibn 'Arabi as 'atavistic.'[68] From some point during

the second half of the 1960s, this relationship came to the fore and began
to direct his life. The resulting reorientation is perhaps best understood
not in terms of an abrupt conversion (as suggested by the account we have
just related), but of the gradual awakening of a mature man, who found in
his cultural–spiritual heritage a basis for meaning in a life marked out by
extraordinary privilege and loss.

What were the immediate influences upon Rauf, and what can be uncovered in the way of his own spiritual life prior to his arrival in London?
Associates project the family milieu of his youth within its broader sociocultural context as an essential aspect of his 'preparation' for his ultimate
vocation. Encapsulating the privileged tastes and refinement of the late
Ottoman elite, it planted in him the seeds of a deep sophistication. This
was a milieu characterised by a cosmopolitan openness to other cultures
and a tolerance of different faiths. For example, there are accounts of Emire
Hanim having entertained guests of diverse backgrounds, including the
Jewish doctor who had delivered her sons and became a close friend. Rauf
recalled overhearing their conversations about religion and spirituality, in
which the doctor had commented that, if God were removed, there would
be great difficulty 'finding something to replace Him'. Such concerns may
have reflected an early flavour of the direction in which mysticism typically
developed among the higher strata of society after 1925, where it sometimes
'merged into spiritualism'.[69] Associates suggest that, although it was rooted
in faith, there was no emphasis in Rauf's immediate family on traditional
Islamic practice, and hence 'no narrowing' in his early experience. This may
be a projection of the Beshara view concerning religion. It is at odds with
Arim's claim that all family members practised Islam, and that it would have
been inconceivable for it to have been otherwise.[70] Given her proximity to
the family, Arim's claim must be given greater weight, but the situation in all
likelihood combined elements of both characterisations.[71]

Emire Hanim occupies a prominent place in associates' perceptions of
the origins of Rauf's spiritual knowledge. Thus, he said that he had learned
'all that he knew' from her.[72] Emire Hanim was indeed the dominant influence in his formative years. His childhood exposure to the world of sufism,
its shaykhs and *dhikr* meetings mainly took place through her.[73] As a young
teenager, he may have read the *Fusus* (reportedly much emphasised within
the family) at home with his brother Mahmut, under Emire Hanim's watchful
eye. It is also possible that he was taken to become a *murid* of the Mevlevis
at this time, but (significantly, according to associates) they did not accept
him.

While all this ended when Rauf left Istanbul aged seventeen, there is a
conviction within Beshara that he continued to nurture a 'spiritual connection', which informed his conduct and choices even before his so-called
conversion of the 1960s. Such claims relating to an individual's inner life
are impossible to evaluate in the absence of any indication of their external
manifestation. In Rauf's case the image that dominates narratives of his life

prior to his 'conversion' is devoid of any such tangible indications. Yet the internal perspective finds evidence of further preparation for his ultimate vocation in the unusual breadth and variety of his experience prior to his arrival in London. This was characterised by extensive travels and encounters with many different cultures, for example. He had himself reportedly come to the realisation that his rich experience of life 'had been necessary for him to develop his spiritual understanding.'[74] It also enabled him later to relate his 'spiritual knowledge' to many fields.[75] In its 'complete absence of narrowing in any way', as one associate puts it, his later life experience had consolidated that of his youth. All this had facilitated the maturing of a vision based on a conviction that the 'narrow path of religion' could not be a viable basis for spirituality in the future. Rauf himself apparently projected the narrative of his life prior to its London chapter as preparation for what was to come in the work of Beshara. He thus reportedly remarked, in one associate's words, that 'nothing (intrinsically important) had happened until his fifties, when he arrived in England.'

After leaving Istanbul, Rauf visited the city perhaps twice, during the years of his marriage to Faize. On later visits, which began some years after his divorce from her in 1962, he encountered the city's sufi personalities, and developed close personal relations with several sufi shaykhs.[76] These included the wandering Melami dervish Shevke Dede, who had told him to return to England during his visit to Istanbul with Culme-Seymour. Rauf reportedly respected him greatly. Among them also were Mevlevi shaykhs, including Suleyman Loras Dede. He was on good terms with Muzaffer Özak (1916–85), the Halveti–Jerrahi shaykh who attracted Western converts and ultimately exported his *tariqa* to the USA.[77] Özkardeş also became a close contact for, according to his daughter, Rauf was his 'spiritual son', and the two men would correspond with each other.[78]

We cannot discount the possible influence of such figures on Rauf, and on the conceptualisation of his spiritual project. Arim indeed recalls that Rauf later discussed Beshara with Özkardeş and Özak (among others), and they understood and respected his vocation.[79] While Özak is well known in twentieth-century Turkish and Western sufism, Shevke Dede, as a Melami, remains inscrutable. We can briefly illuminate the figures of Özkardeş and Süreyya, who are little known beyond Turkey.

The tombs of these two shaykhs in Yildiz Park graveyard, in Beşiktaş, Istanbul,[80] provide evidence of the continuing vitality of the cult that surrounds them.[81] Devotees describe Süreyya as one of the four 'second' *pirs* recognised by the Qadiriyya (the 'first' is 'Abd al-Qadir himself). They deem both shaykhs members of the highest category of saint.[82] Süreyya described himself as Jesus Christ, come on earth again as a great saint with the purpose of matching his spiritual maturity and perfection in the corporeal realm.[83] Accordingly, he asserted that he was endowed as Jesus had been, and could do what he had done, including raising the dead.[84] Özkardeş described himself as 'Mehdi Rasul', the figure who will appear at the end of time to restore righteousness for a period. Devotees report that he heard Ibn 'Arabi telling him that he would assume this position. In Özkardeş' words, Ibn 'Arabi had said 'I am giving the great news: you are Mehdi who I mention in my books.'[85] Devotees believe that, at the Resurrection, Muslims will wait for Özkardeş to intercede for them. Christians will wait for Süreyya, who claimed he would be able to intercede for people of all religions. Reflecting their roles and spiritual identities, the cult surrounding these two saints is marked by a strong eschatological element.[86] Their profound admiration and support for Ataturk deserve particular mention, for Rauf was reportedly familiar with the narratives in which this was expressed.[87]

Rauf had no relationship as *murid* to any particular shaykh and no *tariqa* affiliation that might form the basis of his credentials as Beshara's guiding figure.[88] Such credentials as he had were based instead in two distinct but interrelated spheres. First were his familial spiritual associations, which we outlined above. Young thus writes that, on both sides, Rauf's family was 'steeped in the inner, esoteric knowledge of the Unity not only of God but also of the Unity of all Existence'. Based on this, he indeed suggests that Rauf claimed an 'atavistic' esoteric education.[89] His familial spiritual associations furnished potentially powerful symbolic legitimisation of Rauf's status in Beshara. This was perhaps at its most potent in the case of the proximity of his grandfather's tomb to that of the very saint whose teaching he established in the movement. Equally important, however, was Rauf's descent from Hüdayi, especially given his projection of the Celvetiyye as the *tariqa* that most closely reflects the teaching of Ibn 'Arabi.[90] Yet it seems that Rauf made scant mention of these connections, Young's comment above notwithstanding. Most associates were alerted to his grandfather's physical proximity to Ibn 'Arabi in death (with all that this implied) only when it was mentioned on the inside cover of the *White Fusus* in 1986, and only very few close associates correctly grasped Emire Hanim's genealogy.[91]

In contrast, Rauf made the second basis of his spiritual authority widely known to associates. He shared and emphasised accounts of two momentous visions of saintly figures that had effectively redirected his life, and ultimately would shape Beshara. We relate these two accounts, which convey the Uwaysi character of his spiritual education, below.[92] There were other visions, but it is difficult to convey a clear picture of them, as Rauf largely withheld from associates the details of his spiritual experiences. Most of them relate to Ibn 'Arabi's role in directing him to his destiny in England, and in Beshara. These include the saint's appearance to him following his 'conversion', when he instructed Rauf to make for England. There is an account of a mysterious figure who introduced him to Ibn 'Arabi's writings in a dream. Another narrative has the saint appear to Rauf during his early days in London. Rauf related that he had known that something would be established in England but he had not known what, or the direction it should take. He had been thinking 'should it be along Mevlevi lines, or perhaps Celveti?' Having thought about it from all angles, he had declared: 'None of them! Let it be only for Him!' At this very point Ibn 'Arabi had appeared, standing at the end of Rauf's bed. The saint had exclaimed *in English* 'At last!' Rauf had attributed significance to this choice of language.

There were also visions of the Prophet. Rauf shared an account of one such vision with a very close associate, in correspondence. It took place during the early days of Beshara, in 1973. He had woken before dawn and was calling down prayers and blessings upon the Prophet in his Kastamonu hotel room. He planned to visit the tomb of Shaban Veli (founder of the *tariqa* to which his grandfather had been affiliated) that day. In a vision he saw himself, Culme-Seymour and Münevver Ayaşli transported to the Kastamonu public square. They were browsing through tourist shops and contemplating buying a wooden key-hanger. The prayers and blessings he was repeating were engraved on it. At that moment the Prophet had appeared, in 'Arab dress'. He said he had two key-hangers, one for Rauf and Culme-Seymour, and one for Münevver Ayaşli. They were the same as the key-hangers they had been looking at, but the key-hangers extended by the Prophet bore the name ''Ali' in gold letters, rather than 'Muhammad'. Rauf then recalled the hadith of the Prophet, 'I am the citadel of knowledge and 'Ali is the key to the gate'. He concluded his account by invoking 'Ali to open this gate for himself, and for the associate with whom he was corresponding.[93]

The first vision Rauf emphasised and shared widely with associates was apparently linked with the period of his 'conversion', and may thus have signified an 'initiation' into the mystical way. It took the form of a triple intervention by three towering saints: Ibn 'Arabi, 'Abd al-Qadir al-Jilani and Uways al-Qarani. Rauf alerted associates to the 'responsibility and taste' of these figures in the work of Beshara. It appears that they had always been a part of his life. As a child, for example, he had reportedly called on them for help in times of need. Now they had appeared to him to direct his spiritual way.[94] We have explored Rauf's 'atavistic' relationship to Ibn 'Arabi. His connection with 'Abd al-Qadir can perhaps be understood as a reflection of his mother's strong Qadiri associations. Describing this great saint as *al-ghawth al-a'zam*, Rauf was to cite him at length in his early discourses.[95] Finally, it was apt that Uways in particular should provide spontaneous initiation to a man who had neither living master nor formal spiritual training, for the tradition of auto- (or more precisely theo-) didactic sufism takes its name from him.[96]

The second of Rauf's well-known visions took the form of a dream he had at Chisholme during autumn 1978. This was to provide further direction to Beshara. He found himself in a square room with French windows at one end, giving onto a beautiful garden. At the other end there was an open door. Light streamed in through it.[97] Rauf stood with 'the people of Beshara' in a semicircle in one corner, near the door. On the other side of the room stood 'men of great stature' (*büyükler*, as he conveyed it in Turkish), dressed in robes and large turbans. A man in a robe and turban stood in the centre, facing the door. This was Hüdayi. He was waiting to greet 'the master', his teacher Üftade (d.1580), with whom the Celveti tradition emanated.[98]

Before Hüdayi could greet him, Üftade swiftly walked in, his gold-embroidered multicoloured robe flowing behind him.[99] After all present had greeted him, he turned and gestured to Rauf, saying 'You are of us!' (*sizler bizlerdensiniz*). Rauf explained the significance of the saint's address, which had been in the plural. It indicated that 'the people of Beshara [as a whole] are of the taste of Üftade, Hüdayi, and their followers.'[100] The saint's turn of phrase had been emphatic, moreover, implicitly removing any doubt that may have surrounded this matter.

Following this dream, the Celveti saints came to occupy a special place for Rauf, and by extension for Beshara. He spoke much of them to associates, and visits to their tombs were incorporated into the Turkey trip. His spiritual relationship with Hüdayi was reportedly marked by a subtle veiling. Rauf put this down to his physical descent from the saint, which produced some awkwardness between them.[101] Üftade, on the other hand, 'would come and go' freely to Rauf. He related that he could hear the saint's firm footsteps, and would converse directly with him.

From the early 1970s, Rauf's life story was inextricably tied to the emergence and development of Beshara. Associates describe the first phase of his 'life in Beshara' as one of 'coming together', a reference to the coalescence represented by the Swyre Farm era. The second phase began with the institution of residential courses. This demanded of him an increased intensity of involvement, as he assumed personal responsibility for designing courses and delivering materials. He was generally accessible at this time, and could be found daily in the Mead Hall at Chisholme by any who needed to consult him. The third phase overlapped somewhat with the second. At the end of the 1970s, he began to devote ever more time to translating the Bosnevi commentary. To meet the demands of this work he withdrew a little and was less involved in overseeing courses directly, although 'he kept his finger on the pulse'. The final phase began in the wake of serious illness in 1984. At this point he began to put his affairs and those of Beshara in order, in preparation for death.

Rauf underwent a successful operation to treat cancer of the oesophagus in 1984. Two years later his health began to deteriorate again, and he died in September 1987. His burial in the grounds of Chisholme was a simple affair. Led by Peter Young, associates took turns in carrying the coffin to its resting-place. Some hint at the significance of his passing. They point to the fact that the night marking the end of the fortieth day after this coincided with the worst storms for many decades in the south of England, in October 1987. Associates have made a point of commemorating the date of his passing with a *dhikr* gathering.[102]

Approach as adviser and guide

[Rauf's] great concern was 'the dilemma of modern man's lack of spiritual dimension'.

Beshara associate[103]

Bulent constantly insisted on the intellectual discipline that would not provide easy answers to our dilemmas, but would provide a road map that people could carry with them throughout their life.

Beshara associate[104]

Rauf reportedly described his involvement in spiritual education at Chisholme as 'something he had dreamed about all his life'.[105] How can his role be characterised, and how did he see this? How did he communicate with and guide students? What was the impact of his approach?

The pointer to Unity

Rauf's outstanding characteristic as a spiritual adviser and guide appears to have been his self-effacing manner. He preferred not to speak of himself, spoke of his past only anecdotally and provided information only in answer to direct questions.[106] His systematic deflecting of attention away from himself towards unmediated actualisation of the goal of the spiritual way was the antithesis of many contemporary 'guru-centric' spiritual trends. Although some associates might have perceived him as a guru or some kind of 'holy man' (as Feild appears to have done), Rauf always insisted that he was unimportant.[107] Rather what mattered was associates' certainty of 'their non-separation from God'.[108] All questions and actions 'were transformed towards helping others to appreciate [the] goal [of Union with God]',[109] and he never veered from 'the premise that Union with God was the sole purpose for the existence of Man'.[110] Although he recognised that he served as a conduit for a specific teaching, Rauf did not project himself as the bridge to the ultimate destination of Union. As one associate recalls,

> [Rauf] often said ... he was just a signpost, pointing the way to those who recognised that he knew what they were looking for. He avoided in any way being a teacher or guru figure, and was strongly critical of those who interpose themselves between the seeker and the sought. *"Don't look at me; look at what I see. Don't love me; love what I love."*[111]

He insisted that he was 'just a messenger, a means by which wisdom and knowledge could be passed', and constantly reminded students that he was not some 'sheikh'.[112] He had no interest in titles: associates referred to him by his first name (some adding to this 'Bey' according to the Turkish manner of respectful address). An understating of his personal role was captured in the formalisation of this as 'Consultant' to the Trust. Such understating also underpins associates' outward projections of this role.[113]

While he reportedly saw and projected himself as a student just like them (albeit one who had been 'studying for longer'),[114] associates believe Rauf was 'at the state of Perfect Man.'[115] A perception of his status as realised man was indeed implicit in his role as 'pointer' to Unity,[116] as we described it above, for his knowledge ultimately flowed from this. Thus as one associate puts it, 'We are all mirrors to each other, and we all have in us the inexorable search for the answer to our identity ... A man of knowledge is someone who can show us, through his own knowledge and being, that there is a way to those answers, and who can be a mirror to our inner needs. Bulent was such a man.'[117] 'Through him', another writes, 'we saw what was possible for us, and gained confidence that what had seemed an impossible dream was the reality of ourselves.'[118]

At the court of the unknown king

On the surface, associates led 'a completely ordinary life' with Rauf. They shared a drink, laughed together and functioned as completely free agents. Nothing was singled out, as one associate puts it, for 'religious prohibition'. On the inside, however, what was happening to them 'was not normal'. One associate describes the time he spent with Rauf in Turkey during their early relationship as 'studying at the court of an unknown king'. Looking back, associates refer to Rauf as 'a true friend' and 'a wise counsellor'.[119] His qualities inspired great respect and love in them, yet they also recall fondly his sense of humour and fun, cherishing memories of him and imagining how he would respond to specific situations. They took notice of his wide interests and his 'tremendously polite, generous, thoughtful and tactful' bearing towards all people, regardless of their background.[120] Rauf himself was reportedly 'well aware that [associates] found his company ... sometimes awe-inspiring and difficult to bear, because he was fully present in the moment.'[121] Particularly conscious of the contrast between their own experience and condition and his 'consummate, exquisite' taste,[122] some characterise their early encounters with him in terms of 'raw youth being educated by a cultured man', or 'illiterates in need of civilising'.

In his dealings with students, Rauf was in equal measure compassionate and stern. As they became familiar with his ways and drew closer to him, associates 'found themselves in the company of a person in full possession of that essentially compassionate nature, which is in every individual as their original potential.'[123] Recognising always 'the original behind the image',[124] he believed that 'there was something good in all people, and [that] it was the job of anyone concerned with the well-being of any person to encourage those good qualities, and to place no emphasis on the inessential qualities of negativity'.[125]

On the Oneness of Being and the way: Rauf as communicator and adviser

How did Rauf explain the Oneness of Being and the spiritual way to students? While 'at ease with the most elevated explanations concerning Man's perfectibility', he was reportedly able to express these ideas 'at the level of those who brought the questions'.[126] He actively encouraged questions,[127] and took these as the best indicator of a student's potential for understanding. He would interact with each according to their level, matching his openness to their receptivity, and displaying 'a unique ability to understand and empathise with the needs of each person'.[128] Yet at times, while relaxing with a group, he would be prompted by a passing remark to suddenly come out emphatically with something they all 'had to know and understand'.[129] He sometimes interpreted the significant dreams students brought to his attention. These provided an opportunity to impart spiritual knowledge intensely personal to the dreamer.

As a communicator of esoteric truths and a guide to the spiritual way, Rauf 'was never mystifying'.[130] He reduced mysticism to 'the most simple and practical value based on the absolute Unity of Existence, and the love of that One in knowing itself as the Beautiful'.[131] His talks delivered to students on the early intensive courses (often given 'in response to a particular stage or difficulty' and published in 1986 as *Addresses*)[132] recruited dictionary definitions,[133] quotations from Western literary masterpieces[134] and mundane analogies[135] to facilitate understanding. Intended, in Young's words, 'for those who want to come to understand their relationship to Reality, what their purpose is and how consequently they should proceed',[136] the style of these talks is direct, simple and focused. To explain or illustrate a point, Rauf drew in them on a few authorities and celebrated sufis, but especially Ibn 'Arabi.[137] His brief summaries of themes in the latter's metaphysics written over the years to individual associates or for use in the School and collected in *Addresses II* represented an attempt to render accessible key points in this.[138]

Concerning the challenges of the spiritual way, Rauf spun students no illusions. One recalls that he stressed the intertwining of experiences of divine guidance with those of bewilderment. Another remembers him suggesting good-humouredly that a notice be hung above the door of the study room at the School, with the words 'Abandon hope, all ye who enter here!'[139] Repeatedly, he reminded students of their current reality, 'at the extreme limit of manifestation', and their ultimate destiny as 'the *perfect reflection* of all ... the Ipseity is and means'.[140] He explained to them the mystical psychology elaborated by sufi authorities to chart the possibilities of mystical experience.[141] Delicately but firmly, he guided them through the stages of the way. He identified potential pitfalls and provided prescriptions for avoiding or tackling them, always underlining what was indispensable. For example:

> All and everyone starts at [the] point of ... 'the lowest of the low' – lower than which there is not ... Unless your resolve is unshakeable ... you will never succeed

... You are dead, you are asleep. Until you wake up, unless you come to life before the physical death, you will remain in varying degrees or at the lowest of the low ... How to do this? Through Trust, Certainty, Patience, Resolution and Veracity. How to acquire these? Again, through Service, Knowledge, Meditation and *Zikr*.[142]

Emphasising the 'deep and constant importance' of humility, Rauf posited it as 'the fulcrum of all possible evolution without which no manner of attainment is to be expected.'[143] Realisation of essential oneness, he told students, could thus flow only from

> the complete humility of your ego to accept ... knowledge [of the ego as His individuation as you] and make it its own belief ... *you* as a separate entity do not realise, understand or know anything, or, to tell the truth, exist as such. Can your ego ... allow you to admit such a premise?[144]

They must remain vigilant against even an implicit or tacit denial of the Oneness of Being, as would arise if one were 'to hold personal or subjective views, to have one's own particular knowledge, learning or response.'[145] To avoid this, he advised as a first task

> to hold vivid in our minds the best reference we know to the Unity of Existence ... that essentially there is no other existence or existent than the One and Only ... This ... way of understanding the Unity of Existence with special emphasis on ... the non-existence of anything aught but the Existence of Only the One ... should be indelibly printed before our eyes and stressed in our thoughts at all moments and under all considerations.[146]

Only through perfect servitude, Rauf insisted, could deluded affirmation of separate existence and a denial of the Oneness of Being be finally obliterated. He projected this as

> Perfect ... and total abnegation of the partial human freedom and independence in favour of service to the One ... Complete servitude is the only factor which negates a separate existence than the one served, simply because the perfect servant is imbued with the qualities and attributes of the One served.[147]

What does Union signify, and how can the aspirant arrive at it? Rauf was clear that it signifies more than knowledge alone:

> The meaning of the word ... Union as used by many like Ibnul 'Arabi ... does not ... end with its admitted esoteric vocabulary meaning. For Ibnul 'Arabi and many that think like him ... Union is not a matter of knowing what it means but the act of progression towards the fulfilment of that action and knowledge, to feel an irresistible desire to reach, consciously, that state of being where one is in Union ... [K]nowledge ... is not *per se* enough to allow one to be in the State of Union ... An example ... from Ibnul 'Arabi clarifies what is meant by knowing about it and being it. He says one might know what heroism is but that does not make one into a hero until one actually performs an act of Heroism. Then only is one a Hero. So ... Union is a deliberate act of progression to being One.[148]

On the realisation of Union, he clarified, 'Nothing has happened. Simply, that he who was Essentially Him, came to realise, but not only intellectually, that he was no other than Him.'[149] 'Death during life' is thus 'a completely esoteric transposition'. The beginning of self-knowledge launches the journey according to which 'we change from one state to another until we come to a point of reality which is unchangeable ... the point of Truth.'[150] 'In this world, already here', Rauf explained to students, 'it is Paradise – if one has the predilection and the necessary intention to progress towards and Be no other than that which is unqualified Sheer Beauty.'[151] Thus

> Ibnul 'Arabi sees 'death' as such ... as not existing. He himself goes and comes ... to the other world, converses with the inhabitants of both worlds and advises them, and assumes that such a state is not a unique possibility accessible to him alone. Quite in concordance with the saying of the Prophet 'Die before you die', Ibnul 'Arabi expects all that follow his teachings to ... accede as urgently and as ... soon as each is capable of understanding what it means. He has no patience in this ... He says in his ... *Risalat-ul Wujudiyyah* that he has no converse with those who see illusion as reality since they are ... veiled from Reality. They are not, therefore, ardently in Love and are not consequently intent on Union.[152]

Ultimately, Rauf stressed, 'the good-Taste for it' (*dhawq*) is the prerequisite for the 'unceasing progression towards and finally [arriving at] Being'. Citing the Prophet's prayer for 'taste in vision', he suggested that 'the crux of the matter of Union ... seems to lie in a taste for it.'[153] This concept was central to Rauf's approach to spiritual education, and we will return to it shortly.

Among the specific challenges of the way, Rauf singled out doubt. He described it as a wavering of conviction 'instilled in one to deviate from the path of one's knowledge'. This was most likely to strike *before* students could realise the extensive knowledge they had received during the relatively short time of the course. He advanced an antidote to such doubt. '[O]ne must learn not to judge, oneself, but one must discriminate according to reason and intellect, and then apply oneself to Him for intercession so that one may see the truth in Truth.'[154] He also alerted students to a further kind of doubt that would assault them when they were back in society and away from the support of fellow students: people would try to undermine their certainty. He explained that they need not fear this if they understood correctly the basis of the knowledge they had received on the course.[155] To those daunted by the challenges they faced, he provided reassurance. For example, he suggested that, if they were asked to undertake a task, whatever was needed for its accomplishment would be provided, and if they were asked a question, the answer would be contained within it.[156] He attributed this reality to the interconnectedness of all things.

Rauf's approach to spiritual education and the insights he conveyed fundamentally changed students' relations to things, themselves and others, and to the world at large. The profoundly positive psychological impact of such insights as the following can readily be imagined: 'As a host is to his guests externally, so man is to himself, and in his relationship to reality, internally.'[157] He repeatedly underscored, in one associate's words, 'the very great nature that is man's inheritance – his being in the image of God, and the fact that it is within our capacity to know this nature and to be conscious of it.'[158] By stressing the immediate existential relevance of the Oneness of Being with all its implications for the individual, he offered a powerful antidote to the difficulties posed by their own psychology to those who grasped it.[159] For example,

> The essential is not to falter from one's own essence, which is The Essence ... by permanent, concentrated ... belief that the ... premise [that one's own essence is The Essence] is the only Truth, and that all that is essentially originates from that very same source. All the rest is paraphernalia, 'I feel this,' 'I feel that,' 'I have done right,' 'I have done wrong,' and all such are nothing but sheer tests of strength of your belief. But belief must be verified, reasoned and intuited ... When all this is true then the tests are borne in ease, knowing well that the Essential being is ever untouched by accident or fault ... Then the tests pass over one and leave no mark or scar.[160]

And

> What is the single most important point that must be understood by a person who wants to know? It is that there is only One, Unique, Absolute, Infinite Existence. It must be more than an idea. One has to be so completely certain of it that one adopts it through reason and intuition as the basic unshakeable fact of one's existence. When it is like that in one's existence, then every possible ramification that occurs to one is seen as not being outside the Existence, but as being an aspect of it. Accept and completely adopt the idea that there is only the Unique, Absolute Existence, apart from which there is not. Then constantly, or as much as possible, keep it in mind. Then, as only He can adopt such an idea, you disappear in the face of the awareness of this idea ... Then your consciousness of this idea is your consciousness of His Existence; His consciousness of Himself. Then where are you? You never were. He shows you He is yourself, then bit by bit He shows you how He is all that there is. These showings are His caprices, until all exterior existence is known as Him. He shows you He is you, then shows you (Himself) that all else is Him.[161]

A practical dimension

There was a strong practical dimension to Rauf's approach. He would transform everyday objects and mundane acts into opportunities to convey and illustrate esoteric concepts. Through such clarifications, they took on a new, 'spiritual' aspect. This was at its clearest in relation to two principles. The first of these was to value one's essential nature (and thus one's inherent dignity as man). Rauf emphasised this by setting great store by the proper use of things. He construed the misuse of something (or a lack of its use) as a failure to properly value the object in question, and by extension one's own humanity.

His purpose in this was to warn students against failing to use their humanity, or misusing it.[162]

The second principle relates to the development of *dhawq*, introduced above. Best rendered as 'taste' or 'discernment', Rauf designated by this an inner capacity to recognise and distinguish between multiple levels of being and experience, to align oneself spontaneously with the 'best' or most refined of them, and to savour the quality.[163] As just noted, he projected a taste for Union as a prerequisite for it. He was convinced that humanity as a whole would gradually learn *dhawq* with the passage of time, and conveyed this idea through the French saying 'Le bon-goût s'apprend' ('good-Taste is learnt'), which he repeated often.[164] He explained: 'Good taste is learned, therefore given freely to allow the essential development through the potential of the Self. "Given" is what is "learned". One can only learn what is given, but being given is dependent upon desire to receive for its effect.'[165] He brought the notion of taste home to students (and endeavoured to cultivate it in them) by emphasising *quality*, urging the use of the best as far as was possible in all spheres of life. This emphasis was particularly prominent in relation to food, both in its preparation and enjoyment. As one associate recalls,

> So much to do with Bulent was about food. He realised that if you eat well and are nourished you feel well and this makes you receptive. Consequently, he insisted on the quality of the ingredients and cooking at Chisholme, using food as a tool, catering to people totally, physically and spiritually, by feeding them. He appreciated that there is a continuum between the exercise of *dhawq* in relation to food and in the context of the spiritual experience.

Food has often served as a symbol of spiritual nourishment, and this dimension is apparent in Rauf's attitude towards it.[166] He had an undoubted love for good food.[167] He also had considerable knowledge of cooking, and liked to write on the subject.[168] Those who watched him at work in the kitchen recognised that 'a different level of awareness was involved in his cooking', rooted in 'traditions which have touched upon the very principles of human life'. He has been described by one associate as 'a mystic in the kitchen'. For him, cooking was thus 'a mystical art'. Reflecting the organic connection between the world of the kitchen and that of spirituality, he would emphasise *dhawq* as 'the essential ingredient ... in all cooking, whether referring to food or to the human evolution and education'.[169] Prominent in the School kitchen, his 'Notice to Cooks' synthesises the esoteric symbolism of cooking (prominent in traditional Mevlevi discourse) with his underlining of the proper use and valuing of things and the centrality of *dhawq*:[170]

> Now know this – that cooking is an art. It is also an integral part of esoteric training because it is a twofold means of service: service to humanity and service to the food prepared. There is no higher state than that which a man can reach; all other forms of life in this world find their possibility of reaching a higher state through their conjunction with man. The only possibility for the sublimation of some minerals, vegetables and animals in a higher state of life is through cooking.

That is why ... the Mevlevi [sic] ... refer to the esoteric education of the novices as cooking, and to achievement as taste.[171] Those who use ingredients of food without consideration of providing the best possible means of an ingredient's expression are devaluing service, awareness and value of life. Therefore, cooking is not a mixture of ingredients but a harmonious composition of artistic value, nutrient and transcendent ... It should be undertaken only in an attitude of deep respect and consideration and full awareness of the bounty and clemency in the Divine order. Note – that there is no expression of divine manifestation devoid of beauty. Beauty of taste (*dhawq*) is an absolutely necessary ingredient of the essential (in all senses) composition. Had it been in the Divine order of things that mankind should graze, there would have been no need for cooking at all ... Know then, that cooking is a responsibility in awareness wherein under-cooking or over-cooking are equally reprehensible and a clear oversight ... May the *himma* of the great saint who was Rumi's personal cook until his death, Şemseddin Ateşbaz Wali,[172] be upon you who undertake to serve in this kitchen.

Associates who spent time with Rauf have become accomplished cooks, mastering modern Turkish and late Ottoman cuisine.[173] Emphasising the impact of good food on a person's state, they continue to pay considerable attention to the preparation and presentation of food, and to regular nourishment. The role of good food in spiritual realisation is summed up in one associate's recollection of having been 'so taken by beauty' that he wanted 'to make mayonnaise that was so good that people would cry out and remember God on tasting it!'

On studying Ibn 'Arabi

'The purpose of all your study', Rauf impressed on students during an early intensive course, 'is to bring you to a realisation of your "essential" oneness with the One and Only Absolute Existence.' He added a reminder that 'essential' here 'mainly means "in your essence" as well as your origin and your reality.'[174] Rauf's notion of esoteric education had important implications for the approach to the study of Ibn 'Arabi he instituted. Convinced that the esoteric truths set out in the saint's writings could not be 'taught' any more than knowledge of them could be 'acquired', he insisted that all the student could do was to adopt the right intention and demeanour, and thus to remain open to receive understanding if it were given. "Arabi [sic] *cannot* be taught', he wrote. 'The only teacher in this matter is 'Arabi. It can only be studied, learnt, absorbed – that is if 'Arabi wants to teach.'[175] 'Knowledge is *given to one*, not acquired', he reminded an associate who was experiencing difficulties in understanding *The Twenty-nine Pages*:

> You are studying and trying to learn: this is your volition, and being open to reception – nothing more. If it is not given to you, you may be as open as a door to the north wind, but nothing but cold air will blow through you. *It is given* ... Knowledge is given to each according to other than himself.[176]

He emphasised the importance of the proper approach to study further in relation to the *Fusus*. An associate's words capture this:

> In approach to [the *Fusus*] sentiment is essential, because there is no way of reaching to meanings ... solely with the intellect since it is limited in its capacity and it fixes ... truth by its very nature, and it could not therefore be the central instrument for understanding a book of this calibre ... as it might conceivably be in the case of a purely ... scholarly work. This book is beyond ordinary measure ... This matter is so elevated ... that one could not, however much one studied it or used different methods of approach, arrive at real comprehension without God's help and assistance, and it would seem to be of primary importance to ask for that help and for the aptitude which is capable of receiving the meaning perfectly. It is His own Knowledge and there is no Knower but Him, and if such aptitude or receptivity should become realized in us, it is because He gives it as a gift.[177]

Rauf described 'the knowledge contained in *The Twenty-nine Pages*' as a key. 'If it is given to you', he wrote, 'then you know'.[178] Its pages must thus become 'the constant baggage of those who want to know ... as natural to them as breathing. They must become the embryo of all thought, the matrix of action, the reason of personality and personality difference of those who are one with the One'.[179] This required sustained and measured study, for, as he would say, 'too quick an ingestion may cause indigestion'. He warned students that the *White Fusus* in particular might be 'easily accessible to a too easy understanding', which must be avoided. Responding to the difficulties they encountered with the text, he encouraged students to persevere, for gradually *they* would change in order to understand *it*.

Through continued engagement with the *White Fusus* with its distinctive discursive style, students could also learn to rise to what Rauf posited as the main challenge in studying Ibn 'Arabi's thought. This is the tendency or temptation to 'fix' Ibn 'Arabi's meaning in the endeavour to understand it. 'The moment you become "clear" concerning something [in Ibn 'Arabi's writings],' he warned students, 'you must rest assured that you have *limited* it.' In becoming clear about Ibn 'Arabi's meaning, the reader would thus have lost the author's 'own subtlety and layers of meaning', for what he deals with are 'very subtle realities'. Studying his writings in English translation or summary posed further difficulties in this challenge, for the characteristic precision of the English language imposes an artificial and necessarily limiting 'clarity' on terms and ideas in the original Arabic. In an associate's words,

> Arabic has a profound ambiguity to it that makes it best suited to carry the subtle ambiguities expressed by Ibn 'Arabi. The moment you move out of the Arabic into English, you necessarily become 'clear', and inevitably lose nuances. To avoid 'clarity' or 'fixedness' of meaning, the Ottoman commentators were careful to bring out all possible angles in the text. [Bosnevi's] copious, even exhaustive, commentary approaches the same point from all different angles. The 'clarity' we [in Beshara] strive to avoid because of the 'certainties' it creates is shaken in reading this commentary, for in it meaning always seems to shift.[180]

Reflecting Rauf's emphases, the spirit that informs the study of Ibn 'Arabi
in Beshara is thus, as an associate puts it, 'to say, "this is", and "there is also
this". It is not a question of "this" *or* "that", for that approach issues inevitably
in a loss of nuances.' The either/or approach also manifests the 'clarity' or
'fixedness' Rauf had so strongly rejected. Underlining humility as the key to
study, he had argued: 'If you claim that you have clarity and that you know
something, then you become an *'alim* [having lesser, rational knowledge] *not*
an *'arif* [having spiritual knowledge or gnosis].'[181] As one associate expresses
it, servanthood must thus be 'absolutely at the core' in the study of Ibn 'Arabi.
Bequeathed by Rauf, this is the Beshara approach.

On the identity of Beshara: the final emphasis

Realising that his death might not be far off, in the wake of his serious illness
Rauf turned his attention to the future of the movement he had shaped. He
may have been motivated by a persistent recognition of the implicit tension
between the resources on which he had drawn, and the focus he had specified for Beshara. Alternatively, the assumptions of some students concerning
its identity may have prompted him to address the issue more energetically. Associates relate that he had always made it clear that Beshara 'was
not about sufism'. For example, whenever students had made references to
sufism during courses he would remind them that he was not a sufi shaykh,
Beshara was not a *tariqa*, and they had not been asked to embrace Islam.
In 1984, the need to establish a correct understanding for posterity appears
to have pressed on him with some urgency. He was anxious that 'what was
being understood as Beshara should not be related to a past tradition', as one
associate recalls. For the sake of clarity, he underlined more forcefully that
Beshara was *not* a sufi group. Against this, he projected 'its non-sufi universal
aspect', focusing squarely on its 'universal dimensions'. Projected consistently
and exclusively since his death, this final emphasis was to become the movement's hallmark.

   During the early years, Rauf would take associates to visit Mevlevi shaykhs
and Halveti–Jerrahi sufis in Turkey.[182] Gradually, he began to discourage such
meetings with sufis. At the level of the movement, all contacts with 'sufi-type
organisations' had reportedly ceased by the late 1970s.[183] 'He held us back',
one associate explains, because he felt 'it might confuse the issue, since what
he was bringing *was not sufi*.'[184]

   Rauf's presentation of the fundamental teaching of Beshara evinces a
self-distancing from the sufi tradition across time. We can illustrate this by
comparing the two volumes of his *Addresses*. We described the thrust of
the first volume, which was written for the earliest intensive courses, above.
Rauf framed it in the textual and conceptual universe of Islam and traditional Islamic sufism. He drew freely on the Qur'anic language of Muslim
belief, liberally quoting in transliteration from (and alluding to) Qur'anic and
hadith texts.[185] The tenor is in general one of Muslim devotion, and prayers

specific to Muslim practice are incorporated.[186] He also used sufi terminology in transliteration, and referred repeatedly to doctrinal themes and practice within the *tariqa*s specifically.[187]

Published unedited, the series of Rauf's short texts described as 'Essentials' in the second volume of *Addresses* were written from 1984 to the end of his life, precisely during the period when his concern to clarify the identity of Beshara came to the fore.[188] In contrast with the first volume of *Addresses*, the presentation of the fundamental Beshara teaching here is almost completely shorn of Muslim and sufi allusions and terminology. These fragments represent the distilled exposition of an outlook premised exclusively on the Oneness of Being (projected existentially) that carefully avoids all culture- and religious-specific frameworks, including in particular the Islamic–sufi one. The universal relevance and implications of the essential message are thus immediately accessible.

Legacy

The distinction between his project's universal and sufi(–Islamic) dimensions, recruitment of the latter to serve the former and the successful institution-alisation of a 'universal' as opposed to a 'sufi' identity within the movement represent a significant aspect of Rauf's legacy. In general, his approach and emphases define and direct the framework for Beshara's self-perception, its approach to spiritual education and its specific activities. Certain material dimensions of his legacy can finally be explored.

Publications

Aside from the few translations of works by Ibn 'Arabi and members of his school introduced earlier (and his work as editor of *The Twenty-nine Pages*), Rauf's published legacy is modest.[189] Of particular interest are the two volumes entitled *Addresses* and *Addresses II*, published in 1986 and posthumously in 2001, respectively, to which we have already referred.[190] The first furnishes evidence of his familiarity with sufi doctrine and practice, and the metaphysics of Ibn 'Arabi. The second brings the focused metaphysical fragments we have just described together with brief translations, reflections on aspects of Ibn 'Arabi's teaching, a rare radio interview, various short articles, an autobiographical sketch and an introduction to Turkish cookery. It encompasses Rauf's main interests as a writer: Ottoman and Turkish history, civilisation and culture (explored in *The Last Sultans* and writings on cookery, for example), sufi metaphysics and the endless quest for Union.

Turning: the Mevlevis and Anatolian spiritual history on film

Rauf served as an archaeological/historical adviser, part scriptwriter and part-narrator for a documentary film entitled *Turning*. This was directed and produced by Diane Cilento, and first screened on British television in 1975.[191] It is treasured by associates and routinely shown to students at the School, for while it was Cilento's work, Rauf's ideas stamp its framework and approach.[192] Captured in its title, the focus of the film is the symbolism and significance of the Mevlevi mystical 'dance'.[193] It approaches this through a long view of spiritual evolution illustrated by the Anatolian region, framing the whole in terms of T. S. Eliot's poetic reference to dance and stillness.[194]

Cilento introduces Rumi as a sufi, 'one ... drunk with love who seeks to fill his every breath with ... rememoration of God's name'. 'Mevlana is to Turkey', she explains, 'what Shakespeare is to England, and more: saint, mystic and teacher'. Rauf's narration explains the significance of each movement of the dance, focusing on the 'interior journey'. In turning, he explains, the dervish celebrates 'his reunion with the cosmic order of things'. His turning is not 'a trance or a state of ecstasy, it is ... a higher state of consciousness'. Possibly the first footage of the Mevlevi *sama'* made by Westerners for a Western audience,[195] *Turning* records its public performance on the basketball pitch of a Konya high-school.[196] It also films Mevlevi dervishes at work, for example as craftsmen making the clothes worn during the *sama'*, and as bakers. Rauf explains that 'to undertake the teaching of the way of Mevlana, the *salik* (traveller on the sufi path) must first be accepted after scrutiny as to the real desire he has to love and to learn. He then embarks on a course ... of apprenticeship and dedication'. He learns a skill from an experienced dervish, 'who will guide his ... esoteric development'. Rauf applies Rumi's own image of baking bread to explain his teaching.[197] The raw grain (the *salik*) is hand-ground into flour, mixed with yeast, kneaded, left to rise and then moulded into the shape of the loaf. Then comes the fire, from which he emerges 'metamorphosized, whole, instead of a disintegrated mass of grains'.

Prefacing its treatment of the Mevlevis, *Turning* traces 'the origins of the mystic dance' from ancient times. It does this by mapping the spiritual evolution of Anatolian populations up to Rumi's time. The story begins with the 10,000-year-old ruins of Çatal Höyük near Konya. Excavated during the 1960s, the focus of its fertility cult was the Mother Goddess Kybele ('Big Mama'), 'symbol of the replenishing earth', always pregnant and about to give birth.[198] The story resumes 6,000 years later, with the appearance of female sphinxes at the ancient city of the Hittites, Alacahöyük.[199] Some time after 2000 BC, 'the Hattites and the Hittites ... slimmed our lady down into a twig-like creature'. This was followed by the appearance of the Hittite Amazon, 'the next representation of the all-powerful mother figure Kybele'. Then Artemis appeared.[200] 'Like the Big Mama of Çatal Höyük, who turned into the goddess of the Hittites, she represents endless fecundity. Her domain was once the mighty port of Ephesus.'[201] While Artemis represented 'the mystic image of the mother-lover-wife, but really inaccessible and inviolate', the Romans were 'much more prosaic ... They turned Artemis into Diana ... and worshipped her less as a mother than a body. Her popularity began to wane.'

Referring to St Paul's attempt to preach in the theatre at Ephesus and his ejection from the city due to incitement by artisans who feared the demise of the statue trade, the story turns to the advent of Christianity, which marked 'the beginning of the end for Artemis'. John the Apostle brought Mary to Ephesus, for Jesus had entrusted care of her to him.[202] She is believed to be buried there, 'high on a mountain overlooking the sea'. Here is 'the last of the chain of great mother figures, the virgin mother'. The story turns to the advent of Islam and Rumi: 'a new wave of religious feeling swept through Anatolia ... the religion of Islam. From Balkh ... came a man known today as Mevlana, inspiration of the whirling dervishes.'

The coherence of the narrative in this overview of spiritual history has been somewhat compromised by editing, which has condensed the latter part of the film in particular. We defer consideration of its basis and development to a later discussion, but cite one associate's projection of its thrust here, by way of illumination:

> In every era there was a way to worship God appropriate to it, and this changed in each age. The film provides an overview of the different ways in which God has been worshipped, illustrated through the case of Anatolia. There the first form of monotheism to take hold was Christianity, but people translated this, and saw in the Virgin Mary a continuation of the mother goddess of previous eras, in this case as the Mother of God. Yet Mary represented a transitional phase or paradigm, because people recognised the mother goddess in her, but also had to accept the monotheism of Christianity. With the advent of Islam the mother goddess motif was brought to an end, as there was now 'pure' monotheism. This set the stage for the further evolution of man's approach to God and its final fulfilment.

Preparing for posterity: institutionalisation and continuity

Rauf had frequently remarked that most leaders 'were unwilling to make sufficient preparation for the time after they died'.[203] As a result, their inspiration often died with them. The outward success with which his own death was absorbed (and the continued vitality of Beshara since), which we described earlier, must be counted a dimension of his legacy. The movement's institutions were established at an early stage at his instigation and insistence, and their specific responsibilities and the directives by which they would be run were clarified at the same time. Given his understanding of spiritual education and his role within this, he had never wished to encourage dependence on his own presence and input. The sense that associates must themselves assume responsibility was reinforced when he increasingly withdrew into translation work, and as ill health later took over. Aspects of his role have indeed become institutionalised in the 'people of Beshara' as a whole, for they bear collective responsibility for continually evaluating the movement's orientation and approach against the fundamental premises and principles he established. Rauf considered it important for a particular individual to assume responsibility for the overall process of education at the School, however, and indeed 'prepared' an associate for this role.[204] This was Peter Young, Principal of the School and a *de facto* point of reference within the movement today.

How and when did Young's involvement with Beshara begin? He had attended a talk by Feild while a student at Cambridge,[205] and had dismissed it as 'not for him'. Gradually, some of his university peers became involved at Swyre Farm. After graduating he worked for a time as a nurse in psychiatric care, then as a personal assistant to a 'young tycoon' who was focused on making money. The two men were injured in a car accident: in the aftermath of this he finally agreed to visit Swyre Farm in 1974, at the insistence of an ex-Cambridge friend who had become involved there. He had made a personal pact 'to accept with humility whatever he would encounter' during this brief visit, and experienced 'a great opening' there. This took the form of a sense of 'surrender' he now describes as *taslim* (from the Arabic root used to denote self-surrender to God). Rauf had not been there at the time, so the two did not meet.

On returning home to Leeds, Young studied *The Twenty-nine Pages* with friends there involved in Beshara. In 1975, he went to Chisholme to help with building work. At the end of that year he was invited to join the first intensive course. As he was unable to raise the fees, someone sponsored him. He was then invited to supervise on the next intensive course, the first held at Sherborne House. Young then completed the first of the further courses at Chisholme. Settling locally, he worked as a builder and remained closely involved with the School.

In 1984, Rauf ask Young to serve as Director of Studies for the intensive course, as he planned to be away in Turkey. He advised him to maintain his building work at the same time. When Rauf returned, his health was deteriorating. He hinted that Young might give up his building work and stay with him as a companion. Young nursed him for three months during his convalescence following the operation in August 1984. He spent twenty-four hours a day with him, sleeping in Culme-Seymour's room whenever she was away in order to be close at hand. The two men developed an intimate relationship, for Young 'had to learn everything about Bulent to be able to run Chisholme', as one associate puts it today.

Rauf had reportedly said that he should have died in 1984, but was given three more years 'to do what was needed'. For the remainder of his life, Young relates, he 'put things in order' and 'whipped' Young himself 'into shape'. Rauf taught him continuously during this time. 'It was not formal teaching as such', Young explains, 'just being with him'. Rauf considered knowledge of Ottoman Turkish important to his education, so that he could become familiar with Ottoman commentaries on the *Fusus*. Funds were raised and Young registered for a second-year undergraduate course in Ottoman Turkish at Oxford University (1985–86). In 1986, his position as Director of Studies at Chisholme was expanded to that of Principal. Three days before he died, Rauf asked Young 'to spend three days with him'. He was with him when Rauf passed away.

Young is in no doubt that Rauf had given him a special responsibility for safeguarding and continuing the work of spiritual education he had begun. Associates hold him in high regard, for they believe that Rauf 'had identified a potential in him'. They attribute his authority to his 'training' by Rauf. Thanks to this, they believe that he developed the discernment and qualities indispensable to the task of spiritual guidance (in assigning *wazifas* to students, for example). While the transition on Rauf's death had brought its challenges (for, as one associate puts it, 'Young is not Rauf'),[206] associates are quick to acknowledge that Young has remained faithful to Rauf's approach, and has carried out his responsibilities sensitively. For his part, Young is conscious of a life-long commitment to Beshara.[207]

Physical traces

Rauf's physical mark is evident throughout the School. His two rooms in particular, which open onto each other and are always decorated with fresh flowers, are maintained just as they were when he was alive.[208] Referred to today as 'the library' (they house his modest book collection), they form a special space. Associates take to them for quiet reading and reflection and for intimate discussions, surrounded by the books, furniture, artwork and artefacts Rauf had collected across the years.[209]

Rauf had chosen the location in which he wished to be buried on the estate. The necessary permission for this was sought and, in the event, arrived the day after he died. He had been walking with Young and had traced out an area on the hill looking down on the house, where there was a natural circular indentation in the grass. He had later described and had drawn up by an associate (an architect) a plan of the structure he wished to have raised over his grave. He insisted that the latter be open to the sky. Referring to the *haqiqa Muhammadiyya*, he described the structure he had in mind as a 'Monument to the Reality of Man'. It was built during 1988–89 by associates. A stone base is shaped out of the circumferences of three concentric stepped circles. Rauf is buried within the empty space marked by this, which is covered with grass. Four tall columns support a mirror image of the smallest, innermost circle of the base. Around the circumference of the topmost base step the Qur'anic verse uttered in any reference to death is engraved: 'They are from Him and to Him they return.'[210]

This site represents the highest point of the estate. It has a commanding view on all sides, and captures the silence and beauty of the empty fields and moors to the south. Young suggests that 'it is without doubt a *maqam*, bringing clarity to those who go there'.[211] Associates make a point of visiting it to reflect and meditate, and to pay their respects at Rauf's grave. They do not see it as a monument to Rauf, but a reminder of the potential of man, indeed of their own potential.[212] As a recent web posting makes clear, the Monument is 'neither a tomb nor a grave. It is dedicated to the *reality* of Man which does not die, which is in eternity and forever one with the One, and from which spiritual help and direction flows to all people everywhere.'[213] There is a notable absence at this site of any of the paraphernalia associated with popular expressions of devotion during visits to shrines, be this in the Muslim context or at the shrines of sufi masters in the West.[214] Since Rauf's death, a small number of associates have been buried in simple graves close to the Monument. Others have expressed the wish to join them there.

The message implicit in the Monument to Man, the culture that informs associates' perceptions of it and the manner of their visits to it constitute an eloquent statement of Rauf's legacy for the movement. In particular, it encapsulates his distinctive application of the teaching of Ibn 'Arabi in fashioning the Beshara perspective.

Chapter 5

The Beshara perspective and the teaching of Ibn 'Arabi

Beshara is the certainty that what you thought yourself to be you are not, and what you are, what is 'in' you, is such a treasure, a reality, a mystery, that even a glimpse of it would change your life forever.

Beshara website

Associates believe Bulent Rauf had been singled out for a mission that was not of his own making. Having understood the provenance of the 'order' to make for England on the tongue of the wandering dervish, he had accepted that it was compelling. Aware he had been 'sent' to England, at first he did not know what for, but a 'series of remarkable occurrences' after his first meeting with Feild revealed that 'his real work' had now begun.[1] Referring to his interest in Ibn 'Arabi, sustained 'without at the time being aware of how important it was', according to associates Rauf then 'realised that he had a body of knowledge for which there was great need'. He 'took the light of knowledge as revealed to him in the works of Ibn 'Arabi and brought it to those who thirsted for this in lands beyond the borders of traditional Arab or Turkish culture'.[2]

This brief account captures the fundamental relationship between the Beshara perspective projected by Rauf and the teaching of Ibn 'Arabi. In London, he encountered the yearning of counterculture youth whose mood was influenced by the New Age. He had some knowledge of the teaching of Ibn 'Arabi, however acquired. This resonated powerfully with a crystallising New Age monism and its assumption of the Self as sacred. It also furnished well-trodden experiential paths to the ultimate within. Rauf's task was to creatively apply this resource to construct a perspective relevant to young Western spiritual seekers. How did he adapt Ibn 'Arabi's teaching in forming the Beshara perspective? How did he justify the specific adoption of Ibn 'Arabi's exposition of the Oneness of Being, which became the bedrock of the Beshara perspective, and which he himself projected as common to all esoteric teachings? How did he address the Islamic religious framing of this exposition? How does Ibn 'Arabi's teaching inform and shape the Beshara perspective in relation to perceptions of individual spirituality and the spiritual development of humanity as a whole? What implications has Rauf's application of this teaching had for the perception in Beshara of the significance and quality of the present times? Is there a distinctive vision of a new age in Beshara, and how does it relate to Ibn 'Arabi's teaching? How has this shaped the perception within Beshara of its own responsibility and calling?

Why Ibn 'Arabi?

The Beshara perspective is founded on the notion of the Oneness of Being. Reflecting the perennialism that shapes the movement, Peter Young projects this notion as 'the primary esoteric truth, known to all saints and mystics world wide and throughout humanity's [existence]'.[3] Put otherwise by an associate, 'At the heart of every religious system is the same fundamental premise – the Unity of Being beyond all condition'.[4] Rauf maintained that 'the primordial principle of the Absolute Unity of Existence is expressed with unique clarity and fullness'[5] in Ibn 'Arabi's writings in particular, out of all those that address this theme. As an associate puts it, Ibn 'Arabi's metaphysical teaching thus provides 'the best explanation of the notion of Unity and the most complete form of knowledge of it'. The 'same degree of understanding' cannot be found elsewhere, another maintains, for 'there is nobody else like Ibn 'Arabi'.[6] It was indeed his task, Young explains, 'to bring out the esoteric aspects of the religion into a doctrine of the unity of existence'.[7]

The incomparability of Ibn 'Arabi's exposition of unity flowed ultimately from its author's saintly stature, and this origin constituted a further basis for its embrace.[8] As described earlier, Rauf had personally encountered the saintly Ibn 'Arabi in the imaginal realm. In projecting his saintly stature to associates, he rehearsed aspects of Ibn 'Arabi's own intimations concerning this. 'Ibn 'Arabi is not only a man of Wisdom' or 'Mohammedian Shaykh', he thus wrote, but 'the universal Doctor Maximus, invited to sit upon the silver throne of Mohammedian Sainthood by Jesus'.[9] As 'the Seal of Mohammedian Sainthood', he is 'the most perfect heir to the Prophet Mohammed and revealer of his mysteries'.[10]

Ultimately, Rauf suggested, Ibn 'Arabi served as a conduit for knowledge of Unity by virtue of his vantage point as saint:

> It is to Ibn 'Arabi, who speaks from objective vision of the Unique Existence, that the exposition of Its Self-revelation may be ascribed, as the first Sufi to correlate the 'theory' of *wahdat al-wujud*, of which he is celebrated as the originator and most complete propounder of all time.[11]

As Perfect Man, Ibn 'Arabi 'is one with God, he is essentially no other than God'.[12] The fruit of his realised perspective, his writings thus emanate from 'the most ancient place', and yield an education 'from the interior reality of man to the interior reality of man, without intermediary'.[13] They represent an utterly authentic source, unsullied by the 'interposing of the self (*nafs*) which colours and misrepresents the truth',[14] for 'the saint is in Union and in Union there is the One Unique Self and no other'. As a saint and perfect servant, Ibn 'Arabi is a channel through which knowledge of God could come 'directly from God according to His own manner and wish'. Hence, 'the words of the saint are to be trusted'. Referring to Bosnevi's commentary on the *Fusus*, one associate points out that 'it is made quite clear there ... that ... denial of the words of ... Ibn 'Arabi is the same as denial of the words of the Prophet Mohammed and the words of God.'

Ibn 'Arabi's metaphysics as exposition of Absolute Truth

The counterculture youth Rauf encountered in London were seeking an alternative to established religions and their systems of belief. As he projected this, Ibn 'Arabi's perspective could meet their expectations. Religions capture aspects of Truth in relative forms, but Ibn 'Arabi's metaphysics pointed to Absolute Truth. Rauf had explained to Field: 'We are not involved with religion or with form. We are involved with the ... inner stream of truth that underlies all religion. Our way is not for those who cannot go beyond form. It is for those who wish to go straight to the Essence.'[15] To embark on the journey towards Truth through self-knowledge Rauf did not stipulate a requirement to embrace anything in the way of religious belief. Rather, all that was required was an acceptance of the fundamental premise of the Oneness of Being.[16] In Beshara this premise is grasped and explored through the teaching of Ibn 'Arabi articulated in an existential discourse. No necessary connection to religions or their beliefs and practices is assumed or posited for actualisation of the realities this teaching enfolds.

Two fundamental principles

In Beshara Ibn 'Arabi's teaching is summed up in two fundamental principles, reflecting his best-known propositions. The second flowing from the first, these are the Oneness of Being[17] and the Perfectibility of Man (more commonly denoted by the notion of the Perfect Man). Young recently explained these principles in the following terms:

> The Truth is of One, Absolute and All-inclusive Existence, other than which we are not, and other than which there is nothing. Hence all things are only truly themselves through the One Existence, which gives of Its own Being perpetually. Man alone has the possibility of coming to know fully, through knowing his own existence in depth, that he is no other than the Self-same Unique Existence that existentiated him. And further, once the mystery of one's own existence is uncovered, it can be seen that it is the same Unique Existence which is the underlying reality of everything and that there is nothing other than It in existence.[18]

It is by virtue of his unique capacity for such full knowledge of his essential identity with the One Being that man alone possesses the potential for completion or perfectibility. Made upon God's form, in perfection he is the complete image of Reality, manifesting all the Divine Names and Attributes.[19] The Perfect Man (*al-insan al-kamil*) is a central notion in Ibn 'Arabi's thought:[20] Rauf explained that, while limiting the infinity of the One Being in his capacity as an exteriorisation of this, the Perfect Man's interior is yet 'the Ipseity, which is infinite'.[21]

Major motifs and their projection in Beshara

Beshara presents the contours of Ibn 'Arabi's metaphysical teaching and its major motifs in a simple existential framework.[22] Here, this teaching furnishes an answer to questions concerning the nature, meaning and purpose of existence as such, and of human existence and its potential in particular, without reference to any religious discourse. In this presentation prominence is given to a *hadith qudsi* fundamental to sufi spirituality, which reads: 'I was a hidden treasure and I loved to be known so I created the creatures and made Myself known to them; so they knew Me'.[23] Rauf characterised the approach of Beshara through direct reference to this: 'Our way is knowledge and love, which is the inverse realisation of "I loved to be known …".'[24] Through his interpretation of this hadith Ibn 'Arabi rooted cosmogony, or the origin and development of the universe, in God's desire to reveal Himself. His entire metaphysics may indeed be seen as an elaboration on it,[25] pivoting on the idea of the Self-disclosure of the divine to itself through an apparent 'other'. The corollary of this is that everything in creation constitutes a locus of manifestation (*mazhar*) for the appearance, or theophany (*tajalli*), of the divine.[26]

The four motifs generally emphasised in relation to this cosmogony are knowledge, mercy, love and beauty.[27] Of these, Rauf dwelt especially on the latter two. Many have underlined love, here designating precisely the Divine Love to be known, as the principle of cosmogenesis according to Ibn 'Arabi. It is the driving force behind the Universal Breath, which symbolises the movement of theophanic cosmogony. Love has been described simply as 'the generating force of existence',[28] for it is the first mover and ultimate cause of existence of the universe. Rauf elaborated on the nature of Divine Love thus:

> Love in its purest essential form is 'Divine Love' and this is the motivating principle of all manifestation … Divine Love is neither directional nor relational, for it knows no subject or object other than itself … It is the love that knows and sees that there is nothing other than Him in all things and that there is no existence apart from His existence, and the identification of Divine Love in the human vehicle is only His love of Himself manifested in His image.[29]

He never tired of emphasising the pivotal role of love, reflecting in this a central theme of sufi teaching (especially from the thirteenth century onwards),[30] and drew repeatedly on a love-centred metaphysics. Responding to an associate's question concerning the correct translation of the *hadith qudsi* just mentioned, for example, he wrote:

> The text is this: 'I was a Hidden Treasure and I *loved* to know Myself'. The word of love was at the start of things and 'Arabi [sic] could not have quoted it any other

way ... He did not say 'I was a Hidden Treasure and I wished or wanted to know Myself', but He said 'I loved to know Myself.' For those who understand, there is a great difference and a great explanation in this.[31]

A grasp of this 'great explanation' underpins the centrality of love in Beshara, which is perceived as fundamental and all-encompassing. Thus, Rauf wrote, 'all expression is the expression of love, - since love is the prime motive of manifestation, and manifestation in expression emanating from the original: "... I loved to be known"'.[32] Moreover, 'To arrive at Union man must love. If not, then not. If a man's creed is Love he will crave for, strive for, work for and attain Union.'[33] The primacy of love is crystal clear in Young's response to the events of 9/11, which took the form of a plea entitled 'A Response from Love':

> The reality of Love is that there is only one need: the need for Oneness. When this is realised, we will all see the requirement to ... love one's enemy as oneself. As things are now, we are divided by our differences. Now is for building the bridges that will bring all humanity together under the banner of Universal Love. Many of those about to die in the ... tragedies of 11th September were brought ... to the immediate threshold of clear perception ... On this doorstep, with no time for thought ... They reached for their mobile phones and called their beloved, to say simply, 'I love you.' No anger, incomprehension or blame at what was taking place. Only Love and the urgency of declaring it ... To die truly is to be stripped of irrelevancies and falsehood and to enter into our still centre with only that which belongs to it: affirmation and Love. Death is a change of state, from this relative condition of existence ... into a state ... which is the presence of Absolute Love ... It is the reality of our existence ... Until we wake up to the reality of Who, What and Where we are, it is for us to practise staying on the doorstep, as if we were about to die. Here there is only Love and its affirmation ... There is no necessity of going back to 'normal' after these events. There is on the contrary the total requirement of stepping ... towards the realisation of the Presence of Absolute Love, which even now holds all in Its own Being. This is the possibility for Mankind, which is offered to us now.[34]

Notions of love and beauty are inseparable in Ibn 'Arabi's metaphysics, for beauty is 'the primary and inexhaustible source' of love.[35] It has indeed been suggested that the idea of beauty (and the Divine Love of it) 'modulates [his] thought on Divine love from beginning to end.'[36] The intertwining of these two motifs is encapsulated in a hadith, quoted often by Ibn 'Arabi, in which the Prophet relates that 'God is beautiful and He loves beauty.'[37] Rauf repeated the love/beauty motif throughout *Addresses* and *Addresses II*, sometimes introducing the interconnected notion of mercy (*rahma*): 'Beauty, out of Benevolence [*rahma*], showed Itself to Itself for Love of Beauty, and returned It to Itself.' Some examples illustrate this prominent focus:

> Love is the movement of Beauty and Beauty is He who exposes that beauty through the vehicle of Love.[38]

When one's vision has progressed to a vision of 'no-other', then one sees Him everywhere. From thence, as Ibnul 'Arabi says in his poem: 'O marvel! ... I follow the religion of Love: whatever way Love's mounts take, That is my religion and my faith.' This is seeing Him everywhere, whatever way Love transports, it is necessarily to Beauty and that is his religion and his faith.

Your work will help bring you to a threshold of understanding ... Whatever the way, the gist of the matter is the love-affair, where yearning must be so supreme that it must be stripped of everything but yearning. The aim of this yearning – but an aim only born of this yearning itself, devoid of everything that could be an aim with, alongside, or other than this yearning – is Beauty, the *Jemal*.

The metaphysical importance accorded to beauty has significantly coloured the Beshara perspective and associates' attitudes.[39] Rauf emphasised that the Essence is itself 'sheer Beauty'.[40] As a manifestation of this, the creation is projected and appreciated as beautiful in its entirety (indeed, as Ibn 'Arabi put it, 'there is nothing more beautiful than the cosmos').[41] Rauf's insistence on developing a taste for beauty (*dhawq*) in spiritual education translates into the cultivation of a taste for the One who is Beautiful, and aims at the ultimate goal of union with Beauty. His emphasis on beauty may be partly attributable to the influence of Rumi's thought and Mevlevi teaching,[42] in addition to that of Ibn 'Arabi. It informs the detailed attention to beauty and the beautification of space at the School. It also appears in his prescription of the divine self-descriptive *Dhu'l-Jamal wa'l-Ihsan* (The One Who possesses Beauty and makes Beautiful) in the collective *dhikr*, a formula not commonly recited in the *tariqa*s (see Appendix 4).

Ibn 'Arabi's teaching as universal

Ibn 'Arabi is a figure for the entire world, whose teaching goes way beyond the boundaries of cultures and religions.

Beshara associate

What I have concluded so far is that Ibn al-'Arabi's works are not about him or his ideas, which would make him as culturally anchored as an Ibn Qudamah or Ibn Hajar. His works show processes, open windows, reflect on language and reflection ... He is universal because, while reading his works, our eyes follow his finger pointing to the universal and his finger ceases to exist.

Eric Winkel, p. viii

By projecting Ibn 'Arabi's teaching as an existential (as opposed to a religious) discourse, Rauf implicitly emphasised its universal address, underscoring its relevance to man *qua* man, whatever the particularities of his constructed identity. Set against this, the form of Ibn 'Arabi's teaching, emanating from a particular cultural–religious context and reflecting the norms of his age, presented a potential problem. Ibn 'Arabi wrote, of course, for a Muslim audience (and specifically for Muslims inclined to plumb the esoteric depths of their religion). Some of the subjects he discussed, however, in particular the meaning and purpose of man, are of potentially universal relevance. As Winkel's comment above shows, scholars sympathetic to Ibn 'Arabi often assume or explicitly highlight this universally relevant facet of his teaching.[43] By directly promoting this aspect, Rauf could make it inviting and meaningful to seekers of diverse cultural–religious provenance, while avoiding the imposition of any particularity of belief or identity on those who endeavoured to benefit from it.

Those who uphold the Beshara perspective acknowledge that Ibn 'Arabi wrote from within the Islamic tradition, and that he was himself 'a Muslim who undoubtedly practised the sharia to perfection'. His provenance was appropriate to expressing the essential truths his writings encapsulate, and it reflected the Divine Will. His association with this tradition did not restrict him in any way, however, for his writings emanated from 'a truly universal point of view'.[44] His understanding of man was neither conditioned by his time, nor can it be tied to any specific context: the truth he articulated about man is ever-pertinent. As one associate writes, 'Eight hundred years later, it is apparent that [his] address is ... applicable to all, transcending even the boundaries of time and culture, religions and eras'.[45] According to another associate, long years of study underpin a conviction that 'Ibn 'Arabi's is almost certainly the most complete exposition of human nature which has ever been set out'. Although couched in 'extremely complex texts ... in a difficult foreign language' and replete with cultural references 'which were probably abstruse even in their own time', the fact is that one cannot find 'the same degree of understanding' anywhere else. The difficult task of 'bridging the cultural gap' bears rich fruit for those in search of spiritual guidance, according to this associate: 'although what Ibn 'Arabi is saying may be dressed in the clothing of his time in terms of issues ... which engaged his contemporaries, its meaning transcends those limits and speaks to the eternal human condition'.[46]

As we suggested earlier, Rauf's determined focus on the 'universal' aspects of Ibn 'Arabi's teaching (and the concomitant downplaying of specifically 'Islamic' facets of this) was evident in his preparation of *The Twenty-nine Pages*. Affifi had underlined Ibn 'Arabi's constant resort to Qur'an/hadith texts to support his claims, and provided ample illustration of such references.[47] These references are almost entirely absent from *The Twenty-nine Pages*, and the underlying inter-textuality is thus no longer evident.[48] The outcome is an exposition effectively amputated from its Islamic scriptural and doctrinal matrix,[49] encapsulating the universal teaching of Ibn 'Arabi upheld by Beshara. In further elaborating this teaching, Rauf drew selectively from the author's corpus, applying the notion of the Oneness of Being in determining what to adopt. An associate explains:

Bulent was very careful in what he introduced. He made it very clear that not everything that Ibn 'Arabi wrote is relevant to Beshara ... only certain aspects of Ibn 'Arabi's writings are relevant to the focus of Beshara. Bulent identified the *Fusus* as the major work. He picked out quotations from the *Futuhat* and added commentaries on the *Fusus*.[50] He quite consciously steered us away from aspects of

Ibn 'Arabi's writings. For example, someone would report, 'I have found a book by Ibn 'Arabi', and Bulent would reply, 'It is not relevant to you.' He was very selective, informed by a specific perspective. This does not mean that you cannot read other works [of Ibn 'Arabi] after reaching a certain stage in education and the discipline, but you must have the fundamentals first.

Ibn 'Arabi's writings yield some justification for Rauf's focus on their 'universal' content. There is thus a general sense that, according to Ibn 'Arabi, particular religious forms and beliefs belong to the relative realm while, in contrast, the universal is of the essential. Ibn 'Arabi indeed issued a well-known warning to believers not to restrict God to the form of their own belief and then to reject the beliefs of others as unbelief.[51] As Bursevi commented, 'The knower of God, whatever his origin is ... accepts all kinds of beliefs, but does not remain tied to any figurative belief.'[52] Accordingly, Beshara emphasises the image of Ibn 'Arabi as 'outspoken critic of religious and philosophical dogmatism'.[53] As a MIAS leaflet puts it, Ibn 'Arabi accepted that 'each person has a unique path to the Truth, which unites all paths in Itself'. Such understandings bolster the movement's downplaying of the significance of the specifically Islamic facet in Ibn 'Arabi's teaching. They also underpin its confident dismissal of the possibility that the embrace of Islam could be a prerequisite for drawing guidance from this teaching.[54]

A direct personal message

[T]he subject Ibn 'Arabi offers is ourselves.

Beshara associate[55]

The only agreement required ... is to the premise that Reality is One. That accepted, Ibn 'Arabi's doctrine is shown ... to be ... immediate in its address.

The Twenty-nine Pages, p. 6

In Beshara, Ibn 'Arabi's universal teaching is projected as a message addressed to each individual, and participation in the Absolute Truth to which it points is held up as their personal birthright. The direct focus of esoteric education (in course activities) is that which lies within each individual. Hence, what is studied is projected as being 'about' each student personally. Similarly, as we have seen, the approach to meditation imposes no form, allowing what is 'within' the individual to surface. Further evidence of this approach arises in the fact that Ibn 'Arabi's metaphysics is couched in personalised language in Beshara materials, and brought into the realm of the individual's everyday reality. For example, Young writes:

We are not who we think we are and our lives are not as we believe them to be. The true situation is that we appeared here in this life from another condition of existence. This condition of existence – which is also known as the All-inclusive Truth – is very close indeed; in fact It is so close that we don't see It, it is so simple that we can't believe It can be true. But once exposed to this Truth we perceive that we as such do not exist, nor does the world; what we thought was ourselves is nothing but the moment by moment Self-manifestation of One, Absolute and All-inclusive Truth, the Unity of all Existence. We have never for an instant been separated from This even while being manifested here. We are nothing but This, and there is nothing but This Unique Existence in expressive movement as the world. We are not things and nor is the world. We are on the contrary the Self-expressions of Love, Which **is** the One Reality, and in Whose image we are definitely formed.[56]

The notion of the Oneness of Being serves in Beshara as a personal touch-stone, by which associates can make sense of and navigate through life. Based on long years of supervising students, an associate explains that 'Once people are introduced to it, it allows things to be understood, and this has an imme-diate effect.' Another associate points to its immediate personal relevance thus: 'There is only one Reality. It is God's vision of Himself as He reveals Himself in the infinity of His forms, some of which are *you* and *I*.' The 'reverse side' of the Oneness of Being is the perfectibility of man, the 'return' to the realised state of primordial unity. Hence, as an associate explains, 'in Beshara we say It (the One Reality) is like that – Unity, but *It is also you*.' Once man's essential identity with the One Being is grasped, the direct, personal rele-vance of the abstract notion of the Perfect Man becomes clear. Rauf thus commented: 'through your origin and Reality you are His complete and Perfect image ... since you are His expression ... the Perfect Man potential is in you.'[57] As Young emphasises, each person can come to know the Truth that 'the Reality is wholly and undividedly present' in them, each in their own lifetime, 'because this is our potential; this is what we are for.'[58]

Associates apply the touchstone of the Oneness of Being with striking directness. Long years of viewing life from this perspective, in its capacity as 'a relative condition of existence,'[59] have cultivated in them a distinctive bearing. For example, they face problems and death with relative equanimity and acceptance. They are constantly vigilant against slipping back into the illusion of the reality of the individual self, which results from 'thoughts of separation.'[60] They nurture a passionately open, tolerant, accepting and deeply respectful attitude towards others and the world in general.[61] This arises out of an understanding that, in one associate's words, 'everything you encounter is Reality in appearance', while every person has the potential for perfection by virtue of their humanity. There is a marked tendency to suspend judge-ment, for whatever transpires is construed as what is 'meant to be.'[62] The world is viewed as the stage on which the Divine Names play out their poten-tialities. Hence, even manifestations of the 'darker' Names in acts of tyranny and oppression are explained (while not condoned on the level of human action) as part of the Divine Unfolding.[63] Whatever transpires in the manifest world is posited as the macrocosmic reflection of the drama unfolding in the interior of man:

As we enter the new millennium, the world presents us with an image of great change. It is a picture which reflects the openings ... taking place in the heart of

Man, the place which ... observes events as happening in both exterior and interior worlds. The conflicts and the unions ... the heroic movements, the damnable actions ... all this too takes place in me. In me is the stage on which the fascist holds forth in pride and power over that other part of me which cowers and shrinks from the violence which the borrowed strength of this partiality engenders.[64]

According to Ibn 'Arabi all things, including all creatures, have no being (*wujud*) of their own. Their quality has often been projected in terms of 'total dependence and humility'.[65] Applying to themselves such understandings, associates consciously nurture an attitude of servanthood. This is facilitated by the specific activity of work (service) during courses, discussed earlier. 'In everything', an associate explains, 'we try to take the place of a servant.' This emphasis on servanthood informs the cultivation of the desire to receive, or 'receptivity'. Ultimately the fruit of divine bestowal, the latter can be understood as the attitude which paves the way for the Divine Self-disclosure to unfold through the individual unobstructed by the constructed self, via a state emptied of discursive thinking.[66] An associate explains with reference to Ibn 'Arabi's understanding of servanthood, thus: 'The servant is he who hears that which is enacted through him.' He is not someone who simply obeys a command, for this formulation introduces duality.[67] Associates stress that what is ultimately needed for complete/perfect servanthood is 'the quality of the heart free of every attribute'. As one puts it, the complete servant 'follows the *haqq* [Truth; God; the Real] everywhere and recognises It in everything, because the journey of the heart consists of remaining in the place of total receptivity and constantly facing the Absolute *haqq*'.[68]

The personal appropriation and direct application of such emphases can issue in a particular attitude among associates in which the individual human will is significantly downplayed, and a prepared openness to the Divine Will cultivated.[69] Citing Rumi's announcement that he had 'thrown off the pack-saddle of freewill' by way of elaboration, Young explains that 'we in Beshara recognise that we are under something very profound that has its own order, which we respect and accept'.[70] A student thus relates that, at the end of the nine-day course, he was '*told* to do the intensive course', and had no option but to comply. Young himself suggests that everyone who comes to Chisholme has been 'brought'.[71] Common teleological assumptions reinforce such attitudes, as does the conviction that 'the spiritual governs and controls the material everywhere', these apparently distinct spheres being in reality 'but two sides of the same coin'.[72] In this view, the Divine Will uses individuals as 'tools'. Feild had been used, in Young's words, 'as a catalyst in the fulfilment of Bulent's task'. Ataturk had been used to point the way to a new era in spiritual expression. Through a gift of oratory, Winston Churchill 'had been used as an instrument against Hitler', to embody 'symbols of hope and a free world versus fascism'.

The spiritual evolution of man

In addressing the perfectibility of Man and our potential in coming to the reality of ... unification with God, Ibn 'Arabi tells us that there is also a universal aspect to this, pertaining to the spiritual development, not of individuals, but of mankind as a whole. In this, there is a direction or unfoldment, for which he himself has a responsibility.

Beshara associate[73]

A distinctive concept of the spiritual evolution of mankind lies at the heart of the Beshara perspective. This meta-narrative[74] is developed from Ibn 'Arabi's view of spiritual history, which is synthesised with Biblical themes and those characteristic of New Age thinking. It furnishes a particular understanding of the present times, and informs the movement's perception of its own role in the unfolding cosmic drama. What is the view of spiritual history that forms its starting point?

Ibn 'Arabi on the spiritual unfolding of man

Ibn 'Arabi's view of spiritual history intertwines with his teaching on prophets and saints. He posits successive cycles in the unfolding of man, each with a distinct beginning and ending. All are contained within the sphere of *al-haqiqa al-Muhammadiyya*, the Muhammadan Reality. The first cycle, the 'Adamic' cycle, begins with Adam. It proceeds through a series of prophets until Jesus, who ends it. The appearance of Muhammad, final prophet and Seal of the Prophets, brings to an end the preceding cycle of time for the Divine Name *al-Batin* (the Hidden) and ushers in the cycle of the Name *al-Zahir* (the Apparent). With it begins the cycle after the Adamic one, the 'Muhammadan' cycle. Muhammad's authority had previously been in hidden mode, for all preceding prophets were aspects of the *haqiqa Muhammadiyya* but none expressed it explicitly in its totality. This authority became apparent with Muhammad, which explains why this cycle comes under the Name *al-Zahir*.

After Muhammad's appearance there are no more prophets, but there are saints. At a certain point sainthood upon the heart of Muhammad, which reflects the explicit completeness of sainthood represented by Muhammad himself, is sealed. This arises through the Seal of Muhammadan Sainthood, an office with which Ibn 'Arabi identified himself. Sainthood inherited from the prophets and envoys, an explicitly *particular* form of sainthood (though implicitly complete), continues. Towards the end of the Muhammadan cycle the signs of the end of time begin to appear. Among them is the coming down of Jesus from heaven to earth in his capacity as the Seal of Universal Sainthood, to seal the sainthood of the saints inherited from the prophets and envoys.[75] As the Hour approaches the earth loses all its saints and the time of the Resurrection (*al-qiyama*) draws near, when there is no single believer left on earth.[76]

The Beshara view

The general backdrop to the specific Beshara meta-narrative is a projection of the human story as the direct, ongoing Divine Self-disclosure, based on Ibn 'Arabi's cosmological doctrine. Within this stands Ibn 'Arabi's notion of man's spiritual evolution, the bare bones of which we have just sketched. Rauf did not rehearse all aspects of this, but trained a particular focus on the meanings and roles within it of certain prophets and seals. He also 'completed' it, by mapping its tracks to the present time. As a framework, his interpretation assumed Ibn 'Arabi's concept of a progression from Adam to Muhammad in terms of the disclosure of particular aspects of the Divine Wisdom. (This is implicit in the *Fusus*, and developed explicitly in the Bosnevi commentary.) Based on this, his particular concern was to clarify the underlying evolution in the possibilities of man's relation to God (and the ways in which he can approach God) contained in the pre-established order within the Divine Knowledge, and its fulfilment implied in the notion of a progression. This informed a particular conception of the quality of the present times in terms of possibilities and requirements, yielding ultimate justification for the Beshara perspective and a delineation of the movement's own role in such fulfilment.

Some of the themes encompassed by the Beshara view summarised here are not treated in internal materials. Others are treated very briefly, typically through subtle allusions. Rauf did not suggest that all aspects could be articulated completely or with equal clarity, as some remain beyond the grasp of human knowledge. He was also aware of the complexity and subtlety of the ideas involved, which makes them difficult to grasp but easy to misconstrue.[77] The absence of substantial written development of certain themes is thus at times deliberate: in the words of one associate, 'the only real safety is for one to come to this understanding in oneself. Clues have been provided, but it is then left for the individual to find out for themselves.' Might lack of full written elaboration compromise the possibility for perpetuating this view? Associates think not, for this will be guaranteed 'by its own truthfulness, in the manner appropriate to this'. Of those who have completed courses, perhaps only very few grasp all of the themes discussed here. As far as the movement as a whole is concerned, what is more important is for students 'to submit themselves to an education, and to come to know themselves', rather than to gain such insights. By so doing, they contribute directly to the inexorable unfolding and fulfilment of man's spiritual destiny. Finally, there is awareness that a smattering of knowledge of such weighty issues could be dangerous, and a wish to avoid at all costs encouraging in any way 'a teleological apocalyptic vision without knowledge'.

While an effort has been made to check this against the understandings of long-standing associates, a degree of interpretation is perhaps inevitable in our presentation of the Beshara view here.

Prophethood and sainthood

Rauf elaborated his interpretation in an early paper entitled *Christ*, which was distributed at Swyre Farm.[78] There, he introduced Ibn 'Arabi's concept of the relationship between the prophetic function and sainthood (*wilaya/ walaya*).[79] He defined the latter thus: 'The term "saint" (*wali*) can be applied only to those ... who have become totally absorbed in the Oneness of existence and who have realised their unity with Him.' All prophets (*nabi*) and messengers/envoys (*rasul*) are 'invested with the reality of sainthood by their very nature'. Their intrinsic and inherent nature is that of saint. The prophetic function is 'primarily relative and thus ephemeral in so far as the message contained is applicable only for a certain span of time.' In contrast, the state of sainthood 'is a permanency of being and realisation, for it is the perfection of man ... The knowledge of the saint is universal for it is identifiable with His knowledge of Himself.' The prophetic message is 'fundamentally exoteric'. The prophets thus 'were not allowed and could not reveal all they knew to the masses, for this would have been additional to what they were instructed to say within the limits of a religious doctrinal establishment'. They did not reveal openly 'the intrinsic truths, which were capable of being understood at that time only by a spiritual elite'.

Moses, Jesus and Muhammad: an evolving paradigm of religion

Christ explains that, while the prophets appeared as 'the successive unfoldment of a single principle', the prophetic messages of three prophets in particular represented a paradigm shift in 'the unfoldment of religion' understood as a linear progression. These are Moses, Jesus and Muhammad. Moses' prophetic message was contained in 'a primary attitude of complete submission to a totally transcendent deity'. In this conception, 'God was so far removed from immanent realities ... that the ordinary man had little possibility of achieving any sense of unity with Him.' Relative to Moses, Jesus demonstrated 'a totally reversed perspective ... The fundamental principle in his outward teaching was not based on the unapproachability of God but rather on a religion based on the spiritual realisation of man through his potential love of God.' Accordingly, through Jesus, 'men saw a path that led towards unification, for God appeared to live among them'. Muhammad balanced these paradigmatic opposites. He instigated 'not a new religion but one of synthesis based on the realities of both the immanent and the transcendent nature of God.' He thus preached 'neither the transcendent message of Moses, nor the immanent teachings of Christ exclusively.'[80] Muhammad's origin was 'essentially mortal', while that of Jesus was 'essentially' or 'primarily' divine. It is for this reason that Muhammad 'is said to be the prototype of the "Perfect Man", since Jesus cannot represent that to which he does not completely belong, namely the natural order of this world'.

The special nature of Jesus[81]

Rauf reflected at length in *Christ* on the significance of Jesus' nature and role in the spiritual evolution of man, both in its prophetic cycle sealed through Muhammad, and in the role projected for him thereafter by Ibn 'Arabi. 'The nature and spiritual constitution of Christ is distinguishable from all other prophets and messengers', he emphasised. Being born of only one parent, he has two fundamentally separable natures: 'that which was born from corporal matter through the vehicle of Mary, and that which was transmitted by Gabriel in the form of true spirit'. Rauf drew on the opening lines of the chapter on Jesus in the *Fusus* and quoted John 8: 58 by way of elaboration. Perhaps with an audience of predominantly Christian provenance in mind, he pointed to the historical failure to correctly understand the dual nature of Jesus: 'Men have denied through their misunderstanding of Christ the essential transcendence of the Absolute. It is misleading to call Christ "the Son of God" and a confusion of terms. He was both God and man, a dual nature incorrectly synthesised by many into "the Son of God".'

The part of Jesus' constitution that 'corresponds to pure spirit' is of far-reaching significance. In this aspect, he is identified with Divine Love. As symbol of the act of creation, he is 'necessarily identified with the underlying factor of all creation', which is 'Divine Love'. Rauf thus described Jesus as 'the axis or centre of Divine Love'.

The dual role of Jesus in the evolution of man

Jesus' dual nature, Rauf demonstrated, is tailored to his function in the evolution of man, for his message 'contains [these] two aspects within one essential reality'. When he first appeared, he was 'charged with the exterior duty of a prophet', but he was also 'the complete model of the universal saint, for of all the prophets and messengers Christ manifested more explicitly the saintly nature'.[82] In contrast, in his Second Coming 'the situation will be reversed', for he will represent 'the Seal of the Sanctity of the Prophets and Messengers' (identical with the Seal of Universal Sainthood). When Christ comes again, Rauf wrote, 'he will come on a universal level'. As such, 'he will not found a new religion which could consequently only be viable to a minority, but rather he will bring out the intrinsic saintly truths of all religions'. Citing Revelation 20: 1–3, he discussed the Golden Age ushered in by Jesus in his Second Coming. This is traditionally projected as a thousand-year period of peace when the devil is prevented from misleading people, in stark contrast with all preceding ages and the chaos that will follow. Significantly, Rauf described this as 'the age of the completion of man's spiritual potentiality on a global scale, when Universal nature will exist through Christ as the inner realisation of all men'. As symbol of this completion, Jesus 'will bring the esoteric reality of sainthood into the fulfilment of the global evolution, for he is the leader of all the *walis*'.

On Jesus, Muhammad, Ibn 'Arabi and Rumi: symbolic watersheds

Rauf had spoken of a 'deeply symbolic connection' between Jesus, Muhammad, Ibn 'Arabi and Rumi. This is scantily documented in Beshara materials, but explained by long-standing associates. Rauf traced momentous watersheds, signalled by these figures, through which the course of spiritual evolution was directed and, in the case of the two later Muslim saints, by means of which specific foundations were laid for the path that ultimately will pave the way for Jesus' Second Coming.

Regarding the connection between Jesus and Muhammad, Rauf emphasised that 'it was not possible for there to be a Muhammad before a Jesus, and it was not possible for there to be a full manifestation of a Jesus, before there had been a Muhammad'. The first manifestation of Jesus had opened a new phase in the spiritual evolution of man: this was in spite of it having been a partial manifestation, as the time was not yet right for his full manifestation. Flowing from his special constitution, Jesus in his first coming had opened a door, bringing the possibility of *direct* contact between the human and the divine. Prior to this, priests and other intermediaries had been considered indispensable to such contact. This 'first event of Jesus' had 'allowed' the arrival of Muhammad as the first fully human manifestation of the divine, expressed through a prophetic image.

Turning to the symbolic connection between Muhammad and Ibn 'Arabi, Rauf suggested that Ibn 'Arabi later appeared as an expression of this same fully human manifestation of the divine, 'but without the prophetic cover'. Ibn 'Arabi is thus 'the interior of Muhammad being expressed'. The importance of his role as the Seal of Muhammadan Sainthood lies therein, Rauf argued, for 'he brings the *haqiqa Muhammadiyya* and articulates it'.[83] In other words, Ibn 'Arabi's function was to 'bring out' hitherto implicit esoteric truths as they are encapsulated in Muhammad, in whom the evolution of the esoteric content of religion through all the prophets had reached its culmination and completion.

In addressing the link between Ibn 'Arabi and Jesus, Rauf projected Ibn 'Arabi in his sainthood as an anticipation of Jesus in his capacity as a universal saint. This is because, in the words of one associate, the office of the Seal of Muhammadan Sainthood occupied by Ibn 'Arabi 'relates to Muhammad specifically in his capacity as the Perfect Man'. Otherwise put, as the perfect inheritor of Muhammad as Perfect Man, the Seal of Muhammadan Sainthood reflects the *haqiqa Muhammadiyya* in its entirety. This office thus has to do with 'the Perfect Man as archetype on the one hand, and the perfectibility of man on the other'. Rauf's emphasis was on 'what Ibn 'Arabi brought of universality', by virtue of his position as Seal of Muhammadan Sainthood.[84] To understand this projection correctly, this associate stresses, a clear conception of the difference between the Seals of Muhammadan and Universal Sainthood is indispensable. Thus, unless they are seen to form 'two sides of the same coin', confusion reigns.[85]

Ibn 'Arabi had discussed the symbolic significance of Jesus and Muhammad in the spiritual unfolding of man, and touched on his own role in this as the Seal of Muhammadan Sainthood. Rauf introduced in addition the figure of Rumi. He clarified his nature, the symbolic connection between him and Ibn 'Arabi, and their functions relative to each other in man's spiritual evolution. Rumi's contribution is best understood in relation to the ultimate focus of the Beshara view of spiritual evolution, viz. preparation for the Second Coming. We return to it there.

The Beshara view: further elaboration on a theme

Some years after *Christ*, Young elaborated more explicitly two significant interrelated themes in the Beshara view summarised above. These trace the process of the hidden/interior (*batin*) becoming apparent/exterior (*zahir*), and the making explicit of previously implicit esoteric truths towards the ultimate universalising of knowledge of Oneness. In a paper written in 1976 (and published in the *JMIAS* in 1982), he situates these themes in the context of man's spiritual evolution. He also explicitly frames the latter in terms of the broadest possible context, the process and purpose of cosmogony as driven by the Divine Love to be known:

> the determinations of the *Nafas ar-Rahman* [the Breath of the All-Merciful] necessarily conform to the motive: 'I was a hidden treasure, and I loved to be known'. So it is a movement, principially of Love outward refinding Itself on its return, which is expressed temporally as a cyclic movement. With the exhalation of the 'I' the hidden treasure moves outwards towards the world, which is thus the Truth in Truth. It follows that what happens in time will also conform to this principle of the hidden becoming apparent, the *Batin* Itself becoming *Zahir*. So what was implicit at the beginning of this cycle becomes apparent, explicit. But if the *Batin* becomes *Zahir* it follows that everything is in reality *Batin* and that the external revelation, the Universe, is no way different from the internal revelation. It is this situation which in the history of the world is signified by the Second Coming of Christ, and in relation to this Ibn 'Arabi stands midway between the Seal of Prophets, Muhammed, and Christ in his Second Coming. Muhammed was the perfect symbol, the perfect example to mankind, because he was complete balance, the equal affirmation of transcendence and immanence ... [W]hen we say 'There is no God but God and Muhammed is His Messenger', we are ... saying that Perfect Man is ... the link between the *Batin* and the *Zahir*. The religion of Muhammed demonstrates this by being the most explicitly esoteric religion, summarising the transcendental emphasis of Judaism and the immanence of Christianity in the affirmation, 'there is no God but God'. So the full affirmation implies, 'all existence is His existence', and that the reality of Man is the reality of the relationship of the One with Himself. Consequently, the relationship in the flesh established the matrix for global evolution, and is the appearance of the relationship between *Batin* and *Zahir*. But in establishing the matrix it was necessary that the esoteric truths be implicit, although the most explicitly implicit hitherto. Now one of the names of Ibn 'Arabi is 'Seal of the Muhammedan Sainthood' and

sainthood is in accordance with the knowledge that God has of Himself. So it follows that although the prophet must necessarily be a saint the sainthood is the internal aspect of prophecy; consequently Ibn 'Arabi as Seal of Muhammedan Sainthood was the appearance of that internal reality and his function was the making explicit of what had previously been implicit. This also explains his name Muhyiddin, the Animator of Religion. [Ibn 'Arabi] says ... that following the Seal of the Prophets no new laws would be established but there will be 'prophecy of explanation' revealing the truths inherent in the established laws. This is precisely the function of Ibn 'Arabi himself. Why? He says, 'God first created the entire world as something amorphous and without grace ... but it is a rule in the Divine activity to prepare no place without its receiving a Divine spirit'. In the global evolution, Ibn 'Arabi is the preparation of the place and the Second Coming is the Divine Spirit. He goes on, 'and this is none other (from a complementary point of view to the former) than the actualisation of the aptitude which such a form possesses, having already the predisposition for it, to receive the inexhaustible effusion of the essential revelation'. The place must be prepared to receive the essential revelation of the Second Coming of Christ, and the preparation can only be in terms of knowledge. At the Second Coming, the *Zahir* is seen to be nothing other than the *Batin*. ... Ibn 'Arabi unitively is Universal Man but his distinctive reality is *precisely his universality*, and the manifestation of this man necessarily involved the transmission of knowledge, because his manifestation was that of the reality of Knowledge, and it is that which is meant by the Seal of Sainthood.[86]

In the early 1990s, Young was inspired to synthesise these themes with an interpretation of the prophecy of Jeremiah. He was gripped by the significance of the latter's reference to 'circumcision of the heart'.[87] On exploring this and associated verses, he discovered a resonance with the evolution described above, and 'the bringing out of the esoteric truths, which is the Meaning of Ibn 'Arabi'. Interweaving Biblical motifs with citations from the school of Ibn 'Arabi, he has constructed a clear religious–spiritual history which has caught the imagination of many associates.[88]

Young observes that Abraham had marked his pact with God through circumcision in the flesh, but the people of Jeremiah had contravened it and fallen into idolatry. The prophet admonished them, telling them 'circumcise your hearts'.[89] This indicated the real meaning of circumcision in the flesh, as 'an outward mark of an inward intention to cut away any attachment to anything other than the One'. Although it constituted the real 'work' that 'was to be undertaken', and that had been promised in the original covenant, this had almost been forgotten.

Jeremiah conveyed Yahweh's promise to make a 'new covenant' with the House of Israel: 'deep within them, I will plant my law, writing it on their hearts. Then I will be their God ... There will be no further need for neighbour to teach neighbour ... they will all know me, the least no less than the greatest'.[90] The teaching of Jesus then followed, as 'an education in the more interior dimensions of the covenant which were now to be ... followed by all who accepted his message. What was one keeping company with other than God, what inner idols were there?' The compilers of the New Testament indeed identified Jesus' message with the new covenant promised by Jeremiah.

The advent of Jesus also explicitly introduced love into the understanding of the covenant, as its interior dimension. 'How but through Love could the writing on the hearts, foretold by Jeremiah, take place?' The coming of Jesus 'brought the news hitherto known only by the few – that it is the Reality Itself that exteriorises Itself in a movement of Love, as Its own complete image, Man.' With the final destruction of the Temple, 'the house of God built in stone was gone'. A new truth 'had become prevalent in the consciousness of the era: "I am with you always." It was in the hearts and minds of Man that the Real was to be found.'[91] The awareness of this possibility swept the ancient world, 'opening the way for a new kind of contemplative spirituality for the generality of mankind'.

The 'sons of Ishmael' then rose 'under the banner of the Prophet Muhammad', together with 'all others who followed him'. They swept away 'all accretions to the pure religion of Abraham ... all religious intermediaries and priesthoods'. Gradually, 'the day foretold by Jeremiah was approaching'. Already, 'the possibility of knowing God through ... knowledge of the self, with the covenant written on the heart, had extended far beyond the House of Israel'. The Muslims were thus 'the vanguard for the whole of humanity' in the 'covenant of ... Union'.[92] The mission of Muhammad

> introduced the possibility of a unitive and global spiritual perspective ... The whole earth had become the mosque in which the Real could be worshipped, and by every believing soul irrespective of birth or clan. No priesthood stood between man and his God ...[93] With the swearing of the covenant, now in the form of a simple attestation of the unity of God and the messengerhood of Mohammed, each person took responsibility for their own orientation towards the Real and the condition of their soul. The covenant had become a gateway through which the secure and certain could pass in a journey of self-discovery to their own innermost heart, there to find the Real. In knowing themselves ... they would also know ... the Origin, just as Mohammed reported, that 'He who knows himself knows his Lord'. This was an invitation to ... knowledge of the self and ... of God. To know God was to love Him, since real knowledge necessarily entails love of the Known.

In this way the foundation was laid for the completion of Jeremiah's prophecy that 'all would know God'. What remained was 'elucidation of the esoteric truths hidden in that which had been established, principally through the teaching of ... Ibn 'Arabi and his school, opening the way from a Mohammedian perspective to that which was inclusive of all approaches to truth – from wherever and by whomsoever'. This, Young maintains, has become 'the quality of our time':

> Circumcision of the heart remains the key instruction: that it be cut away even from the particularities of a particular way, and so be free to become completely reflective of the Real whatever form It might take, wherever It might appear.

The work consists not in the bare conformity to the precepts of a religion but in the moment by moment adherence to the covenant of *tawhid*, in the valuing of Oneness and in making no partner to Being at all.

An associate has retraced the Beshara meta-narrative, this time rooting it in *Turning*. She posits the religious–spiritual history of the Anatolian region as 'a progression of more and more expansive revelations ... more and more outwardly expressed invitations to completion'. Such a view of history, she maintains, 'can in some way inform us of the era in which we live'.[94] From the time of Çatal Höyük, designated sacred spaces and temples in the region passed through 'successive religious identities' before and after the rise of Alexander and the Roman Empire. With the spread of the teachings of Jesus, however,

> The era of the temple, the space set aside as holy and administered by priests who mediated between man and the gods, gave way to the ... church – the place of gathering of the community. The locus of revelation of the Divine moved from the temple, into the community ... It was at this time ... that the second temple in Jerusalem was destroyed and the Jewish people began their worship in the synagogue, also a gathering place of the community, without a priest.[95]

Thus, 'the locus of the revelation spread into the earth and through the community. It also spread from the chosen people of Israel to all who embraced Christ's teachings, thus spreading rapidly through the vast empire which had been made ready to receive it'. Her treatment picks up the now familiar progression to the appearance of Islam: 'God said to Muhammad "I have made the whole earth a mosque for you."' The physical location for worship became 'not a temple, not a community, but the correctly oriented prostrated form of the believer'.[96] The author then rehearses the role of Ibn 'Arabi and Rumi. These 'two great poles of Islamic sainthood' came to Konya,

> establishing an education in the Unity of Existence which was to be followed by other great Anatolian saints throughout the centuries[97] ... Their interior knowledge expressed itself through a large range of culture, sensibility and taste ... A very large place had been made ready for them, prepared to receive what ... they brought. 'God knows best where to place His message' it says in the Qur'an, and 'He Who manifests Himself in a form does so only according to the degree of receptivity of that form', as we read in ... the *Fusus*.

The author finally reflects on the 'subsequent reception' of the thought of Ibn 'Arabi in the Ottoman Empire, which provided 'an expansive and fertile ground for a profound interior teaching'.[98] This sets the scene for her recapitulation of the Beshara projection of the present era, to which we now turn.

Preparing for the Second Coming of Christ

This time is about the preparation of a platform for the Seal of Universal Sainthood.

Peter Young

Reality is making Itself known, on a global platform as never before in humanity's history, as the real Existence of each person and of everything.

Beshara website

'Historically', Rauf wrote in *Christ*, 'we now stand at the beginning of a transition to a new cycle.' The anticipated new cycle, the new age, is one marked by the Second Coming, while the transition represents the time of preparation that will make this possible. This view of the present times is rooted in Rauf's reading of Ibn ʿArabi's perspective on his own times. As Chodkiewicz describes it, Ibn ʿArabi's work is thus 'entirely oriented toward the horizon of the *eschata*: revelation is sealed by the Qur'an, prophecy is finished ... the Last Judgement is imminent. "We are presently", he says in the *Futuhat*, "in the third third of the night of the universe's sleep" – a sleep that began "with the death of God's Messenger."'[99] As an associate recently pointed out, 'Chronologically, the modern era is situated somewhere, for Ibn ʿArabi, along the continuum between the time of Mohammed and the Second Coming of Jesus.'[100]

How central and urgent is the theme of the Second Coming to the Beshara perspective? What does it signify? How have the protagonists in man's spiritual unfolding identified by Rauf set in motion processes that will establish the prerequisites for the Second Coming? What must be done in the way of preparation for this today? What is the immediate task for Beshara in this final stage of preparation? Finally, can the Beshara treatment of the Second Coming be compared with those of contemporary apocalyptic and millenarian trends?

The reader who looks for explicit discussion of the Second Coming in Beshara sources in the public domain will be disappointed, for it is little evident.[101] This reflects an image-sensitivity, captured in Young's remark: 'one has to be careful of the audience when referring to the Second Coming, given widespread negative perceptions of "millennial" or "doomsday" cults.'[102] Associates confirm that the theme of the Second Coming was at the heart of Beshara during the early years. It was spoken of openly and often at Swyre Farm, for example.[103] Rauf confided in students thus: 'momentous things are coming, perhaps in your lifetime or that of your children or their children'. To make any sense of this, he added, 'you need to be educated'. He was indeed driven by the urgent need to provide the foundations that would make communication of these truths to students possible and meaningful.[104]

Rauf was not alone in highlighting the Second Coming during the early days of Beshara. A general mood of expectation crystallised during the 1960s and 1970s, as prophecies of Jesus' imminent return gathered pace among apocalyptic and millenarian trends in NRMs and New Age communities.[105] Indeed, as Barrett puts it, 'From the 1960s onwards ... particularly with the publication of books such as Hal Lindsay's *The Late, Great Planet Earth*, there has been an increased expectation of Christ's imminent return, and a strong belief that we are living in the End Times.'[106] Rauf's vision of the Second Coming was not apocalyptic, although as we shall see he did envisage the likelihood of external conflict (reflecting an inner conflict) as the Second Coming drew nearer.[107] The Second Coming appears as a precursor of the end of time in the meta-narrative he conveyed, [108] but he strongly discouraged associates' speculation concerning this. He explained to any who asked about it that it was not their business; their concern must be with preparing for the Second Coming and understanding its meaning exclusively. Knowledge of the timing of eschatological matters such as the End Times was ultimately beyond human grasp, he insisted. There is no sense today among associates of being near the end of time, and the Beshara perspective makes no link between such concerns and anticipation of the Second Coming. Rauf's focus was thus on the Second Coming in its capacity as an open-ended new age in its own right, rather than as a precursor to a Golden Age leading ultimately to destruction, as depicted by Ibn 'Arabi.[109] The vision projected in Beshara paints a resoundingly positive tableau of the final fulfilment of man in his relation to the divine, without worrying about what may or may not lie beyond that.[110]

Explicit internal discussion of the Second Coming in Beshara appears to have faded at some point. It has recently been revived, but remains, as before, almost entirely outside of the public domain.[111] Recalling Rauf's insistence that preparation for Jesus' Second Coming was 'the very crux of the matter of Beshara', some associates express their strong approval of this revived affirmation.

An ongoing preparation: the pivotal role of Rumi

Rauf's projection of the necessary preparation for the Second Coming developed out of his understanding of the significance of this 'event' as the final realisation of human spiritual evolution, and a fulfilment of the possibility (which had earlier been brought by Jesus himself) of direct contact and unification with the divine. We elaborated above his understanding of the symbolic importance of Jesus, Muhammad and Ibn 'Arabi in setting the stage for this, both individually and relative to each other. For Rauf, Rumi played a specific significant role in the fruition and expansion of the possibility brought by Jesus and developed through Muhammad and Ibn 'Arabi. In the single documented reference to this in his words,[112] he explained Rumi's essential nature and his symbolic purpose relative to Ibn 'Arabi:

> There is [a] kind of Qutb[113] whose domain and responsibility is more in the overall spirituality of the universal trends and knowledge, as well as the effects. Rumi's

domain of influence was of this nature, that he had to continue the overall esoteric enlightenment of man and his progress towards a universal esoteric platform. That is why he had to succeed ... Ibn 'Arabi in time, so as to channel what Ibn 'Arabi had pronounced as the Seal of Universal Sainthood into universal flow and direct it in its spiritual context more towards the line of a sainthood which is Christ-like.[114]

An associate sums up Rauf's conception of Rumi's role relative to Ibn 'Arabi more simply: 'He opened another door, viz. the possibility of what Ibn 'Arabi brought coming out in much more global potential.' Young reiterates in a note written to accompany *Turning*:[115]

[Rumi's] task has been to take that which had been brought out from the Interior and established here in the world by ... Ibn 'Arabi ... and to 'turn it into universal flow and effect'. (Bulent Rauf) We do not mean here the transmission and dissemination of the work of Ibn 'Arabi, which was the task of ... Konevi. Rather Rumi's task has been the transformation of a perspective founded irrevocably upon the Unity of Existence into a form capable of being received anywhere by anyone who has a heart and spiritual intelligence.[116]

Rauf hinted that Rumi's effectiveness for his task flowed from his use of poetry to express spiritual truth, and his articulation of this from the Station of Love:

it was appropriate that he should find expression through that form. It is a form particularly fitting to what he wished to say of Beauty and Love. Ibnul 'Arabi had already paved the way for him with his exposition concerning the Unity of Existence, and certainly that very doctrine is the essence of Rumi's expression, illuminated through colourful stories and analogies. He speaks from the Station of Love, of the Station of Love, of the infinite Love Affair and the endless revelations of the Beloved ... His ... Mathnawi is a unique expression of love for the ... Beauty of the Beloved ...[117]

Rumi continues with his task today. Thus,

Rumi is at the still point of the turning of our present world. Despite the fact that his bodily existence came to an end in 1273, his essential reality is permanent and continues to be active as an extension of spiritual help from the Presence of All Help.[118] Unlike the Pole of the Time, who is a living person in the world, Rumi's place may be thought of rather as the axial point of the present era. His responsibility as such is the turning of the overall spirituality of mankind in the direction that of necessity it must take. Thus, he oversees a greater span than his own lifetime.[119]

Rauf explained that the office of the *qutb* of the time designates the 'temporal–spiritual' function of a living saint. In contrast with this, Rumi's *qutb*-ship designates a function in spiritual history, as a force for universalising specific spiritual knowledge encapsulated in Ibn 'Arabi's legacy.[120] This understanding can be seen as a construct forged out of a synthesis of his understanding of the process by which man's spiritual evolution will reach its

imminent fulfilment, and an appreciation of the pertinence of Rumi's continuing *baraka* (manifest in his legacy) to this.

Rauf's projection of Rumi brought together a number of themes. Some,
like that of Rumi's '*qutb*-ship', were of his own fashioning. Others resonate
with more widespread contemporary perceptions of the poet–saint. He
highlighted Rumi's earthly encounter with Ibn 'Arabi and the links between
them, perhaps to underscore their important symbolic connection described
above.[121] To clarify his nature, Rauf explained that Rumi was 'a spiritual
descendant from the line of Christ',[122] reflecting his application to Rumi of
Ibn 'Arabi's notion of a sainthood that is Christ-like.[123] This projection of
Rumi's sainthood links directly to the more commonly held notion of his
strong association with love. His message was thus, in Young's words, of 'the
universal reality of Love'.[124] As Young puts it, the love of which Rumi spoke and
which, 'made flesh, he was', acknowledges 'no racial or religious distinctions
or distance'. Rather it is universal in its remit.[125] This is a frequent emphasis
in projections of Rumi today in the West, where his poetry is mostly read in
translation, 'filtered through the lens of a New Age ... idiom'.[126] Yet Rauf was
careful to avoid the suggestion that Rumi be associated with love alone, or
that his association with love should result in denying such an association to
other saints:

> Some people call Rumi the 'Pole of Love' and Ibnul 'Arabi the 'Pole of Knowledge',
> but one should never be misled into thinking that there is anything other than One
> Perfect Man, or that real Love is ever without Knowledge, or real Knowledge ever
> without Love.[127]

Alluding to the Second Coming, Young suggests that Rumi's influence is
perhaps 'more prevalent since his death, with the approach of that time for
which he was preparing during his lifetime'. He projects Rumi's popularity
in the contemporary West as a fruit of the accomplishment of the saint's
specific task:

> This work has been in progress below the surface for hundreds of years since
> Rumi's lifetime. Today we are witnessing the beginnings of its outward effects,
> not least in the widespread appreciation of Rumi's spiritual perspective and the
> availability of his poetry. His current standing as America's favourite poet cannot
> have come about except through the interior necessities of our time, guided and
> navigated by the extension of spiritual help that is Rumi himself.[128]

For many sufis, Rumi's stature as saint is unmatched. As in the case of other
saints, it is far from unusual for sufis to discern the effects of his *baraka*,
his active spiritual influence, in the personal sphere and beyond.[129] What
is distinctive to the Beshara perspective is the symbolic importance of this
influence within its meta-narrative of spiritual evolution, as well as what it
indicates in the way of the immediacy of the final task of preparation for the
Second Coming, and its illumination of the nature of that task.

The final task: preparing the universal esoteric platform

In his Christic nature and his strong association with love, Rumi prefigures Jesus in his Second Coming, while his specific purpose paves the way for this. In the words of an associate, only in light of Rumi's significance correctly understood is it possible to grasp Beshara 'as an event of our time'. The fruition of Rumi's function in establishing the possibility of a global awareness of the truths Ibn 'Arabi exteriorised confirmed Rauf's projection of Beshara as a vehicle for the final task of preparation for the Second Coming. The parameters of this task, the task of the present times, were drawn in *Christ*:

> Christ is ... the axis or centre of Divine Love. Man must approach love through a universal assimilation of knowledge, for knowledge is essentially prior in terms of any ascent to the complete identification with His Love. This knowledge has been prepared and given but it can only be completed in its universal absorption. In order for Christ to come again man will have to evolve spiritually to a universal level, and through Knowledge a 'platform' for this will be created ... Christ at the time of his Second Coming will speak only on an esoteric level, for ... he will not act in order to found any religion but will demonstrate the intrinsic truth of all religions. As such, he cannot come until a certain degree of knowledge has been established on a global level, for without this his function would have to remain primarily exoteric.

The final task, the task of Beshara, is to create the global 'platform' of knowledge of the Oneness of Being that will make possible the Second Coming. Rauf termed this 'a universal esoteric platform'.[130] He drove home to associates the need to get on with building it. Signifying the assimilation on a universal level of knowledge of the essential nature of man (i.e. of self-knowledge and hence knowledge of God), it is in a sense a precondition for the Second Coming. As such its emergence constitutes the penultimate episode of the meta-narrative, making its conclusion possible.[131]

Rauf appreciated that the transition to a universal assimilation of esoteric knowledge would see 'many changes and disturbances'. Against these, he explained, man must 'establish his determination to fulfil his destiny'. He spoke to Feild of two approaching confrontations. The first will be between 'those who know and those who do not want to know, and the second between those who know and those who will have to know'. Any battle or war that would be waged in the 'outer world' must ultimately be understood as a materialisation of these confrontations *within* man. 'Look inside your self', he told Feild:

> Is it not so that both of these confrontations must take place within? There is a part of you, as there is a part of everyone, that does not want to know, and there are parts that will simply have to know, when the time comes, so that there is no separation any longer. What appears to be outside of yourself is really inside yourself. There is nothing outside, and so the battle is first of all within your own being. As more and more people go through these two confrontations, it is likely that we

will see the battle materialized in the outer world. I don't say that there will or will not be a war. But what I do say ... is that the whole world will one day be raised to know of its complete dependence on God. The choice that each of us must make is to surrender to God now, today ... not at some nebulous future time when we will no longer be granted the privilege of choosing. But one way or another a confrontation will take place.[132]

Rauf urged those who had 'reached the knowledge of their essential unity with God' to 'forge the way', passing on this knowledge to build the platform. He explained that, as the transition towards the Second Coming progressed, more knowledge would be 'released', so that it might be 'preserved and carried on'.[133] He pressed his contacts in possession of esoteric learning in different traditions 'to bring out what they knew', telling them that the time for this had come.[134]

The relationship between the platform and the Second Coming is perhaps most effectively projected in terms of the former as a necessary corollary of the latter, rather than in the causal terms implied by the notion of preparation. The knowledge that will allow Jesus' appearance to be experienced of necessity must be on a universal level, for any denial of this knowledge frustrates its very purpose and obstructs the appearance that symbolises its fulfilment. Rauf did not posit the Second Coming as an external event in the future.[135] (Reportedly inspired by Ibn 'Arabi, he indeed insisted that 'time does not really exist', for 'past and future are contained within the present'.) He explained to Feild, 'although I seem to be talking about an historical event, everything of which I speak is within you and is happening *at this moment*. There is no other; and what happened ... two thousand years ago is part of the unfoldment of this moment'.[136] Just as the confrontations that would lead up to it would take place within man (and might be reflected at the same time in the exterior world), so the Second Coming would take place within man, through the individual development of the necessary receptivity based on knowledge of Oneness. Rauf applied the notion of 'Maryian' receptivity to describe this condition, which would ultimately prepare for the receiving of Christ. Accordingly, the responsibility to build the universal esoteric platform can be understood in terms of the individual arriving at such receptivity here and now.[137] As it becomes preponderant and develops into universal extent, this will ultimately be reflected in a global 'event', the re-manifestation of Jesus on earth.

In Young's words, Rauf was confident that 'there would be sufficient people across the world who have this knowledge to allow the Second Coming to happen'. What was the vision of the new age he saw encapsulated in this global 'event'?

The Second Coming as new age: 'universality' and global unity

Beshara is the news that mankind is evolving to accommodate a universal perspective which is beyond religion, and free from all the constraints of nationality and culture, dogma, political ideology and selfhood.

Beshara website

During this period of time, the evolution of the planet and of humanity has reached a point when we are undergoing a fundamental spiritual change in our individual and mass consciousness. This is why we talk of a New Age. This new consciousness is the result of the increasingly successful incarnation of what some people call the energies of cosmic love. This new consciousness demonstrates itself in an instinctive understanding of the sacredness, and ... interconnectedness of all existence.

William Bloom, cited in Heelas, *The New Age Movement*, Appendix 1

[T]he cosmos is all lover and beloved, and all of it goes back to Him.

Ibn 'Arabi[138]

In the Beshara perspective the new age signified by the Second Coming must be situated within the grand narrative of Ibn 'Arabi's cosmogony. In fulfilment of man's spiritual destiny, the Divine Love to be known will become manifest in the coming of Jesus as the embodiment of the universal reality of Divine Love. If knowledge is the outward face of love in the Self-disclosure of the divine to itself through an apparent 'other', through knowledge of God, man, as no other than God, effectively returns that love to the Beloved Himself. When knowledge of God has become universal, when every person sees the divine in every other person, humanity is in its entirety a mirror to the divine, allowing the universal reality of Divine Love to appear. From the outset, the cosmic drama has gradually set the stage for universalisation of the knowledge of God. Ultimately, then, the construction of a universal esoteric platform is not the work of man alone. Rather, it is itself a reflection of the Divine Self-disclosure, taking place in accordance with the Divine Will for the era. Yet man participates in this transition. Through his own receptivity, he advances the process that directs creation towards its fulfilment, in the advent of the new age.[139]

Why did Rauf project the period from the mid-twentieth century onwards specifically as a time of the universal assimilation of esoteric knowledge? How does the Beshara perspective interpret significant changes during this time, for example in science, politics, and globalisation? In a cosmic sense, the new age symbolises the fulfilment of man's spiritual destiny within the Divine Self-knowledge. What are the tangible characteristics of the *earthly* new age? What will man's self-perception be, and how will this shape human relations and society? Is there a place in the new age for such constructs as ideology and nationalism? What will be the fate of the religions and their spiritual ways?

The sixties as 'event' and the counterculture generation as revolutionary vanguard

At the heart of the Beshara perspective is a notion that man's aptitude for receiving esoteric knowledge has expanded in tandem with its gradual release and exteriorisation across time, in accordance with the Divine Will. Associates link this understanding with Ibn 'Arabi's explanation at the beginning of the first chapter of the *Fusus* that God does not prepare a place without breathing the Spirit into it, and that this in-breathing itself represents an actualisation of the inherent aptitude of the place to receive the Spirit.[140] Rauf believed that the generation born in the West after World War II (the baby boomers) possessed a heightened level of preparedness or receptivity. This was manifest in a more developed aptitude to receive esoteric knowledge specifically, and reflected the culmination of the gradual development to which we have just referred.[141] Young reflected more recently that it was with this generation that a 'revolution in consciousness' began during the early 1960s. Although located 'predominantly in the west', it was to have 'global effects'.[142]

In the Beshara perspective, this revolution is projected as the working-out of a divine impulse. Thus it reflected 'a new, unprecedented movement which repudiates any labelling or appropriation'.[143] Far from being some limited or short-term social or cultural phenomenon, it was in fact 'a movement of unfolding – from the hidden interior to the exterior consciousness of mankind – of the possibility of a universal ... perspective'.[144] As Young explains:

> The primary esoteric truth ... is that Existence is an intrinsic and indivisible Unity. This Unity is the real being of everyone and everything, and it is this Truth that is now in the business of making Itself known – not only to the spiritual giants as in the past, but to the general human consciousness, to whoever wants to know ... The special people – the prophets and saints of the past who discovered this perspective and ... led to it ... were ... building the conditions for the present. That is why in the past this perspective was ... difficult to approach and required stringent spiritual practices and discipline to attain to it. Holy books have revealed it and concealed it at the same time, requiring an esoteric core teaching, and teachers, to take those with special aptitude further into the mystery. While all this has been true, the conditions of the present era are different and its quality entirely new ... where before it was as if we were approaching the Real, now it is rather that the Truth, our interior Reality is approaching us and making itself known. What was before a hidden, guarded truth is now becoming obvious. No longer the jealous preserve of the interior of the religions, now this truth must become known universally throughout mankind. Why? Because this is what Truth wants.[145]

In accordance with its will for the era, the movement of Divine Self-disclosure effected a 'surge of interest in the search for a spiritual perspective' in the sixties. It turned each person involved to 'a new awareness of their interior mysteries of body, soul and spirit'.[146] The resulting revolution in consciousness, which was thus divinely instigated, gradually brought about a 'sea-change in self-awareness'.[147] This amounted to a paradigm shift, encapsulated in a growing consciousness of unity in different spheres of human thought and life. At the same time, it was itself an effect or corollary of the expanding assimilation of esoteric knowledge, the knowledge of Unity.

Young draws on his first-hand experience as counterculture spiritual seeker in characterising this divinely appointed 'revolution in consciousness'. Among its signs, he singles out the feeling that there was 'another way of living, another way to be than simply following the accepted mores of previous generations'.[148] He suggests, too, that there was 'more than a little acknowledgement of the Reality of Love, the real Flower Power behind the scenes'.[149] Through their emerging global consciousness, counterculture spiritual seekers would ultimately blaze the way for the earthly new age built on and reflecting the assimilation of esoteric knowledge.

'Universality' as Beshara leitmotif: paradigm shift and hallmark of the new age

The term universality is prominent in the Beshara projection of the new age. It captures the quality that flows from the notion of the Oneness of Being: implicit within it is a sense of all-inclusiveness. Rauf projected universality as an intrinsic existential quality, rather than one imposed from without in the framework of a particular discourse (including spiritual, theological and religious discourses). In this understanding, each sphere of life and each discipline yields its own expression of universality, its own intrinsic universal meaning, in its own terms of reference.[150] Young posits the 'all-inclusive point of view' that represents the perspective of the Oneness of Being as 'the particular gift that comes from Ibn 'Arabi'. Yet he is quick to point out that this is 'not exclusively a spiritual point of view, unless what is meant by that is the existence of one absolute and all-encompassing reality, which is the only real existence of everyone and everything'. Far from being exclusively or specifically spiritual, he argues, this perspective 'leaves nothing out'.[151] Transcending and simultaneously encompassing all of these, it is 'completely free from all partiality and all qualifying adjectives', and 'from the qualifications of all religions'.[152]

The role of the 'new' science

The perspective that flows from the Oneness of Being is unique in origin (it is 'His vision of the world') and compass, and no humanly constructed perspective can match it in this respect. Yet Rauf believed that one discipline in particular could contribute to the establishment of universality. This is the 'new' science, reflecting a new paradigm based on a holistic perspective.[153] This is how he commented on the work of a prominent philosopher of science and physicist:

In an old article ... entitled *Quarks, Quasars and The Meaning of Life* by Paul Davies, it is quoted ... 'This theme of simplicity, wholeness and beauty – revealed through mathematical formulae or delicate experimentation – recurs again and again as nature's mysteries and subtleties are explored.' If you leave out that which is between the two dashes, what ... Davies marvels at has been expounded upon in exactly the same tone as the quote above and in much greater detail and depth seven to eight centuries ago ... by the one who is known as ... the Shaykh al-Akbar.[154]

Rauf in fact had a dream in which 'he found that the message of what Beshara is was understood not by those whom we consider to be spiritual or religious, but by scientists.'[155] He foresaw an important role for science in an emergent new 'vernacular' of the new age: 'It is the required birthright of today that it should be allowed to benefit from a new expression of both religion and physics in the formulation of a new vision.'[156] Articulated in an existential language, the incontrovertible findings of science would furnish an important medium for expansion of the perspective of the Oneness of Being, while at the same time endorsing this. Put simply by associates, 'The physical sciences show us that we are being offered the witnessing of an order which is single.'[157] And, 'Scientific experimentation is reaching a threshold of a quality of appreciation which concurs with that of people whose ... lives are informed ... by the Unity of Being. What at first may be apprehended as a concept, namely the Unity of Being, and experienced as an evanescent beauty, can be willingly and consciously re-integrated into the being of the individual self.'[158]

Such high regard for the new science is a prominent feature of New Age thought, and Rauf was by no means alone in it. He stressed 'the correlation between mysticism and science'[159] to associates, urging them to keep abreast of developments in scientific thinking and to engage in dialogue with scientists, This emphasis was prominent within the movement for some time.[160] It was reflected in the many interviews with scientific experts and reviews of scientific works in *Beshara Magazine*, and in the Sherborne/Frilford seminar series.[161] There has not been much engagement with the scientific community more recently, but individual associates remain interested in the new science and refer to its findings in their writings.[162]

Notwithstanding its significant potential, Beshara holds that science, like all other disciplines, is ultimately limited in its perspective. This is because it lacks a 'metaphysical framework' within which to situate its findings. Similarly, all contemporary discussions of the relation between religion and science, economics or the environment 'lack the perspective capable of generating the understandings they seek'. In contrast, the perspective of the Oneness of Being makes possible 'strategic metaphysical thinking'. As one associate puts it, 'Ibn 'Arabi ... gives a single vision – a vision both unified and unifying.'[163] The interest in other disciplines fostered by Rauf and evident in *Beshara Magazine* served a process of 'making connections' with potential allies in the emergence of universality. Ultimately, however, these disciplines would have to bow to the all-encompassing perspective of the Oneness of Being. The vision upheld by Beshara is thus all-embracing (it includes 'politics, science and technological achievement', for example), and situates its constituent parts in relation to 'an inner movement, of the spirit or consciousness'.[164]

From the 'tyranny of the self' to the bindings of love

Ultimately, the new paradigm upheld by Beshara, the paradigm of universality, must supplant an entrenched existing paradigm. As Young clarifies, the new paradigm

> does not need to be invented and is already with us ... It is certainly most completely expressed in the teachings of Ibn 'Arabi, in his grand exposition of the height and reality of man. The new paradigm ... is of one absolute and all-inclusive reality in which we, mankind, have a definite and unique role to play ... This is service to Life and to existence, both as the absolute reality and as all the living things that are Its relative expression.[165]

In contrast with this, the prevalent paradigm is summed up in the idea that 'the limited self is the real existence and that this limited existence must be served and maintained'.[166] Mistaking it for the truth, 'ordinary human thought' uses the 'conjecture' of the illusory separate self as a model.[167] It thus underlies pervasive exclusivist constructs in social, religious, political and ideological spheres, and contributes to what Young describes as a perspective of the 'tyranny of the self'.[168] As he explains,

> most of us have derived our sense of identity from accidents of birth, sex and race; from religion, cultural background, personal affiliations, etc.; to these we have added our own ideas and opinions ... We have used all of these techniques ... to endorse the idea of the separate self, the ego, which must necessarily be in competition with others ... for the illusion to be maintained. By extension, this same model of the self is that which most institutions employ, as do nationalists and even religious communities. Yet, all of these are nothing other than an extended ego, self-defined according to an exclusive point of view. Today these extended egos are coming under pressure due to the changing conditions of the era. It is time to see that they are illusory, due to peering through the wrong end of a telescope ... Man must now begin to see completely clearly and look through the lens which gives the big picture. This is the Universal Perspective.[169]

Determined by the Oneness of Being, the universal perspective trains its focus on what might be described as the 'common divine humanity' of all. It leads to 'a holism of identity', to coin a phrase, prioritising the essential reality of each person over contingent, socially constructed identities.[170] Young singles out contemporary nationalist constructs as anathema to this vision.[171] This reflects a prominent theme of what might tentatively be termed New Age political consciousness (taking into account the acute individualism that characterises the New Age), which implicitly posits in opposition to nationalism the vision of a unified world.[172] Religious 'fundamentalists', too, come in for attack by Young:

this conjectural separation has developed many forms in the general human consciousness that cover up the reality of our human situation. Separate existence is the enemy that dwells between the two sides of the forehead,[173] and it is a killer that has killed tens of millions even since fifty years ago. Is it not time ... that the lie of nationalism be called, be it benign in appearance or maleficent? We need to understand that nationality is nothing but a conjectural extension of a purely conjectural existence, and that it is bound by this fact to be self-serving. However much a European Economic Community maintains a face of brotherhood and understanding within its limits, it can only do so by maintaining those limits. Consequently, it is in implicit opposition to the rest of the world. The examples that could be given here are endless. What together they indicate is the unavoidable necessity for the cultivation of a different view, a greater possibility within the reach of the generality of mankind. It is becoming increasingly apparent that, where ... we have been at war or in an uneasy peace with our neighbouring country, it is this enemy within that prevents real peace ... between countries. It is more than ever clear that all so-called and entirely misnamed fundamentalists everywhere, be they nominally Muslims, Jews or southern Baptists, belong to the same religion, and we must perceive that this religion is the binding of oneself to a self-invented conjectural limit ... It is more than ever clear that national boundaries are only being maintained by the same limited and limiting tendency on both sides of the divide. The greatest enemy is within.[174]

In focusing on religious fundamentalists specifically in this text (which is drawn from the public domain), Young was perhaps conscious to avoid alienating Beshara's allies (and potential allies) within the religions, by a frontal attack on these. We defer detailed consideration of the Beshara perception of the religions to a later discussion, but a comment by Rauf concerning their place in the new age is pertinent here. He explained to Feild that the new age 'does not mean the formation of any new religion'. Far from it:

> There will be no more need for any form of religion. All that will have to go. When you come upon the essence, do you still want the form? When you have drunk of the water of life, do you still need the glass to contain it? It has fulfilled its purpose and something new can come about. All I can say is that what will come about will be like nothing that has ever been seen before – not like any of the great civilizations of the past. I am speaking of a completely new way of life ...[175]

Situations of violent conflict involving various nationalist and religious protagonists reinforce perceptions in Beshara of the urgent need for the paradigm shift dictated by the notion of the Oneness of Being. The views of a long-standing Israeli associate illustrate the logic and pull of the case advanced in this regard:[176]

> Ibn 'Arabi pulls you by the forelock and tells you 'look from another angle'. You get a completely different view as a result, and a new possibility of a potentially all-encompassing vision. According to Ibn 'Arabi, there is only one Being and you are no other than that Being, and it is to do with love and knowledge. It is very direct and piercing and there is no doubt in it. The Oneness of Being points to the fact that we all come from the same place. In one respect, nationalism is a bad thing,

for there is room for everyone: if people on both sides [of the Israel/Palestine conflict] could be stopped from clinging to nationalism, and accepted instead the Oneness of Being, compromise and peace could be possible. At the same time, we are now in a new age, when everyone wants recognition, like ethnic groups.[177] What is positive about this is that it demonstrates that people are being connected to themselves. This is positive because, ultimately, when they go beyond ethnic and other boundaries, they can find the Unity within. In another respect, one cannot say that nationalism is entirely bad, because in Ibn 'Arabi's vision nothing is denied and everything has a place. The particularities are God expressing Himself. Thus the One is expressing Itself as a Jew, and the One is expressing Itself as a Palestinian. We all come from One Reality, but because we are so confused, we kill one another. We need to achieve recognition of both levels – the underlying Unity, and the particularisms as Its expressions, which are also to be valued. I think the new age is displaying strong energies of self-recognition: everyone has to be recognised and accepted, in a peaceful manner. In the meantime, however, as this age unfolds, we tend not to go beyond our own particularity. So, the Jews say 'God is mine; He loves me; This is my land', and the Palestinians echo this. The One wants all people to express themselves. The best condition is of people with all of their differences intact, but where these differences do not serve as a basis for conflict, because all are accepted as different faces of the One.

Emphasis on the common underlying identity thus does not negate its particular expressions. Rather, it situates these in a proper perspective. By viewing their differences as 'attributes of a single entity to which there are no exclusive rights except Its own right to Itself', another associate argues, tension and conflict among people disappear.[178] Alternatively, 'Each of us is a unique event in the universe ... and we have the capability to recognise and enjoy the uniqueness in each of us.'[179] As 'Each one of us is His extension, He is our Being, and He it is who inspires us to seek Him in ourselves and others.'[180]

The society envisaged by Beshara is shaped above all by love, and it is love that will ultimately heal a world divided by differences:

> The One All-inclusive Truth has another name, which is Love. Love is the truth that binds us all together, through which we can learn to live and interact, knowing that we are loved by an inexhaustible Love ... We do not have to try to obtain it from others because It is there for us in our very being. We must learn to be connected constantly to the Source. Love Alone is effective; It is the Only Actor.[181]

And

> The reality of Love is that there is only one need: the need for Oneness. When this is realised, we will all see the requirement to rebuild shattered ruins, re-house refugees, and to love one's enemy as oneself ... Now is for building the bridges that will bring all humanity together under the banner of Universal Love.[182]

Signs of a shift

The vision posited in the Beshara perspective is of a world at once unified and encompassing all. It is a vision that is inclusive, participatory and fundamentally empowering. Associates see signs of its materialisation in an emergent universality in several arenas. Many New Agers see a harbinger of the New Age in the world's unification through systems that bring together people previously separated by time and space. The Beshara perspective resonates with this, projecting material processes of globalisation as 'external manifestations of unification' and 'evidence of being in the early stages of universality'. Material globalisation is thus seen as a physical manifestation or effect of the universal assimilation of esoteric knowledge, of man's preparation by the Real to experience the Second Coming. One associate puts it simply: 'People say that global communication has caused a revolution in the way we perceive ourselves ... But global communication is just an effect, a reflection of a deeper matter, the result of a body becoming conscious of itself'.[183] Associates acknowledge that there are problems with globalisation as this is presently driven. Nonetheless, there is a strong perception among them that the infrastructure for a unified global perspective is now in place. This fuels a conviction that the ground has been prepared for its rapid spread. Constituent elements of this infrastructure include the internet, which makes possible instant, global communication, and the establishment of English as the first global *lingua franca*, for example. Transnational corporations, capable of much quicker and more sweeping policy changes than national governments, if their profit-driven interests so require, are also cited. One associate remarks that, whatever its intentions may be, 'the empire of international global capitalism and popular western culture ... is laying the ground' in which certain ideas are 'rapidly communicating themselves'.[184]

What are these ideas, and how have they impacted on attitudes and actions? Young argues that, during the last quarter century, a global consciousness has emerged. The realisation that 'we inhabit one world, each part ... connected to every other' is particularly evident, he suggests, in the now universal appreciation of global economic and ecological interdependence. Meanwhile transnational problems are compelling former enemies to cooperate and multiculturalism within nations forces a questioning of long-held self-identities.[185] Added to this is a growing conviction that 'the individual human being has a value based purely and essentially on their humanity', and that 'differences in human beings deserve recognition and respect'.[186] Awareness of the *need* for a unified and unifying vision is also expanding rapidly.[187] Young construes all this as evidence of Unity 'making itself known from many different sides'. It amounts to 'preparation of the fertile ground ready to receive the "seed" of the knowledge of Union'.[188] In sum, according to the Beshara perspective, the world is now providing 'the conditions for a vastly expanded perception'.[189] In the words of an associate,

We have ... inter-nets and world-wide-webs and the sudden realisation of a mate-rial globalism ... The world has shrunk as our information of it has expanded ... God does not send the Spirit without first preparing the place ... There has been much mention in the media lately of the term globalism to describe the global market system which, in its present form, might be more accurately described as economic imperialism. The globalism of the spirit, the real new dispensation that all the above-mentioned events precurse, requires a preparedness on a global scale, to receive. And what is to be received is the Spirit.[190]

In accordance with the Divine Will for the era and in an unprecedented way the universal perspective is now emerging,[191] as 'we are being turned away from ego-based constructs toward the recognition of our one reality.'[192] Esoteric knowledge has suddenly become generally accessible, and assimila-tion of it is expanding. 'The knowledge of the essential Unity of Existence will become generally known', Young announced at the turn of the millennium, 'exactly according to the well known tradition ... "I was a hidden treasure and I loved to be known."'[193] As the interior Reality makes itself known and esoteric knowledge opens for all, it is met with an unprecedented interest in esoteric matters,[194] and a growing aptitude for assimilating the truth of Oneness.[195] To illustrate this opening up, associates point to the case of the Tibetans. Their long-guarded esoteric teachings have now become accessible across the world, while the Dalai Lama himself openly performs blessings never carried out before in public, or among the uninitiated. They adduce examples of esoteric lore from other traditions published for the first time for general consumption during the last few decades.[196] The success of Beshara itself in its global reach is also cited, especially the 'invitation' it has received to take courses to Indonesia.[197] 'The invitation to completeness', an associate writes, 'can no longer be contained in the order laid out by the temple, the tribe, the community, the followers of the law of a prophet.'[198] Referring to the teaching of Ibn 'Arabi, another writes:

> I believe ... there is now, in the world, a new spiritual dispensation. In the same way that Prophets of old have been the places of dispensation, this new dispensation also takes place in Man ... [but] as the nature of this dispensation is Universality, it is offered to all humankind. We are ... in an age of unveiling ... Everything ... Ibn 'Arabi brought as a distillation into the subtlest of liquors of the essential tastes of the Prophets, distinguished and blended in the recipe par excellence of the *Fusus* ... matured in the oaken casks of his heirs ... this is now bottled and freely avail-able, ready for drinking.[199]

Another associate argues that recent technological developments have brought about

> the possibility of a universal witnessing which is truly new. Things ... always ... known, but interiorly, and only to the elect, have now been made available to the senses of anyone who cares to look ... We are being made aware of an order of Being ... to which we are the witness. This witnessing is increasingly apparent in the exterior; it is direct; it is available to anyone who has the aptitude for it, and

... is not mediated by organisation, hierarchy and exclusivity ... Ibn 'Arabi's aim is bringing knowledge of the Unity of Existence ... [He] directly addresses the ... aptitude for perfection in each person ... In his own times, Ibn 'Arabi wrote only what he was ordered to write by God. In the case of the *Fusus* ... he tells us ... he was specifically ordered to bring it out to those who would benefit by it ... those who had the aptitude for perfection ... [If] in our times, this bringing out can be more universally extended, it will not only be because his works are increasingly being translated into languages spoken throughout the world; nor only because the exclusivity which has surrounded this kind of knowledge in the past has been removed; but because ... conditions actually apparent in our world speak of, or hint at, a readiness.[200]

Such 'signs' strengthen a conviction among associates of the certainty of the fulfilment of man's spiritual destiny, as the new paradigm takes shape in the midst of human society today. Reflecting this (and consistent with characteristic New Age presumptions of the reality of spiritual evolution), some Beshara materials employ the metaphor of 'coming of age' to describe an ongoing spiritual transformation.[201] Through a proper understanding of the self, mankind will reach spiritual maturity, and the spirit of the era will be established. This is 'the spirit of Man's universality, not of religions, nations and philosophies, not of states and gurus, personalities and partialities, traces captured in imaginations of a past time'.[202] Stemming from such convictions, associates have a positive and strongly optimistic perception of the present times.[203] In Coates' words, for example, 'modernity is itself an inseparable dimension of the Unity of Being',[204] and thus all that is part of the modern world has positive meaning. This perception stands in stark contrast with projections of modernity as a deviation and a time of degeneration, characteristic of the Traditionalists/Perennialists, for example.[205] Again, Coates' words illustrate the Beshara perspective:

> there is ... something new in the air ... which is not going to melt away and the need for which is becoming increasingly transparent in an age of globalisation ... Ibn 'Arabi calls it 'the clarification of the mirror of the world'[206] and I suggest that the key to understanding all the unprecedented changes which constitute the modern world ... *is to see* that they are indissolubly inseparable from that same process of universal clarification. One might call it ... a global manifestation of the essential. From such a perspective we can begin to discern the universal, yet unique, grounds of modernity itself ... And this is to begin to recognise that ... modernity ... is indissolubly tied to that movement ... which Ibn 'Arabi describes in the *Fusus* ... as 'the clarification of the mirror of the world'. We can envisage that modern science, technology and economics ... are none other, in reality, than partial aspects of the Self-disclosure of the One Unique Being in its love to be known.[207]

Moreover,

> the interior reality of the era is inescapably a movement of Love. In spite of the inverse appearances of that Love perhaps we stand ... on the brink of an increasing

global actualisation of the full human potential to be the place of Its superlative expression. Which Love in reality is the unfolding from the unseen of God's love to be known and the preparation of the place ... to receive and mirror such a gift in its fullness.[208]

If further grounds for optimism are needed, one associate finds them in the recent appearance of 'one of the first public prophets of those whose religion is true universality of spirit, the reality of the human being'. This is Nelson Mandela, who 'has become in effect a public saint':

Nothing short of a universal love became focused in the person of ... Mandela, a great giving of being which opened the eyes of the world through the painstaking example of his years of submission and then the resolution, integrity, care and patience with which he eventually dismantled the false premise of his enemy's estate.[209]

Beshara as an 'event' of the times and its appointed task

Beshara is the 'good news' that 'Existence is an absolute and all-inclusive Unity'.[210] Situating it within man's spiritual evolution and in light of the purpose of the Divine Will for the era, Young suggests that 'what we have come to know as Beshara' is in fact 'a grand and essential movement of Existence'.[211] It is 'Its movement of Love' that 'gives of Its own Being to us all perpetually'.[212] 'It is His Beshara which He brought about', Rauf wrote early on, 'and there is nothing but Him in any case. You do your best, but ultimately it is up to Him.'[213] On introducing the study of Ibn 'Arabi at Swyre Farm, he indeed projected this not as his own demand, but 'the demand of His Beshara'. In like vein, an associate reflects: 'Beshara came to us. We did not look for it. Bulent was told to go to England, and then the matter started.' As another associate recently explained, 'Those who come to study as students of the School come as part of what is called in the introductory talk on the First Intensive Course "a global plan", the unfoldment of which 'is in the hands of God'.[214] Young puts it simply:

We do not doubt that [Beshara] has come about according to a Will. It has always been very clear that the work of the ... School goes beyond the imagined frontiers of the 'personal' spiritual development of the individual or even of a group of individuals ... It has been clear from the outset that Beshara is concerned with the establishment of an esoteric perspective which is completely in accordance with the Will of the manifestation of this present time.[215]

Beshara came about 'to promote the knowledge in this world of the Unity of Existence'.[216] In the present era, when such knowledge will expand as the Divine Self-disclosure proceeds in accordance with its Will for the times, the task of Beshara is to help prepare the universal platform that will make possible the fulfilment of man's spiritual destiny. In an associate's words, 'It serves as a channel for the Divine Will to manifest itself in accordance with its own determination of the era, and is engaged in preparing for the new era of the realisation of unity and universality.'[217] The establishment of 'a global and unified vision which henceforth will be the context of all humanity' is Beshara's ultimate purpose.[218] In light of this, Rauf's concern to consolidate Beshara's universal identity and to distance it from its early sufi associations, described earlier, becomes clear.

Young recently underlined the demands its appointed task makes on those involved in Beshara:

> there is something happening that is so big, so stupendous, that there is no time for sects, factions, differing units or anything of this kind. Now is the time for us to be united with one aim, one goal, the Unity of Existence as reflected in each of us. It is this Unity which is pointing us in one direction towards universality ... Our intention, which is of course His purpose, is to bring to the knowledge of all who wish to hear, that Union, the recognition of the Unity of being is for everyone. We who are for Union, of all people, must not be parted by our differences but united by our Oneness. There is only One Being, One Self and it is the knowledge of this that binds us together.[219]

The old paradigm based on 'the limited ego, sects and sections all such I-ness' cannot coexist with the expanding new paradigm of 'the One Self, the Universal All-encompassing Truth' which Beshara conveys. They are indeed mutually exclusive.[220] As Young explains,

> This is where our work is so fundamental: the work in exposing the Truth to ourselves, in loving unity, and speaking of It and through It. Thus it becomes established through contagion that there **is** a different way of being, of living in conscious accord with the Real ... that mankind is already a unified totality, and only behaves as if it is not because it has not yet seen it for itself. This can only happen if we are prepared to let go of the past and its hold upon us ... We need even to let go of the form in which we have perceived Reality and each other and to allow that the Real – which is ever in a new configuration – is now announcing Itself in an entirely new way.[221]

By putting forward the 'all-inclusive perspective', Beshara confronts humanity with a fundamental choice, conveying the challenge inherent within the metaphysics of the Unity of Being itself:[222]

> whether to accept to live our lives as **our** lives, under the illusion of separation; or to accept the Truth ... that our lives are not **our** lives but are extensions of Universal Life in a relative form as us. This is the choice that is being highlighted at the present time and its acceptance is crucial. Because from now on we are no longer motivated by self-engendered concerns, but are in proper relation to the Real and closer to ourselves as we really are. From now on we have accepted that this life has meaning and purpose **only** in service to the Real, in loving It and coming to know and see It directly for ourselves.[223]

It is time for all who are moved so to do to turn as one from the small to the great, to our singular reality – the common reality of all of humanity – there to realise and reflect the Unity of all Existence ... In so doing we will be taking a giant step forward towards the real purpose of Man, the Reality of Whom, like an unborn child in the womb of humanity, is only just now beginning to appear. This is the real meaning and purpose of the present era.[224]

Beshara 'as an event of our time' can ultimately be understood in light of the projection of Rumi's hand in man's spiritual evolution, described earlier. As Young explains,

Rumi's language of Love crosses all boundaries with insouciance. This is because the Reality of Love is both above all things and present within all things ... Rumi's well-known invitation, issued from the still-pointed centre of Love to the whole of humanity is to be taken literally, now more than ever before.[225] Who are these people to whom he calls? All who will respond! All who can say in their hearts, like ... Ibn 'Arabi, 'I follow the religion of Love. That is my religion and my faith.'[226] All who select themselves by responding to this universal invitation, these are Rumi's people ... By responding to the invitation they leave behind their self-definition by religions and race, and step into the arena of Oneness and the One Universal Spirit. This is the direction that is opened up for all of mankind; the direction that we must now take.[227]

This quotation points to a defining dimension of the Beshara perspective. We can sum this up in terms of the implications of embracing Rumi's 'invitation' for perceptions of the religions and religious affiliation. In the following discussion we explore the view of religion in the Beshara perspective, and examine how this perspective relates to the Muslim–sufi tradition and culture on which Rauf drew in its construction.

Chapter 6

The spiritual life: culture and practice

Imagine there's no heaven.
It's easy if you try.
No hell below us. Above us only sky.
Imagine all the people. Living for today ...
Imagine there's no countries. It isn't hard to do.
Nothing to kill or die for. And no religion too.
Imagine all the people. Living life in peace ...
Imagine no possessions. I wonder if you can.
No need for greed or hunger. A brotherhood of man.
Imagine all the people. Sharing all the world ...
You may say I'm a dreamer. But I'm not the only one.
I hope someday you'll join us. And the world will live as one.

John Lennon, Imagine

[Beshara] is the name for a spiritual path which is so simple and universal that it cannot even be ... described as a method at all. For it involves merely coming to understand the reality of ... 'He is me, I am no other than Him, though I am not Him.'

Beshara associate[1]

Bulent's aim in Beshara, the aim and taste of the whole enterprise, is witnessing God's beauty and immanence.

Peter Young

The end of religions and spiritual orders: a direct realisation of Truth

As we have hinted before, the Beshara vision of man's spiritual fulfilment symbolised by the Second Coming and captured in the incipient new age pivots not on religion, but a direct realisation of Truth. The Second Coming will not be brought about through the religions themselves, but through their underlying perennial core, which 'unites us all.'[2] Rather than the religions with their accompanying institutions and beliefs, this is what will mark out the new age. The religions did have their purpose in the spiritual evolution of man, as determined by the Divine Will. They may well continue in their core expression and as paths of devotion, and some people may still need their beliefs and practices to approach God. In reality, however, the religions have served their purpose and have had their day.[3] Man's relation to God is so destined for the present age that it is without need of mediation through their offices and institutions, or those of their associated spiritual orders. Far from the aspects of Truth captured in relative form in the beliefs of religions, the bedrock of our era is the experiential grasp of the Oneness of Being, and its direct reflection in self-realisation. As the Truth makes itself universally known, knowledge of the interior reality of man is becoming generally accessible. This poses a challenge to the authority claims of those who were formerly the exclusive repositories of such knowledge within the religions and their spiritual orders, and indeed undermines the very need for them. At the same time, it points to the possibility for every individual to actualise their potential for perfection, when in the past this had seemed beyond the reach of all but the special few.

The problem with religions in the new age and its solution

As the divinely ordained expansion in the direct realisation of Truth proceeds apace, the religions and their dogmas, practices, institutions and offices will ultimately become redundant. Their limitations render them incompatible with new age universality and unity, and indeed a potential threat to this. Rauf had argued that, 'being doctrinal', religions are 'naturally dogmatic and exclusive'.[4] A sense that the religions were implicated in world conflict reflected sentiments that were widespread among sixties youth, who looked forward to a post-theist world marked by peace, justice, unity and freedom. This was captured in the lyrics of *Imagine*, cited above. The song was released in 1970, a year that has been dubbed 'the high-water mark of secularism' in the West.[5] Writing in the late 1980s, an associate remarked that 'countless bloody wars have been waged in the name of a particular belief system professing itself as the "true" and hence universal way'. He argued that even 'the creation of a new universal religion, albeit on a global scale' could not rehabilitate the paradigm of religious belief for the new age, unless people are able to 'penetrate beyond the dichotomy of believer and believed'. Only through self-knowledge rooted in monistic self-realisation might an individual infuse their religious beliefs with a grasp of their relativity, checking powerful tendencies towards exclusivity and misplaced claims to universality. This alone might make it possible for the different expressions of religious belief to coexist harmoniously as 'different faces of the One', rather than as potential sources of conflict.[6] In the absence of self-knowledge, even an imagined universal faith 'upon which everybody globally agreed' would 'degenerate into a particular form of propaganda'. The 'truly universal perspective' starts only in 'the act of self-knowledge ... and can only come about through verifying the reality of things for and in oneself'.[7]

The spiritual orders: the case of the *tariqa*s in Turkey

The problematic nature of the religions as relative forms that are inherently exclusive and potentially divisive also encompasses their spiritual orders. These are yet more exclusive, thanks to the commitment they demand and their formal requirements for admission. Rauf used the Islamic case to illustrate this point. He posited the Islamic religion as a circle. This contains a smaller circle, representing the *tariqa*. Situated beyond both, Beshara encompasses the entire globe (and indeed the cosmos). Furthermore, while religions and spiritual orders encapsulate hierarchical systems of authority and reflect secret knowledge, the Oneness of Being (and hence Beshara) demands an open, inclusive and uncompromisingly egalitarian order.

As we described earlier, Rauf's formative years unfolded in a milieu deeply coloured by the values of sufism and the *tariqas*. Echoing some voices from within the *tariqas* (and reflecting the modernising impulse of his times), as a mature man he fully supported the radical Kemalist agenda. This approval extended to its draconian measures against the *tariqas*, which Rauf deemed necessary and timely. He acknowledged that some spiritually realised individuals could be found within the *tariqas*. As specific forms, however, he considered them devoid of genuine spirituality and increasingly prone to corruption as the end of their finite validity approached. Their termination in Turkey may have had the appearance of 'an act of political repression', but Rauf projected it as 'a real act – an act from the side of the Real'. The Real had used Ataturk as a tool to bring the era of 'formal spirituality' symbolised by the *tariqas* to an end. He had been chosen to play a part in the great changes that would mark the era as determined by the Divine Will, and Rauf suggested that he had been given a particular type of sainthood (*wilaya*) to that end.[8]

Rauf found his conviction that the *tariqa* institution had no place in the unfolding era corroborated by the stance of the final shaykh of the Celvetiyye in Istanbul. Some decades after the reforms, Sirri Dede had ordered the *tariqa* he headed to be closed. He stipulated that after his death there would be neither Celveti shaykh nor *murid*. This decision had followed a dream vision in which Hüdayi had appeared to him and tugged a piece of his clothing, exclaiming 'Enough of this!' Sirri Dede had understood from this that 'the formal situation was finished', and with it the institutions of shaykh and *tariqa*. Rauf had reportedly heard this account from Sirri Dede himself, and related it repeatedly to associates.[9] His special connection to the Celveti saints described earlier can only have underlined its significance for him.

Signs of the demise of religion?

Associates take a particular interest in evidence of the gradual demise of religion in contemporary Western societies, a theme we touched on earlier and to which we will return. For example, one points to 'an upsurge in atheism, materialism and spiritualism following the two World Wars'. Another drew the following conclusion from the findings of surveys relating to Christian belief in Britain during the late 1980s: 'what we may well be seeing is a move away from the outward form of religions towards that which unites them – their interior meaning.'[10] Some associates adduce 'the very strong aversion to religion' they claim to have discerned during very recent years. Alluding to the threat of militant Islamism, one argues that people today 'increasingly identify religion as the cause of world problems'. Others train their attack more carefully on the *misuse* of religion, but the conclusion is one and the same:

> Religion has now become such an issue. Beshara from its very inception has insisted that it is non-religious. Neither is it an amalgam or synthesis of religions. Instead, it focuses on the essence or core from which religions may proceed. Thirty years later, we realise the importance of this. This is what Beshara has to offer.

Religions and esoteric education in Beshara

Given the School's self-projection in publicity materials as 'a spiritual orientation to life without the bounds of dogma or religion',[11] we must consider whether active commitment to a religious tradition can pose an obstacle for the student of esoteric education there. In one associate's words, this is the case only if they are not prepared 'to suspend their preconceptions and to actually undergo an education'. Thus, 'if one accepts the possibility that Beshara is what it is about, one must be prepared to go beyond what one already knows or has'. After completing courses, students are free to 'don whatever clothes they want'. Very few situate their Beshara education within an ongoing religious commitment: for those who do, its strengthening of the latter can find expression in a revitalised religious practice. More typically, however, what brings a student to Beshara is dissatisfaction at some level with a natal religion, or failing commitment to it. At root, the courses thus constitute 'an enquiry', as Young puts it. Young acknowledges that the Beshara perspective poses potential challenges for those who retain their religious attachments. For example, committed Jews and Catholics 'might experience a block in relation to performing the *dhikr* in Arabic'.[12] Such matters aside, the general sense is that those who remain religiously committed can nonetheless benefit greatly from the esoteric education Beshara offers.

As we have seen, the search for a 'living spiritual tradition' offering a direct experience of the Self as sacred had driven many sixties youth into the open arms of gurus and NRMs. Seekers of Christian and Jewish provenance had turned up at Swyre Farm under Feild in almost equal numbers. Those of Jewish background remain a significant constituency for Beshara today. Since the mid-1980s, they have mainly come from Israel.[13] A few associates of Muslim provenance have been visible across the years.[14] However, the main source of Muslim interest has developed since 1999, and is centred on Jakarta.

As we noted earlier, the export of nine-day courses has led to an Indonesian initiative to set up some form of regional representation for the School. The Indonesian experience represents the first time that Beshara 'has been taken to a Muslim country'. While we consider this experience in detail in a later discussion, we cite here the observations of an associate who has run Jakarta courses, to provide some indication of the internal perception of Muslim encounters with the movement. In his experience, practising Muslims have readily accepted one aspect of the fundamental Beshara teaching and the material studied, in their capacity as the 'esoteric core' of Islam. However, they 'need to see and accept that [Beshara] is supra-religious', and they have been uncomfortable with this aspect. The 'limitations' of some Muslim encounters with Beshara are illuminated in terms of Rauf's observation that people in general 'draw from Beshara in accordance with their aptitudes. Some remain within limits, and others go beyond'. From the point of view of Beshara, Muslims nonetheless enjoy what Young describes as 'a beneficial starting point'. Thus 'they are already in a state of submission'. For this reason, the Beshara encounter with them has in some ways proven easier than that with Western individuals who lack 'a developed religious background'. In other respects it has been more challenging, however, given in particular the impact of 'long commitment to the sharia'. The ultimate challenge for Muslims, Young suggests, is thus to make the small but significant shift of consciousness 'from the Seal of *Muhammadan* Sainthood to the Seal of *Universal* Sainthood, in other words, towards a more inclusive perspective'.

Talk of God? Monism versus theism

The call to transcend religion is profoundly disturbing to many Muslims, especially in societies where the traditional remains strong in spite of modernity. In parts of the West, however, it is far less of an issue, as we will illustrate later. For counterculture youth in the sixties, the movement's bold repudiation of religion exerted a powerful pull. Young's own reflections on his early encounter with Beshara are illuminating in this respect. He had understood at the outset that he was 'getting into something that was beyond religion'. His first exposure to the movement came as something of a surprise, however, and he could not see 'why there should be any talk about God at all' in this milieu. His reference to 'talk of God' points to a monistic/theistic dialectic in the movement's perspective. This reflects a paradoxical dimension of Ibn 'Arabi's thought which is encapsulated in his doctrine of the Divine Names and Attributes.[15] For Ibn 'Arabi, God is envisaged at once both monistically and theistically. This arises out of his correlation of the two broad categories of Divine Attributes which Muslim thinkers uphold,[16] with two contrasting definitions of God. These definitions project God on the one hand as incomparable/transcendent (*tanzih*), and on the other as similar/immanent (*tashbih*). *Tashbih* points to the monistic assumption of the sacred Self, and is characteristic of those who receive *kashf* or 'unveilings'.[17] *Tanzih* tends to be typical of rational thinkers who deny *tashbih*, and focus on the 'I–Thou' relationship between God and man.[18] According to Ibn 'Arabi, the *muhaqqiq* or 'verifier' sees through two 'eyes' simultaneously. Through one 'eye', he sees his own uniqueness as a *creature*, and through the other, he sees his genuine *identity with God*.

Returning to Young's early experience of Beshara, he relates that he soon discovered ('through studying Ibn 'Arabi') that 'the Truth has a personal face'.

Depending on the precision of its application, 'God' in Beshara often refers to this 'personal face' of the Essence, encapsulating the theistic facet we have just described. God envisaged theistically as transcendent (and as separated by a gulf from His creatures) is experienced through those Names appropriate to servanthood (or that call forth a response in terms of it). This is expressed through modes of devotion, worship and obedience. In Beshara, such references to God theistically envisaged are solidly embedded in what must be described as an uncompromising, determinative non-dualism. Thus as one associate puts it, 'In Beshara we are not concerned with finding God. Rather what counts is God's vision of Himself and a realisation of what already *is*.'

In Beshara, 'talk of God' can also refer to the ineffable Essence behind the 'personal face', however. Rauf warned that this use of the name 'God' should be only with the greatest caution, for it is inherently limiting:

> In an atmosphere so saturated with His and Only His existence, where even the mention of the Name God is used warily ... used only because there is no other word with which we can express the Sole and Unique Being; and where this name God is used by us, well aware of its inadequacy because we know that to name Him is to limit Him, which is the depth of ignorance for us, since we know and are certain of His Limitlessness; and where consequently, for us the use of the word God is only done apologetically.[19]

Emphatically situating the focus of Beshara on the Essence rather than the theistic God of religion, the following record of a recent discussion at Chisholme is particularly illuminating:

> When you say 'He' or 'Him', to whom, or to what, are you referring? Each of us should look at this question individually, because each of us may mean something different by this pronoun. In particular, do you use it as equivalent to the name 'God', or is it intended for the Ipseity, the Itselfness, of all existence? If the former, then you are referring to the personal face of the Reality. If the latter, what you mean reaches beyond this personal aspect of Reality, into the Essence Itself. Religion is concerned with the relationship of the numerous facets of existence, i.e. me or you, or all of us, with the face of existence that is the Divinity. The education of this School is from beyond religion, beyond the relationship of aspects, and it aims at the Ipseity of all existence. The fruit of this education is that there be witnessed nothing in existence but Him ... don't let this word 'He' refer to another being, because there is no such being. Don't even let your intended meaning stay at the level of the relationships of religion.[20]

A culture of devotion

Frithjof Schuon has argued that 'Man would not be man if there were not within him two incommensurable dimensions, one for devotion and the other for union.'[21] The explicit and relentless focus in Beshara is on union, through realisation of a thoroughgoing non-dualism. Yet at the same time the movement evinces a strong devotional culture, through engagement with the 'personal face' of Reality. As in the case of Ibn 'Arabi's doctrine,[22] in this context we must also use the inherently dualistic notion of devotion (encompassing also notions of worship and praise) with some qualification.[23] Young explains that in Beshara devotion is embraced 'from a position of appreciating the Real beyond the personal face'. From this position, one can see that 'Reality can assume two aspects at the same time: the Worshipper and the Worshipped, the Lover and the Beloved'. The ultimate aim in Beshara is the transcendence of all duality (including that at the heart of the theistic conceptions of religion), so that the return of one's being 'to *Hu*, the Ipseity of all existence', can be achieved as 'a deliberate act'.[24] As Young suggests, 'the metaphysics and the devotion are two sides of the same coin' in Beshara. Ultimately, however, the monistic 'metaphysical side' is determinative, while the devotional culture and its constituent practices serve ultimately as 'an affirmation of Reality'.

Spiritual practices: origins and adaptations

[Bulent's] way was the way of the Sufi, with his own thoughts, feelings, ideas, understandings, his own mysticism on top.

> Angela Culme-Seymour, *Bolter's Grand-daughter*, p. 255

Assuming the character traits of God – that is Sufism.

> Ibn 'Arabi[25]

From 'Desperate Dan' to the Perfect Man is a mighty long leap to make.

> Arthur Brown, 1970s pop phenomenon and early Beshara associate

Which spiritual practices does Beshara recommend? What are their specific origins in Islamic and sufi practice?[26] How did Rauf project their importance for the spiritual way and for spiritual realisation? How did he adapt them for use in Beshara? We describe here the practices that make up what we can loosely designate the Beshara 'way' (the path to perfection practised in Beshara), and explore their relationship to the Islamic–sufi tradition. Certain of these practices are appropriate only to the course context, but some are performed weekly or daily by associates in general, beyond the School.

Dhikr: the remembrance of God

Dhikr signifies simply 'remembrance' in Arabic, but Qur'anic usage ties it specifically to remembrance of God. Rauf saw fit to explain to Feild why it was necessary to adopt a particular form of remembrance of God, and why he himself taught the Islamic–sufi form of this designated by *dhikr*:

> You may wonder why it is necessary to perform *zikr*, particularly since you are not an orthodox Moslem ... There are many ways of performing *zikr*, and the teacher must seek the level of the pupil so that he will give him the correct type ... You

must not take away form if the pupil still needs form. The rule is, if the pupil is not ready to go beyond form, then give him an exercise ... it is necessary for you to learn about *zikr* ... for it is only possible to know the truth if you are in a state of continuous remembrance, if you are always awake. I can only teach from my own experience, so I will instruct you in remembrance of God through *zikr*.[27]

The Qur'an and hadith prescribe *dhikr* as a duty for all Muslims. Traditional sufi authorities have projected it as the *raison d'être* of all Islamic ritual, and it has emerged in its most developed ritual expression as a distinctively sufi practice.[28] Rauf singled out *dhikr* as 'a daily practice for all followers of the Way'.[29] He explained to students that their 'rememoration of Him' should be a major proof of their constant awareness of 'His Uniqueness and Oneness of Existence'.[30] Through it, they could develop certainty and security of heart, for 'Through nothing else but His *Zikr* is the heart satisfied'.[31] He stressed humility as its 'essential ingredient': 'Without the necessary relegation of the "I" to Him, the *Zikr* can never be His *Zikr* by Him, through His own individuation in you. There is no other form of *Zikr*'.[32] This focus on *His dhikr* reflected the notion of God invoking Himself, which arises in certain Qur'anic verses and *hadith qudsi*.[33]

In addition to *dhikr* as a state of constant remembrance, Rauf assigned it to students in the form of two specific spiritual exercises. These are the collective ritualised practice and the *wazifa*.

Dhikr as collective practice

We describe a collective Beshara *dhikr* at the end of this volume (Appendix 3). Such gatherings are held at the School and wherever associates can come together every Thursday evening throughout the year, and also to mark an annual cycle of significant dates.[34]

The collective *dhikr* gathering in the *tariqa*s (which typically involves corporeal movement and sometimes a distinctive respiratory rhythm) is often termed a *hadra*, meaning literally 'presence'. This turn of phrase derives from the fact that, as one scholar of sufism puts it, 'the Name ... pronounced in [such] meetings is the Name of God Himself, *Allah* ... in which God is present and through which He makes Himself present'.[35] In Beshara, gatherings of collective *dhikr* are referred to simply as *dhikr*. There is an understanding of the term *hadra* as 'the presence of God', but this is not linked to the collective *dhikr* for, in the words of one associate, 'we are constantly in the presence of God, and this is not a state brought about by specific activities'.

We cannot speak of a uniform collective *dhikr* in the traditional *tariqa*s, but it is possible to identify features of the Beshara collective *dhikr* that set it apart.[36] First, the sexes are fully integrated with each other in its performance. There is no spatial segregation and they may even be in physical contact, with arms around each other's shoulders and waists.[37] Second, someone is designated on each occasion to 'lead' the *dhikr* (usually Young), but their role does not take in the element of supervision characteristic of the 'presiding' shaykh in the context of the traditional collective *dhikr*. Finally, the Beshara gathering does not integrate the collective *dhikr* with other devotional activity. In the traditional *tariqa*s the *dhikr* generally forms the culmination of the gathering, completing a sequence of other activities which are effectively preparation for it. These include singing religious songs (*anashid*), reciting the *wird* of the *tariqa*, and recounting the story of the Prophet's birth (in one of its celebrated narratives). All this is interspersed with the plentiful calling down of blessings upon the Prophet.[38] The precise elements represented are determined by specific *tariqa* traditions, and the gathering's cultural–social and local contexts. In contrast, the Beshara *dhikr* is 'stripped of all cultural specificity'.[39] It starts immediately with the invocation of Divine Names and repudiates the devotional preamble favoured by the *tariqa*s, with its culturally specific forms.

As is evident from our description of this, the flow of the Beshara *dhikr* is punctuated by a few minutes of silent reflection between its individual phases. This helps to maintain a steady pace throughout, and there is none of the crescendo and climax typical of many *tariqa*-based *dhikr*s. Their most widely used method of invocation, which contributes to this process ('the invocation from the chest' [*dhikr al-sadr*]), is eschewed in Beshara.[40] There is nothing 'ecstatic' in this gathering, which instead exhibits a sober spirit of measured control.[41]

Young emphasises that, in the concluding of the *dhikr*, 'no fixed order is prescribed for the leader to follow'. It is left to their discretion whether or not to include the *takbir* and the *salawat*, and they may recite these alone inaudibly on the breath, or lead the gathering in singing them aloud.[42] Inclusion of the *salawat* in particular appears to be the norm, and the *takbir* is also often included. One or both are recited or sung before the final '*Hu*'.

The *wazifa* and the forms of its practice

Performance of the *wazifa* or 'daily office' is also at its most developed and rigorous in the *tariqa*s. Assigned to the disciple by the shaykh and tailor-made for them, it typically encompasses the *shahada* and the name *Allah* or its substitute, the pronoun *Huwa*.[43] In Beshara, it is a practice in which one or more of the Divine Names is repeated a number of times (the number sometimes determined by their numerological value), and sometimes prefaced by the particle of invocation, *ya*. Rosaries are used for this, and are sold in the School.[44] An abacus is used to keep count of very large numbers of repetitions. While the *wazifa* is an integral part of both intensive and further courses, some form of it is also performed as a daily practice by at least some associates wherever they are.

As we noted in an earlier discussion, the practice of *wazifa*s appears in three different formats in the intensive course. Individual *wazifa*s are assigned by Young following Rauf's practice. Tailored to their state or psychology and level of self-knowledge, they may be changed as students proceed through the course. They are perceived as a 'medicine' for the student, and their impact is therefore closely monitored. The Divine Names are always prefaced in these *wazifa*s by the particle of invocation. Secondly, a collective *wazifa* practised for the course duration also has the format of an invocation. It begins with repetition of *ya Rahman al-Rahim* (O All-Compassionate, Most Merciful One!), and introduces invocation of different Divine Names each week.

Thirdly, a further collective *wazifa* practice proceeds parallel to this one for the six weeks of the course prior to the last two. Based exclusively on repetition of the name *Allah*, it effectively represents a culmination of *wazifa* practice throughout the course. Strictly speaking, it is not an invocation, but an act of remembrance (*dhikr*). Beginning with 1,000 repetitions, it is increased weekly to 3,000, 5,000, 10,000, 15,000 and 20,000. Allowing for the greater amounts of time required by the growing number of repetitions, at a certain point the students' individual *wazifa*s are reduced to a minimum. For the final night and for this one night only, everyone at the School joins the student group to repeat the name 21,000 times. Young holds that this particular practice 'was given by Ibn 'Arabi to his own students'.[45] Its inclusion towards the end of the course and in a collective context is significant, for in the view of the *tariqa*s the power of the supreme name makes it inappropriate as a solitary practice for the beginner.[46]

During the further course, *wazifa* practices build on those of the intensive course, in the context of the week-long retreat setting described earlier. This reflects a long-established association of the *wazifa* with retreat in sufi practice.[47] The day before the retreat is marked with a fast. After breaking this at sunset, students take to their designated rooms and perform the first *wazifa*. This consists of 10,000 repetitions of the *tahlil* (*la ilaha illa Allah*). Each successive *wazifa* involves a very large specified number of repetitions of a particular Divine Name, such that a single *wazifa* might take as much as eighteen hours. On the first day the *wazifa* is *Allah*, on the second *Hu*, the third *Hayy*, the fourth *Qayyum*, the fifth *Rahman*, and the final *wazifa* (making a total of seven in all) is *Rahim*.[48] This practice is one of remembrance rather than invocation, and it is particularly noteworthy that the selection and order of Divine Names prescribed points, as one associate puts it, to 'an implicit progression – a *mi'raj'* (ascension).[49]

Khalwa or spiritual retreat, and preparation for it

Khalwa or spiritual retreat was routinely practised in the traditional *tariqa*s, where it was combined with *dhikr*, vigils and fasts.[50] Its ultimate goal was to experience 'the *dhikr* of the divine Essence',[51] the culmination of an experience of spiritual ascent that calls to mind the Prophet's heavenly journey or *mi'raj*. The guidance of a (living) spiritual director was always considered vital.[52]

Historically, the further course furnished the only framework for the practice of *khalwa* in Beshara, where it has been tied to the *wazifa* practice we
have just discussed. At the time of writing, this looked set to change. A dedicated retreat cell has been a long time in the making at Chisholme. The idea
of such a space did not arise in Rauf's lifetime: the initiative to establish it
'came through' Young. During a six-month 'sabbatical' from the School in
1992 he had cut loose all ties and set off travelling. After some time, he finally
felt able to 'stop and just be'. The question of how this experience might be
made possible for others (indeed of 'how to go away without going away')
arose in him. He 'received' a picture of the retreat building in response, set
into the hillside some distance from the School. When he returned, he asked
an associate (an architect) to measure the hillside and draw up the basic plan.
It emerged that the dimensions of the structure Young had envisaged would
indeed fit there.

Construction of the cell has depended on the skills of associates and
students. Based on four arches with a central dome, it is without windows
apart from a single narrow skylight. Designed to provide self-contained
accommodation for one, it encompasses the necessary ablution and heating
facilities. From the regular rooms where retreats have been held during the
further course the sights and sounds of life have been evident. In contrast,
this dedicated space captures the potent symbolism of the retreat cell as
grave.[53]

Young anticipates that the cell retreat will last for about a week.[54] Supervision arrangements will probably involve daily checks. It is unlikely that
specific activities will be prescribed, for the Beshara *khalwa* is not conceived
in terms of an 'external practice' that is designed 'to take one somewhere'. In
Young's words, its purpose is rather 'to achieve a complete emptiness – an
emptiness of oneself – and the preparation of the place for the vision of the
Divine Beauty, which is the *jalwa*, the coming out of retreat'.[55] Rauf had clarified the nature and purpose of retreat in the context of the further course.
He had urged students to affirm the Oneness of Being (the fact that 'there
is nothing but Him') *within* the world, and to understand the real purpose
of retreat in light of this affirmation. 'As there is nothing other than Him,
who is retreat from?' he had asked them. A practice beyond practice, the
Beshara retreat is simply an opportunity to allow Reality to appear in the
practitioner as it is, their absolute existential 'emptiness' thus 'filled' by the
divine presence.[56]

Given the setting and the absence of specific practices, associates anticipate that cell retreats will be qualitatively different from their experiences
during the further course, and more intense. Young is concerned to ensure
that they will be fully prepared, and to that end has instituted a series of
preparatory weeks. He considers the completion of three such weeks spread
over a period of years indispensable. (This is over and above the completion
of both long courses.) He insists that he must feel complete confidence in an
associate before they enter retreat. Long-term associates have been attending

preparatory weeks in some numbers.[57] These events serve to clarify their aims and intentions, setting the scene for the emergence of questions concerning what it means to enter the cell, what is required for this, and whether an aspirant is ready. Such questions are addressed both in periods of silent solitary contemplation and in discussion. Aspirants may bring up for discussion issues they have encountered during contemplation or in dreams. Isolation is not prescribed as such (meals are taken in the dining hall, for example), but participants are required to remain in a state of contemplation as far as possible, and to suspend contact with the outside world. They must also remain in a state of ablution throughout. They take part in the nightly *dhikr* scheduled for the intensive course group, or perform a nightly *dhikr* as a group themselves if no courses are running. There is no prescribed *wazifa*.

As we have just noted, Rauf had clarified the purpose of retreat. He provided students with specific guidance for its practice, but associates point out that the courses as a whole (and study in particular) had furnished them with appropriate understanding, and they saw the retreat week simply as a practical application of this. Although practised collectively, the six-week 'Allah' *wazifa* during the second half of the intensive course also provided some flavour of the retreat week. Associates emphasise that they did not learn about retreat 'from books'. Rauf indeed told them 'not to concern themselves' with Ibn 'Arabi's treatise on the subject, which one of them had encountered in a 1981 translation.[58]

Meditation and the theophanic prayer

Rauf conceded that there are probably 'as many kinds of meditation as there are people', but those who 'lead' it often impose rules, to avoid 'possible inappropriate or even dangerous happenings'. It may have a designated 'content', such as a focal thought, but some kinds 'eliminate all interference from thought', to achieve 'the perfect void'. As we indicated earlier, he did not prescribe a particular meditation formula or technique himself, and often said that the less said about meditation, the better.[59] He posited concentration as its 'essential point', and 'the criterion by which it should be judged successful, or even deemed to be meditation at all'. Alongside this he considered the 'direction or dedication' of the meditation the only rule with which those who aspire to meditate must comply, for ultimately this is what would bring them to its intended goal.

For practice in Beshara, Rauf recommended a meditation that strives to eliminate all interference, while being properly directed at all times 'from His multifarious individuations to His state of Unity ... His state of being the One and the Unique'.[60] If dedicated to this proper aim and executed with sustained concentration, he assured associates, it will potentially leave the meditator

> in the presence of that supreme quiet centre ... the perfect void wherein resides the essential relationship of immanence and transcendence. Here is the cup, so to

speak, fully open ... to receive the All Creational Impulse, the perfect Theophany and merge it with the matching creaturial receptivity of the in-flowing Most Holy Effusion. This meditation does not aim at reciprocity but to alignment. It is a conscious concentrated dialogue of expression of the Essential Existence and, but not with, its image in active receptivity. At this moment ... there is no time. The meditator is beyond the confines of time ... He is ... aligned to ... his essence, which is His Essence. The only existent there present is the One ... Absolute Existent and His individuation as the perfected man ... Nothing really happens. The meditator has not moved or changed, the Essential Being has not reached down ... In that still point they have 're-met' without ever having separated from each other, they have re-cognised their unity.[61]

It is clear from this that Rauf considered meditation indispensable to what he termed 'real prayer', viz. the *theophanic* prayer. In relation to this concept of prayer he cited Corbin, who had posited it in light of his emphasis on the Theophanic Imagination as creation.[62] It is prayer predicated on conscious recognition of the creation as theophany, and the essential unity of the one who prays and the one prayed to. Thus it is prayer as a modality of the Oneness of Being. As creation is 'nothing other in its reality than the Theophany', Rauf explained, the ensuing prayer is 'no other than the Theophanic Prayer which is the Divine Service, since the Unity of Being is the condition of prayer. It means that the prayer is the expression of a mode of the Being, a means of existing and causing to exist.'[63] He conceded that the 'ritualistic prayer of religion' provides a potential means through which the theophanic prayer can be established. To enable this, however, it must pass beyond its 'ritualistic emphasis', for it is the 'emphasis of form' in the ritual that 'binds and bounds the spirit of prayer to ... performance of the ritual.' This emphasis does not allow the spirit of prayer 'to soar as a mirror-thought to the Theophanic Imagination', but causes it instead to 'remain within the limits set for it in its form.'[64] There is no such limitation in the case of meditation as Rauf projected it. Thus, if ritual threatens to imprison prayer in the relative world of forms, meditation can set a 'tone' for prayer that facilitates its transformation into theophanic mode:

> Where the 'tone' of the prayer is subject to atmosphere, a complete Divine Service seems hopelessly impossible within the realms of relative conditioning which is the atmosphere of our daily normal existence. Concentrated thought, reflection, takes us out beyond the limitations of exoteric relative existence and allows for a moment of intensive thought which can give us the necessary conditions of reaching into, or re-establishing for a while, the Theophanic Prayer, the Divine Service. In this case meditation becomes the necessary atmosphere in which real prayer finds its proper 'tone'.[65]

This 'tone', Rauf explained, was prepared by 'the harmony of the stillness': 'the intensive concentration without qualification or thought has actively prepared the receptivity of the harmonious place wherein alone can take place the Divine Self Revelation, the Theophanic Prayer, the Divine Service.'[66]

Rauf's emphasis on the importance of meditation can be understood in light of this. For example, he cited a hadith of the Prophet according to which 'one moment of meditation' is preferable to 'seventy thousand times of ritualistic prayer.'[67] It was significant, he suggested, that meditation is something 'all religions prescribe, though set aside for the select and not for the masses.'[68] Thus it holds 'a primordial position in the dual unicity of the concept of man and God.'[69] Ultimately, it prepares the way for the theophanic prayer,[70] which Rauf projected as

> the aim and purpose of the Creative Imagination ... this is the sole cause and purpose of there being man at all so he can fulfill [sic] that which is required of him, establishing of that condition of prayer which is the Unity of Being ... There can be no greater prayer and there can be no superior meditation. This is the apotheosis of all prayer and meditation.[71]

A short-lived meditation of ascent: the *tahajjud*

Tahajjud signifies 'to keep a vigil'. In Muslim usage, its usual meaning is to perform the nightly *salat*, or to recite the Qur'an by night. Recommended by the Prophet, it is a supererogatory act that has taken on special importance among sufis.[72] It was practised in Beshara up to 1978, when it was terminated possibly because it was thought to be too much for many students. A particularly powerful practice, it took the form of 'a very special and high level meditation,'[73] modelled on and conceived in imitation of the Prophet's ascension. Each student undertook it once during the second half of the intensive course. They would wake at an agreed time, carry out a full ablution and make for a designated empty room. After performing a *salat* of two *rak'as*, an early associate recollects, they would 'visualise themselves passing through the *hadarat* or Presences, in imitation of the Prophet during his *mi'raj*'. First was the *'alam al-mulk/al-shuhud*, then the *Malakut* and the *Jabarut*. They would finally stand in the Essence, 'in the sense of *al-haqiqa al-Muhammadiyya*.'[74] The student then 'descended' through these same stages, performed two further *rak'as*, and returned to sleep.[75]

As the aim of this meditation was 'Union and closeness', Rauf warned those undertaking it 'not to think of visiting the *Hadara*s or reaching them, but going through them to further levels', making their destination the Essence alone.[76] Thus,

> this meditation is also the *mi'raj* of the person – 'the time when he or she is admitted into the Divine Presence,' – the Presence far beyond the *Hadara*s where even angels may not enter.[77] This is the presence of ... 'Or Nearer' (*Aw Adna*),[78] where only man, made in His image and breathed into of His Spirit ... may enter.[79]

The Beshara *wird*: prayers of Ibn 'Arabi

In the context of sufi devotion and the *tariqa*s the *wird* (pl. *awrad*) designates a special prayer or litany. This is typically associated with a prominent spiritual guide, to whom it is attributed. There are set times for its observance in private, and it can also form part of collective practice in *dhikr* gatherings.[80]

In 1979 the MIAS published Ibn 'Arabi's *Awrad al-usbu'.* This is a collection of fourteen prayers, one for the morning and evening of each of the days of the week.[81] Some associates have taken daily recitation of these prayers as a regular practice, underlining their author's position as supreme spiritual guide in Beshara. The publication provides a facsimile of the Arabic text which Rauf had in his possession during the 1970s (itself a facsimile copy printed in Istanbul). Alongside this is a phonetic transliteration in English, for the benefit of non-Arabic speakers.[82]

The initiative that led to this publication began with an Israeli associate who could read Arabic. Rauf kept his copy of the *Awrad* on his bedside table, and had referred to its contents in some of his talks.[83] This associate had noticed the book and asked to look at it. He then enquired whether it could be made available in transliteration. Rauf agreed that he assume this task and designated a second student with scant knowledge of Arabic to help him. He suggested that they devote their 'work' periods to it (they were at the time engaged on the further course). Having no knowledge of an Arabic–English transliteration system, the associate who could read Arabic first transliterated the text in Hebrew, then from Hebrew into English. Each prayer was read from its English transliteration to Rauf, who corrected as necessary. It was then typed and diacriticals marked by hand.

The completed text was distributed to associates with the instruction to recite the appropriate prayer in private each morning and evening. Their lack of linguistic comprehension was not considered important, and it dampened neither their enthusiasm for the text nor their impressions of its beauty and power.[84] Reminiscing, one associate recently wrote:

> Most of us understood no more than the occasional word, but this did not matter. Here were the words which Ibn 'Arabi himself used, and gave as an example of how best to approach God through prayer, and if we did not know exactly what we were saying, it did not matter. The sounds and the intention to pray – this was what was important. And the rest, we left to God. After all, these are prayers of Union, therefore His prayers. He is the One who prays and the One prayed to. Even had we had a translation then, it may well have been no more understood than the Arabic, and been a distraction from the essential movement of the heart in prayer ... But occasionally Bulent would provide us with a morsel, a fragment from the banquet, translating a line or two which was apposite to the discussion at that moment. Like a mother feeding her children from her own plate, tasting a bit first, then cutting it small so it can be digested easily. In this way, one developed a taste for the richer food.[85]

The associate who assisted in transliterating the *Awrad* has recently contributed to their publication in English translation, drawing on Arabic skills developed since.[86] This publication has made it possible for associates to fully comprehend texts they have long recited. The co-translators underline the contrast between these *awrad* and those of other spiritual masters, like the well-known *Hizb al-bahr* of al-Shadhili. Unlike the latter, Ibn 'Arabi's *awrad*

> are neither devotional in any ordinary sense, nor do they appear to be intended as prayers for communal recitation. On the contrary, they seem to be more private and intimate affairs, where the requests imply a high degree of understanding and self-knowledge. In reading them, one is immediately struck by the precision and depth of their formulation, which is consecrated primarily to the clarification and celebration of Union ... They are founded upon the detailed exposition of spiritual Union, expressing the most intimate of converse with the Divine Beloved, and situating the one who prays as the true adorer. Here the reciter and the one recited to are understood to be two sides of the same reality. What is recited is that which 'arrives in the heart' ... and is 'received' by the adorer, on the one hand, and the request that reaches the Real ... and is responded to, on the other. For the one who reads them, these prayers are as much educational as devotional.[87]

A protective prayer and amulet

Associates also recite in private a protective prayer by Ibn 'Arabi. This is *Hizb al-wiqaya* ('Prayer of Protection'), also known as *al-Dawr al-a'la* ('The Most Elevated Cycle').[88] The associate who set in motion transliteration of the *Awrad* also transliterated this prayer, working on it the same year during the trip to Turkey. When it was ready it was distributed to other associates. Rauf gave no specific guidelines regarding its use, but he did emphasise its protective power. In 1981 the MIAS published the transliteration alongside a facsimile of Rauf's copy of the Arabic text.[89] Leather bound and embellished with gold, the latter had been copied in Istanbul for the personal use of his grandmother Fatma Hanim by the 'Head Calligrapher', apparently in 1922–23.

The MIAS website underlines the prayer's protective powers and indicates how it can be used: 'this prayer ... protects its recipient. In microfiche form, it is frequently carried as an amulet or displayed in a significant place.' Associates wear a microfiche of it in a silver encasement on a chain around the neck (together with the symbol *Hu*).[90] They position a microfilm copy above the inside of doors at home and at work, and often display framed copies of its first page in Arabic. Some read it regularly, while others resort to it in times of particular difficulty, or to ward off a specific perceived evil.

Beshara practices as affirmation of Reality

The practices we have just described serve ultimately as an affirmation of Reality. This is especially clear in the case of *dhikr* and the *wazifa*. As an associate explains in relation to the *wazifa*: 'By repeating *ya 'Alim* (Oh All-Knowledgeable One), for example, one affirms one's ignorance and, simultaneously, one's capacity as a place for the manifestation of knowledge. And one asks for its manifestation through realisation.' Created in God's image, man is in potential the place of manifestation of the Divine Names and Attributes in their totality. In true servanthood, he reflects these as they are, and actualises in perfect equilibrium the divine character traits or qualities latent in his own soul. As Rauf explained to students, 'You have to arrive at a Perfection of imaging Him to be able to acquire all the ninety-nine qualities and attributes in yourself.'[91] Through the spiritual practices of the Beshara 'way', the individual participates in an affirmation of the Real and proceeds towards such an imaging.

Islamic–sufi forms and interior realities

The more one studies Ibn 'Arabi, the more one deals with meanings rather than form.

Beshara associate

Revealed Law is identical to essential reality ... the Law *is* essential reality.

Ibn 'Arabi[92]

As discussed earlier, Rauf's reading of Ibn 'Arabi's exposition of the Oneness of Being had downplayed its Islamic specificity. At the same time, however, he implicitly imported the Islamic–sufi frame of reference of this exposition, by retaining Ibn 'Arabi's terminology. An associate explains that 'a technical language is indispensable if one is to be able to speak of matters of the spirit and devotion. Beshara has adopted specifically the vocabulary of Islamic spirituality as expressed in Ibn 'Arabi's writings.'[93] Mirroring this, the broad outline of the spiritual way in Beshara and its constitutive practices are drawn from Ibn 'Arabi's teaching on the path. This implicit Islamic–sufi frame of reference was reinforced by Rauf's own cultural–spiritual heritage, on which he drew in explicating the way.

Couched in the conceptual vocabulary of sufism and pursued through adapted Islamic–sufi practices, this spiritual way has served as a powerful conduit for Islamic cultural norms and features of Islamic–sufi identity.[94] Rauf's efforts to ensure that the movement would not be characterised in such terms and the inevitable 'dilution' of this cultural element since his death notwithstanding, outsider impressions of Beshara as an Islamic–sufi movement of (practising) Muslims remain strong. This reflects a dialectic within the movement's culture and identity that operates on two fronts simultaneously. First is the embrace of Islamic–sufi forms, set against a bid to transcend *all* particularistic (and thus inherently 'limited') forms. This issue forms the subject of recent debates among associates, and we will return to it later. Second is the tension between those exterior forms adopted in the movement, and their interior signification. External assumptions concerning the significance of these exterior forms for Beshara thus do not necessarily coincide with the Beshara understanding concerning this.

Before exploring this second area, we can sketch a few examples of forms and practices used in Beshara that are clearly part of Muslim culture in its broader expressions, beyond the more focused sphere of the sufi tradition. Most obvious superficially is associates' use of 'Islamic' names.[95] Some early associates had been designated names by Feild or Vilayat Khan. Rauf later changed some of these. Taking note of these names (and motivated by what they were learning during courses), later students were eager to discover their own names (and those of their children). They turned to Rauf, who would assign names by consulting the Qur'an. Sometimes, he felt that more than one name was apt, and would consult in order to confirm a particular one. As an associate explains, these names capture 'the Divine Attribute that is most strongly reflected in the person', in their capacity as a locus of Divine Self-disclosure. They are drawn from the ninety-nine Beautiful Names of God, or reflect a divine quality/self-descriptive beyond these.[96] In Beshara these Names are not prefixed with *'abd* (servant [of]), as they are in Muslim usage. Towards the end of his life, Rauf explained to students that they 'would have to ask Him directly in prayer' for their names. Today names are 'shown' to students in diverse ways. This may be in a dream, or through someone 'accidentally' addressing them by a particular name. Young confirms such indications by consulting the Qur'an.

Consultation (*istikhara*) as practised in Beshara is of course also drawn from Muslim usage, where in essence it consists in entrusting God with the choice between two or more possible options.[97] Associates ask Young to consult the Qur'an on their behalf concerning important decisions: he applies a specific technique acquired from Rauf. The complete fast from sunrise to sunset (obligatory on the opening day of courses/reading weeks) is also modelled on Muslim practice, and some associates apply it at other times too. Application of the protective power of *surat* al-Inshirah (Qur'an 94) by passing the palms over the head and body (performed during the collective *dhikr*, for example) can also be mentioned, as can the practice of ablution we discussed earlier, and that of visiting saints' tombs, which we will consider shortly. Finally, in Young's words, in Beshara 'the importance of beginning any action "in the Name of God" or with the *Fatiha* is stressed': recitation of such formulae and texts (including the *salawat*) thus helps the student to 'focus intention in action'.

Given the prominence of such cultural markers (especially their names and use of characteristic motifs and expressions of Muslim devotion), it is hardly surprising that Muslims who first encounter associates often assume they are engaging with fellow-Muslims, especially as such encounters tend to take place in Muslim settings. This calls forth inevitable questions concerning the identity of such interesting Westerners.

Are you a Muslim?

Associates often met with this direct question during the trip to Turkey, and in sufi circles in the UK. Rauf advised them how best to respond. He suggested they say *al-hamdu li-llah* (thanks be to God), a traditional Muslim

formula of affirmation. This response was respectful of the questioner's feelings. For Rauf, it was also far from disingenuous, notwithstanding the movement's perception of the era and its view of the religions. He hinted at the
thinking that informed it in the following comment:

> anyone who has read the Qur'an knows that the word Moslem has a broader appli-
> cation than purely to the Mohammedans. Pharoah's wife ... who adopted Moses
> and brought him up as an Egyptian prince is referred to in the Qur'an as a Moslem;
> so are equally referred to as Moslems the twelve Apostles of Jesus.[98]

He also implicitly pointed to a key distinction in use of the term 'muslim',
between an original signification, as 'one who surrenders himself to God'
(here with a small m; muslim), and its historical application to membership
in the community that follows the Prophet Muhammad (in this case with
a capital m; Muslim).[99] As Young explains, 'Being muslim does not mean
following the letter of the sharia. The Qur'an is clear on this, describing
Abraham as a muslim. Being muslim is to do with submission to the Real.'[100]

Young highlights in addition the difficulty in judging who is a 'muslim'. To
illustrate this, he relates an account of a gathering in the company of Ahmet
Kayhan (d.2000),[101] during a visit to Turkey. One of those present had asked
him: 'How many Muslims are there in England?' Before he could reply, one
of Kayhan's close associates had interjected with his own counter-question:
'How many Muslims are there in Turkey?' Young reflects thus: 'We do not
know. Those who think they are in the "Muhammadi image" would have to
ask the Prophet Muhammad whether in fact they are.'[102]

Associates of non-Muslim provenance do not consider themselves bound
by the five pillars of Islamic faith or the sharia. Young's position on this matter
is illuminating. If it is 'shown to be necessary' to an individual to follow the
sharia, he argues, then they must do it. What he takes issue with is people
maintaining that it is necessary for *him* to observe it.[103] Personally, he believes
it has been 'shown to be necessary' for him *not* to the follow the sharia or
to declare himself a Muslim, for this would 'limit' Beshara and compromise
its task as determined by the quality of the era.[104] Beshara must thus itself
reflect the universality and all-inclusiveness that mark out the new age. Like
a university, Young suggests, the School must be open to 'all-comers', offering
an education without imposing a particular identity. Sharia observance or
otherwise is simply irrelevant: it is 'not an issue in terms of Beshara being
a School'. Within the School, matters that might appear rooted in application of sharia rules must be otherwise understood. Prominent examples
are abstention from pork, and the exclusion of menstruating women from
specific (aspects of) practices (as in the collective *dhikr* and the one-week
retreat during the further course). Such matters perhaps reflect some perennial or universal notion of ritual cleanliness. At the same time, the fact that
they are upheld at all in Beshara may be seen as evidence of an unresolved
tension between the cultural provenance of its teaching, and its self-projection in detachment from this.

A long-standing associate makes crystal clear Beshara's non-alignment to Islam as an exoteric religion: 'We are not Muslims by any convention, and we do not follow that model.'[105] Another makes the same point by underlining the basis of the importance of the *Fusus* in Beshara in terms of the fact that this text was singled out for condemnation by Ibn Taymiyya:

> Ibn Taymiyya said 'How can they say Ibn 'Arabi is "alright"? They have not read the *Fusus!*' He was right: there is barely any element of sharia in the *Fusus*, or it is only hinted at there. The text represents a de-formalisation of Ibn 'Arabi's teaching, in the sense of distancing it from its formal Islamic context. For this reason, it constitutes a distillation of his teaching for us in Beshara. We do not study everything of Ibn 'Arabi in Beshara, just the *Fusus*, and there is a big difference between that and the rest of his work. This is not to say that the *Fusus* evinces any 'de-Islamisation', for *islam* means submission, *taslim*, and this is the underlying focus of the text.

Several associates define the Beshara approach in contrast with that of the sufi Guénonians.[106] They suggest that these two impulses in the transmission of Ibn 'Arabi's legacy diverge on the question of embracing Islam, issuing in significantly different results. As one associate puts it:

> Beshara is a school of esoteric education. It is not a matter of conversion [to Islam] à la René Guénon. What happened with Guénon and his followers is that people became Muslim, and so this impulse *circumscribed* Ibn 'Arabi's legacy.[107]

Concerning the Prophet Muhammad

The predominant imagining of the Prophet Muhammad in Beshara is one characteristic of sufi thought in general, and largely attributable in its systematised form in particular to Ibn 'Arabi. Mystical veneration of the Prophet grew rapidly after his death. This built on certain hadith,[108] which were taken to signify that he was the meaning and end of creation.[109] Ibn 'Arabi elaborated into a coherent theory this belief in the pre-existent essence of the Prophet (*al-haqiqa al-Muhammadiyya*: the Muhammadan Reality or the 'archetypal Muhammad'), and his spiritual pre-eminence.[110] The Beshara understanding of the Prophet derives from the resulting doctrine of his primordial rank, and his central place in cosmogenesis and the unfolding of the universe.

Yet Muhammad was also a historical prophet, who conveyed a distinctive revealed law (*shar'*). He set a particular example of conduct encapsulated in the Sunna, which became established in part as a source for the elaboration of the law of the community. As Addas puts it, Ibn 'Arabi made it explicit that 'Since Muhammad is the archetype of sainthood, it is in strict conformity to his *sunna*, and by taking nourishment from his example, that the aspirant manages to restore his original nature of *imago Dei*.'[111] Thus, according to Ibn 'Arabi, 'it is in conforming to the Prophet's *sunna* and to the Law that was revealed to him that man re-integrates in himself the divine characteristics that lie dormant deep within him.'[112]

We must evaluate associates' perceptions of the historical Muhammad and their attitudes towards the Sunna and sharia in light of this centrality of the *imitatio Muhammadi* to Ibn 'Arabi's projection of the mystical path, for this projection is claimed by Beshara as its model. Associates evince a basic familiarity with the main features of the Prophet's life and character, as they have encountered aspects of these in relation to the texts they have studied. Their appreciation, indeed veneration, of him is clear.[113] However, prescribed emulation of the conduct of this infallible model (itself also *the* mystical exemplar), which is of the utmost importance to Muslim devotion,[114] does not arise as such in Beshara. The Beshara focus is thus on the interior of Muhammad (Muhammad as the 'Reality of Man', the *haqiqa Muhammadiyya*), rather than the exterior forms of Sunna and sharia associated with the historical Muhammad.[115]

The practice of invoking God's blessings and peace upon the Prophet (known as the *tasliya, al-salat 'ala Muhammad* or simply the *salawat*), which is fundamental to Muslim devotion,[116] is prominent in Beshara education and training. Students are encouraged to 'sing' it while performing ablution, and more generally when beginning any action. We can illuminate the movement's stance concerning the Prophet (and any consciousness of tension in this) by examining associates' projections of this practice. One associate explains that, by calling down God's blessings and peace upon Muhammad, one is in fact 'calling down blessings and peace upon the Reality of Man'. Through recitation of the *salawat*, he elaborates, one thus 'seeks help and intercession from the Source of all Help, the *mamadd al-himam*', which is essentially the 'archetypal Muhammad'.[117] There is a sense that, if the focus on Muhammad as the Reality of Man is properly sustained, acts of emulation will flow naturally. Significantly, in this case such acts are *not* carried out, as one associate puts it, 'because the Prophet instituted them'. Associates additionally suggest that 'conformity to the Reality of Man itself implies conformity to the revealed law (*shar'*) of Muhammad'. One situates the movement's understanding of the Prophet, and of veneration of him, by rehearsing now familiar themes in the Beshara perspective:

> Bulent would stress the Reality of Muhammad, insisting that he is not to be limited to the man who walked on earth and brought the law. The Muhammadan Reality is the important thing, and it is limitless. Its foremost expression is the Prophet Muhammad. However, we were not asked to become Muslims, to perform the *salat* and the hajj. Bulent used to be very emphatic, saying 'You must see that things are different now.' Beshara is the expression of how things are *now*. In the past, we may have had to become Muslim, follow the sharia, and so on, but Bulent would explain that Beshara cuts through all of that. He would say 'Things are different now, and it is not necessary to become a Muslim to understand the height of these matters, of the Muhammadan Reality.' He was not acting under his own steam in this: his approach was part of how the order is for the times we are in. This is because people are quite different today, reflecting the nature of the times. I remember meeting with shaykh Muzaffer Özak when we attended

a Halveti *dhikr* in Turkey. The shaykh had been surprised when he was told that we were studying Ibn 'Arabi, and exclaimed 'You have gone to the top of the tree!' This is an era when Ibn 'Arabi and that height has been made accessible. There are people who can understand it, and at that level. This coincides with the time that it is made available for them: it is one without distinction. Muhammad brought the *Fusus* and gave it to Ibn 'Arabi. It is about the interior, about the Reality of Muhammad. Thus you come to the matter from its inside – the enormity of what Muhammad represents, which is vast and awe inspiring. Therefore when you look at his physical appearance in history, it is even *more* awesome to you. To really know and love something, you do not stop at its exterior or appearance, but learn its reality. This is what you are really attracted to, but this takes time. You see what it constitutes, and so you venerate based on that understanding, and not because you are told to do so, based on the 'outside'. Veneration of Muhammad flows naturally as the outcome of an understanding of his magnitude and all-inclusiveness: it is not through fear or duty, for example. In Beshara, the *salawat* is a fruit of this process. The understanding of the whole matter develops naturally through study. The last chapter of the *Fusus* is the chapter on Muhammad, and this is studied at the end of the course. If it has been working in the student, they will see how everything has built up towards it.

If an associate (of non-Muslim provenance) feels so inclined, they are free to explore the Sunna. The majority do not appear to be so inclined (or perhaps their focus is trained on the less visible sphere of the 'noble virtues' exemplified by the Prophet, rather than on emulating him in specific acts). When the fundamental position occupied in Ibn 'Arabi's doctrine by practice of the Sunna is put to them, associates respond by pointing out that he had been 'brought up following this'. The implication here is that practice of the Sunna must ultimately be located among those aspects of Ibn 'Arabi's teaching that reflect his own contextual realm of exterior forms. These are not relevant to Beshara. By the same logic, the Sunna itself represents an exterior form, and thus one that is culturally bound and temporally limited.

One associate questions whether the content of the sharia as embodied in Muslim settings today would in fact be sanctioned by the Prophet, and suggests that it is not necessarily a faithful reflection of the guidance the Prophet had intended. To elaborate, he points out that, in his Second Coming, Jesus will 'remove a lot of the rules which grew up around what the Prophet intended'. Referring here to Bosnevi's commentary on the chapter on Jesus in the *Fusus*,[118] he infers that the Prophet cannot have instituted all that has been understood as sharia by the Muslim community across its history. To follow this, then, is not necessarily to follow Muhammad.

The cult of saints

The Muslim cult of saints (*wali*, pl. *awliya'*, the 'friends of God') is most visibly expressed through the practice of visiting their tombs (*ziyara*), in search of their blessing (*baraka*).[119] This cult informs a striking dimension of the movement's spiritual culture. Students encounter Ibn 'Arabi's concept of sainthood and the associated teachings at an early stage of the intensive course,[120] and he himself is projected to them throughout as saint par excellence. Three months into the course this encounter is brought into the physical realm, when students visit the tombs of saints during the trip to Turkey. Rauf had stressed to associates his own connections in the imaginal realm, bringing home the reality of saintly intervention in earthly life; he would also credit certain saints with specific blessings. Some associates would later experience such interventions themselves. Many have made private pilgrimages to saints' tombs, especially that of Ibn 'Arabi, and photographs of these tombs embellish their homes. An associate may feel a special bond to one saint or another, but none doubt the saints' presence and power, their invisible hierarchy and their cosmic mediating role.

How did Rauf project sainthood and the importance of the saints for those on the spiritual way? How did he project the practice of *ziyara* and what recommendations did he make concerning it? Which saints form the focus of the cult of saints in Beshara, and how did Rauf describe them? How is the particular association with certain of them understood, and how has it found expression?

The saints and their *himma* or spiritual 'power'

In 'A Trip to Turkey', Rauf described the saints' capacity for helping those who seek God:

> because they themselves are in the station of witnessing the Beauty of Oneness through the witnessing of the plurality of the images of this world and the other world, [they] serve the servants of God by order of the *Haqq*. They guide them and bring them to safety. Their service to those who want to approach God is to lift off the veils which prevent the witnessing, to ease the way for them to approach the station of Oneness.[121]

He explained that the saints' spiritual 'power' or 'will' (*himma*) comes from

> the original *Mamadd al-Himma* (The Place of Extension of all *Himmah*) through the agency and channel of the Archetypal Perfect Man, which is the Reality of Realities, or the Reality of Mohammed.[122]

The saints bring their *himma* to bear upon servants of God who want to approach Him by cleaning their hearts, 'removing the impediments on their way and polishing them and protecting them from all that may cause [their] distancing ... from God.'[123]

Rauf urged associates to think about the saints (and to refer to them) in an appropriate manner. As we noted earlier, he warned against excluding the *himma* of some of the saints by differentiating between them.[124] He insisted on conduct in accordance with the dictates of *adab* (tact) in all matters relating to them.[125] To underline the inscrutability of their knowledge, he pointed out that 'God alone knows what they know and in what way they know it, and that is why we say "God sanctified [sic] their secret".'[126]

The focus of the cult

In addition to Ibn 'Arabi and Rumi, the two saintly giants of 'Turkish' sufism and the most powerful influences on Ottoman religion, Rauf emphasised certain others. We can consider the figures he introduced in 'A Trip to Turkey' in three clusters. First are three saints of the Seljuk era, buried in or near Konya. Alongside Rumi, Rauf introduced students to Rumi's inspiration Shams-i-Tabriz, to his cook Ateşbaz Veli,[127] and to Qunawi, whom he projected in this context, as we have noted, as Rumi's teacher.[128]

He also introduced three saints from the Ottoman period, each the founder of a *tariqa*. First is Haci Bektaş Veli (d.c.1337),[129] founder of the Bektashi order.[130] Second is Haci Bayram Veli (d.1429–30),[131] who founded the Bayramiyye.[132] Third is Shaban Veli (d.1568–69), founder of the Shabaniyye (to which Rauf's grandfather had been affiliated).[133] Both the Shabaniyye and the Bayramiyye emerged within the milieu of the Halvetiyye.[134] This is the third of the major orders originating in Turkey (alongside the Mevleviyye and the Celvetiyye).[135]

The final cluster of saints on whom Rauf focused comprises three later saints of the Ottoman Celveti *tariqa*.[136] These are Üftade (d.1580),[137] Hüdayi (d.1628)[138] and Bursevi (d.1728).[139] Üftade was its 'founder' (the originator of its distinctive teachings and practice), Hüdayi his most important disciple, and Bursevi one of the *tariqa*'s most illustrious later masters.

Ziyara: the practice of visiting the tombs of saints

Rauf had first conceived of the trip to Turkey in terms of 'a very special hagiological trip', on which he might take a small group of close associates.[140] It materialised as a compulsory element of the intensive course, encompassing larger numbers. Organised visits to the tombs of saints form the heart of this trip. The itinerary encompasses the tombs of the first cluster of saints in and around Konya,[141] of Haci Bayram Veli in Ankara, of Üftade and Bursevi in Bursa, and of Hüdayi in Istanbul.[142]

How did Rauf project the purpose of these visits? He conceded that it is not necessary to go to the tombs of saints 'to plead for their *Himmah*', for one can plead for this everywhere. However,

> to make the effort of fully abluting, going especially to visit them at their last worldly abode ... is a sign of determination ... delicacy and ... reverence, so as to put oneself at the mercy and compassion of the 'Friends' of God so that through your plea – which possibly they have provoked – they are moved to respond with clemency and compassion ... and act in one's favour and help to cleanse one and to bring one closer to God.[143]

On this basis, he underlined the importance of such visits.[144] He reminded students that they would be visiting the living presence of a saint and not the tomb of a dead person, for there is no death for the person who has realised Union.[145] Advising them on the proper manner of these visits, he urged them to go in to them

> with reverence, clean, with a pure and trusting heart and ask them for their help through their *Himmah*, and then repeat, for and dedicated to them, the *Fatiha* ... And then the *Ikhlass* [sic], repeat three times.[146]

He added a specific recommendation concerning the visits in Konya. He insisted on a particular order, based on a request reportedly made by Rumi himself, who said that 'no one should come to his tomb without first visiting ... Konevi then Shams ... and lastly himself'.[147]

Rauf first took students to visit the tombs of the three Celveti saints in Bursa and Istanbul in December 1978, as part of the first further course. This trip was under his personal direction and was conducted separately from the one organised for intensive course students. It was after they returned to Chisholme from this trip that he had the significant dream of Üftade, Hüdayi and their Celveti followers we described earlier, probably in January 1979. Since then visits to these three saints have become an integral part of the trip to Turkey.[148]

The special association of Beshara with the Celveti saints

The significance of this sequence of events is projected internally in terms of an emerging clarification of Beshara's orientation in the realm of the saints. An associate suggests it had initially been clear that Beshara's 'drinking-place' was located in Anatolia. This had been reflected in the early visits to saints there. Rauf was then drawn to visit the Celveti saints. Following this, Üftade affirmed his relationship (and that of his Celveti followers) with Beshara, via his encounter with Rauf in the imaginal realm. Once the particular drinking-place of Beshara had thus been identified, Üsküdar (Istanbul) and Bursa became prominent visiting destinations, while Anatolia remained important as locus of six important saints (identified above).[149]

Contrary to the impression this account might create, the notion of a drinking-place is not spatial in reference. Rather, it signifies here the 'ways or manners of imbibing [from the Divine Source]' of different saints, their 'inclination' or 'taste', denoted by the term *mashrab*, which in sufi usage can take on this particular sense.[150] To have the *mashrab* of a particular saint (or to be in their *mashrab*) means to follow their way, to reflect their characteristic taste or temperamental inclination, their own distinctive experience of realisation or manner of education. Rauf had repeated that the Celvetis were closest in manner to the teachings of Ibn 'Arabi. As one associate puts it, they were in his *mashrab*,[151] and as Rauf explained following his dream, Beshara is in *their mashrab*.

As we noted earlier, Rauf claimed descent through his mother from one of the daughters of the Celveti saint Hüdayi. He was to enjoy especially close encounters in the imaginal realm with Hüdayi's master, Üftade. While he may have spoken of these saints to associates before this, most recall that he first mentioned them during the first further course, in one-to-one conversation. Some date this first mention to the preceding summer, spent in Turkey.[152] Published references to the Celvetiyye first appeared in Beshara materials in the mid-1980s, associated with the appearance of the *White Fusus*.[153] The origins and distinctive orientation of the *tariqa* were explained there by way of introduction to Bursevi (to whom the work was initially attributed) as a Celveti saint:

> the Jelvetis emerged in the 16th Century from the Helveti Order through the great Shaykh Mahmud Muhyiddin Uftade instructing his principal disciple ... Hudayi ... in the manner which was to become that of the Jelveti Order, and Hudayi became the first Shaykh of that Order. Ibn 'Arabi did not found a *tariqa* as such, but the Jelveti manner reflected most closely his teaching. The Helvetis are disposed towards retreat (*khalwah*) and seclusion with the Beloved through retirement from this world, but the taste of the Jelveti is at the same time for the return to this world after Union, the coming out of that seclusion adorned with Divine characteristics which is regarded as ... an added gift (the bridal present – *jilwah*),[154] the superlative perfection of expression, and this manner very clearly signifies that which is central to 'Arabi's [sic] teaching and the Mohammedian Way.[155]

In 'A Trip to Turkey', Rauf added:

> [Uftade] was the pupil of the famous Halveti Sheikh, Haji Bayram Weli of Ankara. Although a Halveti, Uftade induced through his teachings the founding of the Jelveti order by his favourite pupil the Hudai ... Helvet means 'privacy', denoting a gnostic's seclusion with the absolute Uniqueness. The Jelveti order prefers the return to expression and immanence after seclusion, without leaving the seclusion, and full participation in all the plurality of the Uniqueness, which is an added gift.[156]

Although it undoubtedly gave rise to prominent figures in sufi thought, there is still relatively little Western (and indeed Turkish) scholarship on the Celveti order, and its main manuscripts remain largely unpublished.[157] Since the 1990s a number of Turkish studies on Üftade, Hüdayi and Bursevi have appeared, drawing on these manuscripts.[158] What then were Rauf's sources? In addition to oral tradition, his knowledge possibly derived from *The Darvishes*, a copy of which had been placed on loan to the MIAS Library by a key associate in 1978.[159] He probably also drew on the few published sources then available in Turkish. Thus, 'A Trip to Turkey' acknowledges its accounts of the Celveti saints as 'an extract from' a 1982 quasi-scholarly Turkish travel book, which provides biographies of spiritual figures associated with particular sites.[160]

Did Rauf's projection of the Celvetiyye and its saints stand the test of recent scholarship? Ballanfat's recent French translation of Üftade's *Divan* (published in English by Anqa Publishing) provides a comprehensive over-view of the life and teachings of this founder of the Celvetiyye and its distinc-tive orientation.[161] We can summarise their main features here.

Üftade and the Celveti way

Ballanfat describes Üftade, who was born in 1490 in Bursa, as one of the greatest figures of Ottoman Sufism. This is mainly for his founding of the Celvetiyye.[162] Üftade began his spiritual life aged ten under the guidance of a Bayrami master,[163] Hizir Dede (d.1507),[164] and served him until his death eight years later. Hizir would evaluate his disciple's spiritual progress by exam-ining his dreams, and advised him accordingly. He instructed him to train in the traditional disciplines. As Üftade studied, all the exoteric sciences were unveiled to him.[165] He did not reach realisation by Hizir's death, and continued on his journey without a living master.[166] Some years later he experienced a spiritual opening, on the strength of which he is described as an Uwaysi. While the influence of his earthly master on his own spiritual teaching is clear, Üftade himself reports that he had been initiated and guided by three hidden masters. These were Ibn 'Arabi, Rumi and Emir Sultan.[167]

Üftade set out the stages and goal of the spiritual journey as he conceived of this. He designated his path 'celveti', and underlined its specificity compared to the other ways in Bursa,[168] particularly the Halvetiyye.[169] The contrasting terms halvet and celvet refer to different types of spiritual practice, each origi-nating in the Prophet's experience. First, he was isolated in retreat (halvet), in the cave at Hira. Later, he directed men by mixing with them, and lit the way for them through his own enlightenment (celvet). While halvet corresponds to annihilation, celvet corresponds to the existence beyond annihilation that is its consummation. The halveti way is hence a pre-condition for the celveti one. In the summation of the halveti way the mystic no longer sees himself. In the celveti way, he is reinstalled and maintained in the contemplation of Divine Beauty, and consequently is able to provide spiritual direction there-after.[170] The accomplishment of the spiritual quest hence ends not in suppres-sion of the mystic's being, but in its transfiguration into 'pure aspiration', for he is effectively recomposed by divine order and participates in the Divine Existence.[171] The summit of spiritual experience is the contemplation of the Divine Beauty in total annihilation, but the station of completion is reached only with the return to creation thereafter, for the purpose of spiritual direc-tion.

Üftade considered the Prophet's mi'raj the model for his way.[172] Just as the Prophet had reached the highest station and then returned to direct men, the mystic on the celveti way re-descends towards the creatures following spir-itual ascension. Üftade upheld the absolute faithfulness of the celveti way to the Prophet's teachings when compared with the methods of other tariqas, and consciously rooted his teaching in the Prophet's example.[173] For him, the particularity of his way lay precisely in the fact that it was the way of the Prophet and his companions (and of the prophets in general).[174]

His concept of the spiritual journey was developed through Üftade's doctrine of the four stages that must be traversed to arrive at realisation.[175] The law, the way, (mystical) knowledge and Reality correspond in turn to the four subtle centres of man's interior.[176] These are his corporeal nature (*tabi'a*), soul (*nafs*), spirit (*ruh*) and secret consciousness (*sirr*). The mystic must build up each subtle centre by that which corresponds to it, at the same time moving beyond each step on this interior ladder through the qualities and impetus released by its purification. Through his traversing of the stages, his subtle centres are put in order by divine intervention, a supreme gift that makes possible union in total annihilation. In the eyes of God he is maintained as other and granted a separate existence, raised up by the theophany of the Divine Essence. For Üftade, spiritual realisation thus consists in elevation to another level of existence. It is a forgetting of the self by the self, through effacement of the *sirr*. Otherwise put, it is a link tying the Essence to the witness, a seeing of none other than God.[177] The return to creation makes possible real knowledge of Unity, in the vision of its multiplicity there.[178]

Üftade taught that purification of the subtle centres is achieved through the affirmation of Unity, which he emphasised as the celveti way. It consists of 'being free of all that is not God, by being His servant.'[179] The invocation of the formula of Unity undoubtedly has incomparable power, but Üftade gave it pride of place also because it is the Prophet's formula.[180] His conceptualisation of spirituality gave a dominant place to the law (sharia), which encompasses the three other stages of the journey.[181] The two principal elements in this are thus the most exterior (the law), and the most interior (Reality). While the way and knowledge unite them, the law is the essential condition for reaching the journey's goal. For Üftade, observance of the law is a permanent requisite of sainthood that can never be abandoned.[182] In fact, he taught that the law can be completely fulfilled only by the mystic who has reached total annihilation.[183] For him, observance of the law is intimately connected to the role of reason in the acquisition of sainthood. He thus maintained that the prophets' conduct rested on the security of reason,[184] while the persistence of reason in the station of perfection is what makes spiritual direction possible.[185]

To reach the level required for spiritual direction, the celveti master must accomplish the double journey, first to the station of total annihilation, then the re-descent from there through existence beyond annihilation.[186] This master upholds the law and recommends that his disciples follow it not by way of imitation, but through their interior knowledge.[187] He guides them through daily interpretation of their dreams, having received the ability to do this for the purposes of spiritual direction 'through the light of God', on the attainment of spiritual realisation.[188]

Üftade, the Celvetis and Ibn 'Arabi

Üftade referred regularly to Ibn 'Arabi. He considered among the most important lessons of the latter's teaching conformity to the law, and the view that everything ultimately lies in its fulfilment.[189] Ballanfat sees the influence of Ibn ʿArabi's characterisation of the Melamis as mystics of the highest rank in Üftade's definition of the ideal celveti as a man who has attained total annihilation, whose state is covered by a veil, and who does not cut himself off from others.[190] Üftade held that, after the Prophet's companions, those who have reached Ibn ʿArabi's rank have been only few.[191] He criticised those who did not grant the saint veneration worthy of this rank, and argued that those who cannot perceive his true status fall into heresy.[192] He understood the doctrine of *wahdat al-wujud* as developed by Ibn ʿArabi's successors from the perspective of the mystical quest, in terms of annihilation and union with God,[193] and thereby connected his understanding of the mystical journey to Ibn ʿArabi's teaching. Üftade clearly considered himself an heir of Ibn ʿArabi,[194] but the saint has also been a significant direct source of influence on later Celveti masters: Bursevi spoke of his own initiatic contact with him, for example.[195] Ballanfat indeed considers the inheritance of a *direct* teaching by Ibn ʿArabi through *kashf* ('unveiling') as a major characteristic of the order.[196]

Üftade and Rumi

Ibn ʿArabi's influence on Üftade notwithstanding, Ballanfat points out that Bistami and Rumi are the mystics most mentioned in his discourse.[197] Of these two, Üftade identified most strongly with Rumi, with whom he had a direct spiritual connection. The *Mathnavi* indeed served as a life-long guide and source of inspiration for him; it is the most frequently mentioned work in his discourse, and he drew many of his teachings from it.[198] Rumi himself told him to use it in his sermons, and he would always quote and comment on several verses from it in opening and closing these. The saint would appear to him in a vision before sermons, and whenever he intended to give advice. Üftade had also learned Persian through Rumi's direct inspiration.[199] Other Celveti masters also enjoyed a privileged relationship with Rumi, and Ballanfat notes the continuing importance of the *Mathnavi* as a reference for them.[200]

Beshara and the Celvetiyye

Ballanfat's work has provided associates with an accessible, reliable source on the Celvetiyye. Their knowledge of the order and its teachings had previously been limited to Rauf's few contributions.[201] They were familiar, for example, with the story of a late-rising Hüdayi who had no time to make a fire, but heated water for his master Üftade to perform the ablution before the dawn prayer by holding the water container against his heart, and invoking God.[202] They were aware of a significant contrast between the names Halveti and Celveti, symbolised by the position of the diacritical that distinguishes the first letter of the two words from each other.[203] Based on this, they have tended to think of the two orders in terms of a strict dichotomy between 'seclusion from the world' and 'return to the world'. In fact retreat was practised in both orders, while the most significance difference between them lay rather in the overall conception of the spiritual journey and its ultimate goal, and the methods employed.[204] Finally, associates have long had a sense of the closeness of the Celvetiyye, out of all the *tariqa*s, to the teaching of Ibn 'Arabi.

Based on his own special connection with Celveti saints and his conviction that 'the people of Beshara' were in their *mashrab* specifically, Rauf had emphasised an affinity between their way and Beshara. Our brief overview above does suggest certain objective affinities, which we can enumerate here. First is the pivotal place of the affirmation of Unity. Second is the centrality of both Ibn 'Arabi and Rumi.[205] Third is the emphasis on 'direct' training, the acquisition of knowledge through inspiration (*kashf*), and the Uwaysi manner of sufi initiation.

An Uwaysi culture?

For the counter culture, all power and authority is conditional, contractual, on trial: it must constantly explain and justify itself.

Frank Musgrove, p. 150

Never forget – there is only one Teacher!
Bulent Rauf, cited in Reshad Feild, *The Last Barrier*, p. 164

Affiliate yourself to God. None of those you have met have authority over you.
Ibn 'Arabi's account of advice given him by the 'Imam of the Left'[206]

The Oneness of Being as cultural essence

The Islamic–sufi facets of the Beshara culture which we discussed earlier are expressed through the distinctively Ottoman/Turkish articulation that shaped Rauf's heritage. Long-standing associates have a particular interest in this heritage, and have developed a deep sympathy for the Ottoman milieu. Young explains this appreciation in terms of Rauf's insistence that 'Ibn 'Arabi was the bedrock of Ottoman culture, even if not everyone knew this.'[207] Ottoman culture was not special in itself, Young insists. Rather, 'it was the order of *wahdat al-wujud* manifest in it that made it important'. For Beshara the significance of Ottoman culture thus lies in its perceived capacity as an actualisation of the implications of the Oneness of Being. This is captured in the successful incorporation of diversity in unity, for example, and in the encapsulation of order and harmony.

The Beshara vision of an age of unity and universality indeed has as its corollary a self-distancing from all specific cultural forms, in favour of that which 'flows' from the order of the Oneness of Being, and thus implicitly encompasses them all.[208] We can illustrate this position, which also entails a repudiation of cultural eclecticism, by an associate's views concerning the sphere of music:

> There is very little, if any, western music that could be said to align itself to a point of view like that of Ibn 'Arabi. Although there is plenty of Sufi music coming out of

various culturally specific regions such as Pakistan and Turkey and to some extent North Africa, all these forms have some traditional cultural root. Even Sufi music recorded in the US tends to adopt traditional eastern musical forms.[209]

Evaluating a compact disk produced by another associate (to which we will return later), he implies that its uniqueness lies in the vocalist's explicit intention 'to serve the expression, rather than simply add some music to some words'. Consequently, 'just as it would be misleading to call it either religious or secular music, so it would be inaccurate to call it eclectic'. The specific musical character of each song rather reflects 'the order it emanates from', and to which it gives expression. There is no 'forcing' into specific cultural forms.[210]

Rauf translated the demands of the order of the Oneness of Being into an emphasis on beauty and harmony; on everything having its appropriate place, use and purpose; on proper conduct and etiquette; and on measured and respectful behaviour. The impact of this is at its most evident in the School, but it is also discernible in associates' attitudes and conduct more broadly. Paradoxically, much of this emphasis can be projected in terms of the ethos, values and norms of dying traditional modes (especially those associated with Rauf's own cultural provenance), in contrast with those of modernity. At the same time, the centrality of the Oneness of Being has shaped a subtle, implicit valuing of a tendency to uniformity in Beshara. This is of particular interest in light of the modern (and quintessentially New Age) emphasis of individuality.

From counterculture to Uwaysi culture

The Beshara culture can also be understood in terms of a characterisation of the movement, following Young's suggestion, as 'essentially Uwaysi, in the sense that no shaykh or intermediary is involved'. Associates indeed describe the Beshara approach as 'the most direct path, based on an intention to go straight up without intermediary'. An emphasis of Uwaysi mysticism served to reinforce salient aspects of the perspective Rauf advanced. It also furnished legitimisation of the Beshara approach in terms of a specific strand of sufism. By exploring these areas, we can illuminate the spiritual culture of Beshara. Furthermore, we can demonstrate the resonance of its perspective with its New Age constituency, both within the sixties counterculture and in the decades since.

As we suggested earlier, an important dimension of Rauf's repudiation of the *tariqa* lay in his resistance to authoritarian religious and spiritual structures. He recognised that some people may be better placed to guide others, by virtue of their longer training and study. However, he insisted that the notion of the Oneness of Being does not admit hierarchy or the exercise of power by one person over another, for its corollary is the principle that *everyone* is in potential a teacher or guide to Reality and has, moreover, the potential for sainthood. This potential may not be realised, but it is every-one's birthright.[211] To illuminate the reality of the spiritual teacher–student or master–disciple relationship (a reality they should aspire to actualise), Rauf pointed associates to the example of Shams and Rumi. He projected this as a relationship between equals.[212] The only 'vertical' relation is thus between man and the Real: all others are immediately and exclusively 'horizontal'.

Rauf's characterisation of the era as one in which esoteric knowledge is becoming increasingly accessible and assimilated highlighted further the necessarily *egalitarian* nature of contemporary spiritual education. Significantly, Rauf's position in this respect appealed to counterculture atti-tudes towards power and authority, which reflected a strong concern with human dignity.[213] It resonated with the New Age notion of the Self as the final locus of authority embraced by elements of the counterculture, for it dove-tailed with an imagining of the incipient/imminent Aquarian age as a time in which open 'brotherhoods' would supplant the hierarchical or vertical struc-tures that had characterised the receding Piscean age. For Rauf, the *tariqa* as a hierarchical organisation, with the authoritarian figure of shaykh at its apex responsible for conveying inherited knowledge and exercising power over his followers (who are required to obey him unquestioningly), was anathema, particularly when seen in light of the divinely appointed ethos of the era. He rejected the emphasis on the shaykh and the deference and submission of some of those who follow shaykhs, which at times issued in what associ-ates describe as a 'cult of the shaykh' among *murid*s. He seemed particularly averse to the practice of *fana' fi'l-shaykh* ('self-realisation in one's teacher', as he put it), which he implicitly posited as the norm within the *tariqa*s.[214] All of this was antithetical to the egalitarianism flowing from the Oneness of Being. As we have noted before, Rauf never projected himself as a sufi shaykh. He explained to associates that he was both 'less than a shaykh and more than a shaykh'.[215] He also repudiated any projection of himself as a guru,[216] and rejected outright the ethos of contemporary guru-centred movements.

We can sum up Rauf's position in the proposition that, while suluki mysti-cism (formalised historically in the *tariqa*s) has fulfilled its function and is inappropriate to the spiritual realities of contemporary man, Uwaysi mysti-cism as 'Self-spirituality' will now find its day. How can the historical rela-tionship between these two strands of sufism be understood? As the sufi quest became institutionalised within the framework of the *tariqa*s centring on the role of the shaykh, by the fourteenth century the need for the shaykh became virtually unquestioned in the eastern Muslim world (although still debated in Muslim Spain and North Africa).[217] Epitomised in the sufi adage (and putative saying of the Prophet) 'He who has no shaykh has the Devil as his shaykh',[218] this emphasis was tied to the notion of the *silsila* or chain of spiritual authority, the ultimate basis of the legitimacy of both shaykh and *tariqa*. Some argue that, already somewhat marginal, the Uwaysi tradition, with its method of transhistorical initiation, was further marginalised by the institution of the *tariqa*.[219] However, more nuanced approaches to the history of sufism reveal that strands of Uwaysi and suluki sufism were frequently found together in any particular sufi's experience. Some may not have identified themselves as Uwaysi by name, but they can be regarded as such based on their declared connections in the unseen world.[220] Across the centuries, many who have been attached to a living shaykh (and through him to a regular *silsila*) have indeed considered a *deceased* saint as their true teacher.[221] Ibn 'Arabi and Üftade, significant sources of Rauf's inspiration, were themselves tutored by Uwaysi figures, although each also had visible earthly teachers, and participated in suluki sufism.[222]

Rauf's focus was on Uwaysi mysticism as the inherently non-institutionalised dimension of sufi experience, beyond the sphere of masters among living men, and conducted in the imaginal realm at the interface between material and spirit worlds. His personal spiritual teachers belonged to the community of saints who had departed this world. Although he encouraged associates to seek the help of such saints, his ultimate concern was with the potential for *direct* transmission and guidance from the Real, as the One Teacher with whom the saint as Perfect Man is in essence identical. This is the divinely appointed channel for the present era. To this end, Young illuminates the fate of the earthly teacher's role as mediator (and the basis of the knowledge that qualifies them as such) in light of the movement of the *batin* becoming *zahir* discussed earlier:

> Now the teacher is a mediator by virtue of knowing himself to be God in his essence and knowing himself to be the manifested consciousness of God. The knowledge of this is the possibility of all men and thus direct application is not a contradiction of the usual order, but a summary of the essential aspects of it. And inasmuch as the movement of the Divine Breath is outwards, the inner revealing itself as outer, in time the need for teachers is perhaps inevitably reduced to its principal, direct application and direct transmission. Whether this situation is realised by the pupil or not, this is the reality of this guidance. How could anything other than Reality be the Guide to the Real?[223]

Direct transmission from the Real to the heart of man is thus his destiny, spiritual guidance emanating 'from above' (or within) without intermediary. This is the Beshara experience, and it adumbrates the profound change that awaits humanity as a whole. It is conceivable that some associates have a connection with Ibn 'Arabi or the great Celveti saints, evident in their dreams, for example. However, the ultimate basis of their Uwaysi mysticism must be projected in terms of a perceived direct connection with the Real as the One Source of initiation, guidance and knowledge.[224] Rauf in fact insisted that there are in reality no 'human' teachers, for 'the teacher you find on earth is just a manifestation of the One who teaches all.'[225] As one associate puts it, 'The unique way of Beshara, brought by Bulent, is the way of no teachers.'

Baldick's (at times contentious) characterisation of the historical Uwaysi tradition points to its advantages in 'overcoming barriers of time, space and language', by providing the individual with a 'direct source of authority' to which they could turn. Its 'dubious appeal' lay also in the justification it furnished for avoiding 'often severe demands of the living [shaykhs] available.'[226] In Beshara, emphasis of this strand of sufi experience provides a framework through which to articulate a personal spirituality built on a direct access to Truth, in which the institution of spiritual teacher/director is redundant and cultural forms are unimportant (even irrelevant). By resorting to the Uwaysi mode Rauf legitimised the Beshara approach in terms of the broad sufi tradition, while implicitly rejecting the suluki mode, *especially* in its institutionalised form in the *tariqa*. In support of this position, he could adduce the historical experiences of Ibn 'Arabi and Rumi, two of his major inspirations, who each marked the high point of the sufi tradition. Both had lived before the crystallisation of the *tariqa*s and the resulting transformation of the sufi quest from an individual endeavour resting on a personal basis, and expressed through a relatively loose and open master–disciple relationship.[227] With regard to Rumi, Rauf emphasised that 'It was his son, Sultan Weled, who, after his father's death, made those things that his father had started into a formal affair, a *tariqa*.'[228] He repeatedly reminded associates that 'one cannot make out of Ibn 'Arabi a *tariqa*.'[229] In this regard, some associates cite Ibn 'Arabi's critical evaluation of his encounters with emergent sufi institutions in the east.[230] Others argue more generally that sufism cannot be conflated with the formal *tariqa*s, and is not dependent for its genuine expression on this framework. They point to its existence well before the rise of formal structures, and insist that its practice can (indeed did) thrive without (in both senses of the word) such structures.[231]

Alluding to Rauf's paradigm of man's spiritual meta-history, associates suggest that 'there are distinct eras, and in each one there is a predominant way in which God is worshipped. With each prophet, a new modality or facet in the worship of God was revealed.' In every new era, the 'predominant facet' of the preceding one is supplanted. 'The spirit leaves it, and only the form or husk remains which then itself deteriorates and falls.'[232] When new facets appear, they can be before their time:[233] their aptness is brought into focus only when the emergent spiritual landscape becomes clarified and is finally established. This is how it is in the case of the *tariqa*s, of which only the 'husk' now remains,[234] and Beshara, by contrast with them. Associates indeed attribute the awkwardness of exchanges during visits to Turkey between Rauf on the one hand and sufi shaykhs on the other to the inherent incompatibility of the old order (represented by the shaykhs and *tariqa*s) and the new (exemplified in Beshara).[235] In the unfolding era the spirit no longer inhabits forms like the *tariqa*s, as the time for 'formality' in spiritual life is over. Instead, the Truth reaches directly to anyone who is prepared to receive it, in quintessentially Uwaysi manner. For this reason, Rauf had greeted associates who had returned enthusiastically from a Halveti–Jerrahi *dhikr* in Istanbul during the early 1970s (which he had reluctantly agreed that they attend 'if they felt they had to') with the reminder that what they had seen was 'part of something that is past.'

Rauf, according to associates, 'could never have been a shaykh, for this is not what is required now'. Effectively, he had added his name to the roll-call of Turkish sufi masters who looked beyond the proscribed formal *tariqa* as framework for spiritual life. In contrast with them, however, his alternative spiritual vision was addressed primarily to a non-Muslim Western audience, and hence involved a more radical departure from the tradition out of which it arose.

Describing Rauf's 'conversion' to the spiritual path alongside those of al-Jilani and Üftade, an associate has suggested that, like them, he too was a 'Muhyiddin', a 'revivifier of religion or faith'. Significantly, he had specifically revived 'an order for his time'.[236] This new order for contemporary man entailed a particular projection of the main source for its exposition, Ibn 'Arabi. We consider next the contents and channels of this projection, and reflect on its implications for perceptions of Beshara among others who are interested in Ibn 'Arabi's teaching and his legacy for today's world.

Chapter 7

Projecting Ibn 'Arabi for today's world

Beshara and Ibn 'Arabi

The importance of Ibn 'Arabi in Beshara

It will be clear by now that Ibn 'Arabi occupies a profoundly important place in Beshara, and that associates share perceptions of his saintly grandeur with Muslims and sufis of many hues. Rauf had successfully resisted a temptation on the part of early associates to make some kind of 'cult figure' out of the mystic. Nonetheless, a few do evince an emotional intolerance towards anyone who is critical of Ibn 'Arabi, or more interested in his historical opponents. For some associates, he has become an intimate life-guide. Describing the diverse community in which she lives, for example, one suggests that Ibn 'Arabi 'not only provided an inner personal guide but also a kind of operating manual for understanding what was in front of me.'[1] A second remarks that the mystic 'answered questions I had not yet begun to ask. His metaphysics empowered me by providing tools for seeing the fundamental issues of life from a new perspective. It challenged my assumptions about everything.' And a third affirms that 'Studying Ibn 'Arabi provides a key to understanding all aspects of life and the human condition. Everything that happens is understood in the light of Ibn 'Arabi's teachings. He is the key.'[2] Associates agree that Ibn 'Arabi has offered them 'a change of perception, of how you see, feel and experience things', and that he has enriched their lives and worlds. A sense of closeness and indebtedness to him has impelled some to make a personal pilgrimage to his shrine in Damascus. One explains that her endeavours to travel to various places had been thwarted: her conclusion was that a journey to Ibn 'Arabi was 'required', before any other might be possible.

Beshara, Ibn 'Arabi and universality

Although Ibn 'Arabi is its main resource, the movement's emphasis on universality informs a concern to avoid conflating Beshara with him. This underpins sensitivity to what one associate construes as 'the question of the primacy of Ibn 'Arabi' within Beshara.[3] Rauf had explained that 'Ibn 'Arabi is of Beshara, but Beshara is not only Ibn 'Arabi'. Young elaborates: 'While Ibn 'Arabi was a vehicle for knowledge, this knowledge did not originate in him. It comes through Ibn 'Arabi, but it is not Ibn 'Arabi himself.' An associate is clearer still: 'Ibn 'Arabi is central to Beshara not because he is Ibn 'Arabi, but because of the universality he communicates. Beshara is not a school for Ibn

'Arabi, but for universality. Because his works in this area are unparalleled, he is the source for education.'

As we have seen, Rauf drew selectively on Ibn 'Arabi's works in accordance with his own particular understanding of universality. As a result associates do not study 'everything of Ibn 'Arabi', for they consider much of what he wrote specific to his function as 'Reviver of the Faith', concerned with 'the refinement of Islam as a religion'. This 'level' of his writings is evident in his treatment of issues like *fiqh*, and it is relevant only to 'people of the religion'. There is a perception that, if studied, such elements in his corpus may lead associates to 'a turn not necessarily espoused by Beshara'.[4]

Beshara's perennialist approach has at the same time guided it to sources from other traditions. In publicising its courses, for example, the School emphasises that 'study material is drawn from many sources and traditions, all pointing to the One Universal Reality which cannot be confined to any one form or way'.[5] Young further underlines that the School curriculum 'is not exclusively Ibn 'Arabi, but starts with Ibn 'Arabi and goes on to the study of texts relating to the essential matter from all the major spiritual traditions'.[6] Finally, while giving pride of place to a poem from Ibn 'Arabi's *Kitab al-Tajalliyat*,[7] the Beshara website library also carries an excerpt from Martin Luther King, a poem by Rabindranath Tagore, a Message from the American Elders, and verses by the third Zen Patriarch Sengtsan.[8]

'Now is the time of Ibn 'Arabi'

Underlining the aptness of his unifying teaching for this conflict-ridden and divided world, associates suggest that 'the time of Ibn 'Arabi' is upon us. One argues that this teaching deserves 'a far wider recognition and application. Founded on a harmonious vision of Reality, integrating all apparent differences without destroying their truths, overflowing with insights into the human reality and true compassion, his writings are singularly appropriate and needed in the world of today'.[9] Another suggests that 'In these times of war and, at the political level at least, increasing disharmony between people of different religious faiths, it seems especially important to affirm the universal vision that Ibn 'Arabi and his followers embody, and the tolerant and compassionate perspective which they expounded so well'.[10]

Such perceptions of the potential relevance of Ibn 'Arabi's legacy to contemporary needs are shared by mainstream scholars, Muslim and other, who identify in it rich resources for constructing a more peaceful global society, or a new 'world civilisation'.[11] Referring to the dangers implicit in notions of a 'clash of civilisations', for example, Mesbahi recently argued that 'The Unity of Existence offers to man a new citizenship: to become a universal citizen ... without the fetters of beliefs and doctrines'.[12] Thus, 'The heart of civilisation is ... big enough to contain all the cultures, ready to accept images of truth, without any preferences, since all that exists is truth. Ibn 'Arabi's voice is therefore useful because it teaches us how to wander within boundaries ...

in order.' to see that others are equal in value in relation to the Absolute.'[13] In a similar vein, Kiliç suggests that 'anyone who is interested in Ibn al-'Arabi's teachings, whatever their culture, will move, step by step, beyond the bound-aries of their locality, nationality and sectarianism, finally reaching, through him, a universal perspective. Ibn al-'Arabi could be an architect for all those who seek to unite, be they part of the Islamic culture, or any other.'[14] More widely known in Euro-American scholarship, Morris projects Ibn 'Arabi's teaching as a potential cure for the ills of Muslim societies, especially where salafis lay claim to a single authentic interpretation of the Islamic sources and understanding of the Divine Will.[15] Beyond these societies, he suggests that the mystic's legacy offers a response to the needs of an emerging global society built on human diversity, furnishing a framework for a new universal spirituality that cultivates mutual understanding among people of all reli-gious backgrounds.[16]

Most scholars share such convictions within the specialist academic milieu, but some occasionally move beyond this to a wider public, through more accessible publications and the media, for example. Alongside the efforts of a few engaged sufis and scholars,[17] it is Beshara associates in particular who have assumed the task of bringing Ibn 'Arabi's message to a non-specialist audience in the West, and transporting this into popular culture there. In what follows, we explore specific examples of their avenues of engagement and efforts at popularisation. Returning then to the specialist arena, we consider the work of the MIAS in disseminating Ibn 'Arabi's works through cooperation with the scholarly community, and assess its implications and impacts.

Discussed earlier, their conviction of the universal relevance of his teaching is what drives associates to bring Ibn 'Arabi into the wider culture. Consonant with this (and implied by it) is an understanding that his message is poten-tially within universal reach, in terms of the qualifications that are required in order to benefit from it. We explore the basis of this view (which some mainstream academics share with Beshara), and situate it against conflicting contemporary perceptions. Finally, we evaluate the Beshara appropriation of Ibn 'Arabi and the image of the man and his legacy implicit within it, and compare this with competing views.

Avenues of engagement: bringing Ibn 'Arabi into the wider culture

Lewis remarks that Rumi has now entered American popular culture, and he indeed writes of a 'Rumi-mania' today.[18] Although a comparable 'Ibn 'Arabi-mania' remains remote, and there is still relatively little popular material on this saint,[19] a belief in the importance of his message has impelled some associates to develop avenues of engagement with the wider culture through his popularisation. The arts and music have provided a successful route of access for sufism in general into Western popular culture, and Western sufi movements have actively fostered these as a sphere of intersection with it.[20] Associates have also used this channel, among others, to popularise Ibn 'Arabi.

Music and audio-media

Let Love love Love (2001) is a compact disk produced by a classically trained vocalist associate.[21] In five of the twelve tracks she sings excerpts from *Stations of Desire*, Sells' translation of Ibn 'Arabi's *Tarjuman al-ashwaq*. A sixth is a section from Ibn 'Arabi's prayer for Sunday morning, as translated in *The Seven Days of the Heart*. The remaining tracks are the vocalist's own songs, which in the words of an associate reviewer are 'clearly informed by a devotional spirit that could only have been expressed by holding on to Ibn 'Arabi's coat-tails'.[22] The reviewer (who also owns the production/recording company behind the disk) continues:

> Naturally the theme is love, and all that is implied in the affair in terms of know-ledge, the pain of separation, and the maturation of the soul ... *Let Love love Love* is an album not of songs but of prayers. And they are prayers which for whatever reason have demanded musical expression.[23]

Perhaps inspired by the success of audio-media in popularising Rumi, associates have also produced a compact disk entitled *A Garden Amidst Flames: Readings from Muhyiddin Ibn Arabi*.[24] Readings from the *Tarjuman, Sufis of Andalusia, The Treatise on Being* and *The Kernel of the Kernel* by associates (and one in Rauf's voice) are set to music, which has also been composed, and is played, by associates. The back cover explains that

> Ibn 'Arabi's linked theses of the Unity of Being and the Perfectibility of Man are universal and enduring concepts which transcend all religious and cultural divi-sions, and draw out the meaning at the heart of every true spiritual teaching. This recording, which uses musical settings, aims to bring a taste of Ibn 'Arabi's universal perspective to English speaking listeners, whatever their cultural back-ground. Ibn 'Arabi said 'Tradition has left us only words; it is up to us to find out what they mean.' He also said, 'The wise man will not allow himself to be tied to one form of belief.' Such a large point of view is a priceless gift, to be strived for and celebrated.

Cultural–spiritual tourism

Associates have designed a series of *In the Footsteps of Ibn 'Arabi* guided tours under the auspices of Anqa Publishing. These aim 'to explore the traces of Ibn 'Arabi's world and follow in his footsteps'.[25] The first such tours were to Andalusia, Spain (2004 and 2005).[26] A third visited Anatolia, Turkey, where Ibn 'Arabi spent several years (2006).[27] In Andalusia the tour group visits the major sites of his youth, reading along the way Ibn 'Arabi's own accounts of 'the places he knew and the people he met'. Participants are encouraged to bring *Sufis of Andalusia* with them, and notes on relevant places and sites are distributed during the journey. Just over half of those who participated in the 2004 tour had a strong connection with Beshara. In addition, there were members of the Sufi Order and the Schuonian *tariqa* Maryamiyya, and individuals who had discovered the tour through the internet.[28] Anqa Publishing aspires to establish such *In the Footsteps of Ibn 'Arabi* tours as an annual event.

Providing an accessible 'flavour' of Ibn 'Arabi in print

Towards the end of the 1980s an American student of contemporary Western spirituality had argued that, in contrast with the case of Rumi, 'we are still waiting for the scholar and writer who can make [Ibn 'Arabi] accessible for our generation'.[29] We can consider Hirtenstein's *The Unlimited Mercifier*, published by Anqa Publishing a decade later, in light of this remark.[30] The author's main aim in the work was thus to produce 'a readable account which will convey something of the *flavour* of Ibn 'Arabi, a sense of his greatness and genius and what spiritual benefits there may be for people today in reading [his] works'.[31] Set apart by its ample use of maps, photographs and illustrations, the volume is not intended to be 'either academic or scholarly'.[32] On the contrary, it endeavours to make Ibn 'Arabi both generally accessible and relevant to contemporary life.

Hirtenstein situates his subject in the broadest possible context of human experience, through references to the lore of diverse spiritual traditions, great historical figures from different religions and civilisations, contemporary personalities, and modern scientific findings. He simplifies aspects of Ibn 'Arabi's life and teaching (as well as general concepts and attitudes) through mundane metaphors and contemporary popular idiom.[33] His style is warm, direct and engaging,[34] making particularly effective use of personalising, inclusive language in presenting the subject.[35] Hirtenstein always points to the immediate implications of Ibn 'Arabi's teaching for the reader willing to follow it. Indeed, at the outset he explicitly invites his readers 'to understand Ibn 'Arabi on a more intimate and personal level'.[36] The title of his work reflects an underlying emphasis on Ibn 'Arabi's universal role. This is accompanied by an attempt throughout the text to unfold the immediate relevance of his spiritual life and teaching for every individual. Aimed at the lay reader interested in practical spirituality, Hirtenstein characterises the work as 'ultimately a personal view' of Ibn 'Arabi.[37] This personal view introduces central Beshara themes and emphases to the framing of the mystic and his teaching in *The Unlimited Mercifier*. These include unity and universality, the immediate personal relevance of Ibn 'Arabi's teaching and its implications for spirituality today, and the nature of the present era in terms of the possibilities for direct knowledge of Truth without intermediaries.

Professional creativity and Ibn 'Arabi as inspiration

It is noteworthy that associates have chosen jobs and careers in the 'expressive professions' such as teaching and counselling, where there is a clear interest in human potential. There are among them a number of complementary health therapists. Several are engaged in the arts, music or creative work. They suggest that their sense of aesthetics has been influenced by knowledge of Ibn 'Arabi. As one puts it, 'the understanding of beauty and the importance of taste absorbed during courses' are carried into their work. This can occasionally be made explicit, in response to an expression of interest in their source of inspiration or a question concerning this. At the same time, however, they believe that their work speaks on a more subtle level to all those who encounter it. This reflects a more general point for, as an associate explains, 'It is not so much the kind of work which is important ... as the quality with which the work is carried out'.[38] Prominent creative professionals among associates include an accomplished London chef,[39] several architects, an actor, a fashion designer, and a landscape gardener who has undertaken projects for the Prince of Wales.

An associate whose first novel won the PEN/Faulkner Award for Fiction (1998)[40] offers a particular example of the creative expression of Ibn 'Arabi's inspiration, and the resulting potential as a channel of engagement with popular culture. Rafi Zabor's *The Bear Comes Home*[41] was not a best seller as such, in spite of excellent reviews. It sold some 30,000 copies in the USA, but fewer in the UK and in its French, German and Spanish translations. However, it quickly became a cult classic. It has been described as an account of the spiritual odyssey of a 'deeply human sax-playing bear', and characterised by one reviewer as 'a modern fable'.[42] Zabor explains that the work has an 'Akbarian understructure' which his own personality and 'the demands of art' led him to conceal.[43] In its author's words, the metaphysics in the novel are derived from his own experience 'as buttressed by' the writings of Ibn 'Arabi. The primary reference in *The Bear Comes Home* is to the chapter on the Five Presences (*hadaras*) in Bursevi's translation of/commentary on Ibn 'Arabi's *Lubb al-lubb*.[44] The characters thus experience their lives in the precisely delineated worlds of the first four of these Presences, each of which is keyed to specific image systems of the author's invention. The World of Eternal Individuations, for example, is associated with stars, constellations and crystalline images. Zabor suggests that the whole book can be seen as its characters' attempts 'to overcome the limitations of dualism and separation from Universal Being'. His hope is that the web-work of imagery he presents will convey to the reader the experiential realities depicted in the story, making the metaphysical material artistically real, for the impact on the reader turns on this artistic realisation.

While many did not grasp its disguised Akbarian symbolism, Zabor explains that a few reviewers made discreet references to the novel's 'implicit mystical thrust'. He explicitly highlighted this aspect during an interview on national American television, in response to the interviewer's characterisation of *The Bear Comes Home* as a 'philosophical' and 'religious' novel.[45]

Scholarly dissemination: the Muhyiddin Ibn 'Arabi Society, Beshara and 'sufi academia'

Hermansen has suggested that 'perennialist' sufi movements have had more of an impact on artistic, cultural and intellectual trends in contemporary religious thought than their 'hybrid' counterparts, and a generally broader impact in mainstream Western culture. According to this argument, movements with an Islamic orientation favour 'translations and commentaries on classical Sufi texts', while universal ones evince a greater inclination to produce the more accessible genres of 'quest narratives, teaching stories and works on transpersonal psychology'.[46] Beshara appears to be something of an anomaly. The attempts at popularisation we have just described notwithstanding, its main arena of engagement with the wider culture is thus arguably through the medium of scholarly work on Ibn 'Arabi fostered by the MIAS.[47]

We must emphasise that our concern here is with the MIAS in its capacity as a particular activity or expression of Beshara, rather than an association of disparate individuals brought together by a common interest in Ibn 'Arabi. Given that associates may take issue with the very positing of such a capacity to the Society (which they project as without any agenda other than to disseminate Ibn 'Arabi's works, as we will discuss below), some clarification is in order. As we noted earlier, the Society was established on the initiative of associates and under Rauf's guidance. Associates exclusively have since served as its officers. The Chairman points out that there is no policy in this regard, for officers self-select.[48] He suggests that the situation has thus arisen accidentally: 'those interested in Ibn 'Arabi happen to have been educated at the Beshara School and to live in Oxford, where the Society is headquartered'. Accidentally or otherwise, however, the outcome has been that core decision-making and the overall directing of the Society have been (and remain) in associates' hands. This furnishes a legitimate basis for considering the Society's achievements in relation to the movement, and for exploring expression of the movement's ethos in the Society's work. How do associates themselves perceive the distinction between Beshara and the MIAS? One explains that 'while the MIAS is for all of Ibn 'Arabi's work and is a scholarly pursuit, the focus of Beshara concerns universality'. Another points to the recommended manner of approaching the *Fusus* (elaborated in the Foreword to the second volume of the *White Fusus*) as 'what sets Beshara apart from the MIAS'; we will discuss this shortly.

Through its activities detailed earlier, the MIAS targets and reaches an audience that is qualitatively different from the constituency of potential Beshara students. In particular, this audience encompasses a high proportion of professional scholars and students of sufism. It thus participates in

the global network of what we term here 'sufi academia', a product of the
expanding interface between professional scholarship on sufism and its practice as a spiritual way.[49] For associates, the activities of the MIAS furnish
opportunities for furthering their knowledge of Ibn 'Arabi's teaching, and a
forum for reinforcing their personal convictions.

In 1989, an associate delivered the following positive assessment of the
Society's achievements:

> This Society can now, I believe, be said to be one of the most important gathering
> points for the study, understanding and promulgation of [Ibn 'Arabi's works] ...
> For, whereas all that is published beyond the Society's embrace is published by
> individual scholars ... at the same time there is a growing co-ordination of all the
> various people involved under the aegis of the Society. The most obvious sign of
> this ... is at the Symposia.[50]

This success had brought to the fore issues of broader interest concerning
attitudes and assumptions within 'sufi academia', and the impact of subjective
belief in this. The MIAS had spelt out its mission from the first, encapsulated
in *The Rules of the Society* (1981). These describe its *raison d'être* as

> furthering a common interest in the study, promulgation, publication, transla-
> tion and furtherance of the works *and ideals* of Muhyiddin Ibn 'Arabi and those
> persons being his students, followers or otherwise who have perpetuated his
> works, interests *and ideals*.[51]

During 1988 the Chairman indicated the implications of this for the Society's
attitude towards scholarship in the field. Acknowledging that it was providing
a forum for scholars (who at least in some cases were otherwise isolated), he
effectively reminded his audience, a Society AGM, of the parameters of the
Society's mission:

> whilst the Society very much wishes to encourage academic research, translation
> and so on, when approaching Ibn 'Arabi it is not just a matter of linguistics, it is
> important also to be able to be in tune with the spirit of what Ibn 'Arabi has written
> and to have a clear understanding of what it is that is being said ... [T]here are
> those who manage to convey the spirit of what is being said into their translations
> and it is our fervent hope that in time even more translators will arrive at this
> point.[52]

The MIAS is founded on the Beshara conception of the 'ideals' of Ibn 'Arabi,
and the 'spirit' of his writings. The core of its mission lies in the furtherance
of these ideals and spirit, and the promulgation of his writings ultimately
serves this end. In its origin and ethos it is not an exclusively objective or
disengaged scholarly society, even if this facet is the one most immediately
encountered by scholars in the field. Another of its facets thus reflects a selective identification with parts of the received tradition of Ibn 'Arabi, who for
Beshara is the exemplar of a particular type of spirituality, characterised by
certain emphases in his life and teachings. This facet has shaped the Society

as an association committed to representing a certain image of Ibn 'Arabi and his teachings.[53] It forms a subtle undercurrent, which occasionally comes to the fore in explicit statements. An example is the following, made by the Society's Honorary Secretary during 1985:

> There is ... a responsibility upon a Society which endeavours to represent a man whose work is so universal that all sects and creeds can find their truth in it. Such sects will exclaim 'This is exactly what we are saying and we must be right because Ibn 'Arabi ... says so.' To which the reply must inevitably be 'Yes, it is so', unless the exclaimer claims exclusivity of correctness – 'It is like this and only like this', to which the proper answer is, 'No, Ibn 'Arabi, who is a man of Wisdom, does not allow himself to be caught up in any one form of belief[54] because he knows his own essence, which is infinite and thereby capable of all forms ... The Society's integrity therefore consists in being entirely non-sectarian in itself, and in not becoming the unwitting tool of anyone or any group whose interest lies in promoting their own viewpoint by limiting the universality of Ibn 'Arabi's work, however rightly guided they may feel themselves to be. This does not prohibit comment but should, on the contrary, encourage it. Ibn 'Arabi is capable of all forms and people will recognise in his work their own beliefs and find them clarified. But here, for this Society, balance and discretion is essential.[55]

An encounter during 1985 between the Society and Charles-André Gilis, a Belgian academic, Muslim convert and disciple of Michel Vâlsan,[56] provided a test case for this approach. Gilis had accepted an invitation to speak at that year's AGM of the MIAS.[57] He had chosen to address a subject he recognised as 'delicate' and potentially controversial: 'the very conception of what should be an organisation aiming to defend and promote Ibn 'Arabi's teaching.'[58] He posited two essential facets to which Ibn 'Arabi's views concerning Islam might be ultimately reduced. First is the idea that 'Metaphysical Truth, as communicated to Man at the origin, is considered in its unity and universality, that is without connection with any particular form, any special revelation or religion.' From this point of view, he explained, 'Islam presents no special excellency [sic] and enjoys no particular privilege.'[59] The second aspect of Ibn 'Arabi's views concerning Islam was no less important but was, he suggested, 'curiously enough, much less seldom [sic] referred to.'[60] In this aspect, Gilis explained,

> the Truth is examined not in itself, but from a formal point of view in relation with the expression of Sacred Law (al-Haqq). From this point of view, the Divine Blessing is attached to a special doctrinal formulation, excluding any other. Naturally, any traditional form may be, in reality, the object of such Blessing, attesting its truth, expediency and spiritual efficiency. However, there is no doubt that Ibn 'Arabi's teaching endows Islam with particular excellence. In fact, he maintains that Islamic tradition enjoys exclusive privileges, so that it really prevails over any other.[61]

Gilis reconciled these two seemingly contradictory aspects in light of Ibn 'Arabi's 'very complete doctrine' and incomparable 'synthetic vision'. He suggested that, therein, the two aspects in reality 'explain themselves one by the other'. On the one hand, 'Islamic Law effectively possesses legal competence and universal supremacy, implying in the field of external forms and action the establishment of a new traditional statute, final and irrevocable ... including the power of abrogating, confirming or submitting to a special status what nowadays remains' of previous traditions. On the other hand, 'this providential privilege can be justified, from a metaphysical point of view, only by the complementary obligation, for the Islamic community, to profess a Faith, as universal and global, in the whole of Divine Revelations effected in this world since its origin'.[62] Citing passages from the *Futuhat* outlining Ibn 'Arabi's teaching concerning the status of Sacred Laws other than the Law of Islam and the reality of 'conversion' to Islam, Gilis concluded

> there can be doubt that there is, between the universal metaphysical Doctrine as expressed by Ibn 'Arabi and the Islamic tradition, an indissoluble link. [Ibn 'Arabi] is ... a traditional author, commissioned to advise Allah's faithful ... constantly referring to the very traditional precepts of Islam or those confirmed by Islam, scrupulously abiding by the slightest prescriptions of the Sacred Law, speaking in the name and in favour of Allah's Religion. His teaching represents a sacred character in view of its origin, expressive modes and aims. Therefore, one cannot underestimate the link between this teaching and Islamic tradition without taking the risk of totally distorting its meaning and significance, and even, in some way, violating it.[63]

At this point he cut to the heart of the matter, as far his addressing the AGM was concerned. He recalled that, when he had expressed this view to Young, who as Society Honorary Secretary had issued the invitation to him, Young had responded that 'The Society is not affiliated to any specific doctrine but to the Truth as expounded by Ibn 'Arabi'. Gilis proceeded to refer to this statement in his talk, thus:

> But it seems that it is precisely there that the whole problem lies. If the Truth, the defence and illustration of which your Society is devoted to, is not Truth in itself, but actually Truth as expounded by Ibn 'Arabi, you cannot, it appears, escape the following dilemma: either you think that there is no necessary relation between Truth as expressed in Ibn 'Arabi's teaching and Islam, and in that case one may rightly consider that you don't know this teaching, or that you know it incompletely and imperfectly; or you acknowledge the existence of that relation and, in that case, I ask the question why your Society refuses to take into consideration that essential element, namely in its statutes and the way of recruiting its members.[64]

Gilis' contribution (which in places clearly showcased his own Traditionalist views)[65] prompted a response from Rauf, included in the Report of the AGM as an additional Note. He suggested that the very invitation extended by the Society to Gilis (who had made it clear that he wished to express his opinions frankly), and the audience's willingness to listen to his talk, bore witness to an attitude of 'complete respectful tolerance' within the Society. This stemmed from the fact that, 'in emulation of the person it represents, [the Society] does not hold to "one form of belief".[66]

This encounter brought to the fore the defining projection of the teaching of Ibn 'Arabi underlying the MIAS, a projection which arises directly out of the Society's origins in Beshara. Rauf suggested that the members of the Society take themselves ('perhaps rather pretentiously') as 'an exemplar or a nucleus of an unlimitable universality as an expression of a Divine intent [which] we respect'. Reflecting its understanding of this 'Divine intent', the Beshara(/MIAS) projection of Ibn 'Arabi's teaching assigns no role to religion in its actualisation and in the fulfilment of man's spiritual evolution, as we have discussed before. This is antithetical to the Traditionalist perspective. In the latter, the great orthodox religions represent forms of divine gnosis adapted providentially to different circumstances. As embodiments of perennial Truth they constitute the valid framework for the spiritual path and ultimately, through their initiatic traditions, for the highest form of spiritual realisation. Given this, it is unsurprising that the encounter between the Beshara(/MIAS) perspective and Traditionalism (as appropriated by a follower of Vâlsan) would end in collision.[67]

Gilis' later response to Rauf's comments regarding the *Fusus* (which we will consider shortly) perhaps strikes a chord with a much broader constituency than his particular line of Traditionalism, however, including many non-Traditionalist Muslims, sufis and scholars. Speaking of the *Fusus* and the approach to it he had encountered during the AGM of the MIAS just discussed (and perhaps prior to that), he wrote:

> this book cannot be interpreted in a way leading to the rejection of the teaching given by [Ibn 'Arabi] in other treaties [sic], *equally written under divine inspiration*, a teaching which lays great stress on the excellence and current primacy of the Islamic form and Law. A Society whose aim is to promote Ibn 'Arabi's teaching cannot, without betraying him, restrict itself to the exclusive defence of some aspects it implies to the detriment of the others. This point is elementary and fundamental.[68]

It is understandable that the articulation of such reservations has not been widespread, however. Many scholars who participate in MIAS activities may not have grasped the Society's original and underlying link with Beshara. Even if there is a broad awareness of this (associates who publish in the field thus self-describe as students of Ibn 'Arabi via the Beshara School), the implications of this for the Society's guiding assumptions are not necessarily apparent or clear. For those who are apprised of these implications, they do not necessarily form an impediment to fruitful intellectual exchange and scholarly cooperation.[69] Indeed, as we hinted above, the interface between sufi affiliation on the one hand and scholarship on sufism on the other has so expanded that it can be largely taken as read that a considerable segment of contemporary scholarship on sufism emanates from distinct sufi perspectives, from which it is inseparable.[70] In this respect, the case of the Society in its capacity as a 'wing' of the movement is no more significant than any number of other cases. Moreover, the exercise of control and selectivity regarding the parameters of its activities and those invited to participate in these is very subtle.

A few years after the 'Gilis affair', the debate concerning the requisite credentials for the 'representation' (and study) of Ibn 'Arabi (the notion of 'who can speak for him', as one associate puts it) resurfaced, during a plenary session of the 1990 MIAS symposium. Associates recall the presence of two camps in the audience that were at odds with the Society's perspective and ethos. One trend argued that, to be able to represent Ibn 'Arabi in such a body as the Society, and to be able to study him, one must be Muslim. (This echoed Gilis' stance but did not emanate from his particular perspective, or that of sufi Traditionalism more broadly.) The second, the voice of 'scholarly elitism' which we will discuss further later, insisted on the requirement of Arabic competence, and conversance with traditional Islamic sciences and medieval Islamic intellectual traditions. A conscious effort engaged at this time to consolidate the Society as an open body that promotes no particular perspective (including that of Beshara, according to one founding officer) appears to have been a response of sorts to this episode, and the challenges it raised. It is notable that symposia continue to evince a certain disjunction between the contributions, approaches and expectations of specialist scholars on the one hand, and those of associates (especially those of them who are less engaged, or not engaged at all, in the scholarly field), on the other.[71]

The Society has undoubtedly had a significant intellectual impact in the Western academic arena, and this has been achieved without Beshara having many professional academicians to call its own.[72] If anecdotal evidence can be taken as indicative, this impact has also begun to reach into the Muslim world. Morris thus suggests that the Society

> has succeeded in creating a remarkable global network of editors, translators, and interpreters of [Ibn 'Arabi's] works which is increasingly effective and influential not only in English-speaking countries and among academic specialists, but also in Muslim countries where intellectuals earlier in the past century had tended to reject aspects of Islam associated with Ibn 'Arabi.[73]

Associates' perceptions of this development resonate with the so-called 'pizza effect' hypothesis. According to this, Ibn 'Arabi is being re-exported to the Muslim world (through the MIAS and also through Beshara courses, as in the case of Indonesia) effectively repackaged, and thus implicitly in a 'new and improved' version, after his earlier 'importation' to the West.[74] Reflecting a characteristic Beshara emphasis, however, the Society does not claim any credit for what it recognises as 'the considerable growth in interest in the work of Ibn 'Arabi both in [the UK] and world wide'.[75] As the Honorary Secretary explains,

It would not be fruitful to endeavour to isolate the contribution of the Society to this ... In any case, for those who have studied Ibn 'Arabi it is certain that if there is any good, if there is any increase in interest in knowledge of the Real, or any real movement it is because He has done it; whether by way of intermediaries, through agencies or not, is immaterial and any such question would be on the same level as whether Shakespeare wrote his plays in his own hand or dictated them to a secretary.[76]

The MIAS joins its voice with those of certain sufi academics in a projection of the 'influence' (or 'role') of Ibn 'Arabi in the contemporary world that is at least in part conviction-driven.[77] The editorial in a 2003 MIAS Newsletter thus maintained:

There is every sign that the Akbarian point of view is becoming more widely known ... [more than] four major conferences ... have taken place in the last year ... There is also a steady increase in the number of new books and papers ... in English, French, German, Czech, Turkish and Spanish ... whilst behind the scenes there are many new research projects starting up which will bear fruit in the future.[78]

Morris is particularly interested in Ibn 'Arabi's contemporary 'influences'[79] (he has also written widely on his historical influence). In support of his claims, he adduces the recent 'profusion' of translations, publications, conferences, etc., relating to Ibn 'Arabi's writings. Mapping this development across the globe, he imbues it with significance well beyond that of a mere symptom of a global information and communication age. 'Interest in Ibn 'Arabi is just about everywhere in the world today',[80] he notes. Meanwhile 'the remarkable degree and sustained duration' of such interest in the contemporary West specifically 'suggests that something else, beyond the history of ideas and concepts, may be involved here'.[81] Lewisohn provides a further example of this confident (and far from sober) assessment of the contemporary 'influence' of Ibn 'Arabi:

Much, if not most, of the scholarly efforts of Western scholars of Islamic mysticism over the past decade have concentrated on Ibn 'Arabi ... Two works by ... Chittick [*Imaginal Worlds: Ibn al-'Arabi and the Problem of Religious Diversity* and *The Self-Disclosure of God: Principles of Ibn al-'Arabi's Cosmology*] have served to illustrate that Ibn 'Arabi has become as much the *Shaykh al-Akbar* of Islamic Sufism in the West as he was and still is in the East.[82]

For their part, associates construe this growing interest in Ibn 'Arabi's works and their expanding dissemination as further evidence of the significance of the present times as projected in the Beshara perspective. One recently commented during a symposium that, thirty years ago,

Idries Shah mentioned Ibn 'Arabi in *The Way of the Sufi*, but at that time you could not find out anything about him – there was nothing in English. Shah would say 'He is too difficult: you would not understand'. In the last thirty years Ibn 'Arabi has emerged as perhaps the greatest thinker we have. It would be astonishing to imagine that he is not aware that the time is right for the dissemination of his ideas.

Ibn 'Arabi and his readers: spirituality for the elite?

As we have seen, the focus and activities of the MIAS brought to the surface competing views concerning the requisite credentials for 'representing', studying and understanding Ibn 'Arabi. Underpinning this debate are divergent notions of his intended audience, shaped by the differing purposes and expectations of those who study his works.

Ibn 'Arabi as 'manual' for universal 'practical spirituality', or as scholarly preserve?

Beshara shares with Morris a perception that Ibn 'Arabi speaks to every individual, regardless of religious, cultural or linguistic backgrounds, aiming ultimately to spark an experiential process within them.[83] Thus, in Morris' words, 'the ultimate aim of all [Ibn 'Arabi's] writings is to support ... his reader's ... uniquely personal process ... of "realisation" (to use one of Ibn 'Arabi's favourite expressions, *tahqiq*), or of evolving spiritual intelligence'.[84] The human process of 'realisation'/'verification' is universal,[85] and all people possess the bases of spiritual intelligence, which they can actively develop. Thus, 'the distribution of particular spiritual gifts ... and forms of spiritual intelligence ... to be found among human beings have nothing at all to do, in their roots, with the outward accidents of age, culture and upbringing'.[86] In this view, Ibn 'Arabi's message addresses every individual regardless of background: humanity as a whole is its potential beneficiary. The task for those who uphold his legacy today is to present his ultimate purpose clarified in such a way that this can be grasped by an audience well beyond those trained to understand the specific historical–cultural–religious expression of his writings. This informs the common focus of Beshara and Morris in 'translating' these writings for the widest possible audience, and especially for those involved in practical spirituality.[87] Thus translated, they can be projected in their focused simplicity as an accessible 'manual' for people of all backgrounds. Thus, Morris writes:

> once we appreciate that the aim of the *Futuhat* is to deepen our spiritual awareness and understanding, and to develop all the wide-ranging dimensions of practical spiritual intelligence, we can better appreciate that reading and studying this work in the spirit in which it was written is not that different in essence ... from reading any of the host of widely available 'manuals' for the various familiar forms of traditional bodily–spiritual disciplines (Tai Chi, yoga, and so on).[88]

The projection of Ibn 'Arabi's writings (appropriately 'translated') as a 'manual for practical spirituality' that can be universally studied and understood is implicitly challenged by those who insist that, while anyone might study these, a proper understanding of them will ultimately elude all but the suitably qualified few. A comment by a contemporary scholar of sufism illustrates this attitude of 'scholarly elitism', which we referred to above, and which is potentially somewhat objectionable to associates. 'To understand Ibn 'Arabi', Radtke recently suggested, 'one must be a good Arabist, and have a sharp mind.'[89] While such credentials may produce a level of scholarly understanding, associates would argue that, on its own, this is not the level of understanding Ibn 'Arabi ultimately intended or wished for his readers. As Hirtenstein puts it, 'studying' his writings 'in the modern ... academic sense ... would perhaps have been rather laughable to Ibn 'Arabi, whose whole purpose in writing was to convey inspiration, to effect an inner transformation of the reader.'[90] Morris, also, implies that to focus exclusively on the scholarly level betrays a failure to grasp the purpose of Ibn 'Arabi and, based on this, his intended audiences:

> since the intellectual comprehension of the *Futuhat* – especially for modern readers (of *any* cultural, linguistic and religious background), who are inevitably unfamiliar with so much of its original cultural context – requires elaborate explanatory and background contextualisation, it is all too easy for most potential readers to assume that Ibn 'Arabi was primarily writing this book as an intellectual (i.e. primarily philosophical or theological) composition which is therefore really accessible only to a handful of specialised scholars and students. With regard to Ibn 'Arabi's own potential and intended audiences, at least, nothing could be further from the truth.[91]

That the two approaches are not mutually exclusive (and that the scholarly approach can play effective handmaiden to that of practical spirituality) is illustrated by the case of several associates who have dedicated themselves to acquiring relevant scholarly skills and linguistic training. For many of those interested in Ibn 'Arabi in terms of practical spirituality, however, the fact remains that use of translations of his works is indispensable. The implication in Radtke's comment (echoed by other scholars in the field) that a proper understanding may elude such students of Ibn 'Arabi is clearly antithetical to Beshara (and to Morris).[92]

Radtke's second assumption (that one must have 'a sharp mind' to approach Ibn 'Arabi) is shared by popular Muslim opinion. This is in awe of the elevated discourse and rich learning evident in Ibn 'Arabi's writings. At his shrine in Damascus, for example, local devotees insist that it would be beyond their capacity even to begin to understand these. Some read fragments (particularly of the *Futuhat*) for the blessings this act confers on the reader, but without deep comprehension. They point to the fact that even scholars they know who have spent long years studying Ibn 'Arabi readily confess they have achieved only a modest understanding, 'not even a drop in the ocean'. As Chittick remarks, Ibn 'Arabi indeed 'expected his readers not only to be practitioners of Sufism but also to be familiar with most fields of learning, especially Koran commentary, hadith, jurisprudence, theology, and philosophy, and he made few allowances for those who did not know these sciences well.'[93]

Ibn 'Arabi's 'elite' in today's world

There is a sense that Ibn 'Arabi never intended his works to be read by the generality of folk, out of a concern that mistaken understanding might cause them to be led astray.[94] Local devotees at his shrine indeed attribute to him a caution expressed in the phrase 'our works are our concern alone (*kutubuna takhussuna*)'.[95] If these works were intended for elite consumption, it is important to clarify Ibn 'Arabi's own understanding of the basis for membership in the intended elite. Perhaps we can best approach this question by identifying those he excluded from it: who, for Ibn 'Arabi, constituted the 'common people' (*al-'amma*; *al-'awamm*)? As Chittick observes,

> All [of Ibn 'Arabi's] works exhibit an extremely high level of sophistication, definitely not for popular consumption. When he refers disparagingly to the '*amma* or 'common people', he usually has in mind the exoteric scholars, the jurists or 'knowers of formalities' (*'ulama' al-rusum*) as he calls them – in other words, the learned class of Muslims in the ordinary sense of the term. But he also uses the term for Sufis who have not yet advanced to the stage of 'verification' (*tahqiq*) and who continue to follow authority (*taqlid*) ...[96]

Implicitly translating this distinction for contemporary audiences (but without explicitly applying Ibn 'Arabi's categories),[97] Morris removes the 'spiritually intelligent' from the 'common people'. In a similar vein, associates separate out those who have 'receptivity', a quality brought about by a process of 'emptying' oneself of preconditioned views concerning the self and the world, and nurtured through spiritual training.[98] In each case, what results from this qualification is preparedness in the reading process for the receiving of *kashf* ('unveiling'), which provides ultimate, true understanding. As we have seen, Morris suggests that the development of spiritual intelligence (and through this spiritual realisation itself) is in potential a universal human process. For its part, Beshara maintains that every person has potential for receptivity, and thus for understanding Ibn 'Arabi's writings as he intended them to be understood: this potential can be actualised through appropriate spiritual training. Lack of familiarity with the exoteric Islamic sciences is not an obstacle, for even those who are proficient in them but do not advance to the stage of 'verification' remain part of the 'common people', whom such understanding will ultimately elude.

We can finally highlight the Beshara view concerning the necessary qualifications/tools for understanding Ibn 'Arabi's writings through an associate's description of the recommended manner for approaching the *Fusus*. In the Foreword to Volume 2 of the *White Fusus* (which we cited earlier), this associate insists that the only way to arrive at 'a real comprehension' of the text is to ask for God's help, and 'for the aptitude which is capable of receiving the meaning perfectly'.[99] The emphasis is thus on the role of receptivity and *kashf* in attaining comprehension (this same emphasis is also represented in Morris' spiritual intelligence), while the limitations of the intellect are underlined.[100] In contrast with this, the author of a recent partial analysis of the *Fusus* remarks that Ibn 'Arabi's thought 'yields itself only to the most strenuous interpretive efforts and then only partially'.[101] For associates the picture suggested by this remark is presumably that of the scholar who in his solitary endeavours calls exclusively on the tools of the intellect (*'aql*), and thereby actively precludes any possibility of complete understanding. An associate sums the matter up simply: 'to understand Ibn 'Arabi one *has to be* a mystic – it *must* be experiential.'[102]

In sum, Beshara and Morris would see Ibn 'Arabi's works read today by anyone who is sincerely so inclined (for such inclination is itself evidence of a certain spiritual aptitude), regardless of their cultural–religious background and formal qualifications. Accordingly, both underline the importance of the translator's task, and both have energetically assumed this.[103] The aim is to make Ibn 'Arabi's writings widely accessible by identifying and removing potentially discouraging or confounding barriers between these writings and the contemporary spiritual seeker–reader. This opens the way for the receptive and spiritually gifted of all backgrounds to benefit from these writings.[104] In the Beshara perspective the importance of this task derives also from the fact that a wider availability of appropriate translations and accessible presentations will facilitate the expanding assimilation of esoteric knowledge, and thus the unfolding of the incipient new age.

While he projected the potential for receptivity (and thus ultimately for understanding Ibn 'Arabi's message) as inherent to humanity as such, Rauf had at the same time insisted that Beshara was (and must remain) an elitist enterprise, in the specific sense of 'an elitism of "receptivity"'. By way of illustration, associates recall preparations for an advertisement campaign during the early 1980s, with a hired media consultant. The discussion had turned to how Beshara might appeal to 'an ordinary person on the London Underground'. Rauf had been adamant that 'Beshara would not appeal to such an "ordinary person", and if it did appeal to them, this would mean that they were in fact no longer an "ordinary person"'. As an associate explains, such a person would have experienced the inner transformation that manifests in the activation of receptivity, and removes them from the ranks of the 'common people'. Rauf had argued that the 'level' of what was presented in Beshara must not be compromised through simplification, which might threaten to reduce what is elevated to something mundane, doing it a disservice in the process. Writing in relation to the aspiration to make Ibn 'Arabi's works known through the encouragement of publication in the context of the MIAS, an associate made the Beshara understanding in this respect clear:

> Publication is a matter of making public ... 'for people' – *publicus* in Latin means 'of the people'. [Ibn 'Arabi's] work is aimed at 'people', at the best in a human being. It is for everyone, but not just anyone. It is not to be made popular in the sense of popularisation to the lowest common denominator. It is popularisation at the level of the elite which exists in potential in all humankind, popularisation to the highest common denominator.[105]

Ibn 'Arabi (re-) constructed?

Notwithstanding such aspirations, there is perhaps an inevitable danger of reductionism through simplification in popularising any complex figure or thought-system deriving from another age and religious–cultural context. At the same time, 'translation' (linguistic but also cultural, through implicit or explicit de- and re-contextualisation) introduces the possibility of distortion. Furnishing an example not far removed from our own focus, the fate of Rumi in the contemporary West sheds light on this issue. It has been argued that Rumi has recently been made 'functional' in the field of contemporary Western spirituality.[106] Lewis' views regarding this development are pertinent: as for the present case, his discussion returns inexorably to the pivotal issue of the central place of Islam in shaping the legacy in question.

'I watched with delight', Lewis recalls, 'as Rumi won a growing following in North America. I watch now with concern as popular culture dilutes and distorts his message'.[107] As a corrective to such dilution and distortion, Lewis provides a succinct 'Rumi background' at the beginning of his work, introducing his subject 'as Muslim', 'as Sunni', 'as Hanafi', and finally 'as Sufi'. On 'Rumi as Muslim', he writes:

> It simply will not do to extract quotations out of context and present Rumi as a prophet of the presumptions of an unchurched and syncretic spirituality. While Rumi does indeed demonstrate a tolerant and inclusive understanding of religion, he also, we must remember, trained as a preacher ... and a scholar of Islamic law. Rumi did not come to his theology of tolerance and inclusive spirituality by turning away from traditional Islam or organized religion, but through an immersion in it; his spiritual yearning stemmed from a radical desire to follow the example of the Prophet Muhammad and actualize his potential as a perfect Muslim.[108]

He continues:

> As a Muslim, Rumi acknowledged Muhammad's prophethood and professed himself submissive to God. Rumi himself states ... what should be obvious to any careful reader of his poems: he performed the five obligatory prayers that constitute one of the central tenets and requirements of an observant Muslim.[109]

Having elaborated the four dimensions of his identity listed above,[110] Lewis' conclusive characterisation of Rumi is as 'a mystically minded Hanafi scholar'.[111]

An 'Ibn 'Arabi background' versus the Beshara Ibn 'Arabi

Following this gentle re-rooting of Rumi in his rightful traditions, we cautiously venture to profile the main inspiration for Beshara thus:[112] 'as Muslim', 'as Sunni', 'as *mujtahid mutlaq*', and finally 'as Sufi-*muhaqqiq*'.[113] Such a characterisation will not remain without challenge on at least three counts, of course.[114] Nonetheless, it can be fruitfully counterposed to the construct of Ibn 'Arabi (and of what he says to a contemporary Western audience) put forward by Beshara and those who share its approach in making Ibn 'Arabi 'functional' in contemporary Western spirituality. What most concerns us here is the first dimension of his identity posited above, and its implications for what he says to contemporary readers. To this we must add the third dimension, the significance of which lies in what it indicates of his deep involvement with matters of the law or sharia (and his denial of any antagonism between this and the eternal truths to which it points).[115] The following observation by Chittick captures the main point:

> In order to turn his concentration towards its ultimate object and actualize its creative power, man must follow the path of purification and perfection. For Ibn 'Arabi, as for all Sufis, the basis of this path is the practice of Islam. He takes the daily prayers, the fast during Ramadan, etc. – in short, the 'pillars' of Islam – for granted. In words of advice to disciples, we even find him telling them, 'Do not play with your beard or any part of your clothing during the ritual prayer ... and make sure that your back is straight when you bow down' ... A work like *Kunh ma la budd minhu'l-murid*, translated into English as *Instructions to a Postulant*, shows that he considered the sincere and scrupulous practice of both the mandatory commands of the *Shari'ah* and the supererogatory acts recommended by the *Sunnah* as the *sine qua non* of all Sufism.[116]

Beshara does not highlight Ibn 'Arabi's Muslim provenance, but it is perhaps unfair to suggest, following Leaman's critique of Coates' *Ibn 'Arabi and Modern Thought*, that associates summarily dismiss this:

> [A credible approach] would treat with respect Ibn 'Arabi's background, in particular his background as a *Muslim* thinker. This should not be airbrushed out as though it were an embarrassing and unfortunate detail.[117]

Ibn 'Arabi as ecumenist

Yet if Ibn 'Arabi, like Rumi, is to appeal to those Lewis describes as 'unchurched Westerners hungry for some form of non-institutional religion or non-traditional spirituality,'[118] concerns such as those just described by Chittick simply cannot be given prominence (and can perhaps have no place whatever) in projections of him. Far from emphasising his Muslim provenance and frame of reference, the appeal of such projections will be enhanced by an image of an Ibn 'Arabi who accepted all religions, and placed them on an equal footing in a fundamentally ecumenical spirit. Beshara's projection of Ibn 'Arabi implicitly highlights this image, and it is consolidated through an emphasis of the Oneness of Being as a unifying theme.[119] To take but one example, however, his celebrated verses from the *Tarjuman*[120] (adduced by many who uphold him as an advocate of religious tolerance, or even of a 'supra-confessionalism') must be understood in light of Ibn 'Arabi's entire teaching.[121] Such an approach suggests that the image of a man who placed all religions on an equal footing does not remain without challenge.[122]

The Oneness of Being and the perfectibility of man

Leaman's critique of Coates' work points to a second important feature of the Beshara projection of Ibn 'Arabi. He suggests that this associate tends to 'repeat like a mantra *wahdat al-wujud* and little else'.[123] This tendency in Beshara perhaps results from a simplification-driven reductionism, which we suggested earlier as the inevitable price of any endeavour to sum up and render accessible a dauntingly complex and subtle system of thought. Consonant with the expectations of its New Age constituency, the early Beshara focus appears to have been squarely on a surface understanding of *wahdat al-wujud*. It is perhaps significant, for example, that one of the first Beshara publications was a reprint of the 1901 English translation of Balyani's *Risalat al-Ahadiyya*, which had been attributed erroneously to Ibn 'Arabi and published in his name. As Chittick observes, this treatise has often been quoted to illustrate Ibn 'Arabi's understanding of *wahdat al-wujud*, but has informed a skewed understanding of the latter. For,

> Balyani's exposition of *wahdat al-wujud* cannot be put into the same category as that of Ibn al-'Arabi and his immediate disciples, who always took care to offset expressions of God's similarity with descriptions of His incomparability. Where Balyani and others like him say 'He', Ibn al-'Arabi and his followers say 'He/not He' ...[124]

A subtle shift in emphasis has been discernible more recently, at least among long-standing associates, from the Oneness of Being to the principle of the perfectibility of man. This reflects two developments. First is an awareness of the problems surrounding the facile attribution of this expression to Ibn 'Arabi and its application as shorthand for his system, following a revisiting of this in recent scholarship as discussed earlier.[125] Second is a realisation that 'the idea of the Unity of Existence is no longer an exclusively Beshara matter'. In contrast with the situation thirty years ago, an associate explains, 'it is now found all over the world, and is widely accepted'. Another associate suggests that, today, this notion 'is the norm and effectively part of [mainstream] culture, while in the 1960s it was utterly alien and considered almost outrageous'.[126] The perfectibility of man, however, is a legacy of Ibn 'Arabi that 'has not been discussed enough and should be made more widely known'. As for any mystic, an associate recently argued, Ibn 'Arabi's emphasis lay on 'the true potential of the human being and the path to realising that potential, which reaches its completion in the Perfect or Complete Man'. Rather than the doctrine of the Oneness of Being, 'the crux of his teaching is perhaps better described as the perfectibility of Man'.[127] As far as the work of Beshara is concerned, associates suggest that 'the perfectibility of man and the process through which one must go to reach it is the challenge for today'.

The *Fusus* as central Beshara text and its discontents

The Beshara emphasis of the *Fusus* represents a particular (for some a contentious) projection of Ibn 'Arabi's legacy. Rauf had described this text as 'the quintessence of Ibn 'Arabi's teachings'. He would refer to it as 'the Prophet's book', and marvelled constantly at its elevation. It seems he also had intimate knowledge of it.[128] Associates describe the text as 'Ibn 'Arabi's major work'.[129] They emphasise the benefit it encapsulates for people.[130] Their explanations of its importance are couched in terms drawn from Rauf's Foreword to the *White Fusus*, Bosnevi's introduction to his commentary and Ibn 'Arabi's own remarks in the text itself. The *Fusus* conveys 'the taste of Muhammad', they elaborate: 'as it was revealed to Ibn 'Arabi we can be sure that it comes from the most ancient place'.[131] Further, 'it comes directly from God according to His own manner and wish'.[132] The fact that it mentions the word 'beshara' is naturally deemed significant. Thus:

> It can be no coincidence that Beshara is mentioned in the *Fusus* ... in the chapter concerning the Wisdom of Uniqueness in the Word of Hud, and arises in conjunction with the meeting of this prophet of the people of 'Ad with the author of the *Fusus*.[133] Hud corroborates the uniqueness of each individuation and the special face that God shows to each individual. We are told that 'for the creation there is no Beshara (good tidings) greater than this, that Hud with the Word of Truth, announced that Truth, God, is the Ipseity (essence) of all things'.[134]

We underlined earlier the place of the *Fusus* in the historical polemics against Ibn 'Arabi and his school. At the same time, as Morris observes, characterisations of Ibn 'Arabi's thought in Western scholarship have until very recently focused on 'the abstract ontological language and insights' associated with this text.[135] In contemporary Muslim contexts perceptions of the *Fusus* as problematic remain widespread, even among those otherwise favourable to Ibn 'Arabi, and it appears that the *Futuhat* rather than the *Fusus* is 'the most widely read, and most often quoted' of all his works in sufi circles.[136] This bears witness to the continuing reservations that surround it. The 'deliberate interpolation' hypothesis was a historical stratagem for dealing with difficulties presented by such texts from the perspective of 'orthodoxy'. It was used to exonerate the author of the *Fusus* by casting doubt on the text's attribution to him in its present form, on the grounds that specific problematic statements have been interpolated.[137] Such forms of argumentation remain widespread in some contemporary sufi circles.[138] An example arises in the case of Mahmoud al-Ghorab, a well-known Damascus-based Egyptian sufi shaykh and author. From a 'systematic analysis' of the text, he had concluded that the *Fusus* in its extant form 'could not have been authored in its entirety by Ibn 'Arabi'.[139] Al-Ghorab relates an encounter with the MIAS. Having already contributed a chapter to *Muhyiddin Ibn 'Arabi: A Commemorative Volume*, in 1996 he submitted an article for publication in the *JMIAS*. This encompassed what he describes as a 'point-by-point proof' of his case concerning the *Fusus*.[140] An exchange of correspondence ensued with the Journal Editor, and the article was not published. In al-Ghorab's view, this outcome was due to the fact that his arguments 'threatened to undermine the foundations of the entire edifice of Beshara and the work of Rauf, in their according of a central place to the *Fusus*'. For his part, the Editor had countered al-Ghorab's arguments concerning the *Fusus* by referring to certificates of audition associated with the copy under discussion.[141]

This episode illustrates contrasting attitudes towards the *Fusus* among a sector of Arab Muslim sufi opinion, and in Beshara. In response to Gilis' insistence cited earlier that it was unacceptable to interpret the *Fusus* in a way that contradicts Ibn 'Arabi's other writings (which he had also received through divine inspiration), Rauf advanced an uncompromising defence of the text's unique and uniquely authoritative status:

> It is an important factor for everyone who is a student of Ibn 'Arabi that, although the actual 'pen to paper' writing of the *Fusus* is by the Shaykh, the contents of the text he puts down on paper is not his own since he affirms that from other than what was given to him to write there is 'nothing added' to the text by him nor 'anything left out' of it by him. The whole book was put into his hands by the Envoy himself ... Consequently a student, a follower or a lover of the Greatest Shaykh is necessarily the follower and lover of what the Greatest Shaykh represents as meaning or mystery of Mohammed the Envoy and the Reality of Realities that the Archetypal man represents. Through the *Fusus* ... Ibn 'Arabi acquires the magnitude of the interior meaning of God and His Self Manifestation as His Beloved. To place the *Fusus al-Hikam*, Ibn 'Arabi's *Magnum Opus*, although less in volume, on an equal footing with any of the other writings of the Greatest Shaykh, is not to give credence to his contention.[142]

For the very reason that it serves well the approach and ethos of Beshara, a primary focus on the *Fusus* as the complete measure of Ibn 'Arabi's teaching (in its capacity as 'a meaning which requires us to move from where we are')[143] potentially alienates some outsiders who might have found common ground with the movement, based on a shared appreciation of his oeuvre. In this regard, Rauf's institution of the 'philosophical' tradition of commentary on the text (which formed a particular strand in the transmission of Ibn 'Arabi's teaching) as the focus of study in Beshara is equally significant. Chittick argues that Qunawi effectively initiated this tradition, for his explicit endeavour had been to demonstrate that the 'school of verification' (as he understood it) was largely in harmony with *falsafa*, and 'to bring Ibn 'Arabi into the mainstream of Islamic philosophy'.[144] It was continued and accentuated by Jandi, Kashani and Qaysari.[145] Later on Bosnevi, whose commentary occupies a key place in Beshara, 'made an especially valuable contribution to the philosophical exposition of Ibn 'Arabi's ideas'.[146]

By focusing on the trend of philosophical exposition of Ibn 'Arabi's teaching expressed in the *Fusus* commentaries, Rauf presented an intellectually demanding, if relatively systematic, exposition of this. At the same time, he established a subtle emphasis in the form in which this teaching is conveyed in Beshara. Not everyone may concur with his argument, but Chittick's evaluation of the impact of Qunawi's purpose and methodology in shaping his exposition of Ibn 'Arabi's teaching is pertinent here. He has argued that Qunawi and his followers 'placed many of Ibn 'Arabi's important teachings in the background'.[147] Moreover, Qunawi's 'relatively systematic exposition and his focus on philosophical issues rather than on Qur'an and *Hadith* do not square with his sources, and presumably not with the oral instructions that he had received from his master [Ibn 'Arabi]'.[148] Chittick cites Chodkiewicz's opinion that Qunawi had thus brought about 'a necessary, though perhaps unfortunate, adjustment of Ibn 'Arabi's teachings to the intellectual needs of the times'.[149] Such observations arguably point to a preference for developing a 'philosophical' or abstract, theoretical elaboration on the content of the *Fusus*. The latter itself encompasses relatively little of an explicitly exoteric Islamic character, dealing rather with the communication of metaphysical Truth to man at the origin, unconnected to any particular form, revelation or religion.[150] Given the character of the text, Qunawi and his followers might have chosen through their commentaries to 'restore' to it the esoteric–exoteric dialectic/balance evident in Ibn 'Arabi's oeuvre as a whole, through a systematic explanatory resort to scripture and the exoteric discourse of Islam.

Through the privileged place accorded to the *Fusus* and the 'philosophical' commentary tradition inaugurated by Qunawi and represented later by Bosnevi,[151] the appropriation of Ibn 'Arabi's teaching in Beshara reflects an 'adjustment' to the times analogous to that which Chodkiewicz posits as the legacy of Qunawi. An associate recently argued that the early propagators of Ibn 'Arabi's works

> undertook their work in a truly Akbarian fashion – not by slavish literality, but by opening their hearts to the inner spirit of [Ibn 'Arabi's] vision, whilst at the same time taking account of outer circumstances in order to express its meaning in the best manner for their time and place.[152]

This is suggestive of the internal perception of Rauf's purpose in his selective approach to Ibn 'Arabi's oeuvre, and his focus on the *Fusus*.

Chapter 8

Beshara and sufism in the modern world

To sum up, we revisit Beshara as a NRM associated with the New Age, and situate it in terms of our typology of sufi spirituality in the West. More speculatively, we then explore possible trajectories of sufi spirituality/sufism in Western and in Muslim majority societies at the start of the twenty-first century, drawing on the Beshara experience to illuminate this broader discussion.[1] In the West, we consider the implications of major cultural shifts associated with modernity for religion and spirituality in general, and for attitudes towards sufism and Islam in particular; accordingly, we flag potential outcomes for universal and Islamic sufism. The twentieth-century sufi experience in Western arenas has been shaped by social and cultural forces generated by distinctive historical circumstances. Giving due notice to historical /cultural specificities (and without positing the Western case as universal paradigm), by reflecting on the Western encounter with sufism we can illuminate aspects of its potential development in majority Muslim arenas. Two factors are particularly relevant here. First is modernisation, which can be framed in terms of an aspiration towards culturally distinctive modernities that draw on indigenous resources in Muslim countries. Second is the accelerating penetration of New Age spiritualities and NRMs from the West into Muslim countries. In all spheres of life processes of economic and cultural globalisation and the accompanying flows of products, ideas and people have generated novel interfaces with local resources and new developments. This is evident in the arena of spirituality/religion as in any other, and has had particularly significant outcomes for sufi spirituality. The processes and trends that concern us are at their sharpest in what may be described as the 'cosmopolitan' arenas of Muslim settings: these are mainly in major cities and their environs (and in some towns), where wealth can be found and where substantial professional middle and upper-middle classes have developed. Such arenas form the focus of the final part of this chapter.

Situating Beshara

Beshara is beyond the limitations of any religion or philosophy and can in no way be placed in any category.

'Beshara: Swyre Farm' leaflet

A new religious movement?

Beshara takes its place within the constellation of NRMs that have emerged in the West during the last fifty years. That it is 'new' is beyond doubt, the manner of its appearance in Britain at the turn of the 1960s placing it squarely within the overall phenomenon of NRMs. Moreover, its application of the tradition upon which it draws is evidently innovative and unconventional.[2] How apt are the two other elements in the term NRM when applied to Beshara? Like some other movements nonetheless classified as NRMs, Beshara explicitly denies that it is a religion.[3] It would indeed be anathema for it to add 'a further source of division' by positing itself, in one associate's words, as 'yet another religion'. Nonetheless, as Barker argues, movements may be regarded as 'religious' if they offer a religious/philosophical worldview, or claim to provide the means by which a higher goal can be obtained (transcendent knowledge, spiritual enlightenment or 'true' development, for example). Understood in this way, the term can be applied to groups which, like Beshara, provide their members with 'ultimate answers to fundamental questions', such as 'the meaning of life' and 'one's place in the nature of things'.[4]

What about the term 'movement'?[5] We have highlighted Beshara's internal cohesion, based on associates' common self-perceptions, worldview and practice, and their shared histories. First-generation associates in particular display consistency in understanding, attitude and opinion, but a degree of uniformity is discernible among all those involved. Drawing on a common set of resources, associates repeat the same analogies, turns of phrase, images and textual quotations. This bears witness to the effectiveness of Beshara education; at the same time, it points to the carefully circumscribed conceptual universe to which students are exposed. The role of the School in Beshara's persistence as a distinct and internally cohesive movement must be underlined. Associates themselves emphasise the life-long bonds that are established among them as fellow students on courses, and the lasting, shared rhythms they acquire.[6] Their shared belonging is reinforced in a number of ways by the network that pivots on the School, itself consolidated by the constant traffic of associates to and fro for visits and events. Worthy of mention are associates' use of designated names and the visible identifiers upon their persons and in their significant spaces (the symbol *Hu* and the *Hizb al-wiqaya*). Important too is their participation in regular joint activities such as *dhikr* and local study groups,[7] and the ample flow of information from the School and across the network. All of this points to the fact that, like other NRMs, Beshara is implicitly separated from the wider society.[8]

Dual identities

Yet associates do not self-identify as members of a NRM (or any other kind of social movement, for that matter). They are averse to any notion of membership in a discrete movement set apart from the remainder of society/humanity. As one puts it, 'Beshara is the announcement of what human beings really are. It is not something invented, produced or created. Anyone involved in it or who sees its value will reject any formulation like membership as incorrect and invidious.' Associates consider themselves participants in an enterprise of an altogether different order which ultimately encompasses all of humanity, and is part of a divine plan.[9] They maintain that Beshara cannot be reduced to the mundane phenomena in which they are visibly involved (the School and Trust and their activities 'in the world' described in this volume), for it is simultaneously a reflection and crystallisation of 'a movement from the side of the Real'. This is by nature universal, and manifests in the relative world in many different forms. Associates' perceptions of the sixties illuminate this understanding of the dual nature of Beshara, by clarifying its origins. One describes the sense of 'opening, optimism and spirituality' of the time as 'something very important and real'. He argues that the many movements appearing during the sixties were themselves the *effect* of a divine impulse, rather than the *cause* of a new search for spirituality.[10] The variety of spiritual trends that appeared at the time is attributed to the fact that this impulse expresses itself differently in accordance with the receptivity of the place of its manifestation (a receptivity it has conferred on each place). Beshara is one of many such forms in the relative world, and is thus by definition limited. At the same time, however, it is an encapsulation of the very essence of the signification of the divine impulse itself, without addition or interpretation. As such, it potentially represents much more than just one out of many such spiritual movements.[11] Young sums up the matter:

> [Beshara] is good news in that it is the perennial announcement from our interior, from our essence, of its essential oneness to ourselves, which is its exterior. If you think about it, this is the good news which can free us from the illusion of self if we are receptive to it. At one point I thought that I understood what Beshara is; now I am quite sure that I don't. And it seems that this not knowing is altogether more satisfactory and healthy, because what we study leads us to the conclusion that Beshara is not at all something which is invented or brought about by people. It is a name for a movement from the one reality to the individual man. Beshara is from the Divine side, and therefore for a human being to claim to understand it would be at best partial. All of us who are involved are still finding out what it is, and I think that will continue. You see, in a sense, what is happening now as Beshara is not new. Ever since there has been man capable of knowing himself, there has been an emergence of what might be called 'the perennial tradition' which has been known to a few. It has emerged in the great figures from time to time, in Socrates, for instance, or in Lao Tzu. What is new about Beshara is that the know-ledge is accessible to all people. This school, for example, is open to anyone, from any tradition.[12]

The dual concept of 'what Beshara is' informs an ongoing internal debate concerning the nature, and consequently the responsibilities and work, of Beshara.[13] The ideal understanding emphasises Beshara as divine impulse in the form of a universal and global movement, of which the School is one manifestation. This perspective informs an awareness of the need ultimately to transcend the relativity of the movement's form, and the cultivation of a self-consciously universal outlook. It also shapes three significant aspects of the ethos and modus operandi of Beshara as a movement.

First is the absence of explicit 'entry' criteria. While most associates have completed a Beshara course and this is seen as the natural step, it is not a formal requirement.[14] Conversely, there is a reliance on voluntary defection from the movement as necessary, and no explicit internal controls operate. Thus, as Young explains, 'people take themselves away from Beshara if they are not at ease, and so it is not necessary to take any steps in relation to them'. (Like others, the movement has had its share of mavericks, who have eventually self-excluded.) Second is a minimalist organisational culture, described in terms of 'a resistance from within to any attempt to make "a corporate organisation" out of Beshara'. Associates characterise its approach to self-organisation as 'a swell in the ocean', for different people come to the fore to carry out a specific task, only to recede once it has been completed.[15] Third is the approach to the administration and development of the movement's institutions and activities. An associate recently summed up thinking on this matter thus: 'There is no one in charge of Beshara except God Himself. Direction will always come "from above".' Accordingly, associates are careful to 'give all power of arrangement and organisation to God'.[16] Perceptions of the property at Chisholme provide a good indication of the attitude informed by such perceptions. Young relates that Rauf 'had been clear that Chisholme House had been given' because of the importance of Beshara's work, and he had realised that 'a physical place is not given to just anyone'. A director of the Chisholme Institute describes the property as 'a gift from the Real for a specific purpose'. Reflecting on how the directors should approach their task, he points out that the purpose behind acquisition of the property

> implies a responsibility of acknowledging its source, and by virtue of that being receptive to what is required and not imposing personal preferences and understandings. It is not for the directors to have opinions at all – it is for them to be receptive to what is required in the discharge of their responsibilities, based on the understanding that the School is a gift from the Real. The directors' job is to take themselves out of the way in terms of personal colouring, and this characterises meetings. We observe ablution before the meetings, in order to be in the correct mode. All business is dealt with in the spirit of asking 'what is the appropriate response?' The directors do not consider themselves to be directing anything: they realise who the Real Director is. The establishment of the Chisholme Institute itself separate from the Beshara Trust was at the time considered the appropriate mode for the reception and use of the gift of Chisholme. There should not be any dissonance between what the metaphysics we study shows plus the four key areas of activity and the five qualities on the one hand,[17] and the running of the Chisholme Institute, on the other. There is a requirement for it all to be consistent.[18]

Strategies for change

As a NRM, Beshara focuses on the individual as the primary arena for the change it seeks to facilitate in preparation for the ultimate goal, actualised in bringing about the new age.[19] A poster put up around the London Underground as part of a publicity campaign during the early 1970s thus read: 'You may not be able to change the world, but can you change yourself?' Real change takes place at the level of the individual, through self-knowledge, and it has 'universal effect.'[20] Starting with the individual, a collective change of heart can eventually be achieved and, ultimately, the world will be changed. As one associate puts it, 'Real change takes place in ourselves – in our hearts, in a change of consciousness, and not at the hands of leaders or politicians, who won't or can't change.'[21] Young emphasises that the 'work' undertaken by students on courses 'does not end with themselves', for its ultimate purpose is expansion of the esoteric vision that will take man to the culmination of his spiritual evolution.[22] As a 'locus of potential receptivity', each person has a part to play in the fulfilment of this destiny.[23]

Associates recognise that there are problems in the current order on earth, the results of the institutionalised domination of the illusory self. There are also hinted perceptions of the responsibility of current modes of socialisation for the sorry condition of the individual, exiled from knowledge of their true nature. Projecting Chisholme and its courses as the proper context for achieving self-knowledge, for example, Young expressed the following oblique criticism: 'It is as if we are brought up nowadays without a context for understanding these things.'[24] However, Beshara does not reject the current order outright, for the phenomenal world is a 'theatre of manifestation' for the One Being, and 'the whole of reality, God's vast earth including ourselves'[25] is thus ultimately theophanic. As Coates puts it,

> The unique configuration of predominating qualities of the modern era which constitute what Eric Hobsbawm described as 'the greatest transformation in history since remote times' are none other than part of the infinity and inherent contents of the Self-disclosure of Being in Its love to be known.[26]

Associates indeed applaud aspects of the present order (such as technological advances), deeming these indispensable to fulfilment of the purpose of Beshara, in accordance with the Divine Will. The movement can thus be described as world-accommodating,[27] bearing in mind that, for associates, the only reality the phenomenal world ultimately has is 'as a forever-in-the-making modality of the One Being.'[28]

Seclusion is not the way of Beshara, for Rauf insisted that associates pursue the spiritual path in the world after their period of spiritual education, building families and careers there. Although 'the way in the world' is more difficult, he explained, it would 'take them further'. He emphasised that, 'whereas some seek wisdom through a retreat from the world, Beshara should offer a place from which to gain a perspective and understanding which ... correlates this world into a coherent picture.'[29] Associates were, as one puts it, 'to penetrate the fabric of existence to uncover what universality means, for, reflecting the progression of the *batin* becoming *zahir*, it is very much something of this world.'[30] The spiritual orientation towards life projected by Beshara indeed becomes meaningful, as another puts it, 'in its expression in the outer world.'[31]

Across the years Young and other associates have occasionally responded from the Beshara perspective to significant world events, typically by calling for a global consciousness. Their efforts in this regard have remained confined to internal media such as the *MIAS Newsletter* or the Beshara website, however. There does not appear to be any effort presently to engage through mainstream media or to apprise the powerful and eminent of the movement's ideas and concerns. Associates are moreover disinterested in participating in conventional politics. The School remains the pivot in the focus on individual change, as the movement's powerhouse. The transformation of the individual is not the only fruit, however, for the very practices undertaken during that process, and thereafter by the transformed, contribute incrementally to preparation for the momentous changes ahead. Young relates that, by 1980, Rauf had said of Chisholme that the work of Beshara 'must be in the walls by now'. He himself recently suggested that it might become possible in the future for visitors to experience 'the work that is being done at Chisholme' simply through their physical presence there.

Kindred spirits

As we suggested earlier, Beshara has projected all contemporary movements involved in comparable work as the varied expressions of the single universal divine impulse. Accordingly, it has perceived kindred spirits – and ultimately itself – in these:

> Beshara ... is the name of a spiritual emergence, and an inclination towards a ... universal perspective, that lies behind so many movements in the world today. Beshara is no-one's exclusive domain ... like the 'yeast in the dough' it is discernible within all movements that aspire to a holistic understanding.[32]

First-generation associates suggest a strong affinity between the ideas and approach they encountered in Beshara, and those of two figures in contemporary spirituality whose works they were more likely to have read than others: Bennett and Krishnamurti. By the late 1960s, Krishnamurti had come to enjoy such celebrity and success that he has been described as *the* Western guru of the time. He had become 'a star of the New Age synthesis' in the campuses of Californian universities, but also enjoyed worldwide popularity.[33] As for Bennett,[34] the following characterisation sums up his spiritual career:

> No one responded more enthusiastically to the late-twentieth-century blend of ecology, esotericism, science and eschatology than J. G. Bennett. Indeed, one might say that [he] was a typical New Age figure ... exploring every possible avenue and ready to unify his discoveries in a personal syncretism. The final decades of his life saw him on a rapidly accelerating trip through all the available alternatives as he rushed from guru to guru in search of the elusive Source – only to find it at last within himself.[35]

A movement of the New Age?

Throughout this volume, we have pointed to aspects of the connection between Beshara and the New Age. Here, we revisit two key areas by way of summing up. Interrelated but separated for the sake of clarity, these are the characteristic New Age worldview, and its modes of affiliation/self-organisation. Before proceeding, two questions must be addressed. First, do those involved object to the association of Beshara with the New Age posited here? And second, how helpful is scholarly use of the term New Age today? Negative media coverage and increasing commercialisation during the 1980s prompted many considered central to the New Age to dissociate themselves from the label by the beginning of the 1990s.[36] More recently, some scholars have joined them in a preference for alternative labels.[37] While such reservations must be kept in mind, we advance two grounds for retaining the term to describe Beshara. First is the historical approach we have adopted in this volume, focusing on the context of its formation in the late 1960s/early 1970s, and mapping its development in the decades since. Second, we maintain that the term effectively captures its distinctive, explicit and central 'millenarian' focus on the coming of a new era.[38] Beshara's history has unfolded within that of a trend comfortably described by its first-generation spokespersons as New Age. Scholars today describe this trend as New Age only with reservations conveyed by use of quotations marks, sensitive to the fact that some now see it as 'a pejorative, even meaningless epithet.'[39] Others argue that it is 'time to drop' the concept of New Age altogether, for, as an 'essentialized category', it can only obscure our understanding of ongoing religious change in the twenty-first century.[40] Reflecting such realities, some associates feel uncomfortable when Beshara is discussed in relation to the New Age, sensing that this detracts from the perceived gravity of their project. At the same time, however, first-generation associates insist that their activities were indeed 'of the New Age', and look back nostalgically on the sixties as its 'fullest expression'.

A New Age worldview

The Beshara worldview evinces a strong affinity with that of the New Age. It shares its metaphysical monism (and accompanying holism and emphasis on unity and interconnectedness), and its Self-spirituality (with the epistemological individualism and emphasis on inner authority that flow from this). It has in common with the New Age its perennialism and its detraditionalised approach. The former furnishes the ultimate rationale for Beshara's focus, projected as what is essential to all the religions.[41] The latter is responsible for the characteristic 'simplicity' of its perspective, as described by associates, and the absence from it of 'anything doctrinaire'. It also underlines the centrality to Beshara of the 'cardinal New Age value', 'real freedom', to be 'who you really are, to be your true self', by 'giving up all the limitations of the illusory ego self'.[42] Prominent too are the characteristic New Age faith in the new science and the presumption of spiritual evolution underpinning the unfolding of a new age. We can look more closely at two of these areas that appear to raise some questions.

Monism supreme

The monistic assumption of the sacred Self in Beshara coexists in a dialectical relationship with a dualistic dimension, expressed in the conceptual language of theism.[43] Individual associates emphasise this theistic aspect to varying degrees,[44] but it always appears as detraditionalised.[45] What is prioritised is not the search for salvation via prescriptions and rites drawn from an established tradition with its texts and authorities, but actualisation, through practices that achieve a 'going within'.[46] The theistic dimension thus does not disqualify the Beshara perspective as a part of the New Age. Moreover, as we suggested earlier, the element of Self-spirituality ultimately wins the day, while 'the dynamics of theistic religiosity' represent only a partial aspect of this.[47] For those who first encounter Beshara, it is undoubtedly the monistic facet that predominates. The Beshara brochure confronts the reader with a direct expression of this hallmark of New Age thinking, through the question 'If you are the Oyster what is the Pearl?' On the facing page is the response that, through self-knowledge, one comes to realise 'that the One Real Being is one's very essence and that oneself is its own "envelope"'. One associate sums it up thus: 'It is not a question of achieving or changing anything, but of unveiling and coming to realise the already-existing perfection, which is also our own perfection.'[48] Another writes:

> I first came across Ibn 'Arabi ... through ... *The Twenty-nine Pages* ... I was immediately struck by the vastness of what had been presented ... when we began to study the *Fusus* ... I began to understand a personal connection to this knowledge ... This was a direct invitation to something other than the heaven proposed by conventional religion or the following of a particular way, and it seemed to be addressed to me no less than to any other human being ... During subsequent years of study ... it seemed that the subject never really left this point: that there was in us an essential condition of identity and that this was not something ultimately realised through intellectual understanding or good actions, was not something we could ever become, but something which had to be ... utterly accepted as what is.[49]

Only as their familiarity with Ibn 'Arabi's thought progresses do associates grasp the nuances embedded in the 'theistic qualification' of the monistic view.[50]

Inner authority

[I]f there is too much external authority ... one can conclude that one is no longer with the New Age ... Messages from without ... must always be mediated by experience or intuition for what is going on to be designated 'New Age'.
                                    Paul Heelas, *The New Age Movement*, p. 35

The Beshara project rests on the conviction that immediate essential knowledge of Reality can be had without intermediary, and with minimal formal apparatus. Thus the concept of esoteric education is premised on the belief that the requisite knowledge is achieved, as the Beshara brochure puts it, 'through our very being, through our own core structure'. A strong emphasis on inner authority is intensified in Beshara by the explicit, principled repudiation of the institution of the teacher as such, which has been evident throughout this volume. In Beshara there are no teachers. On offer instead is a context set up and run by those who have begun to grasp what it means to go within: here, participants are enabled to arrive at their own experiences. Rauf had compared Beshara to a university, where there are no teachers, in contrast with a primary or secondary school, where there are. His radical rejection of the institution of the teacher is projected in some internal accounts of the Beshara founding narrative as an important pull factor. Some of those who became involved may have had unhelpful encounters with spiritual teachers, or were generally repelled by the 'guru-centric' spirituality that had become prominent.[51]

Reflecting Rauf's clear emphasis on inner experience, associates taste and test the Self as compass from the outset. One associate describes his first experience of reading Ibn 'Arabi in the following terms, for example:

> When I first encountered Ibn 'Arabi, I had a sense I was reading something that corroborated what I myself had felt. It felt right, but of course I realised I did not understand it at that time.[52]

During a talk at a career event for young people in 1987, another implicitly described the ethos of the Beshara schools in terms of the New Age emphasis of inner authority:

> At this stage of world history, people are less willing to depend on outside authorities. They want to know for themselves. People need to be ready for a new level of understanding in this shifting world, relying on their own inner certainty as an anchor, not on any temporary external structures or edifices of imposed belief.[53]

Inner authority is underlined to students as the key in approaching the performance of spiritual practices (and the ablution preparatory to them). As Young explains:

> Generally, we encourage our students to cultivate taste and sentiment in practice. Therefore there is no absolute prescription for this. It is for them to find out from themselves what is best, and our advice and recommendations will be geared towards this, rather than performing a ritual correctly.[54]

We can also illustrate Self-referentiality in Beshara through the key concepts of perfect servanthood ('the servant is he who hears that which is enacted through him'),[55] and 'verification' ('seeing for oneself, knowing what arises within at each moment').[56] Such concepts point to the general convergence between the New Age emphasis on the one hand, and mystical or gnostic teachings, which accord primacy to experience over reason/faith and stress that man in his deepest essence is one with divine reality, on the other.[57]

While the clear emphasis on unmediated individualism in Beshara illustrated here points to a strong affinity with the New Age, we must consider two areas of apparent tension within it. First is the possibility that Ibn 'Arabi functions for associates as an 'external' voice of authority.[58] As discussed earlier, in Beshara Ibn 'Arabi's authority is perceived to derive ultimately from his role as a conduit for the expression of Truth. It hinges on his status as realised man, the ultimate aspiration of Self-spirituality. According to the Beshara brochure, 'Students are encouraged not to place their reliance on any external authority, since the best teacher is Reality Itself.' For Beshara Reality Itself, the Reality within, is what speaks through Ibn 'Arabi. Ultimately, then, authority vested in him is vested not in an external authority, but in the Reality within each individual seeker, the Self. Furthermore, while associates describe the ultimate purpose of all of Ibn 'Arabi's teachings as 'the transformation of man' (a central New Age theme), as we have seen, his legacy is applied selectively and in a thoroughly detraditionalised manner.[59]

The second area that calls for investigation concerns the dialectic between the principle of 'no teachers' and the dynamics of group situations, where a natural tendency to defer to greater experience or insight arises. The role of teachers and their status as a locus of authority in New Age groups is diverse, ranging from mere facilitating through de facto authority to a 'benevolent dictatorship'. The influence of the more integrated state of the teacher is personalised by some seekers, who may vest considerable authority in them; this can be the case in spite of the teacher's explicit protestations. Some teachers turn a blind eye to this process, and finally come to embrace the image projected on them by their followers. The issue of authority and its mediation is central to all spiritual groups, but the dialectic of Self-authority and the authority projected on or assumed by the teacher emerges as a particular challenge within the New Age. The absence of an expectation that seekers should 'simply *listen* to what they have to say'[60] without it being mediated by inner experience may indeed be typical of New Age teachers. Nonetheless, human nature produces situations where the teacher's voice all but silences the seeker's Self.

Beshara provides an apt case through which to explore this dialectic because of its explicit repudiation of the institution of the teacher/spiritual guide/guru/chosen figure.[61] Pointing to the issue of authority that is the crux of the matter, one associate describes the importance of the Beshara position in terms of breaking a cycle of claimed authority: 'by attributing things to one's teacher, one can claim authority for oneself'. Such awareness notwithstanding, some associates have yet tended towards an exaggerated emphasis of Rauf as their personal teacher. The most prominent example is Feild: the recent launch of a website dedicated to Rauf under Beshara Trust sponsorship was indeed conceived as a corrective to his continuing claims on the internet that Rauf had been his 'teacher'.[62] Longer-lasting associates than Feild are more careful in projecting their relationship with Rauf, even if some of them have also undoubtedly sought the security of the authority of Rauf (or more recently of Young) over that of the Self.

Modes of affiliation and self-organisation

It is generally accepted that modes of affiliation and organisation (and associated concepts of leadership) form crucial grounds for distinguishing between the NAM as a whole and NRMs. For example, Bruce argues that to call most expressions of the New Age 'movements' is 'to imply a degree of cohesion and structure which they do not possess,'[63] while Heelas suggests that 'Perhaps only as few as 5 or 10 per cent of New Agers belong to and are faithful members of particular New Age organizations.'[64] The relatively few well-organised NRMs that can be associated with the New Age thus form the exception, when compared with the typically looser networks, communities, centres, camps, festivals, etc. that make up the very diverse modes of affiliation within the NAM.

Hanegraaff offers a key to assessing whether a particular NRM might be situated within the NAM, based on modes of affiliation and organisation (which of course have their significant implications for areas of doctrine and practice). He too locates the defining character of the NAM as a whole in an absence of generally recognised leaders and organisations (and hence of normative doctrines and common practices). However, he attaches a significant qualification to this characterisation: 'it cannot be doubted that there exist many clearly organized movements with leaders, specific doctrines and practices which do describe themselves explicitly as "New Age", side by side with movements which are often associated with New Age by others although they refer to themselves by more specific designations.'[65] Hanegraaff projects the NAM as a specific historical stage in the development of what sociologists of religion have termed the 'cultic milieu' in modern Western societies, a feature highly conducive to the spawning of cults. It is a kind of cultural 'underground' current of beliefs and ideas, held by vast numbers of individuals with varying degrees of commitment and without their being expressed in an organised setting, that from the culturally dominant or majority viewpoint seem more or less unorthodox or deviant. This supportive milieu witnesses the continual rise and collapse of cultic movements. These are receptive towards each other's beliefs due to a shared concern with the defence of individual liberty of belief and practice, and the presence of the mystical tradition, which feeds a tendency towards tolerance and syncretism. The cultic milieu is united by 'the shared ideology of "seekership", a concept applied to "persons who have adopted a problem-solving perspective while defining conventional religious institutions and beliefs as inadequate"'.[66]

In specific terms, Hanegraaff suggests that the NAM is 'synonymous with the cultic milieu having become conscious of itself as constituting a more or less unified "movement"'.[67] Schematising the sharply contrasting characteristics of cult and sect based on Campbell's seminal discussion of the cultic milieu,[68] he suggests that a particular actor within the wider field of NRMs may be considered to qualify as New Age 'the more they diverge from sect characteristics and approach the cultic profile'.[69] In applying this paradigm to elucidate the commonalities of Beshara and the New Age, an important qualification must be borne in mind. This is expressed in Campbell's sensitivity to the inherent tension between cultic characteristics and cults themselves, which led him to conclude that 'the organizational form most typical of the cultic milieu is not the cult but the "society of seekers"'.[70] It must also be pointed out that New Age spiritualities have gradually moved into the mainstream, and thus away from the 'disapproval and even outright hostility of the organisations representing cultural orthodoxy' faced by the cultic milieu. We will return to this point below.[71]

In applying Hanegraaff's schematisation of the cult–sect dichotomy to Beshara,[72] we bear in mind features of the movement's self-organisation and modus operandi discussed above. Of the cultic characteristics he lists, Beshara scores at least six out of ten (individualistic; loosely structured; few demands on members; tolerant; inclusivist; rudimentary organisation). In contrast, it scores at most a possible four out of ten of the sectarian characteristics listed (stable; stable belief systems; stable organisation; persisting over time), all of which may require a longer-term perspective for their proper evaluation. This is also the case for those cultic characteristics it may not share (transient; fluctuating belief systems; highly ephemeral). In contrast, those characteristics it does *not* share with the sectarian profile are currently beyond any doubt (collectivist; tightly structured; many demands on members; intolerant; exclusivist). On this basis we conclude that, as a NRM, Beshara must be situated closer to the cultic profile, while it diverges significantly from sect characteristics. This underlines its affinity with the New Age.

On Beshara, sufism and Muslim identity

Drawing on the sufi tradition detached from its Islamic origins and identity, Beshara represents an articulation of the trend we have designated universal sufism. While Rauf is situated in 2b in our working typology (Appendix 1), his explicit distancing of Beshara from *sufism* as well as from Islam sets him apart from other figures there, who have typically claimed to uphold sufism properly understood. For example, Vilayat Khan argued that sufism lies at the heart of every religion while transcending them all: this is the 'sufism' the Sufi Order claims to embrace. In contrast, Rauf did not dwell on the true content and purpose of sufism or its relation to the world's religions. For him, it represented another prisoner of the ephemeral world of forms and traditions. As such, it could not serve as a divinely designated medium for the individual spiritual path and the fulfilment of man's spiritual destiny in the contemporary era, and the attempt to rehabilitate it was thus misplaced. In this respect, Rauf shared elements in common with figures in 2a in our typology, who applied its resources to the end of self-transformation without identifying with the sufi tradition as such (in Rauf's case without the syncretism evident among others.)

The repudiation of sufism in Beshara represents an explicit severing of tenuous connections with the cultural world of Islam that survive among other universal sufis by virtue of their explicit embrace of sufism, however the latter is constructed. Its position in this respect has implications for the potential appeal of Beshara to various constituencies, which we will consider shortly. To conclude our attempt to situate Beshara here, we can finally revisit Rauf's project in terms of his provenance as a Turkish Muslim.

The twentieth century was largely defined in the Muslim experience by the problem of how to construct a Muslim identity for a changing world, as modernity and its nationalist aspects, which had interrupted Muslims' links to the past, had shattered the collective Muslim identity.[73] Rauf did not conceptualise the future in terms of the specific identities of the Muslim *umma* or Turkish society, however. His concern was with humanity as whole, and with constructing a global human identity by retrieving what he believed to be its essential and original articulation. This encompassing perspective reflected the cosmopolitan values of his social and educational background, but it also bore witness to the damage sustained by the Muslim collective identity. The quest for primordial identities is commonly awakened by the experience of exile. Exile did not drive Rauf to Islam, however, but to a universal human identity based on a supra-religious spirituality built on the teachings of a leading light of the sufi tradition. Rauf witnessed the powerful resonance of this emphasis with the changing horizons of the counterculture seekers he met. He may indeed have anticipated that ongoing changes in modes of engagement with the sacred in Western societies would secure its continuing appeal, for he told associates that the spirituality he envisaged would find its place there.

Sufism and the shifting sands of the West

Contemporary society is in a dilemma. It appears to 'need' religion as a container of spirit, but does not want it or, for various historical reasons, cannot accept it in its traditional form.

David Tacey, p. 127

Tradition is now made for self, rather than self for tradition.
Paul Heelas and Linda Woodhead, Homeless Minds Today?, p. 66

For many people today, to set aside their own path in order to conform to some external authority just doesn't seem comprehensible as a form of spiritual life.
Charles Taylor[74]

As suggested in Chapter 1, changes in religion that came to the fore during the 1960s laid significant foundations for the religious architecture of the advanced industrialised societies of the West into the twenty-first century. Sociologists have mapped a gradual shift in religion from a culture of duty and obligation to one of choice in these societies, in an increasingly pluralist religious environment. An image has become established of the individual seeker actively engaged in exploring and experimenting on various paths. Seekers 'shop' (and 'consume'), according to this image, in a (rational-) choice based marketplace, where religions and religious/spiritual providers compete with each other for a share.[75] Religion has become more a matter for personal concern than ever before, while the sacred is becoming 'detached from traditional containers and retainers'.[76]

A critical aspect of the profound changes in attitude towards the sacred in these societies has recently been captured by Heelas and Woodhead *et al.*, in the thesis that they are witnessing a 'spiritual revolution'. This involves specifically a shift *from* religion *to* spirituality.[77] The decline of institutionalised traditional religion (particularly Christianity, with its belief in a personal God), which became significant during the 1960s, proceeds apace.[78] Yet atheism and agnosticism have not increased significantly,[79] for those who leave behind religion in the traditional sense have not abandoned their concern for the sacred. Identifying themselves as 'spiritual' as opposed to 'religious' (and as believers in 'some sort of spirit or life-force'), they are expressing this concern through alternative formulations and channels.[80]

Some characterise the spirituality embodied by this growing sector as 'spirituality of life',[81] but it can also be thought of in terms of the Self-spirituality encountered in the NAM. Its general thrust can be understood in terms of the modern landscape. As touched on earlier, this features a fundamental turn to the self, but also, through its broadening out, to 'here and now' life in general as a value. In particular, this means life experienced as intensely personal, and as encompassing the interior life.[82] The turn to the self/life reflects the corrosive effects of modernity on tradition (understood as 'supra-self' authorities lying outside of the individual self and claiming to be higher than it); this manifests as widespread detraditionalisation.[83] Advanced Western societies are evincing a growing cultural emphasis on subjective life, reflecting what Taylor has termed 'the massive subjective turn of modern culture, a new form of inwardness, in which we come to think of ourselves as beings with inner depths'.[84] As suggested in Chapter 1, the turn to 'subjectivity' was pronounced in the sixties counterculture. The processes that generated 'homelessness' then remain just as active today, as in the case of loss of faith in primary institutions. They continue to fuel the turn to 'subjectivity'[85] to such an extent that the subjective turn has been posited as possibly 'the defining cultural development' of modern Western culture.[86]

Associated with the 'flight from deference'[87] and celebration of the self, the subjective turn/the turn to life constitutes in essence 'a turn away from life lived in terms of external or "objective" roles, duties and obligations, and a turn towards life lived by reference to one's subjective experiences'.[88] It is a shift of emphasis from 'life-as' or 'dictated-life' ('life lived in terms of institutionalized or traditionalized formations *provided by* "primary institutions"') to 'subjective-life' or 'expressed-life' ('life lived in terms of personal, intimate, psychological ... interior experiences *catered for* by "secondary institutions"').[89] As people move away from 'worlds in which [they] think of themselves first and foremost as belonging to established and "given" orders of things' transmitted from the past and flowing into the future, their primary

'sources of significance' shift from collective, supra-self orders to the individual's subjectivities. The goal thus becomes 'to have the courage to become
one's own authority', rather than to defer to higher authority, and to become
'who I truly am', rather than what others want me to be or 'what I should be'.[90]
In the institutional sphere, the turn to self/life is tied to the proliferation of
those institutions that provide 'homes for life' for, and cater to, modernity's
homeless. In contrast with primary institutions, these secondary institutions are relatively less traditionalised. Thus while in primary institutions
'the essential thrust has to do with obedience or deference to what is given
and authoritative', secondary institutions accord value to self-expression, the
experiential, and the exercise of individual autonomy, and are life-affirming/
expanding.[91]

What are the implications of this fundamental shift in modern culture for
attitudes towards engagement with the sacred? Heelas and Woodhead *et al.*
have advanced the 'subjectivisation' thesis as an explanatory framework for
the simultaneous decline of traditional religion and the rise of spirituality in
Western societies. Locating 'religion' (a supra-self tradition) in the sphere
of 'life-as' and 'spirituality' in that of 'subjective-life', through this thesis they
explain the growth in subjective-life forms of the sacred (spirituality), and
the decline of life-as forms (religion). They do this by providing evidence
(drawn largely from Britain) that, if people in Western societies today are
concerned about the sacred, they are more likely to become involved with
forms that emphasise inner sources of significance/authority (and cultiva-
tion/sacralisation of unique subjective-lives), than with those that emphasise
a transcendent source of significance/authority (to which the individual must
conform at the expense of the unique subjective-life).[92] Put simply, spirituality directly caters for subjective-life, while life-as, dictated by deference to
tradition, remains well in evidence in religion.[93] Subjective-life spirituality
itself can be catered for through the secondary spiritual institutions that have
proliferated since the sixties and offer some form of guidance and partner-
ship on the life/spiritual journey, and hence an alternative to the prospect of
individuals 'dredging up meaning from their own subjectivities alone'.[94]

Proceeding from this sketch of the sacred landscape of advanced industrial societies, from the perspective of the early twenty-first century we can
project the NAM as 'the most visible expression and articulation of a spirituality of life'. It is thus a symptom of a much wider phenomenon located within
the mainstream culture ('the most visible tip of the iceberg'),[95] and grounded
in major sociocultural processes pivoting on the ascription of ultimate value
to subjective-life. These processes provide a supportive environment for
the continuing flourishing of its ('New Age') spiritualities of life.[96] Since the
sixties, these spiritualities have indeed increasingly come to be transmitted
by relatively widespread cultural provisions in varied domains. In contrast
with their earlier countercultural association, they have become deeply
embedded, acceptable and even fashionable in the mainstream.[97] Indeed, as
Heelas and Seel recently pointed out, 'many [people] are [now] more likely

to encounter New Age provisions in the culture than they are to encounter Christianity'. Moreover, whereas until the sixties 'it was "natural" for people to turn to Christianity, it is becoming "natural" for increasing numbers to turn to alternative spiritualities of life'.[98] We can conclude that, so long as value is attached to the cultivation of subjective-life (a central feature of late modernity), the future looks promising for New Age spiritualities.[99]

This cultural/religious/spiritual terrain clearly has implications for attitudes towards sufism and Islam in advanced Western societies. Perceived as an apparently clear-cut and highly traditionalised form of 'life-as' religion in which the sacred operates from without, which subordinates the self to a higher authority and which dictates beliefs and modes of conduct (the absence of parallels to the primary institution of the church and its authoritative mediating functionaries notwithstanding), Islam might seem a remote choice for Western seekers. In contrast, the prospects look potentially brighter for sufism, at least in its universal articulation. As the case of Beshara demonstrates, there is an essential convergence between the defining emphases of New Age/subjective-life spirituality and universal sufism framed as detraditionalised, perennialist metaphysical monism.[100] This makes universal sufism a potentially viable choice for the growing numbers of Western seekers who favour the language of (life-) spirituality over that of traditional religion, and whose emphasis on the autonomous individual quest reflects a wariness of highly institutionalised forms.[101] The self-distancing of such sufi spirituality from Islam means that it also remains untouched by popular negative associations of the latter (including life-as ones) likely to repel seekers:

> Perhaps because of Islam's bad press, or maybe merely because outsiders feel that it is a faith characterised by onerous ritual observances, it is to the non-Islamic aspects of Sufism that (non-Muslim) people are drawn ... One reason for the distinctly unIslamic or de-Islamicised ... flavour of much new Sufism is perhaps the image in the popular mind of Islam itself. Islam is generally viewed as dry, intolerant, legalistic, aggressive, fervent, authoritarian. Unglamorous, in short, when compared to other faiths which have more alluring and friendly images. Buddhists are wise, Hindus are joyous, Zen monks are inscrutable. Islam has not fared so well.[102]

Nonetheless, there is evidence that involvement by Westerners in universal sufism can in some cases lead to their attachment to an Islamic *tariqa*.[103] In other cases, individuals have been attracted to and embraced the spiritual teaching of a sufi shaykh, and have later converted to Islam.[104] In such cases, the security and certainties associated with submission to an external authority and the 'onerous' requirements of Islamic ritual practice can be a powerful pull factor. It is difficult to predict outcomes, however, for the trajectories of trends in sufism/sufi spirituality in the West generally mirror the diversity of individual choice and experience arising out of an emphasis of subjectivity. Compare, for example, the contrasting sufi legacies and careers of Rauf and Bawa Muhaiyaddeen, who established his Fellowship in the USA just as the Beshara Trust was formed in Britain. While Rauf moved away from the implicit Islamic–sufi associations of his cultural–religious background, the history of Bawa's emergence as a teacher and the development of his Fellowship constituted 'a movement from a less articulated, implicit identification with Islam to a more articulated, explicit identification'.[105] The contrast is the more striking for the fact that Ibn 'Arabi's metaphysics of Unity was central to what both men sought to impart.[106]

Consistent with its importance for the sixties counterculture, the appeal of the New Age seems to derive in part from the fact that it runs counter to many of the canons and assumptions of modernity, and can thus be projected in one of its facets as a reaction against this.[107] In more general terms, subjective-life spirituality embodies a repudiation of 'life as led in terms of the stresses and strains, ambitions and configurations of [what] capitalistic modernity has to offer'.[108] Those who engage with spiritualities of life/self are profoundly dissatisfied with mainstream modern identities and values, including those of secular humanism. In its capacity as 'a highly optimistic, celebratory, utopian and spiritual form of humanism',[109] the New Age (and spiritualities of life/self more broadly) thus offers liberation from the 'iron cage' of modernity (as it was described by Weber,[110] and as its primary institutions are experienced by its discontents). The discontents of modernity might thus be counted among the potential constituents of universal sufi spiritualities like that cultivated in Beshara. One associate indeed assures us that, 'Unlike that theorist of modernity Max Weber, we need not fear the "disenchantment of the world", for the *wahdat al-wujud* of Ibn 'Arabi reveals a re-enchanted picture of the world as the ever-renewed Disclosure of Being.'[111] Another associate remarks that the movement offered him 'an elevated, "divine" humanism'. Equally, the New Age and spiritualities of life/self, including their sufi articulations, present a welcome refuge for those unnerved by the uncertainties of modern times when, as Marx put it, 'all that is solid melts into air,'[112] for life/self itself forms the basis of an enduring certainty.

Yet, these same discontents of modernity also make their way to Islamic sufi groups, finding both liberation and certainty in the embrace of Islam in its capacity as life-as religion, and in the guidance of the charismatic sufi master.[113] For example, *tariqa*s that build on Guénon's legacy evince a characteristic, acute confrontation with the assumptions and values of modernity. By virtue of their elitism and repudiation of individualism, their focus on spiritual authority embodied in a guide, on direct personal initiation and on the importance of commitment to a valid (exoteric) religious tradition, the Western sufi Traditionalists/Perennialists in many ways embody the antithesis of universal sufism in its nexus with the New Age, as exemplified by Beshara.[114] As one author puts it, according to Schuon, 'The only remedy for our suffering is found in religion, but the entire modern world diverts us from our return. We die of thirst beside a spring because we are persuaded that it has been poisoned.'[115] For Rauf, the salvation of man in the modern world lay not in religion (which for him could certainly become a poisoned chalice), but in a monistic metaphysics and spiritual realisation that require no external 'container' but the individual heart.

What of Muslims born and brought up in societies that evince an increasing cultural emphasis on subjective-life? That second- and third-generation immigrants are turning to Islamism has recently been demonstrated in Britain, for example, with devastating effect. Evidence of a new interest in sufism might eventually be uncovered, however, and it may partly result from repulsion at Islamist violence. Presently, such interest appears to be explored overwhelmingly within a conservative Muslim (and often ethnically and geographically circumscribed) milieu.[116] As for universal sufism, across the decades there has been negligible interest from British Muslim communities in Beshara, for example, and there is no evidence today of approaches from second- and third-generation British-born Muslims. Young Euro-American Muslims alienated from mainstream Muslim communities and transplanted leaderships and imbibing the assumptions and influences of contemporary Western spirituality are probably as likely to find their way to a progressive, highly subjective and personal interpretation of a rationally mediated text-centric Islam associated with individual private practice as they are to universal sufism.

Sufism in the West has undoubtedly served as an important channel for social and cultural engagement between the Euro-American and Muslim worlds.[117] At the same time, it remains 'caught in the cultural wars' between these worlds, 'even as it functions as one of the few viable bridges' between their respective cultures.[118] The Beshara emphasis of the figure of Ibn 'Arabi is a case in point, for it propels the movement into an arena fraught with contention. Conservative Muslims and salafis who reject his apparent monism can be suspicious of the ultimate intentions of Westerners in embracing Ibn 'Arabi and promoting this aspect of his thought, in which they see an undermining of central tenets of Islamic belief. Flowing from their own emphasis of this aspect, associates for their part can project the ritual–legal preoccupations of Muslims, including sufis, and their perceived exclusivism, as evidence of a failure to rise to the spirit of their adopted path. Muslims and Islamic sufis deem universal sufis in general guilty of breaking the sacred bond between the interior and exterior worlds by repudiating the religious–legal framework within which sufism has traditionally been practised, thereby debasing a precious currency. Beshara faces a specific charge of self-deception in its projection of Ibn 'Arabi, levelled by sufi Traditionalists/Perennialists in the West, who likewise draw heavily on his teaching but insist that their sufism, like his, forms the core of Islam, rather than a virtual negation of it.[119]

Muslim rejections of Ibn 'Arabi's apparent monism resonate with the attacks of conservative Christians on the monism at the heart of the New Age, each perceived to lead to a dissolution of moral distinctions.[120] However, neither this nor a shared antipathy towards the absence of obligation to external authority and the central emphasis of the self in the New Age can be taken as evidence of potential common ground, or a budding conservative

Muslim–Christian anti-New Age alliance. American Christian evangelical writer Pearcey thus recently noted that Islam is often described as another Abrahamic religion, implying that it is not very different from Christianity. 'So it may come as a surprise', she argued,

> to learn that the God of Islam is actually more akin to the nonpersonal Absolute of neo-Platonism and Hinduism than the God of the Bible. Yet it is true, and the central reason is that Islam rejects the Trinity. Without that concept, it cannot hold a fully personal conception of God ... That's why it is correct to say ... that Islam is actually akin to neo-Platonism and Hinduism.[121]

Pearcey's purpose is to situate Islam in her effort to defend Christianity. Based on the above argument, she tars it with the same brush as other religious/philosophical systems 'that begin with a nonpersonal force or [spiritual] essence', in contrast with those that 'begin with a personal God'. As such, Islam stands shoulder to shoulder with 'the natural opponent to Christianity', viz., pantheistic spirituality. Today, this enemy of Christianity, deriving from 'an extraordinarily broad religious tendency that has appeared in virtually every age and culture – West, East and Middle East (Islamic)', manifests as the core of the NAM.[122] Pearcey counsels Christians to take note of the true alignment of Islam 'as the world focuses attention on Islamic cultures' in the aftermath of 9/11, if they are to make sense of 'current cultural and political events'.[123] For her, Islam (not sufism, which she does not mention here, references to Perennialism notwithstanding)[124] is guilty of contributing to the bedrock of the NAM, the essence of which it ultimately shares.[125]

Her polemical agenda and simplistic approach aside, Pearcey's arguments tap into a growing recognition of the effects of a process described recently by Campbell as 'the Easternisation of the West'. Built on broadly Weberian categories of religion, this thesis dovetails with that of a spiritual revolution and points specifically to 'the abandonment of the traditional Western conception of the divine as transcendent and personal and its replacement by a view of the divine as immanent and essentially impersonal'.[126] Campbell claims that there has been 'a fundamental sea-change in the relationship between the East and West worldviews'. Whereas formerly the Western view was dominant and the Eastern 'a popular but merely subordinate alternative', this relationship has been reversed, for throughout the developed Western world 'the initiative, and indeed the moral high ground, appears to have passed to those who propound monism and a vaguely spiritual or pan-psychic versions of mysticism'.[127] Significantly, Campbell hints that the resurgence of Islam in the developing world 'could still spark a reaction in the West that could favour a return to traditional forms of Christianity'.[128] This would presumably signal the demise of sufi spirituality there. We turn now to the arenas of this resurgence, which are subject to (and often eagerly welcome) a 'Westernisation' (in the conventional sense of the word, encompassing industrialisation and capitalism) now under serious challenge in the heartland of 'the West' itself from a perspective that is, in Campbell's words, in essence 'Eastern'. It is a perspective that has broken the 2,000-year-old grip of the dominant 'Western' paradigm over the majority of the population in Western Europe and North America.[129]

Modern Muslims, spiritual seekers and sufism

Modernity effectively involves the institutionalisation of doubt.

Anthony Giddens, p. 176

Whether in Jakarta, Tehran, Cairo or Casablanca, a new way of situating oneself vis-à-vis oneself and what is sacred is emerging wherein, often, the interest for the individual has replaced the great causes.

Raphael Voix and Patrick Haenni

Sufism on the shelf of New Age bookstores in New York or Paris differs from Sufism as practised in the suburbs of Cairo or Istanbul.

Hammer, p. 129

Relating to Islam under the conditions of modernity

Programmes of modernisation were launched in many parts of the Muslim world in the second half of the nineteenth century. By the end of World War II, the accelerated rate of change had reached almost every corner of life among Muslims. Modern transformation brought pervasive nation-states with their extensive apparatus of control over social and political life; centralised education and legal systems; telegraph and telephone lines; railways and highways; printing and visual media; and finally satellite dishes, mobile phones and electronic communication. Massive urbanisation and attendant migration profoundly altered Muslims' relations with the land, their patterns of living, employment and consumption, and reached into the very structure of the family and social hierarchy.[130] While the processes of modernisation, once unleashed, became irreversible, the new was never triumphant in the Muslim world and could not obliterate the pre-existing, issuing in a dialectical relationship to it. In many quarters, there emerged a continually evolving project to constitute a modernity informed by the cultural premises, traditions and historical experiences of the societies concerned, and a selective denial of certain premises of the Western cultural programme of modernity.[131]

In majority Muslim countries as elsewhere, modernisation did not bring in its wake a decline in the influence of the sacred. Yet the conditions of modernity (with increasing rationalisation, differentiation, pluralisation and the emphasis of individual autonomy) have generated significant changes in the ways in which Muslims relate to their faith. For example, 'Islam' has become increasingly objectified in the consciousness of many due to the impacts of print, modern mass education and mass communication, but also by the penetration of multiple ideological/philosophical options with which it must compete.[132] Notions of religious authority have been transformed: its scope has been greatly broadened by expanding possibilities for direct access to the primary Islamic texts, while centuries-old traditional systems for learning and transmitting authoritative religious knowledge have broken down.[133] Associated hierarchical concepts of Islamic intellectual authority have been further eroded by the rise to prominence during the twentieth century of the salafi mode of Islam. This upholds a direct 'return' to scripture without the need for specialist credentials (and without the guiding parameters of historical Muslim scholarly consensus). It has reinforced the expansion of intellectual autonomy and the operation of subjectivity in the construction of religious knowledge.[134]

Alongside proliferating print materials on Islam supported by rising literacy rates and levels of education, new media and modes of communication have opened spaces in which self-styled Islamic authorities are hosted, new Muslim identities forged and public debates widened.[135] The upshot has been 'a spectacularly wild growth of interpretations'[136] of Islamic scripture in recent decades. The options have become overwhelming in an era when the notions of 'Islam' and 'Muslim' are subject to as many interpretations as there are individuals willing to interpret, while once taken-for-granted certainties concerning all but the core doctrinal content of Islam (in some cases itself not immune to reinterpretive scrutiny) have been shaken.[137] Contemporary Islam's 'state of virtual anarchy'[138] reflects and intensifies the uncertainties generated by the Muslim experience of modernity. Some take refuge in uncompromising commitment to modern constructions of an all-encompassing Islamic religious code with prescriptive force for private/public and individual/societal spheres, an option often upheld by sociopolitical movements as the route to an 'Islamic' modernity. In contrast, others become convinced of the necessity to exercise personal authority in constructing a Muslim identity and navigating a modern Muslim life, and claim religion as a matter of private individual choice. Reflecting the growing awareness of self that characterises the modern individual, such Muslims have a sense of personal autonomy and vest ultimate authority in the self (even though they may consult external authorities). This is often accompanied by an emphasis on freedom, exploration, experimentation and the establishment of truths through personal experience.

'Intensely modern' Muslims ...

Immersed in processes of modernisation and globalisation,[139] the professional middle and upper-middle classes of the Muslim world's cosmopolitan arenas provide examples of the second response to the 'virtually anarchic' scene sketched here. They have internalised rational–critical norms underpinning modern secular and especially higher education, and display the reflexivity characteristic of intensely modern attitudes,[140] sharpened by the heightened exposure of the cosmopolitan milieu. Often the most dislocated from surviving 'traditional' modes, they may also have the most to lose from the threatened triumph of those who would see an expanded role for Islam in public life, or the creation of an 'Islamic state'. Attitudes towards the sacred among members of these classes illustrate developments shaping the role of sufism/sufi spirituality in modern Muslim life that are of particular interest to a comparative perspective encompassing Western and Muslim arenas. Like many people worldwide, some of these classes evince a revived interest in the sacred. While they draw on Islamic–sufi resources, their modes of engagement with the sacred represent departures from the parent tradition, and resonate with recent shifts in religiosity widely evident in the advanced industrial societies of the West.

It is among such Muslims that we can observe the 'multifarious local identities and criss-crossing frontiers' spawned by globalisation, conceived as a generator of diversity through the reinventing or removal of inherited borders and barriers.[141] They have long been exposed to the cultural contrasts of the cosmopolitan milieu, and are widely travelled and often educated abroad. They are also best placed to take advantage of imported spiritual resources furnished by New Age/NRM providers in the global 'spiritual marketplace', and those issuing from processes in which these become hybridised or are repackaged at home.[142] For some of them, sufism as Islamic 'depth spirituality' provides the answer to a quest fuelled by a sense of the religious–spiritual life-way as the active choice of the individual. For such seekers, it furnishes a culturally resonant discourse that can underpin a modern, cosmopolitan Muslim identity, while accommodating intellectual autonomy, syncretism, an eclectic approach and a turn to the self. While for some the 'traditional' tariqas[143] may provide a frame of reference, for many this form of organised sufism is not a viable port of call on the spiritual journey.

The 'traditional' tariqas and the challenge of modernity

Embodying a mode of traditional religious authority resting on the principle of their safeguarding and transmitting knowledge that derives from the Prophet, the traditional tariqas and their shaykhs have been significantly impacted by the effects of modernisation. Mid-twentieth-century scholarship had predicted that organised sufism would become increasingly marginal to the future of societies in Muslim countries, the tariqas shrinking and possibly disappearing as their social functions declined in a changing environment.[144] Sufism, meanwhile, came in for sustained attack throughout the century on the part of salafis and modernist/liberal intellectuals, for its perceived backwardness, passivity and irrationality.[145] It has also had to compete as one of many alternate 'Islams' within the objectified tradition. Nonetheless, the traditional tariqas have continued to be strong in urban as well as rural settings across the Muslim world. There are even hints that both tariqas and sufi heritages more generally have recently enjoyed something of an induced revival, as some regimes have woken up to their potential importance as a moderate alternative to more problematic embodiments of Islamic identity and piety.[146] A growing interest in sufi spirituality as an expression of Islamic piety is perhaps propelled by disillusionment with the dry legalism and ritualism of other Islamic approaches (and repulsion at the actions of extremists). Meanwhile, sufis are increasingly visible in intra-Muslim debates, as some assert themselves as true heirs and representatives of traditional Islam with its inherent pluralism and tolerance, especially in constructing a united defence against the attacks of salafi opponents.[147]

Such signs of sufi vitality notwithstanding (and bearing in mind that generalisations cannot capture complex diversities on the ground), we must underline the potentially deleterious long-term impact of modernisation processes on traditional sufi life and attitudes towards it, especially in urban contexts. Pressures of global economic forces, experiences of social and geographical mobility and the fluidity of social relationships can each put under strain the traditional framework for sufi life. The latter is thus centred on the personal role of the shaykh figurehead, and a shared community 'constructed largely through direct contact, ritual interaction and oral teaching'.[148] Anecdotal evidence from such historical sufi strongholds as Syria and Turkey suggests that, when great living shaykhs pass away today, more often than not they leave behind no successor (or no successor of calibre), signalling a precarious future for some shaykh-centric traditional frameworks. There are cases of traditional *tariqa*s in urban contexts where the head shaykh possesses neither substantial knowledge nor spiritual training (or inclination), but has assumed a familial inheritance on a shaykh's death for the status and advantages it brings. There are other cases where the main body of *tariqa* membership is made up of illiterates. Coupled with cases of suspect behaviour, such examples fuel the vehement rejection of the *tariqa*s among those who see them as corrupt, backward and threatening to the autonomy of the individual (as indeed to the wellbeing of the vulnerable). The shaykh (even if well-informed and spiritually advanced) is redundant in the eyes of those for whom the modern emphasis on intellectual autonomy dovetails with salafi assumptions concerning modes of religious knowledge. As an accomplished young USA graduate in Damascus of implicitly salafi orientation put it, the Qur'an and hadith provide whatever is required for their own comprehension (the latter, where necessary, elucidating the former). Hence, only someone who is 'weak' will seek out a shaykh for help in understanding them, acquiring in the process the shaykh's ideas *rather than his own*. A young Muslim should study the contents of the Qur'an and hadith himself, he explains. Eventually, he will advance to the Qur'anic sciences, although for most this is unlikely before the end of their earthly life, given the enormity of the primary task. The thrust of these comments was aimed at religious authorities more broadly, but directed with greatest vehemence at the traditional sufi shaykh.[149]

Alongside its undermining effects, modernity (and globalisation) at the same time offers indispensable tools for the expansion and propagation of sufism. The availability of English as a global vernacular and fast communications and travel provide pertinent examples. Paradoxically, the traditional *tariqa*s may use these tools to their own advantage, while simultaneously sustaining the further undermining effects associated with them.[150] This is particularly clear in relation to mass printing and new media, which have made the traditional sufi 'secret' accessible to all, without initiation or training. Such developments point to an expanding extra-*tariqa* arena for sufi life. This is characterised by more individual, text-centric and self-tailored modes, and more tenuous links, if any, to a shaykh figurehead. The inner self emerges as ultimate authority in this alternative sufi future, perhaps mediated through the experiential guidance of past sufi masters in imaginal or textual realms. In the institutional realm, counterparts to such developments can be seen in the emergence of looser, egalitarian associations that provide pre-packaged resources and offer support and companionship on the spiritual journey. The ethos here is marked by a sharing of experiences, rather than the demand for obedience to a master in a hierarchical situation.

Seeking sufism: cosmopolitan Muslims and the spiritual quest

These new forms of sufi life are illustrated by intensely modern Muslims in the professional middle and upper-middle classes in cosmopolitan arenas throughout the Muslim world, who are engaging with sufi spirituality detached from the *tariqa*s. This is resourced through accessible products and media and takes place via new forms of association, some of them in syncretic or distinctly non-Islamic (and at times non-religious) settings. The influx of products and influences associated with the New Age[151] has produced significant interfaces between global and local spiritual marketplaces,[152] generating new religious spaces and identities among the cosmopolitan middle classes and elites. Drawing on global New Age/NRM and local sufi resources, newly constructed religious identities are emerging, involving a self-distancing from the perceived dangers/irrelevancies of Islamist/traditional Islamic modes in favour of modern, individualist and pluralist values. Reflecting this, multiple paths to the sacred are often acknowledged (and tested), and non-Muslims are accepted not only as fellow seekers in sufi practice but even as spiritual teachers.

To explore these developments, we introduce three country studies. Morocco provides an example from the Arab world, while we have selected Indonesia and Turkey for their particular relevance to this volume, the former the only Muslim arena where Beshara has a clientele, the latter the origin of its guiding figure and home to the sufi tradition upon which he drew. We confine our discussion to the major cities of Casablanca and Rabat, Jakarta, and Istanbul, respectively. In all three countries, sufism was a major (if not the predominant) articulation of Muslim religiosity prior to the twentieth century.[153]

From the New Age to sufism and Islam in Casablanca and Rabat

A recent study of religious attitudes among the highly cosmopolitan and largely secularised 'Frenchified' bourgeoisie of Casablanca and Rabat demonstrates the role of sufism in new approaches to the sacred.[154] The study identifies factors that have contributed to a reconfigured religiosity within this stratum since the 1990s. Growing disappointment with leftist, nationalist or Pan-Arab political ideals has coincided with involvement in the New Age among some of its members, leading to a new-found fascination with Islam. This has not brought them to Islamism, however, but to an 'Islam' reconstituted along New Age lines, in which sufism serves as a pivotal resource.[155] Individuals interviewed in the study have either experimented with the New Age during spells in the West, or sampled it in Morocco (in such forms as yoga, zen and various personal development therapies), where the movement took root among the indigenous population during the 1980s.[156] Reflecting 'a strong temptation to reformulate foreign spiritual influences by indexing them to Islam as well as the search for local equivalences', Moroccan New Agers have then been drawn to sufism as local mysticism, whether as an individual pursuit or in the context of a *tariqa*.[157]

Significantly, such 'migrants' to Islam have included individuals who had no previous inclination to follow it.[158] While their fresh interest in the sacred mediated through sufism might be projected in terms of 're-Islamisation' experienced as identity reconciliation, the study emphasises that it cannot be understood in terms of a simple 'return to the roots'. Their new interest in sufism thus often results from attraction to what is perceived as the 'modern' discourse it offers (in its affinity with the 'modern' experiential religiosity of many in the contemporary West, and in opposition to traditional Moroccan Islam, for example). Moreover, some claim a right to multiple spiritual commitments of which sufism is but one, pointing to a relativist perspective. They may also evince a syncretistic approach in spheres of practice and theory (using zen meditation to prepare for *dhikr* or performing *dhikr* in the *zazen* position, for example), reflecting a cosmopolitan acceptance of pluralism. Finally, it must be acknowledged that, given their educational background and cultural orientation, for many there simply are no such putative religious roots to which they might return.

The 'reconstituted religiosity' of this cosmopolitan bourgeoisie is a private, individual affair. Indeed it strongly affirms the centrality and autonomy of the individual. Having 'self-realisation' as its goal, it posits inner harmony and wellbeing as the ultimate objectives of a personal spiritual quest, typically premised on a monistic worldview and mediated through inner experience. To use a term from our discussion above, its emphasis is thus to cultivate and sacralise the unique subjective-life. A new relationship to the sacred is thus (re-)conceptualised along the lines of spiritualities of life in contemporary Western societies. It avoids the problems posed by the authority of religious institutions/traditions, marginalises the legal aspect of the faith, and situates itself outside of the political sphere. Through syncretism, spiritual

journeys mediated via international networks, and lives lived in full engagement with globalisation, cosmopolitans interested in the sacred reconfigure
an Islam that also transcends the problematic of the West as civilisational
other. Bearing no relation to the notion of an Islamic state (the defining
Islamist concern and goal), such an Islam as theirs has been projected as
'post-Islamist'.[159] The Moroccan case demonstrates that, in a context marked
by disillusionment with grand political narratives and collective identities,
the New Age can function as a pathway to this reconstituted Islam, while sufi
spirituality unlocks the gate.

Sufism in Indonesia and the Beshara clientele in Jakarta

Combined with its substantial religious diversity, the twentieth-century
Indonesian experience of modernisation makes for a particularly rich context
within which to map changes in sufi life. Recent research highlights important new departures in cosmopolitan Indonesian contexts that help explain
the existence of a clientele for Beshara courses in the capital city Jakarta.[160]

Sufism has enjoyed increased vitality as part of Indonesia's Islamic revival
since the 1970s.[161] Significantly, this upsurge of interest in sufi activity encompasses 'cosmopolitan sophisticates' as much as provincials.[162] Since the mid-
1980s, well-educated middle-class urban Muslims of all ages have been
attracted to the traditional *tariqa*s, associated with their institutional homes
(*pesantren*). From the 1990s, they have also been turning to 'a whole range of
novel activities identified with "Sufism"'[163] now popular in Indonesia's major
cities, and manifest in newly emerging urban sufi networks. The tastes of the
new urban Muslim middle class, newly enthusiastic about and committed to
Islam, reflect the highly cosmopolitan attitudes and lifestyles that have spread
across urban Indonesian society particularly from the 1990s. Such attitudes
and lifestyles have been stimulated by intensified economic development
and social modernisation, within an international environment characterised by growing involvement in global systems of production, exchange and
communication.[164] The new-style sufi activities in which these cosmopolitans
participate range from

> reading reflective and 'how-to' spiritual books, to attending academically-styled
> private courses, to joining informal prayer groups or healing groups using *dzikir*
> chanting, to accepting the spiritual direction of non-traditional teachers outside
> the conventional *tarekat*.[165]

Proponents and observers distinguish these new forms of sufi activity from
older ones through such terms as 'Neo-Sufism' and 'Practical Sufism'.[166] Key
features include 'pursuit of an experiential or "inner" dimension to religious
life and a moving away from, or even rejection of, the supposed hierarchy,
authoritarianism and "other worldliness" of conventional *tarekats*'.[167] Activities
of 'Practical Sufism' are premised on an implicit disengagement of sufism as
teaching/practice from *tariqa* as traditional institutional form. The new sufi
activities thus take place in new institutional forms that have emerged in

urban settings as an alternative to the *tariqa*. These furnish resources through which cosmopolitan Muslims estranged from the social milieu of traditional sufism can engage with sufi teaching/practice.[168] As such, they respond to new social needs generated by the turn of an expanding new middle class of cosmopolitan Muslims to privatised styles of religiosity, under the impact of global economic and cultural forces and social and geographical mobility.

Prominent among the new urban sufi networks are 'such international cultural forms as the "foundation", "institute", "seminar series", "intensive course", or "spiritual workshop",'[169] each marked by an informal and egalitarian ethos.[170] New-style commercial private adult Islamic education foundations such as the prototypical and highly liberal Paramadina Foundation and the Indonesian Islamic Media Network/Intensive Course and Networking for Islamic Sciences (ICNIS) offer short courses in sufism within broader curricula. These are modelled on university courses and use the academic lecture format and an intellectually rigorous approach, drawing faculty from State Islamic Institutes, for example. Some link their students to *tariqa*s to provide support for spiritual development and experiential opportunities (if students so wish).[171] Tazkiya Sejati Foundation, founded specifically for the purpose, offers short courses in sufism set in a more devotional or reflective tone, and also encourages students to connect with a *tariqa* (while not deeming this absolutely necessary for sufi practice). Some short-course graduates have helped shape other frameworks within which to continue their study and practice of sufism outside of the *tariqa*s.[172]

The existence of a clientele for Beshara and the invitation to hold courses in Jakarta must be situated against this background. Beshara was first discovered by ex-students of Paramadina and Tazkiya in Jakarta who had been particularly attracted by lectures on Ibn 'Arabi.[173] During the late 1990s, they had searched the internet for further resources. As we have seen, since 1999 Beshara has been invited regularly to run short courses there.[174] Indonesians have joined the trip to Turkey, and are also engaged in negotiations to establish Beshara South East Asia. We use the Jakarta courses (and particularly that held during summer 2005) to explore the motivations and nature of Indonesian participation in Beshara.

Jakarta courses are open to everyone, and it has been stipulated that all future activities and meetings held there under the aegis of Beshara must follow this principle. Most of the clientele have been Indonesian Muslims (some of the women wearing the Islamic headscarf). The head of a Jakarta Brahma Kumaris Centre[175] and a few Christian-origin (Western) non-Indonesians living in Indonesia or elsewhere in Southeast Asia have also attended Jakarta courses. In summer 2005, Muslims of both sexes and mixed ages attended. They were on the whole university-educated (some in the USA/Europe) middle- and upper-class professionals (or the wives of such professionals),[176] encompassing the very well-connected and members of national elites. It seems they were for the most part without prior experience of sufism or exposure to sufi teaching.

The course comprises study sessions, meditation periods, and a Thursday evening collective Beshara *dhikr* (its movements simplified somewhat for ease of performance).[177] Given the widespread use of domestic help, work, a key course activity through which a taste of service is acquired, has been dropped from the schedule. Out of further consideration for the context, time and space are allocated for performance of the five daily prayers and for attendance of the Friday collective prayer for those wishing to do this.[178] To convey the teacher-less approach, participants are seated in a circle for study, and it is emphasised that guidance proceeds not from a particular individual, but potentially from all present, each in their capacity as 'a face of the Real'. The aim is to encourage engagement, based on recognition that the feelings and experience of each individual are relevant and important. The setting is thus far from that of the academic lecture, the tone fully reflective, and the style participatory. Participants have more recently been divided into two or three groups depending on how many courses they have previously attended. First-time participants study extracts from *The Twenty-nine Pages*, poems by Rumi and short papers by Rauf, Young and other associates, for example.[179]

During the summer 2005 course, only a third of the Muslim participants performed the daily and Friday prayers. The others remained in the study room to chat. None seemed to be uncomfortable with the fact that the *dhikr* was not an exclusively Muslim gathering,[180] and that it encompassed both sexes (the circle spontaneously self-segregated according to gender, with physical contact where male and female sections met). Personal motivations for involvement were matched by an explicit shared concern over the threat to tolerance and pluralism posed by some radical Islamist groups, especially since the fall of the New Order in 1998, and a commitment to protect and nurture these values.[181] In the course summing-up, participants convey what they feel they have gained from it. Some have reported experiences of 'extraordinary openings'. One has described the course as 'teaching them what their religion means'.

If the appeal of Beshara in Jakarta can be situated within the milieu of 'Practical Sufism' and its new urban networks, we must flag a point of difference with the latter. A fundamental characteristic of 'Practical Sufism' is its 'stated link with *shari'a*-based Islam',[182] mediated through an explicit emphasis on Muslim identity and the sharia as the basis for Islamic spirituality.[183] Howell argues that this emphasis has served to distance the new sufi activities from the modern mystical/spiritual groups not identified with the teachings of a single recognised religion (the *kebatinan*). These are often highly syncretic or eclectic, or centre on a new religion/revelation/self-sufficient approach to spiritual life, and typically draw to some degree on sufi traditions. Proliferating in the cities especially from the mid-twentieth century and gaining legal recognition as (semi-denominational) 'faiths' in 1973, these groups have not yet fully escaped certain negative associations, including that of occultism.[184] Such independent mystical groups have faded in popularity

among Muslim middle classes and educated elites as the changing composition of these strata under New Order development programmes means that
they have become more uniformly, and more piously, Muslim. As a result,
these strata have increasingly preferred to explore inner spirituality *within*
the bounds of orthodox Islam, rather than outside it.[185] In contrast with the
Islamic self-identification of 'Practical Sufism' that makes it acceptable to
this constituency, Jakarta Beshara courses open with a statement that 'the
Beshara School is areligious, and does not prescribe any religious way'.

The interest in Beshara described here further illustrates a new readiness
among cosmopolitan Muslims to make use of resources for spiritual enrichment that have no linkage with Islam. This is evident in their 'patronising
a new array of imported growth movement and New Age-style products
available through city bookshops, workshops, locally-based representatives of international New Religious Movements and internet web-sites'.[186]
For example, Howell maps moves by graduates of academic-style sufism
short courses to explore techniques for personal development or spiritual
enrichment offered by New Age resources unconnected to Islam. Often
introduced to them through these same courses, such resources include
the Brahma Kumaris, Raja Yoga, Reiki, Emotional Intelligence and Parent
Effectiveness Training. Those who explore them 'are prepared to see them
offering techniques ... that are essentially "Sufi" in the sense that they may
enhance self-reflection ... or deepen meditative awareness'.[187] International
New Age resources are thus effectively understood in terms of a religiously
de-contextualised and rather chic 'spirituality' (*spiritualitas*), assimilated to
sufism. This strategy is facilitated by the fact that many such resources are
packaged as generic spiritual or psychological tools, and can be treated as
such.[188]

The evidence suggests that the majority of Jakarta Beshara students find in
its courses (including those at Chisholme in the case of the student who has
made his way there after completing two Jakarta courses) a resource through
which to explore the inner depths of a specifically *Muslim* spirituality, while
rejecting the perennialist supra-religious context. Thus many students have
felt a strong need 'to assert and defend Islamic practice', and they frequently
raise this issue during discussions. It has repeatedly surfaced in relation to the
failure in Beshara to uphold the five daily Muslim prayers, for example. Their
sense has been that, in the words of a course supervisor, 'what the School
teaches is very good, but it goes wrong in not embracing sharia Islam'. In
contrast, some younger Muslim participants have been receptive to the idea
of 'moving beyond religion as a whole', and regarding the sharia as a (relative)
form. They have 'found a taste' for Beshara, as a course supervisor puts it.
This fits with Howell's description of the willingness of some Paramadina and
Tazkiya short-course graduates who remain committed Muslims to cham-
pion home-grown, local spiritual groups that now 'model radically perennialist and universalist understandings of spiritual life'.[189] Examples are the
perennialist Anand Ashram established in Jakarta in 1991 as a 'Center for

Holistic Health and Meditation,[190] and the perennialist and radically universalist Salamullah, which allows for a wholesale shedding of particularistic
religious identities and an affirmation of the New Age as an expression of the
Divine Wish.[191]

To sum up, the sufism that appeals to well-educated cosmopolitan
Indonesian urbanites is in many cases a new sufism, one that responds to the
quest for 'a depth spirituality drawing on Islam's Sufi heritage' that is 'fully
compatible with modern careers and family life and need not stifle independent critical judgement'[192] through submission to an authoritarian master.
This new sufism also serves at times as 'inspiration for "late-" or "ultra-
modern" forms of religiosity ... that may embrace religious universalism or
the confident appropriation of techniques and inspiration from diverse traditions into an enriched, even perennialist, Islamic faith'.[193] In this way, urban
sufism in early twenty-first century Indonesia has become for many 'a bridge
to other religions, spiritualities and therapies'.[194] Indonesian Muslims have
generally drawn on non-Islamic resources which they feel can be integrated
into their own construction of Islamic faith through a process of abstrac-
tion. In exceptional cases, however, the potential exists for this same process
'to eventuate in a radically universalist construction of Islam and even [to]
propel the seeker outside the bounds of Islam altogether'.[195] Beshara in Jakarta
provides an additional international resource through which this exceptional
case might arise.

Seekers and journeys to sufism in secular Istanbul
Under the Turkish Republic Kemalism adopted secularism, projected as a
necessary condition for modernisation, as an authoritarian state ideology.
Based on the conviction that Islam must be kept under strict state control
or confined to the personal conscience, an attempt was made to impose
secularism as a way of life on the people. As is the case elsewhere, however,
secularisation has not led to the decline or extinction of religion in this
constitutionally secular majority Muslim country, but to its creative transformation. This transformation has encompassed the promotion of alternative 'Islamic' versions of modernity by Islamic social movements in the face
of forced modernisation, experienced as opposition to religion, under the
hegemonic secularist project.[196] In this sense, religious revival has become
'the internal dialectic of Kemalist modernity,'[197] and sufism has played an
important part in it.

The impact of the deep-rooted sufi past on post-revolutionary Turkish
society has not been fully evaluated. However, there is widespread evidence of
ongoing sufi influences on Turkish attitudes and sensibilities, and in continually shaping Turkish culture.[198] The role of sufism in creating 'Turkish Islam'
('a particular way of crafting and creating one's own way of being Muslim'
or reproducing religious knowledge in daily life among those raised in a
Turkish milieu)[199] must thus be highlighted. As Yavuz puts it, 'The first factor
... that defines the Turkish understanding of Islam and makes it unique is the

enduring tradition of Sufism that formed its foundation and has managed to remain a dominant force despite various efforts towards its subjugation and elimination.[200]

During the last two decades, sufi traditions appear to have blossomed within the reconstituted framework of the 'traditional' *tariqa*s. Kafadar thus highlights the ongoing appeal of the urban Qadiri, Rifa'i and Halveti *tariqa*s to professionals and artisans from more traditional family backgrounds, and their new appeal to individuals brought up in secular Westernised homes. He cites the much-commented-on role of the Naqshbandiyya as a major force in Turkish political and social life, and its large, visible following in both rural and urban areas (especially eastern Anatolia, Konya and the Fatih district of Istanbul). He points also to the widespread influence of Mevlevi traditions, which continued to be respected even in leftist secularist circles under the Republic, and the semi-legitimate status of the Mevleviyye as a cultural institution.[201] Under the continued ban on their activities, the *tariqa*s remain for the most part underground and invisible, holding their meetings and ritual gatherings in private residences, for example.[202] Recent anecdotal evidence suggests the existence of numerous circles of very modest proportions formed around individual sufi masters in urban contexts, their members ranging from educated professionals to the illiterate.[203]

Evidence of *tariqa* vitality notwithstanding, their proscribed status and the strong suspicion surrounding them inculcated by the state and its media has deterred many from involvement. Images of the later *tariqa*s as degenerate persist, while the sustained tarring of *tariqa*s with the same brush as the Islamists by secularist leftist intellectuals has produced widespread negative perceptions of them.[204] The cultural struggle generated by aggressive secularisation has forced many engaged in the perpetuation of sufi traditions to develop alternative frameworks to the *tariqa*s, and approaches more congenial to new generations that are thoroughly modern, secular-educated, Westernised and wary of anything overtly traditional. Two important recent examples are Ahmet Kayhan (1900–2000)[205] and Hasan Lutfi Shushud (1903–88).[206] Based respectively in Ankara and Istanbul, these sufi masters held teaching sessions and assigned personal prayer practices to students in the context of completely informal circles.[207] These encompassed men and women, conservative and overtly very 'modern' Muslims,[208] Turks and non-Turks, and sometimes non-Muslims. Neither Kayhan nor Shushud self-projected as shaykhs or countenanced suggestions that their activities had any affinity to the formal *tariqa*s (of which they were indeed critical).[209] Some of the strategies invoked by such teachers in accommodating to the secular milieu and the non-observant lifestyles of many of their students are comparable to those adopted by some of the 'Islamic' sufi teachers in Western contexts. Kayhan, for example, would counsel some students to hold on to the formal Islamic prayers, 'even if just twice a day'.

A contemporary illustration of this approach which we can consider in more detail arises in the case of sufi teacher Cemalnur Sargut (b.1952).

Sargut is Head of the Turkish Women's Cultural Association in Istanbul and co-founder of Cenan Education, Culture and Health Foundation, a *waqf* dedicated to social and cultural education, provision of charitable and educational support, and individual 'realisation and enhancement' through 'historical Turkish spiritual values'.[210] A thoroughly modern woman and popular sufi teacher in the progressive line of Kenan Rifai (d.1950),[211] she believes that sufism must be taught today in an academic rather than a *tariqa* framework, 'like in a university', but bearing in mind that 'lessons in sufism never end'.[212] What is intended is no dry academic approach, however, for Sargut argues specifically that teachers 'who teach and live sufism together with their students' such that they form 'one body' must take the place of traditional forms. She has a warm, compassionate and relaxed relationship with her own students, and makes a point of always being available to them. 'I am their servant', she explains, 'when they need me I must be there'.[213] They meet twice a week, one session devoted to studying sufi understandings of the Qur'an, another to the text of the (sung) religious poems (*ilahiyat*) of Kenan Rifai.[214] Sessions are day-long affairs, very relaxed, strongly participatory and involving lengthy discussion.[215] Additionally, Sargut engages with students individually whenever she feels they need this, discussing what has arisen in the study sessions. Like Kayhan and Shushud before her, she welcomes non-Muslim attendance at her sessions, and has accepted Christian and Jewish students.[216]

The approach of the Rifa'i line in which Sargut participates is modern, liberal and open as a matter of principle.[217] Sargut stresses the inevitability of social change: 'Everything must change, for God is in change every moment, and shows a new Face'. Regarding the sharia, for example, while she claims to underline its meaning and importance to students, her approach focuses its parameters on the individual, such that its prescriptions sit comfortably in a secular environment and have currency among modern takers. A long-term student thus lists the following as the 'content' of the sharia: 'to pray and fast; to abstain from drinking, lying, gossiping and thinking badly of others; to help others; to obey the law of the time'. Any association of the headscarf with the sharia is vehemently rejected. This principled position and its embodiment in teachers like Sargut (and her teacher, the late Ayverdi) is undoubtedly part of their appeal to cosmopolitan young Turkish women, for whom the headscarf signals a socially backward tradition associated with repressive patriarchal norms, a relinquishing of personal freedom and a threat to personal identity.[218] It is equally attractive to those young men unaccustomed to the restrictive patterns of interaction associated with 'Islamic' dress and the imperatives of gender segregation.

With regard to the few sharia prescriptions upheld, Sargut is careful to avoid any imposition on her students. In the case of the formal prayers, for example, she reports that students often express their desire to begin to perform them once they have heard her explanation of their meaning and purpose; alternatively, some simply report to her that they have begun to perform them. She does not herself recommend any additional devotional practices, such as the repetition of particular invocations to accompany the practice of *tasbih*. A student may choose a specific invocation of their own and share it with her or not, and she is accepting of this.[219] Members of the group have performed the collective *dhikr* only in Medina on the Night of Power, during an *'umra* visit led by Sargut, and in conjunction with another Rifa'i and a Jerrahi teacher.[220] It is not part of their regular activities.

In informal circles such as those described here, the master's physical presence plays a defining and central role. In the absence of the clear patterns of institutionalisation associated with the *tariqa* and the office of successor, they can become vulnerable to disintegration and their members to a loss of direction following the master's death, except in cases where a teacher-successor has been successfully prepared and established in advance.[221] The potentially precarious situation of such circles contrasts strongly with the case of the *Risale-i Nur* movement/community, formed around the legacy of Bediuzzaman Said Nursi (1877–1960).[222] Through its extensive infrastructure, this has become a major element in the religious dynamic of Turkish society.[223] It has been argued that Nursi's teachings have 'helped to create a neo-Sufism' in Turkey,[224] as part of a shift from a '*tekke*-centric' to a 'text-centric' understanding of Islam, imposed on the *tariqa*s by government oppression since the 1920s.[225] Nursi's *Risale-i Nur* forms the focus of the movement. Students study and reflect upon the text regularly, in group settings and in private. Some carry it with them, and quote it chapter and verse to explain an opinion or clarify a view. It has been described as functioning as 'a pocket shaykh'[226] and, as such, it constitutes a spiritual guide that will never depart this earth.[227]

While pointing out that not everyone participating in it is aware of this, students agree with a characterisation of the *Nur* movement in terms of an involvement with sufi spirituality 'as a reality without a name'. They thus 'drink deep from the cup of sufism', through their embrace of teachings embodied in a text steeped in the imagery, frames of reference and terminology of the sufi tradition, notwithstanding its author's self-distancing from that tradition under the Republican regime. In contrast with *tariqa* sufism, as Islamic depth spirituality sufi spirituality in the *Nur* way is tailored to the expectations and tastes of the ordinary Muslim; at the same time, it serves as the engine for a reconstructed religious identity that is viable in a modern, secular milieu. The sufi conceptualisation of the spiritual path as 'a means of working the heart' with the aim of 'making man into a true human being' has been simplified, so that it is accessible to all. It is shorn of its excesses and potential pitfalls, and firmly bonded to the requirements of the Prophetic example and the sharia.[228] In the *Nur* movement, one finds none of the elaborate and rigorous practices associated with the *tariqa*s (we note, however, that special *awrad* can be read after the prayers if students desire). The authority of the shaykh is replaced by the authority of the individual student who, in engaging with the text, draws from it in accordance with their own level of understanding,[229] projecting the personal spiritual journey in terms of individual capacity, inclination and aspiration. In Turkey, Nursi represents 'the seismic shift from *tekke* ... to text and from oral Islam to print Islam'.[230] His legacy has driven the construction of a socially conservative Islam defined by the broad path of the Sunna but infused with individual sufi spirituality. Significantly, given the absence of the *tariqa*, in the *Nur* movement the individual traveller on the sufi path none-theless enjoys the benefits of a supportive community and dedicated social institutions.[231]

Some young Turkish spiritual seekers perceive available religious options in stark terms, as a choice between a repressive Islamism or backward *tariqa*s on the one hand, and 'militant' secularism on the other. They may not have encountered organised resources such as the *Nur* movement and sufi groups like that of Sargut, or may feel deterred by the Islamic practices or intrusive social context perceived to be associated with them. Some prefer the solitary quest, looking to popular publications addressing sufi spirituality for guid-ance. While drawing on sufi texts, symbolism and practice, many of these are by authors without any connection to the traditional Turkish sufi milieu. The writings of Ahmed Hulusi, formerly a well-known journalist in Turkey who is currently based in North Carolina (USA), provide an example. These have a large popular following in Turkey.[232] Hulusi has never been associated with the *tariqa*s and rejects any such connection.[233] Yet he is described by his English translator as a 'Sufi Master',[234] and one of his readers suggests that his writings 'bring together something from all the *tariqa*s'.[235] His approach synthesises a modern understanding of Islam that recruits arguments from science,[236] with a monistic sufi teaching ('Open your heart and be inspired by the Voice of the Universal Essence that is within us all')[237] that seems to resonate with the New Age.[238] Written in a simple conversational style, his writings aim to guide readers to a proper understanding of Islam and spir-itual realities,[239] based on the author's own spiritual experiences.[240] Hulusi also offers his readers 'daily messages for meditation' on his website, and reminds them that, in matters spiritual, 'everyone should define a path for himself'.[241] Readers sometimes meet and share views concerning 'the master's' writings at his publisher's bookstore.

Hulusi's offerings remain tied to the conceptual world of sufism and Islam. In contrast, a new interest in spirituality played out far from the parameters of Islamic belief and practice has exploded in Turkish cities during the past ten, and more particularly five, years. This has mirrored the visible rise of new spiritual resource providers, going hand in hand with the emergence of a competitive market of ideas and identities in the country by the mid-1990s, as the public sphere was gradually freed from the ideological domination of the state.[242] Alienation from Islamic culture, a love of all things 'Western', and a conscious self-identification with modernity have combined to propel affluent middle- and upper-class (and some less privileged) young cosmo-politan Turks, plagued by 'meaning and purpose of life' questions, into the arms of the Turkish New Age Movement. The latter, dubbed by some Turks 'esoterica' (or the more familiar 'spirituality'), has enjoyed considerable mainstreaming in Turkish culture.[243] Major booksellers bear witness to the 'esoteric boom' in the Turkish publishing industry,[244] and to reader demand for the global range of New Age and occult literature in Turkish translation, in addition to a growing number of relevant works by Turkish authors.[245] Until recently, associated activities took place in private homes, but today Istanbul has a handful of 'spiritual centres' (as described by those involved), and many yoga schools, meditation courses, and offerings in massage and psychological therapies.[246] OWO, the city's biggest spiritual centre, established in an affluent district in 2002 by the young daughter of a hotel magnate, reports a burgeoning interest in its resources and regular positive media coverage. Collectively, 300–400 people a week attend sessions and workshops typically delivered in English by some twenty-five experts from abroad in yoga, breath therapy, tai chi, reiki, varieties of massage (including Ayurvedic), several meditation techniques (including the range developed by OSHO), bio-energy healing, primal and co-dependency, astrology, tarot, kabbalah and shamanism, for example.[247] Members of the clientele range from the ages of fifteen to seventy, and are generally religiously non-observant and from secular backgrounds. Session and workshop prices are affordable only for the better-off, but some free sessions without appointment are provided by healers. Those drawn to these include women wearing the Islamic headscarf, seeking to improve a child's health or performance in school examinations, for example. One of its administrators suggests that the resources offered by OWO are not perceived as 'not Islamic', because clients understand that 'spirituality is not a religion'. These resources rather offer an opportunity to 'open a space in the mind' and reduce stress, and are 'totally removed from the religious sphere'. The centre aspires to provide an all-round service, offering an Ayurvedic menu in its café, providing a range of relevant literature and goods for sale, and recommending reading on its website.[248] It has also pioneered the export of workshops in yoga, percussion and other therapies to Turkish companies, following initial successes with foreign companies in Istanbul.

Among their many resources, OWO and its sister organisation KUN[249] also offer opportunities to explore sufi spirituality through sessions, workshops and summer camps. Sargut delivers a monthly two-hour seminar at OWO, which is free and regularly attracts over a hundred attendees. Sufi workshops and summer camps organised by both centres are led by non-Turkish, non-Muslim women associated with OSHO. A German first 'trained' in Afghanistan and Iran who then found OSHO and held sufi workshops in India, Zahira leads the OWO Sufi Camp that is split between Istanbul and Antalya. Videha, an Italian who is a former student of hers, leads an OSHO Sufi Camp near Bodrum, organised through KUN. These events aim at an international clientele. For example, OSHO Sufi Camp publicity materials make much of the fact that this is held in 'the land of the Sufis'. Using an image of Rumi, a 'Pilgrimage to Konya' is promised.[250] But young Turks are also drawing on these resources. In 2005, for example, six of the twenty-eight participants in the OWO Sufi Camp were Turkish (the remainder were from

Germany, Italy and Russia, for example). At an earlier OWO sufi workshop, fifteen out of the forty participants were Turks. Zahira has created what one participant describes as 'a type of OSHO sufi line', building on the fact that 'OSHO loves sufism'.[251] Participants in sufi workshops and camps led by these teachers encompass *dhikr*, OSHO meditations (especially, under Zahira at OWO, the 'no-dimensions' meditation and the whirling meditation),[252] reading stories and poems from Rumi, Hafiz and Iqbal, a large dose of 'love' (expressed through 'frequent hugs', according to one participant), and 'plenty of free dance', including with disco music.[253]

The involvement of Turkish youth with such imported spiritual activities is explained by some Turkish observers in terms of 'moda' or a fashion, dictated by the burgeoning (and celebrity/artist-endorsed) Western interest in spirituality and copied by self-consciously 'modern' or 'Western' Turks.[254] Young people from secular families are ignorant of their country's rich sufi legacy, and have no natural sense of identification with it.[255] Some assume that it is backward or dangerous. In the Turkish New Age, their first personal encounter with sufi spirituality is in its re-imported form, repackaged by Westerners as a self-help activity, a floating aid to inner harmony. Thus freed from its negative Turkish associations, it is also very trendy. Yet this encounter has led some to explore home-grown forms of sufi spirituality, issuing in a reconstituted modern sufi self that can accommodate a progressive Islamic identity and practice. As one young woman recently attracted to OSHO puts it, when she read all his discourses they served for her as 'a gate to Rumi'. The indexing of the imported to the local points here to reappropriating the local, but this is by no means in its traditional forms.[256] At the same time, a 'rediscovered modern but authentic' sufism among young people effectively constitutes one more youth sub/counterculture, emerging in provocation to and deconstructing the dominant culture (especially when it draws on the cultural legacy of the Ottoman past).

For their part, and consistent with their tolerant attitudes, contemporary Turkish sufi teachers are not critical of the appetite for imported spirituality among the young. Given the long period of 'militant' secularism, they see a positive development in any opening to spirituality. That involvement with such importations leads some to their door is an added boon. As Sargut suggests, it is not their fault that young Turks today do not know that their country is 'the very soil on which sufism has grown'. In Appendix 5 we illustrate spiritual journeys among young cosmopolitan Turkish Muslims that bring them back to this soil, highlighting the seeking mode that underpins them, and the role of the New Age in this. There, the life story of one such man in his thirties reveals how traumatic events triggered a journey from a strongly Westernised, secular background to a newly constituted Islamic identity and practice in the context of Sargut's sufi group, via an encounter with New Age spirituality and sufi workshops in Istanbul's new spiritual centres.

At the start of the twenty-first century, Muslims are engaged in 'reframing the basic narratives of their faith and identity'.[257] As we have seen, for Turkish and Moroccan cosmopolitans without strong Islamic roots, the global New Age plays a significant role on the path to a fresh Muslim identity and newly constructed relationship to the sacred, mediated through sufi resources. This takes place against a backdrop coloured by alienation from traditional, Islamist and secular identities and the grand causes animating the politics of nation and *umma*, and via thoroughly modern modes of religiosity. For them as for their Indonesian counterparts, reformulated sufi resources meet both individual spiritual needs and the demands of cosmopolitan modernity. Adapted from its traditional forms, sufism plays a key role in the construction of an intensely modern and cosmopolitan Muslim self, in its capacity as a culturally authentic yet highly accommodating resource.

Through an adapted sufism, we see a religiosity in certain Muslim settings that resonates with modalities now widespread in the advanced industrialised societies of the West, pointing to significant commonalities between the two worlds. Ways of relating to the sacred such as those described here call into question an over-hasty assumption that the subjective turn (and associated 'ethic of subjectivity')[258] is remote to societies in Muslim majority countries. Life-as religion indeed remains central in these societies, and is flourishing (as are other forms of life-as roles that serve supra-self orders). Yet while this is the main focus and concern of outside observers, it is far from the whole story.[259] The resonance highlighted here can be situated in the context of what Heelas describes as 'theistic spiritualities of life' *within* religion. Evident both in the advanced industrial societies of the West and beyond, it is characterised by a mixing of the traditionalised with the detraditionalised, and the *retention* of faith in the personal God of theism. These spiritualities serve to carry themes that are strongly resonant with those of the New Age (and are in many cases identical to them in functional terms), but are situated within a 'softened' tradition.[260]

It has been suggested that economic development fuels 'life-cum-spirituality concerns' and a movement away from the *constrictively* traditionalised.[261] As growing numbers enjoy the benefits of such development (and as religious markets are gradually deregulated), religious transformations such as those described above may become increasingly widespread in Muslim settings. In the context of the global cultural arena, this development would signal the strengthening of an inclusivist religious/spiritual ethos among Muslims, one that emphasises the common ('divine') humanity of all, in contrast with an ethos that underscores exclusivism and sociocultural differentiation.[262] What the Muslim seekers discussed here demonstrate is that visions of 'Islamic modernities' are not the monopoly of those who advocate a future of normative fundamentalisms dividing the world into believers and unbelievers. For these seekers, visions of an Islamic modernity within a global future are of multicultural, pluralist societies, and religious–secular accommodation. Old polarities are transcended and boundaries redrawn, while the interconnectedness of different societies and cultures is accepted not only intellectually, but as lived personal reality.[263] The 'thunderous vitality of contemporary Islam' may indeed be 'in direct proportion to modernization.'[264] As a paradigmatic orientation within it and a response to globalisation, the attitudes of such modern Muslim seekers, mediated through a sufism recovered from tradition, deserve substantial attention.

Epilogue

Flowing from the story of Beshara, we pick up three questions in this epilogue. First, how does this story illuminate broader issues relating to the study of sufism in the West and that of modern Islam and NRMs? Second, what is the significance (and implications) of the sufi–New Age nexus exemplified by Beshara in the arena of global culture and cultural exchange? Third, how might we project the future of Beshara, and how might this shed light on future religious–spiritual landscapes and the future of sufism?

On studying sufism, modern Islam and NRMs

Some approaches to the study of sufism in the modern West assume or seek out evidence of continuities with categories of the pre-modern sufi tradition in the Muslim world. The facile application of such categories to the study of contemporary trends and figures in the West creates an artificial sense of a reified tradition, and can obscure proper understanding.[1] Greater illumination of many Western sufi movements can be achieved by approaching these as products of the modern present, taking into account any preferences for self-projection in terms of the historical tradition but assessing their application as potentially fresh constructs. We have demonstrated in this volume that, as a movement of sufi spirituality in the modern West, Beshara can be illuminated by locating it within the arena of its emergence, rather than against the backdrop of pre-modern Islamic sufism or by projecting it as an example of the ongoing influence of prominent figures within this. It must thus be located at the interface of late Ottoman sufism as projected by Rauf (who was exposed to its fading rays), and shifts in religiosity in Western societies as manifest in sixties Britain. In this perspective, we understand the movement's self-description in terms of the category of Uwaysi (Theo-didactic) sufism as an attempt to clarify and seek legitimacy for its own approach. While we do not deny the possibility of a continuing strand of sufi experience capturing the Uwaysi spirit, the interpretive approach here is determined ultimately by the changed context of Western modernity.

We have commented in passing that there are relatively few studies of NRMs in the West that draw on Islamic–sufi resources. In more general terms, scholars of NRMs have shown little interest in Islam and Islamic groups, regardless of geographical location. At first sight, the relatively few entries relating to Islam in surveys of NRMs can be attributed to their exclusively or heavily 'West'-centric focus, which is occasionally made explicit.[2] Certain assumptions and anomalies arise in surveys of this nature, however, and these serve to illuminate entrenched attitudes towards Muslim religiosity within NRM studies.

We can illustrate these through the example of the *Encyclopedia of New Religions: New Religious Movements, Sects, and Alternative Spiritualities* (2004). The editor's introduction to the section 'New Religions [NRMs], Sects and Alternative Spiritualities with Roots in Islam' explains that 'many trends and movements within contemporary Islam that can be described as new religions or alternative spiritualities are Sufi in orientation'. Entries in the section have been selected to bear out this claim.[3] The editor hints at the reasons for the success of sufism in inspiring Westerners (where Islam has failed): 'although many new groups and movements within Islam maintain conservative attitudes and, particularly in the West, seek to distinguish themselves from the surrounding culture, there are developments such as the Haqqani Naqshbandis ... that are far more accommodating and innovative'. That he thus effectively dismisses the numerous movements (some of them sufi in orientation, but many decidedly not) that emerged within mainstream Islam during the twentieth century, a period of unprecedented religious dynamism among Muslims, is perhaps explicable in terms of the primary focus and resulting scope of his work. As the inside cover explains, the *Encyclopedia* provides readers with 'a comprehensive map of the significant religious and spiritual groups functioning in today's world, *especially in the West*' (our emphasis). However, a glance at the 'Roots in Judaism' section begs the question, for it encompasses, among others, Gush Emunim, a religious nationalist settler movement geographically contained within Israel. If a strictly Western focus is intended, this should be upheld consistently (as in the case of Islam/sufi-derived movements engaging people of non-Muslim provenance in the West). If something else is admitted (for example, Judaism-derived movements for Jews in a Jewish majority setting, as in the case of Gush Emunim), then surely *Islamic* movements appearing during the second half of the twentieth century (and earlier) *in Muslim majority settings* must be seriously represented?[4] Their summary dismissal reflects an assumption that they are relevant only to specialists on the closed and separate world of Islam (or to Muslims themselves). It has the unfortunate effect, in such a broad survey work, of perpetuating an impression that 'Islam' is both monolithic and bereft of impulses of dynamism, differentiation and adaptability that have brought change and development to other religious traditions. The exclusion of Muslim homologues of movements like Gush Emunim is all the more surprising for the fact that many of them have had a profound impact (direct or indirect) on Western arenas (*vide* the obvious example of al-Qaʻida and the dominant salafi trend in modern Islam from which it emanates), and have evidently recruited Westerners, including those born into Islam and, significantly, converts.[5] The overlooking of Turkish-origin groups such as the *Nur* movement and its derivatives, emanating from a secular context at a physical interface with Europe and engaging millions of people (including many in Western Europe and the USA) is further evidence that, for many in this somewhat confused field, 'Islam for Muslims' simply evinces no parallels with the religious experience of any other peoples in the modern world, and thus cannot be situated or treated within the same frameworks.

We have hinted at some such parallels in this study, but our purpose here is to underscore the need for a more inclusive and integrated approach that acknowledges the importance and dynamism of modern movements in Islam, irrespective of whether they appeal to Westerners or draw on sufism. The conflation of 'Islamic' religious dynamism with sufism implicit in the *Encyclopedia's* approach[6] merely reinforces the suggestion implicit in the Orientalist projection of sufism as 'discovered' 200 years ago, viz. that this part of the Islamic tradition is worthy of particular attention – coinciding with the assumption that it is, ultimately, extrinsic to it, and can hence function as a potential resource for Westerners.

As J. Gordon Melton recently hinted, 9/11 highlighted the need to 'overcome the barriers between NRM studies and Islamic studies',[7] each of them a relatively insular field. An integrated approach might enable a better understanding of the nature of immediate threats of violence associated with some Islamist movements. More importantly, it may also facilitate the erosion of increasingly dangerous long-standing misconceptions (and ignorance) surrounding the religious impulses of modern Muslims. Such misconceptions have partly shaped the present crisis, and they are perpetuated by the isolation and perceived otherness of Islamic studies. While our subject lies squarely within the Western arena of NRMs, through a necessary marriage of the fields of NRM studies and Islamic studies in this volume we have sought to make a contribution, however modest and indirect, to breaking down the barriers to which Gordon Melton refers.[8] Most recent years have seen a new acknowledgement of the importance of a truly global perspective in NRM studies. This is accompanied by a gradual paradigm shift towards situating NRMs within the larger field of social movements, moving away from the earlier emphasis on their newness and *sui generis* religious nature.[9] Both developments augur well for future integration of the field with Islamic studies.[10]

On the sufi–New Age nexus and global culture

As part of the modern globalisation of religion in general, the New Age demonstrates the ease of cultural interaction and interchange in the modern world.[11] At a time that calls for investment in positive cultural engagement between Western and Muslim worlds, the sufi–New Age nexus in the West, illustrated by the case of Beshara, deserves particular investigation. It has been suggested that, where the New Age has adopted oriental conceptions, this has been '*as perceived by*' those Westerners involved, and '*only* to the extent that they could be assimilated into already existing Western frameworks'.[12] The selective reconstruction of traditions implied in this comment is a universal feature of the cultural migration of ideas. It is well illustrated by the example of Rauf, himself arguably a Westernised 'Oriental', who imported an 'oriental' conception that was remoulded for its assimilation into Western frameworks marked by countercultural discontent with modernity and the turn to subjectivity. Under Young, and within the changing British spiritual landscape of the last two decades, this process has advanced further, and the nature of Beshara's relationship to the world of sufism and Islam has perhaps become clearer (although not every associate may agree with this assessment, it might be noted). Yet the very presence and activities of Beshara contribute to a gradual broadening of familiarisation with sufi (and by extension Islamic) motifs, images and terminology in society at large. The New Age has been acknowledged as an important indicator of contemporary cultural change. Most striking is its resort to a universal reservoir of resources for understanding and celebrating what it means to be human, implicitly divesting the modern West of its claim to universal cultural validity and breaking the monopoly of divisive cultural and religious paradigms. As sufism takes its place in the global repository of spiritual wisdom, the sufi niche in the global New Age (through movements, practices, literature, tourism, the arts, etc.), while perhaps outwardly insignificant, thus represents a potentially important contribution to the gradual erosion of Western perceptions of Islam as other, and the 'detailed ignorance' that accompanies such perceptions.[13]

The sufi–New Age nexus illuminates the complexities and paradoxes of the experience of modernity in diverse cultures. As we have suggested, for some of those drawn to it in the advanced industrial societies of the West, the embrace of sufism (whether in its New Age appropriation or otherwise) represents a reaction *against* modernity. In Muslim contexts, the New Age (perceived as 'modern', but itself implicitly refusing to bow to a blanket privileging of the modern) and sufism (originally the heart of traditional, pre-modern Islamic piety) are tapped as resources in exploring culturally resonant paths to modernity. The dialectical relation of the New Age to Western culture is of particular interest when it is exported as a global product to cultural contexts where local traditions have furnished resources for its original self-expression. As illustrated in this volume, following its export to the West, Muslim arenas have seen sufism re-imported and embraced by youth in a 'Westernised' New Age form.[14] This can ultimately be applied as a resource in constructing a modernity implicitly indexed to Western patterns, but conceived as distinct from them. In the absence of such repackaged 'Western' forms, some of those concerned, who have then gone on to develop a deeper commitment to *Muslim* culture, may never have become thus involved. Against earlier prejudices, such findings further underline the importance of the New Age as a field of academic enquiry.

On the future of Beshara, religious–spiritual landscapes, and sufism

Like other sixties counterculture New Age seekers, first-generation associates who make up the core of Beshara are now in their fifties (and sixties).

They have grown older in the mainstream: while remaining deeply involved, they have settled down, found jobs and established families.[15] Brought up within a milieu influenced by their parents' involvement, the older offspring of these associates are now adults. Given their characteristic aversion to imposing anything, associates are disinclined to frog-march their offspring to Chisholme. Some of these offspring have become deeply involved, and have answered a recent call for 'the next generation' to come forward, so that responsibility within the movement can be handed on.[16] A considerable number of them (perhaps half, according to one associate) are disinterested, and others look disdainfully upon their parents' involvement.[17] Whether or not they have grown up within the movement, younger associates have not on the whole equipped themselves linguistically to study first-hand the works of Ibn 'Arabi or other sufis (through choices in higher education, for example).[18] This points to an inevitable further distancing from the cultural context of Beshara's source of inspiration in the future, as numbers of first-generation associates who are thus equipped (and who had personally encountered Rauf) decline with time. Some first-generation associates indeed now sense the necessity to reassert consciously and explicitly the universal thrust of Beshara over (perhaps somehow *without*) its 'Muslim–sufi' casing (somewhat as Rauf had done towards the end of his life), if there is to be a true expression and perpetuation of its original message that will be universally accessible.

The expectation of a new age appears to be less of an immediate preoccupation within the movement today than during the early 1970s. Yet the coming of a new era remains central to associates' understandings of the world, and the tone of Young's discourses in particular serves to underline the urgent need for the changes that will help pave its way. This expectation is clearly evident in the movement's projection of its view of the present times in the public domain, where it appears repeatedly, if without specific detail. It must thus be deemed part of its appeal to those who approach it. Associates have registered with quiet confidence the burgeoning interest in all things spiritual in Western societies in recent years, and the growing challenge mounted by 'spirituality' to traditional religious frameworks, the very social and cultural changes of which the movement itself might be construed as a product, and to which it owes its continuing appeal. Projected as harbingers of the approaching materialisation of their utopian vision, such observations have served to vindicate their worldview.

It is noteworthy that Beshara very quickly established an international presence. It has also made good use of opportunities offered by globalisation for enhancing its work. For example, while it is unclear how successful NRMs in general have been in using the internet for self-publicity and recruitment of new members, and although some sociologists suspect that the 'disembodied' interface will fail given the importance of social networks in the recruitment process,[19] Beshara has received a steady flow of students via this particular route, which has also taken it to Indonesia. In general, the movement scores well against Stark's ten propositions specifying the necessary or sufficient conditions for the success of religious movements.[20] The first of these deserves particular attention: 'New religious movements are likely to succeed to the extent that they retain cultural continuity with the conventional faith(s) of the societies in which they seek converts.'[21] This suggests that, by drawing on resources associated with a religious tradition perceived as extraneous to the Western cultural context that represents its primary sphere of operation, Beshara competes from a position of relative weakness compared with Judeo-Christian-based movements. In its embrace of key New Age themes, however, it simultaneously taps into an expanding undercurrent in modes of engagement with the sacred in this arena. In the context of the New Age/spirituality of life, notions of cultural capital and its expenditure on conversion demand particular assessment, for the ultimate index is the self and its wellbeing and freedom, rather than the cultural straitjackets of society. It can of course be argued that the New Age represents a particular cultural expression, but its eclecticism points to a confident cultural borrowing and synthesis that defies the logic of Stark's first proposition. Moreover, Campbell's thesis of the 'Easternisation of the West' must also be placed in the balance.

Beshara's viability as spiritual resource provider becomes clear when viewed alongside the experience of Rauf's contemporaries among Turkish sufi masters, which we illustrated earlier. Several twentieth-century Turkish sufi masters shared with Rauf a general ethos and aspects of approach to the spiritual life, and their followers' perceptions of them resonate closely with associates' perceptions of Rauf. Such masters have often emphasised love and ethics over law, and common humanity over religious divides, for example, and they have eschewed formal institutionalisation. The 'ever-colonizing Turkish dervishes'[22] who have brought their teaching to the West have tended to export a pre-determined formula, however, adapting this ad hoc as necessitated by its new milieu. What sets Beshara apart from their endeavours is the fact that this project was conceived outside of the Muslim milieu: it took shape in response to the search of Western seekers specifically, while Rauf was in the West. This circumstance has served as a powerful counterbalance to the 'alien' cultural–religious provenance of the resources upon which he drew.

A study of the religious–spiritual orientations of the cohort of first-generation associates must reflect on the findings of research on their baby-boomer counterparts mapping developments from the 1960s to the present, as they move beyond late middle age. This may add to our understanding of religious–spiritual trends in this influential generation (which significantly altered the religious–spiritual landscape of the USA).[23] Beyond this specific cohort, the growing Beshara clientele points more generally to the widespread spiritual quest and search for meaning in the West today. The movement's existence, teaching and approach reflect the impact of transformations associated with modernity on religious life throughout contemporary Western societies, highlighting among others changing understandings of authority and the turn to the self, re-sacralisation, and the 'Easternisation of the West'. At the same time, its success points to the potency of its message of 'Oneness' in its capacity as an integrating, 'totalising' foil to the fragmenting impacts of modernity.

From a broader perspective, the strong resonance between the narratives of those who have come to Beshara in Britain and seekers in majority Muslim societies who have arrived at a 'new' sufism must be underlined. Differences in starting point, context and destination notwithstanding, the underlying commonalities of motivation and process, reflecting universal impacts of modernisation and characteristic influences of late modernity, are striking. As they search for that which transcends them and gives meaning and purpose to their lives, some of the 'intensely modern' Muslim seekers we have described evince the same emphases as their Western counterparts. They too 'value experience over beliefs, distrust institutions and leaders, stress personal fulfilment yet yearn for community, and are fluid in their allegiance'.[24] All are actively engaged as individuals in 'creating an ongoing personal religious narrative in relation to the symbolic resources available'.[25]

Beshara illuminates facets of the place and role of sufi spirituality in the contemporary world. For example, close collaborative relationships that have developed between associates and 'recent' Turkish Muslim sufis illustrate the strong bonds to which a shared sufi heritage can give rise, notwithstanding significant differences with regard to religious framing, and the potential of the sufi heritage as a channel for cultural rapprochement between Muslim and Western worlds. It is undeniable that modernity imposed unprecedented pressures on sufism as the heart of traditional Muslim piety. Yet it has also occasioned transformations and revitalisations of this in ways unimaginable a century ago. Some Westerners involved with sufism suggest that, when its spiritual treasures began to lose their currency in a modernising Muslim world (where its fate would increasingly be sealed by the triumph of an 'exoteric' Islam),[26] these were providentially rescued by Western souls who lamented a parallel earlier loss in their own societies. While not everyone will agree with this projection, the resuscitation of sufism in its lands of origin and its continued expansion and metamorphosis in the West have undoubtedly been facilitated by the shrinking of space and cultural difference in the modern world, which has made possible strategic alliances aiming to preserve and perpetuate its heritage. Meanwhile, the detachment of sufism from its Islamic and *tariqa* matrix has had profound implications for the diffusion, democratisation, and, according to some, degradation of sufi traditions. The story of Beshara gives form to one outcome of the profound changes that mark out the sufi experience in the modern world.

Notes

Chapter 1

1 All terms in this study are ultimately employed in their capacity as heuristic devices and as having permeable borders, rather than as clear-cut and fixed labels. This approach is especially apt in fields of study where it cannot be taken for granted that any term has a clear definition upon which all will agree, and where claims to authoritative definitions invariably serve ideological and/or political ends.

2 Arthur Marwick argues that 'the evidence ... is indisputable that some time between the mid-fifties ... and the world recession of 1973 changes so important in major aspects of British society took place as to establish the phrase "cultural revolution" in the legitimate realm of hyperbole'. See Arthur Marwick, *Britain in Our Century: Images and Controversies* (London, 1984), p. 163. On the contentious nature of this argument, see his *Culture in Britain since 1945* (Oxford, 1991), pp. 67–8. As the most characteristic elements of the period he lists: (a) an outburst of individualism; (b) the rise of young people to positions of unprecedented influence, 'youth subculture' having a steady impact on the rest of society; (c) advances in technology and massive improvements in material life; (d) 'permissiveness' and sexual liberation; (e) unprecedented international cultural exchange; (f) the emergence of 'a participatory ... popular culture, in which rock music, its central component, effectively became a kind of universal language'; (g) original developments in elite thought associated with structuralism/post-structuralism; (h) new concerns for civil and personal rights; (i) the appearance of 'the first intimations of the ... challenges implicit in the concept of the entire West as a collection of multicultural societies'. See *Culture in Britain*, pp. xvii–xx; cf. Arthur Marwick, *The Sixties: Cultural Revolution in Britain, France, Italy and the United States, c. 1958-1974* (Oxford, 1998), pp. 3–4.

3 While this is the common projection of the period, which we uphold here for purposes of simplicity, Marwick questions whether there was a single unified cohesive counterculture at this time. He also doubts the accompanying notion of a dialectical process whereby one type of culture was in direct confrontation with, and about to take the place of, another. He holds that the essence of sixties developments was rather in the coalescence of a large number of subcultures and movements. All were somehow critical of the established order, and all expanded, interacted and ultimately permeated and transformed society, thanks partly to the existence and expansion of a liberal, progressive presence within the institutions of authority, that was prepared to tolerate them. See Arthur Marwick, Introduction: locating key texts amid the distinctive landscape of the sixties, in Anthony Aldgate, James Chapman and Arthur Marwick, eds, *Windows on the Sixties: Exploring Key Texts of Media and Culture* (London, 2000), pp. xii–xiii.

For classic overviews of the counterculture, its origins, concerns and activities, encompassing Britain and the USA, see Frank Musgrove, *Ecstasy and Holiness: Counter Culture and the Open Society* (London, 1974), and Thoedore Roszak, *The Making of a Counter Culture: Reflections on the Technocratic Society and its Youthful Opposition* (Berkeley, 1995/1969). See also J. Milton Yinger, *Countercultures: The Promise and Peril of a World Turned Upside Down* (London, 1982).

4 See Roszak, *The Making of a Counter Culture*, p. xxix, and Paul Heelas, *The New Age Movement: The Celebration of the Self and the Sacralization of Modernity* (Oxford, 1996), p. 56, for example.

5 See Peter Berger, Brigitte Berger and Hansfried Kellner, *The Homeless Mind: Modernization and Consciousness* (New York, 1973). For a summary of its main thesis (on which we draw here), see Paul Heelas and Linda Woodhead, Homeless Minds Today?, in Linda Woodhead with Paul Heelas and David Martin, eds, *Peter Berger and The Study*

of Religion (London, 2001), pp. 43ff. For a classic discussion of 'the maelstrom of modern life', see Marshall Berman, *All that is Solid Melts into Air: The Experience of Modernity* (London, 1981). For institutional transformations associated with it, see Anthony Giddens, *The Consequences of Modernity* (Oxford, 2000).

6 See Heelas and Woodhead, Homeless Minds Today?, pp. 44–6.

7 See Heelas, *The New Age Movement*, p. 51. He identifies two parallel orientations, one directed at changing the mainstream (exemplified in political activism in the form of civil rights or anti-Vietnam demonstrations), the other aiming at living the hedonistic life through the world of 'sex, drugs and rock-and-roll'. As we will pick up in Ch. 8, the 'turn to the self' or to 'subjectivity' has been posited as possibly the defining cultural feature of modern Western culture as a whole, and its countercultural expressions must be situated within the longer view of modernity. Charles Taylor, *The Ethics of Authenticity* (Cambridge, MA, 1991), traces the 'birth' of the powerful moral 'ideal of authenticity' that characterises contemporary culture (usually couched in terms of goals of self-fulfilment or self-realisation) to the end of the eighteenth century, mapping key developments and articulations of this and its underlying conception of the self in philosophy and art, for example (see pp. 25–9, 81–91). This ideal 'accords crucial moral importance to a kind of contact with myself, with my own inner nature … it greatly increases the importance of this self-contact by introducing the principle of originality: each of our voices has something of its own to say' (p. 29). He observes that, since the sixties, 'the individualism of self-fulfilment' has grown particularly strong in Western societies (p. 14). Taylor originally explored 'the radical turn inward' as a defining influence on the development of modern self-identity in his *Sources of the Self: The Making of the Modern Identity* (Cambridge, MA, 1989).

8 On the situation of religion in post-war Britain, see Grace Davie, *Religion in Britain since 1945* (Oxford, 1994), and Steve Bruce, *Religion in Modern Britain* (Oxford, 1995). Detailed statistics concerning church membership and attendance can be found in Bruce, pp. 35–41. The historian A. N. Wilson recently suggested that the most striking feature of 1960s Britain was the *absolute* decline of religion (*The Moral Maze*, BBC Radio 4, 19 June 2004). Such statements require some qualification. Thus, while post-war statistics in general demonstrate a decline in religious membership and practice, indices of religious belief have remained relatively high, pointing to a pattern of what Davie terms 'believing without belonging' in post-war Britain. Significantly, this disjunction has been accentuated in each post-war generation. Regarding the American context, the well-known *Time Magazine* article 'Is God Dead?' (8 April 1966) in fact demonstrated that denominational allegiance had risen country-wide during the preceding few years, while almost half the adult population claimed membership in a church or synagogue.

9 In 1968, for example, Peter Berger told *The New York Times* that, by the twenty-first century, 'religious believers are likely to be found only in small sects, huddled together to resist a worldwide secular culture'. See R. Stark, 'Secularization: R.I.P.', *Sociology of Religion*, 60: 3 (1999), pp. 249–50, for this and further examples of the contemporary mood.

10 Gerald Parsons, Expanding the Religious Spectrum: New Religious Movements in Modern Britain, in Gerald Parsons, ed., *The Growth of Religious Diversity: Britain from 1945*, 1: *Traditions* (London, 1993), p. 277, cites an estimate that, between 1945 and 1990, over 500 new movements of religious expression emerged in Britain. For the sake of a balanced picture it should be noted that, even taken together, the numbers participating in such new movements have come nowhere near the segment of the population estimated to have remained actively committed members of traditional Christian churches (15% in 1993: p. 278). Nonetheless, added to the various New Age expressions (on which see below), the number of those who have had some involvement with new movements of religious expression in post-war Britain would appear to be far from insignificant. This remains a contested point, however; see for example Bruce, *Religion in Modern Britain*, pp. 95, 117ff.

The secularisation thesis upholds the necessary connection between the onset of modernity (associated with the rise of individualism and rationality) and the demise of traditional forms of religious life. Put simply, it posits secularisation (a process in which religion diminishes in importance in society and the individual consciousness) as a necessary part of modernisation, indeed as the direct result of it. Religiousness is expected to decrease as industrialisation, urbanisation and rationalisation associated with modernisation increase, and in tandem with the pluralisation caused by modernity and the progressive differentiation of modern institutions. Founders of the sociology of religion and their successors had expected secularisation to succeed ultimately in eradicating religion altogether from modern culture and conscience. Their vision was of a world that would become increasingly and inescapably more rationalised and disenchanted. Evidence of expanding (re-)'sacralisation' ('growth in the territory of the sacred') or 'de-secularisation' is now increasingly cited to critique and counter theories of secularisation. See, for example, Paul Heelas and Linda Woodhead with Benjamin Seel, Bronislaw Szerszynski and Karin Tusting, *The Spiritual Revolution: Why Religion is Giving Way to Spirituality* (Oxford, 2004), p. 9; Peter L. Berger, Secularization and De-Secularization, in Linda Woodhead, ed., *Religions in the Modern World: Traditions and Transformations* (London, 2002), pp. 291–6; Peter L. Berger, ed., *The De-Secularization of the World: Essays on the Resurgence of Religion in World Politics* (Washington, 2000).

As far as Britain is concerned, it is now widely accepted that there is no evidence of a decline in religiosity or experiences of a transcendental kind among post-war generations. These have clearly persisted, if at times in new formulations and expressions; see further, Gerald Parsons, Introduction: Persistence, Pluralism and Perplexity, in Parsons, *The Growth of Religious Diversity*, pp. 13–17, and Grace Davie, 'Believing without Belonging: Is this the Future of Religion in Britain?', *Social Compass*, 37 (1990), pp. 455–69.

For the arguments of a die-hard proponent of the secularisation thesis, see Steve Bruce, ed., *Religion and Modernization* (Oxford, 1992) and *From Cathedrals to Cults: Religion in the Modern World* (Oxford, 1996). For the ongoing debate concerning the aptness and applicability of the thesis, which Berger, Secularization and De-Secularization, p. 292, suggests has been abandoned by the majority of contemporary sociologists of religion (if understood as a simple equation between modernity and secularisation), see Grace Davie, *Religion in Modern Europe: A Memory Mutates* (Oxford, 2000), pp. 24ff., and Danièle Hervieu-Leger, The Twofold Limit of the Notion of Secularization, in Woodhead *et al.*, eds, *Peter Berger and The Study of Religion*, pp. 112ff. For a powerfully argued call to 'declare an end to social scientific faith in the theory of secularization' based on a range of evidence, see Stark, 'Secularization: R.I.P.', pp. 249–73; see also David Martin, 'The Secularization Issue: Prospect and Retrospect', *British Journal of Sociology*, 42 (1991), pp. 465–74.

For an overview of religious diversity in contemporary Britain (to which waves of immigration have also contributed significantly, especially from the 1960s), see Paul Weller, ed., *Religions in the UK: A Multi-Faith Directory* (Mickleover, Derby, 1993).

11 This neutral term (along with 'minority' or 'alternative' religions) is the preferred one in the scholarly literature given that the term 'cult' (itself a technical term in the sociology of religion, in contradistinction to 'sect' and 'church') has taken on unhelpful associations and negative connotations due to the propaganda efforts of the anti-cult movement and media views. On the use of these terms, see Eileen Barker, 'New Religious Movements', *Farmington Papers, Modern Theology*, 12 (The Farmington Institute for Christian Studies, Oxford), November 1999, p. 1; David V. Barrett, *The New Believers: A Survey of Sects, Cults and Alternative Religions* (London, 2001), chapter 2; George D. Chryssides, *Exploring New Religions* (London, 1999), p. 4; Elisabeth Arweck, New Religious Movements, in Woodhead, ed., *Religions in the Modern World*, pp. 279–81.

12 This definition draws on Barker, 'New Religious Movements', p. 1 and Barrett, *The New Believers*, p. 26. Some assume Western societies as context. Others refer explicitly to

North America and Western Europe, while recognising that the appearance of NRMs is a global phenomenon. See for example Arweck, New Religious Movements, p. 269.

Challenges arise in mapping NRMs in relation to the classical religious traditions to which they present connections, and in drawing boundaries between a 'traditional religion', a 'new variant' of this, and a NRM. Equally, there are problems in applying the term NRM to all the groups it seeks to define, given the numerous and important differences between them. As put by Lorne L. Dawson, ed., *Cults and New Religious Movements: A Reader* (Oxford, 2003), p. 2, 'some are no longer new, some never were movements, and the religious status of some is a matter of dispute'. John Coleman, Editorial, in John Coleman and Gregory Brown, eds, *New Religious Movements* (Concilium: Religion in the Eighties) (Edinburgh, 1983), p. vii, elaborates that 'NRM' serves as 'a mantle for an extraordinary variety of diverse groups. In general, sociologists … join together under this rubric the three fastest growing sectors of religion in the West: neo-orthodox or neo-fundamentalist versions of Christianity and Judaism …; neo-Orientalism in Europe and the United States; [and] various human potential movements which have been influenced by neo-Oriental ideas such as … EST and forms of trans-personal psychology.' See also Parsons, Expanding the Religious Spectrum, pp. 279–80, 285–7; Chryssides, *Exploring New Religions*, pp. 11ff.; Harvey Cox, *Turning East: The Promise and Peril of the New Orientalism* (London, 1979), pp. 18, 20. Given this diversity, it is impossible to generalise about NRMs, as underlined, for example, by Bryan Wilson, Introduction, in B. R. Wilson and J. Cresswell, eds, *New Religious Movements: Challenge and Response* (London, 1999), p. 7, and Eileen Barker, New Religious Movements: Their Incidence and Significance, in ibid. pp. 20, 29. The present discussion focuses mainly on those NRMs dubbed by some 'neo-Oriental' (or 'Eastern-derived'): see following note.

13 Coleman, Editorial, p. vii, uses the term to designate groups that draw exclusively or substantially on 'Oriental' (as opposed to 'Western') religious traditions: there are of course problems with this approach. On typologies of NRMs, see below.

14 Important qualitative and quantitative differences between the wave of interest in 'Oriental spirituality' from the 1960s and earlier waves beginning in the nineteenth century must be underlined. In contrast with the 'mere imbibing of ideas from books and lectures' on the part of intellectuals, the more recent wave involved greater numbers, and a characteristic insistence on direct experience through practice. See Cox, *Turning East*, pp. 9, 18; Coleman, Editorial, p. ix; Heelas, *The New Age Movement*, pp. 47, 55. Western intellectuals had turned to Oriental spiritual traditions during the nineteenth century either to expand upon the meaning of Christian truths, or out of a rejection of Christianity and loss of faith in the ability of Christian institutions to answer to contemporary spiritual needs. Some travelled east, but Eastern teachers also began to arrive in the West, where intellectuals provided a receptive audience. New trends emerged in the West around teachers drawing on Oriental religious teachings and practices. The eventual popularisation of this interest was possibly fed by a growing loss of faith in the project of Western modernity after 1914. This early wave of interest in Eastern spirituality is exemplified by personalities behind the influential Theosophical Society. On Madame Blavatsky (d.1891) and Annie Besant (d.1933), for example, see Barrett, *The New Believers*, pp. 344–7, and Emily B. Sellon and Renee Weber, Theosophy and the Theosophical Society, in Antoine Faivre and Jacob Needleman, eds, *Modern Esoteric Spirituality* (London, 1993), pp. 311–29. René Guénon (d.1951), whose writings inspired a new movement founded on a rejection of modernity and reconstruction of the 'perennial philosophy' encapsulating the central truths behind all major world religions, is another important example. His works stressed 'the urgent need for the West's remaining spiritual and intellectual elite to find both personal and collective salvation in the surviving vestiges of the ancient religious traditions', i.e. the Eastern religions. See Mark Sedgwick, 'Traditionalist Sufism', *ARIES*, 22 (1999) and www.Traditionalists.org. On his broad influence, see 'Guénon', in Wouter J. Hanegraaff with Antoine Faivre, Roelof van den Broek and Jean-Pierre Brach, eds, *Dictionary of Gnosis and Western Esotericism* (Leiden, 2005), 1, pp. 442–5. See also

Robin Waterfield, *René Guénon and the Future of the West: The Life and Writings of a Twentieth Century Metaphysician* (Wellingborough, Northamptonshire, 1987). For further nineteenth- and early twentieth-century examples of Western intellectual interest in Eastern spirituality, see Robert Ellwood, 'Asian Religions in North America', in Coleman and Brown, eds, *New Religious Movements*, pp. 17ff.

15 From the early 1970s, counter-cultists contributed substantially to literature on NRMs, fuelling a propaganda war against them and adding to their public stigmatisation within the general population. On the overwhelmingly negative popular perception of NRMs in Britain, at least until the late 1980s, see Chryssides, *Exploring New Religions*, pp. 22ff., and Parsons, Expanding the Religious Spectrum, pp. 289ff.

16 See for example Parsons, Expanding the Religious Spectrum, p. 277, and Davie, *Religion in Modern Europe*, p. 116. Interest in NRMs continues to inspire a steady stream of publications, reflecting a disproportionate interest in a phenomenon that may be relatively small quantitatively, yet points to important underlying social issues. For examples see Peter Clarke, ed., *The Routledge Encyclopaedia of New Religious Movements* (London, 2005); Christopher Partridge, ed., *Encyclopaedia of New Religions* (Oxford, 2004); James R. Lewis, ed., *The Oxford Handbook of New Religious Movements* (Oxford, 2003); Eileen Barker, *New Religious Movements: A Practical Introduction* (London, 2000) and *Of Gods and Men: New Religious Movements in the West* (Macon, GA, 1983); Timothy Miller, ed., *America's Alternative Religions* (Albany, NY, 1995); Diane Choquette, *New Religious Movements in the United States and Canada: A Critical Assessment and Annotated Bibliography* (London, 1985); Wilson and Cresswell, eds, *New Religious Movements*; Lorne L. Dawson, *Comprehending Cults: The Sociology of New Religious Movements* (Oxford, 1999); Elisabeth Arweck and Peter Clarke, eds, *New Religious Movements in Western Europe: An Annotated Bibliography* (Westport, CT, 1997). There are several detailed studies of individual groups/gurus. For these and further bibliographies, see Dawson, ed., *Cults and New Religious Movements*, pp. 3–4, 34–5.

Several typologies of NRMs have been advanced. See, for example, Peter B. Clarke, Introduction: Change and Variety in New Religious Movements in Western Europe, c.1960 to the Present, in Arweck and Clarke, eds, *New Religious Movements in Western Europe*, pp. xxxiiff. Two contrasting approaches can be mentioned by way of illustration. J. Gordon Melton, ed., *The Encyclopaedia of American Religions* (Detroit, 1993), distinguishes eight 'family groups' according to a largely descriptive and historical approach. Roy Wallis, *The Elementary Forms of the New Religious Life* (London, 1984), offers an analytical categorisation in terms of movements that are world accommodating, world affirming or world rejecting, based on how they view their relationship to the rest of society. These differences in attitude, he suggests, account most fully for differences in organisation and behaviour among NRMs. Wallis' scheme has been widely applied: see, for example, Parsons, Expanding the Religious Spectrum, p. 280; Ali Kose, *Conversion to Islam: A Study of Native British Converts* (London, 1996), pp. 145–7. Cf. Bruce, *Religion in Modern Britain*, pp. 96–101, and Chryssides, *Exploring New Religions*, pp. 26–8. Eileen Barker, 'New Religious Movements and Political Orders', Centre for the Study of Religions and Society, Pamphlet Library no. 15 (1987), points out that NRMs are often too complex to fit into such clear-cut categories. For further discussion of typologies and the development of 'ideal types', see Arweck, New Religious Movements, pp. 265, 270.

17 See Cox, *Turning East*, pp. 93–4; Coleman, Editorial, p. ix; Dawson, Who Joins New Religious Movements and Why: Twenty Years of Research and What have we Learned?, in Dawson, ed., *Cults and New Religious Movements*, pp. 121–3. The latter notes the ambiguity surrounding joiners' religious backgrounds, specifically whether or not they tend to be 'unchurched'.

18 See Coleman, Editorial, pp. ix–x. This 'direct and personal experience' of the sacred is contrasted with 'beliefs'. The comment of a joiner cited in Cox, *Turning East*, p. 96, underlines this contrast: 'All I got at any church I ever went to were sermons ... *about* God, *about* "the peace that surpasses understanding". Words, words, words. It was all up here (pointing to the head). I never really *felt* it ... it seemed lifeless. It was like reading the label instead of eating the contents.' It is noteworthy that most neo-Oriental NRMs show new initiates techniques of prayer or meditation without delay, so they can begin their new spiritual venture at the level of practice immediately. See ibid., p.97.

19 Paul Heelas, The Spiritual Revolution: From 'Religion' to 'Spirituality', in Woodhead, ed., *Religions in the Modern World*, p.358, provides a working definition of these two terms: '"Religion" is ... very much God-centred, with no mention of affirmation of life in the here-and-now ... [E]specially since the 1960s, "religion" has increasingly come to be seen as that which is institutionalized: involving prescribed rituals; established ways of believing; the "official", as regulated and transmitted by religious authorities; that which is enshrined in tradition ... the voice of the authority of the transcendent. For many, it has also come to be associated with the formal, dogmatic and hierarchical, if not the impersonal or patriarchal.' Spirituality, in contrast, 'has to do with the personal; that which is interior or immanent; that which is one's experienced relationship with the sacred ... At heart, spirituality has come to mean "life" ... Life, rather than what transcends life, becomes God.' On the growing awareness of the sharp distinction between organised religion and spirituality in the USA from the 1960s (and the defection of young people from one to the other), see Robert Wuthnow, The New Spiritual Freedom, in Dawson, ed., *Cults and New Religious Movements*, pp.102–4.

20 The 'guru-quest' was so significant that, in Britain, the 1960s have been dubbed the beginning of the 'age of the modern guru'. Heelas, *The New Age Movement*, p.51, suggests that there were only relatively few gurus, masters and organised spiritual paths in the West during the 1960s. Yet at this time The Beatles (and Bob Dylan) fell under the spell of the Mahareshi Mahesh Yogi (see below), and their patronage gave his movement a massive publicity boost. The example of Bede Griffiths (who has been described as a 'Christian guru') points to the ethos of the times. Formerly a monk of Prinknash Abbey and Prior of Farnborough Abbey, he based himself at an ashram in Tamil Nadu which had been founded in 1950 by two Frenchmen as a Christian community following the customs of a Hindu ashram. Among Griffiths' best-known works is *The Marriage of East and West* (London, 1982).

By the early 1970s, the guru phenomenon was becoming, as Ziauddin Sardar, *Desperately Seeking Paradise: Journeys of a Sceptical Muslim* (London, 2004), p.69, suggests, 'a general epidemic'. On the rise of the Western guru from the late nineteenth century, see Peter Washington, *Madame Blavatsky's Baboon: Theosophy and the Emergence of the Western Guru* (London, 1993), and Anthony Storr, *Feet of Clay: A Study of Gurus* (London, 1996).

21 See Cox, *Turning East*, pp.97–8.

22 The expression derives from the title of the work by Berger *et al.*, cited earlier. As they pointed out, the 'homeless mind', unable to tolerate the continuous uncertainty associated with radical de-institutionalisation, seeks out 'secondary institutions', which are less strongly institutionalised and relatively detraditionalised compared with primary institutions experienced as 'iron cage meaninglessness and rigidity'. Among such secondary institutions, they identified psychoanalysis and psychotherapy, 'occultism, magic and mystical religion', Pentecostalism and the Jesus People. See Heelas and Woodhead, Homeless Minds Today?, pp.46–7; for further characterisation of 'secondary institutions' (among which the type of movements discussed here can be located), see pp.53ff.

More detailed motives for joining specific NRMs included concern for health and the planet, a perception of Eastern spirituality in terms of an unspoiled purity, and a bid to get away from religious forms perceived to be male dominated. See Cox, *Turning East*, pp.98–100; cf. Kose, *Conversion to Islam*, pp.147–8. Motives can be generally illuminated by viewing NRMs as 'laboratory specimens of counter-cultural ideals'. For example, Steven M. Tipton, *Getting Saved from the Sixties: Moral Meaning in Conversion and Cultural Change* (Berkeley, 1982), p.20, cited in Coleman, Editorial, p.viii, presents four sets of contrasts that encompass the cultural conflict between NRMs and the 'dominant Western culture'. These are: (a) ecstatic experience v. technical reason; (b) holism v. analytic discrimination; (c) acceptance v. problem-solving activism; and (d) intuitive certainty v. pluralistic relativism.

   23 Clarke, Introduction, p. xviii, citing D. Bell, 'The Return of the Sacred?', *British Journal of Sociology*, 28: 4 (1977), pp. 419–49, and R. Stark and W. Bainbridge, *The Future of Religion* (Berkeley, 1985).

   24 Clarke, Introduction, p. xix. Such views are illustrated by B. R. Wilson: see, for example, his *Contemporary Transformations of Religion* (Oxford, 1979) and Secularization: Religion in the Modern World, in S. Sutherland and P. B. Clarke, eds, *The Study of Religion: Traditional and New Religions* (London, 1991), pp. 195–208. See also Coleman, Editorial, p. vii. On the British case specifically, see Parsons, Expanding the Religious Spectrum, pp. 298ff.

   25 See for example Robert N. Bellah, New Religious Consciousness and the Crisis in Modernity, in Charles Y. Glock and Robert N. Bellah, eds, *The New Religious Consciousness* (Berkeley, 1976), pp. 333–52. See further Ch. 8.

   26 See Wuthnow, The New Spiritual Freedom, pp. 89–111.

   27 The priorities and strategies of 'seekers' within the American baby-boomer generation (as opposed to those of its members who have retained childhood religious affiliations and remain connected to a community of memory) are explored in Wade Clark Roof, *A Generation of Seekers: The Spiritual Lives of the Baby Boom Generation* (San Francisco, 1993), which underlines the defining nature of choice and experience. His *Spiritual Marketplace: Baby Boomers and the Remaking of American Religion* (Princeton, 1999) posits 'seeking' or an open 'questing mood' (in contrast with an earlier 'unquestioned belief') as the major characteristic of the current religious situation.

   28 See for example Colin Campbell, A New Age Theodicy for a New Age, in Woodhead *et al.*, eds, *Peter Berger and the Study of Religion*, p. 77.

   29 Wouter J. Hanegraaff, *New Age Religion and Western Culture: Esotericism in the Mirror of Secular Thought* (Leiden, 1996), p. 12, and Chryssides *Exploring New Religions*, p. 315. The term NAM came into use in the latter part of the 1970s, and developed into the dominant label during the 1980s. Elements and concerns that are characteristic of the New Age significantly pre-dated this, however. For example, Heelas, *The New Age Movement*, pp. 42–9, identifies seventeenth–eighteenth-century harbingers. His historical survey proper begins in the later nineteenth century, when 'a certain resurgence of New Age activities' took place. The twentieth century up until the 1960s saw a lull in development of the New Age, but Heelas construes this as a time of 'consolidation', as intellectuals began to explore characteristic New Age themes and a number of New Age organisations were established. Indeed he claims that, by the 1920s, 'much of the repertoire of the current New Age was in evidence'. Wouter J. Hanegraaff, The New Age Movement and the Esoteric Tradition, in Roelof van den Broek and Hanegraaff, eds, *Gnosis and Hermeticism from Antiquity to Modern Times* (Albany, NY, 1998), pp. 361–3 (and his *New Age Religion*, pp. 95ff.) offers an overview of the development of the New Age, beginning in the 1950s with apocalyptic UFO cults ('a proto-New Age movement'). During the 1960s, an idealistic expectation of a New Age developed in communities and trends rooted in England ('the New Age in a restricted sense'). The 1980s saw the emergence of 'the New Age in a general sense', as increasing numbers began to perceive an inner connection between the different kinds of alternative ideas and practices that had flourished since the 1960s. See also 'New Age Movement', in Hanegraaff *et al.*, eds, *Dictionary of Gnosis and Western Esotericism*, 2, pp. 859–60 (hereafter cited as 'New Age Movement').

   While the New Age expanded with the 1960s counterculture, it was not until the 1980s that it became established as a recognisable movement, through a process of institutionalisation involving the emergence of large numbers of practices, groups, networks, seminars, centres, retreats, exhibitions, forms of music and books, etc., compared with numbers at the end of the 1960s. Alternatively, this process can be thought of in terms of a movement out of the counterculture and into the mainstream, such that its effects are felt in many aspects of life. See Heelas, *The New Age Movement*, p. 68. The term 'movement' in NAM should not be taken to imply that the New Age 'is in any sense an organized entity. Far from being centrally administered, it is comprised of diverse modes of operation.' These include relatively few well-organised NRMs, communities, networks, centres, camps, weekend training seminars, festivals, shops, businesses, banks, and the individual pursuing a solitary spiritual quest. See ibid. p. 16.

The relationship between NRMs and the NAM must be clarified, given that some approaches conflate NRMs collectively (often excluding explicitly Christian ones) with the NAM, while others suggest that the NAM is itself one NRM among others (see for example Parsons, Expanding the Religious Spectrum, pp. 283–4). The NAM doubtless encompasses some NRMs, which either self-identify as New Age or are associated with it by external observers, but the NAM as a whole must be distinguished from NRMs, the crucial distinction turning on modes of affiliation and organisation (see Ch. 8). Note also that, while the NAM gained momentum in the 1980s, some suggested in the mid-1980s that NRMs were in decline (this latter view has itself been contested).

30 Significant changes during the 1970s introduced differences in the emerging NAM, when compared with the New Age of the earlier period. According to Hanegraaff, *New Age Religion*, pp. 11–12, (a) The early New Age as found in the counterculture was dominated by youth rebelling against the values of the older generation. In contrast, the NAM of the 1980s (onwards) attracts people of all ages. (b) The left wing political ideals of the counterculture and its commitment to radical action are absent from the NAM of the 1980s. (c) The widespread use of psychedelic drugs characteristic of the counterculture is strongly discouraged or forbidden in the NAM of the 1980s. See also Douglas R. Groothius, *Unmasking the New Age: Is there a New Religious Movement trying to transform Society?* (Dowers Grove, IL, 1991/1986), p. 45.

31 See Hanegraaff, *New Age Religion*, p. 3. Such studies include works by Heelas and Hanegraaff cited here. See further Wouter J. Hanegraaff, New Age Religion, in Woodhead, ed., *Religions in the Modern World*, pp. 249–63; Michael York, *The Emerging Network: A Sociology of the New Age and Neo-Pagan Movements* (Lanham, MD, 1995) and 'The New Age Movement in Great Britain', *SYZYGY – Journal of Alternative Religion and Culture*, 1: 2–3 (1992), pp. 147–57; James R. Lewis and J. Gordon Melton, eds, *Perspectives on the New Age* (Albany, NY, 1992); Campbell, A New Age Theodicy for a New Age, pp. 73—84; 'New Age Movement', pp. 855–61; Dominic Corrywright, *Theoretical and Empirical Investigations into New Age Spiritualities* (Oxford, 2003); Olav Hammer, *Claiming Knowledge: Strategies of Epistemology from Theosophy to the New Age* (Leiden, 2000). For a Christian anti-New Age polemic based on a perception of the New Age as an implicitly post-Christian force that subverts Judeo-Christian values and morals, see Groothius, *Unmasking the New Age*. For an introductory anthology of New Age writings, see William Bloom, ed., *The New Age: An Anthology of Essential Writings* (London, 1991).

32 For example, one list of topics encountered on the shelves of a New Age bookshop encompasses meditation, visualisation, dream interpretation, astrology, self-improvement, Tarot, crystals, ESP, clairvoyance, divination, channelling, angels, and Eastern religions. See Chryssides, *Exploring New Religions*, p. 315; cf. Groothius, *Unmasking the New Age*, p. 18; Hanegraaff, *New Age Religion*, p. 1; Bruce, *Religion in Modern Britain*, p. 105.

33 Throughout this volume, we supplement Heelas' analysis with the work of Hanegraaff, and refer also to certain of the works cited in the note above. For alternative summaries of the underlying vision/unifying beliefs of the New Age, see 'New Age Movement', p. 856; Campbell, A New Age Theodicy for a New Age, pp. 77–9; Hanegraaff, *The New Age Movement and the Esoteric Tradition*, pp. 370–2. We note that both Heelas and Hanegraaff's approaches to the New Age (among those of other scholars) have recently been criticised as essentialist. We uphold their usefulness to the present study, however, as these approaches highlight key features of religious change recognised even by scholars who have more recently questioned the usefulness of the concept/label New Age itself. (We address reservations surrounding use of this label in Ch. 8. For critiques of the concept of New Age and of essentialist approaches to this, see Lisolette Frisk, 'Is "New Age" A Construction? Searching a New Paradigm of Contemporary Religion', www.cesnur.org.) Note, finally, that we use the capitalised version (New Age) to refer to the broad phenomenon introduced here, and the small case version (new age) to refer specifically to the Beshara imagining of an incipient/imminent era, i.e., its own envisioning of the new age, in later chapters.

We are also heavily indebted to the work of Heelas and his collaborators in characterising the contemporary religious scene in the West, and shifts of emphasis and discourse within this; this is evident throughout the volume and particularly in Ch. 8.

34 This paragraph draws on Heelas, *The New Age Movement*, pp. 2, 16–20.

35 See also Groothius, *Unmasking the New Age*, p. 22.

36 The term originates with Roy Wallis, *The Elementary Forms of the New Religious Life*, p. 100, cited in Heelas, *The New Age Movement*, p. 21.

37 Spirituality for New Agers thus is 'not a matter of accepting doctrines formulated by others, but rather a highly individual quest, that can (and perhaps should) be based primarily on personal experience.' See 'New Age Movement', p. 856.

38 Tradition here is understood as 'supra-self' authorities that lie outside of the individual self, and claim to be higher (it is clear from the context when this specific emphasis is indicated in our use of the term); see further Ch. 8. Following Heelas, *The Spiritual Revolution: From 'Religion' to 'Spirituality'*, p. 375, detraditionalisation in this context thus signifies 'the shift of authority from faith in, or reliance/dependency on, that which lies beyond the person to that which lies within.'

39 Heelas, *The New Age Movement*, p. 23. The related issues of authority and the role of the teacher are subject to particular variation on the ground in New Age groups. Thus there are examples in which obedience towards the teacher-figure (who can be credited with special powers and can be regarded as above conventional morality) is stressed. This echoes a wider paradox within the New Age, captured in the following remark ('New Age Movement', p. 860): 'the notion of an entirely individual spiritual quest can imply participating in rituals scripted by others and adopting explanatory frameworks expounded by authoritative spokespersons.'

Note that not all conceptualisations of the New Age insist on Heelas' emphasis on Self-authority (with its resulting promotion of equality and egalitarianism) as a defining issue. Some indeed give prominence instead to the role of the authority figure. For example, Jonathan Garb, 'The Image of the Saint in Twentieth Century Jewish Mysticism' (Lecture delivered at Hebrew University of Jerusalem, 4 August 2004; we are indebted to the author for providing a copy of this), suggests that 'the centrality of the chosen figure or spiritual guide or "Guru"' is 'a common component of "New Age" discourse'. At some level, this reflects the continuing absence of consensus concerning what is, and is not, New Age. See also Chs. 6 and 8.

40 Heelas, *The New Age Movement*, pp. 21–2.

41 Ibid., p. 23.

42 Ibid., pp. 23–4, 26.

43 Campbell, A New Age Theodicy for a New Age, p. 84.

44 Ibid.

45 Heelas, *The New Age Movement*, pp. 27–8, 33.

46 See for example Hanegraaff, *New Age Religion*, pp. 119ff.

47 Groothius, *Unmasking the New Age*, p. 9, identifies monism (contrasted with 'a sound theistic world and life view') as 'the terminal disease at the heart of the New Age Movement'. Campbell, A New Age Theodicy for a New Age, p. 78, suggests that 'the basic ontological New Age position is probably best described as metaphysical monism'.

48 Dualism is associated with the legacy of mainstream Christianity. Reductionism is associated with modern forms of scientific rationalism that issue in materialism and fragmentation. See Hanegraaff, *The New Age Movement and the Esoteric Tradition*, p. 371. Note that New Agers frequently afford centrality to intuition and the 'heart', compared to rationality: see Heelas, *The New Age Movement*, pp. 5, 37.

49 Hanegraaff, *The New Age Movement and the Esoteric Tradition*, p. 371.

50 Heelas, *The New Age Movement*, pp. 27, 33.

51 Hanegraaff, *The New Age Movement and the Esoteric Tradition*, p. 367.

52 See Campbell, *A New Age Theodicy for a New Age*, pp. 77–8. Note that humanity's spiritual evolution is in some cases perceived to be facilitated by a special force. The latter is often tied to a notion of the current accessibility of previously secret knowledge, which makes possible a quickening of the evolutionary process.

53 Heelas, *The New Age Movement*, pp. 49–50. The 'upsurge in Self-spirituality' had already got underway during the 1950s with the 'beatniks', members of the generation that came to maturity in the 1950s who rejected the West's social and political systems, and expressed this through contempt for regular work, possessions, etc. The beatnik movement was small until it coalesced with the hippies of the counterculture.

54 These included music, literature, spontaneous gatherings and the widespread use of hallucinogenic drugs like LSD. On the latter, see Jay Stevens, *Storming Heaven: LSD and the American Dream* (London, 1989).

55 For examples, see Heelas, *The New Age Movement*, pp. 51–4. For surveys of the period, see those listed in ibid., pp. 71–2 n. 14, especially Glock and Bellah, eds, *The New Religious Consciousness*; Robert Wuthnow, *The Consciousness Revolution* (Berkeley, 1976); Robert Ellwood, *Religions and Spiritual Groups in Modern America* (Englewood Cliffs, NJ, 1973). For an overview of Eastern spirituality specifically in the West at the end of the 1960s, see Jacob Needleman, *The New Religions* (New York, 1984).

56 On The Beatles' encounter with him, see Bruce, *Religion in Modern Britain*, p. 98, and Kate Allison, 'Egos Searching for Answers', *The Times*, Mysticism Supplement, 26 October 2002, p. 5.

57 According to a contemporary New Ager, the song 'became the "anthem" of the New Age, summing up its vision ... and the newly-born hopes of a generation.' See Caryl Matrisciana, *Gods of The New Age* (Basingstoke, Hampshire, 1986), p. 14. The early part of this work provides a first-hand description of the mood and motifs of the New Age in 'swinging London' of the late 1960s.

58 The reference is to zodiacal ages that last for approximately 2000 years, each marked by the earth's domination by one of the twelve zodiacal constellations, bringing certain characteristics, values and ideals to bear upon the world as a whole. As Chryssides, *Exploring New Religions*, pp. 315–16, points out, no precise date can be given for the changeover from Pisces to Aquarius, and dates posited have ranged from the late nineteenth to the late twenty-first century. Some believe the Age of Aquarius has already come, others that the point of changeover is upon us, and yet others that it is still expected. See also Hanegraaff, *New Age Religion*, p. 102.

While belief in the dawning Age of Aquarius is long established, it was popularised during the 1960s, perhaps due in part to a growing awareness of the approaching new millennium. Feeding into this was much apocalyptic talk concerning the price that economic progress was inflicting on the environment.

59 They attributed to the zodiacal Aquarius, the Water Bearer, the appearance of new modes of communication and mass movements in the form of egalitarian brotherhoods and networks, supplanting hierarchical structures. Even the growing accessibility of jet travel was explained in terms of the quality of Aquarius as an air sign. Some construed the Aquarian age as one of synthesis (in contrast to the preceding Piscean age of conflict), while others stressed its significance as a symbol of man's determination to take control of his destiny. Some saw the Piscean age as dark and violent, in contrast with projections of the Aquarian age as 'a millennium of love and light'. Conflating the Piscean age with the Christian one (for it began with Jesus' birth), others held that when the Piscean age reached its end (2000 years later), Christianity would become something of the past. On this, see Matrisciana, *Gods of the New Age*, pp. 21, 24; Chryssides, *Exploring New Religions*, p. 316; Hanegraaff, *New Age Religion*, p. 102. Some argued that the Aquarian age began specifically on 4 February 1962: see www.home.earthlink.net/~gnosisla/February5.html.

60 Leonard Lewin's preface to an anthology of Idries Shah's writings and interviews published in 1972 reflects this climate: 'In the ... ever more rapidly changing setting which is today's world ... it is far from clear what it is that is taking place ... When the present upheaval ... has finally disclosed the true nature of the world of tomorrow, we can all then participate in that knowledge of the further evolution of the human state. But meanwhile, in the present uncertainty and confusion, many must be asking such questions as, "What *really* is happening?" ... Mankind is now preparing to emerge from the chrysalis ... the quality of his consciousness is about to undergo a transformation to a new condition long latent within. The protective casing which must be breached is a mental prison-shell compounded of vanity, self-love, self-deceit, greed, mental arrogance, prejudice, selfishness, and years and years of conditioning. In all cultures, and at all times, a few, a very few, individuals have been able to free themselves, and have helped others to escape. Now this opportunity is being made available to all who are able to perceive its reality. The social turmoil of our times can be seen as an external manifestation of this process.' See Leonard Lewin, ed., *The Diffusion of Sufi Ideas in the West: An Anthology of New Writings by and about Idries Shah* (Boulder, CO, 1972), pp. 8–10.

61 See for example Annemarie Schimmel, *Mystical Dimensions of Islam* (Chapel Hill, NC, 1975), p. 3; William C. Chittick, *Sufism: A Short Introduction* (Oxford, 2000), pp. vii, 1–20 and 'Sufi Thought and Practice', *The Oxford Encyclopaedia of the Modern Islamic World* (New York, 1994), 4, p. 103; Ron Geaves, *The Sufis of Britain: An Exploration of Muslim Identity* (Cardiff, 2000), pp. 5–6.

Additional introductory studies on sufism are Julian Baldick, *An Introduction to Sufism* (London, 1989); Carl Ernst, *The Shambhala Guide to Sufism* (Boston, 1997); Alexander Knysh, *Islamic Mysticism: A Short History* (Leiden, 2000). Examples of introductory works by authors with diverse sufi orientations are Sara Sviri, *The Taste of Hidden Things: Images on the Sufi Path* (Inverness, CA, 1997); Titus Burckhardt, *An Introduction to Sufi Doctrine*, trans. D. M. Matheson (Lahore, Pakistan, 1971); Martin Lings, *What is Sufism?* (Cambridge, 1995/1975). See also *Teachings of Sufism*, selected and trans. Carl Ernst (Boston, 1999), and *Principles of Sufism* by al-Qushayri, trans. B. R. von Schlegell (Oneonta, NY, 1990).

A comprehensive treatment of all aspects of sufism (largely contributed by authors whose approach is shaped by that of Traditionalism/Perennialism, on which see below) can be found in Seyyed Hossein Nasr, ed., *Islamic Spirituality: Foundations* (London, 1987) and *Manifestations* (London, 1991). For the twentieth-century development of sufism, see Elizabeth Sirriyeh, Sufi Thought and its Reconstruction, in Suha Taji-Farouki and Basheer M. Nafi, eds, *Islamic Thought in the Twentieth Century* (London, 2004), pp. 104–27. For internet resources, see the comprehensive listing in Alan Godlas, *Sufism's Many Paths*, www.uga.edu.

62 For an introduction to this debate, see Ernst, *The Shambhala Guide to Sufism*, chapter 1, and Ron Geaves, *Aspects of Islam* (London, 2005), chapter 7.

63 This approach is not without its problems. See for example Chittick, *Sufism: A Short Introduction*, p. 1, and Ernst, *The Shambhala Guide to Sufism*, pp. xvii, 132. Geaves, *The Sufis of Britain*, pp. 6–7, 11, 75, assesses the relative prioritisation in self-application of the labels 'Muslim' and 'sufi' among Muslim practitioners of sufism. Exploring the label 'mystic' in relation to the definition of sufism as 'Islamic mysticism', he concludes that there are many Muslims who self-define as sufi but cannot be defined as mystics in any sense. Cf. Lings, *What is Sufism?*, p. 15: 'Sufism is none other than Islamic mysticism, which means that it is the central and most powerful current of that tidal wave which constitutes the revelation of Islam.'

64 See Chittick, 'Sufi Thought and Practice', p. 102 and *Sufism: A Short Introduction*, p. 18.

65 Historically, Abu Hamid al-Ghazali (d.1111), a major architect of the subsequent development of Islam, is credited with having integrated the sufi tradition with the Islamic disciplines of philosophy, theology and law. Islam emerged as 'a complete body with ... Sufism as the heart, theology as the head, philosophy as its rationality binding the different parts together, and law as the working limbs.' See Cyril Glassé, *The Concise Encyclopaedia of Islam* (London, 1991), p. 138.

Since their emergence as major social organisations in the Muslim community after 1100, participation in sufism has generally been through initiation into one of the sufi orders or *tariqa*s (although alternative sufi traditions persisted outside of their framework). Note that the term *tariqa* (meaning 'path' or 'way') is used both for the social organisation and the special devotional exercises that form the basis of the order's ritual and structure. The sufi oral tradition that underpins the *tariqa*s draws on knowledge deriving originally from the Prophet (via 'Ali or Abu Bakr), transmitted through generations of shaykhs in an unbroken chain of authorisation. On the emergence of the *tariqa*s, see Marshall G. S. Hodgson, *The Venture of Islam*, 2: *The Expansion of Islam in the Middle Periods* (Chicago, 1977), chapter 4, and J. Spencer Trimingham, *The Sufi Orders in Islam* (Oxford, 1971). For an overview encompassing the modern period, see John O. Voll, 'Sufi Orders', *The Oxford Encyclopaedia of the Modern Islamic World*, 4, pp. 109–17.

66 For a survey of historical opposition to sufism, see Frederick de Jong and Bernd Radtke, Introduction, in de Jong and Radtke, eds, *Islamic Mysticism Contested: Thirteen Centuries of Controversies and Polemics* (Leiden, 1999), pp. 1–21, and Josef van Ess, Sufism and its Opponents: Reflections on Topoi, Tribulations and Transformations, in ibid., pp. 22–44. (The importance of a contextual approach to understanding particular anti-sufi expressions in specific times and places must be stressed, for there has never been a clear or uniform pattern of enmity towards sufis in Islamic history. See van Ess, Sufism and its Opponents, p. 34.) For modern Islamic critiques of sufism, see Elizabeth Sirriyeh, *Sufis and Anti-Sufis: The Defence, Rethinking and Rejection of Sufism in the Modern World* (London, 1998), and Geaves, *The Sufis of Britain*, chapter 4. On the operation of such ideas at the popular level today, see Ernst, *The Shambhala Guide to Sufism*, p. xi, and Garbi Schmidt, Sufi Charisma on the Internet, in David Westerlund, ed., *Sufism in Europe and North America* (London, 2004), pp. 119ff.

67 Ernst, *The Shambhala Guide to Sufism*, pp. 8–17.

68 During the early twentieth century, Hinduism was of greatest interest to the Western reading public. Later, especially during the late 1960s, India was the most popular destination for counterculture seekers travelling east. For NRMs in the Hindu tradition and forms of Buddhism in the West, see Chryssides, *Exploring New Religions*, chapters 5–6; Frederic Lenoir, 'The Adaptation of Buddhism to the West', *Diogenes*, 47/3 no. 187 (1999), pp. 100–9; Heelas, *The New Age Movement*, pp. 54–5. Japanese and Tibetan traditions also emerged as an important resource.

69 Alan Williams, 'Hearing Voices, Seeing Visions', *The Times*, Mysticism Supplement, p. 3, appears to concur with the sentiment behind this. He thus suggests that sufism recently 'has become sexy. And cool, too, through the endorsement of A-list celebrities.'

70 See, for example, Gisela Webb, Tradition and Innovation in Contemporary American Islamic Spirituality: The Bawa Muhaiyaddeen Fellowship, in Yvonne Y. Haddad and Jane I. Smith, eds, *Muslim Communities in North America* (Albany, NY, 1994), pp. 75–6, and David Westerlund, Introduction, in Westerlund, ed., *Sufism in Europe and North America*, p. 8. The field has in cases suffered from problems of hostile attitudes and axe-grinding or polemics (if at times executed with such subtlety that this may pass unnoticed by the uninformed). See for example Peter Wilson, The Strange Fate of Sufism in the New Age, in Peter B. Clarke, ed., *New Trends and Developments in the World of Islam* (London, 1997), p. 180. Difficulties are also associated with the high degree of discretion surrounding some figures and organisations, raising ethical dilemmas concerning disclosure of information. See for example Mark Sedgwick, *Against the Modern World: Traditionalism and the Secret Intellectual History of the Twentieth Century* (New York, 2004), p. 9.

71 Representative survey studies are Andrew Rawlinson, 'A History of Western Sufism', *DISKUS*, 1: 1 (1993), pp. 45–83 (Web Edition, 37 pp., referred to here); Marcia Hermansen, In the Garden of American Sufi Movements: Hybrids and Perennials, in Clarke, ed., *New Trends and Developments*, pp. 155–78 and 'Hybrid Identity Formations in Muslim America: The Case of American Sufi Movements', *The Muslim World*, 90 (Spring 2000), pp. 158–97; Geaves, *The Sufis of Britain*; Westerlund, ed., *Sufism in Europe and North America* (in particular Westerlund, The Contextualisation of Sufism in Europe, pp. 13–35; Marcia Hermansen, What's American about American Sufi Movements?, pp. 36–63, and Olav Hammer, Sufism for Westerners, pp. 127–43); Carl A. Keller, Le Soufisme en Europe occidentale, in Jacques Waardenburg, ed., *Scholarly Approaches to Religion: Interreligious Perceptions and Islam* (Bern, 1994), pp. 359–89. Jamal Malik and John Hinnells, eds, *Sufism in the West* (London, 2006) was not yet available at the time of writing.

72 For example, Hermansen introduces a garden metaphor to distinguish between groups that identify closely with an Islamic source/content ('hybrids') and those that do not ('perennials'). Rawlinson uncovers the origins of organised twentieth-century Western sufism in antithetical trends tied to two prominent figures, Guénon (who became the seminal figure for Shadhiliyya-associated Traditionalists/Perennialists) and Hazrat Inayat Khan (founder of the Sufi Order): while the former identified with Islam, the latter did not. A parallel dichotomy is applied by Hammer, Sufism for Westerners, p. 139, and its importance underlined by Westerlund, The Contextualisation of Sufism in Europe, pp. 16–17. Of course, as Ernst's comment at the head of this section suggests, the requirement for sufi groups to position themselves explicitly in relation to Islamic identity is a distinctively modern phenomenon. Naturally, it is an issue that takes on particular significance in the Western context. Note, finally, that Chittick's application of the internal typology of 'intoxicated' and 'sober' sufism to its Western expressions stands in contrast to an approach pivoting on Islamic identity. See for example *Sufism: A Short Introduction*, pp. 26–31, esp. 30–1; 'Sufi Thought and Practice', pp. 105–6.

73 Hermansen, In the Garden of American Sufi Movements, pp. 155–7. Her examples of 'hybrids' (Islamic sufis) include the Halveti–Jerrahi order under Muzaffer Özak, the Naqshbandi–Haqqani order under Nazim al-Haqqani, and the Bawa Muhaiyaddeen Fellowship. On these see also Geaves, *The Sufis of Britain*, pp. 138ff., 148ff.; Kose, *Conversion to Islam*, pp. 163ff.; Webb, Tradition and Innovation, pp. 75–108.

74 Examples include Hazrat Inayat Khan (and the Sufi Order), Idries Shah (and the Society for Sufi Studies), and Irina Tweedie (and the Golden Sufi Center).
On Inayat Khan and the Sufi Order, see Geaves, *The Sufis of Britain*, pp. 174–80; James Jervis, The Sufi Order in the West and Pir Vilayat 'Inayat Khan: Space-Age Spirituality in Contemporary Euro-America, in Clarke, ed., *New Trends and Developments*, pp. 211–60. For an example of his writings, see *The Heart of Sufism: Essential Writings of Hazrat Inayat Khan* (Boston, 1999).
On Shah's controversial journey to the rank of sufi authority, see James Moore, 'Neo-Sufism: The Case of Idries Shah', *Religion Today*, III: 3 (1987), pp. 4–6. For the cases of his supporters and detractors, see Wilson, The Strange Fate of Sufism, pp. 182–95. Shah's writings (which succeeded in disseminating knowledge of sufism to a broad Western audience) promote it as a non-confessional, individualistic tradition belonging to the universal quest for truth and spiritual wisdom. See also Geaves, *The Sufis of Britain*, pp. 166–8; Hermansen, In the Garden of American Sufi Movements, p. 156; Hammer, Sufism for Westerners, pp. 136–8.
On Irina Tweedie and the Golden Sufi Center (currently under Llewellyn Vaughan-Lee), see www.goldensufi.org. The group self-projects as 'the vehicle for the work of the Naqshbandiyya–Mujaddidiyya Order of Sufism', and describes its purpose as being 'to

make available this lineage of Sufism.' There is no requirement to embrace Islam and 'very few specific practices', apart from the silent *dhikr*, are prescribed. See 'Beliefs and Ethics of the Naqshbandi Path', points 26 and 17, www.goldensufi.org. On Tweedie's journey to sufism and the encounter with her teacher (a Hindu who had a Muslim teacher with a Naqshbandi–Mujaddidi lineage) in India, see her *Daughter of Fire* (Nevada City, CA, 1986); Sara Sviri, *Daughter of Fire* by Irina Tweedie: Documentation and Experiences of a Modern Naqshbandi Sufi, in Peter B. Clarke and Elizabeth Puttick, eds, *Women as Teachers and Disciples in Traditional and New Religions* (Lewiston, KY, 1993), pp. 77–90.

The case of Guénon and associated Shadhili–Perennialist Frithjof Schuon (expositor of the *religio perennis*) has caused some confusion. While Rawlinson counter-poses him to Khan based on his insistence that truth resides in Islam as a whole, Hermansen initially situated him as a 'perennial' (read 'universal'), but later conceded that he upheld adherence to the sharia. On Schuon, see Seyyed Hossein Nasr, Biography of Frithjof Schuon, in Seyyed Hossein Nasr and William Stoddardt, eds, *Religion of the Heart: Essays Presented to Frithjof Schuon on his Eightieth Birthday* (Washington, DC, 1991), pp. 1–6. Jean Borella, René Guénon and the Traditionalist School, in Faivre and Needleman, eds, *Modern Esoteric Spirituality*, pp. 330–58, provides a succinct introduction to the ideas of Guénon, Schuon and prominent Shadhili–Perennialists Burckhardt, Lings and Nasr. See also Jane I. Smith, Seyyed Hossein Nasr: Defender of the Sacred and Islamic Traditionalism, in Yvonne Y. Haddad, ed., *Muslims of America* (New York, 1993), pp. 80–95.

75 Note that the term is in some cases self-applied, as in the sympathetic exploration of Inayat Khan's teachings by a life-long student of these: H. J. Wittevene, *Universal Sufism* (Shaftesbury, Dorset, 1997).

76 Ian B. Draper, From Celts to Kaaba: Sufism in Glastonbury, in Westerlund, ed., *Sufism in Europe and North America*, pp. 148–50, 152, 155, describes exclusion of the issue of Islamic identity as part of the self-adjustment of the Naqshbandiyya–Haqqaniyya to the town's setting and discourses. He suggests that such strategic changes have issued in a move 'towards a universal Sufic stance, not dissimilar to ... Inayat Khan'. Meanwhile, as Hermansen, In the Garden of American Sufi Movements, p. 158, and Jervis, The Sufi Order, pp. 216–17, 249 n. 30 indicate, the debate continues as to whether Inayat Khan harboured aspirations of gradually bringing his followers into Islam, given that he instructed 'higher initiates' to perform the Islamic ritual prayers.

77 For example, Fadhlalla Haeri, *The Elements of Sufism* (Shaftesbury, Dorset, 1997), pp. 41–3: 'In pseudo-sufi movements we find much euphoria and temporary states of excitement which are achieved by utilising certain practices and techniques ... However, such states are not lasting ... Although inner development is possible to a certain degree without following the outer laws, if a person wishes to develop himself fully, then he has to participate in the Islamic Law and way of life fully.' Based on a prophetic hadith projecting a tripartite division of the Islamic religion into *islam* (submission), *iman* (faith) and *ihsan* ('doing the beautiful', the 'special domain' of the sufis), Islamic sufis thus insist that access to *ihsan* is built on the safeguards of right practice (*islam*) and right understanding (*iman*). *Ihsan* here can be understood as 'spontaneous virtue and spiritual perfection', encapsulated in the ideal of 'worshipping God as if you see Him'. See Chittick, *Sufism: A Short Introduction*, pp. 4–5, 20–1, 30. See also Ernst, *The Shambhala Guide to Sufism*, p. 26, on the threefold rhetorical formula of organically connected aspects of Islamic religion: *shari'a* (law), *tariqa* (inner path) and *haqiqa* (God as Reality).

78 Cf. Wilson, The Strange Fate of Sufism, p. 199.

79 For example, Alan Godlas, 'Sufism, the West and Modernity', www.uga.edu/islam/sufismwest.html, distinguishes (a) Islamic sufi orders, sharing an avowed adherence to Islam and the sharia, from (b) Quasi-Islamic sufi organisations/orders, in which the shaykh may adhere to the sharia but such adherence is not made a condition for entering the sufi path (thus encompassing both Muslim and non-Muslim aspirants). Sedgwick, 'Traditionalist Sufism', posits three types of 'Islamic' sufi group: (a) immigrants' *tariqas* (transplants from Muslim contexts); (b) 'standard' *tariqas* (e.g. the Naqshbandiyya–

Haqqaniyya, where the shaykh has a 'standard' Islamic education but is at home in the West and has numerous Western convert members); (c) 'novel' *tariqa*s: note his significant positioning of the 'sufi Guénonians' here, for his typology is geared to answering the question of 'how traditional they really are'.

80 Rawlinson, cited in Wilson, *The Strange Fate of Sufism*, p. 179.

81 Cf. Jervis, *The Sufi Order*, p. 211.

82 Historically, the preference was for other kinds of terminology to self-describe or to describe individual sufis. See Ernst, *The Shambhala Guide to Sufism*, pp. 26ff.

83 Associates themselves, it must be noted, favour use of the term 'student' or 'ongoing student', or refer to a 'serious involvement' with Beshara. We reserve the term student to refer more narrowly to the context of courses at or associated with the School.

84 Most published sources that describe it (magazines, web postings, etc.) have been produced under its own auspices. The few external sources identified here and in the following notes form the exception.

We must first mention a recent PhD thesis: Isabel J. Jeffrey, *The Contemporary Influences of Muhyiddin Ibn 'Arabi in the West: The Beshara School and the Muhyiddin Ibn 'Arabi Society* (University of Exeter, February 2003). Referring to this work (at the time still in progress), James W. Morris, 'Ibn 'Arabi in the "Far West": Visible and Invisible Influences', *JMIAS*, XXIX (2001), p. 112 n. 35, observed that 'even the generally "external" description of such a relatively limited spiritual group is in itself a daunting task'. Morris here refers to Beshara in its capacity as a vehicle for the 'influence' of Ibn 'Arabi: the work of Jeffrey, his former student, is shaped by this approach. While illuminating in some respects, it does not in itself make for a satisfying methodological framework within which to analyse a complex phenomenon that demands careful contextualisation.

Second, the two and a half pages devoted to Beshara in Stephen Annett's study of the 'non-establishment spiritual state of Britain' deserve special mention for what they capture of Beshara's earliest years, based on discussion with participants at the time (errors of interpretation and some misrepresentation notwithstanding). See Stephen Annett, ed., *The Many Ways of Being: A Guide to Spiritual Groups and Growth Centres in Britain* (London, 1976), pp. 84–6.

85 For example: (a) Hermansen, 'Hybrid Identity Formations', p. 171, lists 'The Beshara Foundation' among the cluster of groups stemming from the Mevlevi Order, describing it as 'a Sufi-inspired movement ... which is characterized as primarily gnostic rather than devotional'. Cf. In The Garden of American Sufi Movements, p. 171 n. 9, where she characterises 'The Beshara Foundation' as a 'Sufi-inspired perennialist movement'. (b) Moore, 'Neo-Sufism: The Case of Idries Shah', p. 7 n. 1, includes Rauf in a list of figures articulating various 'dervish traditions' in Britain of the 1980s. (c) Godlas, 'Sufism, the West and Modernity', includes Beshara among 'Organizations or Schools related to Sufism or Sufi Orders'. He notes that it regards itself 'as a school for realising esoteric truth, a school that is independent of religion'. He includes the Muhyiddin Ibn 'Arabi Society (on which see below) as a separate entry in the same category. (d) Annett, ed., *The Many Ways of Being*, places Beshara among 'Eastern Oriented Groups' under the sub-section 'Sufism'. (e) Heelas, *The New Age Movement*, p. 71 n. 15 lists it among the 'earlier eastern imports' in the UK as a 'Sufi centre'. (f) Beshara publications appear under the heading 'Beshara School of Intensive Esoteric Education', listed as a 'Sufi group in America', in Sufism in North America: A Bibliography, in Michael A. Koszegi and J. Gordon Melton, eds, *Islam in North America: A Sourcebook* (New York, 1992), pp. 228–9. 'Beshara' is also mentioned here as a sufi periodical (p. 242).

86 In addition to (a) in note 85, for example: (i) Wilson, *The Strange Fate of Sufism*, pp. 199, 208 n. 111, mentions Rauf as Feild's teacher, and notes that the former went on to establish Beshara. (ii) Hülya Küçük, 'Sufism in the West: Its Brief History and Nature' (paper presented at First WOCMES Conference, Mainz, Germany, September 2002; we are indebted to the author for providing a copy of this), p. 23, mentions Rauf in relation to Feild and highlights his 'Mevlevi connections'. (iii) Jeffrey Somers, Whirling and the

West: The Mevelvi Dervishes in the West, in Clarke, ed., *New Trends and Developments*, p. 270, describes Beshara as perhaps the earliest of the UK-based organisations 'that have maintained some sort of relationship with the Mevlevi [sic]'. His description of Beshara is essentially based on Annett's, but he adds that part of their practice involves 'whirling like the Mevlevi [sic]'. (iv) Rawlinson, 'A History of Western Sufism', p. 26, mentions Rauf in the context of a discussion of Feild: 'he definitely had Mevlevi connections, though he never claimed to be a Mevlevi sheikh; he also taught the way of Ibn 'Arabi'. Annett, ed., *The Many Ways of Being*, pp. 84–6, breaks the mould, mentioning neither Feild nor the Mevlevis in his treatment of Beshara.

87 See, for example, Hermansen, 'Hybrid Identity Formations', p. 179 and In the Garden of American Sufi Movements, p. 167; Godlas, 'Sufism, the West and Modernity'; Kose, *Conversion to Islam*, p. 143.

88 Clarke, Introduction, p. xxiv, mentions Beshara as 'a less well-known group', while Arweck, New Religious Movements, p. 265, lists it among NRMs that are 'derived from esoteric teachings'.

89 'Sufism and the "Modern" in Islam': International Conference organised by Griffith University (Brisbane), ISIM (Leiden) and the PPIM (Jakarta), September 2003; conference publicity.

90 See Martin van Bruinessen, 'Sufism and the "Modern"', *ISIM Review*, 13 (2003), p. 62.

91 See for example Hermansen, What's American about American Sufi Movements?, p. 52; Draper, From Celts to Kaaba.

92 The following thus touch on this connection without analysis: Wilson, The Strange Fate of Sufism; Hermansen, In the Garden of American Sufi Movements, p. 172 n. 34 and What's American about American Sufi Movements?, p. 62; Webb, Tradition and Innovation, p. 75. Michael M. Koszegi, The Sufi Order in the West: Sufism's Encounter with the New Age, in Koszegi and Gordon Melton, eds, *Islam in North America*, p. 211, suggests that sufism 'has had a great influence on the formation and character of the New Age', and that 'a study of the full scope of sufi influences on the New Age would be a major work'. His argument addresses specifically the perceived contribution of the Sufi Order, mapping aspects of its thought that harmonise with the 'New Age mindset' (see further Ch. 8). Westerlund, The Contextualisation of Sufism in Europe, pp. 32–4, sheds some light on the commonalities between the attitudes of 'the broad contemporary religious current that is often referred to as "New Age"', and 'universalistically oriented forms of Sufism'. A major shortcoming of the allusions and brief comments listed here stems from their failure to provide a working concept of the New Age (reflecting in all likelihood the difficulties discussed above). This makes possible only a limited understanding of the bases and significance of the connection identified.

93 An important avenue that cannot be pursued here would be to compare the sufi encounter with the New Age and that of other mystical traditions. A comparison of the twentieth-century trajectories of sufism and of Jewish mysticism or Kabbalah in the West is a fertile and under-explored area, for example.

94 Cf. Webb, Tradition and Innovation, pp. 77–8.

95 Claude Addas, *Quest for the Red Sulphur: The Life of Ibn 'Arabi*, trans. Peter Kingsley (Cambridge, 1993), pp. 292–3.

96 We use 'man' (with a small m) throughout this volume to denote both humankind as a whole (as in the present case) and the individual male person; the intended sense will be clear from the context.

97 Following scholarship in the field, we use the term metaphysics to describe Ibn 'Arabi's system of thought, while reflecting that this term has been used to denote different things in the long history of Western philosophy, and that the content and purpose of metaphysics is the subject of continuing debate.

98 On the history of the expression and the various meanings that have been given to it, see William C. Chittick, Rumi and *wahdat al-wujud*, in Amin Banani, Richard

Houannisian and Georges Sabagh, eds, *Poetry and Mysticism in Islam: The Heritage of Rumi* (Cambridge, 1994), pp. 70–111. His 'The Central Point: Qunawi's Role in the School of Ibn 'Arabi', *JMIAS*, XXXV (2004), pp. 25–46, represents the fruit of long years of reflection on the issue; we draw on this here. For his earlier treatments, see *Imaginal Worlds: Ibn al-'Arabi and the Problem of Religious Diversity* (Albany, NY, 1994), chapter 1; Ibn 'Arabi, in Seyyed Hossein Nasr and Oliver Leaman, eds, *The History of Islamic Philosophy* (London, 2001), pp. 504–5; more recently, 'Wahdat al-shuhud/al-wudjud', *Encyclopaedia of Islam*, 2nd edn (hereafter EI²), XI, pp. 37–9.

99 See Ronald L. Nettler, *Sufi Metaphysics and Qur'anic Prophets: Ibn 'Arabi's Thought and Method in the Fusus al-Hikam* (Cambridge, 2003), p. 8. As Schimmel, *Mystical Dimensions of Islam*, p. 26 puts it, the Oneness of Being in Ibn 'Arabi's thought does not involve a 'substantial continuity' between God and creation. Nonetheless, we would underline the fact that some of the many parallel levels on which his polyvalent texts operate offer ammunition for those who would characterise Ibn 'Arabi as heterodox (or worse) from the perspective of normative Islamic belief.

100 See David Perley, 'Vagueness: An Additional Nuance in the Interpretation of Ibn 'Arabi's Mystical Language', *American Journal of Islamic Social Sciences*, 22: 4 (2005), pp. 57–8.

101 We allude here to apophasis as a mode of discourse. See ibid, and Michael Sells, *Mystical Languages of Unsaying* (Chicago, 1994), chapters 3–4.

102 The latter as translated in William C. Chittick, *The Sufi Path of Knowledge: Ibn al-'Arabi's Metaphysics of Imagination* (Albany, NY, 1989), p. 212.

103 Chittick, 'The Central Point', p. 28, 5 n. 2 and Rumi and *wahdat al-wujud*, pp. 76–7; cf. Nettler, *Sufi Metaphysics*, p. 8, noting that Ibn 'Arabi thoroughly denied an 'either/or' approach.

104 Chittick, 'The Central Point', p. 32.

105 Michel Chodkiewicz, *The Spiritual Writings of Amir 'Abd al-Kader*, trans. J. Chrestensen, T. Manning, *et al.* (Albany, NY, 1995), p. 16.

106 A celebrated Naqshbandi, Jami was a leading literary figure at the Timurid court in Herat, best known as author of the sufi biographical dictionary *Nafahat al-uns* and his poetic masterpiece *Lawa'ih*: see Chittick, Ibn 'Arabi, p. 512; 'Djami', EI², II, pp. 421–2. Note that if *wujud* is understood to mean *al-wujud al-haqq* (the Real Being), it is a truism to state that Ibn 'Arabi believed in *wahdat al-wujud*. Divested of any technical meaning, the notion of *wahdat al-wujud* (the proposition that Real Being, the Being that is God, is one) is thus identical to *tawhid*. See Chittick, 'The Central Point', pp. 31, 29.

107 It was thus applied as a term of praise to designate an expression of *tawhid* typified by the writings of Ibn 'Arabi and his followers. See Chittick, Rumi and *wahdat al-wujud*, p. 87.

108 Qunawi was Ibn 'Arabi's son-in-law and close disciple, whom he gave permission to teach all of his works. By the time of his death in 1274, he was recognised as the chief transmitter of Ibn 'Arabi's teaching. On him see Jane Clark, 'Early Best-sellers in the Akbarian Tradition: The Dissemination of Ibn 'Arabi's Teaching through Sadr al-Din Qunawi', *JMIAS*, XXXIII (2003), pp. 22–53. Note that the adjective 'Akbarian' is derived from the title used by his followers to refer to Ibn 'Arabi, al-Shaykh al-Akbar ('The Greatest Master').

Chodkiewicz, *The Spiritual Writings of Amir 'Abd al-Kader*, p. 193 n. 55, describes Qunawi's major contribution to the reception of Ibn 'Arabi's teaching as having given this a structure and coherence that was 'largely determinative' in how it was read by later generations. Chittick, The School of Ibn 'Arabi, in Nasr and Leaman, eds, *The History of Islamic Philosophy*, pp. 511, 513, agrees that, of all his immediate disciples, Qunawi deserves most credit for determining how Ibn 'Arabi was later interpreted.

109 Chittick, 'The Central Point', pp. 29–30 and The School of Ibn 'Arabi, pp. 513–14.

110 Chittick, 'The Central Point', p. 30; cf. Chodkiewicz, *The Spiritual Writings of Amir 'Abd al-Kader*, p. 193 n. 55.

111 Chittick, 'The Central Point', p. 30. For Ibn Taymiyya's attack on Ibn 'Arabi's school, see Alexander Knysh, *Ibn 'Arabi in the Later Islamic Tradition: The Making of a Polemical Image in Medieval Islam* (Albany, NY, 1999), chapter 4. On the fate of this attack and the eventual triumph of the doctrine of *wahdat al-wujud*, see Basheer M. Nafi, '*Tasawwuf* and Reform in Pre-Modern Islamic Culture: In Search of Ibrahim al-Kurani', *Die Welt des Islams*, 42: 3 (2002), pp. 313, 329.

112 Chittick, 'Wahdat al-shuhud/wudjud', p. 39 and Rumi and *wahdat al-wujud*, pp. 85–7, 89–90. Such accusations are based on the assumption that those who speak of *wahdat al-wujud* understand by it the absolute identity of God with creation/the cosmos (and hence of God with man).

113 Claude Addas, *Ibn 'Arabi: The Voyage of No Return*, trans. David Streight (Cambridge, 2000), p. 80. As shorthand, Chittick, 'The Central Point', p. 28 n. 5, suggests that what *wahdat al-wujud* might mean for Ibn 'Arabi and his immediate followers is that 'the Real Being is One, and everything else is uniquely itself, different from the Real Being and from every other thing. In each unique thing, the Real Being discloses a unique face of its infinite reality while remaining One and Unique in itself. We, on the other hand, remain forever ourselves in our own realities, forever other than the Real Being, while we simultaneously remain conjoined with the Real Being inasmuch as we find and are found.'

114 Chodkiewicz, *The Spiritual Writings of Amir 'Abd al-Kader*, p. 16.

115 See Schimmel, *Mystical Dimensions of Islam*, p. 267. As Chittick, Rumi and *wahdat al-wujud*, p. 88, recently pointed out, it would take a major study to survey views of Ibn 'Arabi and of *wahdat al-wujud* projected by various orientalists over the past century, as well as the contributions of more recent scholars. Cf. Franklin D. Lewis, *Rumi: Past and Present, East and West: The Life, Teachings and Poetry of Jalal al-Din Rumi* (Oxford, 2000), chapters 12–14.

116 Chittick, 'The Central Point', p. 31. Mahmoud al-Ghorab, Muhyiddin Ibn al-'Arabi amidst Religions (*adyan*) and Schools of Thought (*madhahib*), in Stephen Hirtenstein and Michael Tiernan, eds, *Muhyiddin Ibn 'Arabi: A Commemorative Volume* (Shaftesbury, Dorset, 1993), p. 219, comments thus: 'The reader will find that whosoever tries to clarify what [Ibn 'Arabi] ... wrote about the Oneness of Being, always ends up making it more obscure, and had he left the Shaykh's own words as explicit as he wrote them, the matter would never have been confused.'

An example of an explicit statement of the 'content' of *wahdat al-wujud* and the rejection of its attribution (thus understood) to Ibn 'Arabi arises in a comment by a contemporary Naqshbandi author in Damascus (which possibly reflects a familiarity with Western scholarship on the subject): 'Perhaps the most famous misrepresentation of the Shaykh ... is the attribution to him of the doctrine of "oneness of being" (*wahdat al-wujud*) in the pantheistic sense of the immanence of the Deity in everything that exists ... This attribution and others of its type are evidently spurious, and Ibn 'Arabi's '*aqida* flatly contradicts them.' See Gibril F. Haddad, '*Aqidat al-'awamm min ahl al-Islam* (translation with introduction of part of the Introduction to *al-Futuhat al-Makkiyya*: 'Common Doctrine of the Muslims') [Credo of the Masses and People of Submission and *Taqlid*, vol. 1: 162–17], p. 7, www.abc.se/~m9783/n/iarabi_e.htm (accessed December 2004).

Cf. Chittick, Rumi and *wahdat al-wujud*, p. 91: the author cites the example of a contemporary Egyptian scholar and fervent supporter of Ibn 'Arabi who writes that those who attribute *wahdat al-wujud* to him commit a grievous error, yet fails to define what he understands by the term. Cf. Th. Emil Homerin, 'Ibn 'Arabi in the People's Assembly: Religion, Press, and Politics in Sadat's Egypt', *The Middle East Journal*, 40: 3 (1986), p. 471.

117 As Morris argues, his 'esotericism' can be properly understood only in light of his firm adherence to the defining principles of the Islamic tradition. See James Winston Morris, 'Ibn 'Arabi's "Esotericism": The Problem of Spiritual Authority', *Studia Islamica*, LXXI (1990), pp. 37–64.

118 Chittick, Ibn 'Arabi, p. 497; see also his *The Sufi Path of Knowledge*, p. x. Cf. James Winston Morris, *Orientations: Islamic Thought in a World Civilization* (Sarajevo, 2001), p. 63.

119 See Knysh, *Ibn 'Arabi in the Later Islamic Tradition*, p. 1.

120 Among other self-styled salafis, Wahhabis are the major modern opponents of Ibn 'Arabi. Muhammad Ibn 'Abd al-Wahhab himself declared Ibn 'Arabi an unbeliever: see for example Epistle 28, *Mu'allafat al-Shaykh al-Imam Muhammad Ibn 'Abd al-Wahhab*, ed., 'Abd al-'Aziz b. Zayd al-Rumi *et al.* (Riyadh, Saudi Arabi, n.d.), 5, p. 189.

121 See for example Homerin, 'Ibn 'Arabi in the People's Assembly', pp. 462–77; Michel Chodkiewicz, 'The Diffusion of Ibn 'Arabi's Doctrine', *JMIAS*, IX (1991), p. 36. Cf. Muhammad Sa'id Ramadan al-Buti, *Hadha walidi* (Damascus, 1998/1995), p. 111. The author recalls the attitude of his father, the respected shaykh Mullah Ramadan al-Buti, concerning the *Futuhat*: 'Someone once offered to sell him the *Futuhat*, but he refused to buy it. Then some volumes of it sneaked into a book lot he received from auction. I remember that he leafed through one volume, then put the whole thing in a far corner of his library. When he heard that some of the ulama of Damascus were gathering to study it among themselves and that many common folk would join them he became angry ... making clear his disapproval.'

122 See for example Chodkiewicz, 'The Diffusion of Ibn 'Arabi's Doctrine', p. 49.

123 See Addas, *Quest for the Red Sulphur*, pp. 291–2, for example.

124 Chodkiewicz, *The Spiritual Writings of Amir 'Abd al-Kader*, pp. 7, 22; cf. his *Seal of the Saints: Prophethood and Sainthood in the Doctrine of Ibn 'Arabi*, trans. Liadain Sherrard (Cambridge, 1993), p. 140 and 'The Diffusion of Ibn 'Arabi's Doctrine', p. 49.

125 Chittick, The School of Ibn 'Arabi, pp. 510–11; cf. Chodkiewicz, 'The Diffusion of Ibn 'Arabi's Doctrine', p. 51 and *Seal of the Saints*, p. 140.

126 Chodkiewicz, 'The Diffusion of Ibn 'Arabi's Doctrine', pp. 37–8, 40. The author attributes the exceptional influence exercised by Ibn 'Arabi (in contrast with other representatives of the 'learned tradition' of sufism) to the fact that his work (p. 51) 'has an answer for everything. Ontology, cosmology, prophetology, exegesis, ritual, it encompasses without exception all the domains on which the *ahl al-tasawwuf* [the sufis] need a trusted guide.'

127 For examples, see ibid., pp. 44ff.

128 For examples of the life of the shrine complex and relations with the saint among those who live and work in the neighbourhood, see Suha Taji-Farouki, *At the Resting-place of the Seal of Saints: Ibn 'Arabi and his Shrine Complex in Contemporary Damascus* (forthcoming).

129 Cf. Thierry Zarcone, 'Rereadings and Transformations in Sufism in the West', *Diogenes*, 47/3 no. 187 (1999), p. 112.

130 For an introduction to the phenomenological approach, see 'Phenomenology of Religion', *The Encyclopaedia of Religion*, ed. in chief, Mircea Eliade (New York, 1987), 11, pp. 272–85.

131 Thus we deliberately cite Beshara 'texts' (both written and oral) frequently, and often at length.

132 The empirical approach to the study of religion, which recognises that it is impossible to answer the question of ultimate religious/metaphysical truth on scientific grounds (and hence insists that it cannot be the researcher's business 'to adjudicate on the validity of the believer's truth'), is thus integrated. On this approach, see Hanegraaff, *New Age Religion*, p. 4; for elaboration, see his 'Empirical Method in the Study of Esotericism', *Method and Theory in the Study of Religion*, 7: 2 (1995), pp. 99–129.

133 Cf. Eileen Barker, The Scientific Study of Religion? You must be Joking!, in Dawson, ed., *Cults and New Religious Movements*, pp. 7ff.

134 We noted earlier the tendency for sociological studies to predominate in the discussion of NRMs. One of its consequences has been 'a singular lack of serious academic studies that have treated the ideas of a new religion as a topic of study in its own right'. This is in spite of the fact that an NRM's teachings are 'the fuel by which [it] is driven, and without which it would fail'. See Chryssides, *Exploring New Religions*, pp. 2, 4; also Hanegraaff, *New Age Religion*, p. 3.

On the social attributes of those who join NRMs, see Dawson, Who Joins New Religious Movements and Why.

135 For a discussion of the study of conversion in the psychology of religion (and an example of a theoretical model), see Benjamin Beit-Hallahmi, 'The *Varieties* as an Inspiration: Confessions of a Slow Learner', *Cross Currents*, 53 (Fall 2003), and Beit-Hallahmi and M. Argyle, *The Psychology of Religious Behaviour, Belief and Experience* (London, 1997). See also Dawson, Who Joins New Religious Movements and Why, pp. 124–5, and Saul Levine, The Joiners, in Dawson, ed., *Cults and New Religious Movements*, pp. 131–42. Note that the therapeutic effects of group entry and membership depend on pre-conversion psychological state, and the nature of the group as social network.

136 See Kose, *Conversion to Islam*, pp. 83, 149–57, 168–73, for an example of the kind of research in question.

137 Apart from the exceptions pointed to below, such oral sources remain unnamed throughout, reflecting associates' general preferences.

138 We address the question of the status of the contents of the *Journal of the Muhyiddin Ibn 'Arabi Society (JMIAS)* and its *Newsletter* in Chs. 2 and 7.

139 All named authors of published materials who are associates are explicitly identified as such in our text/notes, so that it is clear that the source in question is treated as an internal one. In some cases, the author's connection with the movement is evident from references to Beshara/Rauf in biographical details and acknowledgements. Where this is not the case, their status as associates has been otherwise verified. The Bibliography lists all works by associates under 'Internal sources': even when not published by Beshara (or explicitly produced in its name), their writings nonetheless convey their understandings *qua* associates, reflecting the holism of their own worldview, which is not confined to specific areas of their lives. The matter is somewhat more complicated in the case of associates who have published in scholarly media, and who on questioning explicitly claim that they were *not* writing in their capacity as Beshara associates. It is unthinkable for there to be any conflict in such cases with the fundamental Beshara worldview, however, even though explicit mention of certain of its more distinctive motifs may have been judiciously eschewed. Nonetheless, when used as sources in this study, the multiple aspects of some such texts must be underlined; reflecting this, we have listed some under both 'Beshara sources' and 'Other sources' in the Bibliography.

140 It will simplify matters to provide a few comments concerning specific internal sources here.

A. Published Sources: (a) An autobiographical fragment arises in Bulent Rauf, *Addresses II* (Beshara Publications, Chisholme House, Roxburgh, 2001), pp. 79–96. (b) Contributions by Rauf's second wife, Angela Culme-Seymour, arise in the Foreword to Bulent Rauf, *The Last Sultans*, ed. Meral Arim and Judy Kearns (Cheltenham, 1995) and, more importantly, in her *Bolter's Grand-daughter* (Oxford, 2001), chapters 26ff. This autobiographical account writes of Rauf as her companion/husband, rather than his role within the movement: as such, it represents a unique (if somewhat limited) source. (c) Rafi Zabor, *I, Wabenzi: A Souvenir* (New York, 2005); the author thanks him for providing an unedited pre-publication version of this. The work is the first part of a lengthy memoir (he calls it 'a souvenir') that can be situated in the autobiographical 'quest narrative' genre. Part of the text documents the year Zabor spent at Swyre Farm (mid-1972 to mid-1973), and provides a first-hand account of day-to-day life there under Feild. We were able to usefully compare associates' oral accounts concerning this early period against this narrative (especially given Zabor's impressive memory, his own research, and his admission whenever he is unsure concerning his recollection of some point). As *I, Wabenzi* was at the time of writing still under publisher's consideration we have not quoted it directly, and leave it to the interested reader to pursue. Zabor is presently preparing the first of three further volumes, which will address specifically the problems that led to Feild's departure and the subsequent transformation of Swyre Farm. (d) Reshad Feild, *The Last Barrier: A Journey into the Essence of Sufi Teachings* (Great Barrington, MA, 2002), can be considered an internal source with some qualification. First published in 1976, this work is an account of his time with Rauf during the late 1960s–early 1970s, at the time of the emergence of Beshara. Wilson, *The Strange Fate of Sufism*, p. 199 (also p. 208 n. 113), describes it as 'a New Age classic'; its reappearance in 2002 in a twenty-fifth anniversary edition (with a Foreword by Coleman Barks) would appear to substantiate this. Wilson considers the work of questionable status as a document, suggesting there is substantial evidence that it is 'a fictionalised account'. However, he cannot tell 'why or to what extent' Feild has 'creatively mythologised' the narratives here and in his other works. (To illustrate such 'fictionalisation', he points to Feild's claim that, when he first met Rauf, he knew 'virtually nothing' of sufism. In the preface to the later edition, however, Feild does refer to his early meeting with Vilayat Khan and hints at the start of a significant relationship with him.) An external source close to Feild during his early relationship with Rauf cautions that he tended towards exaggeration in his narratives, particularly in relation to episodes described in *The Last Barrier*. Some associates doubt the accuracy of the narrative he presents here (for the most part without having read it), and are generally suspicious of the work. However, the Principal of the Beshara School considers it 'largely a good book', while a well-informed associate underlines the fact that, here as elsewhere, Feild had been 'a good communicator of what Rauf said'. These latter two comments provide adequate justification for drawing on this source in presenting Rauf's views, especially when this account of them clearly resonates with that documented in Beshara materials. The work is indeed particularly valuable for the glimpses it furnishes of Rauf directly engaged with a 'student'.

B. **Unpublished Sources:** Personal correspondence from Rauf to a close associate from the early 1970s provides further autobiographical glimpses and an insight into his style of communication.

C. **Oral Sources:** Among long-standing associates consulted, three deserve specific mention: (a) Rauf's distant cousin and life-long friend Meral Arim, who completed a course at the School and for a time taught Turkish there at his request. She also transmitted information concerning Rauf's second cousin Hatice Münevver Ayaşli. (b) Grenville Collins, Chairman of the MIAS, who was particularly close to Rauf. (c) Peter Young, Principal of the Beshara School. Given his status within the movement post-Rauf, his presentations of Beshara self-perception and worldview can be considered 'authoritative' (we use the term advisedly: see below).

141 These include surviving elderly members of the khedival family in Istanbul, who provided information relating to Rauf and his immediate family (for this we thank Sinan Kuneralp, who served as a channel of communication). Thanks are also due to Peter Dewey (first Chairman of the Board of Trustees of the Beshara Trust) and Joanna Brown (secretary to Feild during the early Swyre Farm period) for their oral narratives, and for providing early documentation.

142 The rationale set out here for the selection of sources results in the exclusion of associates who have become involved in Beshara more recently, amongst whom there are naturally younger associates. The ages of most associates consulted are thus clustered at just above fifty years (and some a little older), representing the baby-boomer generation that came of age during the sixties, reaching its twenties by the end of the 1960s/early 1970s. By way of compensation, insights concerning the engagement of younger and/or more recent associates can be found in descriptions of aspects of recent life at the School (in Appendix 3, for example), and in certain of the life stories in Appendix 5.

143 This is the case for certain associates involved in the MIAS and especially those with knowledge of Arabic, which may have been culturally acquired (as in the case of an Iraqi Jewish associate and an Israeli associate), or the result of (formal or private) study.

144 This situation is compounded by the emphasis placed on individual experience within the movement, reflecting the tendency towards 'epistemological individualism' discussed earlier.

145 Additionally, they may reveal information in the context of a formal interview, only to request its withdrawal later for reasons of privacy or other sensitivities.

146 As awareness of the project spread in Beshara circles (and as a growing number of associates encountered the researcher), this feeling began to subside.

147 Such positive perceptions and expectations can exercise a subtle pressure on the researcher: while aspiring to avoid selectivity in the secondary construction of the subject, they may nonetheless find themselves swayed at some level by a desire not to upset informants with whom personal relationships have developed in the course of the research.

148 In analysing all data, we have brought to bear an awareness of the impact of the questions posed on the formulation of associates' responses.

149 This bearing can exercise an inhibiting impact on the researcher. Often the line of questioning pursued in such settings had to be constructed opportunistically, in light of 'on the spot' evaluations of interviewees' potential for openness in relation to different areas.

150 Such occasions arose during various social gatherings, at Chisholme House and during the MIAS symposia in Oxford, for example.

151 We have endeavoured to take into account the possible impact of our own presence and participation in specific settings and activities. As Barker, The Scientific Study of Religion, p. 9, remarks, it is increasingly recognised that 'detached observation is not only difficult but methodologically inappropriate for the kind of research that is needed for an acceptable secondary construction of NRMs. There is some information that one can acquire only by becoming part of the data'.

152 Specific refusal of access arose in relation to a further course 'conversation' session at the School: see Ch. 3. Heelas, The New Age Movement, pp. 8–10, raises the general question of difficulties posed for the outside researcher in the case of the New Age, given that it is claimed to be about experience: 'From the point of view of the New Ager, the academic frame of inquiry – with the importance attached to intellectually-informed distinctions and other modes of analysis – is likely to be seen as doing more harm than good. The objection, quite simply, is that the "ego-operations" of the academic cannot do justice to what the New Age is all about – the wisdom of the experiential. The academic, however, can take refuge in the fact that New Agers talk and write ... It is thus possible to convey their experiences, by way of quotations, as well as they do themselves.' The same can be said of the study of mysticism and spirituality more generally: in each case, the situation is compensated by the existence of materials reflecting a first-hand perspective.

153 For example, Peter Coates, Ibn 'Arabi and Modern Thought: The History of Taking Metaphysics Seriously (Oxford, 2002), p. 28, argues: 'there is enough translated material of sufficiently high quality available now in English, to arrive at a rounded picture of the world-view of Ibn 'Arabi. Importantly, mis-descriptions of his viewpoint and clear errors of understanding have been cleared up.' In his recent review of this work Atif Khalil agrees, but adds an important qualification: 'There is such a wide range of excellent secondary literature available today on [Ibn 'Arabi] that one can acquire a fairly accurate conception of his worldview relying solely on Western scholarship – to the extent possible for one not proficient in Arabic, as Ibn 'Arabi's ideas are intricately tied to subtle nuances of the language.' See Journal of Religion and Society, 7 (2005), at http://moses. creighton.edu/JRS/.

154 Chittick, Ibn 'Arabi and His School, in Nasr, ed., Islamic Spirituality: Manifestations, p. 57. A comprehensive study of his thought giving due attention to a diachronic analysis of his oeuvre as a whole is yet to be achieved.

155 A case in point is the doctrine of the Seals. For example, compare expositions of this in Chodkiewicz, Seal of the Saints, chapters 8–9, and Souad Hakim, 'The Spirit and the Son of the Spirit: A Reading of Jesus ('Isa) according to Ibn 'Arabi', *JMIAS*, XXXI (2002), pp. 1–28.

156 See for example Nettler, *Sufi Metaphysics and Qur'anic Prophets*, p. 2. Chittick, Ibn 'Arabi, p. 497, observes that Ibn 'Arabi wrote 'at an exceedingly high level of discourse, making him one of the most difficult of all Muslim authors.'

157 Cf. James Morris, 'Ibn 'Arabi's Rhetoric of Realisation: Keys to Reading and "Translating" the *Meccan Illuminations*, 1: Ibn 'Arabi's Audiences and Intentions', *JIMAS*, XXXIII (2003), p. 85.

Chapter 2

1 We derive legitimacy for this 'dichotomous' approach from the fact that the movement itself implicitly upholds it. In an interview, for example, the Principal responded to the seemingly straightforward question 'Can you tell me how the School began?' thus: 'Perhaps we won't be able to talk here about what happened ... except at the observable level.' 'Courses at Chisholme House', *Beshara Magazine*, 8 (n.d.), p. 27.

2 See Obituary, *JMIAS*, VI (1987), p. 1; *Ismail Hakki Bursevi's Translation of and Commentary on Fusus al-Hikam by Muhyiddin Ibn 'Arabi*, rendered into English by Bulent Rauf with the help of Rosemary Brass and Hugh Tollemache [from the 1832 Bulaq edition of a manuscript written in Turkish and Arabic c.1700] (MIAS, Oxford and Istanbul, 1986), 4 vols, 1, inside cover. This text is hereafter referred to as the *White Fusus* (for an explanation, see Ch. 3). Note that Rauf retained his Turkish passport and could have settled in Turkey or elsewhere.

3 Christopher Ryan, Conversion to the Essence, in Turan Koç, ed., *International Symposium on Islamic Thought in Anatolia in the XIIIth and XIVth Centuries and Daud al-Qaysari* (Ankara, 1998), p. 339. Ryan is a long-standing associate.

4 See Obituary; *White Fusus*, 1, inside cover.

5 Culme-Seymour, *Bolter's Grand-daughter*, p. 251; cf. her 'Translating Ibn 'Arabi': A Personal Recollection by Angela Culme-Seymour, *MIAS Newsletter*, September 1988, p. 4, where she suggests they first met in 1967. They did not marry until autumn 1977: see *Bolter's Grand-daughter*, p. 316; cf. Hugh Tollemache, 'An Obituary of Bulent Rauf', *Beshara Magazine*, 3 (Autumn 1987), p. 3, which suggests this was in 1973. Culme-Seymour, *Bolter's Grand-daughter*, pp. 253–4, paints the following picture of Rauf during the earliest part of their friendship: 'He knew a lot of people in London and often went out to dinners and dancing, in spite of his broken hip, and he loved to kiss beautiful girls. It was not surprising that [he] was sought after and a success with so many people. He had an unusual and distinguished appearance, great charisma and he could talk well and knowledgeably about almost any subject you could think of.'

6 Culme-Seymour, *Bolter's Grand-daughter*, p. 271.

7 This was condensed into a chapter on the Eastern Mediterranean in Jennifer Feller, ed., *Great Dishes of the World in Colour* (London, 1976). See ibid., pp. 271–2; *Beshara Newsletter*, Autumn 1996, pp. 5ff., and Rauf, *Addresses II*, p. 108.

8 Culme-Seymour, *Bolter's Grand-daughter*, p. 293.

9 Münevver Ayaşli; on her, see Ch. 4.

10 Culme-Seymour, *Bolter's Grand-daughter*, p. 266.

11 Ibid. Rauf's cousin Arim and Young identify him as Shevke Dede. Arim suggests he was a Melami sufi and a poor man who sold postcards in the main Istanbul post office. She describes how his exclamation (which had been accompanied by a hand gesture) had fallen far short of acceptable Turkish norms of etiquette. Yet Rauf was not offended and smiled, having understood its significance. Her version of the episode has Shevke Dede say 'we have been thinking of England for five years'. Other versions (including Young's) suggest 'forty years'. Tollemache, 'An Obituary of Bulent Rauf' (mistakenly?) dates this episode to 1966.

12 It is unclear when he assumed this name, which he presumably received from Vilayat Khan, on whom see below. Feild, *The Last Barrier*, p. 184, has Rauf refer to him by it during his first visit to him in Turkey, in November 1969.

13 The group had 'Top Ten' hits in the USA and the UK: see Rawlinson, 'A History of Western Sufism', p. 3. On Dusty Springfield's significance as a pop artist, see Marwick, *Culture in Britain since 1945*, p. 96.

In general, musicians featured prominently among spiritual seekers of the counterculture. Cf. Sardar, *Desperately Seeking Paradise*, p. 68, recalling that many of the followers of 'Abd al-Qadir al-Sufi he encountered in London during 1972 were musicians and singers (including Richard Thompson, who sang with Fairport Convention). Note also pop phenomenon Arthur Brown's involvement with Beshara. On the role of music in the counterculture, see Steve Turner, *Hungry for Heaven: Rock and Roll and the Search for Redemption* (London, 1995).

14 Culme-Seymour, *Bolter's Grand-daughter*, p. 293; Feild, *The Last Barrier*, p. xiii.

15 Feild, *The Last Barrier*, p. xiii.

16 Hermansen, 'Hybrid Identity Formations', p. 171, also maintains that he studied 'in the Gurdjieff-Ouspensky tradition, including Druids and other occult movements', in London. On Gurdjieff and Ouspensky, see below.

17 The Sufi Order in the West was the creation of Vilayat's father Inayat Khan (d.1927), Indian Chishti sufi and distinguished musician. His pioneering activities in the West were carried out during extensive travels there in the 1910s–1920s. These introduced fundamental innovations to his Chishti heritage, such that the Sufi Order emerged as an independent phenomenon reflecting an effective detachment of sufism from Islam. See Rawlinson, 'A History of Western Sufism', pp. 8–9, and Jervis, The Sufi Order, pp. 216–17. Geaves, *The Sufis of Britain*, pp. 65–6, 164, 174, suggests that the Chishti *tariqa* was in any case 'the most eclectic of the subcontinent *tariqas*', historically open to Hindu and Sikh communities due to 'its universal message'. He points in addition to Inayat's development in 'an environment of tolerance, universality and music'. According to Inayat's grandson Zia (Sufi Order head since Vilayat's death in June 2004), his work in the West expressed a deep commitment to ecumenism 'under the sign of the "Universel", the archetype of the spirituality of the future as he envisioned it, a Temple of Light in which all faiths converge in polyphonic glorification of the One Being'. See Pir Vilayat Inayat Khan, *Thinking like the Universe: The Sufi Path of Awakening*, ed. Pythia Peay (London, 2000), Foreword, p. ix.

Inayat had reportedly designated his son Vilayat as his successor while the latter was still a child. Vilayat was later trained and confirmed as a sufi master by the son of Inayat's teacher. See Khan, *Thinking like the Universe*, p. ix. He studied psychology and philosophy in Paris and Oxford. In 1956, he assumed his position as head of the Sufi Order (comprising a major part of the original organisation which had suffered splits on Inayat's death due to competing claims to leadership; see Jervis, The Sufi Order, pp. 217ff.), and set himself to continuing his father's work in Euro-America. From the early 1970s, he centred his focus on the USA. The Sufi Order is arguably the most prevalent and the best known (at least on a popular level) of the sufi groups in Euro-America today; see Jervis, The Sufi Order, p. 212.

Zia characterises Vilayat's contribution to Inayat's legacy as 'reconciliation of the hallowed tradition of Sufism with the contemporary spirit of egalitarianism and advances in science and technology'. He describes the purpose of his work as having been 'not to propagate doctrines so much as to beckon the awakening of the inner faculties possessed by each of us'. See *Thinking like the Universe*, p. ix. As the ideal framework for such 'unveiling' is the group spiritual retreat, in 1975 Vilayat established 'The Abode of the Message' in New Lebanon, NY, as a retreat centre (see www.sufiorder.org/abode). *Thinking like the Universe* is based on his teaching during such retreats. It delineates the spiritual path and details its practices. First is withdrawal from the demands of the world, second the expansion of ordinary consciousness, and third a move towards 'transcendent states of unity'. To facilitate this transition, he recommends that disciples choose three teachers (masters, saints or prophets) from different traditions. This reflects a conviction that 'The message of Sufism today points to the importance of the spirituality of the future calling upon understanding and integrating into a meaningful pattern the essential contributions of the world religions.' Following 'the transcendent states of unity', the path requires a return to the world: Vilayat recommends 'whirling' and *dhikr* to deepen the process of 'awakening in life'. Finally, disciples are urged to take steps towards creating a spiritual value system in the service of 'a more conscious and compassionate' human future.

18 Feild, *The Last Barrier*, p. xiii. Some of his associates suggest this encounter had been at a New Age Conference on Healing and Spirituality at Attingham Park, supported by George Trevelyan; Vilayat had been a keynote speaker.

19 The following account is based on the recollections of associates who joined the group at this time. Their journeys to Feild's doorstep offer glimpses of the mood of the young people concerned. A textile designer in her early twenties tells how she had been 'looking for something', reading avidly on Hinduism, Buddhism, 'anything that might help me develop a clearer sense of who I was'. An architect in his early twenties describes how he had been 'searching all over for spiritual guidance'. Both had been introduced to the group through a mutual friend, who was a close associate of Feild.

20 On this practice (known also as the 'Dances of Universal Peace'), and the role of American Chishti sufi Samuel Lewis in inspiring it, see Jervis, The Sufi Order, p. 224; Hermansen, In the Garden of American Sufi Movements, pp. 160–1 and 'Hybrid Identity Formations', pp. 181–2. On Lewis, see Andrew Rawlinson, *The Book of Enlightened Masters* (Chicago, 1997), pp. 396–403. For a description of the dance as performed in Britain today, see Geaves, *The Sufis of Britain*, pp. 177ff.

21 On the *wazifa* in sufism, see Ch. 6. On its use in the Sufi Order, see Jervis, The Sufi Order, p. 236.

22 Wilson, The Strange Fate of Sufism, p. 208 n. 109, believes Feild appears 'leading communal Sufi dancing in the film *Glastonbury Festival*' with Vilayat. An early associate of Feild's confirms his participation in this event, which took place during the second Glastonbury Festival. The dance was 'a Rainbow dance' they had made up on the spot. Rauf was also at the Festival, but did not participate in the dance.

23 Culme-Seymour, *Bolter's Grand-daughter*, p. 293.

24 Feild, *The Last Barrier*, pp. xiii, 1. An account of his relationship with Rauf appears in this record of his journey on the spiritual path, published a few years after their ways had parted. Although he did not identify him explicitly, it was evident that his teacher here ('Hamid') was Rauf. Any doubts were put to rest in the twenty-fifth anniversary edition. In a new Preface, Field thus writes of Hamid (p. xi): 'His real name was Bulent Rauf, and he was one of those masters who chose to remain virtually anonymous during his lifetime ... Only now, in this new edition of *The Last Barrier*, will his name be known.' The last page of this edition also carries a photograph of Rauf.

25 Feild's account suggests that it took place in autumn 1968; Culme-Seymour's in spring 1971. Associates suggest that, after an initial encounter, Feild went away, and later reappeared. Precision may elude us, but it is clear that a significant meeting took place between the two men at some point during the end or turn of the 1960s, and led to a relationship with important consequences for the emergence of Beshara.

26 Feild, *The Last Barrier*, p. xiii. One external source points out that the owner of the antique shop where Feild encountered Rauf was a close friend of Feild's: this might explain why Feild took to Rauf so quickly.

27 Ibid., p. 2.

28 This is surprising, given his relationship with Vilayat. The claim might be understood in light of Vilayat's Indian provenance, if not as part of Feild's 'creative mythologisation'.

29 Culme-Seymour, *Bolter's Grand-daughter*, p. 294.

30 Feild, *The Last Barrier*, p. 4.

31 Ibid., p. 13.

32 Ibid., p. 14; chapters 2 and 3 (to p. 31). The shaykh in Istanbul remains unnamed; the saint was Haci Bayram Veli, buried in Ankara (see Ch. 6).

33 Ibid., pp. 39ff.

34 Ibid., pp. 53–4.

35 Ibid., pp. 70–2.

36 See ibid., pp. 83, 133, for example; cf. p. 66. Regarding the depiction of Rauf here, Wilson, *The Strange Fate of Sufism*, p. 208 n. 112, observes that, 'As with many other popular depictions of Sufi training, the Teacher is portrayed as relying heavily on disorientatingly affecting caprice.'

37 Feild names Loras explicitly in the preface to the new edition of *The Last Barrier* (p. xiv). On his encounter with him, see p. 141. Loras reportedly asked him to 'bring the line of the Mevlevis ... to the West'. Feild also has Rauf say to him 'You have a special link with Mevlana; that is why you were sent to Konya, and why you were received as you were.' (See pp. xiv and 165.) He was finally initiated as a Mevlevi (reportedly as a shaykh) in Los Angeles in 1976 by Loras, whom he had helped to bring to the USA (and Canada). See Rawlinson, 'A History of Western Sufism', p. 26. As we noted earlier, his Mevlevi connections are generally prominent in perceptions of Feild: Hermansen, In the Garden of American Sufi Movements, p. 171 and 'Hybrid Identity Formations', p. 171, reports that he founded the 'Mevlana Foundation' in 1976 (this apparently went by the name of the 'Institute of Conscious Living/Life' to begin with). See Wilson, *The Strange Fate of Sufism*, p. 199, and Lewis, *Rumi: Past and Present*, pp. 518–19. Feild has acted more recently as 'spiritual adviser' to the Foundation (currently centred on Boulder, Colorado) and to the Turning Society in British Vancouver. Kabir Helminski, an American currently regarded as a Mevlevi shaykh, was first introduced to the Mevlevis through him. See *Rumi: Past and Present*, pp. 518, 522.

38 Culme-Seymour, *Bolter's Grand-daughter*, p. 294.

39 Feild, *The Last Barrier*, p. 5.

40 Ibid.

41 Ibid., p. 6.

42 Ibid.

43 Culme-Seymour, *Bolter's Grand-daughter*, p. 294.

44 Ibid.

45 Feild's account in *The Last Barrier* makes occasional reference to Rauf's 'students', some of whom travelled to Turkey to study with him. Feild also has Rauf himself refer in this text to a young man in London who was 'a student' of his. See pp. 169 and 62, respectively.

46 A quintessentially 1960s rock band that was internationally acclaimed if somewhat controversial, its music has been described as capturing some of the optimism of the decade. For a time during the mid-1960s (with the breakthrough 1964 hit 'You really got me'), it rivalled The Rolling Stones as the second most popular British group behind The Beatles; it was also very successful in the USA. The Kinks' early singles set a standard for rock that reverberated for decades.

47 Feild, *The Last Barrier*, p. 164; cf. p. 47: 'I want to pass on to you some of the knowledge that I have been given, so that you can go back and teach others.'

48 Difficulties in tracing these steps arise from contradictions between dates recorded by Feild on the one hand, and those put forward by Culme-Seymour, Beshara sources, and others involved at the time, on the other. Complications also arise out of the variances of individual recollections, and the impact on narratives of the conflicting agendas of involved parties. The following account relies on Beshara associates' narratives, but we have balanced these by the version of events advanced by Peter Dewey, first Chairman of the Board of Trustees of the Beshara Trust that was soon established. In this capacity, he was at the heart of things. As Dewey did not go on to become part of the Beshara movement, this version can be deemed 'external'.

49 Shah published some twenty titles on sufism, which have been translated into many languages and sold in millions. Among the best known are *The Sufis* (London, 1964) and *The Way of the Sufi* (London, 1968). By his own admission, he was moved by a concern to make available in the West 'those aspects of Sufism which shall be of use to the West'. See Pat Williams, 'An Interview with Idries Shah', in Lewin, ed., *The Diffusion of Sufi Ideas in the West*, p. 17. He is credited with having 'reclaimed' the study of sufism in the West from the orientalist disciplines, which had made it inaccessible and irrelevant to ordinary people.

50 In contrast, a Beshara associate who was a member of Feild's early London group suggests that the initiative to establish a centre emanated from a constellation of personalities and the founders and leaders of a range of spiritual groups (among them Rauf). They were united by a conviction of the need to draw their various strands together and to facilitate dialogue and joint activities, motivated by their recognition of the groundswell of interest in spirituality. This version downplays the lead role of the Sufi Order suggested by Dewey. Nonetheless, this same associate relates that the Sufi Order was by this time well established in the USA and France, and news of its successes there was drawing increasing numbers to Feild's London group. Sufficiently broad-based to absorb diverse traditions and ways, the latter operated within a fluid network of groups, some of which were associated with specific religions (such as a kabbalah study group under Warren Kenton, on whom see Ch. 5, and a Christian meditation group). Members of Feild's group attended other groups with his blessing and encouragement, while retaining their Sufi Order attachment.

51 At about the same time, Dewey joined in efforts to locate and purchase a venue for a parallel centre in Scotland, resulting in the establishment of the Salisbury Centre in Edinburgh.

52 According to Dewey, Feild had supplanted Vilayat's existing representative (a woman), causing some tension. Following in Inayat's controversial footsteps (see Hermansen, In the Garden of American Sufi Movements, p. 164) and apparently those of Vilayat, too, Feild appointed a woman to serve as his chief assistant. (This appears to have been the same woman [a healer] who later assisted him in his role as centre director.) Rawlinson, 'A History of Western Sufism', p. 26, records Feild's claim to have received twelve initiations from Vilayat, 'the equivalent of being made a sheikh'.

53 Dewey dates this to late 1969 or early 1970. A leaflet presenting Feild's credentials (referred to earlier, dating from 1970 or 1971), and alluding to his imminent opening of 'a large country centre to which people can go for training and retreat', specifies his relationship to the Sufi Order. According to this, he was 'of the London Branch of the International School of Esoteric Studies, a branch of the Sufi Order founded in the West by Pir-O-Murshid Inayat Khan in 1910'. This leaflet (which carries the Sufi Order symbol) confirms that Feild had been working for the past few years with Vilayat. It claims that he had by this time 'visited many of the Pirs and Sheiks [sic] of the Sufi tradition' in Turkey and Pakistan.

54 Dewey remains active today in promoting religious ecumenism.

55 Promotional leaflet 'Beshara: Swyre Farm', n.d. (probably from mid-1970s), and 'Courses at Chisholme', p. 27. The Trust was Registered Charity No. 296769.

56 The Arabic noun *bishara* signifies 'good news', 'glad tidings' or 'annunciation' (see further Ch. 5).

57 It is unclear precisely when this happened, or when the name became reflected in legal documentation relating to the charity.

58 Feild, *The Last Barrier*, pp. xvi–xvii, cites a letter from Rauf (September 1973) that speaks of 'founding a Beshara'. An internal circular of 20 June 1972 issued in advance of a planned open day/fête there refers to Swyre Farm as the 'Beshara centre' or 'Beshara'.

59 Reshad Feild, *Going Home: The Journey of a Travelling Man* (Shaftesbury, 1996), p. 1.

60 On Glastonbury and the Glastonbury Festival, see Chryssides, *Exploring New Religions*, pp. 325ff.

61 Associates offer a classic counterculture understanding of the motives behind drug use at the time, and the search for alternative ways of living that motivated it.

62 Dewey's comment is borne out by research on the subject, for there is an acknowledged link between drug experimentation (and the resulting psychedelic experiences which changed many young users' frames of reference) and the attraction of Eastern spirituality (including 'sufism'), which offered comparable results through techniques like meditation. See, for example, Musgrove, *Ecstasy and Holiness*, p. 141. Moreover, the negative consequences of drug use may have fuelled a search for a substitute that could offer natural methods of 'getting high'. Cf. Geaves, *The Sufis of Britain*, p. 141, and Hanegraaff, *New Age Religion*, p. 11. Vilayat Khan has indeed observed that the drug period 'was a good time for Sufism and Sufi dancing – the intoxication of the dervish was very attractive'. (Cited in Jervis, The Sufi Order, p. 232. He himself made prohibition of drug use a condition for Sufi Order membership in the 1960s: see Geaves, *The Sufis of Britain*, p. 176, and Koszegi, The Sufi Order in the West, p. 213.) Lings, *What is Sufism?*, p. 96 (writing in 1973), offered an explanation for 'some of the current illusions about what can be obtained through drugs', in terms of the limited consciousness of 'profane man'.

63 Kose, *Conversion to Islam*, pp. 150–1, indicates that drug use was indeed characteristic of many who went on to join NRMs. According to his findings, those who had used LSD/marijuana three or more times were twice as likely to join NRMs as those who had never used these drugs, or had used them less intensively. Such drug use appears to have been even higher among joiners of Eastern NRMs specifically. Cf. authoritative New Age writer Marilyn Ferguson, *The Aquarian Conspiracy: Personal and Social Transformation in the 1980s* (Los Angeles, 1980), p. 89: 'It is impossible to overestimate the historic role of psychedelics as an entry point drawing people into other transformative technologies. For tens of thousands ... the drugs were a pass to Xanadu, especially in the 1960s ... The annals of the Aquarian Conspiracy are full of accounts of passages: LSD to Zen, LSD to India, psilocybin to Psychosynthesis.' See further Susan Love Brown, Baby Boomers, American Character, and the New Age: A Synthesis, in Lewis and Gordon Melton, eds, *Perspectives on the New Age*, pp. 94–5.

64 For a colourful account of this early period and those involved, see Zabor, *I, Wabenzi*.

65 On the over-representation of Jews in NRMs based on the American case (explained in terms of the relatively greater secularisation of the American Jewish community), see Dawson, Who Joins New Religious Movements and Why, p. 123. Note that several of the Jews involved in Swyre Farm at this time were indeed American.

66 Field, *The Last Barrier*, p. xiv. Associates corroborate this figure.

67 This reflected his own interest in meditation, but possibly also its centrality within the Sufi Order. Jervis, The Sufi Order, p. 227, describes it as 'the fulcrum of Vilayat's esoteric methodology', and 'the principal means of self-transformation' he upheld. Vilayat is indeed perhaps best known for his inventive style of meditation; see pp. 223, 235.

68 'The Path to Unity', p. 5: undated text of a lecture delivered at Swyre Farm, 9 pp. Feild, *The Last Barrier*, p. ix, recently explained that, although 'steeped in the Sufi tradition', he is not a sufi, nor is he 'tied to any other of the world's spiritual lifelines': 'I have no labels, but I travel with all true seekers.'

69 An associate recalls that one of the *dhikr* forms Feild recommended was that of Hasan Lutfi Shushud, Bennett's final teacher, who had directly taught him this form. On him, see Washington, *Madame Blavatsky's Baboon*, p. 399, and Ch. 8.

70 The practice of turning or whirling has commonly been instrumentalised in Western contexts in recent decades, where it is projected as a self-sufficient practice, the 'success' of which is independent of the practitioner's beliefs/religious background. In Britain, it is closely associated with a Mevlevi group operating under the auspices of the Study Society. Among the original participants are 'non-Muslim Mevlevis', who follow practices associated with Advaita Vedanta teachings and TM (they are also heirs to the work of Ouspensky). See Geaves, *The Sufis of Britain*, pp. 168ff. On whirling in contemporary Muslim contexts, see Ch. 8.

71 The leaflet presenting his credentials (referred to earlier) states that he had developed techniques for healing the 'subtle bodies' through the use of 'sound and the Mantrum, called by the Sufis the Wasifa [sic]'.

72 'The Path of Initiation', p. 2: undated text of a lecture delivered at Swyre Farm, 4 pp.

73 See for example 'The Path to Unity', p. 4, and below.

74 See ibid., p. 2, for example. On Krishnamurti and his early connections with Theosophy, see Barrett, *The New Believers*, pp. 345–6. See further J. Krishnamurti, *Total Freedom: The Essential Krishnamurti* (New York, 1996).

75 See 'The Path to Unity', p. 8: the reference here is specifically to his *Secret of the Golden Flower*. The importance of this and other pioneering works of Richard Wilhelm (d. 1930) was in opening up to the West the spiritual heritage of China. Among others, his 1923 German translation of the *I Ching* (later translated into English as *I Ching: Book of Changes*) was crucial in this regard.

76 'The Path to Unity', pp. 6, 8. Heelas, *The New Age Movement*, pp. 46–7, emphasises Jung's general significance for the development of the New Age and his impact on its thinking. Drawing on 'the perennial – "archetypal" – components found in religions east and west', he thus developed 'all the great themes of Self-spirituality'. Hermansen, 'Hybrid Identity Formations', p. 179, observes that Jungian psychology has been of particular interest to Western sufis because it 'incorporates a spiritual dimension and involves dream work'.

77 Feild quotes from Herman Hesse's novel *Steppenwolf* in 'The Path to Unity', p. 3, for example. Hesse's *Siddhartha* was especially popular with the counterculture generation: see Heelas, *The New Age Movement*, p. 51.

78 After Feild's departure, Dom Sylvester Houédard (1924–92) became a frequent speaker and established a lasting relationship with the movement. A concrete poet and Benedictine monk at Prinknash Abbey (Gloucestershire), he became known for his vision of 'wider ecumenism'. His articles appeared in the *JMIAS*, and his *Commentaries on Meister Eckhardt Sermons* was published by Beshara Publications (2000).

79 'Beshara: Swyre Farm', and Feild, *Going Home*, p. 1.

80 The *mihrab* is a niche built into the wall of a mosque to designate the direction of Muslim prayer (towards Mecca).

81 Feild, *Going Home*, p. 2. The absence of Muslim religious leaders is noteworthy.

82 He was called Khojasti Mistri.

83 Feild, *Going Home*, p. 2.

84 'The Message of Dedication': Khidr's Day, 6 May 1973 (Swyre Farm communique).

85 On this, see Ch. 5.

86 An allusion to Qur'an 36: 82.

87 On this significant figure of Islamic mysticism, see Ch. 4.

88 Alice Bailey and Djawal Khul, *A Treatise on the Seven Rays* (5 vols.): 2, *Esoteric Psychology*, appeared in 1942. The overall title reflects the premise that the nature, quality and interrelationship of seven streams of energy pervade the solar system, the earth and all that lives and moves within its orbit. The first two volumes explore the psychological make-up of humans as the appearance of an incarnating, evolving spiritual entity. Bailey's works were reportedly dictated and transmitted to her telepathically by the Tibetan Master Djawal Khul over a period of thirty years, in the first half of the twentieth century. She is associated with the Arcane School, an early twentieth-century offshoot of Theosophy; see Heelas, *The New Age Movement*, p. 45. Hanegraaff, *New Age Religion*, p. 95, underlines her pervasive influence in the New Age movement, especially in its early phase. For examples of the lasting impact of her 'Plan', see Groothius, *Unmasking the New Age*, pp. 119–20.

89 Huey P. Newton (d. 1989) was an African-American who co-founded the Black Panthers with Bobby Seale in 1966. The group became a political force that was both

admired and feared for its militant stance, which reflected a shift from Martin Luther
King's commitment to non-violence in the African-American struggle for civil rights.
See Hugh Pearson, *The Shadow of the Panther: Huey Newton and the Price of Black Power
in America* (Reading, MA, 1994).

90 Sri Aurobindo (d.1950) was closely associated with The Mother (Mirra Alfassa,
d.1973). Together they are associated with the Sri Aurobindo Ashram at Pondicherry,
with Auroville (inaugurated in 1968), and with 'Integral Yoga'. See www.miraura.org for
their teachings, writings and legacy. Heelas, *The New Age Movement*, p.43, provides an
insight into Alfassa's background. He describes Auroville as 'one of the best-known of
New Age centres' today.

91 Thomas Traherne (d.1674) was an English metaphysical poet. His great theme
has been described as the visionary innocence of childhood, inspiring comparison
with William Blake. Some characterise his approach as a delicately balanced fusion of
nature mysticism and Christian mysticism. The resonance of his vocabulary with that of
Buddhism has also been noted.

92 A celebrated female Muslim mystic and saint (d.801); on her see Widad al-
Sakkakini, *First among Sufis: Life and Thought of Rabia al-Adawiyya, The Woman Saint of
Basra* (London, 1982).

93 Rabindranath Tagore (d.1941) was an Anglo-Indian poet, playwright, essayist
and Nobel laureate for literature (1913). Among his famous statements is: 'Temples and
mosques obstruct thy path'. For examples of his work, see Rabindranath Tagore, *Collected
Poems and Plays* (New York, 1943). Heelas, *The New Age Movement*, p.48, situates him
among those intellectuals who began to explore New Age themes and assumptions
during the early twentieth century.

94 On this celebrated Muslim sufi saint, see Ch. 4.

95 'Devotion to Him is studying Him in every aspect. Understanding Him is knowing
all you can of Him. Serving Him is teaching what you know of Him to others.'

96 Jervis, *The Sufi Order*, pp.236–7, describes this aspect of the Sufi Order, which
is symbolised outwardly by a building, 'The Universel' (built by Vilayat, its foundation
stone was laid by Inayat). In the Universal Worship, scriptures from six world religions
are placed upon an altar. Candles are lit for each tradition, with a central one symbolising
the One God. Selections from the scriptures and from Inayat's teachings are read out,
dhikr and *wazifa*s chanted, and songs or hymns sung. Its underlying theme is unity in
diversity. See also Koszegi, *The Sufi Order in the West*, p.214.

97 Associates suggest that Rauf had responded positively to the idea of establishing a
dedicated centre, put to him by Feild before the purchase of Swyre Farm.

98 From the summer of 1970, he was engaged in research towards a commissioned
volume on the late Ottoman sultans (published posthumously as *The Last Sultans*); see
Culme-Seymour, *Bolter's Grand-daughter*, p.295. One associate recalls that Rauf did not
visit the centre throughout its first year.

99 Relations seem to have been harmonious. For example, Rauf suggested that Feild
take a small number of Swyre Farm residents to the public performance of the Mevlevi
sama' in Konya on the 'nuptial' night of Rumi (commemorating his death) in December
1972. Feild lectured to the group during the trip, and they stopped off to visit Rauf,
himself in Turkey at the time.

100 Perhaps significantly, a one-page leaflet distributed at Swyre Farm under Feild's
direction depicted the Sufi Order symbol, accompanied by Inayat's explanation of its
various elements' significance: Hazrat Pir-o-Murshid, 'The Symbol of the Sufi Order', n.d.
(This symbol is a winged heart encompassing a five-pointed star surmounting a crescent.
On its significance, see Jervis, *The Sufi Order*, p.217.)

By the time of the 'dedication ceremony' (May 1973), a new symbol had emerged.
Represented on the front cover of 'The Message of Dedication' leaflet, it depicted the
Arabic *Hu* (a contraction of the sacred pronoun *Huwa* designating the Divine Essence),
enclosed by a circle formed out of the second letter (*w*). Associates suggest that this

circle signifies completion of the 'cycle of existence'; for Rauf's treatment of this theme as actualised by the Perfect Man, see for example Rauf, *Addresses II*, p. 28. The symbol was at some early stage fashioned into a pendant and worn on a neck chain by Swyre Farm residents: there is a reference to it thus worn in Bennett, *Intimations: Talks with J. G. Bennett at Beshara* (Beshara Publications, Swyre Farm, Aldsworth, 1975), p. 97, for example, on which see below. Wearing it has since become firmly established in Beshara, and it has emerged as the movement's distinctive motif. The arrival of a silversmith at Swyre Farm saw the introduction of the silver versions that are worn by associates today, typically with a small rectangular silver case holding the text of a prayer of Ibn 'Arabi (*Hizb al-wiqaya*), on which see Ch. 6. On the possible origins of the symbol, see Ch. 3.

101 Misunderstandings arose over a number of issues. For example, Feild had virtually depleted the Sufi Order's local funds during a lecture tour of the USA as Vilayat's representative, causing him much inconvenience.

102 Feild himself captures some of the difficulties during this visit in the later parts of *The Last Barrier*.

103 For example, Rauf may have been behind the gradual reorientation of collective *dhikr* that removed earlier forms of movement (including turning): one associate suggests that the collective *dhikr* was thus made 'more rigorous'.

References to Ibn 'Arabi in Feild's talks at Swyre Farm may also reflect Rauf's input. This is difficult to confirm, however, for they might equally have originated in his Sufi Order orbit. (As Jervis, The Sufi Order, p. 229, notes, the philosophical foundations of the Sufi Order also lie in theosophical sufism, which is greatly indebted to Ibn 'Arabi.) Of these references, the following in particular may reflect Rauf's input: 'In the path of the mystic, whatever label they may be given, whether they are called Christian or Jewish or Moslem, there are ... various stages along the journey ... To explain these stages, we need some sort of language, and so it is in the language of the Sufis and particularly Ibn El Arabi that I would like to explain some of these stages which we call FANA.' See 'The Path of the Mystic', September 1972, p. 3.

104 The idea of introducing formal study of Ibn 'Arabi's thought at Swyre Farm appears to have been discussed some months before this: personal correspondence from Rauf to a close associate (May 1972) thus mentions Vilayat's reaction to the suggestion. Having originally thought that it was 'too soon' for such study, he had later 'come round' to the idea.

105 While fundamentally critical of him, associates acknowledge that activities under his lead were 'very powerful: he touched people's hearts and drew them to him, including the openly sceptical'. 'He could weave a spell,' one associate recalls, 'but if you wrote it down it did not necessarily make sense.'

106 In *The Last Barrier*, Feild depicted his own relationship with Suleyman Dede (as that with Rauf) in terms of a sufi shaykh and his disciple. His attitude towards the Swyre Farm community may well have evinced expectations of his own status as shaykh. (Presently, it seems that Feild 'does not present himself as a Sufi sheikh but rather as an esoteric healer and a teacher of the science of the breath'. See Rawlinson, 'A History of Western Sufism', pp. 26–7.)

107 Feild himself likely conveyed to associates Rauf's insistence that there were 'no teachers' at Swyre Farm, even if aspects of his own demeanour may have contradicted this in practice.

108 Feild dates this letter to late September 1973, somewhat later than might have been expected. He includes it in the Preface to the new edition of *The Last Barrier*. Rauf opened it with an oblique reference to his dissatisfaction with Feild, thus: '[T]his is a reminder that one should be aware of His being with you and so harmonize all your actions with His wish. In other words, it is a reminder to confide oneself to His Will so that all personal direction, desire, and action is in complete accordance with His plan' (p. xv). He reminded Feild further that he had been chosen 'to do God's work for Him'. He then instructed him to 'Tell the people of Vancouver and Canada that man, who is the complete image of God, is eternally linked to Him ... and that they were not invented to be a lot of footloose and fancy-free robots, unguided, irresponsible' (p. xvi). This letter also appears with minor variations in Feild, *Going Home*, pp. 4–5, where he writes: 'When I left England in 1973, after spending some years with my teacher, many people thought I had been thrown out of the circle. The fact is I left with the blessing of my teacher.'

109 See Field, *The Last Barrier*, p. xiv. For his activities after leaving Swyre Farm, see the second and third volumes in the trilogy that opens with this work. These are *The Invisible Way: A Time to Love – A Time to Die* (Wiltshire, 1979), which is a sequel to *The Last Barrier*, and *Going Home*, a lifelong collection. Insights into his perception of his relationship with Rauf at this time can be gleaned from these works: see for example *The Invisible Way*, pp. 21–38, 54, and *Going Home*, pp. 4–5, 42ff., 178. In Canada, Feild started a study group using *The Twenty-nine Pages* (see *Going Home*, pp. 6–7). Thereafter, he joined forces with the leader of an esoteric school, mobilising people through spiritual training to launch centres for the 'Work of Accelerated Transformation' in Mexico, Canada and California. 'Transformation' here signified 'psychological and spiritual development', achieved by imparting knowledge that would sustain the individual, humanity and the planet (see *Going Home*, p. 13). Accounts of this early spell indicate the extent of interest in esoteric learning among young people in these societies. When he gave his first 'class' in Canada at 5.30 a.m., for example, thirty people travelled a long distance to attend (see ibid., pp. 6–7). Feild visited Suleyman Dede in Turkey during his spell abroad. When he finally returned to London, he wrote to Rauf (whom he had not seen for two years), and went to meet him in Turkey. On this encounter (probably during the mid-1970s), see *The Invisible Way*, pp. 21–37. On Feild's more recent activities, see Rawlinson, 'A History of Western Sufism', p. 27. Hermansen, 'Hybrid Identity Formations', p. 171, notes his lasting influence on some American sufi movements (we touched on the Mevlevi arena above).

110 Beshara associates disagree with this characterisation. Instead, they describe the alternative vision as one of 'a centre that would offer the type of education Rauf wanted to establish, which was "universal"'. For his part, Dewey interpreted Rauf's focus on Ibn 'Arabi in terms of an alleged confession that 'he knew nothing about other mystical traditions'. Even in the context of sufism, he had reportedly confided to Dewey that his knowledge 'was confined to Ibn 'Arabi's teaching'. Associates' projections of Rauf naturally disagree with this. Tollemache, 'An Obituary of Bulent Rauf', thus maintains he was able to express himself 'equally clearly in the language of Christian, Moslem, Jew, Zoroastrian ... and many looked to him to explain the meanings of their own traditions'.

111 This was Hugh Tollemache, who was later succeeded by Peter Yiangou. Yiangou remains active in Beshara; on Tollemache, see below.

112 R. A. Nicholson, *Rumi: Poet and Mystic*, ed. A. J. Arberry (London, 1950). Attesting to its popularity, this work was reprinted half a dozen times during the 1970s. See Lewis, *Rumi: Past and Present*, p. 533.

113 'Love and Knowledge' by Rauf; 'The Necessary Realisation of a Universal Perspective' and 'Christ', each attributed to an associate (Rashid [Richard] Hornsby), but virtually dictated to him by Rauf.

114 For a succinct introduction to him (and an assessment of his importance in the twentieth-century spiritual landscape), see Jacob Needleman, G. I. Gurdjieff and his School, in Faivre and Needleman, eds, *Modern Esoteric Spirituality*, pp. 359–80, and 'Gurdjieff', in Hanegraaff *et al.*, eds, *Dictionary of Gnosis and Western Esotericism*, 1, pp. 445–54. For a comprehensive discussion of his life, ideas, their putative sources and the teachings and methods that constitute the Gurdjieff 'work', see J. G. Bennett, *Gurdjieff: A Very Great Enigma* (New York, 1974). See further his autobiographical writings in G. I. Gurdjieff, *Meetings with Remarkable Men* (London, 1963), and James Moore, *Gurdjieff: Anatomy of a Myth* (Shaftesbury, Dorset, 1991). After extensive travels encompassing the Middle East and Central Asia, Gurdjieff (who was of Armenian Greek ancestry) returned to Russia on the eve of World War I with the principles of an esoteric teaching. In 1922, he settled in France with a dedicated group. In 1924, he suffered a near-fatal accident;

following this, his plans for the recently established Institute for the Harmonious Development of Man were abandoned, and he focused on the written development of his ideas. See J. G. Bennett, *Gurdjieff Today* (Sherborne, 1974), pp. 39–40. Proceeding from the conviction that man has become blind to what is real, his teaching was designed to encourage (or force) people to develop, 'in spite of themselves'. Pupils were expected to follow his instructions to the letter, to study his writings and to learn complex dance/posture exercises. Some argue that Gurdjieff's philosophy was substantially based on sufi ideas, while the exercises/methods he advocated derived from sufi practice. On the alleged sufi origins of 'virtually every point in his "system"', see Shah, *The Way of the Sufi*, p. 40 n. 35. Others downplay the role of sufi thought in shaping this: see, for example, Wilson, The Strange Fate of Sufism, pp. 180–1.

115 Ouspensky, a mathematician who set up groups to study what he had learned from Gurdjieff, broke with him in 1924. He revolted against the 'enigmatic' character of Gurdjieff's teachings, seeking an alternative to the master–pupil bond as the medium for their communication. On his work as Gurdjieff's pupil, see Ouspensky, *In Search of the Miraculous: Fragments of an Unknown Teaching* (London, 1950).

116 A mathematician and career scientist, Bennett first met Gurdjieff and Ouspensky in Turkey in 1920, while serving as head of British military intelligence there. They had a profound influence on his life. Following their deaths, he kept alive the spirit of their teachings (at a centre based at Coombe Springs near London from the early 1940s), but gradually developed his own path through additions, culminating in the establishment of the Academy, which attracted as many as 200 students per course. On his life and writings, see publisher's note in Bennett, *How We Do Things* (Sherborne, 1974), and *Witness: The Autobiography of John G. Bennett* (London, 1975).

Bennett described the approach of the ten-month long Academy course in the following terms: 'people of all ages may study [here] techniques of Transformation. By this is meant the realization of the potential latent in human beings for self-perfecting … The teaching and methods of Gurdjieff occupy an important place in its work'. See Bennett, *Gurdjieff Today*, Preface. In his autobiography (*Witness*, Preface, p. v.), he writes: 'In 1970, I became aware that I must do what I could to show that this training is possible. Fifty years of search had convinced me that Gurdjieff's method brought up to date and completed from other sources was the best available technique for giving just the training that the world needs. In October 1971, the … Academy … started its first course … The results show that the method works for those who can commit themselves to an all-out effort'. The 'transformation' achieved through this training is defined as unification of the individual's natural and spiritual elements by breaking through the barrier of illusion that separates them. Bennett believed the need for 'transformed' people would soon become critical. Thus, as only they could respond to the spiritual forces that seek to help mankind, only they could help it survive the imminent catastrophe he predicted; see Bennett, *Gurdjieff Today*, p. 1.

As for his connections with sufism, Bennett met with certain sufi teachers during his early travels in Asia. His interest in the region resurfaced towards the end of his life, when he paid particular attention to the spiritual legacy of the Khwajagan (sufis of eleventh to sixteenth-century Central Asia) in their capacity as 'Masters of Wisdom', members of a special class of men who bear a higher intelligence. See Bennett, *The Masters of Wisdom* (London, 1977). On this specific *silsila* within the Naqshbandiyya, see Trimingham, *The Sufi Orders*, pp. 62–4. His interest in sufi teachings was also evident in his association with the Subud movement. (Founded by the Indonesian Muhammad Sukarno Sumohadiwidjojo, 'Subuh' [d.1987], its procedure is based on adaptation of Naqshbandi–Qadiri methods which, in Shah's opinion [*The Way of the Sufi*, p. 21], have been 'turned upside down'. On Subud see Bennett, *Witness*, chapter 25; Barrett, *The New Believers*, pp. 353–5; Chryssides, *Exploring New Religions*, pp. 259–69.) Bennett's relationship to sufism is best conceived in terms of the application of sufi resources divorced from their Islamic framework as techniques in human transformation, in an eclectic synthesis with other ideas and practices. Cf. Rawlinson, 'A History of Western Sufism', p. 24: his was 'a sufism that was non-Moslem and universal ... Sufism is the Islamic name for the True Way and is hence part of Islam only accidentally and not essentially.' Following a visit to Turkey shortly before his death, Bennett expressed delight at the re-establishment of sufism there. However, he remained convinced of the potency (superiority) of his own eclectic approach (*Witness*, p. 378): 'I could also see for myself how much more we have at Sherborne, where we have brought together ideas and methods from all parts of the world and so have a repertory of techniques that allows much more rapid progress for those who are willing to work.'

117 Bennett had attended the Glastonbury Festival with members of the community under Feild's watch at Swyre Farm. He had later conveyed his profound misgivings concerning the conduct Feild had sanctioned there, during a talk at Swyre Farm (*Intimations*, pp. 96–7): 'I must tell you, because I am no friend of yours if I don't speak to you truly. I came with many of you who are here ... to that festival that was near Glastonbury. And I saw people dancing round and joining hands with people ... and chanting *Ya Hu* or *Allah Hu*. You know the words *Allah Hu* cannot be spoken like that. It is not right. If the word *Allah Hu* is pronounced, the whole depth of one's being must be stirred by it. You, all of you, wear symbols, symbolising this breath of life, this breath which is far more than that, the word *Hu*. But you've chosen and you've taken this supreme symbol of the source of everything, the ultimate that is beyond everything and you are not respecting it as you should ... You will have to use the word, but I came here to beg you to remember, that you have chosen the holiest syllable that there is and if you've done that, you've taken on yourself a great responsibility. If you treat it without this respect, it is sacrilege. It is only the fewest of the few, the rarest of the rare actually come to the reality of Hu. The very great chosen ones, chosen and sent; messengers. Only they really can say the word Hu.'

118 *Intimations*. Rashid Hornsby had studied at Bennett's Academy before he met and established a close relationship with Rauf. His characterisation of Bennett's attitude towards Beshara may reflect an attempt to demonstrate a continuity of approach between the two, an exaggeration of the extent of Bennett's approval of Beshara, or a projection of Rauf's ideas onto him.

119 Ibid., p. x; according to Hornsby, Bennett was 'painfully aware' that those who seek gurus and teachers often 'seek only an identification of their own personality'. Later in life, he became adamant 'in his belief that the old system of teacher and pupil ... should not continue in the form that it had taken in the past. He saw that it was not possible or desirable in the present world situation, where the necessity for the dissemination of esoteric knowledge had obviously to take place on a global scale, if it is to prove affective [sic].'

120 See Annett, ed., *The Many Ways of Being*, p. 86. The author noted that those involved at this time were aged under thirty, and came from 'a broad spectrum of educational and class backgrounds'.

121 Cf. 'Courses at Chisholme', p. 27.

122 In one account, an associate came upon the property 'by chance' (an incident later construed from a teleological perspective as part of the unfolding of Beshara). In another account, the search for a venue had focused deliberately on the north of England and Scotland (given that Swyre Farm was in the south), and an associate living in Scotland heard of Chisholme House and went to look at it.

123 See Beshara website. One associate relates that it had been completely abandoned for eighteen years.

124 Ibid. This land was repurchased in 1986 at the price of its value in 1973. Further lands were also added, bringing the total to 187 acres. For an overview of the 'remarkable offers' that made these transactions possible, see Beshara website.

125 Some of the more Islam-oriented Western sufi movements have established mosques, others *khanqa*s and *zawiya*s modelled on the traditional sufi 'convent': see, for example, Hermansen, 'Hybrid Identity Formations', pp. 182–3. The Sufi Order currently maintains a school at the Abode of the Message, run by a residential community of adults and children. See ibid., and Jervis, *The Sufi Order*, pp. 238–40, on its additional 'Esoteric School', of which all Order initiates are *de facto* members, and its training and study programmes.

126 These included Oxford, Cambridge, Brighton, Blackburn, Leeds, Leicester, Bristol and Canterbury. See 'Beshara: Swyre Farm', and Annett, ed., *The Many Ways of Being*, p. 252. At this time, Annett (p. 35) suggested that, although thousands may have had contact with Beshara, 'only about a hundred people' were 'totally committed'.

127 Ibid., p. 86.

128 'Beshara: Swyre Farm'.

129 See Annett, ed., *The Many Ways of Being*, p. 86.

130 Following Bennett's death late in 1974, his widow decided to see the course in progress to completion and then sell the property. Dewey had made a bid to purchase it with the intention of introducing his own courses there. When his attempt fell through, the Beshara Trust moved swiftly to buy it.

131 Registered in Edinburgh, No. 69001.

132 Culme-Seymour, *Bolter's Grand-daughter*, p. 317.

133 *Beshara Magazine*, 5 (Spring 1988), p. 40.

134 See ibid., and *Beshara Magazine*, 10 (Winter 1989/90), p. 42, and 8, p. 15.

135 *Beshara Magazine*, 5, p. 5. The first courses held there, which offered education 'according to the dictum "Know Thyself"', were advertised in *Beshara Magazine*, 9 (n.d.), p. 51.

136 'Reaffirmation of Intent', *Beshara Magazine*, 1 (Spring 1987), p. 29.

137 Peter Young, 'News from Chisholme', *Beshara Magazine*, 1, p. 31.

138 'Reaffirmation of Intent', p. 29.

139 In all, thirteen issues appeared (three a year). The magazine represented a development of the 'Beshara News Bulletin', circulated for some time to everyone associated with the Trust. It thus continued to provide information about the Trust and its activities.

140 *Beshara Magazine*, subscription/promotional leaflet, n.d. The front covers of later issues state that the magazine is 'concerned with unity', and provides 'a unified perspective in the contemporary world'.

141 See *Beshara Magazine*, 1, p. 30; 2 (Summer 1987), p. 32; 4 (Winter 1987/88), p. 8. Well-known speakers included poet and literary critic Kathleen Raine ('Nature – House of the Soul') and Keith Critchlow ('The Sacred Order') (on him see Ch. 5). Subjects addressed included 'The New Cosmology' and 'Science, Religion and the Symbolic World'.

142 'Reaffirmation of Intent', p. 29. For the basis of the emphasis on science at this point (and for examples of scientists showcased in *Beshara Magazine*), see Ch. 5. *Beshara Magazine* featured specifically those economists who were outlining 'a new economics for a new age'. For example, *Beshara Magazine*, 4, pp. 22–8, features Paul Ekins under the title 'The Living Economy – The Makings of a New Economics': this title refers to his edited volume *The New Economy: A New Economics in the Making* (London, 1986), which had its origins in the work of The Other Economic Summit (1984–85). The work was reviewed in *Beshara Magazine*, 2, pp. 23–5, where it was suggested that, in contrast with the established system, this 'Living Economy' reflects 'the wholeness and interconnectedness of human activity and natural processes'. In it, 'the personal, social, ecological and spiritual dimensions of the whole cannot be arbitrarily disjoined from their "economic" significance'. For another example, see *Beshara Magazine*, 6 (Autumn 1988), pp. 14–18, which features the work of 'futurist' Willis W. Harman under the title 'For a New Society – A New Economics'.

143 *Beshara Magazine*, 1, p. 29; see also 4, p. 8.

144 See *Beshara Magazine*, 1, p. 30.

145 Particular emphasis was placed on continuing and expanding the Sherborne/ Frilford seminar series, with a view to ensuring that Beshara 'set the pace and the example of thought trends and directions'. See ibid., pp. 29–30. The idea of establishing a Beshara preparatory school for children was also mooted at this time.

146 In this context, a reference to the Australia School initiative specifically.

147 Specifically, 'keeping informed of progress in scientific thought, allied to continuous exchange of ideas with the scientific community'. This derived from a conviction that 'At the frontiers of science, knowledge of our universe is undergoing a radical reappraisal. The conclusions emerging are consistent with the spiritual wisdom of God as universal being, thus preparing the way for the emergence of a vision which unites the spiritual and physical universes'. See *Beshara Magazine*, 1, p. 29; cf. Ch. 5.

148 New measures and the rationale for these were described as follows (ibid.): 'Over the past years, finance (economics) has come to assume a far greater unifying role in world affairs. In line with this, the Beshara Trust has adopted radical new approaches to financing the expansion of Beshara and its existing activities. All financial needs will now be handled by The Beshara Company Ltd., an investment company set up and wholly owned by the Trust'. The launch of a Chisholme Endowment Fund, based on a bank loan, was also announced at this time. The hope was that it would meet Chisholme's financial needs and provide student scholarships. This apparently later gave way to a 'covenants fund'; on the latter and a further financial project that had an unfortunate outcome, see below.

149 Ibid., p. 31. This focus was explicitly tied to the primordial affirmation expressed by future humanity ('Indeed, we bear witness to it!'), called out of the loins of the not-yet-created Adam in response to the divine question 'Am I not your Lord?' (Qur'an 7: 171). *Beshara Magazine*, 3 (Autumn 1987), p. 26, thus notes that the reaffirmation course proceeded 'in the light of this original affirmation'. On this primordial covenant and its significance in sufi thought, see Schimmel, *Mystical Dimensions of Islam*, p. 24. On the new course, see further *Beshara Magazine*, 2, p. 30. For the reflections of an associate who participated in it, see Elizabeth Roberts, 'Reaffirmation. A Course at Chisholme House during the Summer of 1987', *Beshara Magazine*, 3, pp. 26–7.

150 *Beshara Magazine*, 1, p. 31. The associate in question is Peter Young.

151 *Beshara Magazine*, 5, p. 38.

152 On his health in the preceding few years, and the months leading to his death, see Culme-Seymour, *Bolter's Grand-daughter*, chapter 33.

153 It is Muslim practice to mark the fortieth day following a death. The Trust organised a special lunch at Chisholme on this occasion, attended by more than 250 people from across the world. See *Beshara Magazine*, 4, p. 10. A parallel event was held in the USA. The Chairman of the Trust at the time was Hugh Tollemache. Some close associates suggest that Tollemache had been closer to Rauf than any other associate: Rauf had reportedly been 'training' him to assume significant responsibility in Beshara, and indeed considered him his 'deputy'. However, it seems that he had withdrawn from active involvement in the movement by the mid-1980s. After reappearing to speak at the Rememoration lunch, he then withdrew completely. Tollemache had been the owner and director of Beshara Press (which originally printed Beshara Publications titles) for many years.

154 Hugh Tollemache, 'The Future of the Beshara Trust' (a speech given at the Rememoration for Bulent Rauf luncheon on 16 October), *Beshara Magazine*, 4, pp. 39–40.

155 Cf. 'Rememoration for Bulent Rauf' (edited extracts from a tribute by Richard Hornsby), ibid., p. 11: 'If there is one thing I think that [Bulent] would like me to reiterate today ... it is that no-one should think that Beshara has anything to do with any person. We all have roles ... let us realise the evidence of our need for each other as a community of friends'. (We refer to this source as 'Rememoration' hereafter.)

156 A reference to activities at Sherborne, as well as those in Australia and the USA.

157 MIAS Information leaflet (undated), and MIAS website.

158 As Grenville Collins, a close associate of Rauf and Society Chairman, puts it, the idea to establish a Society ('down to the wording of its constitution') appeared spontaneously to him at Sherborne House, where he was acting as 'Head of Islamic Studies'. A week later, Abdullah Binzagr (a Saudi who was acting as course supervisor) met with him and told him he had had an idea. He relayed to him word for word the very same thoughts he had had. They decided to bring the matter to Rauf, and asked him whether they should go ahead: he encouraged them, and officers were identified straight away. For a brief note on the Society's origination and Rauf's contribution to its establishment, see *JMIAS*, VI (1987), p. 2. On Binzagr, see Ch. 6.

159 *MIAS Newsletter*, September 1988, p. 2.

160 She is first identified as President in *JMIAS*, VIII (1989), p. 70, and as Honorary Life President in *JMIAS*, XXX (2001), p. 106. It is unclear when the new title was first applied.

161 See for example *JMIAS*, VI (1987), p. 50. This early list of branches also refers to what appears to have been a short-lived branch in Surrey Hills, Sydney (Australia).

162 See for example *JMIAS*, XXIV (1998), p. 90. The Seville branch functioned for a few years but became inactive with the relocation of its Secretary.

163 Seven to date: (a, b) Ibn 'Arabi's *Wird* and *Hizb al-Wiqayah* (see Ch. 6). (c) A translation of and commentary on the *Fusus al-Hikam* attributed to Isma'il Hakki Bursevi (see Ch. 3). (d) Stephen Hirtenstein and Michael Tiernan, eds, *Muhyiddin Ibn 'Arabi: A Commemorative Volume* (MIAS and Element Books, 1990). (e–g) Three special issues of the *JMIAS*: Stephen Hirtenstein, ed., *Prayer and Contemplation* (1993); John Mercer, ed., *The Journey of the Heart* (1996); Stephen Hirtenstein, ed., *Praise* (1997). See further MIAS website.

164 The first was held in Durham (1984), the second in Aberystwyth (1985), and thereafter in Oxford (with the exception of 1994 [Durham] and 1995 [Chisholme House]). Commemorating the 750th anniversary of the death of Ibn 'Arabi, the 1990 symposium was on a particularly grand scale: spanning three days, it attracted a broad international spectrum of scholars.

165 The first was convened at Berkeley, CA in 1987. The MIAS claims it was also 'the first two-day event dedicated to Ibn 'Arabi in the United States, where a significant portion of the current scholarly work is being done'. See *MIAS Newsletter*, September 1987, pp. 3–4.

166 Apart from a brief period early on, the collection has been housed in associates' homes. From the early 1980s, the Society has endeavoured to build up its holdings, especially digital copies of manuscripts from the major Turkish (and Syrian) collections. See for example Minutes of the AGM of the MIAS, 22 September 1984, pp. 1–2.

167 Both the *Newsletter* and the *Journal* present contributions from a range of authors. When referring to their contents, we point out when a particular author is a Beshara associate. Broadly speaking, contributors are of three types: (a) Beshara associates. (b) Scholars whose awareness of Beshara stems from their close relations with Society officers, and who are sympathetic to the movement's commitment to Ibn 'Arabi's legacy. (c) Scholars who are unaware of the Society's connection (at least in its origin) with Beshara. It is noteworthy that a substantial number of contributors not associated with Beshara are also personally engaged with the subject by virtue of a sufi affiliation or sympathy (as distinct from an exclusively scholarly interest).

An indication of the growing contribution to the *JMIAS* by scholars not involved in Beshara arises out of a comparison of the contents of its first ten issues (1982–99) with those of ten more recent ones (XXIV–XXXIV; 1998–2003). In the former over 50% of the authors are associates, while in the latter the figure has dropped to just over 20%.

168 See for example *JMIAS*, XVIII (1995), p. 67.

169 Contributions of time and effort in organising symposia, and in several other aspects of the Society's activities, are on a voluntary basis. As the Treasurer noted in 1988, 'This is, after all, a matter of love.' See Minutes of the AGM of the MIAS, 19 November 1988, Treasurer's Report, p. 4.

When it became clear during the early 1980s that an expansion in activities could be expected, the need for a full-time administrator was recognised. Although fundraising efforts were engaged to that end these were unsuccessful, and the Society has continued to rely mainly on volunteers. See Minutes of the AGM of the MIAS, 15 January 1983, p. 3.

By 1984, Society members who had joined through the UK branch numbered 140; another 20 had joined via the USA branch. By 2004, these figures had risen to 300 and 81, respectively. The UK remains the centre of gravity, and in recent years the USA branch has found its small pool of human resources stretched. See Minutes of the AGM of the MIAS, 1 November 2003.

170 Two Honorary Fellows must be singled out for their connection to Beshara: Münevver Ayaşli and (for a time) Abdullah Binzagr.

171 A cursory look at recent issues of the *MIAS Newsletter* substantiates this observation. For a specific example of the level of cooperation, see *MIAS Newsletter*, 18 (Summer 2002), p. 9. This announced an initiative to produce a supplement to the now-dated bibliography of works by Ibn 'Arabi (Osman Yahia, *Histoire et classification de l'oeuvre d'Ibn 'Arabi* [Damascus, 1964]), which will also provide a detailed consideration of questions of attribution. Involving some twenty scholars in the field, the project is coordinated by Society officers and the Society aims ultimately to publish the supplement.

172 As a cursory look at the internet suggests, this is one of an expanding number of publishers of sufi books, several of which are affiliated to specific *tariqa*s or specialise in a particular sufi orientation.

173 According to its website, 'Anqa Publishing was formed as an independent company in Oxford, UK, in 1998. It works in close collaboration with the MIAS and the partners, Stephen Hirtenstein and Michael Tiernan, are involved in producing the Society's Journal. Both have been students of the Beshara School in Scotland.' It is dedicated to 'bringing out the works of ... Ibn 'Arabi ... and his line.' These writings, it holds, 'contain some of the most beautiful and comprehensive depictions of the vision of One Reality in all its facets.' The company aims to produce quality translations and new, authoritative editions of Arabic texts (using the best manuscripts available), as well as original studies of Ibn 'Arabi's teaching. It takes its name from the legendary bird 'described by Ibn 'Arabi as "the dust-cloud within which God opens up the forms of the universe".' Up to the time of writing, six titles had appeared: Stephen Hirtenstein, *The Unlimited Mercifier: The Spiritual Life and Thought of Ibn 'Arabi* (1999); *The Seven Days of the Heart: Prayers for the Nights and Days of the Week*: translation of Ibn 'Arabi, *Awrad al-usbu'* (*Wird*), by Pablo Beneito and Stephen Hirtenstein (2000); *Contemplation of the Holy Mysteries*; translation of Ibn 'Arabi, *Mashahid al-asrar*, by Cecilia Twinch and Pablo Beneito (2001); Peter Coates, *Ibn 'Arabi and Modern Thought: The History of Taking Metaphysics Seriously* (2002); Stephen Hirtenstein and Martin Notcutt, *Divine Sayings: The Mishkat al-Anwar of Ibn 'Arabi* (Arabic text and English translation) (2004); *The Nightingale in the Garden of Love: The Poems of Uftade*, Paul Ballanfat, trans. from the French by Angela Culme-Seymour (2005). For forthcoming titles, see Anqa website. The distribution of Anqa publications is significantly wider than that of Beshara Publications.

174 On this, see for example *MIAS Newsletter*, 17 (Autumn 2001), pp. 2–3; 18, pp. 6–9; 19 (Autumn 2003), pp. 4–6; Minutes of the AGM of the MIAS, 1 November 2003; 20 November 2004. This initiative aims to establish a comprehensive catalogued digital archive under the auspices of the MIAS. It was given further impetus by the theft of manuscripts from a Konya library.

175 See Jane Clark, 'Summer Gathering: Sunday, August 22nd 2004', p. 3, Beshara website.

176 See Peter Young, 'United by Oneness: Global Considerations for the Present', p. 6, Beshara website.

177 Guests are asked to make a donation for each day's board and lodging (guidelines as to appropriate levels are provided). Such donations are also required from those attending a retreat preparation, reading week, etc.

178 Associates situated abroad (especially those in the USA and Australia) send regular donations to the Institute; writing in 2000, Hermansen, 'Hybrid Identity Formations', p. 171, suggested that about thirty graduates of the School live in the USA. A leaflet outlining the covenant system is not shy of stressing the importance of this (and other financial gifts) as a measure of associates' commitment: 'beyond any financial value, a donation however small or large is a tangible token of your support and participation. If you value the perspective offered through the education at Beshara, please, if you can, make a monthly, quarterly or annual covenant to the Institute.' (It adds that 'The capital costs of acquiring, renovating, maintaining and upgrading Chisholme House and estate are met entirely by gifts.') In one associate's words, 'Beshara is eternal and ongoing, a covenant with God to be a faithful servant. The financial covenant has the purpose of sustaining places for the education to continue and be perpetuated.'

179 He points out that the Beshara brochure currently in use is now fourteen years old: one must thus consider 'whether it requires to be refreshed.'

180 'News – Summer 2004', Beshara website. An account of the August 2005 gathering can also be viewed there.

181 Of the four students on the intensive course 2003–04, for example, two belonged in this category.

Chapter 3

1 See Shah, *The Way of the Sufi*, p. 34. Associates recall that Rauf had agreed with Bennett's assessment of the importance of Shah's work. Bennett thus regarded him as 'the Krishnamurti of Sufism', for he had 'broken down people's illusions' and reached a very wide audience. See Bennett, *Gurdjieff Today*, p. 40.

2 In addition to the specific accounts related below, see for example Peter Young, 'Ibn 'Arabi: Towards a Universal Point of View', *JMIAS*, XXV (1999), p. 95.

3 The earliest Western language translations of Ibn 'Arabi's works and studies of his life and thought include: R. A. Nicholson, 'The Lives of 'Umar Ibnu'l-Farid and Muhyi'ddin Ibnu'l-'Arabi [from the *Shadharat al-Dhahab* of Ibn al-'Imad]', *Journal of the Royal Asiatic Society* (1906), pp. 797–824; ed. and trans., *The Tarjuman al-Ashwaq: A Collection of Mystical Odes by Muhyi'ddin Ibn al-'Arabi* (London, 1911); *The Mystics of Islam* (London, 1914), and *Studies in Islamic Mysticism* (Cambridge, 1921); Hendrik S. Nyberg, ed., *Kleinere Schriften des Ibn al-'Arabi* [critical editions of three texts] (Leiden, 1919); Miguel Asín Palacios, *El Islam Cristianizado: Estudio del sufismo a través de las obras de Abenarabi de Murcia* (Madrid, 1931); and Michel Vâlsan, trans., 'L'Investiture du Cheikh al-Akbar au centre suprême' [from Ibn 'Arabi's prologue to the *Futuhat al-Makkiyya*], *Études Traditionelles*, 311 (1953), pp. 300–11. For a brief overview of the history of Ibn 'Arabi studies in Europe, see Michel Chodkiewicz, Ibn 'Arabi dans l'oeuvre de Henry Corbin, in Mohammad Ali Amir-Moezzi, Christian Jambet and Pierre Lory, eds, *Henry Corbin: Philosophies et sagesses des religions du livre* (Turnhout, Belgium, 2005), pp. 81ff.

4 First published in 1939, by Cambridge University Press.

5 Published by Muhammad Ashraf, Lahore, 1970. Schimmel, *Mystical Dimensions of Islam*, p. 270 n. 25, describes this as 'a sober collection of texts with translations.'

6 The associate still keeps this underlined copy of Affifi's book.

7 In sufi circles it is a common belief and experience that aspirants encounter incidents designed to keep them from the path, when they first turn towards it. In the conceptual universe of traditional sufism 'the whole complex of forces, thought in an ultimate sense to constitute as well as to govern the world', still persists. Thus, 'There are maleficent powers to be warded off by the saints, by amulets, talismen, verses of the

Qur'an, the virtuous life, and trust in God ... All these elements are "givens", accepted principles of the universe of meaning.' Michael Gilsenan, *Saint and Sufi in Modern Egypt: An Essay in the Sociology of Religion* (Oxford, 1973), p. 34.

8 For a personal impression of Nicholson by another authoritative scholar, see An Autobiographical Sketch by the Late Professor A. J. Arberry, *Mystical Poems of Rumi 2 (Second Selection, Poems 201–400)*, trans. A. J. Arberry, ed. E. Yarshetar (Chicago, 1991), pp. x–xii.

9 Schimmel, *Mystical Dimensions of Islam*, p. 266.

10 Affifi addresses the whole of Ibn 'Arabi's thought, encompassing 'his ontology, doctrine of the Logos, epistemology, psychology, mysticism, religion, ethics, eschatology and aesthetics'. See *The Mystical Philosophy*, p. xii. He draws principally on Ibn 'Arabi's *al-Futuhat al-Makkiyya* and *Fusus al-hikam*, in addition to twenty-one of his other works.

11 He published an edition of al-Sulami's *Risalat al-Malamatiyya* (Cairo, 1945), and a widely used edition of *Fusus al-hikam* (Cairo, 1946), with substantial introduction and comments. His later contributions reportedly included an English translation of the *Fusus* intended for publication in the UK (in the event, possibly published in the Middle East). There were various articles in international journals and in the *Bulletin* of the Faculty of Arts, Alexandria University, including 'The Works of Ibn 'Arabi in the Light of a Memorandum drawn up by him [*Fihrist al-mu'allafat*]', *Bulletin*, 8 (1954), pp. 109–17, 193–207. Later publications include *Fi'l-Tasawwuf al-Islami wa ta'rikhihi* and *al-Malamatiyya wa'l-sufiyya*. He refers to both these works in a third, based on his undergraduate lectures: *al-Tasawwuf al-Islami: al-thawra al-ruhiyya fi'l-Islam* (Beirut, 1963). Citing this, Muhammad al-Shaykhani, *al-Tarbiya al-ruhiyya bayna'l-sufiyyin wa'l-salafiyyin* (Damascus, 1995), pp. 273–5, maintains that Affifi considered sufism 'the spiritual depth' of Islam, and the 'true religious, spiritual expression among Muslims'. Did Affifi himself later develop more than a scholarly interest in mysticism? At least one of his former pupils at Alexandria sees no basis for such a possibility. The author thanks Professor Abdelhamid I. Sabra for this information.

12 In line with this, he assumes Hellenistic philosophers such as Plato, Plotinus (and the Neoplatonists) and Philo, and the more recent Spinoza, as points of departure and reference in explaining Ibn 'Arabi's system, and draws explanatory parallels with these. Of course he also draws parallels with the Muslim mystical tradition, especially its 'heterodox' strands exemplified by al-Hallaj (a 'pantheistic sufi'), but also with 'Muslim ascetics', and with Muslim philosophical and theological trends. For his views concerning the sources of influences for Ibn 'Arabi's thought, see *The Mystical Philosophy*, pp. 183–94. He argues that 'On the philosophic side Ibnul 'Arabi is chiefly Neoplatonic ... it was Neoplatonism *as understood* by the Ikhwanus-Safa that he knew.' See ibid., p. 184.

13 Affifi, *The Mystical Philosophy*, pp. 31ff., accuses Ibn 'Arabi of treating the existential proposition as a predicational one and systematically misusing the verb 'to be'. For an associate's analysis and rebuttal of this critique, see Coates, *Ibn 'Arabi and Modern Thought*, pp. 31–2. Coates points out that for Ibn 'Arabi 'existence' (which for him is synonymous with 'being') is to do not with a property, but with human possibility, potentiality, and ultimately perfectibility. Construing Affifi's philosophical critique as his 'main attack' on Ibn 'Arabi, Coates attributes it to the possible impact on him of logical positivism (in general terms in its radical hostility to metaphysics, but especially in its argument with existentialism), in vogue during his years at Cambridge. (Interview with the author, November 2004.)

14 Affifi, *The Mystical Philosophy*, p. 194.

15 Cf. Chittick, *The Sufi Path of Knowledge*, p. xv: 'Ibn al-'Arabi places himself squarely in the mainstream of Islam by basing all his teachings upon the Koran and the Hadith. In this respect he parts company with the philosophers and proponents of Kalam, who were far more likely to derive their sciences from other sources. Ibn al-'Arabi confirms his own logocentrism by claiming repeatedly that the knowledge gained through opening

pertains to the meaning of the Koran. This is a point of fundamental importance, too often forgotten in studies of the Shaykh.'

16 We can illustrate the persistence of such views through the example of Landau's work, based partly on Affifi's text and published twenty years later: 'Conscious of the dangers threatening an unorthodox thinker setting his views against those of the theologians representing authority, Ibn 'Arabi deliberately complicated his style. He would try to make an outrageously heterodox piece of argumentation look irreproachable by expressing it in the language or imagery of orthodoxy.' See Rom Landau, *The Philosophy of Ibn 'Arabi* (London, 1959) p. 24.

This tendency to downplay the importance of the traditional Islamic framework of Ibn 'Arabi's thought has long permeated Western scholarship, and even scholars who have explicitly acknowledged it have often failed to bring it to bear in their interpretation of his writings. The relative lack of interest in this aspect may reflect its cultural remoteness for Western scholars (and, in the case of some Muslim scholars, the influence of Western scholarship on them). Together with an English translation of his own account of his milieu and the company he kept in Andalusia (Ibn 'Arabi, *Sufis of Andalusia: The Ruh al-Quds and al-Durrat al-Fakhirah*, trans. R. W. J. Austin [London, 1971]), the appearance of a French/English biography of unprecedented detail (Claude Addas, *Quest for the Red Sulphur: The Life of Ibn 'Arabi*, trans. Peter Kingsley [Cambridge, 1993]) has perhaps contributed to a broader appreciation of his immersion in the traditional Islamic universe. In contrast with an earlier focus on the *Fusus*, more recent interest in the *Futuhat* has also served to construct a broader view of his thought and life, and their rigorous Islamic dimension. See further Ch. 7.

17 Affifi, *The Mystical Philosophy*, p. xi.

18 Ibid., p. xviii.

19 Ibid., p. 192.

20 Ibid., p. 194.

21 *The Twenty-nine Pages: An Introduction to Ibn 'Arabi's Metaphysics of Unity* [Extracts from *The Mystical Philosophy of Muhyid Din Ibnul Arabi* by A. E. Affifi] (Beshara Publications, Chisholme House, Roxburgh, 1998). Throughout this study references to *The Twenty-nine Pages* are to this version. It is eighty pages in all, including a contents list and index.

Since Rauf first prepared it seven versions of the text have been produced for internal use, each one with minor editorial changes. We consulted two of the earlier versions, neither of which indicates the text's origins in *The Mystical Philosophy*. One of these, with the same sub-titling as the 1998 published version, is quite late: here index entries are restricted to Arabic names and terms. The other is a very early (possibly the first) version. The text here is divided into four untitled chapters with numbered sub-sections, the prose is fuller and more explanatory in style than in the published version, and there is no contents list or index. The streamlined 1998 published version has deleted several paragraphs and a diagram from this. Adapted from *The Mystical Philosophy*, p. 114, the latter is based on Ibn 'Arabi's illustration in *al-Futuhat al-Makkiyya* of his vision of the internal and external aspects of the Divine Essence. According to associates, the symbol of the *Hu* they wear is based on this. Rauf may have taken it directly from *al-Futuhat al-Makkiyya*, for it was probably in use before his encounter with *The Mystical Philosophy*.

Dutch and Hebrew translations of *The Twenty-nine Pages* have been produced. The Hebrew version ('prepared and printed by Beshara Israel', Jerusalem, 1992) was translated by a group of Israeli associates. The Dutch one appears as *'Wie Zichzelf kent ...'* (Beshara Publications, The Netherlands, 1978). A German translation, as yet unpublished, has also been prepared.

22 *The Twenty-nine Pages*, p. 5. See Chodkiewicz, Ibn 'Arabi dans l'oeuvre de Henry Corbin, p. 82, for another assessment of Affifi's analysis and contribution.

23 We can get an idea of Rauf's opinion of Affifi's contribution from Coates' assessment of this (acquired exclusively through the medium of Beshara, Coates' understanding of

Ibn 'Arabi's thought is thus ultimately based on Rauf's projection of this). Expressing his gratitude to Affifi for 'making it available', Coates describes his exposition of Ibn 'Arabi's thought in *The Mystical Philosophy* as 'scrupulous and remarkable for its time'. Forgiving his criticisms of Ibn 'Arabi as 'misconstructions and misunderstandings', he maintains that 'when [Affifi] forgets he is being critical there is a certain admiration and sympathy for Ibn 'Arabi'. As examples of such 'misconstructions and misunderstandings', Coates cites Affifi's projection of Ibn 'Arabi's 'pantheism', his 'systematic misuse of the verb "to be"', and his 'determinism'. He points also to Affifi's mistaken objection to Ibn 'Arabi 'universalising from what may be phenomenologically (and thus subjectively) true for him'. (Interview with the author, November 2004.)

24 Affifi's approach in this respect can be compared with that of a contemporary scholar of Ibn 'Arabi, Claude Addas. In explaining Ibn 'Arabi's thought sixty years after Affifi, she draws explanatory parallels not with Hellenistic philosophers but with the Christian mystic Meister Eckhart. See her *Ibn 'Arabi: The Voyage of No Return*, pp. 86, 93–4. On Eckhart's teaching, see Meister Eckhart, *The Essential Sermons, Commentaries, Treatises, and Defense*, trans. and intro. Edmund Colledge and Bernard McGinn (New York, 1981). Affifi makes a single reference to him. (Note that Eckhart's work was less generally accessible when Affifi was preparing his study.)

Addas, *Ibn 'Arabi: The Voyage of No Return*, p. 80, also argues explicitly that 'Ibn 'Arabi was not a philosopher; his knowledge of philosophy, be it Greek or Arab, does not appear to surpass that which any cultured individual of his time might have gleaned, for example, from the writings of al-Ghazali'. In this view, Ibn 'Arabi's conceptual language borrowed from philosophy simply reflects the practice of a certain cultural *lingua franca*. Compare this assessment with Affifi, *The Mystical Philosophy*, p. 185: 'It is true that Ibnul 'Arabi seems to have been acquainted with more Greek philosophy than what is contained in [*The 'Epistles' of the Ikhwanus-Safa*], e.g., the philosophy of Philo Judaeus and the Stoics ... He seems also to have learnt a great deal from the Muslim Neoplatonists and al-Farabi'.

Addas' approach reflects a more recent general discrediting of the idea that Ibn 'Arabi was a philosopher, and that his philosophical theories can be traced back to certain strands in the Greek tradition. See for example Chittick, Ibn 'Arabi, pp. 497–8: 'If we take the word *falsafah* to refer to the specific school of thought in Islam that goes by the name, then Ibn 'Arabi cannot properly be called a *faylasuf*. But if we consider philosophy as a much broader wisdom tradition, rooted both in Islamic sources and in various pre-Islamic heritages, then Ibn 'Arabi certainly deserves the name *faylasuf* or, as he would probably prefer, *hakim*.' He notes that Ibn 'Arabi himself distinguishes between these two senses of the term by speaking of those who truly deserve the name *hakim* (among whom are the messengers, prophets and saints) and those who have adopted the title ('the *falasifah* proper'). See further al-Ghorab, Muhyiddin Ibn al-'Arabi amidst Religions (*adyan*) and Schools of Thought (*madhahib*), pp. 206–13.

For their part, some Beshara associates emphasise that the crucial distinction here relates to the sources of wisdom and their respective methods. According to Stephen Hirtenstein, 'Ibn al-'Arabi', *The Biographical Encyclopaedia of Islamic Philosophy* (London, 2006), 1, p. 223, for example: 'It has been tempting for scholars to characterise [Ibn 'Arabi] as a mystical philosopher, a term which is definitely at odds with his own teachings on the limitations of rational thought'. This is a reference to Ibn 'Arabi's distinction between the acquisition of knowledge through the intellect or rational faculty (the way of the *falasifa*, *hukama*' and *ahl al-nazar/al-fikr*), which is necessarily limited, and that given by divine inspiration (*kashf, ilham, mubashshira*, etc.). The latter is the way of *tahqiq*, 'verification' or 'realisation'. Chittick, Ibn 'Arabi, pp. 500ff., explains the differing epistemological potential of reason (and reflection) on the one hand, and imagination (in which *kashf* or 'unveiling' is primarily rooted) on the other. He sums up Ibn 'Arabi's position thus (p. 503): 'The rational endeavours of the philosophers and theologians, though useful and sometimes necessary, need to be subordinated to the direct knowledge that is made accessible through the prophetic messages and is actualized through unveiling.

The Verifiers, who see with both eyes [the eye of reason and the eye of imagination], realize perfect knowledge through the heart ... which "fluctuates" ... between reason and unveiling'.

25 We note a passing rejection of the characterisation of Ibn 'Arabi's position as pantheistic in 'What is the Difference? A Reaffirmation', *Beshara Magazine*, 2, p. 30: 'There is no question of pantheism here ... Ibn 'Arabi stresses that "things" are illusory. What is *in* all things is the Essence of the Truth. Such announcement lies at the core of Beshara'.

26 Such as 'monism' or 'non-dualism', as introduced by Landau in his discussion of Ibn 'Arabi's thought. Landau at the same time points to the complexities involved in precisely capturing his doctrine through such terms. *The Philosophy of Ibn 'Arabi*, p. 23, thus argues: 'Ibn 'Arabi's philosophy is usually described as pantheistic. Pantheism, however, as commonly understood, is little more than an ennobled form of materialism. Only in recent years have scholars begun to call Ibn 'Arabi a monist. Yet the term monism, as applied to him, seems not sufficiently qualitative to provide an adequate label for [his] theosophy. The term that might possibly suit his doctrine best is non-dualism, a term that implies not merely its monistic character but also its complete overcoming of all dualistic concepts ... If it can be said that one single consideration preoccupied Ibn 'Arabi more than any other it was the necessity for proving the non-duality of everything concerning God and His universe.' Cf. p. 27: 'If Ibn 'Arabi is usually described as a pantheist, there is ample justification in his own arguments. For while the Qur'an declares: "There is but one God", Ibn 'Arabi maintains that "there is nothing but God". His abandonment of the Islamic conception of God as the creator and cause of the universe, in favour of a God who *is* everything, definitely suggests a step from monotheism to pantheism ... Though again and again he tries to reconcile his "pantheistic" God with the unitarian God of the Qur'an, his God "Who is everything" must needs differ greatly from the Quranic God "like unto whom there is nothing". His God is not one who creates or from whom anything but Himself emanates, but a God who *manifests* Himself in an infinity of forms.'

On the unsuitability of terms such as pantheism, monism and non-dualism for describing Ibn 'Arabi's thought, see Schimmel, *Mystical Dimensions of Islam*, p. 267. In like vein, Chittick, Rumi and *wahdat al-wujud*, p. 73, remarks that 'any attempt to explain the meaning of *wahdat al-wujud* as understood by Ibn al-'Arabi will be deficient and misleading, all the more so if one tries to classify his teachings as pantheism, panentheism, existential monism, pantheistic monism, or the like.' On the use of such labels by orientalists, see also ibid., pp. 87–8, 90.

27 The text of *The Twenty-nine Pages* is divided into sections with the following sub-titles: 'Being', 'The One & the Many', 'Immanence & Transcendence', 'Causality', 'The Divine Names', 'The A'yan al-thabita', 'The Self-Revelations of the One', 'The Reality of Realities', 'The Perfect Man', 'Sainthood', 'Knowledge', 'The Heart', 'The Soul', 'Khayal', 'Fana' & Baqa', 'Beliefs', 'Good & Evil', and 'Love & Beauty'.

28 See for example *The Twenty-nine Pages*, p. 10, where the following explanatory comment has been added after the first mention of the term 'awalim (sing. 'alam): 'The word 'alam (universe) is often used in esoteric language to denote a global, unlimited, in-depth system.' Cf. *The Mystical Philosophy*, p. 7. Similarly, see *The Twenty-nine Pages*, p. 30, where a comment has been added following a quotation from Ibn 'Arabi in which he insists that the individual's seclusion (khalwa) be based upon absolute unification and a denial of all causes and intermediaries, in order to avoid falling into polytheism. It reads: 'He denies becoming one with God. There is no "becoming" whatever, but there is the realisation of the already existing fact that you are one with God.' Cf. *The Mystical Philosophy*, p. 56.

29 *The Twenty-nine Pages*, p. 9. Appearing in various other Beshara materials, the analogy of the pyramid originated with Rauf. (See Rauf, *Addresses II*, p. 29, for example.) This opening statement is not present in the early versions of the text consulted.

30 For example, *The Twenty-nine Pages*, p. 63: 'The supreme happiness of the mystic is in realising, by means of mystic intuition, his essential unity with God.' Further: 'To worship the Real God is to contemplate Him in everything, including yourself' (p. 66); 'There is only one Reality – and a non-existent subjective multiplicity and non-existent subjective relations which limit and determine the One' (p. 27). Finally: 'The basis and cause of all love is Beauty' (p. 72).

31 *The Twenty-nine Pages*, p. 5. The sentence continues: 'particularly those aspects of his doctrine which refer to the Unity of Being and the Perfectibility of Man.'

32 Ibid., p. 5.

33 Spinoza (ibid., p. 45); the context is a discussion of different kinds of knowledge. Plotinus (pp. 29, 34, 48, 51). Philo (p. 40): Affifi's comparison of his terminology (from his description of the philosophy of the Logos) and that of Ibn 'Arabi is retained, with minor simplifications and the insertion of English renderings of some Arabic and Greek terms. Cf. *The Mystical Philosophy*, pp. 91–2.

34 Given here as they appear in the index, these are Bayazid, Hallaj, Suhrawardi al-Muqtul, Ibn Farid, 'Abd al-Qadir al-Gilani, Abu Madyan, Abu Sa'id al-Kharraz, Abu Talib al-Makki, Abu-l Su'ud Ibn Shibl, Jami, Jili, Junayd and Ghazali.

35 *The Twenty-nine Pages*, p. 6.

36 Writing in the mid-1970s, Annett, ed., *The Many Ways of Being*, p. 85, conveys an impression of their attitudes in this regard: 'Initially it is very difficult to come to grips with this sort of philosophy, which is intensely intellectually demanding and requires great clarity of mind. But members of Beshara claim that the writings do justify the effort, and that once the unfamiliar concepts are understood, the noble nature of the writings may be perceived.'

Reflecting on why NRMs tend to attract the better-educated, Dawson, Who Joins New Religious Movements and Why, p. 122, cites a common argument that 'To be properly understood, the teachings [of most NRMs] demand literate intelligence, a willingness to study, and lack of fear in the face of unfamiliar concepts and language.'

37 See Affifi, *The Mystical Philosophy*, p. xi, and Ibn al-'Arabi, *The Bezels of Wisdom*, trans. and intro. R. W. J. Austin (London, 1980), p. 18. According to the latter, it is 'clearly a most important ... synopsis of Ibn al-'Arabi's principal themes and ... must be counted as perhaps his greatest work, apart from the much larger and more diffuse *Meccan Revelations*. Distributed throughout the work are the main topics of his teaching, the nature of God and man and their relationship, the divine Mercy, the Creative Imagination, and so forth.'

38 Nettler, *Sufi Metaphysics and Qur'anic Prophets*, pp. 5–6. Ibn 'Arabi claimed divine inspiration for all his works, but that he had received only the *Fusus* in this manner. The fact that he appears to have forbidden his disciples from having the work bound with any other perhaps also points to its special status. See Chittick, The School of Ibn 'Arabi, p. 515.

39 Chittick, 'The Central Point', p. 7.

40 Austin, *The Bezels of Wisdom*, p. 16.

41 Ibid. This characterisation has been elaborated in Nettler, *Sufi Metaphysics and Qur'anic Prophets*. Highlighting the work's 'Qur'an-centredness', the author demonstrates Ibn 'Arabi's adoption of Qur'anic 'framework stories' as the 'core' around which 'he builds and explicates his sufi metaphysics' (p. 14).

42 Austin, *The Bezels of Wisdom*, p. 19.

43 For example, James W. Morris, Introduction, in Ibn al-'Arabi, *The Meccan Revelations*, ed. Michel Chodkiewicz, trans. William C. Chittick and James W. Morris (New York, 2002), 1, p. 10, refers to 'the notional "doctrines", slogans and ostensible teachings so often connected with the name of Ibn 'Arabi' in later Islamic polemical contexts. He argues that these stereotypes 'usually reflect the profound influence of ... the ... *Fusus al-Hikam*'. In efforts to 'summarise' his thought, Ibn 'Arabi is thus 'somehow identified uniquely with a few paradoxical formulae supposedly drawn from the *Fusus*'.

The *Fusus* has indeed occupied centre stage in historical polemics against Ibn 'Arabi and his school, beginning with Ibn Taymiyya, whose favourable attitude towards Ibn 'Arabi 'underwent a dramatic change after his acquaintance with the *Fusus*'. See Knysh, *Ibn 'Arabi in the Later Islamic Tradition*, p. 96 and *Islamic Mysticism*, pp. 167–8.

44 Yahia, *Histoire et classification*, 1, pp. 241–56, lists 120 commentaries on the *Fusus* up to the nineteenth century, in comparison with only 15 on *al-Futuhat al-Makkiyya* (the last of which is that of Jili, d.1417) (see pp. 232–3); cf. Chittick, The School of Ibn 'Arabi, p. 515. As major commentaries appeared, the practice of reading the text alongside at least one of these became established. See Clark, 'Early Best-sellers in the Akbarian Tradition', pp. 48–51. The author traces the production of the earliest commentaries from al-Tilimsani (d.1291) through al-Jandi (d.1299), al-Kashani (d.1329) and al-Qaysari (d.1350). Chittick, The School of Ibn 'Arabi, pp. 515–19, discusses the content and approach of these and certain later commentaries. See also his 'The Chapter Headings of the *Fusus*', *JMIAS*, II (1984), pp. 41ff.

45 Chittick, 'The Central Point', p. 27.

46 Muhyi-d-din Ibn 'Arabi, *La Sagesse des prophètes*, trans. Titus Burckhardt (n.p., 1974/1955). Burckhardt (d.1984) was renowned for his work on the sacred art of different civilisations. Borella, René Guénon and the Traditionalist School, p. 352, notes that he was considered 'one of the foremost European metaphysicians and ... greatest authorities of Sunni Sufism'. Burckhardt continued the work of Traditionalists/Perennialists Guénon and Schuon. He was initiated into the Darqawiyya–Shadhiliyya in Morocco during the late 1930s. See Rawlinson, 'A History of Western Sufism', p. 17, and Sedgwick, *Against the Modern World*, p. 88. Seyyed Hossein Nasr recently suggested that the extensive interest in Ibn 'Arabi manifested in the West during the past fifty years owes much to Burckhardt's works, including his *La Sagesse des prophètes*. See Nasr, Foreword, in William Stoddardt, ed., *The Essential Titus Burckhardt: Reflections on Sacred Art, Faiths and Civilizations* (Bloomington, IN, 2003), p. xvi. For an introduction to Burckhardt's work, see William Stoddardt, Titus Burckhardt: An Outline of his Life and Works, in Titus Burckhardt, *Mirror of the Intellect: Essays on Traditional Science and Sacred Art*, trans. and ed. William Stoddardt (Cambridge, 1987), pp. 3–9.

Other works by Burckhardt on Ibn 'Arabi and his school would later be translated for use in Beshara. It seems that Rauf had arranged to meet him in London, perhaps during 1974, in relation to the translation and publication of *La Sagesse des prophètes*.

47 Culme-Seymour recalls a visit to a Konya library with Rauf, also in spring 1973: 'That afternoon we went to try and find some original writings of ... Ibn 'Arabi. Bulent told me he was possibly the greatest sheikh of all time; it was very important ... I have remembered that afternoon for many years, but at that time I did not, of course, know, nor have any idea of how the Sheikh's work would become such a part of our, and so many other people's, lives.' See Angela Culme-Seymour, 'Bulent and the Blue *Fusus*: The Story of a Translation', *JMIAS*, XXVI (1999), pp. 36–7; also her *Bolter's Grand-daughter*, p. 284.

48 For her own account of this work's materialisation, see Culme-Seymour, 'Bulent and the Blue *Fusus*', pp. 34–42 and 'Translating Ibn 'Arabi', pp. 4–5. There are discrepancies in dates between these two narratives.

49 Muhyi-d-Din Ibn 'Arabi, *The Wisdom of the Prophets (Fusus al-Hikam)*, trans. from Arabic to French with notes by Titus Burckhardt; trans. from French to English by Angela Culme-Seymour (Beshara Publications, Swyre Farm, Aldsworth, Gloucestershire, 1975), p. xi.

50 Due to its striking blue cover: see Culme-Seymour, 'Bulent and the Blue *Fusus*', Editor's note: p. 34.

51 Two further English translations of the complete text followed in 1980: *The Seals of Wisdom*, trans. 'Aisha 'Abd al-Rahman at-Tarjumana (Norwich) and Austin's *The Bezels of Wisdom*. An anonymous abridged translation under the title *The Seals of Wisdom: From the Fusus al-Hikam* was published by Concord Grove Press (Santa Barbara) in 1983, apparently based on the existing English versions. For a more recent translation, see

The Ringstones of Wisdom: Ibn 'Arabi's Fusus al-Hikam, trans. and intro. Caner K. Dagli (Chicago, 2005).

52 *La Sagesse des prophètes*, pp. 9–18; rendered into English by Culme-Seymour in *The Wisdom of the Prophets*, pp. 1–7.

53 *La Sagesse des prophètes*, p. 15; *The Wisdom of the Prophets*, p. 5.

54 Specifically those by Kashani, al-Nabulusi and Jami; *La Sagesse des prophètes*, p. 6.

55 Ibid., p. 18, as translated in *The Wisdom of the Prophets*, p. 7.

56 Austin, *The Bezels of Wisdom*, p. xvii. On the difficulties and dilemmas facing the translator of Ibn 'Arabi's writings in general and the threat of distortion, see, for example, William C. Chittick, *The Self-Disclosure of God: Principles of Ibn al-'Arabi's Cosmology* (Albany, NY, 1998), pp. xxxvff., and James W. Morris, 'Ibn 'Arabi's Rhetoric of Realisation: Keys to Reading and "Translating" the *Meccan Illuminations*, 2: Rhetoric, Language and the Challenges of Translation', *JMIAS*, XXXIV (2003), pp. 103–44.

57 Cf. Schimmel, *Mystical Dimensions of Islam*, pp. 265–6: 'A translation of the *Fusus* into a Western language is extremely difficult; the style is so concise that ... it needs a detailed commentary for the non-Muslim reader.'

58 *The Wisdom of the Prophets* is thus separated from the original text by more than one layer of translation/interpretation. It shares this in common with certain other Beshara study texts, including *Universal Man* (also from Arabic to French to English) and *Kernel of the Kernel* (from Arabic to Ottoman Turkish to English). On these, see below.

59 Ya'qub Ibn Yusuf, 'Ibn 'Arabi for Our Generation', *Gnosis Magazine*, 7 (Spring 1988), p. 31. He judges *The Seals of Wisdom* 'awkwardly literal', and *The Bezels of Wisdom* 'the best translation available'.

60 'Abd al-Qadir al-Sufi al-Darqawi, Introduction, *The Seals of Wisdom*, p. 4 ('Abd al-Qadir was at the time head of the Norwich-based branch of the Darqawiyya–Shadhiliyya, with which at-Tarjumana and Diwan Press were connected). While it is not mentioned by name, it is clear that this attack was directed at *The Wisdom of the Prophets*, as it was the only English version then available.

61 Culme-Seymour, 'Translating Ibn 'Arabi', p. 6, identifies this as 'No. 11' in the Sahaflar Çarşisi, above the covered bazaar.

62 'Chapters from the *Fusus al-Hikam*', 88 pp. The Introduction occupies pp. i–xxxiii.

63 Part II (72 pp.) encompasses chapters on Jethro (Shu'ayb), Ezra and Jonah (Yunus), Part III (34 pp.) chapters on Lot and Job, and Part IV (70 pp.) chapters on Salih, Loqman, Aaron and Khalid.

64 The same associate whose role had been catalytic in the emergence of *The Twenty-nine Pages*. According to Culme-Seymour, 'Translating Ibn 'Arabi', p. 6, this associate said 'he would like to see libraries all over the world filled entirely with 'Arabi [sic].' A proportion of the profits from the publication was promised to the MIAS: see 'Additional Procedural Committee Meeting of the MIAS', Sherborne, 3 August 1985, p. 2.

65 The *White Fusus*, 1, Foreword, pp. v–vi. We refer to this text as the *White Fusus* following Beshara practice, where it is thus described to distinguish it from the *Blue Fusus*.

Mustafa Tahrali, 'A General Outline of the Influence of Ibn 'Arabi on the Ottoman Era', *JMIAS*, XXVI (1999), p. 51, notes that, alongside the one-volume Bulaq edition (Cairo, 1832), used by Rauf, the text was also published in two volumes in 1873 in Istanbul.

66 Note from MIAS AGM, *JMIAS*, VI (1987), p. 2; also 'Translating Ibn 'Arabi', p. 6.

67 Examples of explanatory footnotes in the early translations arise in chapters on John and Elijah, and provide background information for readers unfamiliar with the Qur'an and Arabic. In the chapter on John (Yahya), for example, Rauf added a note that Yahya is 'St. John the Baptist, who is considered a Prophet and Envoy according to the Koran. The word John is Yahya in Arabic, which derives from the root hayy meaning "life"'. Another provides the Qur'anic narrative concerning the birth of Jesus. See 'Chapters from the *Fusus al-Hikam*', I, pp. 43, 47. In the chapter on Elijah, a note explains

'The word Idries comes from the Arabic root D-R-S, the same root gives DERS, which means a lesson or learning. Idris, Idrs, is a superlative form derived from the same root.' See ibid., p. 63.

68 See the *White Fusus*, 1, Foreword, pp. v–vi.

69 For a description of his working arrangements, see Culme-Seymour, *Bolter's Grand-daughter*, p. 332, and 'Translating Ibn 'Arabi', p. 6.

70 On him, see Ch. 6.

71 The MIAS published volumes 2, 3 and 4 in 1987, 1989 and 1991, respectively. A substantial number of copies of the first volume were sent as gifts to libraries around the world: *MIAS Newsletter*, September 1987, p. 4, gives a figure of over 160.

72 Victoria Rowe Holbrook, 'Ibn 'Arabi and Ottoman Dervish Traditions: The Melami Supra-Order', II, *JMIAS*, XII (1992), p. 31 n. 14. She accounts for the general scarcity of scholarship on the Ottoman Turkish tradition of commentary on Ibn 'Arabi's works in terms of a politically motivated avoidance of a specific sector of history, an 'international prejudice' against the Ottoman past. The modernist educational institutions of the Turkish state suppressed the Ottoman reception of Ibn 'Arabi's works, with the result that the latter was rendered 'difficult' for its scholars to understand. She lists these among other means by which a general ignorance of Ottoman humanities has been produced. See ibid., pp. 17–19.

Reflecting recent changes in this respect, during the last decade Turkish scholars have begun to address this commentary tradition. There has been a major conference on Da'ud al-Qaysari, for example, and all of Qunawi's works, including his *Fusus* commentary, have been published in modern Turkish.

73 On Bosnevi, see Christopher Shelley, 'Abdullah Effendi: Commentator on the *Fusus al-Hikam*', *JMIAS*, XVII (1995), pp. 79–83 (the author is a long-standing Beshara associate self-taught in Ottoman Turkish), and Tahrali, 'A General Outline', p. 51. The full title of the commentary is *Şerhu Fususi'l-hikem el-müsemma bi tecelliyati 'ara'isi'n-nusus fi minassati hikemi'l-fusus*. Shelley suggests that Bosnevi wrote perhaps sixty books and pamphlets.

74 Volumes 3 and 4 each bear an explanatory note indicating that when Rauf died the text of the *Fusus* had not yet been distinguished from the commentary in some chapters. In accordance with his wish at the time of his death, they were published just as he had left them.

75 Holbrook, 'Ibn 'Arabi and Ottoman Dervish Traditions', II, p. 31 n. 14. Cf. Tahrali, 'A General Outline', p. 51.

76 These are *Kitab al-Fukuk fi asrar mustanadat hikam al-fusus* by Qunawi (see for example the *White Fusus*, 1, p. 60), the first full commentary by his student Mu'ayyid al-Din al-Jandi, and the commentary by Da'ud al-Qaysari (see for example ibid., pp. 171–2.) As in the latter case, Bosnevi sometimes provides his own assessment of these earlier commentators' opinions, and may agree with one and disagree with another.

77 See for example the *White Fusus*, 1, pp. 50–1, 74–5.

78 Ibid., p. 6: 'Several times some of the ... brothers and gnostic people repeatedly asked from this poor man to annotate this book in the Turkish language and demanded the explanation of its mysteries'. Eventually, he agreed. Hence, 'the words of the book were translated into Turkish and were commented upon for the benefit of the people and for the manifestation of the Knowledge of God'.

79 Ibid., pp. 7–20. He also refutes here the suggestion that Ibn 'Arabi belonged to the Maliki *madhhab*.

80 Ibid., pp. 6–47. Rauf translates Bosnevi's *asl* (pl. *usul*) as origin(s). Bosnevi writes (p. 6): 'to make the realities of this book understood and to indicate the complexities and meanings and to teach them, the commentary was arranged according to twelve origins (*asl*)'. The discussion here elaborates on Ibn 'Arabi's cosmogony (the descent from the Absolute Unknowable [*al-ghayb al-mutlaq*] to the degree of the coming close of the two arcs [*qaba qawsayn*]); the Divine Names and Qualities; the 'established potentialities' (*a'yan thabita*); the Divine Presences (*hadarat*); Being and the Perfect Man; the letters and words (the Divine Letters and Words and those of being); prophethood, envoyship and sainthood; knowledge (apparent and interior); the supreme status of the station of love; the Way, and the Reality of Muhammad (*al-haqiqa al-Muhammadiyya*). For most of these concepts and terms, see Chittick, *The Sufi Path of Knowledge*, index, and Ibn 'Arabi and His School; Addas, *Ibn 'Arabi: The Voyage of No Return*.

81 For example, the commentary on the Preface (itself little more than a single page in the original) occupies forty-three pages. The first seven words in its first sentence give rise to fourteen pages of commentary, where the meaning of each word is explored. The chapter on Adam (nine pages in *The Bezels of Wisdom*) occupies over eighty pages in the *White Fusus.*

82 Shelley, 'Abdullah Effendi', p. 81; he adds that the commentary was so well received that Bosnevi later translated it into Arabic. Chittick, Ibn 'Arabi and His School, p. 52, suggests that the Arabic version has been published, but does not provide details. Yasushi Tonaga is presently working on this text.

83 Tollemache, 'An Obituary of Bulent Rauf'.

84 The *White Fusus*, 1, Foreword, p. v.

85 Ibid., inside cover. In the *White Fusus*, 1, Foreword, p. v, Rauf introduced Bursevi as a Celveti shaykh who had produced his commentary only after encompassing all existing commentaries. He had conversed with Ibn 'Arabi, and had been tested by the Prophet regarding his knowledge of the language and meaning of the *Fusus*. His status as a saint thus qualified 'to draw out the meanings intended by Ibn 'Arabi' is elaborated further in Rosemary Brass, Foreword, the *White Fusus*, 2 (Brass is an associate who had assisted in the translation). The point is also made here (p. vi) that while Ibn 'Arabi did not found a *tariqa* as such, 'the Jelveti manner reflected most closely his teaching'; this furnished further evidence of Bursevi's credentials as commentator. *MIAS Newsletter*, September 1985, p. 1, characterises the commentary as 'perhaps the summum and summation of all the commentaries which the *Fusus* ... inspired.' On the Celvetiyye, see Ch. 6.

86 Holbrook, 'Ibn 'Arabi and Ottoman Dervish Traditions', II, p. 31 n. 14.

87 Ibid. The author describes the Ottoman Melami as a 'supra-order', considering it inappropriate to project it as a *tariqa* because the Melami 'did not employ the material and disciplinary accoutrement which to a great extent define a *tarikat* as such'. Her term also captures the reality that the Melami were substantially an order of shaykhs who had generally 'completed' a course of inculcation in a 'regular' *tariqa* before their Melami initiation. See ibid., pp. 15–16, and I, pp. 25–6.

88 On the Bayramiyye, see Ch. 6. This order was nurtured within the same tradition as the Halvetiyye, from which the Celvetiyye also later emerged.

89 Shelley, 'Abdullah Effendi', p. 79. He notes that the teacher of Hasan Kabadoz was Ömer Dede Sikkini, to whom the founding of the Melami 'order' is attributed (p. 84 n. 3). Sikkini had been a pupil of Haci Bayram Veli: see below.

90 On the mystical tradition of Melamet, see 'Malamatiyya', EI^2, VI, pp. 223–8, and Schimmel, *Mystical Dimensions of Islam*, pp. 86–8. Its basic doctrine is that 'all outward appearance of piety or religiosity, including good deeds, is ostentation': it requires that the Melami 'struggle continuously against his desire for divine reward and ... approval by man'. The founding of the tradition has been attributed to Hamdun al-Qassar (d. 884–85): see 'Malamatiyya', p. 223, and Yaşar Nuri Öztürk, *The Eye of the Heart: An Introduction to Sufism and the Major Tariqats of Anatolia and the Balkans*, trans. Richard Blakney (Istanbul, 1995), pp. 114–16. Melamet can be thought of as 'a kind of ... disposition that can be found in each Sufi order': see Hülya Küçük, 'Sufi Reactions against the Reforms after Turkey's National Struggle: How a Nightingale turned into a Crow', p. 3. (Paper read at the workshop 'The Triumphs and Travails of Authoritarian Modernisation in Turkey and Iran', International Institute of Social History, Amsterdam: September 2003. We are indebted to the author for providing a copy.) Otherwise put (Holbrook, 'Ibn 'Arabi and Ottoman Dervish Traditions', II, p. 16), it is 'a taste in the spiritual life anyone, regardless

of affiliation, might share'. As a set of characteristics, it is best thought of in terms of a deprecation of the self: this may be a 'denial of being to the self in a philosophical sense', or a more practical 'concealment of spiritual virtue'. See ibid., pp. 16–17.

Within the Ottoman context specifically, the Melamis (more precisely Bayrami–Melamis) first branched out from the Bayramiyye (which had itself just emerged as a *tariqa*) in the fifteenth century, with a disciple of Haci Bayram, Ömer Sikkini. See Victoria Rowe Holbrook, 'Ibn 'Arabi and Ottoman Dervish Traditions: The Melami Supra-Order', I, *JMIAS*, IX (1991), pp. 18–35; II, pp. 13ff.; 'Malamatiyya', pp. 225ff.; Ahmet Yaşar Ocak, Religion, in Ekmeleddin Ihsanoğlu, ed., *History of the Ottoman State, Society and Civilisation*, (Istanbul, 2002), 2, pp. 223–6; Halil Inalcik, *The Ottoman Empire: The Classical Age, 1300–1600*, trans. Norman Itzkowitz and Colin Imber (London, 1973), pp. 191–2; Nathalie Clayer, Alexandre Popovic and Thierry Zarcone, eds, *Melamis–Bayramis: Études sur trois mouvements mystiques musulmans* (Istanbul, 1998). As Holbrook, 'Ibn 'Arabi and Ottoman Dervish Traditions', I, p. 18, observes, Ibn 'Arabi has been associated with the Turkish Melamis 'both by the Melami themselves and in the popular mind'. The Turkish Melami claim self-deprecation 'as the purest practice of Ibn 'Arabi's teachings'. Centuries of popular understanding attribute to them 'a radical observance of the *vahdet-i vücud* (unity of being) philosophy most often associated with Ibn 'Arabi' (ibid., II, p. 17).

For an example of Ibn 'Arabi's references to the Malamatiyya in the *Futuhat* cited by the Turkish Melami in defining their way, see Chodkiewicz, *Seal of the Saints*, pp. 109–11, and Hirtenstein, *The Unlimited Mercifier*, pp. 135–6. See further Michel Chodkiewicz, Les Malamiyya dans la doctrine d'Ibn 'Arabi, in Clayer *et al.*, eds, *Melamis–Bayramis*, pp. 15–25.

91 In the *White Fusus*, 1, p. 79, for example, the author refers to his having joined a campaign to settle an insurrection in 1594 CE, while Bursevi was born in 1653 CE.

92 On the manner of addressing the issue of attribution, see also *MIAS Newsletter*, 19 (Autumn 2003), p. 2. (Note also that Bosnevi is still described here as Bursevi's 'fellow Jelveti'.) Associates recall with distaste an MIAS symposium during which a visitor stated bluntly that the text could not be attributed to Bursevi. They appreciate scholars who have addressed the question of attribution more tactfully.

93 Peter Yiangou, 'Ismail Hakki Bursevi's translation of and commentary of [sic] the *Fusus al-Hikam* by Muhyiddin Ibn 'Arabi', *JMIAS*, VII (1988), p. 86.

94 Culme-Seymour, 'Translating Ibn 'Arabi', p. 7. Associates describe as 'part of the divine subtlety and economy' the fact that the Ottoman commentary was thus 'brought out' by an Ottoman Turk educated in the West, and hence able 'to speak to people there'. Without him, they believe it would not have been possible for it to be 'brought to life', although its contents may have been conveyed 'on an exclusively intellectual plane'.

An associate relates the opinion of an unnamed authority on Ottoman and Arabic literary traditions intimately familiar with the commentary. He reportedly described Rauf's translation as very faithful to the spirit of the original, making it 'an extraordinary work'.

95 Examples arise in 'What is the Difference? A Reaffirmation', p. 30; Roberts, 'Reaffirmation', p. 26; Ryan, Conversion to the Essence, pp. 339–40; John Mercer, Introduction, in Mercer, ed., *The Journey of the Heart* (Oxford, 1996), pp. 1–3.

96 'A Selection from The *Tarjuman al-Ashwaq* of Muhyiddin Ibn al-'Arabi, in a literal translation with an abridged version of the author's commentary by Reynold A. Nicholson, with further annotations by Bulent Rauf'. Rauf's annotations question Nicholson's choice of word or phrase, or provide further explanation. For example, in Commentary LX, he points the reader to *The Merchant of Venice* to illustrate the reference to rain as mercy. In Commentary XX, he suggests that 'it is not quite correct to be so categorical' on the question of whether the Divine Essence enters into Creation: Nicholson states that it does not.

97 Titus Burckhardt, *Mystical Astrology According to Ibn 'Arabi*, trans. from the French by Bulent Rauf (Beshara Publications, Swyre Farmhouse, Aldsworth, Gloucestershire, 1977).

98 *Kernel of the Kernel*: translation of Ibn 'Arabi, *Lubb al-lubb* with a Commentary by Ismail Hakki Bursevi, trans. into English by Bulent Rauf (Beshara Publications, Chisholme House, Roxburgh, 1981). For an elaboration of his approach as translator (avoiding scrupulously 'any interference in the personal understanding of the reader' by eschewing all explanations and checking that 'any influences derivable from the construction of a sentence or the usage of a word' have been expunged by collaborators), see Rauf, *Addresses II*, p. 23.

99 *Universal Man*: 'Abd al-Karim al-Jili, *al-Insan al-Kamil*, Extracts translated with Commentary by Titus Burckhardt as *L'Homme Universel*, trans. from the French to English by Angela Culme-Seymour (Beshara Publications, Sherborne, Gloucestershire, 1983).

100 For a full listing of Beshara publications, see Beshara Publications website.

101 *Sufis of Andalusia*: Ibn 'Arabi, *Ruh al-Quds* and *al-Durrat al-Fakhira*, trans. R. W. J. Austin (Beshara Publications, Sherborne, Gloucestershire, 1988, published with the support of the MIAS; 2002 reprinting). This was originally published in 1971 by George Allen and Unwin.

102 Ibn 'Arabi, *"Whoso Knoweth Himself ..."*, from the Treatise on Being (*Risale-t-ul-Wujudiyyah*), trans. T. H. Weir (Beshara Publications, Frilford Grange, Abingdon, Oxfordshire, 1976; reissued 1988) (reprinted from Weir's 1901 translation). The title is a reference to the hadith 'Whoso knoweth himself knoweth his Lord.'

Michel Chodkiewicz has since demonstrated that this text is the work of the slightly later Awhad al-Din al-Balyani. See Chodkiewicz, *Awhad al-Din Balyani: Epître sur l'unicité absolue [Kitab al-Wahda al-mutlaqa]* (Paris, 1982), discussed in James W. Morris, 'Ibn 'Arabi and his Interpreters', Part II: 'Influences and Interpretations', *Journal of the American Oriental Society*, 106: 4 (1986), pp. 736–41. See also Chittick, The School of Ibn 'Arabi, p. 519 and Rumi and *wahdat al-wujud*, pp. 83–4; Ch. 7. The text is also known as *Risalat al-Ahadiyya*.

103 'Courses at Chisholme', pp. 27–8.

104 Ibid., p. 28.

105 Ibid., p. 27.

106 Beshara website.

107 Beshara School Application Form: Six-month Intensive Course (1 October 2003 – 31 March 2004). This also requests information concerning applicants' understanding of love, and asks whether they have been in love. It seeks to understand what prompted their 'search for a spiritual perspective', and their view of 'the basis for hope for the future of the world'.

108 Beshara website.

109 Ibid.

110 Ibid.

111 This is related to the purpose of spiritual education in the following terms: 'We need to differentiate between that which is holding on to the Real and facing the Real, and the idea of "myself", which is fixity. The student's movement is that of disengaging, from the fixity of his idea of himself, towards the Real.' See 'Disengaging from Fixity' (Notes from the Mead Hall, 6 June 2004), Beshara website.

112 Beshara website.

113 Young explains that lentils and beef are avoided at the School at certain times 'due to their earthy and grounding effect', but are recommended when such qualities are beneficial, when there is 'a tendency to headiness' or after a retreat, for example. (Correspondence with the author, March 2006.)

114 'Warning and Reminder': a notice hung in a hallway used by students at the back entrance to the house.

115 Notice hung in the back entrance hallway. This refers to 'silent meals, silent days, silent fast days, and silent fasts', to be announced as and when required.

116 'Know this: that the child does not belong to the parents but is lent to them by God ... The child is God's and His alone, and represents the potentiality for perfect individuation of Him and the consequent possibility of becoming a perfect mirror in which the Absolute may contemplate Himself. Therefore, also understand that being given the chance to be of service to a child, if carried out in full awareness, is one of the most direct ways of proper service to one's Lord ... In service to a child you serve the movement and receipt into this world of the image of God, as yet not having reached the furthest point in its descent ... This then is your service in the nursery to care and look after, protect and guide a living human image of the Truth, and for you in this activity there is a possibility of knowledge and benefit, of service to the child and gratitude to your Lord. So remember: the child is not simply someone's offspring – it is an individuation of God and when you look after it ... you look after Him ... for He in His rich independence has assumed the guise of dependence as a model and a lesson to you. Your relationship to Him is like the child's to you.'

117 'Cleanliness is next to Godliness'.

118 Some of these positions, like gardener and estate manager, are long term. Others are for more or less specified periods, allocated to individuals in such a way as to make best use of available resources.

119 An associate recalls the case of a kitchen manager who became overwhelmed by the pressure of the responsibility. Her state reportedly lay behind a mysterious stomach complaint that struck the majority of students, and for which no 'physical' cause could be found.

120 Since January 2004, edited highlights of one of these 'conversations' (scheduled for half an hour after breakfast on weekdays) have been posted on the Beshara website each week. The site invites responses to these 'Notes', and offers to post parts of them. Recent titles illustrate subjects discussed: 'Disengaging from fixity'; 'First relax, then concentrate!'; 'I can't stand it anymore'; 'Find the root of it in yourself!' These offer a valuable insight into the tenor of these discussions, and associates' preoccupations. Note the site disclaimer concerning 'exclusivity of truth or comprehensiveness' in the viewpoints expressed.

121 The gardens incorporate a lake with waterfowl and walled and vegetable gardens. There are also poultry, on which Rauf had reportedly been an expert (he had served as a poultry judge while in Switzerland during World War II). Correspondence from Rauf in Turkey to associates advised them how to treat the poultry and waterfowl at Chisholme.

122 These include several by Culme-Seymour, an accomplished water-colour artist.

123 The Beshara brochure describes the Chisholme estate as 'a many-faceted jewel'. It adds that its setting 'in the vibrant beauty of the Scottish Borders' is perfect for 'an education which is attuned to the essential beauty of the One'.

124 A quality appropriate for such activities can be conferred on any space through cleaning and ablution, accompanied by the conscious intention of whoever undertakes this preparation. Thus, a room in an associate's home is rendered appropriate for study (or discussion of Beshara business) through such preparation, which is often completed by sprinkling rosewater.

125 Ablution is also performed in spaces where something has taken place that might distract from the purpose of the School and those within it. An example of such an incident (the traces of which must be removed) is an argument.

126 A visitor to Chisholme noted that 'The manner of cooking, serving and eating food is considered very important, and it is always of a very high standard.' Angela Holroyd, in *Beshara Magazine*, 8, p. 29.

127 Beshara website.

128 Ibid.

129 'Beshara: Swyre Farm'.

130 'My saintly wife, Maryam bint Muhammad b. 'Abdun, said, "I have seen in my sleep someone whom I have never seen in the flesh, but who appears to me in my moments of ecstasy. He asked me whether I was aspiring to the Way, to which I replied that I was, but that I did not know by what means to arrive at it. He then told me that I would come to it through five things, trust, certainty, patience, resolution and veracity." Thus she offered her vision to me (for my consideration) and I told her that that was indeed the method of the Folk.' See Ibn 'Arabi, *Sufis of Andalusia*, pp. 22–3. For references to these qualities, see 'Beshara: Swyre Farm', and Bulent Rauf, *Addresses* (Beshara Publications, Chisholme House, Roxburgh, 1986), pp. 17, 24, 42. (Note that we refer throughout to an early printing of *Addresses*, which may differ in page numbering from more recent ones.)

131 See 'Beshara: Swyre Farm'.

132 Aaron Cass, 'Notes on the Reality of Nourishment', *Beshara Newsletter*, Autumn 1996, p. 8. Cf. Young's comment ('Courses at Chisholme', p. 28) that even during the one or two 'days off' during the course 'there should be no slacking off of awareness'. Rauf, *Addresses II*, p. 52, explains that 'a man's spiritual growth' is judged by 'the constancy of the awareness … not the quantity.'

133 See 'Courses at Chisholme', p. 28.

134 There is typically a cycle of three or four such courses during the summer, in addition to introductory weekend courses in late spring and summer. In 2003, the fees for weekend introductory, nine-day introductory and six-month intensive/further courses were £60, £250 and £3,450, respectively (these cover board and lodging but exclude the trip to Turkey in the case of the intensive course). Potential students are reminded that it is part of the preparation and resolve to attend that they overcome difficulties in securing necessary funds. It is also made clear that the fees do not include payment for 'teaching', for 'there are no teachers'.

135 'Courses at Chisholme', p. 28.

136 Beshara website.

137 Ibid.

138 Preparation of a second essay is required towards the end of the course.

139 See the *White Fusus*, 1, inside cover.

140 *Extracts from the Mathnawi of Jalalu'ddin Rumi*, trans. and commentary by R. A. Nicholson (London, 1926).

141 On this, see Ch. 4.

142 *The Mawaqif and Mukhatabat of Muhammad Ibn 'Abdi'l-Jabbar al-Niffari*, ed. and trans. Arthur J. Arberry (Cambridge, 1987/1935). Al-Niffari was a tenth-century sufi to whom Ibn 'Arabi referred.

143 During the first intensive course in 1975–76, Martin Lings, the Kabbalist Warren Kenton and a Zoroastrian were invited to speak. In the late 1980s, 'scientists, biologists and physicists' were invited: see 'Courses at Chisholme', p. 28.

144 Beshara website.

145 See 'Courses at Chisholme', p. 28.

146 Beshara website.

147 Across the years there has also been provision of Greek.

148 Beshara website. As the Beshara brochure emphasises, a member of staff serves in such contexts 'as a navigator rather than as a leader'.

149 This represents an ideal: in reality, the text's complexity and students' lack of background knowledge can render explanation indispensable. During a study session we attended in early 2004, for example, the pages of *Mystical Astrology According to Ibn 'Arabi* which students were then reading required considerable explanation and indeed point-by-point paraphrasing by the supervisor. Given its complexity and length, this was felt to be necessary if students were to complete the book on time. Supervisors try to remain close to the text when providing explanation, however, and refer heavily to Beshara sources. During this *Mystical Astrology* session, for example, the supervisor explained that 'Universal Nature' was precisely that called 'Big Mama' in the film 'Turning', which the students had viewed. (See Ch. 4.)

150 Beshara website.

151 Ibid.

152 'Beshara: Swyre Farm'. Cf. notice of forthcoming course, *Beshara Magazine*, 4, p. 8: 'This course is for all those who want to know their reality, verifying for themselves the true position of Man in the universe and his relationship to God'.

153 Cf. Rauf's advice to Feild: 'When we have the courage to realise that life itself is the teacher, the timeless truth lying within the moment can come forth from the knowledge written in the great books ... The difficulty is that ... studying books, including the sacred scriptures, is useless without your own inner experience. The major problem for Westerners ... is that they are always trying to copy the experiences of others. This is ridiculous'. See Feild, *The Invisible Way*, pp. 26–7.

154 There is indeed little time for reading during the schedule. The School holds a very modest library collection. In addition to Rauf's small private collection (to which a few additions have been made), there is a limited collection in the Mead Hall, which remains more or less as it was during Rauf's lifetime (with the exception of a few more recent donations).

155 An early indication of Rauf's emphasis on the importance of ablution arises in his comments to Feild in *The Last Barrier*, pp. 59–60. He drew an analogy with the process behind producing a good jar of olives, explaining: 'The jar, which must be carefully cleaned in all ways, is either your body or the space occupied by you or the group. Water takes on the color of the vessel that contains it, and we want this water to be as clear as a mountain stream. That is why ritual washing is so important'.

156 The *ghusl* or 'major' ablution in Islamic practice requires the uninterrupted washing of the whole body, including the hair, after the declaration of intention. This must follow acts or states that produce major ritual impurity (*janaba*), such as menstruation and certain sexual acts. See 'Ghusl', EI², II, p. 1104.

157 'First Course Timetable', 2003–04.

158 In Islamic tradition *wudu'* (literally 'cleansing') denotes the 'minor' ablution, necessary when a person's state of ritual impurity comes from a 'minor impurity', which would render performance of the obligatory prayer invalid. Examples of such causes are sleep and contact with anything 'from the two natural orifices'. The acts making up the *wudu'* derive from Qur'an 5: 6 and the hadith; the law schools differ on details and on which of these should be considered obligatory and which recommended. The Shafi'i al-Ghazali lists six acts that make up the *wudu'*: the intention; washing of face; washing of hands; rubbing of head; washing of feet, and respecting the order of these acts as listed. Understood as an act of putting oneself in a state of purity, it is considered one of the five acts (*'ibadat*) that make up the foundations of Islam. See 'Wudu'', EI², XI, pp. 218–19.

159 Annett, ed., *The Many Ways of Being*, p. 85.

160 'Courses at Chisholme', p. 29. Cf. Rauf, *Addresses II*, p. 49: 'Real service is without the self being self-indulgent in serving people. It has to be completely without the mixation of the person into the service rendered'.

161 'Courses at Chisholme', p. 28.

162 This trip is also open to associates, who join it whenever they can.

163 *Beshara Newsletter*, Autumn 1996, p. 8.

164 See Ch. 6.

165 'A Trip to Turkey arranged by the Beshara School of Intensive Esoteric Education, Chisholme House'. Originally prepared by Rauf, the document has been added to and slightly amended over the years. We refer to versions dated December 1999 and December 2003.

166 Examples of sites visited are the House of Mary and the Basilica of St John at Ephesus. Marking the disciple's grave, the Basilica was one of the most important pilgrimage destinations in the Christian world throughout the Middle Ages. The House of Mary is a shrine visited by both Christians and Muslims. On these two sites, see Ekrem Akurgal, *Ancient Civilizations and Ruins of Turkey*, trans. John Whybrow, 8th edn

(Istanbul, 1993/1969), pp. 144–6. Other places visited are the Green Mosque and the Ulu Cami in Bursa and the Aya Sofya (Haghia Sophia) in Istanbul, for example.

167 *Beshara Newsletter*, Autumn 1996, p. 8.

168 See 'A Trip to Turkey', pp. 7ff. In introducing Rumi, for example, Rauf reiterated the varying degrees and qualities of sainthood, and the concept of the *qutb*. See ibid., p. 10. For the saints discussed in the document, see Ch. 6.

169 Ibid., p. 12.

170 During the late 1980s, Young suggested ('Courses at Chisholme', p. 28) that one in twenty to thirty students leave before completing the six-month intensive course, usually during the early weeks/months. Leavers include those who have completed a nine-day introductory course.

171 Ibid., p. 31.

172 Students on the further course describe the challenge they face in applying themselves as guests, in sensing what needs to be done in the house while not feeling guilty if they need time to themselves.

173 Six months before it is due to begin, he writes to invite all those who have not yet attended the course and might be expected to benefit from it (including those he knows will be unable to attend at that time for practical reasons).

174 Conversation in this context is projected as 'one of the primary methods' of the School. See 'First relax, then concentrate!' (Notes from the Mead Hall, 24 January 2004), Beshara website.

175 Ryan, Conversion to the Essence, p. 342.

176 Cf. 'First relax, then concentrate!'

177 Conversation is projected as ultimately 'between the Real and the Real', based on an acknowledgement that 'the One Reality is manifest and present in each person … and conversation is not with other than It'. This recognition must shape the demeanour of all those who participate in a conversation session. See ibid.

178 Accounting for such possibilities, Young might suggest to an individual to wait before joining the further course. In practice, however, the necessity for such action has reportedly been very rare.

179 In later years, this was substituted with the chapter on Shu'ayb (Jethro).

180 E. H. Winfield and M. M. Kazwini, trans., 'Abd ar-Rahman Jami, *Lawa'ih [The Book of Flashes]* (London, 1906).

Chapter 4

1 There is a single published autobiographical fragment, viz., The Child Across Time, *Addresses II*, pp. 79–96.

2 See, for example, Ira M. Lapidus, Sufism and Ottoman Islamic Society, in Raymond Lifchez, ed., *The Dervish Lodge: Architecture, Art and Sufism in Ottoman Turkey* (Berkeley, 1992), p. 28; Gilles Veinstein and Nathalie Clayer, L'Empire ottoman, in Alexander Popovic and G. Veinstein, eds, *Les Voies d'Allah: les ordres mystiques dans le monde musulman des origines à aujourd'hui* (Paris, 1996), p. 339; Inalcik, *The Ottoman Empire*, chapters 18–19; Barbara Rosenow von Schlegell, *Sufism in the Ottoman Arab World: Shaykh 'Abd al-Ghani al-Nabulusi (d.1143/1731)* (D. Phil thesis, University of California, Berkeley, 1997), p. 77.

It must be noted that we are still very far from a comprehensive history of sufism, sufi social institutions and sufi thought (and indeed of Islam and religion in general) in the Ottoman era, and certain long-standing assumptions in this field are ripe for reconsideration. See for example Ocak, Religion, pp. 177, 236; Cemal Kafadar, The New Visibility of Sufism in Turkish Studies and Cultural Life, in Lifchez, ed., *The Dervish Lodge*, pp. 308–9; Victoria Rowe Holbrook, *The Unreadable Shores of Love: Turkish Modernity and Mystic Romance* (Austin, TX, 1994), pp. 10–11.

There are divergent approaches to studying the history of Ottoman Islam and sufism. For example, Ocak posits four working categories of official, popular, *medrese* and *tekke* Islam as a framework. Inalcik suggests a twofold division of the orders between established and secret. Veinstein and Clayer suggest a further division between 'orthodox' orders (accepted by the Sunni 'orthodox' state) and those it condemned, pointing to the blurring of lines between these types in the case of certain of their branches.

There are significant sources in Turkish on aspects of Ottoman sufism, by Mehmed Fuad Köprülü, Abdülbaki Gölpinarli and Ocak, for example. We can mention some further overviews in English/French: Ahmet Yaşar Ocak, Opposition au soufisme dans l'empire ottoman, in de Jong and Radtke, eds, *Islamic Mysticism Contested*, pp. 603–13; John P. Brown, *The Darvishes or Oriental Spiritualism*, ed. H. A. Rose (London, 1968/1927); Ahmet T. Karamustafa, *God's Unruly Friends: Dervish Groups in the Later Middle Period, 1200–1550* (Salt Lake City, 1994), chapter 6; Hazrat-i Pir-i Üftade, *Le Divan*, trans. Paul Ballanfat (Paris, 2001), pp. 10–14 [hereafter cited as Ballanfat, *Le Divan*]; John Robert Barnes, The Dervish Orders in the Ottoman Empire, in Lifchez, ed., *The Dervish Lodge*, chapter 2 (Lifchez's volume as a whole provides an excellent overview of sufi life in late Ottoman Turkey, taking the *tekke* as its focus). See finally Holbrook, *The Unreadable Shores of Love*.

American diplomat/translator Brown offers insights concerning the experience and practice of the orders in late Ottoman Turkey based on personal acquaintance with their members. His approach and aspects of his treatment and interpretation are outdated (it was written in 1868), but the work remains useful for his detailed observations. Karamustafa's discussion focuses specifically on those dervish groups that formed part of a movement of socially deviant renunciation. Ballanfat provides a brief but informative overview of relations between certain Ottoman sultans and sufism, and sketches the latter's changing fortunes.

For the state of scholarship on Ottoman Arab sufism specifically, see von Schlegell, *Sufism in the Ottoman Arab World*, p. 15 n. 45. On this area see also Eric Geoffroy, *Le Soufisme en Egypte at Syrie sous les derniers Mamelouks et les premiers Ottomans: Orientations spirituelles et enjeux culturels* (Damascus, 1995).

3 See for example Inalcik, *The Ottoman Empire*, pp. 183, 199; Holbrook, 'Ibn 'Arabi and Ottoman Dervish Traditions', I, p. 23; II, p. 17; Tahrali, 'A General Outline', pp. 42–54; Mahmud Erol Kiliç, '"The Ibn al-'Arabi of the Ottomans", 'Abdullah Salahaddin al-'Ushshaqi (1705–82): Life, Works and Thoughts of an Ottoman Akbari', *JMIAS*, XXVI (1999), pp. 111–12.

4 On Ibn 'Arabi as 'patron saint' of the Ottomans, see Ryad Atlagh, 'Paradoxes of a Mausoleum', *JMIAS*, XXII (1997), pp. 15ff.

5 Holbrook, 'Ibn 'Arabi and Ottoman Dervish Traditions', II, p. 17, explains the possible origins of the 'current academic amnesia' concerning this fact. She suggests that, in reality, 'Ottoman thought became organized in ways Ibn 'Arabi initiated, just as Christian thought remained for centuries organized in ways Saint Thomas Aquinas articulated.' See Şeyh Galip, *Beauty and Love*, trans. Victoria Rowe Holbrook (New York, 2005), p. x. See also Ballanfat, *Le Divan*, p. 40; von Schlegell, *Sufism in the Ottoman Arab World*, p. 244; A. Yaşar Ocak, 'Les réactions socio-religieuses contre l'idéologie officielle ottomane et la question de *Zendeqa ve Ilhad* (hérésie et athéisme) au XVIe siècle', *TURCICA*, 23 (1991), p. 78.

6 For examples of the impact of the last sultans' modernising policies on sufism and the *tariqa*s (and of Abdülhamid II's Pan-Islamic policies), see Sirriyeh, *Sufis and Anti-Sufis*, chapter 3; Raymond Lifchez, Introduction, in Lifchez, ed., *The Dervish Lodge*, pp. 6–9.

7 The decree stated: 'from this day forth, there are no *tarikat*s, or *dervishes* and *murid*s belonging to them, within the boundaries of the Turkish Republic.' Cited by Hamid Algar, 'The Naqshbandi Order in Republican Turkey', *Islamic World Report*, 1: 3 (1996), p. 55; cf. p. 65 n. 23.

8 Ataturk opened his famous speech thus: 'Gentlemen and fellow countrymen, know that the Turkish Republic cannot be a nation of sheikhs, dervishes, and mystics. The

truest path is the path of civilization; it is necessary for one to be a man who does what civilization dictates. I could never admit to the civilized Turkish community a primitive people who seek happiness and prosperity by putting their faith in such and such a sheikh, a man opposed to the sparkling light of civilization, which encompasses all science and knowledge. In any case, the lodges must be closed.' Cited by Barnes, The Dervish Orders, p. 46.

9 The following few paragraphs draw on Küçük, 'Sufi Reactions against the Reforms'. Based on her sample, she argues that instances of opposition and support encompass sufis from all kinds of *tariqa*s, with no single *tariqa* emerging as a particular centre of opposition or support.

10 Annemarie Schimmel, Sufism and Spiritual Life in Turkey, in Nasr, ed., *Islamic Spirituality: Manifestations*, p. 224 and *Mystical Dimensions of Islam*, p. 343.

11 Küçük identifies two significant elements of sufi belief and attitude which possibly contributed to the majority position of silent assent to the reforms. First is the 'sufi rule' or 'station' according to which 'everything, good or bad, is from God. His grace, as well as His punishment is nice.' Hence, 'to be a good Sufi, man has to say to everything "By Allah, it is good"'. See 'Sufi Reactions against the Reforms', pp. 3, 23 n. 20. Second is the notion encapsulated in the sufi saying that 'the sufi is the son of his time, and he does what must be done'. See ibid., pp. 19, 30 n. 178.

12 Ibid., p. 12.

13 Ibid., pp. 12–13.

14 Ibid., p. 18.

15 Ibid. Such attitudes remained strong. For example, the Melamis encountered by Holbrook in Istanbul during the 1980s were 'staunch supporters' of the Kemalist reforms, and projected them as timely and necessary for Turkey's welfare. See Holbrook, 'Ibn 'Arabi and Ottoman Dervish Tradition', II, p. 16.

16 Algar, 'The Naqshbandi Order in Republican Turkey', p. 61; cf. Lings, *What is Sufism?*, p. 118 n. 43.

17 As Holbrook, 'Ibn 'Arabi and Ottoman Dervish Traditions', I, p. 18, notes, 'far from promoting sufism as a national treasure … republican discourse has discouraged scholarly interest in it'.

Studies of specific orders in the twentieth century can be found in Sencer Ayata, Traditional Sufi Orders in the Periphery: Kadiri and Nakşibendi Islam in Konya and Trabzon, in Richard Tapper, ed., *Islam in Modern Turkey: Religion, Politics and Literature in a Secular State* (London, 1991), pp. 223–54; Thierry Zarcone, 'Les Naqşibendi et la république turque: de la persécution au répositionnement théologique, politique et social (1925–1991)', *TURCICA*, 24 (1992), pp. 133–51; Hakan Yavuz, The Matrix of Modern Turkish Islamic Movements: The Naqshbandi Sufi Order, in Elisabeth Özdalga, ed., *Naqshbandis in Western and Central Asia: Change and Continuity* (Istanbul, 1999), pp. 129–46. See also Thierry Zarcone, La Turquie républicaine (1923–1993), in Popovic and Veinstein, eds, *Les Voies d'Allah*, pp. 372–97, and Kafadar, The New Visibility of Sufism, pp. 310–22. There are a growing number of studies in Turkish (the works of Mustafa Kara deserve particular mention), but the oral tradition remains a rich source largely still to be excavated. Based on attendance of Melami activities in Istanbul during the 1980s, Holbrook, 'Ibn 'Arabi and Ottoman Dervish Traditions', II, pp. 15–33, is unusual for its use of field material.

For comments concerning the relative numerical strengths of various *tariqa*s during the last decades of Ottoman rule and the Republican period, see Algar, 'The Naqshbandi Order in Republican Turkey', pp. 62, 54; Zarcone, La Turquie républicaine, pp. 373ff.; Kafadar, The New Visibility of Sufism, pp. 310–12; Knysh, *Islamic Mysticism*, pp. 227–8; Öztürk, *The Eye of the Heart*, pp. 92, 134 n. 1; Lifchez, Introduction, p. 5. On transformations in *tariqa*s, see David Shankland, *Islam and Society in Turkey* (Huntingdon, Cambridgeshire, 1999), pp. 64–8, and Holbrook, 'Ibn 'Arabi and Ottoman Dervish Traditions', II, p. 28 n. 5. M. Hakan Yavuz, *Islamic Political Identity in Turkey* (Oxford,

2003), p. 56, suggests that they undertook an 'internal migration' from the public domain to the household/family sphere.

On the place of Islam more generally in Republican Turkey during the last few decades, see Richard Tapper, 'Introduction', in Tapper, ed., *Islam in Modern Turkey*, pp. 2–9; Mehmet Hakan Yavuz, 'The Return of Islam? New Dynamics in State-Society Relations and the Role of Islam in Turkish Politics', *Islamic World Report*, 1: 3 (1996), pp. 77–86 and *Islamic Political Identity in Turkey*.

18 Ayata, Traditional Sufi Orders in the Periphery, p. 224.

19 While it became illegal to represent oneself as a shaykh in the sense of a functionary within a *tariqa* after their prohibition, the law has never been entirely enforceable. See Holbrook, 'Ibn 'Arabi and Ottoman Dervish Traditions', I, p. 16. Kafadar, The New Visibility of Sufism, pp. 310–12, observes that even during the period of martial law in the 1980s the *tariqa*s more or less openly received visiting journalists, tourists and scholars.

20 Kafadar, The New Visibility of Sufism, p. 313.

21 Committed to modernising Egypt along European lines and in association with Europe, Ismail fell into huge debt to foreign bankers. To safeguard their interests, the European powers imposed financial control, which seemed likely to develop into political control, as European ministers took office in the 1878 government. When Ismail dismissed them and showed an inclination to shake off European control he was deposed by the sultan under European pressure. His autocratic rule and the high taxation he imposed had made him unpopular at home, and he became one of the most controversial figures in Egyptian history. Some have seen him as an extravagant incompetent, others as a far-sighted, if unlucky moderniser. See M. E. Yapp, *The Making of the Modern Near East, 1792–1923* (London, 1987), pp. 155–7, 214–15, and Albert Hourani, *Arabic Thought in the Liberal Age 1798–1939* (Cambridge, 1989), passim. See also Family Tree of Mehmet Ali Bulent Rauf, *The Last Sultans*.

22 See Rauf, The Child Across Time, p. 90. She was the sister of Mehmet Tevfik Pasha, who succeeded his father Ismail as khedive, and of Ahmet Fuad I Pasha, who would become the first king of Egypt. Princess Fatma was also known as Fatma Zeyneb, according to khedival family sources.

23 Rauf's earliest memories of Fatma Hanim are related in *Addresses II*, pp. 81–3, 90–2, where he describes something of her lifestyle and great wealth. Although he had been born in Beylerbeyi, he relates that his parents settled in a property in Emirgan (on the European shore of the upper Bosphorus), which Fatma had inherited from Ismail Pasha and where she lived. They lived in the fifteen-room *Selamlik* (male reception-house) of the main house, which was set in a wooded park, having considered this a more manageable home than the latter (the main house was tended by 200 women). Fatma Hanim bequeathed a quarter of her fortune to the University of Cairo: she loved Egypt and had spent winters there. See ibid. pp. 91–2, 94, and Foreword, *The Last Sultans*.

24 Rauf, *Addresses II*, p. 86.

25 Ibid., p. 89. Rauf reports that she had two children by this marriage. According to Arim and khedival family sources, this first husband was Fatma Hanim's cousin Mehmet Tosun Pasha, son of Said Pasha, viceroy of Egypt before Ismail Pasha. Her daughter by this marriage was reportedly Princess Emine Indji, who married Said Halim Pasha.

26 Ibid. Rauf fails to name him here.

27 Ibid. Arim relates that, reflecting his Circassian origins, Mahmut Sirri was widely referred to as 'Çerkez Mahmut Pasha'. Khedival family sources describe him as an Egyptian, but this is probably a misunderstanding arising out of his spell at al-Azhar.

28 Ibid., p. 90.

29 There was also a son, Cemaleddin.

30 Khedival family sources.

31 Culme-Seymour, *Bolter's Grand-daughter*, p. 252.

32 Arim relates that he soon separated from Emire Hanim, possibly following an affair, and moved to Mersin, where he died.

33 Khedival family sources. Tebuk is 685 km from Damascus, south of 'Aqaba; pilgrims would travel to Mecca overland from Turkey through Syria.

34 Discussions with local residents of the Shaykh Muhyi'l-Din Quarter, Damascus, March 2003.

35 The mausoleum was constructed with its adjacent mosque and facing *takiya* [*tekke*] (with a soup kitchen and rooms for the use of visiting sufis and pilgrims) by the conquering Sultan Selim in the early sixteenth century. For an account of its construction, see Atlagh, 'Paradoxes of a Mausoleum', pp. 8–15, and von Schlegell, *Sufism in the Ottoman Arab World*, pp. 236ff. For a contemporary description, see Taji-Farouki, *At the Resting-place of the Seal of Saints*.

36 Outermost is the tomb of 'Abd al-Qadir al-Jaza'iri (d.1883), empty since the return of his remains to Algeria following independence. The middle tomb marks the place where Shaykh Muhammad Amin al-Kharbutli (d.1937), a Hanafi imam at the adjacent mosque, is buried. On the other side of the wall in the Ibn Zaki graveyard outside of the building, a late nineteenth-century Ottoman governor of the Province of Syria, Ishdid Pasha, is buried. The composite headstone set in the inside wall at the middle tomb gives details both of this governor and of al-Kharbutli. On the outer side of the mausoleum, closest to its door onto the mosque courtyard, are the tombs of the two sons of Ibn 'Arabi and, as centrepiece, that of Ibn 'Arabi himself. For more details, see Taji-Farouki, *At the Resting-place of the Seal of Saints*.

37 Personal observations (July 2001); by March 2003, these had been cleaned and a notice posted asking women to refrain from writing on tombs.

38 Personal correspondence from Rauf to a close associate (26 September 1973), describing his visit to the tomb of Shaban Veli. On this founding saint of the Shabaniyye and the *tariqa* itself, see Ch. 6. The tomb is the focus of a large complex that continues to draw visitors from the order. For a description, see 'Sha'baniyya', EI², IX, pp. 154–6.

39 On this complex, see Raymond Lifchez, The Lodges of Istanbul, in Lifchez, ed., *The Dervish Lodge*, pp. 113–17. Hüdayi was effectively the first shaykh of the Celvetiyye. On him and this *tariqa*, see Ch. 6.

40 H. Kamil Yilmaz, *Aziz Mahmud Hüdayi: Hayati, Eserleri, Tarikati* (Istanbul, 1999), p. 262 and n. 20 (note that Rauf Pasha is here described as 'the Lame' [*Topal*]). The author cites two sources. First is Osman-Zade Hüseyin Vassaf, *Sefine-yi evliya*, III/2, written between 1923 and 1925 (published in Latin letters 1990 [Part I] and 1999 [Part II]; Vassaf himself lived 1872–1929). It has not been possible to consult this. Second is Kemaleddin Şenocak, *Kutbu'l-arifin Seyyid Aziz Mahmud Hüdayi* (Istanbul, 1970): the latter (p. 30 n. 2) is repeated virtually word for word by Yilmaz.

It is difficult to ascertain exactly when the restoration in question took place, but it would appear to have been some years after 1910. (If Vassaf refers to it, then it took place before the completion of his work in 1925.) Held in the Ministry of Culture, documentation relating to the Hüdayi *waqf* can only be accessed by special permission, and may not yield relevant information. The author thanks Kamil Yilmaz and Suleyman Derin for this information, and John Norton for translations from the Turkish.

41 Şenocak, *Kutbu'l-arifin*, p. 30 n. 2.

42 The description by Yilmaz and Şenocak of the benefactor appears to confuse Fatma Hanim and Emire Hanim. Fatma Hanim was thus daughter of the khedive Ismail. She died after World War I. Her daughter Emire Hanim, who died some time after 1963 (there is evidence up to then of her correspondence with Rauf and others) may have helped her mother, who was a widow advancing in years by the time of the restoration. Emire Hanim's father-in-law was Rauf Pasha, and this fact is the possible source of the error in the accounts in Yilmaz and Şenocak. Furthermore, while Fatma Hanim owned the house in Beylerbeyi to which these authors allude, it seems she did not settle there but in the Emirgan property referred to above, on the opposite shore of the Bosphorus. A joint mother–daughter initiative is the most plausible scenario.

43 Khedival family sources were unable to substantiate this claim. In contrast with it, other associates suggest that Emire Hanim had been 'in the direct line of' Rumi, referring either to physical ancestry, spiritual genealogy, or both.

44 On the Qadiriyya, see Khaliq Ahmad Nizami, The Qadiriyyah Order, in Nasr, ed., *Islamic Spirituality: Manifestations*, pp. 6ff., and 'Qadiriyya', EI², IV, pp. 380–4. Trimingham, *The Sufi Orders in Islam*, p. 44, points out that the *tariqa* 'was only introduced in any definitive fashion into Istanbul' through the initiative of the seventeenth-century Isma'il Rumi. On the founder of the order, 'Abd al-Qadir al-Jilani, a great twelfth-century saint universally venerated in the Muslim world, see Knysh, *Islamic Mysticism*, pp. 179–84.

After 1925, the Qadiris were possibly affected more adversely by the closure of the *tekke*s than other *tariqa*s, as their ritual performances required a dedicated place. On their recent situation in Turkey, see Zarcone, La Turquie républicaine, p. 376. Zarcone notes that, while they are numerous, they are not as influential in urban environments as the Naqshbandis and Halvetis, but are found especially in the Kurdish region and at Trabzon. He mentions a Qadiri shaykh in Istanbul, Misbah Efendi, who leads a small group there.

Özkardeş' writings, some of which have been translated into English, include *Insanin asli ve Hz Mevlana Celaleddin Rumi* (Istanbul, 1963, trans. as *The Essence of Human and Mevlana Jalaluddin Rumi*); *Bütün dünya insanlarinin umumi sulhu için Allahi doğru olarak bilmeli öğrenmeli ve tapmalidir* (Istanbul, 1969); *Kuran'a göre Islam dininin: hakiki çehresi ve tarifi nedir ve bir ilahi ihtar* (Istanbul, 1970); *Some Considerations about Material and Moral Life* (Istanbul, 1971); *What is the Meaning of the Word Laic which can be Suitable to Divine Knowledge?* (Istanbul, 1973; English/Turkish); *Mağzi-i kur'an: kur'an'in özü* (Istanbul, 1978; trans. as *The Essence of the Qur'an*); *Kur'anin Hakikati (Kalamullah)* (Istanbul, 1979). Certain of these texts were sent as open letters to statesmen and world religious leaders. Özkardeş reportedly taught himself English over nine months, after retiring in 1953 from his position as chief technical inspector of postal and telegraphic training in Istanbul. His devotees claim he was competent in nine languages.

45 Interview, Istanbul, November 2004. Özkardeş' daughter recalls playing as a child with Rauf, himself then a child, when Emire Hanim brought him along on these visits. It might be noted that Özkardeş' daughter is presently the focus of at least part of the cult that surrounded Özkardeş and Süreyya, and is seen as a great saint in her own right.

Evidence of Emire Hanim's association with Özkardeş arises in a copy of a letter from him dated 3 September 1963 to Pope Paul VI, discussing the concept of the Trinity. Özkardeş addresses this copy by hand to Emire Hanim with a note signed 'your *fakir*'.

46 Writing in 1988, Öztürk, *The Eye of the Heart*, pp. 92–3, maintained that, 'In Turkey today … the Shabani, Jarrahi and the 'Uşşaqi groups are still active. The collective membership of these three Khalwati groups is larger than that of any other *tariqat* active in Turkey today'. De Jong, 'Khalwatiyya', EI², IV, pp. 992–3, holds that there is no data on the Khalwatiyya in Turkey after 1925, but there were reportedly twenty-five active *tekke*s of the Shabaniyye in Istanbul in 1921. See also Knysh, *Islamic Mysticism*, p. 268, offering the more recent observation that there are at least fifteen mosques in Istanbul where Shabani dervishes meet for their weekly *dhikr*s. A well-known twentieth-century member of the Shabaniyye is Elmalili Hamdi Yazir, who was commissioned to produce the official Republican translation of the Qur'an into Turkish, with commentary.

47 Khedival family sources. Associates' suggestions that Abdul Rauf Bey was related to Shaban Veli are probably best dismissed as the result of their confusing him with Mahmut Sirri Pasha.

It should be noted that the Mevlevis, by now well integrated into the state, were particularly influential among the upper segments of late Ottoman society, and the order had close ties with the reformist–progressive elite. See for example Brown, *The Darvishes*, p. 294; cf. Veinstein and Clayer, L'Empire ottoman, p. 339.

48 Her mother Hayriye Hanim was a first cousin of Rauf's father. Hayriye Hanim's maternal uncle was thus Rauf Pasha, whose son was Abdul Rauf Bey (Bulent Rauf's father). Cf. Meral Arim, 'Mme Hatice Münevver Ayaşli, 1906–1999', *JMIAS*, XXVII (2000), p. 65: 'Mme Ayaşli's uncle's son, Abdülrauf, was Bulent Rauf's father.' The discussion of Ayaşli here draws on Arim's oral and published accounts (2003 and 1999, respectively), between which there is some discrepancy. Associates met Ayaşli with Rauf during visits to Istanbul. She served as an Honorary Fellow of the MIAS for twenty-two years.

49 His brother Mahmut, with whom he had a close relationship, can only be mentioned in passing. Associates who met him in Turkey describe him as 'much more of a dervish' than Rauf. On his lifestyle, see Culme-Seymour, *Bolter's Grand-daughter*, chapter 26ff., passim.

50 She was named Esma Nail.

51 Arim, 'Mme Hatice Münevver Ayaşli', p. 65, situates this episode in the context of a dream (rather than a waking vision) while Caferi was positioned in Cairo. Caferi reportedly recognised Ibn 'Arabi immediately, as 'he had already seen him several times in dreams'.

52 Ibid. The date of death cannot be ascertained, but it was before the family's departure from Damascus for Istanbul in 1897. During World War I, the family returned to Damascus and visited the tomb of Ibn 'Arabi and that of Esma Nail, which reportedly remained intact. Details conveyed by Arim from Münevver Ayaşli, *Gördüklerim Bildiklerim ve Işittiklerim* (n.p., n.d.). Arim suggests that the little girl was buried at the other side of the window close to the head of Ibn 'Arabi's tomb. This is difficult to imagine given the layout of the mosque, as this area forms the mosque *sahn* (courtyard area). The child may have been buried in the Ibn Zaki graveyard within which the mausoleum stands.

53 Arim, 'Mme Hatice Münevver Ayaşli', p. 67.

54 Ibid. This claim is difficult to reconcile with the fact that Massignon himself had no sympathy for Ibn 'Arabi: see Sedgwick, *Against the Modern World*, pp. 134–5, and Chodkiewicz, Ibn 'Arabi dans l'oeuvre de Henry Corbin, pp. 81–3.

55 Cf. Culme-Seymour, *Bolter's Grand-daughter*, p. 275.

56 Especially after the success of her first novel, *Three Daughters of Pertev Bey*. Twelve other novels were to follow. See Arim, 'Mme Hatice Münevver Ayaşli', p. 67.

57 Culme-Seymour, *Bolter's Grand-daughter*, p. 264, describes her as 'deeply involved in her Mevlana Way', and tells of the young visitors who would come to see her. Rauf reportedly described her as a 'Mevlevi dervish' (see ibid., pp. 262–3). Rauf's unnamed cousin, whom Feild met during his spell in Turkey as Rauf's 'pupil', is apparently Ayaşli. See Feild, *The Last Barrier*, p. 136.

58 Cf. Culme-Seymour, *Bolter's Grand-daughter*, p. 293.

59 The term 'imaginal' is used widely in discussions of sufism to denote an intermediate world between the material world (the world of the senses) and the world of the spirit. It is a realm 'where the spiritual takes body and the body becomes spiritual' (Henry Corbin, *Alone with the Alone: Creative Imagination in the Sufism of Ibn 'Arabi* [Princeton, NJ, 1997], p. 4), and where 'invisible realities become visible and corporeal things are spiritualised' (Chittick, *The Sufi Path of Knowledge*, p. ix). Originally coined by Corbin, the term is used to set this 'imaginational' reality (*'alam al-khayal/al-mithal*) apart from an 'imaginary' one that might be associated with fantasy and 'imaginings'. See further Henry Corbin, *Mundus Imaginalis or the Imaginary and the Imaginal* (Ipswich, England, 1976).

60 Rauf, *Addresses II*, pp. 92–3, describes the affluent surroundings of his childhood. In addition to this autobiographical fragment, a taste of this can be gleaned from personal correspondence to a close associate from the early 1970s. In this Rauf wrote: 'I saw the Sultan sitting on his golden throne in the Dolmabahçe Palace when I was seven or eight years old.' The nostalgic tone of Rauf's descriptions of his childhood can be compared with an account of Kenan Rifai's early life: 'He experienced the pleasure of

seeing and living through the glory and plenty of the last years of a great civilization …
To see bags of gold being brought into the mansion … and to watch his grandfather …
present a small bag … to each guest when bidding him farewell, were commonplaces to
this growing child.' See Samiha Ayverdi, *The Friend* (Collected Works 23), trans. Ismet
Tümtürk (Istanbul, 1995), p.9. On Kenan Rifai, see above and Ch. 8.

61 Faize's father, Ahmet Fuad Pasha I, was the brother of Bulent's maternal
grandmother, Fatma. Both were children of Ismail Pasha. Faize's elder sister, Fevziye,
married Reza Pahlavi, Shah of Iran; see further below.

62 See for example 'Rememoration', p.10.

63 Ryan, Conversion to the Essence, pp.338–9.

64 Ryan locates this in Italy, Arim in Greece.

65 See also 'Rememoration'.

66 Ryan, Conversion to the Essence, p.335.

67 Ibid., p.339.

68 This description appears in the *White Fusus*, 1, inside cover. One associate
rephrases it in terms of Rauf's 'birthright'.

69 Schimmel, *Mystical Dimensions of Islam*, p.337.

70 Note Rauf's memories of the annual performance of a grand celebration of the
Prophet's birthday in the family home: see *Addresses II*, p.95.

71 Muslim urban elites were in general first to relinquish traditional patterns and
embrace a progressive interpretation of Islam, in line with modernising policies in the
Muslim world. In Istanbul, the Kemalist reforms gave this trend further impetus.

72 This statement should perhaps not be taken too seriously, for one associate implies
that it was Rauf's standard response to the question put to him by Turkish shaykhs/
sufis during visits there when they learned that he had no shaykh: 'Where did you learn
everything you know?' On the other hand, compare with the case of Kenan Rifai, whose
followers underline the pivotal role of his mother in his spiritual development. See for
example Ayverdi, *The Friend*, pp.12–13.

73 An indication of the close bond between mother and son arises in Rauf's account
(*Addresses II*, p.85) of a dream his mother had when she was heavily pregnant with him:
'She saw a name written in a light which reminded her of lights used in those days for
celebration illuminations, and wondered what festivity was being celebrated. She was
told in her dream that the light she saw written in the sky over the hills on the opposite
side of the Bosphorus was the name of the son she was bearing in her womb.'

74 'Rememoration', p.10.

75 Tollemache, 'An Obituary of Bulent Rauf'.

76 One internal account (Ryan, Conversion to the Essence, p.339) suggests that
he made 'unsuccessful attempts to be received into a formal *tariqa* in Turkey' *after* his
conversion. Arim rejects this, other associates question it, and Rauf's attitude towards the
*tariqa*s as later conveyed would not support any such overture on the part of the mature
man. It probably represents a confused version of the account of Rauf's introduction to
the Mevlevis as a youth.

77 Özak first visited America in 1980, when he led a city tour performing the
distinctive Halveti–Jerrahi *dhikr* there. Prior to that, his Istanbul bookshop had functioned
as a meeting point, and many Western students of sufism made contact with him by
visiting it. For details and sources on Özak and the activities of the Halveti–Jerrahis,
particularly in New York and California, see Hermansen, 'Hybrid Identity Formations',
p.164. For a general introduction to the Halveti–Jerrahis, see Shams Friedlander, A Note
on the Khalwatiyyah–Jerrahiyyah Order, in Nasr, ed., *Islamic Spirituality: Manifestations*,
pp.233–8. See also Zarcone, La Turquie républicaine, p.376. Özak is credited in strands
of Turkish oral tradition with an instrumental role in convincing the Turkish authorities
to permit resumption of public performance of the Mevlevi *sama'*; cf. Ira Friedlander,
*The Whirling Dervishes – Being an Account of the Sufi Order known as the Mevlevis and its
Founder the Poet and Mystic Mevlana Jalalu'ddin Rumi* (Albany, NY, 1992), p.112.

78 His daughter recalls Rauf meeting Özkardeş later in life.

79 Arim relates that she had conveyed to Özkardeş her intention to travel to Chisholme to teach Turkish at the School, at Rauf's request. He had reportedly responded by encouraging her to 'go and do her duty'.

80 These are close to the *waqf*–tomb complex of Yahya Efendi (d.1570), adviser to Suleyman the Magnificent and Selim II. See M. Baha Tanman, Settings for the Veneration of Saints, in Lifchez, ed., *The Dervish Lodge*, p. 149.

81 Apart from Yahya Efendi's, theirs are the only tombs marked from the entrance to the graveyard for ease of location by visitors. Fridays in particular witness a steady stream of visitors, while devotees take it in turns to sweep and clean the tombs.

82 Described by devotees as the *zat-i veli*, which is characterised by the spirit's return to the body forty days after death and their departure together from the tomb to travel at will, the body thus effectively taken up into the spirit. Such saints can also communicate directly with God, both in life and after death. One devotee reports that, before his death, Süreyya instructed that his coffin be closed with a metal sheet and locked. Sixteen years later when his son died, the coffin was opened to put him with his father. In place of Süreyya's body, clothes and hat was a single rose covered with dewdrops.

In contrast with this category of saint, the lower categories which devotees describe are: (a) the *ef'al-i veli*, whose spirit only remains after death, and (b) the *sifat-i veli*, whose body does not decompose after death. Alongside Süreyya and Özkardeş, devotees point to Süreyya's wife as a *zat-i veli*, and to Özkardeş' daughter as the only *zat-i veli* alive in the world today, after whose death there will be no others, as the End Times are approaching.

83 Özkardeş consistently refers to Süreyya in his writings as the *qutb al-wujud* appearing under the names *al-ghawth al-a'zam* and *sahib al-Rahman* (see Özkardeş, *What is the Meaning of the Word Laic?*, p. 5, for example). He attributed Süreyya's claim concerning the purpose of Jesus' Second Coming to 'Abd al-Qadir's *al-Fath al-rabbani*. His maturation and perfection in the corporeal realm were to be achieved through his marriage to a descendant of the Prophet and his fathering of two children. Through this second life, he would have direct experience of joy and suffering. Özkardeş underlined Islam's rejection of the notion of transmigration of the soul (but pointed to the cases of the prophets Idris and Jesus as exceptions). See undated open letter from Özkardeş to state rulers, Pope Paul VI and the Mormons.

84 Devotees relate that, when he was twenty-six, Özkardeş fell ill and the doctor pronounced him dead. A relative of his went to Süreyya (who was still alive at the time) and asked for his help. He asked for her hand, which he touched, and instructed her to return to Özkardeş and touch him while saying 'with the hands of Süreyya'. She returned and did as he had instructed, and the patient was restored to life, having been dead for seven hours.

85 Özkardeş, *The Essence of the Qur'an*, p. 12.

86 Süreyya indeed declared in 1921 that there would be ninety-nine years to the Resurrection, pointing to a date of 2018 or 2020 depending on whether Gregorian or Hijri calendars are used as the basis for the calculation.

87 Arim relates such an account from Özkardeş, illustrating Süreyya's attitude towards Ataturk: 'While working in the main post office in Istanbul he was informed that he was to be sent to Ankara for a spell. When he went in some distress to bid goodbye to his shaykh Hz. Süreyya, then a very old man, the latter comforted him by telling him that he should not worry if he did not see him again. Nor should he worry for the future of the country, which was experiencing troubled times, for a certain man by the name of Mustafa Kemal had been chosen by God to save Turkey. Hz. Süreyya died soon after, but his prediction was fulfilled in the rise of Ataturk.'

Devotees of Özkardeş claim that Süreyya described Ataturk as a 'true person'. Süreyya reportedly believed that Ataturk had won the war of independence with his help, but insisted that this fact be kept from him. He said: 'the body is from Ataturk, but the spirit is from me'. As Özkardeş, *What is the Meaning of the Word Laic?*, p. 5, put it, in his capacity as *al-ghawth al-a'zam* and *sahib al-Rahman*, Süreyya 'endowed moral courage and protection to Ataturk ... in the days of his performance in the independence war ... and he has given the good news for Ataturk's victory'.

Presumably based on such accounts, Arim suggests that Süreyya was Ataturk's 'spiritual mentor'. This claim is difficult to uphold and does not sit well with an image of Ataturk lacking in sympathy for sufi spirituality and rejecting the *tariqa*s as a symbol of reactionary forces holding Turkey back. Andrew Mango, *Atatürk: The Biography of the Founder of Modern Turkey* (London, 2004), p.45, provides a glimpse of his religious background and attitude: 'Mustafa Kemal had a pious mother. He had been subjected to years of religious instruction and practice, and he knew how to use the language of piety. Not only had he practised the rites of official, orthodox Islam, but during his home leave in Salonica he is said to have attended the ceremonies of whirling dervishes, and to have taken part himself, crying out *"Hu! Hu!"* ... as he whirled around. But it was during the same home leave that Atatürk went to dancing lessons and learnt to waltz. If he did visit the dervishes, he seems to have set little store by the experience. Mustafa Kemal's behaviour during his youth provides no evidence of religious conviction, while his adult life presents clear evidence of the contrary. Most Turkish officers and gentlemen accepted Islam as a general framework for their lives and the life of their society. Others, like Atatürk and many of his friends, seem to have been freethinkers from their earliest years. Islam had to be taken into account as a fact – sometimes an inconvenient fact – of other people's lives. In the eyes of many educated Muslims in Turkey ... religion was the province of women; the sincerity of men who showed religious enthusiasm was suspect. Most of the cadets rejected the indoctrination to which they had been subjected.' See also Patrick Balfour Kinross, *Ataturk: A Biography of Mustafa Kemal, Father of Modern Turkey* (New York, 1965).

88 Associates are very clear that although he 'came out of a tradition that was very rich', Rauf had not himself been part of a *tariqa*.

89 See Young, 'United by Oneness', p.2.

90 See for example Brass, Foreword, the *White Fusus*, 2, and Ch. 6.

91 Even some of these associates have confused Rauf's familial spiritual associations. Believing that his father was related to Shaban Veli, for example (and adding this to his mother's descent from Hüdayi), they have concluded that Rauf 'descended from a Perfect Man or saint from both sides'. Associates who personally encountered Rauf differ greatly in their knowledge of his family background, and relatively few facts circulate widely either orally or as published fragments.

92 Uwaysi sufism can be thought of as a spiritual transmission or connection conferred on a living person by an apparitional spirit body (of a dead saintly figure or shaykh), or by another living but physically absent person (by the spirit body of a living shaykh, for example). See von Schlegell, *Sufism in the Ottoman Arab World*, p.188. The tradition of Uwaysi sufism must be contrasted with that of 'suluki' sufism, which takes place through direct living human contacts. The term suluki (from *suluk*, 'travelling' on the sufi path), which we borrow from ibid., pp.131–2, denotes sufism as we have come to expect it, taking place in the context of a master–disciple relationship. A significant aspect of this is to spend time in the presence of a shaykh (*suhba*). As von Schlegell notes (p.188), while Uwaysi teaching is often 'non-verbal and spontaneous ... very many times it mimics the worldly forms of Suluki Sufism such as the inculcation of *dhikr* and the rites of initiation'. Note finally that Uwaysi sufism is often portrayed in the historical sources as an active process, in which the individual prepares himself to receive spirit bodies by visiting them at tombs, for example. See 'Uwaysiyya', EI², X, p.958. On the saint after whom the tradition of Uwaysi sufism is named, see below.

93 Personal correspondence from Rauf to a close associate (1973).

94 One associate argues that a dimension of the lives and characters of each of these saints had been prominent in Rauf's life: 'Abd al-Qadir had been very wealthy, Uways very poor, and Ibn 'Arabi 'a fountain of knowledge'.

95 Personal correspondence from Rauf to a close associate (early 1970s). For his references to 'Abd al-Qadir, see Rauf, *Addresses*, pp. 36, 38. Rauf conveyed to associates a popular account of the 'common root' of 'Abd al-Qadir and Ibn 'Arabi, making the latter the 'spiritual son' of the former. Told especially by Qadiris and thus possibly conveyed to him by his mother, it is repeated today by devotees of Süreyya and Özkardeş, for example. This account can be found in Ibn 'Arabi, *Journey to the Lord of Power: A Sufi Manual on Retreat*, trans. Rabia Terri Harris (London, 1981), Introduction by Muzaffer Özak al-Jerrahi, pp. 15–16. It relates that Ibn 'Arabi's father travelled to Baghdad at an advanced age, dearly wishing for a son. He visited 'Abd al-Qadir and sought the saint's intercession. Having understood that Ibn 'Arabi's father was not destined to have a descendant while he himself was, 'Abd al-Qadir asked if he would like to have *his* son. They stood back to back, and later Ibn 'Arabi was born: his father named him Muhyi al-Din, as 'Abd al-Qadir had instructed. (See also Friedlander, *The Whirling Dervishes*, p. 39, narrating the story of 'Abd al-Qadir having left his *khirqa* for 'a man he said would be coming from the west and would be called Muhyi-d-din', fifty years before Ibn 'Arabi went to Baghdad [and before he was even born].) Note that Ibn 'Arabi apparently received the *khirqa* in Mecca from 'Abd al-Qadir via the latter's disciple Yunus b. Yahya al-Hashimi; see Addas, *Quest for the Red Sulphur*, pp. 145, 214.

96 Uways was a younger Yemeni contemporary of the Prophet who never met him but shared an affinity with him, communicating with him through visions and intimations. For later sufis, Uways the 'proto-sufi' became 'the archetype of the autodidactic (or, what is, in essence, the same – *Theo*didactic) saint who achieved initiation spontaneously, without need of human mediation of a teacher, or *shaykh*. His intuition … was proverbial, so that he was believed to have divined the essential principles and practices of Islam, spending his nights in prayer and every day in almsgiving, and even the soundest *hadiths* portray him as wielding an extraordinary power of intercession with God.' See Gerald Elmore, 'The *Uwaysi* Spirit of Autodidactic Sainthood as the "Breath of the Merciful"', *JMIAS*, XXVIII (2000), pp. 43–4, 46–7; A. S. Hussaini, 'Uways al-Qarani and the Uwaysi Sufis', *The Muslim World*, 57 (1967), pp. 103–13; 'Uways al-Qarani', and 'Uwaysiyya', EI², X, p. 958; Julian Baldick, *Imaginary Muslims: The Uwaysi Sufis of Central Asia* (London, 1993), Introduction.

Note that Ibn 'Arabi was himself 'a perfect example of the Uwaysite *mysticus auto-didacticus*, with no (visible) master among men'. See Elmore, 'The *Uwaysi* Spirit', p. 47.

Rauf's (implicit) self-projection as an Uwaysi is not unique in contemporary Western sufism. As Webb, Tradition and Innovation, p. 106 n. 43 notes, for example, Bawa Muhaiyaddeen 'clearly identifies with [the Uwaysi] form of attainment of knowledge'.

97 Several associates are quite clear that this room was the Mead Hall, while others disagree or are unsure.

98 On him, see Ch. 6.

99 Rauf had explained that this attire was in deference to Yusuf, as this dream (like all dreams) had taken place in the imaginal realm, which is associated with him. On Yusuf and the realm of *khayal* (and his association with dreams and the understanding of these), see *The Bezels of Wisdom*, chapter IX.

100 The notion 'taste' here signifies specifically *mashrab*. On this term, see Ch. 6.

101 He would put his upright palm to the side of his face to illustrate the subtle veiling he experienced between himself and Hüdayi.

102 We can get an idea of the importance of this date for associates by comparing it with the occasions Rauf had himself singled out for an annual *dhikr*: see Ch. 6. The sufi perception of the saint's death as the point of his or her union with God, often projected through the notion of nuptials, should be noted here.

103 Tollemache, 'An Obituary of Bulent Rauf'.

104 Hornsby, 'Rememoration for Bulent Rauf'.

105 Culme-Seymour, *Bolter's Grand-daughter*, pp. 317–18.

106 Compare with Ryan, Conversion to the Essence, p. 342.

107 According to 'Rememoration', p. 11, Rauf 'endured with patience and fortitude being stared at by many like ... a Sphinx about to give up its secrets. I remember him once insisting on putting on a ... patchwork shirt to visit Swyre Farm. "You see", he said, "they think I am something else, something holy, and I want to show them that that is not what I am."' For him, '"holiness" and knowledge of God were never to be equated ... he never wanted people to be "holy" in their quest for spiritual or self knowledge'.

108 Ryan, Conversion to the Essence, p. 342.

109 Tollemache, 'An Obituary of Bulent Rauf'.

110 John Brass, Foreword, in Rauf, *Addresses II*, p. vi. On facing his own death, he had reportedly explained to an associate that he was not interested in entering heaven, but yearned to go beyond that, 'to be like the love that passes between Him and His complete image'.

111 Tollemache, 'An Obituary of Bulent Rauf'.

112 Culme-Seymour, *Bolter's Grand-daughter*, p. 318.

113 Annett, ed., *The Many Ways of Being*, p. 84, most likely reflected his informants' turn of phrase when he wrote in 1975–76 that Rauf was 'still around in the wings' and helped things along 'behind the scenes'. Young's suggestion that Rauf served as Consultant to the Trust, 'but in a very retiring position', is also noteworthy: see 'Courses at Chisholme', p. 27.

It might be tempting to see features characteristic of Melamism in Rauf's repudiation of the role of shaykh and the formal aspect of sufism, in his self-effacing manner, his dislike of making a show of his spiritual attainment and his immediate emphasis of the Oneness of Being. (In the latter regard, for example, we can reflect on a comment by Holbrook, 'Ibn 'Arabi and Ottoman Dervish Traditions', I, p. 30, concerning the Melami way, where the method is based upon the Oneness of Being: '[This] mystery, the last teaching of other orders, is the first teaching given to aspirants in the Melami *tarikat* ... The emphasis ... placed upon individual perception in this discourse is not the exposition of a theory but a discussion of actual experience.') There is no ground for such speculation, however, in spite of the high esteem in which Ibn 'Arabi held Melamis. Far from hinting at any particular sympathy or affiliation, Rauf indeed barely mentioned the Melami tradition to associates.

Speculation of this kind in Geaves, *The Sufis of Britain*, pp. 167–8, with regard to Idries Shah is equally questionable. 'In many ways', Geaves writes, 'Shah's career and personality epitomised the *Malamati* tradition ... The descriptions of Idries Shah's vision of Sufism clearly indicate his natural empathy for the Malamati school of mysticism.' See further Epilogue.

114 For his views concerning 'students' and 'teachers', see Rauf, *Addresses II*, pp. 52–3 (for example: 'Today what we call a student may be at a certain point in his capacity to absorb knowledge, but tomorrow he can even surpass the teacher.'). See also p. 46, where he refers to associates as his 'co-students'.

115 Cf. the perception of Bawa Muhaiyaddeen among his followers: see Webb, Tradition and Innovation, p. 93.

116 A realised man has arrived at the station of completion designated by the notion of the Perfect Man (*al-insan al-kamil*), such that their identification with the essence of the latter has been actualised. See Ch. 5. Ryan, Conversion to the Essence, p. 342, writes that Rauf had 'intimate knowledge of the most profound spiritual stations'.

117 'Rememoration', p. 11.

118 Tollemache, 'An Obituary of Bulent Rauf'.

119 Ibid.; 'Rememoration'. The term friend is also an English rendering of the Arabic *wali* (saint).

120 See for example Culme-Seymour, 'Bulent and the Blue *Fusus*', pp. 40–1.

121 Brass, Foreword, *Addresses II*, p. vi.

122 Ryan, Conversion to the Essence, p. 339; Obituary, p. 1.

123 Brass, Foreword, *Addresses II*, p. vi.

124 Ryan, Conversion to the Essence, p. 342.

125 'Rememoration', p. 10.

126 Brass, Foreword, *Addresses II*, p. vi; cf. Ryan, Conversion to the Essence, p. 342.

127 Associates relate that Rauf invited to the first further course specifically those who would ask him questions, so that appropriate knowledge 'could be drawn out from him'. To this end, he scheduled one-to-one conversation as part of the course.

128 See 'Rememoration', p. 10. Disciples commonly experience the capacity of spiritual guides to convey what is necessary when it is needed, and in an intelligible form. See Webb, Tradition and Innovation, p. 81, for example.

129 During the trip to Turkey in December 1984, for example, Rauf was resting in his room surrounded by students. He said emphatically: 'Ibn 'Arabi is the archetypal meaning of the Perfect Man. Mark what I said. He is the meaning of the prophets from the first to the last.' One associate recalls rushing out on this occasion (and similar ones) to write down in a personal notebook what Rauf had said, so he could be sure of an accurate record.

130 See Christopher Ryan, 'Bulent Rauf: A Mystic in the Kitchen', *Beshara Newsletter*, Autumn 1996, pp. 3–4.

131 Ibid.

132 See Peter Young, Foreword, *Addresses*, p. ii. Some essays thus refer to the experiences and attitudes of the students to whom they were originally addressed. For example (p. 19): 'It has been noticed that through your studies and through the lectures you hear you come to conclusions which you find contradicted by other readings and lectures. Consequently, certain assertions and predictions will seem ... confusing ... You know very little yet, therefore – and this is for your own good – do not attempt judgements upon what you hear and what you read, at this point in your studies – and for some time to come. I am afraid you will have to take what is given even if you find yourselves confused, and blame nothing but your ignorance, because eventually, with more knowledge you will begin to see how two aspects – though seemingly opposite – make one.' And (p. 34): 'During this period when so many forms of belief are being exposed to us through lectures and through readings, it is of course natural that the mind, and consequently the heart, strays from the central idea for which we have all come here'. The longest address comprises ten small pages.

133 Examples arise in a discussion of Ibn 'Arabi's conception of unity, for example (p. 63), and in an explanation of the meaning of meditation (p. 30).

134 Shakespeare's *The Merchant of Venice* (p. 57) and Milton's *Paradise Lost* (p. 24), for example.

135 In explaining 'Veracity', for example (p. 16), Rauf draws an analogy with an alcoholic's realisation of his need for Alcoholics Anonymous through an honest appraisal 'of that part of his inner composition which constitutes his ego'. He compares the expansive expression that is the outcome of the exhalation of the *Nafas al-Rahman* to the journey of the subject matter of a painting, from the mind of the artist to the museum (p. 58; also 60–1). He likens the evolution of states to climbing a ladder (p. 6), and suggests the idea of 'looking through the right end of the telescope' in order to comprehend the dual nature of man as Eternal, Absolute and Infinite, and as temporal, relative and finite (p. 21). He likens Truth (and the 'immutable Essential '*ayn*' which is the individual) to an ocean, which changes in temper and action but not in its 'ocean-ness' (p. 47). Finally, he compares the Unity of Being in relation to its multiple manifestations to the facets of a jewel or the colours refracted by a prism (pp. 63–4).

136 See Young, Foreword, p. i.

137 He cited Einstein (on relativity) (pp. 20, 22, 28, 65), Philo (on the relationship between Man and God) (pp. 51, 57) and Henry Corbin (on the Theophanic Imagination) (p. 29). Rauf referred to stories on Bayazid (pp. 8, 54, 69) and Rumi (pp. 9–10), introduced quotations from popular fourteenth-century Anatolian mystic poet Yunus Emre (p. 10) and 'Abd al-Qadir al-Jilani (pp. 36, 38), and referred to Bursevi (pp. 54, 64–5) and Qunawi

(p. 57). For references to Ibn 'Arabi, see pp. 20, 56–7, 64, 67, for example: specifically, Rauf referred to the *Wird*, the *Fusus, Kernel of the Kernel* and *Whoso Knoweth Himself*.

138 See especially Rauf, *Addresses II*, pp. 21–8, 33–8. Some of the texts collected in *Addresses II* are nonetheless dense and challenging in places.

139 Jane Carroll, 'Notes from a Student' (paper delivered at MIAS Symposium, May 2004). Thanks are due to her for providing a copy of this.

140 Rauf, *Addresses*, p. 23.

141 On this, see for example Ernst, *The Shambhala Guide to Sufism*, pp. 98ff., and Knysh, *Islamic Mysticism*, pp. 301ff.

142 Rauf, *Addresses*, pp. 24–5. The expression 'lowest of the low' is from Qur'an 95: 5. On the five qualities listed here and the four course activities, see Ch. 3.

143 Ibid., pp. 17–18.

144 Ibid., pp. 9–10.

145 Ibid., p. 35. Their mistake is in believing they have their 'own' knowledge, achieved through their own effort, when it is 'nothing other than a gift and an intercession by Him' (p. 42).

146 Ibid., p. 35.

147 Ibid., p. 54.

148 Ibid., p. 64.

149 Ibid., p. 70.

150 Ibid., pp. 46–7.

151 Ibid., p. 71.

152 Ibid., p. 67. *Risalat-ul Wujudiyyah* is known also as *Whoso Knoweth Himself*: on the question of its authorship, see Ch. 3.

153 Ibid., p. 70. Thus (pp. 68–9), 'to wake up or not is … a matter of taste', and 'It is true that the way one goes, towards Union – or not, and which way, is a matter of Taste'.

154 Ibid., pp. 40–1.

155 Ibid., p. 42.

156 As Clark, 'Summer Gathering', writes, 'Experience has shown us that "the task itself educates you in what is needed"'.

157 Brass, Foreword, *Addresses II*, p. vi.

158 See for example Rauf, *Addresses II*, p. 46: 'Surely it is true that God has made man in his own image … [S]urely man is of a superlative magnitude. No other can reach the development and height that man can reach'.

159 Although Rauf implicitly emphasised the importance of self-observation for students and treated spiritual psychology in the sense of potential ascending levels of consciousness, he seems to have had no particular interest in the contribution of contemporary psychological approaches to personal growth (not to mention psychotherapeutic discourse). This was unlike many other sufi guides in the West who evinced an explicit interest in such subjects (e.g. Vilayat Khan and Shah), reflecting and responding to a culturally pervasive popular psychology (often appropriated by the New Age) that in some cases inspired a virtual translation of sufi teachings into contemporary psychological discourses. See Hermansen, What's American about American Sufi Movements?, pp. 47–54, 'Hybrid Identity Formations', p. 179 and In the Garden of American Sufi Movements, p. 167; Jervis, The Sufi Order, p. 231; Webb, Tradition and Innovation, pp. 102 n. 8, 107 n. 57.

160 Rauf, *Addresses II*, p. 3.

161 Ibid., p. 9.

162 Explaining this approach, Young recalls Rumi's words: 'Do not use your precious sword as a coat hook'.

163 In sufi discourse, the sense of the term is best captured as 'intuitive spiritual savoring', following Gerald T. Elmore, *Islamic Sainthood in the Fullness of Time* (Leiden, 1999), p. 231 n. 28. Ibn 'Arabi explains its signification in the *Futuhat* in the following

terms (cited in Chittick, *The Sufi Path of Knowledge*, p. 220): 'It could be imagined that when man possesses the knowledge of something, he possesses the "tasting" of it, but such is not the case. Tasting derives only from a self-disclosure. Knowledge may be gained through the transmission of a true, sound report.' *Dhawq* is thus tied to direct, personal experience on the one hand, and Divine Self-disclosure (*tajalli*) on the other.

For Rauf, such 'intuitive spiritual savoring' represented the ultimate 'application' of *dhawq*. He used the term in a broader sense, intending first to cultivate in students a general sense of good taste and a direct savouring of quality and refinement. As it developed, their capacity for *dhawq* would equally find its expression in the context of 'spiritual savouring'.

164 See for example 'Rememoration', p. 10.

165 See Rauf, *Addresses II*, p. 58.

166 *Beshara Newsletter*, Autumn 1996, is dedicated to the theme of nourishment. The Editorial employs its symbolism within the context of the Oneness of Being thus: 'Hunger is for Being alone and our nourishment is only Him. Powerless to bring ourselves into existence or to be maintained in it we hunger for Him who nourishes us with His being.'

167 Note that the topic of food receives considerable attention in Islamic culture generally, and the Qur'an describes it as one of the greatest divine blessings, inviting man to contemplate the food God provides as a sign of His wisdom and generosity.

Sufi writers in particular have understood food as a gift and an expression of divine love. As it reflects man's dependence on God, an appropriate attitude towards food and the proper conduct at meals (*adab al-sufra*) form an expression of both gratitude and devotion. See Ayla Algar, Food in the Life of the Tekke, in Lifchez, ed., *The Dervish Lodge*, pp. 296–303, and Gabriel Said Richards, 'The Sufi Approach to Food: A Case Study of Adab', *The Muslim World*, 90 (Spring 2000), pp. 198–217. Note that Ibn 'Arabi treats *adab* while at a meal in several small treatises, translated by Asín Palacios in his *El Islam Christianizado*: see Richards, 'The Sufi Approach to Food', p. 216 n. 78.

A parallel emphasis on the kitchen and cooking arises in the case of Bawa Muhaiyaddeen, who would cook for his followers: he also taught them to cook and encouraged them to cook for each other as a way of fostering servanthood. As Webb observes, the kitchen at the Fellowship is still part of 'an almost-sacred space' there: see Tradition and Innovation, pp. 93–4.

168 Such writings are his chapter in Feller, ed., *Great Dishes of the World*; an unpublished manuscript tracing the origins of Ottoman cuisine, the introduction to which is excerpted in *Beshara Newsletter*, Autumn 1996, and Introduction to Turkish Cookery, in *Addresses II*, pp. 67–78. Bawa Muhaiyaddeen's recipes have also been collected in a book: see Webb, Tradition and Innovation, pp. 93–4.

169 Ryan, 'Bulent Rauf: A Mystic in the Kitchen'.

170 For the full text, see Rauf, *Addresses II*, pp. 65–6. The Notice is prominent in associates' homes.

171 As Annemarie Schimmel, *The Triumphal Sun: A Study of the Works of Jalaloddin Rumi* (London, 1978), pp. 138–52, observes, Rumi's poetry encompasses numerous images taken from the kitchen, food, cooking and eating. The act of eating is a symbol of spiritual nourishment, while cooking represents preparation of the *murid* (in relation to which 'one should not act too hurriedly, for cooking requires slow and careful action, otherwise the stew will boil over and get burnt'). See p. 139, also 320ff., on the metaphor of cooking chickpeas specifically. This complex of images leads (p. 146) 'to the feeling that man is constantly in a kitchen, being treated like one of the ingredients of food ... [Rumi] compares almost everything to a kitchen: the soul, the heart, the head, the stomach and even intellect in whose kitchen the poor Sufis remain hungry'. See further Friedlander, *The Whirling Dervishes*, pp. 107–8.

Algar, Food in the Life of the Tekke, p. 297, suggests that the Mevlevis evince 'a distinctly Turkish emphasis on the kitchen, the preparation and consumption of food'.

172 Ryan, 'Bulent Rauf: A Mystic in the Kitchen', describes him as 'a sort of patron saint of cooks in Turkey'. For an account of his legendary faith, see Friedlander, *The Whirling Dervishes*, p. 58.

173 Ryan, 'Bulent Rauf: A Mystic in the Kitchen', encompasses an account of this associate's experience of learning to cook with Rauf. Rauf 'suggested … that it would be better to serve the food, not from the centre of the dish, but from the edge, so as to preserve the "bereket", the "grace" inherent in the food prepared … In the kitchen itself, one rarely received a scientific explanation for the occasional hints and warnings that he would let drop while cooking. For instance, he once scolded me for using a metal spoon for stirring onions in the pan. He didn't explain why … I noticed the difference when I changed over to a wooden spoon, the relationship between the cook and the onions was somehow different, somehow it "felt" more appropriate.'

174 Rauf, *Addresses*, p. 9.

175 Personal correspondence from Rauf to a close associate (10 July 1972). The comment arises in his endeavour to remind this associate, who was leading a study group focusing on *The Twenty-nine Pages*, that he was not teaching. Rather, all were studying and learning together.

176 Personal correspondence from Rauf to a close associate (1973). Rauf had relayed the same conception of study to Feild, emphasising its difference from the 'Western' approach, which posits it as 'a way of gaining knowledge or assimilating information'. Thus, 'knowledge cannot be acquired; it must be given. It is given to you at the right moment, but really it is all there within you. "Education" comes from the Latin word *educare* … "to bring forth". It does not mean to stuff down some extraneous bits of information from some outside source. The study I mean is the study of essential truths in love and in awareness so that what is within you, waiting to be born, may begin to unfold.' See Feild, *The Last Barrier*, p. 45.

177 Brass, Foreword, the *White Fusus*, 2, p. v. On the emotional reception of this piece when it was read out at an AGM of the MIAS in 1986, see Culme-Seymour, 'Translating Ibn 'Arabi', p. 7.

178 Personal correspondence from Rauf to a close associate (1973).

179 Ibid. (10 July 1972).

180 Associates describe Bosnevi's approach as a juxtaposing of two apparently opposed elements with a third that unites them.

Ibn 'Arabi's own insistence on the multiple meanings of the Word of God is noteworthy. His general rule was expressed thus: 'When it is revealed in the language of a certain people, and when those who speak this language differ as to what God meant by a certain word or group of words due to the variety of possible meanings of the words, each of them – however differing their interpretations may be – effectively comprises what God meant, provided that the interpretation does not deviate from the accepted meanings of the language in question. God knows all these meanings, and there is none that is not the expression of what He meant to say to this specific person.' *Futuhat*, IV: 25, as translated in Michel Chodkiewicz, *An Ocean without Shore: Ibn 'Arabi, The Book, and the Law*, trans. David Streight (Albany, NY, 1993), p. 30. 'Given the rich polysemy of Arabic vocabulary', Chodkiewicz adds, 'rigorous fidelity to the letter of Revelation does not exclude but, on the contrary, it implies a multiplicity of interpretations. Ibn 'Arabi insists on this point.'

181 Rauf used the term *'alim* with derogatory intent. On the concepts of *'ilm* (knowledge in its 'lower', rational sense) and *ma'rifa* (distinctively spiritual knowledge, often translated as 'gnosis') in sufism, see Reza Shah-Kazemi, 'The Notion and Significance of *Ma'rifa* in Sufism', *Journal of Islamic Studies*, 13: 2 (2002), pp. 155–81.

Sensitivity to multiple layers of meaning has come to characterise associates' approaches to Ibn 'Arabi's writings. For example, one associate recalls his strong unease on reading Chodkiewicz's translation in *Seal of the Saints* of a passage from the *Futuhat* suggesting that there can be no Muhammadan attainment (i.e., no saint 'upon the heart of Muhammad') after the Muhammadan Seal. (A reference to *Futuhat*, II: 49, trans. in *Seal of the Saints*, p. 118, thus: 'no other saint [after the Muhammadan Seal] will ever be "on the heart" of Muhammad'.) While acknowledging the accuracy of the translation, the associate 'had a feeling of the need not to shut off possibilities', for he believes that 'those [saints] we visit in Turkey, for example, are Muhammadian through and through'. His point is that the text can carry multiple layers of meaning.

On the general problems of translating Ibn 'Arabi's writings, especially in cases where a translator knowingly/unconsciously 'renders a particular passage as they have understood it ... from the restricted level of their particular individual beliefs, conceptual understanding, or an inadequate "unveiling"', see Morris, 'Ibn 'Arabi's Rhetoric of Realisation', 1, pp. 81ff. On the personal dialectic between the reader and text which Morris considers to have been fashioned deliberately by Ibn 'Arabi, and which inevitably leads to multiple readings, see ibid. pp. 97–8.

182 Associates relate accounts of their participation in more than one *dhikr* in Turkey during the early 1970s. These included one at the home of Suleyman Dede in Konya (on whom see Ch. 2), and another with Özak's Halveti–Jerrahis (on this episode, see Ch. 6). A third, held after the Mevlevi *sama'* in a private apartment in Konya, was attended by 300 people from several *tariqa*s.

183 Associates recall early encounters with sufis who had confronted them with difficult questions and critical opinions, often leading back to the question of Muslim identity (see Ch. 6). For example, Ralph Austin had been invited to lecture at Swyre Farm during 1975. A little later, the Schuonian Martin Lings, with whom Austin was at the time associated, had presented a talk at Chisholme. Both speakers 'had been very critical, and had argued that what we were doing in Beshara was not valid'. Thereafter, 'there were only very limited attempts to find common ground or to fraternise with sufis'. (Austin's attitude later changed, and he became 'a good friend of Beshara'.)

184 Sensitivity to the issue of sufi identification was likely to have been present from the early years, perhaps from after Feild's exit. Writing in the mid-1970s, Annett, ed., *The Many Ways of Being*, p. 84, thus noted that 'although Sufi in inspiration', Beshara chose 'not to use the phrase about itself'. While his projection of the basis of Beshara's self-distancing from sufism reflects its perennialist assumptions, views concerning sufism he attributes to associates seem more characteristic of the Sufi Order approach. Annett thus writes that Beshara associates 'differentiate between two types of Sufism. The first is the traditional Sufism, which is a religion connected to Islam. The second they refer to as the "real" esoteric Sufi tradition, which is free from religions, and it is with this that they associate themselves ... they see themselves as the possessors of the true Sufi esoteric tradition'. He records a belief among associates that 'the word [Sufi] has become devalued in the West', because of 'fake Sufi orders'.

185 For Qur'anic quotations and allusions, see Rauf, *Addresses*, pp. 5, 19, 23–4, 36, 38–9, 45, 47, 53, 56, 58, 65. For examples relating to hadith and *hadith qudsi* (a special category of hadith), see pp. 16, 38, 51, 60, 66.

Qur'anic language used includes, for example, *wiswas, shirk, tawhid, asfal al-safilin* and *al-muqarrabun. Wiswas* (pp. 39ff.), literally 'whisperer', designates the power of evil aimed at weakening human will through Satan, for example. *Shirk* (p. 35) is to associate with God other than Him, while *tawhid* (p. 64) designates the unicity of God, the bedrock of Islam. *Asfal al-safilin* (pp. 24–5) describes the condition of a man who betrays his true nature. *Al-muqarrabun* (p. 38) refers to 'those brought close'.

186 Examples are Fatima's prayer (p. 8), and the Prophet's prayer (p. 36). Note also the recommended integration of the Islamic formal prayer or *salat* at the beginning and end of the *tahajjud* practice (on which see Ch. 6) (p. 39). Most talks end with an invocation (*ya Hadi, ya Hakim*, for example: p. 8) or a supplication (for example, 'May God help us all': p. 25; and 'May God make it easy for us all': p. 49).

187 For example, the sufi terminology of *fana'/baqa', nafs* and *maqam* (station): see ibid., pp. 9–10, 14–15, 46–8. Discussing Union, Rauf observes that the point he makes applies 'in all Sufi esoteric lore' (p. 63). He describes the practice 'in the *Tarikas*' of 'self realisation in one's mentor or teacher' as a stage in 'the evolution of the *nafs*' (pp. 47–8). Describing how one proceeds through the stages to Union, he notes that 'Some *tarikas* give you twenty-one thousand *Ismi Jelal* as a minimum to start with' (p. 49). Finally, regarding the practice of *tahajjud*, he observes that it is 'used in many of the *Tarikas*' (p. 35).

188 'The Essential', 'Response to Sheer Beauty', 'That which Is, always Is', 'What is the single most important point': see Rauf, *Addresses II*, pp. 3–9. These texts 'were for use in the School, or embodied in letters written in response to particular queries, and subsequently more widely circulated.' See 'Note on the texts', ibid., p. vii. Young and another long-standing associate brought together the volume's contents.

189 For a complete bibliography, see ibid., pp. 107–8; Rauf, *The Last Sultans*, pp. 364–6. Two unpublished works entitled *Sultan's Delight* (a collection of Ottoman recipes) and *Turkish Proverbs* must be added to these. There are also a few unpublished articles, and some published in the *JMIAS* under associates' names that are actually Rauf's work. As a learning process for those concerned, he would ask associates to draft an article incorporating certain points, and then invariably rewrite it substantially himself. We have pointed up such cases in the notes. (Note the contrast of this approach with that of a figure like Rajneesh: some of the writings published in the latter's name were thus in fact compiled by his followers. See Arweck, New Religious Movements, p. 271.) Pointed out earlier, Rauf's modest written legacy can also be contrasted with the case of other sufi guides in the West, who have left substantial written (and audiovisual) records of their discourses. This modest legacy might be understood in light of Rauf's intense dislike of personal attention, and his uncompromising focus on direct individual realisation.

190 Of the twelve short essays in the 1986 volume, the final one is reproduced from *JMIAS*, III (1984). The 2001 volume reproduces four articles from the *JMIAS*, and three from the Beshara Trust *Newsletter* and *Beshara Magazine*.

191 This was screened in the 'Everyman' series by the BBC in a forty-five minute version, edited from a much longer original which is now lost. It is difficult to gauge how widely it has circulated, but the film has found its way to the non-print section of the University of North Carolina Undergraduate Library. See Ernst, *The Shambhala Guide to Sufism*, p. 242 n. 29.

Cilento (who was married to Sean Connery from 1963 to 1975) appears to have had a sustained interest in Ibn 'Arabi, and to have retained her connection with Beshara/the MIAS well beyond the film's production. In 1985, for example, she helped convene a symposium on 'The Sufi Legacy of Muhyiddin Ibn 'Arabi' at the University of Melbourne (in collaboration with the late Nasih Mirza), inviting the MIAS to send a speaker. See 'Additional Procedural Committee Meeting of the MIAS' held at Chisholme House, 3 March 1985, p. 4. It seems she also established a centre in Australia ('Karnak', in north Queensland), where Beshara courses were held for a time.

The British archaeologist James Mellaart served on the film as an additional archaeological adviser, and Cilento as an additional scriptwriter/narrator. In her narrative Cilento introduced Rauf as a Yale-educated archaeologist interested in 'the earliest forms of religious consciousness ... so strangely concentrated' in the Anatolian region. She added that he was also 'a dervish and a sufi'.

192 Some associates use it as a resource in their own writings: see for example Jane Carroll, 'Timelessness and Time', *JMIAS*, XXIX (2000), pp. 78–80, and Ch. 5. Rauf himself referred to it in his talks (for example, *Addresses*, p. 69).

193 *Turning* may be partly responsible for perceptions of a strong Mevlevi connection in the few scholarly references to Rauf noted earlier.

On Rumi and the Mevlevi *tariqa*, see William C. Chittick, Rumi and the Mawlawiyyah, in Nasr, ed., *Islamic Spirituality: Foundations*, pp. 105–26 and *The Sufi Path of Love: The Spiritual Teachings of Rumi* (Albany, NY, 1983); Schimmel, *The Triumphal Sun and Mawlana Rumi: Yesterday, Today and Tomorrow*, in Banani *et al.*, eds, *Poetry and Mysticism in Islam*, pp. 5–27; Friedlander, *The Whirling Dervishes*.

194 The film opens with a meditation on a line from a T. S. Eliot poem: 'At the still point of the turning world. There the dance is ... and there is only the dance.'

195 The film might be compared with Friedlander's *The Whirling Dervishes*, which also appeared in 1975 (when it was first published in New York), for the same dervishes appear in the film and the photographs in Friedlander's study. In Lewis' assessment (*Rumi: Past and Present*, p. 526), Friedlander 'recounts popular and legendary anecdotes of Rumi's life, reflecting the information purveyed to tourists in Konya'. For other examples of 'Rumi on video', mostly from the 1970s and 1990s, see ibid., pp. 637–8.

196 On the stages in the resumption of public performance of the *sama'*, see Friedlander, *The Whirling Dervishes*, pp. 112–14. (Note that Lewis, *Rumi: Past and Present*, p. 637, dates the filming of *Turning* to 1973, during the commemoration of the 700th anniversary of Rumi's death, celebrated on 17 December.)

197 See above, and Schimmel, *The Triumphant Sun*, p. 146.

198 On the Çatal Höyük settlement, its fertility cult and Mother Goddess, see Akurgal, *Ancient Civilizations and Ruins of Turkey*, pp. 3–4. The author suggests that the settlement dates from approximately 6,000–5,650 BC. Mural paintings at Çatal Höyük furnish evidence that activities anticipated 'the bull dance ... made famous by the Minoans of Greece', prompting the narrator of the film to ask 'is this where the dance begins?'

199 See ibid., p. 317, and plate 93. The author notes that Alacahöyük was an important centre from the fourth millennium onwards, experiencing glorious times in the Early Bronze Age and Hittite eras.

200 On reaching Ephesus, Akurgal notes (ibid., pp. 142, 147), 'the Greeks found that the mother goddess, Kybele, held sway as chief deity, as in almost every part of Anatolia. In order to placate the indigenous peoples, they adopted a policy of syncretism and introduced the worship of Artemis and Kybele in the same deity'.

201 On Ephesus, see ibid., pp. 142ff.; on the Temple of Artemis there, p. 147.

202 For the Church of the Virgin Mary in Ephesus, see ibid., p. 144.

203 Tollemache, 'An Obituary of Bulent Rauf'. Associates recall Rauf having warned them to be vigilant after he was gone, particularly in case other figures or movements attempted a 'takeover' of Beshara.

204 At a meeting after a Trustees' gathering at Sherborne House just before his last illness, he had confirmed the arrangements that had been put in place and suggested that certain associates keep a check on things. This included a confirmation of Young's particular responsibility.

205 He studied archaeology and architecture.

206 This statement betrays a clear recognition among some associates of the difference between Rauf and his 'successor'. Such sentiments can be understood in terms of Weber's dichotomy of charismatic versus rational–legal modes of authority and leadership (charismatic leadership being of course essential for many, if not all, forms of cultural innovation). See, for example, Chryssides, *Exploring New Religions*, p. 6. In contrast, one associate who is critical of how Beshara has developed since Rauf's death suggests that some associates *failed* to grasp this distinction, and 'quickly put Young into "a quasi-Bulent" role', having misunderstood what had been expected of him. For a discussion of the potential impacts of the death of the founder in the context of NRMs relating these to Weberian categories, see Barrett, *The New Believers*, pp. 58ff.

207 Young has delivered talks across the years, several of which have been published in the *JMIAS*. These are 'Ibn 'Arabi', *JMIAS*, I (1982), pp. 3–19; 'Between the Yea and the Nay', II (1984), pp. 1–4; 'Universal Nature', VI (1987), pp. 21–32; 'The Straight Path', XXIII (1998), pp. 9–18; 'Ibn 'Arabi: Towards a Universal Point of View', XXV (1999), pp. 88–97. He has also contributed brief essays and comments posted on the Beshara website. His work draws on a repertoire of Beshara sources, and typically refers to Qur'anic verses and hadith cited therein.

208 The bed has been replaced with his favourite armchair.

209 Cf. Hermansen, 'Hybrid Identity Formations', p. 184, observing that Bawa Muhaiyaddeen's room at the Fellowship in Philadelphia 'has become a sort of sacred space or shrine ... where disciples may engage in private reflection and meet ... to discuss spiritual matters'. This is in addition to his tomb–shrine (*mazar*) in Coatesville, a simple white room with a cupola. For further detail, see Webb, Tradition and Innovation, pp. 96–7.

On the broader sacralisation of space in Britain brought about by the presence of living and dead sufi masters, see Geaves, *The Sufis of Britain*, pp. 68–9, 129.

Displays of devotion such as those observed at Bawa's room at the Fellowship (where members often kiss his pillow as they enter, for example) do not arise in the case of Rauf's rooms at Chisholme. Indeed the latter are sometimes put to 'mundane' use, for receptions, for example, when food and drink are served. The difference is a simple reflection of the contrasting styles of Bawa and Rauf as spiritual guides. Bawa echoed the approach of the popular sufi shaykh, while Rauf self-consciously repudiated this.

210 Qur'an 2: 156. Photographs of the Monument are displayed alongside those of Rauf in associates' homes.

211 A *maqam* is a sacred place. It often designates the tomb of a sufi saint, but may also designate a space dedicated to a saint in a location where they are not buried (and may not necessarily have visited in the flesh). The belief is that spiritual benefit can be derived from visiting a *maqam*, emanating from the saint's *baraka* or blessing. See further Ch. 6. For examples of tombs of (and *maqam*s dedicated to) sufi figures in the USA that serve as places of visitation, see Hermansen, 'Hybrid Identity Formations', pp. 183–4.

212 In fact there is no name plaque, and Rauf did not specify whether or not he wished there to be one.

213 See www.bulentrauf.org.

214 See, for example, Hermansen, 'Hybrid Identity Formations', p. 183, on the objects left by pilgrims on the grave of Samuel Lewis in New Mexico.

Chapter 5

1 Tollemache, 'An Obituary of Bulent Rauf'. Cf. Annett, ed., *The Many Ways of Being*, p. 84: 'Beshara began in Britain five years ago, when a mysterious Turk was sent here with the sole purpose of initiating the group.'

2 Ryan, Conversion to the Essence, p. 342.

3 Peter Young, 'Reorientation for the New Era', Beshara website.

4 Stephen Hirtenstein, 'The Basis of a Universal Religion', *Beshara Magazine*, 1, p. 6.

5 See *The Twenty-nine Pages*, back cover.

6 Jane Clark, 'Fulfilling Our Potential: Ibn 'Arabi's Understanding of Man in a Contemporary Context', *JMIAS*, XXX (2001), p. 29; cf. Coates, *Ibn 'Arabi and Modern Thought*, p. 29.

7 Young, 'Ibn 'Arabi: Towards A Universal Point of View', p. 94. For elaboration on this 'task', see below.

8 For example Chodkiewicz, *Seal of the Saints*, p. 47 n. 1, points to the organic connection between the 'purely metaphysical' content of Ibn 'Arabi's work (his metaphysical 'doctrine') and his initiatic teaching. These two inseparable, complementary and alternating perspectives inform his entire oeuvre in such a way that his doctrine can be described as 'the written translation of a visionary knowledge and a personal experience of sainthood' (p. 18).

9 See the *White Fusus*, 1, pp. v–vi. The reference is to Ibn 'Arabi's preface to the *Futuhat*: see Layla Shamash and Stephen Hirtenstein, 'From the Preface to the *Futuhat al-Makkiya* by Ibn 'Arabi', *JMIAS*, IV (1985), pp. 4–5. On Ibn 'Arabi's typology of sainthood and the role of the Seals, see below.

10 Brass, Foreword, the *White Fusus*, 2, p. vi.

11 See the *White Fusus*, inside cover. Note Young's clarification: '[I]n speaking of Ibn 'Arabi, we must speak first of his reality, his real place in the Ipseity of God. His life history, like the relative world, is illusion; only from the viewpoint of Reality is it the truth in Truth.' Peter Young, 'Ibn 'Arabi', p. 3.

12 Young, 'Ibn 'Arabi', p. 6.

13 Jane Carroll, *MIAS Newsletter*, 16 (Autumn 2000), p. 5.

The phrase 'from the most ancient place' (based on Ibn 'Arabi's own claim to this effect: Ibn 'Arabi, *Fusus al-hikam* [Cairo, 1946], p. 47) is frequently quoted by associates in their projection of his teaching; see for example Carroll, 'Timelessness and Time', p. 86. As we noted earlier, Ibn 'Arabi claimed to have been divinely inspired in his writings, whether directly or via the Prophet, as in the case of the *Fusus*.

Compare associates' claims with those of its founder concerning the origin of Subud: 'Subud is not foreign. It did not "originate" in the East and it did not "come" to the West … It comes from the Spirit of God.' (See Barrett, *The New Believers*, p. 354.)

14 This and the following quotations: Brass, Foreword, the *White Fusus*, 2, pp. v–vi. Cf. Coates, *Ibn 'Arabi and Modern Thought*, p. 11: 'What is clear is that the metaphysics of Ibn 'Arabi is not a personal intellectual construction of his own … it avoids the accusation of being based on the extravagances of the human intellect.'

15 See Feild, *The Last Barrier*, pp. 71, 93–4.

16 See for example *The Twenty-nine Pages*, p. 6.

17 Ibid, p. 9, introduces concepts of (Absolute) Reality, Existence and Being separately, clarifies relations between them, and implicitly points to their interchangeable usage: 'Absolute Being, or Absolute Existence, or Absolute Reality, which is Entire, Indivisible, Universal and Infinite, is the Origin of all that follows.' Examples of their interchangeable use can be seen in quotations from Beshara materials throughout the present study.

As Chodkiewicz, *The Spiritual Writings of Amir 'Abd al-Kader*, p. 193 n. 55, argues, it is unacceptable to translate the expression *wahdat al-wujud* as 'unity of existence': 'unity of being' or 'oneness of being' is preferable. Addas, *Ibn 'Arabi: The Voyage of No Return*, p. 80, elaborates: 'It is preferable to avoid the frequent use … of "unicity of existence"; the word "existence" implying, etymologically, a relationship to an origin and is thus appropriate, properly speaking, only in reference to what is "outside God".' See further Chittick, 'The Central Point', p. 20 n. 2, stating a preference for 'Oneness of Being' to its alternatives, including 'unity of existence'.

18 See Young, 'Reorientation for the New Era'.

19 On this nature of man, see for example Chittick, *Sufism: A Short Introduction*, pp. 82–3.

20 For a brief introduction, see Chittick, Ibn 'Arabi, pp. 506–7 and Ibn 'Arabi and His School, pp. 65–8; also 'The Central Point', pp. 33ff.

21 See Rauf, *Addresses*, pp. 50–1. See further pp. 22–3, 8, 37, 61.

22 For an introduction to the fundamentals of Ibn 'Arabi's metaphysics, see Addas, *Ibn 'Arabi: The Voyage of No Return*, pp. 79–102; Chittick, Ibn 'Arabi and His School, pp. 58ff. For a more detailed treatment and translations, see Chittick, *The Sufi Path of Knowledge*.

23 Translated in Claude Addas, 'The Experience and Doctrine of Love in Ibn 'Arabi', *JMIAS*, XXXII (2002), p. 32. A *hadith qudsi* is a hadith that has been transmitted by the Prophet directly from God. As Addas, *Ibn 'Arabi: The Voyage of No Return*, p. 91, notes, jurists have often denied the authenticity of this particular one.

For examples of references to this hadith in Beshara materials, see Rauf, *Addresses II*, p. 28; 'Beshara: Swyre Farm'; Young, 'Between the Yea and the Nay', p. 3, 'Ibn 'Arabi', p. 8 and 'Ibn 'Arabi: Towards a Universal Point of View', p. 96; Roberts, 'Reaffirmation', p. 26; Alison Yiangou, 'Facing the Unknown: Some Reflections on the Importance of Ibn 'Arabi to Today', *Muhyiddin Ibn 'Arabi A. D. 1165–1240: His Life and Times (Proceedings of the 7th Annual Symposium of the MIAS, Oxford, March 1999)*, p. 33. Feild, *The Last Barrier*, p. 74, has Rauf prescribe the hadith for him as the basis for a daily contemplation.

Implicit within this hadith, the two major principles of Ibn 'Arabi's teaching just described are elaborated by Rauf thus: 'there is nothing else or other than that Only One and Unique existent, wherein the plurality is a relativisation of the Absolute Oneness – looked at from the uniqueness towards multiplicity … [T]he devolution of the absolute uniqueness of the Ipseity to the multiplicity of immanence … is like a grand staircase thrown down from above at man's feet, and where the man stands ready to ascend towards his origin and essence'. See Rauf, *Addresses II*, pp. 22–3.

24 See Rauf, *Addresses*, p. 18.

25 Ibn 'Arabi implicitly adopts the hadith as the starting point of the chapter on Adam in the *Fusus*: see Ibn 'Arabi, *Fusus al-hikam*, pp. 48ff.

Ryan, Conversion to the Essence, pp. 339–40, incorporates this opening statement in the context of a comment on Ibn 'Arabi's fundamental teaching. He writes: 'Ibn 'Arabi was given to pronounce in the very first sentence of the first chapter of his *Fusus* … "God wanted to see [the] essence of His most perfect Names whose number is infinite" – and if you like you can equally well say: "God wanted to see His own essence in one global object which having been blessed with existence summarized the Divine Order so that there He could manifest His mystery to Himself."' In this, Ryan follows the Bosnevi commentary: Bosnevi concludes his introduction with the observation that 'the Divine tongue … spoke the words: "I was a hidden treasure and I loved that it be known".' See the *White Fusus*, 1, p. 92.

As Addas, 'The Experience and Doctrine of Love', p. 31, notes, 'Several works – those of Corbin in particular – have shown that Akbarian cosmogenesis is nurtured entirely by this Divine saying.' For a succinct introduction to this cosmogenesis and Ibn 'Arabi's ontological theories, see Chittick, Ibn 'Arabi and His School, pp. 60–5.

26 Cf. Reza Shah-Kazemi, The Metaphysics of Interfaith Dialogue: Sufi Perspectives on the Universality of the Qur'anic Message, in James Cutsinger, ed., *Paths to the Heart – Sufism and the Christian East* (Bloomington, 2002), pp. 152–3 n. 28.

27 On knowledge, see Chittick, *The Sufi Path of Knowledge*, pp. 180–1. This cites the *Futuhat*, where Ibn 'Arabi writes immediately after the *hadith qudsi*: 'They only came to know God through that which He reported about Himself: His love for us, His mercy towards us, His clemency, His tenderness, His loving-kindness, His descent into limitation that we may conceive of Him in imaginal form.' Speaking of the 'internal revelation of Reality to Itself', Young, 'Ibn 'Arabi', p. 7, notes that 'while never ceasing to be Love, Knowledge becomes the turning point of Love, or Knowledge is the outward face of Love.'

Regarding mercy, James W. Morris in Chodkiewicz, ed., *The Meccan Revelations*, 1, pp. 77, 258 n. 47, counts Qur'an 7: 156 ('My mercy extends to all things') and the *hadith qudsi* 'My mercy has preceded My anger' among the key leitmotifs of Ibn 'Arabi's thought. As Chittick, Ibn 'Arabi, p. 502, notes, 'Ibn 'Arabi constantly comes back to the theme of mercy as the underlying, all-embracing, fundamental quality of reality.' Pablo Beneito, 'The Presence of Superlative Compassion (*Rahamut*)', *JMIAS*, XXIV (1998), p. 56, demonstrates that, in one respect, *rahma* (benevolence, mercy and compassion) in Ibn 'Arabi's thought can be equated with existence (*wujud*): from the metaphysical perspective, Ibn 'Arabi thus gives it 'all the attributes of existence'. See also the discussion of this theme by an associate: Layla Shamash, 'The Cosmology of Compassion or Macrocosm in the Microcosm', *JMIAS*, XXVIII (2000), pp. 18–34.

28 Addas, 'The Experience and Doctrine of Love', p. 34. The place and meaning of love in Ibn 'Arabi's thought have been widely discussed. See for example ibid., pp. 25–44, especially pp. 25–6; Corbin, *Alone with the Alone*, pp. 105–35; Maurice Gloton, 'The Qur'anic Inspiration of Ibn 'Arabi's Vocabulary of Love: Etymological Links and Doctrinal Development', *JMIAS*, XXVII (2000), pp. 37–52; Elmore, 'The *Uwaysi* Spirit of Autodidactic Sainthood', p. 39; Pablo Beneito, 'The Servant of the Loving One: On the Adoption of the Character Traits of al-*Wadud*', *JMIAS*, XXXII (2002), pp. 1–24.

As Gloton, 'The Qur'anic Inspiration', p. 41, puts it: 'Although indefinable, according to Ibn 'Arabi, Love can be considered as the internal movement, the interior attraction which allows a reality – the Divine Being or any other entity – to exteriorize its possibilities, to open up the seed of which it consists and to become a fully developed tree capable of ... bearing fruit in the image of the divine Life to which it is intimately bound.'

On the role of the Divine Breath or 'Spirit' (often termed by Ibn 'Arabi 'the Breath of the All-Merciful' – *Nafas al-Rahman*) in the act of creation, see Chittick, *Sufism: A Short Introduction*, p. 78 and *The Sufi Path of Knowledge*, pp. 127–30.

29 See *Christ*: internal paper attributed to Rashid Hornsby, n.d.

30 On love in sufi teachings in general, see Chittick, *Sufism: A Short Introduction*, pp. 61ff.

31 Personal correspondence from Rauf to a close associate (1973).

32 Rauf, *Addresses*, p. 5.

33 Rauf, *Addresses II*, pp. 46–7.

34 Peter Young, '11th September 2001: A Response from Love', Beshara website.

Associates enjoy psychological benefits from this emphasis of love: it furnishes a basis for a reflexive attitude that is accepting and compassionate, and a wholesome perspective on the operation of desire. Cf. Hirtenstein, *The Unlimited Mercifier*, p. 195.

35 Addas, 'The Experience and Doctrine of Love', p. 33.

36 Ibid., pp. 28, 33; see further Pablo Beneito, 'On the Divine Love of Beauty', *JMIAS*, XVIII (1995), pp. 1–22.

37 For this hadith, see *Sahih Muslim: Iman*, hadith 147; also Addas, 'The Experience and Doctrine of Love', p. 33. For a reference to it in the *Futuhat*, see Ibn 'Arabi, *Les Illuminations de la Mecque/The Meccan Illuminations, textes choisies/selected texts*, trans. Michel Chodkiewicz, Denis Gril and James W. Morris (Paris, 1988), p. 97 ('On the Beauty of God and the Beauty of the World').

38 For this and the two following examples, see Rauf, *Addresses*, pp. 61, 71, 49; for further examples, pp. 44, 60–1, 66–7, 69. Concerning Rauf, *Addresses II*, a reviewer remarks: 'It is beauty and the love of Beauty that is mentioned throughout the book, whether dealing with cooking, personal reflections, history or the most essential matters concerning Being and the "movement" of Being'. See Arthur Martin, *MIAS Newsletter*, 18 (Summer 2002), p. 6.

39 A comparable concern for beauty is discernible in the case of Schuon and his followers: see for example Sedgwick, *Against the Modern World*, pp. 122–3.

40 Rauf, *Addresses*, p. 66.

41 Chittick, *Sufism: A Short Introduction*, p. 65, sets out Ibn 'Arabi's argument to this effect.

42 As Chittick, *Rumi and the Mawlawiyyah*, p. 120, writes, 'Probably no Sufi order emphasises beauty in theory and in practice as much as the Mawlawis. Certainly Sufis in general are the first to recall the Prophet's saying "God is beautiful and He loves beauty", but the Mawlawis have been especially thorough in drawing all the consequences of this teaching for the spiritual life.'

43 Kiliç, '"The Ibn al-'Arabi of the Ottomans"', p. 110, writes: 'How [Ibn 'Arabi's] universality was understood and interpreted in a particular locality is a very important subject in the history of Sufism, and one that awaits more research.' James Winston Morris, '"... Except His Face": The Political and Aesthetic Dimensions of Ibn 'Arabi's Legacy', *JMIAS*, XXIII (1998), p. 26, adds: 'the real complexity and distinctive subtlety of Ibn 'Arabi's thought best emerges when he is compared with such figures as al-Ghazali and ... Suhrawardi – both of them likewise "mystics" and "philosopher-theologians" deeply grounded in Islamic theology. In this contrast, we can quickly grasp that what is unique in Ibn 'Arabi, in contrast with al-Ghazali, is the *explicit*, truly universal focus of his metaphysical framework ... The appeal to Islamic tradition and the depth of familiarity with that tradition is equally central in both figures, but ... Ibn 'Arabi renders explicit what remains largely implicit in al-Ghazali's writing – and therefore becomes accessible and potentially useful to readers of every spiritual tradition, not simply Muslims.'

44 Yiangou, 'Facing the Unknown', p. 30.

45 Christopher Ryan, 'On the Brink', *MIAS Newsletter*, 18 (Summer 2002), p. 1.

46 Clark, 'Fulfilling Our Potential', p. 36.

47 See especially Affifi, *The Mystical Philosophy*, pp. 191–4.

48 There is explicit mention of one specific Qur'anic verse only, on which Ibn 'Arabi commented. See *The Twenty-nine Pages*, p. 66.

49 Michel Chodkiewicz, *An Ocean without Shore*, p. 24, suggests that Ibn 'Arabi's work in its entirety can be considered as 'a Qur'anic commentary'. Similarly, Morris, '"... Except His Face"', p. 29, describes as 'extraordinary' the extent to which Ibn 'Arabi's writings are 'inextricably embedded in their Islamic scriptural and cultural matrix'. Rauf's own focus notwithstanding, he too argued (*Addresses II*, p. 41) that Ibn 'Arabi follows the Qur'an 'assiduously, without ever deviating, even when scholars and "doctors" find divergence in the words of Ibn 'Arabi from the practice of the Muhammedan religion, thus "missing" the depth of the Muhammedian way'.

50 This associate continues that Rauf added also works of Rumi, 'Abd al-Karim Jili and 'Abd al-Rahman Jami 'that are relevant to bringing out a particular perspective'. While he disagreed with him on certain details, Jili systematised the thought of Ibn 'Arabi and contributed to making his major ideas more widely known: on him see Schimmel, *Mystical Dimensions of Islam*, pp. 281–2. On Jami, see Ch. 1.

51 If they really understood, 'they would recognize God in every form and in every belief'. See *The Bezels of Wisdom*, p. 283. On Ibn 'Arabi's notion of the 'god created in belief(s)' (as opposed to the Absolute God/Real/Truth) and its ramifications, see Chittick, *The Sufi Path of Knowledge*, pp. 335ff.; also Shah-Kazemi, The Metaphysics of Interfaith Dialogue, p. 150.

Ibn 'Arabi's argument is cited in MIAS publicity materials. There is also an allusion to it in 'A Note from Mr. Bulent Rauf in addition to the Minutes of the AGM', Report of the AGM of the MIAS, 26 October 1985, p. 14.

52 See *Kernel of the Kernel*, p. 1. This is repeated in various paraphrases by associates: see, for example, Hornsby, in *Intimations*, p. x.

53 See the *White Fusus*, 1, inside cover.

54 'A Note from Mr. Bulent Rauf' cites Qur'an 5: 48 (which Rauf translates 'Had we wished we would have made you all of one religion ...') by way of confirmation of 'the intentional diversity of belief'.

55 Stuart Kenner, *MIAS Newsletter*, 15 (Spring 2000), p. 2.

56 See Peter Young, 'United by Oneness: Global Considerations for the Present' (paper delivered at MIAS Symposium, August 2000), Beshara website. For further examples of the direct and personal application of the basic thrust of Ibn 'Arabi's teaching, see Notes from the Mead Hall, Beshara website.

57 See Rauf, *Addresses*, p. 54; also *Addresses II*, p. 46. Cf. Rauf's comment to Feild (*The Last Barrier*, p. 184): 'Love is brought to life within you as you surrender to God so that there is only Him, and thus the possibility of perfected man.'

58 See Young, 'United by Oneness'. This has always been the case, he explains: those who have come to self-knowledge have been known as 'saints, mystics, the spiritual giants'.

59 Young, '11th September 2001'. Cf. Rauf, *Addresses*, p. 39.

60 See, for example, 'Who will die today?' (Notes from the Mead Hall, 11 March 2004); 'Questioning the Question' (Notes from Tel Aviv, 10 April 2004), Beshara website.

61 See for example Coates, *Ibn 'Arabi and Modern Thought*, p. 13. The author describes as a general feature of Ibn 'Arabi's metaphysical outlook the fact that this has 'nothing to do with the petty and mean-spirited, or the dogmatic and the intolerant. It ... continually reaffirms the great nature which God has essentially bestowed upon the human Self in creating man in His image.'

62 This can translate into a tendency to deflect responsibility away from the individual, even though associates in principle recognise individual responsibility. A 'bad' act is understood as one based on 'a limited belief'.

63 The implications of the monistic perspective for attitudes to such issues have been subject to continuous debate among associates.

In Islamic culture one of the most powerful arguments against the monistic worldview pivots on what is seen as its inherent threat of moral relativism. The following comment by Fazlur Rahman (cited in Schimmel, *Mystical Dimensions of Islam*, p. 273) sums up the point: 'A thoroughly monistic system, no matter how pious and conscientious it may claim to be, can not, by its very nature, take seriously the objective validity of moral standards'. Schimmel explains thus: 'For [in a thoroughly monistic system], both good and evil are from God, and as much as Muhammad is the manifestation of the name *al-Hadi*, "who guides right", so much is Satan the manifestation of the name *al-Mudill*, "who leads astray". Everything is in perfect order – that is the meaning of God's *rahma*, "mercy".'

64 Christopher Ryan, 'Globalisation of the Spirit: Prerequisite for a New Dispensation', *MIAS Newsletter*, 17 (Autumn 2001), p. 16.

65 Cf. Hirtenstein, 'Ibn al-'Arabi', alluding to the conversation between Bayazid al-Bistami and the divine.

66 Cf. Coates, *Ibn 'Arabi and Modern Thought*, p. 30. For another associate's reflections on the 'incessant stream of thought which constitutes the illusion that is "my life"', and its absence as a condition for 'how we as Human Beings are meant to be, like the rest of nature, places of expression of the Real', see '"I" and "my life"', response to 'Questioning the Question' (Notes from the Mead Hall, 10 April 2004), Beshara website.

Underlining the importance of receptivity, Rauf associated it with 'complete inaction'. He referred to Beshara among other esoteric schools as 'a system of receptivity' to which one submits, which can take the aspirant more directly to 'learning' through 'being given'. See Rauf, *Addresses II*, pp. 37 and 58 respectively.

67 Cf. Roberts, 'Reaffirmation': 'In choosing to make himself a servant, a man must … take his cue from the one served. To do this, it is necessary to adopt the point of view of the one served … service leads to identification with the lord, which is union'. On Absolute Servitude according to Ibn 'Arabi, see Addas, *Ibn 'Arabi: The Voyage of No Return*, pp. 37–8.

68 This is a reference to Bosnevi's remark that 'the heart of the *'arif* has no definite conditioning so that the *haqq* reveals Itself to it according to that non-condition'. See Mercer, Introduction, p. 3.

For a discussion of the Beshara concept of servanthood as 'emptiness', see 'My Life: The Movie' (Notes from the Mead Hall, 4 March 2004), Beshara website.

69 As the Divine Will speaks ultimately through the emptied/receptive heart or the true Self, the individual can become preoccupied with their own feelings and thoughts, for it is in these that the thrust of the Divine Will can be ascertained.

70 Cf. Hirtenstein, *The Unlimited Mercifier*, p. 77.

71 See 'Courses at Chisholme', p. 29.

72 'What is Beshara?' Cf. Yiangou, 'Facing the Unknown', pp. 30–1, which argues that recent changes in thinking in the political arena, science and ecology, and the environmental crisis all suggest that 'the traditional barriers between the spiritual and the material are beginning to seem like Berlin Walls'.

73 Yiangou, 'Facing the Unknown', p. 31.

74 As used here, the term describes a particular way of integrating reality through an overarching, story-like plot.

75 This is *khatm wilayat al-anbiya' wa'l-rusul*, identical to *khatm al-wilaya al-'amma*.

76 See Hakim, 'The Spirit and the Son of the Spirit', pp. 18–24, which draws mainly on the *Futuhat* and occasionally the *'Anqa' mughrib*. Chodkiewicz, *Seal of the Saints*, chapters 8–9, reproduces relevant passages from the *Fusus*. See also Gerald T. Elmore, 'The "Millennial" Motif in Ibn al-'Arabi's *Book of the Fabulous Gryphon*', *Journal of Religion*, 81: 3 (2001), pp. 410–37, especially pp. 415ff. For a straightforward treatment of this complex area, see Hirtenstein, *The Unlimited Mercifier*, chapter 10. As we noted earlier, presentations of Ibn 'Arabi's doctrine of the Seals differ in details.

77 For example, in his only explicit mention of Rumi's role in the spiritual evolution of mankind, in 'A Trip to Turkey', p. 10 (discussed below), Rauf wrote: 'But these considerations are not yet easily appreciable to students of esotericism, and it is here mentioned simply to give you an intimation of the unfathomable deepness of the presence that ... Rumi represents.' Rauf possibly alludes here to his belief that, as 'time' advances, such concepts will be grasped with increasing ease.

An associate describes Rauf's statement concerning Rumi as 'a pearl' embedded in the document, which not all students might appreciate.

78 This is attributed to Rashid Hornsby but was 'essentially dictated to him' by Rauf. The version cited here has been edited slightly by Young. It has not been published but is used internally.

79 On the interchangeable use of these two vocalisations, and for discussions of each, see Elmore, *Islamic Sainthood in the Fullness of Time*, p. 110 n. 7. Following the tendency in Beshara, we use only the form *wilaya* in this volume.

80 In Ibn 'Arabi's discussion the three paradigms are represented by the terms *jalal* with regard to Moses (Majesty, representing transcendence), *jamal* for Jesus (Beauty, referring to immanence) and *kamal* for Muhammad (Perfection or Completeness). See Ibn 'Arabi, *Kitab al-Jalal wa'l-jamal*, trans. Rabia Terri Harris, *JMIAS*, VIII (1989), pp. 5–32.

81 For perceptions of Jesus in Muslim piety, see Tarif Khalidi, ed. and trans., *The Muslim Jesus: Sayings and Stories in Islamic Literature* (Cambridge, MA, 2001). For a contemporary sufi treatment, see Javad Nurbakhsh, *Jesus in the Eyes of the Sufis* (London, 1983): Nurbakhsh claims (p. 9) that 'It is the Sufis who have attempted to preserve the memory of Jesus as he really was, alive in their minds, and in the minds of others, and to keep him in their hearts.' For further contemporary examples, see Westerlund, *The Contextualisation of Sufism in Europe*, p. 27. For sufi celebration of Jesus more generally, see Kenneth Cragg, *Jesus and the Muslim: An Exploration* (London, 1985), pp. 59–63.

82 This is a reference to the fact that, as a prophet, Jesus was the epitome of saintliness, while his prophetic message did not take the form of a law, but of love. For further discussion of Jesus' saintliness, see below.

83 On the significance of this role in relation to the Prophet Muhammad, see for example Addas, *Ibn 'Arabi: The Voyage of No Return*, p. 45.

84 On 'universality' as 'the distinctive reality of Ibn 'Arabi', see Young, 'Ibn 'Arabi', p. 11; also Rauf, *Addresses II*, pp. 39–41.

85 In this associate's opinion, Chodkiewicz's treatment in *Seal of the Saints* (which brings together the many passages dealing with the Seals in the *Futuhat*, the *Fusus* and elsewhere) suffers from such confusion.

86 Young, 'Ibn 'Arabi', pp. 8–11. Emphasis in original; footnotes omitted here. Young had written this text in 1976 at the end of the intensive course he had attended at Chisholme, and delivered it at Swyre Farm and an Edinburgh Festival Fringe event during that summer. Rauf heard about the paper on his return from Turkey and expressed his appreciation of it; he later suggested that it appear in the first volume of the *JMIAS*.

87 He read this in an article by Dom Sylvester Houédard in *MIAS Newsletter*, Summer 1990, later published as 'Notes on the More Than Human Saying: "Unless You Know Yourself You Cannot Know God"', *JMIAS*, XI (1992), pp. 2–3.

88 See Peter Young, 'The New Covenant', Beshara website.

89 Jeremiah 4: 4.

90 Ibid., 31: 31.

91 The quotation is from Matthew 28: 20.

92 Young cites Bursevi (without providing a specific reference in the *White Fusus*) to explain the nature of this covenant: 'that they may not pray to or face anything other than God'.

93 This is illustrated through a citation from Ibn 'Arabi: 'each person was the imam (leader in prayer) of his own microcosm'. Again there is no specific reference, but we can trace this to *The Wisdom of The Prophets*, pp. 128–9 (see also Ibn 'Arabi, *Fusus al-hikam*, p. 223).

94 Carroll, 'Timelessness and Time', p. 78. Note that 'completion' here is synonymous with 'perfection'.

95 Ibid., p. 79.

96 Ibid.

97 Presumably an allusion to the saints visited during the trip to Turkey.

98 Carroll, 'Timelessness and Time', pp. 80–1.

99 See Michel Chodkiewicz, 'The Endless Voyage', in Mercer, ed., *The Journey of the Heart*, p. 83.

100 See Peter Coates, 'Ibn 'Arabi: The Unity of Existence and the Era' (paper presented at the MIAS Symposium, Oxford, May 2003), p. 7.

101 In addition to *Christ*, there are two other significant sources in the public domain: Feild, *The Last Barrier*, pp. 89–91, 166–8, and Young, 'Ibn 'Arabi'.

A review of Young's paper 'United by Oneness' in an *MIAS Newsletter* refers explicitly to the Second Coming, while the text of his talk posted on the Beshara website does not. See Mhairi MacMillan, *MIAS Newsletter*, 16 (Autumn 2000), p. 6; cf. Young, 'United by Oneness'.

102 An allusion to the title of John Lofland's well-known study of the methods of the Unification Church in its early years in the USA, published in 1966: *Doomsday Cult: A Study of Conversion, Proselytization and Maintenance of Faith* (Englewood Cliffs, NJ).

103 Writing in the mid-1970s, Annett, ed., *The Many Ways of Being*, p. 85, reported that 'the long-term aim of [Beshara] is to prepare for the Second Coming of Christ'. This event, he explained, 'will herald the end of a great cycle in man's evolution – whereas the First Coming brought the possibility of going straight to the Creator, the Second Coming will see the fulfilment of this'. His informants were evidently willing to talk about this.

Rauf's very choice of the name Beshara for the emerging spiritual project both reflected the widespread eschatological preoccupations of the time and served to underline this concern within the movement. (The noun *bishara* is thus used by Christian Arabs to denote the Annunciation or Good News of Jesus; the author thanks Michel Chodkiewicz for highlighting this point.) Later, associates would describe the 'good news' denoted by the term as 'the truth that God is One and no other Being exists'.

104 Rauf's sense of urgency was evident in the following comment, reportedly made to Feild in the course of an explanation of the meaning of the Second Coming: 'You may feel that I'm rushing you, that you can't possibly grasp everything that I'm telling you now. But the situation is more urgent than you understand'. See Feild, *The Last Barrier*, p. 166.

105 At this time many NRMs, New Agers and New Age communities held such views. As the predicted apocalypse failed to arrive, the apocalyptic element was gradually replaced in many New Age communities by a vanguardist attitude of living 'as if the New Age had already come'. See Hanegraaff, *New Age Religion*, pp. 96–103.

106 See Barrett, *The New Believers*, p. 80. He adds: 'Wars, earthquakes, famines, climatic changes … all are used as evidence that these are the End Times'.

Bennett's convictions furnish an example of the mood of the time, apt for the perceived affinity between his views and those of Beshara. Writing in 1974 in the preface to the American edition of *Witness* (published in 1975), he commented on the development of his understanding since the appearance of the first edition: 'in 1965, I gave my reasons for believing that we are in the early stages of … the Second Coming of Christ which heralds the end of the present world. I am often asked if this is … to be taken literally, and if so, whether I still hold the same conviction. The answer to both questions is that I am no less convinced than … ten years ago and … discern growing evidence that the great event is in progress. We have to separate fact from fantasy, figurative representation of real signs from interpretations made a thousand or two thousand years before the time of change arrived. The facts are plain.' See *Witness*, p. iii; also Paul Davies, 'The End of the World according to William Blake and J. G. Bennett', *Sacred Web*, 8 (2001), pp. 105ff. Washington, *Madam Blavatsky's Baboon*, pp. 389–90, reports that during his visits to a Naqshbandi shaykh in Damascus in the early 1950s, Bennett was repeatedly told he had a vital role to play in the imminent Second Coming.

For an introduction to apocalyptic beliefs in NRMs and their origins in Jewish and Christian thought, see Barrett, *The New Believers*, chapter 7. We might point to the contrasting terms in which the Golden Age is imagined in Beshara and contemporary Christian millenarian thought/movements. For the sake of clarity, it should be emphasised that the millennium in Christian thinking refers to the Golden Age, the 1000-year period of rule which Christ will establish on earth, and has nothing to do in origin with the 1000-year calendraic period beginning January 2000 or 2001. The Christian and calendraic millennium are two quite different things, although for some people they do tie in neatly together: see ibid. p. 71. Beshara does not appear to have set special store by the approach of the new calendraic millennium, and regular New Year celebrations were organised at Chisholme. More importantly, in its capacity as a 'new beginning', the movement adopted the transition as an opportunity to reinforce the aptness of the Beshara perspective for the needs of humanity, as it 'set sail into the new millennium'. See Young, 'Reorientation for the New Era', p. 1.

107 A working distinction between apocalypticism and millenarianism is helpful here. Hanegraaff, *New Age Religion*, pp. 98–9, suggests that, in the typical apocalyptic vision, the existing worldly order is replaced by 'a radically different, *transcendent* order': it is thus destroyed and passes away. In contrast, the typical millenarian dream 'is one of a perfect, *earthly* realm', and is thus conceived in terms of immanence.

108 Islamic doctrine identifies Jesus as the one by whose descent the approach of the Hour (the Resurrection) is known. See 'Isa', EI², IV, pp. 84–5, and Arthur Jeffrey, The Descent of Jesus in Muhammadan Eschatology, in S. E. Johnson, ed., *The Joy of Study: Papers on the New Testament and Related Subjects presented to honour Frederick Clifton Grant* (New York, 1951), pp. 107–26. For examples of hadith concerning the Second Coming from the canonical Sunni collections, see Muhammad 'Ata' ur-Rahim and Ahmad Thomson, *Jesus, Prophet of Islam* (London, 1997), pp. 271–6.

Note the neglect in the Beshara vision of the figure of the Mahdi, closely associated in Islamic doctrine with the Second Coming. 'al-Mahdi', EI², V, pp. 1230–8, argues that belief in the Mahdi never became an essential part of Sunni doctrine in spite of the support it was given by some prominent hadith scholars and sufis. In later tradition the eschatological role of the Mahdi became more pronounced, and it became commonly accepted that he would rule the Muslim community at the time of Jesus' descent. Jesus would pray behind him, and he would help Jesus slay the anti-Christ. The absence of the anti-Christ (al-Dajjal) from the Beshara vision is similarly noteworthy. For an analysis of contemporary popular Muslim literature treating the anti-Christ, see Roberto Tottoli, 'Hadiths and Traditions in Some Recent Books upon the Dajjal (Anti-Christ)', *Oriente Moderno*, XXI (LXXXII): 1 (2002), pp. 55–75.

For Ibn 'Arabi's discussion of the Mahdi, see Chodkiewicz, *Seal of the Saints*, chapter 8, passim, and James W. Morris, At the End of Time, in Chodkiewicz, ed., *The Meccan Revelations*, 1, pp. 65ff. (a translation of chapter 366 of the *Futuhat*).

Note that some contemporary Islamic sufi views uphold the imminence of the Second Coming and the Last Days, seeing in the world today materialisation of the signs of the Hour and the forces of the anti-Christ. See for example Geaves, *The Sufis of Britain*, pp. 151–2, describing the apocalyptic and millenarian perceptions of Nazim al-Haqqani. The Perennialists/Traditionalists also advance a clear analysis of present conditions (which some project as 'extremely late times') in terms of the End Times: see below.

109 Quoting from the chapter on Seth in the *Fusus* (*The Wisdom of the Prophets*, p. 31), in *Christ* Rauf described the gradual degradation of the human mentality and the complete loss of knowledge of spiritual reality following the Golden Age, leading to the destruction of the earth. Students also read this chapter in *The Wisdom of the Prophets* in its entirety: its contents worried some of them, prompting them to ask him about eschatological issues. In this chapter Ibn 'Arabi predicted the fate of man after the Second Coming. As Austin, *The Bezels of Wisdom*, pp. 61–2, explains: 'He says that the last true human, in the line of Seth, will be born in China and that he will have an elder sister. He goes on to prophesy that thereafter men will become beasts, bereft of spirit and law, until the coming of the Hour. Thus, he indicates that that particular synthesis of spirit and nature, of which we are all a part, will come to an end and the link will be broken.'

110 This focus echoes a common tendency within New Age millenarianism towards a marked lack of interest in systematically developing the 'macro-historical' view of astrological cycles. Thus as Hanegraaff, *New Age Religion*, p. 102, puts it, 'All attention goes to the coming New Age and its contrast to the preceding one. Ideas about preceding cycles are extremely vague and sketchy at best, and the question what kind of period will follow the Age of Aquarius is apparently considered irrelevant.'

111 During the Summer Gathering at Chisholme in August 2004, for example, Young assured the audience of associates that the Second Coming remained a certainty, even if it did not take place during their lifetime or that of their children.

It is notable that the summary of the conversation on this occasion (written by an associate and posted on the Beshara website) alludes to the Second Coming but stops short of explicit reference to it: see Clark, 'Summer Gathering'.

112 See 'A Trip to Turkey', p. 10.

113 Rauf distinguished the kind of *qutb* he described here from the office of '*qutb* of his time'. The *qutb* (pl. *aqtab*) (pole or axis) is the highest member in the hierarchy of saints posited by sufis, a system which can be traced back at least to al-Hakim al-Tirmidhi (d.932). See 'Kutb', EI², V, pp. 543–6, and Richard Gramlich, *Die Schiitischen Derwischordern Persiens*, 2: *Glaube und Lehre* (Wiesbaden, 1976), pp. 158–81. For Ibn 'Arabi's treatment of this office, see Chodkiewicz, *Seal of the Saints*, pp. 53–4, 58, 92–8, 106, 125, and Hirtenstein, *The Unlimited Mercifier*, pp. 130–1.

114 See 'A Trip to Turkey', p. 10. At first sight, the wording here (repeated in the 2003 version of the document) appears to suggest an identification of Ibn 'Arabi himself with the Seal of Universal Sainthood. He of course alluded to himself as the Seal of Muhammadan Sainthood, responsible for the ongoing spiritual guidance of the Muslim community. (See for example Chodkiewicz, *Seal of the Saints*, chapters 7–9; M. Vâlsan, L'Investiture du Cheikh al-Akbar au centre suprême, in *L'Islam et la fonction de René Guénon* (Paris, 1984), pp. 177–91; Shamash and Hirtenstein, 'From the Preface to the *Futuhat al-Makkiya*', pp. 4–6.) Rauf's statement is properly understood by reading 'as' to indicate 'in the matter of' or 'concerning', rather than 'in his capacity as'. Nonetheless, the emphasis on the universal dimension of Ibn 'Arabi's own Sealhood in Rauf's presentation and in the analysis of the associate cited above (in particular his insistence on seeing the two Sealhoods as aspects of each other) must be noted.

Elmore sums up the implications of Ibn 'Arabi's own treatment of his relation to Jesus as the Seal of Universal Sainthood thus: 'The important point to establish is that Jesus and Ibn al-'Arabi are virtually equated as partners in the *khitam*-ate of saintship – whether the former is conceived as a spiritual, metahistorical archetype and the latter his existential instantiation, or "incarnation", as it were, or whether Ibn al-'Arabi is taken to be the more perfect realization of his forerunner's Christic sanctity.' As the author explains, the modes or categories of universal/general sealhood, represented by Jesus, and particular/specific sealhood, which Ibn 'Arabi exemplified, were also denominated 'absolute' and 'Muhammadan' respectively. The latter dichotomy was ambivalent, in that the term 'Muhammadan' could be understood 'either formally in the sense of "historically specific" or significatively, when it would connote something like "complete, perfect, ultimate"'. The textual evidence, Elmore points out, 'definitely supports both interpretations'. See Elmore, 'The "Millennial" Motif in Ibn al-'Arabi's *Book of the Fabulous Gryphon*', p. 420. Elmore's exploration of the 'septicentennial' motif in the *'Anqa' mughrib* exposes the centrality of the parallelism between Ibn 'Arabi and Jesus in Ibn 'Arabi's theory of the seals of prophecy and sainthood: see ibid. pp. 428ff.

It is noteworthy that *The Wisdom of the Prophets*, p. 26 n. 12, translates an apparent error by Burckhardt concerning the nature of the Sealhoods of Jesus and Ibn 'Arabi: see *La Sagesse des prophètes*, p. 50. In a note to his translation of the passage in the chapter on Seth introducing the Seal of Saints, Burckhardt thus identifies the 'Seal of Muhammadan Sainthood' with the 'Seal of Universal Sainthood' (instead of identifying this last Seal with the 'Seal of the Sainthood of the Prophets and the Messengers'). This error is recognised as such by well-informed associates consulted and does not appear to have shaped their understandings, in spite of the important place of this translation in study within the movement.

Note also that Burckhardt's reference here to *Futuhat*, IV: 57 is also apparently an error. Whether he used the Bulaq edition of the text (Cairo, 1293, 4 vols) or the later Beirut edition, the page cited and immediately preceding and following pages do not appear to discuss the Seals.

Finally, it is noteworthy that Rauf's explanation of Jesus' role and purpose in the Second Coming (outlined above) resonates closely in the manner of its expression with Burckhardt's paraphrase of the (incorrectly referenced) passage in the *Futuhat* where Ibn 'Arabi describes this. As noted earlier, Rauf appears not to have known the *Futuhat* well. Given that the nature of Jesus' role in the Second Coming is not clearly explicated in the *Fusus*, he may have relied in his own treatment on Burckhardt's sketch of this (perhaps among others). As translated in *The Wisdom of the Prophets*, Burckhardt thus writes: 'the "messenger" who will "seal" the present great cycle of humanity ... evidently cannot carry a new sacred law, which would only have sense for a collectivity having to exist as such, but will, on the other hand, bring forth the intrinsic truths common to all the traditional forms; he will address himself, then, to humanity in its entirety, which he will be able to do only by situating himself to a certain degree on an esoteric plane, which is that of the contemplative saint (*al-wali*):

115 'At the Still Point', n.d. The title of the note is drawn from the line of a poem by T. S. Eliot, with which *Turning* opens.

116 On the concept of spiritual intelligence, see Ch. 7.

117 See 'A Trip to Turkey', p. 12.

118 The *mamadd/mumidd al-himma*: see Ch. 6.

119 'A Trip to Turkey', p. 12.

120 Ibid., p. 10. It has not been possible to locate a reference to Rumi as *qutb* in literature surveyed, and scholars and Mevlevis consulted were unable to provide any such reference. 'Kutb', p. 545, observes that the special status as *aqtab* of four later sufis in particular is often upheld: 'Abd al-Qadir al-Jilani, Ahmad al-Rifa'i, Ahmad al-Badawi and Ibrahim al-Dasuqi.

For Rumi's teaching on the *qutb* and his view concerning the possible identity of its holder during his own time, see Lewis, *Rumi: Past and Present*, p. 410: 'We may conclude that Shams and then Salah al-Din and then Hosam al-Din, or perhaps Rumi himself as mirrored through the latter two, functioned as the *axis mundi* of Rumi's spiritual world.' Salah al-Din Zarkub was effectively a successor to Shams for Rumi, and Rumi selected him as his own successor. Upon Salah al-Din's death, Hosam al-Din became Rumi's successor; see pp. 206ff.

As Hirtenstein, *The Unlimited Mercifier*, p. 131, notes, in addition to the singular *qutb* around whom the exterior and interior universes turn, Ibn 'Arabi sometimes speaks of the *qutb* of a particular station; see also Chodkiewicz, *Seal of the Saints*, pp. 94–5. It is unlikely that Rauf's concept of Rumi's special *qutb*-ship can be related to this category, however.

Finally, the following comment by Friedlander, *The Whirling Dervishes*, p. 51, is noteworthy: 'Each day of their relationship, Shams subtly showed Jalalu'ddin that his spiritual powers had to be used on a universal level.'

121 Rauf related the encounter between the two when Rumi was a boy, telling of Ibn 'Arabi's celebrated observation as he watched him walk away behind his father: 'How strange! There goes a sea followed by an ocean.' He pointed to the 'link' made between them 'through ... Konevi, whom 'Arabi [sic] had taught while he was in Konya ... Rumi studied under him and became his intimate friend' (See 'A Trip to Turkey', pp. 10-11; cf. Feild, *The Last Barrier*, p. 107). In personal correspondence to a close associate (1973), he referred to the well-known account of Qunawi having invited Rumi to sit with him on the sheepskin that symbolised his position. When Rumi remarked that two could not sit on one sheepskin, Qunawi rose and flung the skin away. This account is repeated in Friedlander, *The Whirling Dervishes*, p. 44, where the author explains: 'This act of eliminating the separation represented the passing of the 'Arabi [sic] teachings to Rumi, linking the 'Arabi and the Mevlevi line.'

Omid Safi, 'Did the Two Oceans Meet? Connections and Disconnections between Ibn al-'Arabi and Rumi', *JMIAS*, XXVI (1999), p. 57, points out that the relationship between Rumi and Ibn 'Arabi 'has been depicted in a full spectrum of ways ranging from discipleship to pure antagonism'. He suggests that scholarly attempts to establish connections and comparisons between the two great mystics have issued in theories that are 'highly problematic', as they 'are often more reflective of the scholars' own philosophical and doctrinal pre-commitments than they are of the data available in the historical sources'.

Many scholars deem unlikely the possibility of Ibn 'Arabi's influence on Rumi. For example, Schimmel, *The Triumphal Sun*, p. 19, maintains that 'although Ibn 'Arabi's main interpreter ... Qunavi ... was Rumi's colleague, the possible influence of his teaching or of his whole attitude upon Jalaloddin was probably counterbalanced by Shams' aversion to these theories as well as against all theoretical burden'. Chittick, Rumi and the Mawlawiyyah, pp. 113–17, agrees with her conclusions: 'It ... needs to be stressed that there is no evidence in Rumi's work of influence by Ibn 'Arabi or al-Qunawi.' See also Lewis, *Rumi: Past and Present*, p. 26.

Rauf's projection of Qunawi as Rumi's teacher (and as a conduit for the transmission to Rumi of Akbarian teachings) is questionable. See Safi, 'Did the Two Oceans Meet?', pp. 56–63.

122 See 'A Trip to Turkey', p. 10.

123 This characterisation of Rumi's sainthood must be understood in terms of Ibn 'Arabi's saintly typology, positing categories of saints who are heirs ('upon the heart' or 'in the footsteps') of different prophets. On this doctrine, see Hirtenstein, *The Unlimited Mercifier*, pp. 131ff.

As Hakim, 'The Spirit and the Son of the Spirit', p. 26, notes, the 'Isawi (Christic, Christ-like) type of saint, one who inherits from and thus participates in Christic knowledge, is 'in most cases, clear and apparent to ordinary people. We can even say that he is the saint *par excellence* in people's minds ... the image of an ascetic man, tolerant, never hurting others although getting hurt himself ... the sainthood of the 'Isawi saint cannot be hidden'. The author lists some of the signs of this type of sainthood identified by Ibn 'Arabi. The 'Isawi character of certain of Ibn 'Arabi's early teachers has been underlined: see for example Hirtenstein, *The Unlimited Mercifier*, pp. 74–8.

Both Rauf and Young have stressed the sympathies of Rumi's Christian contemporaries for him. Rauf thus wrote: 'It is said that there were more Christians than Muslims' at his funeral (see 'A Trip to Turkey', p. 10). Young, 'At the Still Point', suggests that Christians in particular 'saw in his humility and poverty, and in his breadth and scope of teaching a Christ-like spirituality'. F. W. Hasluck, *Christianity and Islam under the Sultans* (Oxford, 1929), 2, p. 372, observes that, in his own life, Rumi had been 'conciliatory in his attitude towards Christianity and Christians'. He provides specific evidence of friendly relations between the Mevlevis and the Christians, relations that have obtained 'throughout their history'. See ibid., pp. 371, 373ff.; also Shah-Kazemi, The Metaphysics of Interfaith Dialogue, pp. 185–6.

124 See Young, 'At the Still Point'. On the idea of love in Rumi's thought, see Schimmel, *The Triumphal Sun*, pp. 332–52, and Chittick, *The Sufi Path of Love*, pp. 194–231.

125 Young, 'At the Still Point'. Cf. Friedlander, *The Whirling Dervishes*, p. 58: Rumi 'spoke of universal love and was the living example of his words'. The essence of Rumi's teaching was 'the cultivating of conscious impressions manifesting as a brotherhood of all mankind based on love'. See also ibid., pp. 152, 60.

126 Lewis, *Rumi: Past and Present*, p. 592, with reference to the translations of Rumi by Coleman Barks. Of several contemporary translators, Barks has been credited with stimulating much of the contemporary interest in Rumi in the USA. See ibid., and Huston Smith, cited in Margaret Doyle, 'Translating Ecstasy: Coleman Barks on Rumi with a Side of Curry', www.newtimes.org. Barks' anthology (with John Moyne) *The Essential Rumi* (New York, 1995) sold half a million copies in a few years. See 'The Soul of Rumi: A Conversation with Coleman Barks', www.gracecathedral.org.

Doyle's discussion yields a clear picture of Barks' personal spirituality and his projection of Rumi: 'He describes his own practice of spirituality, his worship services: "I go for lattés and I go riding in my '72 Dodge convertible. Everything is church, isn't it?"' On Rumi, Barks comments that he was 'without boundaries. He would say that love is the religion and the universe is the book, that experience as we're living it is the sacred text that we study, so that puts us all in the same God club'. Reflecting on Barks' views, Doyle concludes: 'Rumi's words offer an all-encompassing spirituality relevant to our times: being present in the moment, finding the holiness in laughter'.

Lewis, *Rumi: Past and Present*, pp. 589–92, offers an incisive evaluation of Barks' translations and his 'disciple's devotional attitude toward Rumi'. For him, Rumi is 'a great spiritual teacher, who "can see what each soul needs at any particular moment"'. He presents Rumi as 'a guru calmly dispensing words of wisdom capable of resolving, panacea-like, all our ontological ailments ... This view of Rumi as sage leads [Barks] to teleport [Rumi's] poems ... out of their cultural and Islamic context into the inspirational discourse of non-parochial spirituality, all of which makes for a Rumi who shares the social assumptions of a modern American audience'. At times, Barks 'fudges culturally or religiously specific details'. At best, Lewis concludes, his translations provide 'accessible contemporary versions, filtered through the lens of a New Age and particularly American idiom', of a selection of Rumi's poetry.

127 See 'A Trip to Turkey', p. 12. As Safi, 'Did the Two Oceans Meet?', notes, 'Simplifying matters somewhat, certain scholars have come to identify Rumi's legacy as the pinnacle of the "school of love" in Islam, and to represent Ibn al-'Arabi as the zenith of [the] "school of knowledge"'. On this tendency, see also comments by Addas, 'The Experience and Doctrine of Love', pp. 25–7, and Chodkiewcz, *Seal of the Saints*, p. 45.

For an example of this simplified approach in the context of a discussion intended for popular consumption, see 'Lyrics for the Soul', *The Times*, Mysticism Supplement, p. 14, where Schimmel introduces Ibn 'Arabi in contrast with Rumi thus: 'We should not forget that Sufism has also another aspect. Theosophical Sufism ... is largely concerned with ... gnosis, not so much with the longing of the burning heart'.

Rauf referred specifically to a 'Line of Love' in correspondence with a close associate (25 January 1984), in what can be seen as a response to such categorisations. In explaining this 'line', he stressed its inclusiveness, thus: 'Towards the end of *The Twenty-nine Pages*, you will read that Love in itself is nothing: its value is that it leads to Beauty. Its aim is Beauty. Without aim, it is nothing ... Love is no other than the movement of Beauty. Sheer Beauty is ever an expression. Its expression is vehicled by Love. Expression is a movement, and movement is obviously in motion. In this case, that which carries this movement is Love, just like the fluidity of water is what carries it downstream, aided by the slope of the land and gravity – its object is to give life. In the case of Beauty, its object is to give the Reality to all existence, among other things ... Now, when one says the "Line of Love", it means that the emphasis put on the fluency is through the temperament of Love. There is no access to Beauty except through Love. When you say of Christ "He is in the Line of Beauty", the answer is "Naturally." The same with Rumi; the same with Muhammad; the same with the Hüdayi Aziz Mahmud Efendi, who wrote an obituary poem for his master the "Üftade" saying that he was the Nightingale of the Gardens of Love. There is no arrival at Reality without that Love. The same is also true of Ibn 'Arabi since it is he who wrote *The Interpreter of Ardent Desires* and that mentioned in *The Twenty-nine Pages*. What I mean is that one should not differentiate and categorise or "pigeonhole" into sections, appellations, etc., because that sort of thing, that sort of differentiation, makes the people exclusive and determines over them and thereby excludes others and the *himma* of the excluded is barred, which must not be.' On *himma*, see Ch. 6.

128 Many have remarked that Rumi has become the best-selling and most read poet in America during the last decade. See for example Doyle, 'Translating Ecstasy'; Leonard Lewisohn, ed., *The Heritage of Sufism*, 2: *The Legacy of Medieval Persian Sufism, 1150–1500* (Oxford, 1999, 2nd edn), Preface, p. xiv, and 'How Rumi took US by Storm', *The Times*, Mysticism Supplement, p. 2. For an example of the familiarity of Rumi in popular culture today (in this case in popular fiction), see Iyer, *Abandon*. As Schimmel, Mawlana Rumi: Yesterday, Today and Tomorrow, p. 6, observes, 'No other mystic and poet from the Islamic world is as well known in the West as Rumi.' See also her *The Triumphant Sun*, chapter 4, and the detailed treatment in Lewis, *Rumi: Past and Present*, chapters 11–15.

On his influence in the Muslim world, as Schimmel, Mawlana Rumi: Yesterday, Today and Tomorrow, p. 5, notes, 'It would be impossible to enumerate all the translations of and commentaries on Mawlana's work which have been written since his death ... in various languages of the Islamic world ... We find his name everywhere ... Indeed, it would be difficult to find any literary and mystical work composed between Istanbul and Bengal which contains no allusion to his thought or quotation from his verse.'

129 For example, one disciple was recently quoted as saying that Rumi is 'the major-domo of the Muslim mystical tradition, and we taste it through his mediation.' See *The Times*, Mysticism Supplement, p. 6.

130 Writing in 1975, Friedlander, *The Whirling Dervishes*, pp. 113–14, described the times as 'an important bridge-period for the Mevlevis', for their resumed public *sama'* (now attended by '25,000 people from all over the world') had regained something of its earlier flavour. He continued: 'This authentic flavour has yet to become a full meal and take its place in the preparation of a completely universal esoteric platform.' Friedlander knew Rauf quite well at the time he was writing the first edition of *The Whirling Dervishes*, and it is quite likely that his reference to the notion of a universal esoteric platform had originated with him (personal correspondence with the author). Jervis, The Sufi Order, p. 260 n. 203, remarks that Friedlander's *The Year One Catalog* (New York, 1972) 'was inspired by the Pir 'Inayat Khan': his interest in sufism appears to have ranged wide at this time.

131 In light of this, the significance of the movement's name as 'the word the angel Gabriel said when he announced the coming of Christ to Mary at the Annunciation' (as Young in 'Courses at Chisholme', p. 26, recently explained) should perhaps be underlined.

132 See Feild, *The Last Barrier*, pp. 166–7.

133 Ibid., pp. 166, 168.

134 Compare with Hornsby's account (*Intimations*, p. ix) of Bennett's reported conviction of the 'need to talk as freely and openly as possible on matters that would have perhaps remained more secret in the past'. Hornsby added: 'There are those who feel that greater restraint should be exercised in these matters, but this is because they have not yet understood the changes that must come about, and what we are in preparation for.'

Young recalls three specific individuals Rauf encouraged to 'bring out their esoteric knowledge': Khojasti Mistri (a Zoroastrian involved at Swyre Farm), Keith Critchlow and Warren Kenton. Critchlow was a co-founder (with Kathleen Raine and others) in 1980 of *Temenos: A Review of the Arts of the Imagination*. This attracted the interest of

Prince Charles (heir to the British throne), who in 1992 encouraged the establishment of a Temenos Academy, for which he provided accommodation in the Prince's Foundation in London. Critchlow is a Fellow of the Academy who is presently Director of Islamic Arts at the Prince of Wales Institute of Architecture (also established within the Prince's Foundation in 1992); he also leads the Visual Islamic and Traditional Arts Programme (VITA), which joined the Foundation in 1993 and offers postgraduate courses. Described by Sedgwick, www.Traditionalists.org; *Against the Modern World*, pp. 214–16, 328 n. 49, as a Schuonian writer and the 'key Traditionalist' in the Prince's Foundation, among his best known works on art and design is *Islamic Patterns: An Analytical and Cosmological Approach* (London, 1976). He is a MIAS Fellow for life.

Also a Fellow of the Temenos Academy, Kenton (better known by his Hebrew name Z'ev ben Shimon Halevi) is one of the best-known contemporary Kabbalists. He presents himself as a teacher of the Toledano Tradition of Kabbalah (which began in Toledo in medieval Spain) and he is its principal author. (By some assessments his work is not in its entirety traditional Rabbinic Kabbalah, but reflects a mixture of influences.) He offers courses and workshops in several countries through his Kabbalah Society in London, which has groups in all continents. Translated into several languages, his works include *Tree of Life: An Introduction to the Kabbalah* (York Beach, ME, 1972); *Kabbalah: Tradition of a Hidden Knowledge* (New York, 1980); *Kabbalah and Exodus* (York Beach, ME, 1988). See further www.kabbalahsociety.org. An associate claims that Kenton in fact 'brought out' the Kabbalah (which is traditionally treated as secret and not intended for disclosure to anyone under the age of forty) 'under Rauf's direction'.

135 Associates recall that he was nonetheless clear that Christ would appear in his Second Coming as a man; cf. Feild, *The Last Barrier*, pp. 167–8. Hanegraaff, *New Age Religion*, p. 101, observes that, in New Age messianism (which has arisen mainly in the earlier part of the New Age), 'the Christ' denotes a superhuman spiritual agency, 'often described as a "principle" or "energy"'. He continues: 'although New Age believers may talk about "the second coming of the Christ", they do not necessarily believe that this event will involve the appearance of a visible person. Some of them do ... but others expect the second coming to be a purely spiritual event which will be felt and experienced within, rather than seen with physical eyes.'

136 See Feild, *The Last Barrier*, p. 89.

137 In ibid., pp. 91–2, Rauf explained the 'inner meaning' of the Virgin Mary as 'the matrix of all divine possibility in form ... in our world'. 'One day when Mary is recognized again', he continued, 'there will be a reappearance of the Christ, manifested in the outer world.' Cf. Young, 'Universal Nature', p. 27: 'In her maternal aspect [Mary] is active in giving birth and nourishment to her child, which is also a natural passivity to the demands of its intrinsic needs. From the other side, she is the paradigm of perfect receptivity, both in her knowledge and in her state.' He explains the manner in which this 'state of receptivity' came about, according to 'the Qur'anic account and amplified and expounded by Ibn 'Arabi'.

138 *Futuhat*, II: 326, cited in Chittick, *Sufism: A Short Introduction*, p. 67.

139 This understanding fits with the 'post-millenarian' perspective posited by Hanegraaff, *New Age Religion*, p. 100, as dominant in the NAM, in contrast with the 'pre-millenarian' scenario. In the latter, 'the coming of the Kingdom of God is abrupt and violent, as a result of a one-sided otherworldly intervention. Human beings can only react to this event when it happens, but of themselves they can do nothing to bring the kingdom closer.' In the post-millenarian perspective, the millennium comes after a collective human effort, which is one of its prerequisite conditions, as part of a process of evolution. The dominant view in the NAM is thus that 'the New Age will emerge, carried by human commitment, as the result of a (super)natural evolutionary process – although probably steered during the critical transition by superhuman assistance'.

140 See *The Wisdom of the Prophets*, p. 9, and *The Bezels of Wisdom*, p. 50. This point is cited in Ryan, 'Globalisation of the Spirit', p. 16, for example.

141 According to Hornsby, *Intimations*, p. ix, Bennett too was convinced that 'post-war generations are by their nature capable of assimilating certain spiritual realities at a greatly accelerated rate … It is as if by necessity that the possibility of understanding what had previously been hidden and esoteric has been made easier for them.' Cf. Bennett, *Witness*, p. iii. Associates recall certain academics who during the 1970s expressed their surprise that young Beshara students could gain an understanding of Ibn 'Arabi's ideas after studying these for only a few months, in spite of their complexity.

Associates themselves posit a qualitative difference between baby boomers and the preceding generation (that had lived through World War II). As one associate puts it, they had been conceived 'by a generation that longed for a different world of peace and security, in contrast with the conflict and suffering they had experienced during the war'.

142 Young, 'United by Oneness'.

143 See Young, 'Reorientation for the New Era'. Carroll, 'Timelessness and Time', p. 82, alludes to this understanding: 'Many … who participated in the civil rights movement of the sixties in America describe the experience as a spiritual awakening rather than political or social action, and that it was something which seemed to be happening to them, not something which they brought about.' (Carroll is an Anglo-American associate.)

144 See Young, 'Reorientation for the New Era'.

145 Ibid.

146 Ibid. Reflecting familiar New Age interests, Young points out that the new quest 'was widely seen as going beyond the confines of established religion to incorporate such things as health and healing, meditation and traditional wisdom'.

147 Young, 'United by Oneness'.

148 Ibid. Among other signs, he lists questioning the established order, the growth of feminism, political unrest, student power, anti-war demonstrations and a change in music.

149 Ibid.

150 As one associate puts it, far from looking at disciplines to see how spiritual principles can be 'grafted onto' these, the education Beshara provides allows one 'to bring out the intrinsic universal meaning of any discipline. Thanks to his unity and universality, swimming in Ibn 'Arabi's universe unlocks what is real in all areas'. Cf. Editorial, *Beshara Magazine*, 8, p. 3, which argues that integration comes through 'an understanding of the essential principles from which all knowledge springs'.

One associate acknowledges that the 'first generation' within Beshara remains largely 'conditioned by religious thought: their ideas of God and spirituality are theologically based'. Younger associates have generally been less exposed to such conditioning.

151 Young, 'Ibn 'Arabi: Towards a Universal Point of View', p. 90. He notes that this 'is not a Judeo-Christian or Islamic perspective, but it is this which has informed and given rise to the Abrahamic line and to all spirituality everywhere'.

152 Ibid.

153 There is a perception within the New Age of the 'new' and the 'old' science as radical opposites, the latter seen to be materialistic, conducive to human alienation and based on a reductionist paradigm.

What some term 'New Age science' is also referred to as 'New Paradigm science', as some of its key figures call for a radical new paradigm to replace the old mechanistic Newtonian–Cartesian one. Its best-known exponent is Fritjof Capra, who called for a 'holistic and ecological "systems view" of reality': the 'physics–mysticism parallelism' he posited has become a cherished New Age belief. This is elaborated in his popular book *The Tao of Physics: An Exploration of the Parallels between Modern Physics and Eastern Mysticism* (Glasgow, 1983/1975), which argues that a view of the world is beginning to emerge from modern physics that is harmonious with ancient Oriental mysticism. This implies a criticism of current (non-holistic) assumptions about the nature of reality, and issues in a holistic view of the universe as an interconnected web of relations. See Hanegraaff, *New Age Religion*, pp. 62ff., 107, 128–30.

The work of influential theoretical physicist David Bohm serves to illustrate why the writings of the new science are attractive to the New Age even where the unified worldview is only implicit within them. Bohm thus argues that relativity and quantum theory 'imply the need to look on the world as an undivided whole, in which all parts of the universe, including the observer ... merge and unite in one totality'. Cited in Groothuis, *Unmasking the New Age*, p.97; see also pp.94, 98. See further David Bohm, *Wholeness and the Implicate Order* (London and New York, 1980).

As Hanegraaff, *New Age Religion*, pp.63–4, indicates, the popular literature of 'New Age science' suggests that science can shed light on the workings of the divine in the cosmos. Typically characterised by the search for unified worldviews, it emphasises the ubiquity or immanence of the divine in the cosmos. As the worldviews upheld thus represent a particular *interpretation* of the research data provided by the writings of the new science, New Age science might more accurately be described as 'New Age philosophy of nature'.

154 See Rauf, *Addresses II*, p.61 ('To Suggest a Vernacular ...', first published in *Beshara Magazine*, 1). Davies is author of over twenty books, including *God and the New Physics* (London, 1983) and *The Mind of God: Science and the Search for Ultimate Meaning* (London, 1992).

155 See 'Rememoration', p.11. As Hanegraaff, The New Age Movement and the Esoteric Tradition, p.367, remarks, the New Age ultimately believes that 'science and spirituality are simply different roads leading to the same goal'.

156 Rauf, *Addresses II*, p.61. He identified this 'new vision' as Beshara, 'the good omen for the coming age, where the equally entrenched dogmatic insistence upon religion and a denial of religion and God come together with clenched fists'. Implicit here is his criticism of the failure of some scientists to extrapolate intuitively from their findings to this new vision. He reiterated the pivotal relationship between religion and science in a radio interview: 'I think in the future it must be that religion and science begin to complement each other: that science without religion will find future development extremely difficult. Religion without science equally will come to an impasse'. See ibid., p.55.

Evident also in his frequent references to Einstein in *Addresses* and parts of *Addresses II*, Rauf's singling out of (theoretical) physics reflected the appeal of this field specifically (and of relativity theory and quantum physics in particular) in New Age thought, given that its findings could be interpreted to legitimate a particular spiritual worldview. See Campbell, A New Age Theodicy for a New Age, p.79; cf. Jervis, The Sufi Order, p.233: 'Bridging the thirteenth-century "unity of being" monism of Ibn 'Arabi with the leading-edge of twentieth-century science, Vilayat 'Inayat Khan writes that "The best credo of all times is that of modern physics – that everything is an unbroken, undivided wholeness."' See also Coates, *Ibn 'Arabi and Modern Thought*, pp.12–13. For a thoroughgoing New Age exploration of the 'mystical and philosophical ramifications' of quantum theory, see Diarmuid O'Murchu, *Quantum Theology: Spiritual Implications of the New Physics*, rev. and updated edn (New York, 2004).

157 Yiangou, 'Facing the Unknown', p.31.

158 'Beshara Trust Seminar Series', *Beshara Magazine*, 2, p.32.

159 See 'Rememoration'. Cf. with Capra's exposition, above.

160 See, for example, 'Reaffirmation of Intent', p.29.

161 Examples of interviews are those with mathematical physicist Roger Penrose (issue 11, pp.20–6) and biologist Brian Goodwin (issue 12, pp.16–23). Examples of seminars are those by Rom Harré, 'Ontology and Science: The Case of Quantum Theory' (issue 3, pp.8–15); John D. Barrow, 'The New Cosmology' (issue 6, pp.19–25; on him, see Hanegraaff, *New Age Religion*, p.173). Features include Nobel Prize winning chemist Ilya Prigogine, 'The Rediscovery of Time: Science in a World of Limited Predictability' (issue 9, pp.28–32; on his work as New Age inspiration, see Hanegraaff, *New Age Religion*, pp.163–8. He is author, with Isabelle Stengers, of *Chaos out of Order: New Dialogue with Nature* [London, 1985]).

162 Reflecting a particular interest, associate Jane Clark has co-edited a substantial volume in the field: Willis Harman with Jane Clark, eds, *New Metaphysical Foundations of Modern Science* (Sausalito, CA, 1994). See also Clark, 'Fulfilling Our Potential', pp. 50–51 n. 29, where she suggests that what many scientists 'come up with' is 'completely compatible with what Ibn 'Arabi says'.

163 Yiangou, 'Facing the Unknown', p. 30.

164 See Editorial, *Beshara Magazine*, 10, p. 3.

165 See Young, Ibn 'Arabi: Towards a Universal Point of View', p. 91.

166 Ibid.

167 Ibid., p. 92.

168 Young, 'Reorientation for the New Era'.

169 Ibid.

170 'The root of both union and division is identity', a recent conversation explained: 'It is my choice to identify myself either with the small or the great ... when I separate myself from others, or make myself another, a wall is created in my heart'. See 'Walls in the Heart' (Notes from the Mead Hall, 19 February 2004), Beshara website.

171 New Age activists attribute nationalism to 'the false consciousness of separation and exclusiveness'. See Groothius, *Unmasking the New Age*, p. 116. Like Beshara, Krishnamurti also considered nationalism (and religion) a divisive force: see *Total Freedom*, p. 344, for example. (For somewhat different reasons, religious fundamentalism has also perceived modern nationalism as its main enemy and as anathema to its vision. For a classic treatment, see Bruce Lawrence, *Defenders of God: The Fundamentalist Revolt against the Modern Age* [London, 1990], pp. 83–9.)

172 Arising out of its monistic assumptions, the New Age often views the world as a single interlocking system in which the unity of humanity forms the basis of a political reality towards which one must strive: it thus calls for a realisation of unity and interdependence that transcends boundaries between people. See Groothius, *Unmasking the New Age*, pp. 116ff. Some signal the desired-for transformation through a notion of 'planetisation'; cf. comments in Hirtenstein, *The Unlimited Mercifier*, pp. 157–9, concerning the implications of the 'lunar view' of astronauts and the Space Age as 'the threshold of a new vision'. Ryan, 'Globalisation of the Spirit', identifies the nature of the challenge as achieving a recognition that 'the concept of brotherhood of man is not some vague ideal to which we condescend under some idea that there are "others" whom we need to placate in order to create some concept of peace, a concept based upon an impossibility of trying to unite opposites at a level of opposites, while we strive to maintain our separate castles of material security, personal and national'. Note the space dedicated in *Beshara Magazine* to the work of the Club of Rome, and to the ideas of Robert Muller (former Assistant Secretary General of the UN popular among New Agers for his calls for a 'global spirituality'). See *Beshara Magazine*, 8, pp. 4–6; 5, pp. 19–22; 11, pp. 27–31. See also Yiangou, 'Facing the Unknown', p. 31, referring to the Global Forum of Parliamentary and Spiritual Leaders for Human Survival.

173 The image of the self as 'your worst enemy', located 'between your two sides', derives from a hadith with which Young and associates are familiar via the medium of the Bosnevi commentary: see the *White Fusus*, 4, p. 892.

174 Young, 'Ibn 'Arabi: Towards a Universal Point of View', p. 93. Strikingly similar arguments arise in Shah-Kazemi, The Metaphysics of Interfaith Dialogue, pp. 144, 149–50, 160: these dwell on the 'idolatry of selfhood'; 'fixations on selfhood that give rise to pride and arrogance'; 'the innate holiness, the divine "face", within the "neighbour"'; and 'a mode of tolerance that is organically related to an awareness of the divine presence in all things'.

175 See Feild, *The Last Barrier*, pp. 167–8.

176 He first encountered Beshara in Israel during the early 1980s through a Palestinian who set up study circles there (see Ch. 6), and soon found Ibn 'Arabi's teaching 'greatly enlightening' and a positive contrast with what he had encountered in previous study in Israel based on the Gurdjieff teaching. As he had encountered it, this latter approach was to focus mainly on study of the problems, psychology and emotions of the self, with the aim of developing into what Gurdjieff had termed 'a real man'. Recalling the latter's remark that 'Life is real only when I am', he suggests that the perspective offered by Ibn 'Arabi makes the same point but from a significantly different angle.

His views have motivated this associate to gain exemption from life-long compulsory annual one-month military service. They also make it difficult for him to stay in Israel, and he spends as much time as possible at Chisholme. When in Israel he organises study sessions and *dhikr* gatherings. From his perspective, the growing interest in spirituality in Israeli society and people's desire 'to progress from their narrow situations' represent 'an invitation from God to step out of our limitations'; he sees grounds for optimism in this.

177 He alludes to the rise of ethnic nationalisms especially since the demise of the Soviet Union.

178 See Carroll, 'Timelessness and Time', p.84.

179 See Ryan, 'Globalisation of the Spirit', p.17.

180 See Young, 'United by Oneness'.

181 Ibid. Cf. Beshara website.

182 Young, '11th September 2001'.

183 Young, 'United by Oneness'. Cf. Hakim, 'The Spirit and the Son of the Spirit', p.23: 'Spiritual globalisation has preceded or is a mirror to the direction the apparent world is taking today towards concrete globalisation ... spiritual globalisation has gone further than material globalisation, because it has rendered the world as a unified whole.'

184 See Carroll, 'Timelessness and Time', p.81: the author draws an analogy with the roads of the Roman Empire, which allowed 'the spread of the ideas of Christ at the beginning of the first Christian millennium'.

185 See Young, 'United by Oneness'.

186 See Carroll, 'Timelessness and Time', pp.82–3: she argues that this conviction is manifest in the demand for recognition 'as they are' among groups 'not formerly represented' in the prevailing culture, in government or in education, such as gays, women, ethnic minorities, the disabled, etc.

187 Yiangou, 'Facing the Unknown', pp.31–3, suggests that this is strongest among scientists: 'Whether we look at the very small through quantum mechanics, or at the medium scale through chaos theory ... or at the very large through cosmology, we find equally the limits to partial knowledge, and the need for a unified vision ... Certain biologists go so far as to call our age the Age of Biology, because they believe that this provides a model for the whole universe. The whole universe can be regarded as an evolving, living being ... Once again, we are faced with an order of being which is single'. The ecological crisis is also adduced as evidence of an awareness of the need for a single vision.

Yiangou's comment concerning biology alludes to the stance of those who (like James Lovelock, author of the well-known 'Gaia hypothesis', assessed in *Beshara Magazine*, 5, pp.8–10) suggest that the earth behaves like a living, self-regulating organism, or a living system containing smaller living systems. See Hanegraaff, *New Age Religion*, p.108; see also interview with biologist Brian Goodwin on the emergence of the 'new biology', *Beshara Magazine*, 12, pp.16–23, and 'Reanimating Nature', *Beshara Magazine*, 8, pp.16–25. Based on such ideas, New Agers conclude that the earth *is* a living, even intelligent, organism: see Hanegraaff, The New Age Movement and the Esoteric Tradition, p.368.

188 See Young, 'United by Oneness'. 'The way Reality arranges things', Young explains, 'is that It does not impose It's [sic] mysteries and It's presence upon people without their wanting It and requesting It. This is one of It's mysteries. It is like the fact that the guest does not come into your house without being invited.'

189 See Carroll, 'Timelessness and Time', p.82.

190 See Ryan, 'Globalisation of the Spirit', p.16.

191 See Young, 'United by Oneness'.

192 'A Global Viewpoint', Beshara website.

193 Ibid.

194 Ibid.

195 Regarding the latter point, in 1999 Young, 'Ibn 'Arabi: Towards a Universal Point of View', p. 95, cites his own observations of students at Chisholme over a twenty-four-year period.

196 There has been an explosion of such literature from diverse traditions. Examples cited by associates include Carlos Castaneda, *The Teachings of Don Juan: A Yacqui Way of Knowledge* (Berkeley, 1968) (on the Amerindian Shamanistic worldview); *Zen Flesh, Zen Bones: A Collection of Zen and Pre-Zen Writings*, compiled by Paul Reps and Nyogen Senzaki (Rutland, 1957); Martin Prechtel, *Secrets of the Talking Jaguar: A Mayan Shaman's Journey to the Heart of the Indigenous Soul* (New York, 1998) (the latter dubbed the 'first [work] ever to offer an authentic insider's view of contemporary Mayan spirituality').

The fate of sufism and its 'secret' content (traditionally reserved for the initiated elite) has also been one of inexorable exposure during the last century. See Ernst, *The Shambhala Guide to Sufism*, pp. 215ff. As Sirriyeh, Sufi Thought and its Reconstruction, p. 124, observes, during the last century, 'Ever wider access was granted to esoteric Sufi teaching ... beyond the confines of carefully prepared and initiated *murid*s. By the 1990s any seeker, or simply the curious, could learn about supposed Sufi mysteries via a range of popular books and magazines, film and music recordings and through the great explosion of information on the World Wide Web. Some groups, such as the Naqshabandi–Haqqanis, showed extraordinary readiness to disclose detailed information on what would normally in the past have been considered knowledge to be kept hidden from outside view.' For examples associated with this *tariqa*, see Gary Bunt, *Virtually Islamic: Computer-mediated Communication and Cyber Islamic Environments* (Cardiff, 2000), pp. 58ff. (the order provides open opportunities to experience *dhikr* and other sufi practices by downloading files). See also Schmidt, Sufi Charisma on the Internet, pp. 113ff.

Kabbalah has experienced comparable exposure and popularisation during the twentieth century, having become transformed 'from an esoteric phenomenon into an international movement' and 'from a rather esoteric lore to a marketed product of mass culture'. Garb, 'The Image of the Saint in Twentieth Century Mysticism'; see further his *Yehidei ha-segulot yihiyu le-'adaraim: 'iyunim be-kabbalat ha-meah ha-'esrim* (*'The Chosen will become Herds': Studies in Twentieth Century Kabbalah*) (Jerusalem, 2005).

197 Young, 'United by Oneness'. He observes: 'We have tried in the past to arrange such things, but unless these are from Him, all such efforts are so much wasted energy. Only He can put His own work in place, in His own time.'

198 See Carroll, 'Timelessness and Time', p. 85.

199 Ryan, 'Globalisation of the Spirit', pp. 15–16.

200 See Yiangou, 'Facing the Unknown', pp. 33–5.

201 See for example 'A Global Viewpoint'. As Young puts it ('Courses at Chisholme'), 'I think that we are at the point of history of a *rite de passage*, about to go through – or maybe already going through – an extremely crucial isthmus. In terms of maturity, this could be described as something between the teenager and the responsible adult'.

202 Ryan, 'Globalisation of the Spirit', p. 17.

203 As part of the unfolding of the Divine Will, no time/era can be without meaning or good. Associates are indeed given to citing the hadith 'Revile not the era, for I [God] am the era.' See, for example, Coates, *Ibn 'Arabi and Modern Thought*, p. 83.

204 Ibid., p. 181.

205 For the classic Traditionalist treatment, see René Guénon, *The Reign of Quantity and the Signs of the Times* (Ghent, NY, 2001), 4th rev. edn, trans. Lord Northbourne.

206 A reference to a phrase used by Ibn 'Arabi in the first chapter of the *Fusus*: see

The Wisdom of the Prophets, p. 10. Coates explains this in terms of 'an awareness of the theophanic nature of the world'. (Interview with the author, November 2004.)

207 Peter Coates, 'Ibn 'Arabi and Modern Thought', *MIAS Newsletter*, 18 (Summer 2002), p. 10. Cf. Young, 'United by Oneness': 'a clarification and unfolding from the Interior has been taking place without interruption, such that the focus of Unity and Union becomes ever clearer'.

208 Coates, 'Ibn 'Arabi: The Unity of Existence and the Era', p. 9. Cf. Young, 'Ibn 'Arabi: Towards a Universal Point of View', p. 96: 'When we look towards the future ... with the confidence that the entire movement of the world is a movement of love, unfolding from the unseen, then what can lie ahead of us is all the fullness of human potential, on a global scale.'

209 Ryan, 'Globalisation of the Spirit'.

210 See Beshara website.

211 See Young, 'United by Oneness'.

212 See Young, 'Reorientation for the New Era.'

213 Personal correspondence from Rauf to a close associate (early 1970s).

214 Clark, 'Summer Gathering'.

215 See Young, 'United by Oneness'.

216 Ibid.

217 The sense of such grand responsibility is common among New Age groups. For example, as Jervis, The Sufi Order, p. 214, notes, 'Hadrat 'Inayat Khan wrote and often referred to the purpose of the Message [of the Sufi Order] as "the awakening of the consciousness of humanity to the divinity of man." That awakening is essential in constructing "the coming spiritual world", in which spirituality would be directed to "collective awakening" of mankind instead of individuals only."'

218 Young, 'United by Oneness'. As James A. Beckford, New Religious Movements and Globalization, in Phillip Charles Lucas and Thomas Robbins, eds, *New Religious Movements in the 21st Century: Legal, Political, and Social Challenges in Global Perspective* (New York, 2004), pp. 255–6, observes, many NRMs have made strenuous efforts to crystallise forms of global consciousness, deliberately aspiring to overcome boundaries of ideology, religion, etc. in their drive toward a peaceful, harmonious world unified by what they consider to be universal values.

219 Young, 'United by Oneness'.

220 Ibid., and Young, 'Ibn 'Arabi: Towards a Universal Point of View', p. 90.

221 Young, 'United by Oneness'.

222 Coates, *Ibn 'Arabi and Modern Thought*, pp. 181–2, describes this challenge (for 'citizens of the new millennium') as 'to reconceptualize its epistemological and theoretical co-ordinates and adopt as its *axiomatic* descriptor the *very idea* of the Unity of Existence'.

223 Young, 'United by Oneness'.

224 Young, 'Reorientation for the New Era'.

225 He cites the much-repeated verses: 'Come, come, whoever you are. Wanderer, worshipper, lover of leaving. Even if you have broken your vow a thousand times. It doesn't matter! Ours is not a caravan of despair. Come, come, yet again come.' In personal correspondence with a close associate (1973), Rauf had suggested that Love 'comes down' to the present through what was passed to Rumi, 'which from then on was to be the greatest exponent of Love, which is the tradition of Jesus'.

226 This is from the famous verses of the *Tarjuman al-ashwaq* beginning 'My heart has become capable of every form'.

227 Young, 'At the Still Point'.

Chapter 6

1 Jane Clark, 'Summer Gathering', Beshara website.

2 Rauf, cited in Feild, *The Last Barrier*, p. 167.

3 It is important to reflect the nuanced attitude towards the religions displayed by some associates. Although the focus is on a supra-religious future as embodiment of the Divine Will, there is nonetheless an acceptance of the religions in their capacity as part of the unfolding divine project. This can translate into a position distinct from the thoroughgoing rejection of religion typical of many New Agers (O'Murchu, *Quantum Theology*, p. 13, describes religion as 'one of the greatest anomalies of our evolution as a human species', for example). Some associates do appear passionate in their denunciation (at least of the negative effects) of the religions, however.

4 See Rauf, *The Last Sultans*, p. 297. This remark arises in a discussion of Sultan Abdülhamid II: 'what escaped Hamid [sic] was that the Caliphate was a religious institution and religions'. Cf. *Addresses II*, p. 98: describing sixteenth-century Mughal India, Rauf comments that its religious communities were 'as always, inclined towards separatist tendencies, prompted by the dogmatic and formalised religious exclusivity'. And p. 60 (cf. also p. 54), where he suggests that 'a formalised religion' is 'very akin to a medieval concept of a town with its keep and encircling walls to which one either belonged or was excluded from "intrusion" to its embracing, exclusive form'. Tollemache, 'An Obituary of Bulent Rauf', reflects that Rauf 'had no time for the religious bigot or dogma'.

5 Alister McGrath, *The Twilight of Atheism: The Rise and Fall of Disbelief in the Modern World* (New York, 2004), pp. 173, 190.

6 As Rauf, *Addresses II*, p. 60, puts it, the perspective necessitated by the present era 'would need to break down the walls of dogma and creed, enlarging its periphery to allow ... all other forms of belief by the sheer fact that all belief must irrevertibly concern the same one and only ... existence'.

7 Hirtenstein, 'The Basis of a Universal Religion', p. 6. He continues: 'To reach such a viewpoint is the pressing need of our times, and demands an education unbounded by any fixed dogma.' This piece comments on an article in *The Guardian* newspaper discussing the possibility of establishing a universal religion.

8 Associates explain that this type of *wilaya* confers certain gifts on individuals with the aim of bringing about a strong effect: they are driven in an extraordinary way and enjoy an unshakeable sense of destiny, enabling them to achieve their purpose.

In light of this perception of Ataturk, associates find it natural that 'those of spiritual inclination' (like the Turkish sufi shaykhs mentioned in Ch. 4) had been aware of Ataturk's 'importance and destiny' in the spiritual sphere, although he himself had been unaware of it.

Rauf, *The Last Sultans*, pp. 356–7, describes Ataturk's quality in apparently more mundane terms, thus: 'Ankara is modern Turkey's capital, centrally chosen by a genius. Genius has wisdom at its service and true wisdom cannot be confined to any one form; therefore genius has no form of action and, consequently, is not bound by the moral obligations which demand formal binding allegiances. Genius does not obviously fit into patterns, therefore it does not borrow laws of action, but makes its own laws. Its sole judge is its consequences, and its only rule is the aim it has set itself. It is like building a major, vital highway; a few trees, even centuries old, may have to be sacrificed. Along those grand lines, genius is, above all, the use of vision with adaptability as its tool ... Atatürk had this vision peculiar to people known as geniuses. Turkey, which had withered in a death agony for dearth of a statesman for over half a century, had suddenly produced a genius.'

9 He possibly died during the 1970s. Some versions of this account have Sirri Dede as a postman: the item of clothing was his postman's hat, knocked off his head by the saint.

Perhaps more reliable is a version that has him working in the postal service but not as a postman, and well known for his immaculate dress, typically a white suit and tie. In this account, the saint pulled his tie. After the dream, he never wore a tie again.

Sirri Dede's reported interpretation of the signification of Hüdayi's intervention is particularly interesting given the symbolic importance of attire in general in Republican Turkey, and of the hat versus traditional headgear (the turban and fez) in particular, in the aftermath of the famous 'hat reform'. (See for example the poem by Mevlevi shaykh and erstwhile MP for Kastamonu Veled Çelebi [d.1953], who was among the first to wear a hat, cited in Küçük, 'Sufi Reactions against the Reforms', p. 17, encompassing the refrain: 'Don't touch my hat, O khoja!', and asking whether the Prophet had worn a turban.) Given this background, one might be forgiven for speculating that knocking off the hat (and at a stretch pulling the tie) could have signified a concern with the secular Turkish order, rather than a comment on the *tariqa* form.

10 *Beshara Magazine*, 8, p. 12, commenting on the findings of a survey conducted in December 1988, which had concluded that Britain 'is not only not a Christian country; it has become one in which Christianity is almost impossible for most people to imagine ... Words like "spirituality" and "soul" seem meaningless.' The author cited two facts that contradict this view: first, mystical literature was one of the fastest-growing sectors in the book market; second, the survey revealed that 70% of people believed that 'no one church or faith can be the only true religion'. Their conclusion was that the term 'spirituality' was in fact 'far from meaningless. It is, on the contrary, that which people are seeking to understand in a way which is both more universal, in that it encompasses other beliefs, and also more particular, in that at its heart is their own relationship to the universe and to God.'

11 Poster for the Beshara School.

12 See, for example, Story 1 in Appendix 5.

13 An interest in Palestine/Israel first emerged under Feild's watch at Swyre Farm, possibly following a visit to Jerusalem by an American Jew who had become involved in Beshara. In 1972, a few associates travelled to Jerusalem and set up a Beshara centre in a rented flat for about a year before it folded. Some of them made contact with a local Naqshbandi shaykh.

Young estimates that, across the years, two to three hundred Israelis have passed through the School on nine-day or six-month courses or visits. There are usually one or two Israeli students on each long course (in 2003, for example, there were three on the intensive course). The necessity to take Beshara courses to Israel has not been felt: it is easy for Israelis to travel to Chisholme, and they are 'glad of the opportunity for a break from a very depressing and difficult situation', as Young puts it, and 'to see that there is a different way to live'.

Beshara's present link with Israel originated with Samir al-Haigha, a Palestinian Muslim from near Haifa who had moved with his parents to Germany as an adolescent. Having completed his studies in philosophy at the start of the 1980s he heard of Beshara, travelled to the UK and completed the intensive course at Chisholme. He sought Rauf's permission to introduce Beshara to Israel by establishing study circles there, with the ultimate aim of setting up a school. Considering this an important arena, Rauf had agreed. By 1983–84, al-Haigha was travelling across Israel, contacting potentially interested parties and setting up study circles in Jerusalem, Tel Aviv and other cities. Some who joined him had studied under a Gurdjieff teacher whom al-Haigha had approached and who had encouraged his students to meet him, explaining that he had 'something important' to extend. Circles studied Beshara materials in English (including *The Twenty-nine Pages*), initially under al-Haigha's supervision. *Dhikr* gatherings were also organised, and attracted as many as fifty people: one took the form of a large circle by the river in Tel Aviv at night by torchlight. Responding to the interest in Beshara in Israel at this time, in 1985 Rauf encouraged the School to invite three members of the first cadre of al-Haigha's students to attend an intensive course at Chisholme, and found sponsors to meet their course fees. When they returned to Israel, these associates also set up study circles and organised *dhikr* meetings.

While these activities are ongoing (and possibly expanding), relations with al-Haigha, who had set the process in motion, soon broke down. Associates imply that he had not managed his own charisma successfully. By one account he had also behaved towards Rauf, who was then ailing, as a *murid* towards his shaykh (he sought his constant guidance and would act only on his direct instruction or with his explicit approval, for example). He was eventually asked to stop putting himself forward as someone working on behalf of Beshara.

There has been at least one 'Beshara trip' to Israel, in 1990, when a group of associates visited various sites. One Israeli associate's reflections from that time provide an indication of perceptions of Israel in Beshara. This associate wrote (in personal correspondence to another associate): 'Israel is a very powerful place, where there is but a very thin partition between the *Zahir* and the *Batin*. This place seems to be an open heart, reflecting ... all opposites.' He suggested that the task of Beshara in Israel might be to bridge two different groups/approaches: religious people, and those secular groups 'engaged in inner work for self-knowledge and for the uplifting of inner veils.'

The interest in Beshara among Israelis must be situated in the context of the rise in Israel of NRMs (both home-grown and imported) and the engagement of growing numbers in these and in New Age spirituality, especially since the 1970s. Benjamin Beit-Hallahmi, *Despair and Deliverance: Private Salvation in Contemporary Israel* (Albany, NY, 1992), examines the fast-growing search for 'private salvation' among thousands of Israelis since 1973 through one of four routes: the return to Judaism (non-observant individuals joining the orthodox minority); psychotherapeutic movements; occultism; and new religions. He lists among the latter ISKCON, TM, Scientology, The Divine Light Mission, Zen, Theosophy, the Gurdjieff-inspired movement and Messianic Judaism, for example (pp. 11ff.). The author contentiously projects this overnight 'conversion epidemic' as a desperate response to a collective crisis/trauma in the shape of the 1973 war, which he maintains exposed uncertainties concerning Israel's future: as the low point of Zionism in history (experienced in terms of a loss of hope about the future), it had 'cataclysmic psychological consequences.' He construes the rejection of Jewish identity via new religions (and the rejection of Zionism via extreme Judaisation) as variant exit strategies in response to this crisis surrounding Zionism (pp. 134–40, 154).

Beit-Hallahmi suggests that the reaction to NRMs in Israel is 'in accordance with the threat they present to Israeli and Jewish identity', given that a relinquishing of Jewish identity signifies undermining Zionist claims concerning Palestine. The claim to preserve Jewish identity is thus one way in which NRMs can 'remain within the pale' (pp. 46–7). The repudiation of exclusivist religious identities and simultaneous pragmatic acceptance of religious affiliation in Beshara make it an interesting case: its appeal to Israelis indeed makes it worthy of comparative study alongside the movements described by Beit-Hallahmi.

14 We can mention two in addition to al-Haigha. First is Rauf's cousin, Arim. Second is Binzagr, a Saudi reportedly affiliated to a Rifa'i shaykh in Jeddah. In London as a student, he had attended one of Feild's meetings and from there became involved in Beshara. He taught Arabic and served as a staff member on the first two intensive courses held at Sherborne House. Associates indicate that his involvement with Beshara had been with the permission of his shaykh, but when he travelled to Jeddah for a visit during 1979 his shaykh 'did not let him return', and he has had no contact with Beshara since (Rauf had valued his involvement and wanted this to continue). He was a founding member of the MIAS and remains an Honorary Fellow in recognition of this. Associates suggest he viewed Beshara as a forum through which the sufi (and possibly by extension Islamic) presence in the West might be strengthened.

Associates mention four other Muslims who have completed six-month Beshara courses: (a) An eighty-year-old Egyptian married to an English woman and living in the

UK. (b) A young man from Mauritius. Both completed the intensive course in 1977–78. (c) A Turkish medical doctor from Germany who completed intensive and further courses during the second half of the 1980s. (d) A young man who is the son of a Libyan colonel and his English wife, and who completed the intensive course in 1983. The Turk alone has remained in contact with Beshara. We must add recent Indonesian Muslim students to these four: see below and Ch. 8.

15 See Chittick, Ibn 'Arabi, pp. 501–2.

16 The two categories are Mercy (*Rahma*) and Wrath (*Ghadab*), or Bounty (*Fadl*) and Justice (*'Adl*), or Beauty (*Jamal*) and Majesty (*Jalal*), or Gentleness (*Lutf*) and Severity (*Qahr*). The Qur'an and hadith associate the gentle and beautiful Attributes (Names of immanence) with God's nearness to His creatures, and connect the majestic and severe ones (Names of transcendence) with His distance from creation.

17 On *kashf* (which produces *mukashafa*, literally 'the lifting of the veil' in the sense of an 'illumination' or 'epiphany') as a foundation of sufi epistemology, see Knysh, *Islamic Mysticism*, pp. 311–14. It is 'the generic term for suprarational vision of God's presence in the world and the soul', expressing the sufi notion of true understanding as 'the lifting of the veils that obscure the face of the heart'. See Chittick, *Sufism: A Short Introduction*, pp. 24–5, 138; chapter 10 generally.

18 The central tenet of theism is that God must be addressed, worshipped and obeyed as a personal Creator distinct from the creation. Otherwise put, it is the 'I–Thou' relationship between God and man. Inasmuch as He is inaccessible, God is grasped in terms of *tanzih*; inasmuch as He is 'closer to man than his jugular vein' (Qur'an 50: 16), He is grasped in terms of *tashbih*. See also Chittick, *Sufism: A Short Introduction*, pp. 9–11, 25, 104.

19 Rauf, *Addresses*, pp. 34–5.

20 'Beyond Religion' (Notes from the Mead Hall, 22 April 2004), Beshara website.

21 Frithjof Schuon, *Esoterism as Principle and as Way*, trans. William Stoddardt (Middlesex, 1981), p. 232.

22 Corbin, *Alone with the Alone*, p. 246, comments: 'Some have thought it paradoxical that prayer should perform a function in a doctrine such as that of Ibn 'Arabi, and what is more, an essential function, while others have denied that this was so.'

The seemingly paradoxical nature and purpose of praise (analogous to *dhikr*, prayer, worship and devotion in general) in Ibn 'Arabi's doctrine is explored in the articles in Stephen Hirtenstein, ed., *Praise* (Oxford, 1997). See in particular Gerald Elmore, '*Hamd al-hamd*: The Paradox of Praise in Ibn al-'Arabi's Doctrine of Oneness', pp. 59–94, especially pp. 72–3, 92. The author comments (p. 62) that 'the real irony of praise is that in Ibn al-'Arabi's doctrine it seems to have an ultimate significance almost diametrically opposite to the ordinary concept as understood by the exoteric scholars of religion'.

See also comments concerning the character of Ibn 'Arabi's *Awrad* in comparison with the well-known devotional prayers of other prominent sufi figures, below.

23 In this context we must emphasise again that the notion of devotion takes on a somewhat different hue from its ordinary sense.

Annett, ed., *The Many Ways of Being*, p. 85, has captured something of the apparently paradoxical wedding of a thoroughgoing monism with devotion: 'Beshara does not claim to be a spiritual path, but a means of bringing oneself to see what is already there.' On the same page, he observes that, in Beshara, 'The aim of *zikr* is to give praise and worship.'

24 See 'Beyond Religion'.

25 *Futuhat*, II: 267, cited in Chittick, *The Sufi Path of Knowledge*, p. 283.

26 Occasionally we separate out general 'Muslim' from specific 'sufi' practice for the sake of clarity only: no suggestion of any discontinuity between these spheres is intended.

27 Feild, *The Last Barrier*, p. 71.

28 For examples of the clear divine injunctions relating to it, see Qur'an 18: 24 and 33: 41. On its practice and history within sufism, see 'Dhikr', EI², II, pp. 223–6; Jean-Louis

Michon, The Spiritual Practices of Sufism, in Nasr, ed., *Islamic Spirituality: Foundations*, pp. 275–7; Constance E. Padwick, *Muslim Devotions: A Study of Prayer Manuals in Common Use* (Oxford, 1996), pp. 13–20; Schimmel, *Mystical Dimensions of Islam*, pp. 167–78; Chittick, *Sufism: A Short Introduction*, chapter 5; Knysh, *Islamic Mysticism*, pp. 317–22.

29 Feild, *The Last Barrier*, p. 70.

30 Rauf, *Addresses*, p. 17.

31 Qur'an 13: 28. On the heart as spiritual organ, see Seyyed Hossein Nasr, The Heart of the Faithful is the Throne of the All-Merciful, in Cutsinger, ed., *Paths to the Heart*, pp. 32–47.

32 Rauf, *Addresses*, p. 17.

33 Rauf's singling out of *His dhikr* reflects the notion of God invoking Himself, developed in the Qur'an and *hadith qudsi*. For examples, see Souad Hakim, 'Invocation and Illumination (*al-adhkar wa'l-anwar*) according to Ibn 'Arabi', in Stephen Hirtenstein, ed., *Prayer and Contemplation* (Oxford, 1993), p. 22. These include: 'God has said: "Invoke Me and I will invoke you"' and 'Oh my God I cannot enumerate all Your praises, as You have praised Yourself.' As Hakim shows, Ibn 'Arabi elaborates on this type of *dhikr* and concludes that, while God invokes Himself, by Himself, for Himself, and for Himself equally in the creature, 'the greatest and highest [*dhikr*] in the universe is [that] of God of Himself, by Himself, for Himself.' See pp. 24ff.

34 Possibly during the Swyre Farm period, Rauf instituted *dhikr* gatherings for the nights of the Prophet's night-journey (*mi'raj*) and his birthday, the Night of Decree (the middle night of Sha'ban), the Night of Power (*laylat al-qadr*: the night on which the Qur'an was revealed, traditionally celebrated on the night of the 27th of Ramadan), Rumi's 'nuptual night', and the Night of Closeness. Some associates add the night of Khidr's day to this list. Short readings specific to each occasion and explaining their significance are reportedly available to accompany the gatherings, but these are not often used.

The Night of Closeness designates the first Friday night of Rajab (the first of the three holy months, followed by Sha'ban and Ramadan). It is widely marked by Sunnis and celebrated by Turkish Muslims and sufis in particular (the latter commemorate it with gatherings of *dhikr* and praise of the Prophet). It is believed to bring increased blessings and forgiveness and is spent in fasting and intensified prayer. Thanks are due to Suleyman Derin for this information.

35 See Michon, The Spiritual Practices of Sufism, p. 281. 'Hadra', EI², III, p. 51, notes that the term is used broadly in mystical practice as a synonym of *hudur*, 'being in the presence of Allah'. Cf. Geaves, *The Sufis of Britain*, p. 46, suggesting that it 'usually refers to the presence of the Prophet who is believed to bless the gathering rather than the presence of Allah'.

36 Conversely, it is difficult to identify any specific *tariqa* sources on which Rauf may have drawn for the elements of the Beshara *dhikr*. For descriptions of *dhikr* as performed by the Khalwatiyya, Qadiriyya, Naqshbandiyya and Rifa'iyya, see Öztürk, *The Eye of the Heart*, pp. 102, 105–6 and 111–13 respectively. See also 'Dhikr', pp. 224–5. Walter Feldman, Musical Genres and Zikir of the Sunni Tarikats of Istanbul, in Lifchez, ed., *The Dervish Lodge*, pp. 196–7, identifies 'rotation' (moving in a circle) and 'seated zikir' (on the knees), both evident in the Beshara collective *dhikr*, as among the basic types performed by Turkish *tariqa*s. Ballanfat, *Le Divan*, p. 81 n. 194, observes that *Hu*, used in the *dhikr* of many *tariqa*s, is especially prominent in the Celvetiyye, where it forms part of the more advanced invocations; on this *tariqa* see below.

37 In the traditional *tariqa*s, the *dhikr* gathering is strictly a male affair. When it is held in a mosque it may be possible for women to listen from behind a curtain in a designated 'balcony'. For an example, see Taji-Farouki, *At the Resting-place of the Seal of Saints*.

'Hybrid' *tariqa*s in the West hold mixed-sex *dhikr*s with varying degrees of proximity, some providing defined areas for men and women within the same room (with women behind the men, as in the performance of the *salat*). See also Hermansen, In the Garden of American Sufi Movements, pp. 159, 164; Zarcone, 'Rereadings and Transformations of Sufism in the West', p. 115; Ernst, *The Shambhala Guide to Sufism*, p. 227.

38 See, for example, Annemarie Schimmel, *And Muhammad is His Messenger: The Veneration of the Prophet in Islamic Piety* (Chapel Hill, NC, 1985), p. 94.

39 This comment was made by a British Muslim convert and Naqshbandi *murid* who had been visiting friends at Chisholme and had observed the Beshara *dhikr*. The case of British Naqshbandi converts furnishes a further relevant comparison. According to Geaves, *The Sufis of Britain*, p. 154, they believe their own practice of Islam to be 'untouched by cultural accretions', and hence to be 'purer' when compared with that of Nazim al-Haqqani's followers of other nationalities (presumably born Muslims). Zarcone, 'Rereadings and Transformations of Sufism in the West', p. 115, comments that the preliminary prayers usually read before the *dhikr* in the Naqshbandiyya are significantly reduced when this is performed in London, as they 'bore the converts'.

40 This is named after the fact that, 'after having begun by pronouncing the name Allah in its entirety ... the participants finish by pronouncing only the final ha', in a breath that no longer uses the vibration of the vocal chords but only alternating contraction and expansion of the chest'. This method is used particularly by Shadhili and Qadiri *tariqa*s: see Michon, The Spiritual Practices of Sufism, p. 282.

41 A comparison between *dhikr* meetings held by Nazim al-Haqqani's British disciples and those held by his Turkish followers furnishes some illumination: see Geaves, *The Sufis of Britain*, p. 154. The former are 'quieter and more meditative in atmosphere and display none of the more exhibitionist manifestations of individual ecstasy' found in the latter. The author claims that a prior background in meditative practices associated with Buddhism/Hinduism makes many Western followers 'more inclined to contemplative practice to achieve peace and tranquillity', far from other modes of *dhikr* that seem to work by 'arousing emotions'.

42 In the Beshara *dhikr* the *takbir* and *salawat* follow specific formulae. For the *takbir*: *Allahu akbar la ilaha illa Allah wa li-llahi al-hamd*; for the *salawat*: *Allahumma salli 'ala sayyidina Muhammad al-nabi al-ummi wa 'ala alihi wa sahbihi wa sallim*. The same formula is adopted when the *salawat* is repeated in other contexts.

43 See Michon, The Spiritual Practices of Sufism, p. 287, and Padwick, *Muslim Devotions*, p. 22.

44 The rosary is used widely by Muslims (with the exception of some who deem it an innovation) to count repetitions of Divine Names or devotional formulae; see 'Subha', EI[2], IX, pp. 741ff.

45 He is unable to provide a reference to it in Ibn 'Arabi's writings, but is aware of this 'from oral tradition'. Rauf, *Addresses*, p. 49, maintains that Ibn 'Arabi 'used to prescribe as much as ninety thousand' repetitions of *Allah* 'as a starter'.

46 As Michon, The Spiritual Practices of Sufism, p. 277, notes, 'Given its incomparable grandeur, the invocation of the Supreme Name can only be practiced under certain conditions, with the authorization of the *murshid* and under his control. Thus, the authorization to practice invocation outside of collective gatherings is ... generally granted to the *murid* ... at a later stage, when the shaykh has sufficiently tested the disciple's qualifications. If such precautions are necessary to avoid the dangers to which novices could expose themselves by wrongly performing *dhikr*, they are not needed at collective sessions. [There] the presence of the ... experienced shaykh ... provides a security against excesses and ... undesirable psychic manifestations to which ... beginners on the Sufi path could be subjected.'

47 Ibid: 'the [*dhikr*] performed in retreat ... is the most often recommended mode ... When 'Ali ... asked the Prophet the shortest way to God the Prophet answered, "'Ali, always repeat the Name of God in solitary places."'

48 The use of seven formulae comprising the Shahada and six Divine Names is found, for example, in the *dhikr* of the Halvetiyye (where the Names are specifically *Allah, Huwa/Hu, Haqq, Hayy, Qayyum, Qahhar*) and the Suhrawardiyya (using the same

Names, but substituting for the final two *Rahman* and *Rahim*). See ibid., pp. 287–8, and Brown, *The Darvishes*, pp. 274–5; also Ballanfat, *Le Divan*, p. 49.

49 The term *mi'raj* designates the Prophet's nocturnal ascension to the heavens and finally the Divine Presence. On this see 'Mi'radj', EI², VII, pp. 97–105, esp. 97–100, and Schimmel, *And Muhammad is His Messenger*, chapter 9. For an early description in traditional sources, see Alfred Guillaume, *The Life of Muhammad, A Translation of Ibn Ishaq's Sirat Rasul Allah* (Oxford, 1998), pp. 181–7.

As Seyyed Hossein Nasr, The Qur'an as the Foundation of Islamic Spirituality, in Nasr, ed., *Islamic Spirituality: Foundations*, p. 3, observes, the *mi'raj* is 'the model of all spiritual realization in Islam'. In sufism in particular it became the model of mystical experience, expressed in the image of the soul's ascension through the heavens to the Divine Presence. For a general introduction, see Nazeer el-Azma, 'Some Notes on the Impact of the Story of the *Mi'raj* on Sufi Literature', *The Muslim World*, LXIII (1973), pp. 93–104, and Abu'l-A'la 'Affifi, 'The Story of the Prophet's Ascent (*mi'raj*) in Sufi Thought and Literature', *Islamic Quarterly*, 2 (1955), pp. 23–9. An elaborate internal recapitulation of the Prophet's journey to the Divine Presence arises in two important Persian sufis. First is Abu Yazid al-Bistami (d. 874): Schimmel, *And Muhammad is His Messenger*, p. 173, describes him as 'possibly the first to utilize this symbolism'. Second is Ruzbihan Baqli (d. 1202): the symbolism of ascension forms the most important structure underlying his visions. See Ruzbihan Baqli, *The Unveiling of Secrets: Diary of a Sufi Master*, trans. Carl W. Ernst (Chapel Hill, NC, 1997).

Ibn 'Arabi discussed the spiritual ascent in *Kitab al-Isra' ila maqam al-asra*, analysed in el-Azma, 'Some Notes on the Impact of the Story of the *Mi'raj*'. He described his own *mi'raj* as an exact imitation of the Prophet's. For this description, see James W. Morris, Ibn 'Arabi's Spiritual Ascension, in Chodkiewicz, ed., *The Meccan Revelations*, 1, pp. 201–30 and 'The Spiritual Ascension: Ibn 'Arabi and the *Mi'raj*', *Journal of the American Oriental Society*, 107 (1987), pp. 629–52; 108 (1988), pp. 63–78. See also Chodkiewicz, *Seal of the Saints*, chapter 10; Hirtenstein, *The Unlimited Mercifier*, pp. 117–23; Addas, *Ibn 'Arabi: The Voyage of No Return*, pp. 65–6.

50 On *khalwa*, its possible origins, evolution and institutionalisation in the history of sufism, see 'Khalwa', EI², IV, pp. 990–1, and Knysh, *Islamic Mysticism*, pp. 314–17. The Suhrawardiyya, Shadhiliyya, Qadiriyya and Khalwatiyya place special emphasis on this practice, which was traditionally conducted once a year. For a twelfth-century treatise on *khalwa*, see Hadrat 'Abd al-Qadir al-Jilani, *The Secret of Secrets*, interpreted by Tosun Bayrak al-Jerrahi al-Halveti (Cambridge, 1992).

51 See 'Khalwa'.

52 Ibn 'Arabi (*Journey to the Lord of Power*, p. 30) wrote: 'do not enter retreat until you know what your station is, and know your strength in respect to the power of imagination. For if your imagination rules you, then there is no road to retreat except by the hand of the shaykh who is discriminating and aware. If your imagination is under control, then enter retreat without fear.'

53 According to sufi practice, 'Being in a cell should evoke the idea of being in the grave. The cell should be a dark room prohibiting the entering of daylight, as the purpose is the "closing up of the external senses" and the "opening up of the internal senses".' See 'Khalwa'.

For a description of the cell traditionally used by the Halvetis, see Rabia Terri Harris, 'The Relevance of Retreat: A Reflection on the Religious Imagination', *JMIAS*, XXV (1999), p. 7.

54 The forty-day period traditionally prescribed within the *tariqa*s is widely considered unfeasible today, and there is also fear that the contrast on emergence would be dangerously stark. Some *tariqa*s have reduced its length and others no longer prescribe retreat at all. See for example Harris, 'The Relevance of Retreat', pp. 11–12, citing a statement of a contemporary Halveti–Jerrahi authority in Istanbul that 'the time of halvet has passed'.

For a first-hand contemporary account of a retreat, see Michaela M. Özelsel, *Forty Days: The Diary of a Traditional Solitary Sufi Retreat with an Accompanying Interdisciplinary Scientific Commentary* (Brattleboro, VT, 1996).

55 On *jalwa* and its importance in the Celveti conceptualisation of the spiritual path, see below.

56 See, for example, 'For You Alone' (Notes from the Mead Hall, 2 July 2004), Beshara website.

Compare with the practice of retreat in the Sufi Order. According to Geaves, *The Sufis of Britain*, pp. 179–80, Sufi Order retreat utilises 'a range of methods including Buddhist practices'. Moreover, music 'plays a significant role in creating atmosphere'. See also Jervis, *The Sufi Order*, p. 236.

57 Twenty-five attended a preparatory week held during March 2004, for example.

58 Ibn 'Arabi's *Risalat al-Anwar fi-ma yumnah sahib al-khalwa min al-asrar* provides a direct treatment of *khalwa* and its proper conditions. Written in response to the questions of a spiritually advanced colleague, its treatment traces the ascent experienced by the spiritual elite in *khalwa* through the degrees of existence to the Divine Presence. This has been translated by Harris as *Journey to the Lord of Power*: note that the sub-title she provides (*A Sufi Manual on Retreat*) is misleading. See also 'On Withdrawal' (a translation with comments of chapter 205 of the *Futuhat al-Makkiyya*) in Chodkiewicz, ed., *The Meccan Revelations*, 1, pp. 158–61.

59 According to Annett, ed., *The Many Ways of Being*, p. 85, 'Meditation is not thought of by Beshara members as being a particular technique, and the less emphasis laid on technique the better. At first students are introduced to meditation through very simple methods, learning to slow down the breathing rate. Gradually individuals develop their own techniques, which suit them best, but ... these will be very simple.'

60 Rauf, *Addresses*, p. 37.

61 Ibid., pp. 31–2.

62 See Corbin, *Alone with the Alone*, pp. 246ff., esp. pp. 257–8.

63 Rauf, *Addresses*, pp. 28–9.

64 Ibid., p. 29.

65 Ibid., p. 30.

66 Ibid., p. 32.

67 Ibid., p. 30. In full: 'the Mohammedan religion ... has it from the mouth of its Prophet ... who himself instituted and made compulsory the ritual of ... daily quintuple prayer, that a single moment of meditation is preferable to seventy thousand times of ritualistic prayer.' He cites three versions of this hadith (p. 36). These describe a moment of meditation as more beneficial than (a) a year, (b) seventy years, and (c) a thousand years of prayer, respectively. Rauf cites an interpretation of the third version by 'Abd al-Qadir al-Jilani. A further version of this hadith ('An hour of true reflection [*tafakkur*] is better than a night of standing in prayer.') is reported from Abu Darda' via his wife; see Ibn 'Arabi, *Divine Sayings*, trans. Hirtenstein and Notcutt, p. 118 n. 15.

Fikr (intellectual reflection or meditation) is habitually used in contrast to *dhikr* in sufism. In *fikr*, the sufi concentrates upon a religious subject and meditates 'according to a certain progression of ideas or a series of evocations which he assimilates and experiences'. (Typical examples are al-Hallaj's meditations on the Prophet's *mi'raj*, and the practice of the scrutiny of conscience.) Early sufis debated the merits of *fikr* relative to *dhikr*. For example, al-Hasan al-Basri insisted on *fikr* as 'the mirror which makes you see what good there is in you, and what evil'. In commenting on al-Hallaj's words, al-Kalabadhi argued that while by means of *dhikr* the sufi 'is almost certain to succeed in obtaining subjective spiritual states ... *fikr* tends to put him within the possibility of experiencing transcendent truths'. In the course of Islamic history, 'it was the superiority of *dhikr* to *fikr* which was to be most generally affirmed ... Monographs were written on *dhikr*, its techniques and achievements, but not on *fikr* and its methods.' See 'Fikr', EI², II, pp. 891–2, and Knysh, *Islamic Mysticism*, p. 317.

68 Thus, 'It is wrong to think like most Westerners that meditation is a regional practice necessitating an extreme Far-Eastern mind, a deeply Oriental attitude to religion incompatible with ... Western thought forms'. See Rauf, *Addresses*, p. 29.

69 Ibid., p. 30.

70 Rauf may also have projected meditation as preparation for *dhikr*. Annett, ed., *The Many Ways of Being*, p. 85, thus writes: 'Meditation is regarded very much as preparation for *zikr*, helping to make the individual calm, so that *zikr* can be practised in the correct manner.'

71 Rauf, *Addresses*, pp. 32–3. Alongside the ideal of the theophanic prayer, Rauf emphasised (Feild, *The Last Barrier*, p. 53) 'the prayer of the heart, the state where all of life has become a prayer'.

The prayer of the heart (*qalb*, a spiritual organ) is prominent in sufi writings. It is an internal prayer serving to purify the heart. Without fixed time, it should ideally be continuous and constant. If it is neglected, the prescribed formal prayer (*salat*) becomes merely an external show, for it should be an external manifestation of the prayer of the heart. Among others, 'Abd al-Qadir al-Jilani elaborated on its nature and purpose. See Syed Ali Ashraf, The Inner Meaning of the Islamic Rites: Prayer, Pilgrimage, Fasting, Jihad, in Nasr, ed., *Islamic Spirituality: Foundations*, pp. 112–14.

72 For the roots of this practice in the Qur'an, see 'Tahajjud', EI², X, pp. 97–8. For its treatment in the hadith, see *Translation of the Meanings of Sahih al-Bukhari*, by Muhammad Muhsin Khan (Lahore, Pakistan, 1979), II {'The Book of *Tahajjud* (Night) Prayer'}.

The *tahajjud* was recommended by 'Abd al-Qadir al-Jilani in his *Sirr al-asrar* (trans. as *The Secret of Secrets*: for details see n. 50 above) as a specific practice during *khalwa*. As Harris, 'The Relevance of Retreat', pp. 4–5, notes, he recommended for it 'specific petitions, invocations, and Qur'anic recitations, and twelve cycles of formal prayer'. For examples of further elaboration by sufi authorities on night worship, its format and underlying spirit, see Ernst, *The Shambhala Guide to Sufism*, pp. 86–8.

73 Rauf, *Addresses*, p. 36: he referred to it as '*Tahajud* meditation'.

74 On this concept, see below.

75 Rauf, *Addresses*, p. 38. The five 'Divine Presences' are enumerated in order of 'descent' as (p. 23) the *Ghayb*, the *Jabarut*, the *Malakut*, the *Shuhud* and 'the Presence of the Perfect Man, who holds in himself all of the five Presences'. See further 'The Necessary Realisation of a Universal Perspective', undated anon. paper, written by Rauf.

Turan Koç, 'All-Comprehensiveness according to Daud al-Qaysari, and its Implications', *JMIAS*, XXVII (2000), pp. 57–8, offers a helpful explanation of the Presences: 'The sum total of all existent things, when taken as other than God, is the universe or the cosmos. But when they are considered as not other than God, or somehow identical with Him, then they are referred to as "the Presences" (*hadarat*) in Sufi tradition. The followers of Ibn 'Arabi ... talk about five Divine Presences, in which God is present or His presence is perceived.'

For references to the concept/types of the *hadarat* (sing. *hadra*) in Ibn 'Arabi's thought, see Chittick, *The Sufi Path of Knowledge*, index (p. 452). His followers Qunawi, Farghani, Jandi, Kashani and Qaysari developed the concept systematically. For Qaysari's treatment, for example, see Koç, 'All-Comprehensiveness according to Daud al-Qaysari', p. 58. See further 'Abd al-Razzaq al-Qashani, *A Glossary of Sufi Technical Terms*, trans. Nabil Safwat, rev. and ed., David Pendlebury (London, 1991), pp. 44, 57. Bosnevi's definitions arise in the *White Fusus*, 1, p. 29; Bursevi's discussion can be found in *Kernel of the Kernel*, pp. 9–14.

Note that Chittick, 'The Five Divine Presences: From al-Qunawi to al-Qaysari', *The Muslim World*, 72 (1982), p. 107, describes the teaching of the 'Five Divine Presences' as 'probably the most famous teaching of the School of Ibn al-'Arabi after the "Oneness of Being" ... and the "Perfect Man"'.

76 Ibn 'Arabi repeatedly advised the aspirant 'not to stop' at any of the levels revealed to him during his journey of ascent in *khalwa*, each of which constitutes a test: he should stop only when he reaches his ultimate destination. See Ibn 'Arabi, *Journey to the Lord of Power*, pp. 36–48 passim. Reflecting this, Young explains that the Beshara *tahajjud* practice was terminated in response to a concern that students may become 'waylaid' in some state from which they may not want to return; they may also be exposed to influences with which they are not equipped to deal. (Personal correspondence with the author.)

77 This is an allusion to the notion that even Gabriel could not accompany the Prophet once he had reached the proximity of the Divine Presence during his *mi'raj*. See Qur'an, 53: 14, and Ja'far Qasimi, The Life of the Prophet, in Nasr, ed., *Islamic Spirituality: Foundations*, p. 78.

78 Qur'an, 53: 9: 'He was two bows' lengths off, or nearer.' Rauf alludes to the sufi understanding of verses 5–18 as a reference to the Prophet's heavenly ascent. According to the early view, they referred to Gabriel bringing the revelation, and were thus seen as an account of the Prophet's vision during a revelation. Later views, and those of sufis above all, see the passage rather as a description of his vision during the *mi'raj*. See Schimmel, *And Muhammad is His Messenger*, pp. 162–3. Qasimi, The Life of the Prophet, pp. 78–80, cites a passage from al-Suyuti (d.1505) describing the final stage of the Prophet's journey to the Divine Presence. This sets out the interpretation of the verses in question as a reference not to Gabriel, but to God Himself.

79 Rauf, *Addresses*, pp. 38–9.

80 See 'Wird', EI², XI, pp. 209–10; Padwick, *Muslim Devotions*, pp. 20–2; Michon, The Spiritual Practices of Sufism, pp. 277–8, 287. It is widely believed that many of the *awrad* were originally received by the great sufi masters directly from prophets or saints.

81 Muhyiddin Ibn 'Arabi, *Wird* (MIAS, Oxford); reprinted 1988.

82 See MIAS website.

83 See for example Rauf, *Addresses*, p. 70.

84 In contrast, associates quickly acquired an understanding of the meaning of Arabic formulae repeated in the context of *wazifa*s and *dhikr*.

Participants in other universal sufi groups do not necessarily grasp the meaning of the Arabic formulae they use in devotional practices, and such lack of comprehension is considered unimportant. See, for example, Geaves, *The Sufis of Britain*, pp. 173, 183 n. 40.

85 See Christopher Ryan, 'News from Scotland', *MIAS Newsletter*, 16 (Autumn 2000), p. 8.

86 This is Muhiyddin Ibn 'Arabi, *The Seven Days of the Heart: Awrad al-usbu' (Wird), Prayers for the nights and days of the week*, trans. and presented in English by Pablo Beneito and Stephen Hirtenstein (Anqa, Oxford, 2000).

87 Ibid., pp. 2–3.

88 On the term *hizb* (pl. *ahzab*), see Padwick, *Muslim Devotions*, pp. 23–5, and 'Hizb', EI², III, pp. 513–14. Applied in Muslim usage to any single group of supererogatory liturgical formulae (often interchangeably with *wird*), the term has come to have 'an unacknowledged tendency towards semi-magical protection'. A *hizb* thus often functions as an amulet: 'Many famous *ahzab* have directions for use in order to quell or subdue ... hostile forces of men or nature.' For a discussion of historical perceptions of such properties associated with *Hizb al-wiqaya* (as well as its historical transmission and contemporary use, and a translation and critical edition of the text), see Ibn 'Arabi, *A Prayer for Spiritual Elevation and Protection, al-Dawr al-a'la (Hizb al-wiqaya)*, study, translation, transliteration and Arabic text by Suha Taji-Farouki (Anqa/MIAS, Oxford, 2006).

89 *The Hizbu-l Wiqayah of Muhyiddin Ibn 'Arabi* (MIAS, Oxford); reprinted 2003.

90 These can be ordered and purchased from the School, tailor-made by an associate in silver or gold.

91 See Rauf, *Addresses*, p. 54.

92 *Futuhat*, II: 562–3, cited in Addas, *Ibn 'Arabi: The Voyage of No Return*, p. 121.

93 Some associates are now very familiar with this vocabulary, whether relating to the technical expressions of Ibn 'Arabi's metaphysics, or his treatment of the mystical path of devotion. A few make use of his Arabic terminology, but more use English translations of these exclusively, which can result in clumsy and even abstruse results in their written expositions.

Associates appreciate that there are other spiritual vocabularies besides that of Ibn 'Arabi, explaining that they have encountered certain of these in the course of their study. Some mention specifically the language of Meister Eckhart (Elizabeth Roberts, 'Reaffirmation', p. 27, draws on this, for example).

94 As Wilson, *The Strange Fate of Sufism*, pp. 202–3, notes, 'one cannot practise Sufism without inevitably adopting an orientation towards things which might be characterised as being "Islamic"'. Cf. Geaves, *The Sufis of Britain*, pp. 162, 173, 179.

95 Visually, this is mirrored in the prominent examples of Islamic calligraphy in associates' homes.

96 On the ninety-nine Beautiful Names, see al-Ghazali, *The Ninety-Nine Beautiful Names of God: al-Maqsad al-asna fi sharh asma' Allah al-husna*, trans. with notes by David B. Burrell and Nazih Daher (Cambridge, 1992). Examples of associates' names drawn from these are Rahim (from *al-Rahim*, The Most Merciful), Karim (from *al-Karim*, The Generous) and Wadud (from *al-Wadud*, The Loving–Kind). Such names are adapted for women by adding the feminine suffix: for example, Karima from Karim and 'Aliya from *al-'Ali* (The Most High).

Associates named after significant prophets (for example David) retain their names: John and Jane are also retained, for both represent the Arabic Yahya derived from the root *hayy*, itself one of the Names of God.

97 See 'Istikhara', EI², IV, pp. 259–60. The Prophet's own practice was to perform two *rak'a*s of the *salat*, followed by a special prayer including a reference to the subject of the consultation. The inspiration revealing the decision to be taken would be perceived immediately. The practice has also been interpreted in Muslim understandings in a sense making it comparable with incubation, in which case the revelation is received in dreams.

98 'A Note from Mr. Bulent Rauf', p. 15; for the context in which this comment was made, see Ch. 7.

99 Cf. Shah-Kazemi, The Metaphysics of Interfaith Dialogue, pp. 17ff.: the author cites Muhammad Asad's comment that the Prophet's contemporaries would have understood the words *islam* and *muslim* in their original sense ('man's self-surrender to God' and 'one who surrenders … himself to God'), 'without limiting these terms to any specific community or denomination'.

Rauf perhaps again refers implicitly to this understanding of 'islam' as the primordial state of submission in his comment that 'there is no proselytising permitted' in the religion. See 'A Note from Mr. Bulent Rauf', p. 14: it may also be an allusion to Qur'an 2: 256, 'There is no compulsion in religion.'

100 Young uses the term 'muslim' with a small 'm' in the sense of 'submission' in his writings: for example, he describes the all-inclusive point of view as being 'completely *muslim* to the Truth'. See Young, 'Ibn 'Arabi: Towards a Universal Point of View', p. 90.

Cf. Stephen Hirtenstein, 'Muhyiddin Ibn 'Arabi: The Treasure of Compassion', MIAS website: 'It would belittle [Ibn 'Arabi's] greatness to limit his message to Muslims in any strict sense, unless we were to take the word Muslim in its literal meaning – as Ibn 'Arabi so often encourages us to do – i.e. those who have surrendered their will to the will of God.' See also *The Unlimited Mercifier*, p. 69.

101 A sufi master based in Ankara who had an informal circle of followers: see Ch. 8.

102 The claim to be 'in the Muhammadi image' might be made by someone professing to follow the Prophet Muhammad (as someone professing to follow Jesus might advance the claim to be 'in the 'Isawi [of Jesus] image'). The metaphor is one of a mirror image which may not necessarily reflect reality: Young's point here is that an individual's claim to belong to the community of a particular prophet does not in itself indicate that the prophet concerned would embrace them as a member of his community.

The historical Muslim *umma* has suffered doctrinal schisms and political conflict in relation to the fundamental issue of 'who is a Muslim'. Today, competing interpretations divide expressions of Islam (among salafis, traditionalists and modernists, for example), issuing at times in exclusivist definitions. Two extreme-type positions can be posited: the 'minimalist' requires simple but sincere verbal affirmation of the *shahada* or witness of faith, while the 'maximalist' demands that this affirmation be lived out through strict adherence to a consensual spectrum of expression within the doctrinal, ritual and legal legacy of Islam, i.e. to a specific form of Islamic tradition and law.

103 Associates have experienced such pressures in encounters with British Muslim converts, and during visits to Muslim countries.

104 Such limitation must be understood in terms of aligning Beshara with an apparently exclusivist exoteric religious identity, and in light of the following observation by Rauf ('A Note from Mr. Bulent Rauf', p. 15): 'In the Qur'an it is said: "Had we wished we would have made you all of one religion ..." This definitely confirms the intentional diversity of belief, as again God may say: "I conform to the idea my servant has of me."'

105 There is nonetheless evidence of one or two associates having embraced Islam, although they may not always be open about this.

106 Offered without prompting, this definition can possibly be attributed to encounters with sufi Guénonians, converts to Islam who did not take kindly to the Beshara stance: see Ch. 7.

As Zarcone, 'Rereadings and Transformations of Sufism in the West', p. 112, notes, 'Ibn Arabi was the favourite Sufi author of Guénon and his followers.' Moreover, 'it is by the intermediation of the Guénonian converts (Schuon, Vâlsan) that the Sufism of Ibn Arabi has been presented to Westerners ... for almost a century, as the Sufism par excellence, the only, the true'. For sufi Guénonians, Ibn 'Arabi is a central figure as interpreter of Islam (particularly in furnishing resources that justify a view of the equal status of all religions). Sedgwick suggests that Guénon himself did not know Ibn 'Arabi's work well (and perhaps could not read classical Arabic), and that Vâlsan developed the theory that (like his own) Guénon's work was founded on Ibn 'Arabi's thought: see *Against the Modern World*, pp. 77, 135–6. Cf. Waterfield, *René Guénon and the Future of the West*, pp. 41, 85; citing Vâlsan, the author underlines the profound significance of 'Abd al-Rahman 'Illaysh as Guénon's link with Ibn 'Arabi.

The connection of Guénon and the sufi Traditionalists with Ibn 'Arabi can be traced back to the initiation in 1907 of Ivan Aguéli (d. 1917), a Swedish artist, member of the Paris Theosophical Society and 'proto-Traditionalist', as a disciple of 'Illaysh (d. 1921), head of the 'Arabiyya–Shadhiliyya order in Egypt. Aguéli (henceforth 'Abd al-Hadi) was later appointed the shaykh's *muqaddam*. On 'Illaysh's spiritual lineage, life (including a spell in Damascus as guest of the Amir 'Abd al-Qadir), and status as Azharite scholar and sufi shaykh, see Meir Hatina, 'Where East Meets West: Sufism as a Lever for Cultural Rapprochement' (unpublished paper), pp. 3ff. (thanks are due to the author for providing this). Through 'Abd al-Hadi, 'Illaysh controversially formed close ties with Italian government agent Enrico Insabato. The latter was an editor of the Italian/Arabic periodical *Il Convito/al-Nadi* (1904–14), published in Cairo and devoted to Islamic and sufi subjects (especially the thought of Ibn 'Arabi), and having the declared mission of creating bridges between East and West. 'Illaysh was a regular contributor and 'Abd al-Hadi an editor: on this see Michel Vâlsan, *L'Islam et la fonction de René Guénon* (Paris, 1984), pp. 33ff. Among other motives, it seems 'Illaysh may have seen Italian patronage as a means to rejuvenate the 'Arabiyya–Shadhiliyya, which had fallen from prominence at the turn of the century due to a lack of resources and internal rifts. 'Illaysh has been described as a major protagonist of an 'Akbarian current' during the second half of the nineteenth century: see Chodkiewicz, *Seal of the Saints*, pp. 22, 195–6 n. 71. (Rawlinson, 'A History of Western Sufism', indeed dubs the line established through 'Abd al-Hadi the 'Western Shadhiliyya-cum-Akbariyya'.) 'Abd al-Halim Mahmud, *al-Madrasa al-Shadhiliyya al-haditha* (Cairo, 1968), p. 254, describes him as 'a mirror reflecting an image of ... Ibn 'Arabi'. The sufism 'Illaysh practised and promoted was strictly contained within the parameters of the law. (Cf. Rawlinson, 'A History of Western Sufism', pp. 13,

17, which suggests that he was interested in 'Islamic universalism', traced to the teachings of Ibn 'Arabi. His attractiveness to foreigners, especially Christians, and the relations he forged with them perhaps underlie this projection.)

'Illaysh sent 'Abd al-Hadi to Europe in 1911 to further spiritual dialogue; he met Guénon in Paris, and through him the latter established a strong bond with 'Illaysh via correspondence. As a result of this, in 1912 Guénon (henceforth 'Abd al-Wahid Yahya) accepted Islam. Sedgwick, *Against the Modern World*, pp. 59–63, 66–8, suggests that on 'Illaysh's death (which he puts at 1929) 'Abd al-Hadi joined the Hamidiyya–Shadhiliyya; 'Abd al-Wahid also joined this order after moving to Cairo in 1930. From then on, he devoted himself to research on sufism and the works of Ibn 'Arabi.

The emphasis placed on Ibn 'Arabi continued with Schuon (d.1998), who was initiated in 1932 into the 'Alawiyya–Shadhiliyya by Ahmad ibn Mustafa al-'Alawi, to whom he had been directed by Guénon. He was later appointed as an 'Alawi *muqaddam*. This emphasis was also taken up by Vâlsan, Schuon's erstwhile *muqaddam* in Paris, who had taken the 'Alawi *tariqa* from him in 1938.

The breach between Schuon and Guénon from the late 1940s led to a reconfiguration among the main sufi Traditionalists. Guénon's comment from 1950 (cited in Zarcone, 'Rereadings and Transformations of Sufism in the West', p. 116) concerning Schuon's group, resulting from the observation that at the time Islamic ritual observances within it had been reduced to the bare minimum, is noteworthy in the present context: 'soon this group will not be a *tariqa* but a "vague 'universalist' organization"'. (For their part, Schuonians emphasise Guénon's continued respect for Schuon's work 'until his dying day'. See William Stoddardt, Introduction: Titus Burckhardt and the Perennialist School, in Stoddardt, ed., *The Essential Titus Burckhardt*, p. 2.) On the Guénon–Schuon split, Lings (d.2005, a close associate of Guénon who had joined the 'Alawiyya in 1938) followed Schuon (having apparently become the latter's *muqaddam*), while Vâlsan followed Guénon. Schuon (who can be said to have inherited Guénon's position as the leading Traditionalist/Perennialist) and his followers in particular draw heavily on Ibn 'Arabi in their justification of their view of the transcendent unity of religions (which Schuon developed further than Guénon). For Schuon's exposition of this notion, see his seminal work *The Transcendent Unity of Religions* (London, 1953). For an assertion of its validity from the point of view of the Islamic tradition, see Seyyed Hossein Nasr, *Sufi Essays* (London, 1972), pp. 123–51. For a recent 'Schuonian' application of the metaphysics/hermeneutics of Ibn 'Arabi and his school, see Shah-Kazemi, The Metaphysics of Interfaith Dialogue, pp. 140–90, passim. See further his *The Other in the Light of the One: The Universality of the Qur'an and Interfaith Dialogue* (Cambridge, 2006), especially chapter 1, where an understanding of Ibn 'Arabi's 'inclusivist hermeneutic' is set out (thanks are due to the author for providing a pre-publication version of this). For a refutation of the appropriation of Ibn 'Arabi by Guénon and Schuonian writers by a contemporary Shadhili, see Nuh Ha Mim Keller, 'On the Validity of All Religions in the Thought of Ibn al-'Arabi and Emir 'Abd al-Qadir: A Letter to 'Abd al-Matin', 1996, www.masud.co.uk. See also Zarcone, 'Rereadings and Transformations of Sufism in the West', p. 117. For a brief overview of the sufi Guénonians including especially the Schuonian *tariqa* Maryamiyya, see Sedgwick, 'Traditionalist Sufism', pp. 2ff., and Rawlinson, 'A History of Western Sufism', pp. 13–14, 17–19.

Vâlsan (d.1974) effectively became head of the first 'non-Schuonian' Guénonian *tariqa*, and endeavoured to reconcile Guénon's doctrine with the imperatives of Islam and those of the sufism of Ibn 'Arabi. Vâlsan (and more recently his followers, including Chodkiewicz, Gril and Gilis) have applied themselves to translating and publishing studies of Ibn 'Arabi's corpus: they constitute a major force in contemporary French Akbarian studies. Since Vâlsan's death, Chodkiewicz has served as the group's leading figure (he is also a major authority on the *Futuhat*, which he studied with various shaykhs in Syria).

We might finally draw attention to the continuing traditional Shadhili interest in Ibn

'Arabi: in contemporary Damascus, for example, circles devoted to reading the *Futuhat* and mosque lessons in which parts of its final chapter (published separately as *Kitab al-Wasaya*) are read are all led by shaykhs of Shadhili sub-branches. See Taji-Farouki, *At the Resting-place of the Seal of Saints*.

107 This comment may reflect a superficial evaluation of the Guénonian legacy regarding the real nature of Islam as *the* (universal) religion. Many sufi Guénonians thus emphasise Islam in its all-encompassing and universal aspect (as well as in its capacity as a specific historical tradition: compare with comments by Gilis, Ch. 7). Rauf implicitly recognised this understanding of Islam (in his insistence that the Qur'an applies the term 'Moslem' beyond 'the Mohammedans', for example, but equally in his reference to the universality of 'the originally non-dogmatic religion preached by Muhammed'; see Rauf, *Addresses II*, p. 98, also p. 30). He thus reflected Ibn 'Arabi's projection of Islam as encompassing all other religions (set out in *The Twenty-nine Pages*, pp. 42, 65, for example). The parting of company arose in relation to historical Islam: for Rauf the defining imperative was to repudiate *all* historical religions (given that these are not the divinely designated receptacle for the spirit in the present age). An associate elaborates thus: 'All religions expound the same essential truth, but if you embrace a particular one it is of necessity an external form and so is in contradistinction to other forms. Ibn 'Arabi wrote of religion (*din*) being of two kinds: the religion instituted by God, and that which has developed through human transmission. The religion instituted by God is what underlies all the historical religions, and that is what we focus on.' He refers here to *The Bezels of Wisdom*, p. 113 (Ibn 'Arabi, *Fusus al-hikam*, p. 94), where the key distinction between 'the religion of God and those whom God has taught His religion' and 'the religion of created beings, which God acknowledges' is introduced.

For associates, then, the embrace of Islam signifies a divisive and exclusivist closing off to other religions that does not sit well with the 'religion instituted by God', itself destined to be understood by all today. For many sufi Guénonians, in contrast, the embrace of Islam signifies an opening up to the preceding religious traditions, and an implicit encompassing of these (of course it also reflected Guénon's emphasis on the unique quality of tradition/orthodoxy as a channel for salvation). Islam is here understood (at least following Schuon) as the 'quintessential religion' or 'religion as such' par excellence. Quintessential 'Islam' is Islam understood as universal submission to God, rather than only as a particular religious denomination. See, for example, Lings, *What is Sufism?*, pp. 22–3, and Shah-Kazemi, The Metaphysics of Interfaith Dialogue, pp. 142, 160ff., 168–9. According to the latter, '"Islam" encompasses all revelations, which can thus be seen as so many different facets of essentially one and the same self-disclosure of the divine reality'. Cf. p. 174: 'The "Islam" revealed to the Prophet Muhammad is unique, and thus a religion; but at the same time, it is identical in its essence to all religions, and is thus the religion – in other words, it is both such and such a religion, and religion as such'. For Rauf, we reiterate, the embrace of Islam represented a closing off from other religions in an exclusivist form that was (in any case) destined among them all to lose its relevance as a conduit for spiritual vitality.

The associate's analysis cited in our text at the same time fails to take into account the complexity of at least some sufi Guénonians' relationship to Islam, as perceived by at least some commentators. As Zarcone, 'Rereadings and Transformations of Sufism in the West', p. 114, puts it, for example, 'Those who followed [Guénon] into Islam and those who today still continue to espouse this religion comprise two groups: the first gathers together the Guénonians who have chosen to adhere to Sufism while only "passing" by Islam, by in fact "settling" in this religion; the second by contrast unites the people who were fully converted to Islam and have embraced Sufism. In this latter group, some converts have only preserved a distant attachment to the Guénonian system. They have tried to have direct access to the essential texts of Sufism, thanks to knowledge of the Arabic language ... and have links with shaykhs in the East.' He contrasts Schuon (who 'virtually separated himself from Islam while remaining a Sufi') with Vâlsan (who 'consolidated his bond with Islam and sought the most perfect orthodoxy while remaining faithful to Guénon's thought'): see p. 116.

Finally, for examples of the recent impact of Guénon's legacy in bringing Europeans to Islam and sufism, see Loïc Le Pape, Communication Strategies and Public Commitments: The Example of a Sufi Order in Europe, in Stefano Allievi and Jorgen Nielsen, eds, *Muslim Networks and Transnational Communities in and across Europe* (Leiden, 2003), pp. 232–4.

108 For example, the *hadith qudsi* 'But for your sake, I would not have created the spheres', and the prophetic hadith: 'I was a prophet while Adam was between water and clay', 'The first thing that God created was my spirit', and 'Who has seen me, has seen *al-haqq*.' See Schimmel, *And Muhammad is His Messenger*, pp. 130–1.

109 Ibid., pp. 124ff. The author suggests that the interpretation by theologian Muqatil ibn Sulayman (d.767) of 'the light verse' (Qur'an 24: 35) as referring to the Prophet was the first of its kind. This vision was developed by Sahl al-Tustari (d.896), who 'first expressed the entire *Heilsgeschichte* in the terminology of the Light of Muhammad'. Three centuries later, Ibn 'Arabi 'is largely responsible for the central role of this [pre-eternal Muhammadan] light in later Sufism'. Further (p. 132): 'belief in the preexistence of Muhammad's essence, first elaborated by Sahl al-Tustari and Hallaj, praised in eloquent words by authors like Tha'labi, and systematized into theory by Ibn 'Arabi, permeates Sufism.' See also Chodkiewicz, *Seal of the Saints*, pp. 60ff.

110 Schimmel, *And Muhammad is His Messenger*, p. 132. On the specific nature and function of *al-haqiqa al-Muhammadiyya* in the doctrine of Ibn 'Arabi, see Chodkiewicz, *Seal of the Saints*, pp. 67ff. Note the aspect of Muhammad in this doctrine as the Perfect or Complete Man (*al-insan al-kamil*): ibid., pp. 70ff. See also Addas, *Ibn 'Arabi: The Voyage of No Return*, pp. 21–5. Note also the nature of *al-haqiqa al-Muhammadiyya* as the fountainhead of all prophetic activity: see Schimmel, *And Muhammad is His Messenger*, p. 132.

111 See Addas, *Ibn 'Arabi: The Voyage of No Return*, p. 23.

112 Ibid., p. 25. The importance of this notion to Ibn 'Arabi's teaching cannot be overemphasised. Addas, 'The Experience and Doctrine of Love', pp. 27, 38, elaborates further: 'in the Islamic tradition, it is the Prophet Muhammad – and he alone – who constitutes the *exemplum*, the infallible model that the pilgrim of God should imitate to the highest degree. This axiom provides the basis and structure for Ibn 'Arabi's hagiological doctrine; it also governs his spiritual journey.' And: 'Of the nine spiritual virtues ... he takes into consideration out of all those that the Qur'an mentions as unfailingly suited to evoke God's love ... it is the *ittiba' al-nabi* (following the Prophet) that he puts at the top of the list. He emphasizes that in addition to following the Prophet by observing what is legally obligatory ... this implies imitating him also in what is supererogatory ... and, consequently, in the "noble virtues" which he exemplified.' Finally, she adds (*Ibn 'Arabi: The Voyage of No Return*, p. 21): 'for Muslim mystics conformity to the Muhammadan example is the *sine qua non* of all spiritual realisation, being both its means and its end ... Imitation of the Prophet cannot be reduced to copying his deeds and his movements; it implies in-depth knowledge of his "customs" (*sunna*) ... Ibn 'Arabi ... was well aware of this ... [he] would continue his study of hadith until the day he died. It should be emphasised that the importance he placed on this study ... on *practising* the *sunna*, was ... not a pious concession in conformity with the Islamic society in which he lived: it was part and parcel of his hagiological, as well as his initiatory teaching.'

113 For an introduction to the veneration of the Prophet in sufi circles, see Geaves, *The Sufis of Britain*, pp. 28–35.

114 On the Prophet as beautiful model in Muslim piety in general, see Schimmel, *And Muhammad is His Messenger*, pp. 32ff. The matter of how best to understand and effect this emulation has been the subject of persistent debates, and there are important differences of understanding. See for example ibid., pp. 31–2, and Daniel Brown, *Rethinking Tradition in Modern Islamic Thought* (Cambridge, 1999), chapter 1.

115 Cf. Hirtenstein, *The Unlimited Mercifier*, p. 100.

116 On the origins and practice of the tradition of *tasliya* in Muslim devotion (which dates back to the time of the Prophet himself), and its development at the hands of certain mystics, see Schimmel, *And Muhammad is His Messenger*, pp. 92ff. See also Padwick, *Muslim Devotions*, pp. 152ff., noting that 'the *tasliya* has become an essential, sometimes it would seem, *the* essential of the life of salvation and devotion'.

117 Souad al-Hakim, *al-Mu'jam al-sufi: al-hikma fi hudud al-kalima* (Beirut, 1981), p. 1018, describes *mumidd al-himma* (note spelling) as 'one of the functional names of the Perfect Man (the Prophet Muhammad)'.

118 The *White Fusus*, 3, p. 697: '[When Jesus descends again] he will remove some of the determinations, which are established through religious legal opinion of the individuals and which are ambiguous, which were at the time of the Envoy, and were not necessarily according to the determinations of the Envoy (S.A)'.

119 For an introduction to saints and sainthood in Islam, see Ernst, *The Shambhala Guide to Sufism*, chapter 3; Frederick M. Denny, 'God's Friends': The Sanctity of Persons in Islam, in Richard Kieckhefer and George D. Bond, eds, *Sainthood: Its Manifestations in World Religions* (Berkeley, 1988), pp. 69–97; 'Wali', EI², XI, pp. 109ff. For an important early treatment of the subject by sufi al-Hakim al-Tirmidhi (d.c.910), see Bernd Radtke, The Concept of *Wilaya* in Early Sufism, in Leonard Lewisohn, ed., *The Heritage of Persian Sufism*, 1: *Classical Persian Sufism from its Origins to Rumi (700–1300)*, pp. 483ff. For Ibn 'Arabi's treatment, see Chodkiewicz, *Seal of the Saints*.

On the Muslim cult of saints and the practice of *ziyara*, see 'Ziyara', EI², XI, pp. 524–39, on Turkey specifically pp. 534–5: the author notes that, with the relaxation of Kemalist doctrines since the 1950s, the practice of *ziyara* has been reconstituted on new foundations, while retaining connections to the old traditions. For an example from contemporary Egypt, see Nadia Abu Zahra, *The Pure and Powerful: Studies in Contemporary Muslim Society* (London, 2000); from contemporary Damascus, see Taji-Farouki, *At the Resting-place of the Seal of Saints*. For discussion of the medieval cult and practice, see Josef W. Meri, The Etiquette of Devotion in the Islamic Cult of Saints, in James Howard-Johnston and Paul Anthony Hayward, eds, *The Cult of Saints in Late Antiquity and the Middle Ages* (Oxford, 1999), pp. 263–86, and Christopher S. Taylor, *In the Vicinity of the Righteous: Ziyara and the Veneration of Muslim Saints in Late Medieval Egypt* (Leiden, 1999). On the concept of *baraka*, see 'Baraka', EI², I, p. 1032.

120 See *The Twenty-nine Pages*, pp. 41–2, for example.

121 'A Trip to Turkey', p. 7.

122 Ibid. Note that *himma* is sometimes translated as 'spiritual concentration'.

123 Ibid.

124 Note also his comment (ibid., p. 8) that, while demands of geography and time necessitated that Hüdayi be visited before Üftade during the trip, yet 'the magnitude of Üftade is in no way comparable or secondary to any'. (Rauf had also warned associates not to make comparisons regarding authorship of the *White Fusus*, and for this reason later volumes retained the work's attribution to Bursevi).

125 For example, in correspondence to a close associate (early 1970s), Rauf insisted that it was not fitting to describe his own visit to the tomb of Hüdayi. In 'A Trip to Turkey', p. 10, he remarked that to perceive the manner in which the *qutb* of the time exercises his power requires a fine and delicate discernment, 'which will come about only with a growing awareness of tact (*adab*)'.

The term *adab* might be translated as courtesy, culture or correct comportment. According to Denis Gril, *Adab* and Revelation or One of the Foundations of the Hermeneutics of Ibn 'Arabi, in Hirtenstein and Tiernan, eds, *Muhyiddin Ibn 'Arabi: A Commemorative Volume*, p. 228, in Arab–Islamic tradition it describes 'the right attitude in any situation, whether it be a matter of doctrine, path of initiation, religious practice or of comportment towards any being whatsoever'. In sufism, it is often used in the plural to mean 'rules of conduct', the directing principles of the sufi's outward life (parallel to the inner stages of the mystical path and modelled on the example of the Prophet). In the classical literature of sufism it tended to refer more specifically to the attitude that should be observed in respect of God, or in relations between master and disciple. Ibn 'Arabi's treatment of *adab* insists especially on its exercise towards the Qur'anic and Prophetic message: he describes the *adib*, the one who knows and respects *adab*, as 'the wise man'. See ibid., pp. 228–9.

An associate describes tact or *adab* as 'understanding what is due to God and what is due to the servant'. Young, 'Universal Nature', p. 21, elaborates: 'It is said that if a discussion arises concerning the Divine Nature, tact requires that one breaks the circle of conversation and leaves the room, since such a conversation would assume that the Ipseity of God, known only to Itself, were subject to logic, speculation or opinion'. In 'Between the Yea and the Nay', p. 3, he adds that tact is 'action consequent to the perception and appreciation of the order of things … It is difficult to see how that which is not tactfully expressed can convey anything significant of Truth since lack of tact is non-conformity to the order of how things are in Reality'. Such concerns are underlined in 'What is the Difference? A Reaffirmation', pp. 30–1, pointing to the 'delicacy and tact' necessary in talking of what is unlimited and cannot be defined.

126 'A Trip to Turkey', p. 10.

127 Rauf referred to Ateşbaz Veli in his 'Notice to Cooks': his tomb is just outside Konya. On Rumi, Shams and the Mevlevi *tariqa*, see Chittick, Rumi and the Mawlawiyyah, pp. 105–26 and *The Sufi Path of Love*; Schimmel, *The Triumphal Sun* and Mawlana Rumi: Yesterday, Today and Tomorrow, pp. 5–27; Friedlander, *The Whirling Dervishes*.

128 On him, see Clark, 'Early Best-sellers in the Akbarian Tradition', pp. 22–53; Chittick, 'The Central Point' and The School of Ibn 'Arabi, pp. 511–14. For Rauf's projection of Qunawi as Rumi's teacher, see Ch. 5.

129 Trimingham, *The Sufi Orders in Islam*, p. 81; A. T. Karamustafa, Early Sufism in Eastern Anatolia, in Lewisohn, ed., *The Heritage of Persian Sufism*, 1, p. 187, puts the date of death considerably earlier: 'around the same time as Jalal al-Din Rumi (in 1273), or soon thereafter'.

130 On this, see Trimingham, *The Sufi Orders in Islam*, pp. 81–2, 59, 188; Ocak, Religion, pp. 208–10; J. K. Birge, *The Bektashi Order of Dervishes* (London, 1987).

131 The patron saint of Ankara, buried in a shrine beside the mosque he had built (abutting on the Temple of Augustus). He first taught at a *medrese* in Ankara, but abandoned his theological career when invited by Hamidüddin Aksarayi (d.1412; a significant Halveti saint of Bursa known popularly as Somuncu Baba) to join him as his disciple. Following Hamidüddin's death he was regarded as his spiritual successor; returning to Ankara, he gained a large following there. On him, see 'Hadjdji Bayram Wali', EI², III, p. 43, and Fuat Bayramoğlu, Haci Bayram-i Veli: Yaşami, Soyu, Vakfi (Ankara, 1983). Öztürk, *The Eye of the Heart*, p. 115, describes him as 'the man who firmly implanted the Malami way in Anatolia' (see below). All that remains by Haci Bayram Veli are some poems and the *wird* of his master, which he expanded; see Ballanfat, *Le Divan*, p. 19 n. 37.

132 Deriving from the Halvetiyye, the Bayramiyye was founded in Ankara. As touched on earlier, Haci Bayram Veli's disciples included Aq Şemseddin and Ömer Sikkini, who headed the two branches into which the order split after his death. One adopted the manifest *dhikr*, following Aq Şemseddin. The other (under Sikkini of Bursa) abandoned the *dhikr*, *wird*, individual costumes and *tekke*s of the order: these are the Melami–Bayramis.

Characterisations of this latter branch as a blend of the Halvetiyye and the Naqshbandiyya are based on its preference for the hidden *dhikr* (a feature of the Naqshbandis). In fact, this practice is rather a product of its Melami origins. Its chief doctrinal peculiarity (another mark of these origins) is that the devotee was introduced to the concept of *wahdat al-wujud* at the beginning of his spiritual career (rather than at its end, as was the case in other *tariqa*s). The Melamiyye recognised more than one

Bayrami shaykh as the *qutb* of the time. See 'Bayramiyya', EI², I, p.1137; Trimingham, *The Sufi Orders in Islam*, pp 75, 78; Ocak, Religion, pp.204–5. Ballanfat, *Le Divan*, p.19 n.37, notes that the order occupied an important place in Ottoman sufism, particularly through its branches. Like the Naqshbandiyya, its spiritual lineage goes back to both 'Ali and Abu Bakr.

133 See Trimingham, *The Sufi Orders in Islam*, p.76; Knysh, *Islamic Mysticism*, pp.266–7; 'Sha'baniyya'. Shaban Veli left no written works. His successors propagated his way within Anatolia and its influence soon spread far beyond, reaching the Ottoman capital. His significant disciple Shaykh Shuja' (d.1588) had influence on Sultan Murat III. A new branch of the order was established by 'Ali Qarabash (d.1685), author of several works on sufism.

134 On this, see Trimingham, *The Sufi Orders in Islam*, pp.74ff.; 'Khalwatiyya', pp.991–3; B. G. Martin, A Short History of the Khalwatiyya Order of Dervishes, in N. R. Keddie, ed., *Scholars, Saints and Sufis: Muslim Institutions since 1500* (Berkeley, 1972), pp.275–305; Ocak, Religion, pp.205–6.

De Jong, 'Khalwatiyya', notes that the first shaykh in its *silsila* was either 'Umar al-Khalwati (d.1397) or his shaykh Muhammad b. Nur al-Basili, also called al-Khalwati because of his frequent retreats. A third possibility is that the real founder of the *tariqa* was Yahya al-Shirwani al-Babuki (d.1464). In contrast, Ocak identifies the actual founder as Ibrahim Zahid Gilani. The *tariqa* spread in Anatolia under Bayazid II and experienced a florescence under Suleyman the Magnificent and Selim III, when many prominent figures in the administration had links to it or favoured it. While it self-characterised as the *tariqa* of Junayd, De Jong observes that the influence of Ibn 'Arabi's thinking is manifest in varying degrees in its shaykhs' writings. He adds that most of the Khalwati *tariqa*s consider periodic retreat (*khalwa*) a requirement for the *murid*: they differ in their views concerning the stage at which it is prescribed.

Fragmentation of the *tariqa* resulted from the absence of a centralised structure. Öztürk, *The Eye of the Heart*, p.91, writes: 'By the end of the 19th century, the Khalwati *tarikat* consisted of no less than fifty separate brotherhoods, each of which has often been regarded as a distinct *tarikat*. If, however, we consider that all of these brotherhoods hold a basic set of beliefs and ceremonies in common, it seems better to regard them all as members of one great unity: the Khalwati *tarikat*. The *tariqa* is reputed to have attracted fifteen sultans. See further Brown, *The Darvishes*, pp.449ff.

135 See Ocak, Religion, pp.200–2, 205–6.

136 Note that Haci Bayram Veli is linked to this cluster through his connection with the spiritual master of Üftade, Hizir Dede: see below.

137 Trimingham, *The Sufi Orders in Islam*, p.78, refers to him as Muhammad Jilwati 'Pir Uftade'. On him, see below.

138 On him, see 'Huda'i', EI², III, p.538; Lifchez, The Lodges of Istanbul, p.113; Brown, *The Darvishes*, p.87 n.2, 227; Ballanfat, *Le Divan*, p.77 n.192. Having preached in Edirne and Bursa (his native village was Koçhisar), Hüdayi came to Istanbul and eventually settled in Üsküdar (at the site of his *turbe*-mosque complex), possibly in 1593. By 1577, he had become a disciple of Üftade (founder of the Celvetiyye), and would emerge as his most important successor. In addition to producing original works of his own, Hüdayi collected those of Üftade. He served in the imperial mosques of three sultans, and was particularly influential during the reign of Sultan Ahmet I (having reputedly gained his respect following a miraculous interpretation of a dream: he also married into his family). Ballanfat, *Le Divan*, p.6, translates a religious song composed by Hüdayi in honour of Üftade, used in a number of Turkish orders.

139 Bursevi was a student of Osman Fazli, then head of the Celvetiyye, who had initiated him into the *tariqa* and whom he succeeded as its head on Fazli's death in 1691. A celebrated Ottoman scholar and poet, he left more than a hundred works, including a Qur'an commentary (*Ruh al-bayan*) and a commentary on part of Rumi's *Mathnavi*. Lewis, *Rumi: Past and Present*, pp.479–80, 547, notes that the latter (*Ruh al-Masnavi*), covering only the first 738 lines but occupying two volumes, was published in 1860/1870 in Istanbul. Young hopes to commission an English translation of it. For a rendering into modern Turkish, see Ismail Güleç, *Mesnevi Şerhi: Ruhü-l-Mesnevi* (Istanbul, 2004). Bursevi's influence extended beyond Ottoman literature and art to its music: he set Hüdayi's poems to music, composed music himself and left a treatise providing details of the musical performances of the later Mevlevis.

On him, see 'Isma'il Hakki Bursevi', EI², IV, pp. 191–2, and EI¹ (*Encyclopaedia of Islam*, 1ˢᵗ edn [Leiden, 1934]), II, p. 547; Friedlander, *The Whirling Dervishes*, pp. 129–30; Brown, *The Darvishes*, p. 456. Beshara Publications has published as *Kernel of the Kernel* an English translation of Ismail Hakki Bursevi's commentary on and translation of Ibn 'Arabi's *Lubb al-lubb*.

140 Personal correspondence from Rauf to a close associate (26 September 1973).

141 Associates recall that there were few visitors to Qunawi's tomb during the early years of their visits, in contrast with those of Shams and Rumi. On this tomb, see Clark, 'Early Best-sellers in the Akbarian Tradition', pp. 41–2.

142 Limitations of time make it difficult to encompass visits to the tombs of Haci Bektaş Veli and Shaban Veli in the south and north of Anatolia respectively.

143 'A Trip to Turkey', p. 7.

144 For a summary of the opinions of various sufi authorities concerning the special quality of saints' tombs and the effects of pilgrimage to them, see Ernst, *The Shambhala Guide to Sufism*, pp. 72–4.

145 'A Trip to Turkey', pp. 7–8.

146 The references are to Qur'an: 1 (traditionally recited for the dead in Muslim practice) and 112, respectively. 'A Trip to Turkey' provides English transliterations of these texts.

147 'A Trip to Turkey', pp. 12, 2. Implicit in this order is an emphasis of Qunawi's importance in Rumi's life consistent with Rauf's projection of this. Feild's memory presumably let him down when he wrote that Rauf conveyed the proper order for these visits as beginning with Shams, then Qunawi and then Rumi (*The Last Barrier*, p. 107).

Based on several visits to these saints, one associate suggests that the order given in 'A Trip to Turkey' is well known: 'Everyone follows it; it is passed from generation to generation by the Anatolian people.' Note the comment by Friedlander, *The Whirling Dervishes*, p. 66, that 'It is correct to visit Shams and then proceed to [Rumi].'

148 The very first trips had been 'basically a trip to Konya, centring on attendance of the *sama*.' The first time associates went in any number was December 1973, the 700th anniversary of the death of Rumi; on this event, see Lewis, *Rumi: Past and Present*, p. 466.

Up to 1978, trips had encompassed only the following saints: Rumi, Shams and Qunawi in Konya, and Haci Bayram Veli and Haci Bektaş Veli in Ankara and southern Anatolia respectively. In addition, the trip had always arranged a visit to Mary's House at Ephesus.

149 On the very western edge of the Anatolian plain, Bursa cannot be considered part of it.

150 The term *mashrab* appears in Qur'an 7: 160 ('All peoples know their drinking-place'), referring to the twelve tribes of Israel in the desert. Through divine guidance, Moses had struck a rock with his staff, and twelve springs of water appeared for his thirsty people. Ibn 'Arabi incorporates this Qur'anic phrase into a rhyming verse in the *'Anqa' mughrib*, translated in Elmore, *Islamic Sainthood in the Fullness of Time*, p. 308: '"All peoples know their drinking place (*mashrabu-hum*)," and realize their own method and their manner (*tariqu-hum wa-madhhabu-hum*).' Developing the analogy, Ibn 'Arabi writes of the 'churned cream' of sufi wisdom, which Elmore explains as 'the common libation of the various separate *masharib*'. For a further use of the term, see Ibn 'Arabi, *Fusus al-hikam*, p. 61, where he remarks that the meaning of a particular phrase is not as imagined by 'he who is not of this *mashrab*', here signifying the way (of understanding) of the *muhaqqiqun*. For an example of Bosnevi's use of the term (which he ties to *dhawq*), in the context of an explanation of why it was specifically Hud who spoke to Ibn 'Arabi in a vision of all the prophets, see the *White Fusus*, 3, p.570. Note that 'Djilwatiyya', EI², II, p.542, describes *jalwa* and *khalwa* as distinct practices, which the author renders *mashrab*. Finally, the term *mashrab* is also used for theological (and philosophical) 'schools'.

151 Cf. the example of Osman Fazli, seventeenth-century Celveti shaykh and teacher of Bursevi, as projected by Christopher Ryan, 'In Search of Osman Fazli', *MIAS Newsletter*, 20 (Spring 2004), p.4.

152 Inspired by what he heard, one associate arranged a private visit to Bursa and gained access to the tomb of Üftade, then permanently locked. He describes an overwhelming sense of familiarity on entering the tomb: 'I felt as though I was standing before my grandfather.'

153 Minutes of the MIAS AGM, 26 October 1985, provides a two-page biography of Bursevi (citing the EI¹ article on him referred to above): Young's Foreword to the *White Fusus*, 3 (1988) draws on this. Much later (1997), Ryan, Conversion to the Essence, pp.336–8, repeats accounts relating to Üftade and Hüdayi and provides biographical details.

154 According to 'Djilwa', EI², II, p.542, Ibn 'Arabi uses *jilwah* (*jalwa*) (literally the 'ceremony of raising the bride's veil') as 'the name of the state in which the mystic is on coming out of the *khalwa*: filled with the emanations of divine attributes, his own personality has disappeared and mingles with the being of God'. See further Chodkiewicz, ed., *The Meccan Revelations*, 1, pp.157–61, especially p.158, and Brown, *The Darvishes*, p.87 n.3.

155 See Brass, Foreword, the *White Fusus*, 2, pp.vi–vii.

156 See 'A Trip to Turkey', p.8.

157 Thanks are due to Paul Ballanfat for this assessment. For a brief introduction, see 'Djilwatiyya', pp.542–3, and Veinstein and Clayer, L'Empire ottoman, pp.327, 331.

158 For example, Mustafa Bahadiroğlu, *Celvetiye'nin Piri Hz. Üftade ve Divan'i* (Bursa, 1995); Yilmaz, *Aziz Mahmud Hüdayi* (1999); *Menakib-i Üftade*, ed., Abdurrahman Yünal (Bursa, 1996), and Mustafa Utku, *Ismail Hakki Bursevi'den Dersler: Şerh-i Hadis-i Erbain* (Bursa, 1999).

On such recent Turkish publications and the rendering of Celveti texts into modern Turkish from Arabic or Ottoman Turkish, see further *MIAS Newsletter*, 16 (Autumn 2000), p.3.

159 This provides fragmented information. The author notes that Celvetis would wear their hair long and describes their clothing. He remarks that 'They perform on their knees the *zikr* and the *ism-i-jalal*': pp.274, 227, 87, 61. He provides the line of descent (p.87; cf. p.456), and lists fourteen convents in Constantinople of his day, giving the days of the week on which the Celvetis would meet (pp.460–2). Finally, he observes that the order was also known as the 'Hudayis', suggesting that the name derives from the notion of guidance (*huda*) and may also allude to *hadi*, 'a bride when conducted home in public procession'.

160 'A Trip to Turkey' (December 1999), pp.8–10. The reference is to Hasan Turyan, *Bursa Evliyalari ve Tarihi Eserleri* (Bursa, 1982). Holbrook, 'Ibn 'Arabi and Ottoman Dervish Traditions', I, p.33 n.17, characterises this as a doctoral thesis 'combining oral tradition with philological techniques' and 'pious enthusiasm with academics'. It is a modern source for the biographies of spiritually influential figures in the framework of a travel book for those visiting historical sites, providing biographies of the people associated with these.

161 Ballanfat, *Le Divan; The Nightingale in the Garden of Love*. Ballanfat's substantial introduction draws on major Celveti manuscripts, including the significant journal by Hüdayi recording his spiritual education at the hands of the master, *Waqi'at-i Üftade* (of which Ballanfat and Mustafa Bahadiroğlu are currently preparing a critical edition.) See further Yilmaz, *Aziz Mahmud Hüdayi*, pp.186–90, and Bahadiroğlu, *Celvetiye'nin Piri Hz. Üftade*, pp.33ff. References in the present study are to the French publication.

162 See for example *Le Divan*, pp. 45, 47.

163 Given the difficulty in reconciling the life spans of Haci Bayram Veli (d.1429) and Hizir Dede (d.1507), Ballanfat (ibid., pp. 21, 45) suggests he may have acquired this initiation through Uwaysi channels, rather than at the hands of a living Haci Bayram.

The *silsila* of the Celvetiyye given by Ballanfat (ibid., pp. 44–5), starting with the Prophet through 'Ali, lists at its nearer end Hamiddüdin Aksarayi (Somuncu Baba) (d.1412), Haci Bayram Veli (d.1429), Akbiyik Meczub (d.1455), Hizir Dede (d.1507) and Üftade (d.1580). To recap, the Bayramiyye split into two upon the death of its founder: (a) the line of Aq Şemseddin (the Bayramis); (b) the line of Ömer Sikkini (the Melami–Bayramis); a little later, through the line detailed here, it gave rise to (c) the Celvetis.

164 Apparently hailing from a Christian family from Moldavia, Hizir Dede excelled in dream interpretation, had a profound knowledge of pharmacopoeia, and lived a life of retreat; ibid., pp. 19ff.

165 Ibid., pp. 33–4.

166 Ibid., pp. 39.

167 The mention of Emir Sultan is based on a passing remark by Hüdayi concerning his master Üftade (ibid., p. 46). In contrast, Üftade repeatedly makes clear his direct connection with Ibn 'Arabi and Rumi. Emir Sultan was a celebrated Kubrawi saint of Bursa and a contemporary of Somuncu Baba. Üftade had spent half of his life serving at the Emir Sultan mosque as preacher: the saint is buried in the mausoleum attached to it.

168 Ibid., p. 47.

169 Ibid., pp. 47ff.

170 Üftade and Bursevi explained at length the differences between the two ways based on their specific methods, critiquing aspects of the halveti way and demonstrating the superiority of the celveti way. A prominent theme centres on the invocation of the Names of God in halveti practice, in contrast with the emphasis on the affirmation of Unity in the celveti way (which also encompasses invocation of the Names). Üftade suggested that, as spiritual direction for the halveti is linked to a specific Divine Name that guides the mystic in (the seventh stage of) his ascension and descent, this limits its capacities, for the spiritual direction in question is a function of that specific Name. In contrast, the celveti focus on the affirmation of Unity allows comprehension of all the Names: because it reunites them, it is incomparably more efficacious than the halveti way. As it is based on invocation of the Names and not the formula of Unity, the latter cannot lead to perfection. Going directly to the places of manifestation of the Names before passing through annihilation, it can never arrive at true illumination by the Names, for this necessitates first the mystic's total annihilation.

Üftade also faulted the halvetis for displaying their *kashf* ('unveiling'). In contrast, he upheld the rank of the Melami (who hide their states) as the highest. Furthermore, he deemed the *kashf*s of the halvetis artificial: in contrast, those of the celvetis constitute graces, which flow naturally from the station they have reached. Unlike the halveti way (the seven states in which can be traversed during seven years), Üftade pointed out that the celveti way never ends, for spiritual effort is a way of life rather than a technique. He argued that the method of spiritual exercises is limited per se, for as soon as they are neglected, one's rank declines; see ibid., pp. 47–53, and below.

171 Ibid., p. 60.

172 Ibid., p. 29.

173 Ibid., pp. 46–7.

174 This point is made repeatedly: for example, ibid., pp. 28, 46, 63.

175 Ibid., pp. 53–6; see further pp. 58ff.

176 Ibid., pp. 58–9.

177 Ibid., pp. 55–6.

178 Ibid., p. 72, 53.

179 Ibid., pp. 69, 37, 52, 59.

180 Ibid., pp. 69, 73.

181 Ibid., p. 27.

182 Ibid., p. 28.

183 Ibid., p. 60. Üftade's strong attachment to the law is further evident in his upholding of conformity with it as the essential criterion for the validity of *kashf* (pp. 23, 25).

184 Ibid., p. 28.

185 On this basis, Üftade faulted Hallaj: the result of his neglect of reason as an essential principle of spiritual perfection was that he remained 'on the shore of the ocean of annihilation' (ibid., p. 28).

186 Another point of criticism of the halvetis relates to their designation of a successor to a spiritual master without considering whether his spiritual development is complete (i.e. whether he has passed through the four stages): see ibid., p. 48. On the double journey, see pp. 29, 59.

187 Ibid., pp. 25–6.

188 Ibid., p. 24.

189 Ibid., p. 28.

190 Ibid., p. 57.

191 Ibid., p. 40.

192 Ibid., pp. 27–8.

193 Ballanfat quotes the *Waqi'at* thus: 'The meaning of *wahdat al-wujud* is that once the traveller has passed beyond the stages of corporeal nature, soul, spirit and secret consciousness, and has annihilated everything, nothing is shown to him other than the One whose existence is necessary ... There remains nothing but the existence of the necessary Being.' See ibid., p. 76.

Note that an associate familiar with this text cites Üftade's conceptualisation of *wahdat al-wujud* in terms of the mystical experience in the context of the debate concerning the signification of the term profiled in Ch. 1.

194 Ibid., p. 77.

195 Ibid., p. 39 n. 94.

196 He describes the occurrence of 'direct training' through inspiration in general as a fundamental element of the Celvetiyye, which confers a particular identity on it: see ibid., p. 46.

197 Ibid., p. 40.

198 Ibid., pp. 35.

199 Ibid., p. 34.

200 Ibid., p. 35 n. 84. Bursevi is said to have received the first volume of his commentary on the *Mathnavi* in a dream, the night after his disciples had requested that he write one.

For an example of the strong feeling for Rumi among Celvetis, see Lewis, *Rumi: Past and Present*, p. 471. This relates how the Celveti Khalil Pasha (d. 1629), Ottoman Grand Falconer and Commander of the Janissaries, stopped at Rumi's tomb in 1607 on his way to Aleppo to put down a Syrian revolt. The story goes that Khalil produced some poetry inspired by the saint.

201 Associates have added to these across the years. For example, an appendix to 'A Trip to Turkey' (1999) provides a detailed overview of Üftade's life, spiritual development and achievements based on accounts by Hüdayi and Bursevi (the source of these is unclear). There is also a translation of the poem on Üftade's tomb, and a description of this and the adjacent mosque. More recently, an associate has written on Celveti shaykh and teacher of Bursevi Osman Fazli: see Ryan, 'In Search of Osman Fazli'.

In light of recent publications such as Ballanfat's, some associates have remarked on the accuracy of what Rauf had conveyed to them concerning the order and its prominent figures.

202 See Ballanfat, *Le Divan*, p. 78.

203 See Brass, Foreword, the *White Fusus*, 2, pp. vi–vii. As Ballanfat, *Le Divan*, p. 47, notes, both Üftade and later Bursevi explored in full the significance of the diacritical point of the first letter that distinguishes the two names from each other.

204 As Ballanfat, *Le Divan*, p. 43, points out, Üftade put his disciples through forty-day retreats to assist in the purification and opening of the heart. On the practice of *khalwa* among the Halvetis, see Brown, *The Darvishes*, p. 288.

205 Historically, the lines of transmission of these great saints' teachings became intermingled following their death, with the appearance of commentaries on the *Mathnavi* by followers of Ibn 'Arabi and the use of Ibn 'Arabi's works in the development of its metaphysical understanding within the Mevlevi order: cf. Clark, 'Early Best-sellers in the Akbarian Tradition', pp. 39–40.

206 *Futuhat*, chapter 270, cited in Addas, Abu Madyan and Ibn 'Arabi, in Hirtenstein and Tiernan, eds, *Muhyiddin Ibn 'Arabi: A Commemorative Volume*, p. 178.

207 On the importance of the Ottoman realm as an arena for transmission and assimilation of Ibn 'Arabi's doctrine, see Ch. 4; a comprehensive critical assessment of such claims awaits further scholarship.

208 This theoretical ideal notwithstanding, there is something of a Turkish/Middle Eastern 'flavour' to aspects of Beshara culture. A simple example is the liberal use of Turkish cologne, which is found in bottles placed prominently in several rooms at the School and in associates' homes. It is used to wipe the face and hands during study or serious conversation.

209 See Aaron Cass, 'Music Review', *MIAS Newsletter*, 17 (Autumn 2001), pp. 6–7.

210 See ibid. With respect to his own musical endeavours with other associates, Cass emphasises that 'The traditional audience is not ours. The *'ud* and the *ney* are not our instruments, since we are not doing this to firm up or adopt a tradition.' (Correspondence with the author, 2005.)

211 With appropriate spiritual training, associates hold that anyone can become a *mazhar* (place of manifestation) of the specific qualities required to guide others. Such qualities are exemplified in the Divine Names *al-Rashid* and *al-Hadi*: the property of no single person, they belong to Reality. For example, Young developed the discernment necessary to prescribing *wazifa*s through his training by Rauf. Similarly, others in positions of responsibility involving a direct training of students (supervisors, correlators and those responsible for courses in Jakarta) have developed the requisite qualities through their own spiritual training on courses.

212 As Chittick, Rumi and the Mawlawiyyah, p. 109, notes, Shams reportedly stated explicitly that there was no master–disciple relationship, in either direction, between himself and Rumi. See also Lewis, *Rumi: Past and Present*, p. 34. Cf. Ibn 'Arabi's characterisation of his own relationship with his 'teacher' al-Kumi: see Addas, *Quest for the Red Sulphur*, p. 91 ('He was for me simultaneously master and disciple, and I was the same to him.').

213 See, for example, Musgrove, *Ecstasy and Holiness*, pp. 149, 197.

214 See Rauf, *Addresses*, pp. 47–8: 'In the *tarikas* ... the student would have to come to realise himself in his ... *Shaikh* or mentor, before he could advance much further'. For an example of the developed practice of *rabita* ('the linking of one's heart to a being, both perfect and perfection-bestowing, who has attained to certain knowledge of the attributes of the Divine Essence and reached the station of witnessing; and the maintaining of the form of that being in the treasure-house of the imagination, whether one be present with him or absent from him') on the road to *fana' fi'l-shaykh* as preliminary to the final goal, see Hamid Algar, Devotional Practices of the Khalidi–Naqshbandis of Ottoman Turkey, in Lifchez, *The Dervish Lodge*, pp. 216–18.

For an overview of sufi leadership traditions and styles and their historical development, see Arthur F. Buehler, *Sufi Heirs of the Prophet: The Indian Naqshbandiyya and the Rise of the Mediating Sufi Shaykh* (Columbia, SC, 1998), chapters 1–2. On *suhba* or keeping the company of the shaykh as a means of spiritual transformation (and on the norms that govern the disciple's behaviour towards his shaykh), see for example Algar, Devotional Practices, pp. 214–16. For a contemporary example of the attitude of *murids* towards their shaykh, see Kose, *Conversion to Islam*, pp. 163–4, discussing Nazim al-Haqqani: 'It is believed that through obedience, the Shaykh will take one up and his secrets will go from his heart to that of his follower.' He is 'the central figure who determines spiritual and structural guidelines and is the ultimate source of authority as well as being the supreme role model for his followers'.

215 An associate had broken the fast with Shaykh Muzaffer Özak and his followers in Istanbul, and had been struck by his followers' deferential and submissive attitudes towards their shaykh. He brought these impressions to Rauf and commented on the different styles of the two men, and the contrast in their circumstances. Rauf had responded by way of this comment.

216 Annett, ed., *The Many Ways of Being*, p. 84, reflected associates' emphases in his description of Rauf and their views of leadership from the mid-1970s: 'he is in no sense a guru, a concept which absolutely contradicts the Beshara philosophy. Members of the group believe that no single figure should dominate, and this idea is a central concept which is regarded as an idea of the coming age.'

217 For a succinct overview of the institutionalisation of sufism, see Karamustafa, *God's Unruly Friends*, pp. 86–90; see further Trimingham, *The Sufi Orders in Islam*, chapters 1–2, and Knysh, *Islamic Mysticism*, pp. 169–179. Hodgson, *The Venture of Islam*, 2, pp. 204ff., sketches the historical development of sufism from 'the individual piety of mystically-minded Muslims'. On dervish groups that rejected the main institutional features of sufism in the form of the *tariqa*s (while themselves mimicking these in their own loose structures, in spite of their strongly individualistic core), and the tension between them and the *tariqa*s, see Karamustafa, *God's Unruly Friends*, especially pp. 90ff. Notable among these and predating the *tariqa*s was the loose movement of the Qalandariyya, for example; see 'Kalandariyya', EI², 4, pp. 473–4.

218 Entering a *tariqa* has traditionally meant forging a bond with a shaykh. On the importance of the shaykh and submission to him in sufi thought, see Ernst, *The Shambhala Guide to Sufism*, p. 124, and Michon, The Spiritual Practices of Sufism, pp. 271–3. Michon explains that, without a master, 'all illusions and all distractions are to be feared'. He cites the opinion of Seyyed Hossein Nasr, thus: 'Man may seek the fountain of life by himself. He may seek to discover the principles of spiritual regeneration through his own efforts. But this endeavour is in vain ... Only the power of the *shaykh* can deliver man from himself ... to enable him to ... rejoin the sea of Universal Existence.' Finally, Harris, 'The Relevance of Retreat', p. 25, cites a 'Turkish dervish hymn': 'You can't travel without a guide: the roads are full of bandits.'

219 See, for example, Baldick, *Imaginary Muslims*, p. 7. Note that the Naqshbandi *tariqa* has successfully integrated the Uwaysi tradition/method within its own framework and practice.

220 See von Schlegell, *Sufism in the Ottoman Arab World*, pp. 132–3. For the example of al-Nabulusi and his own perception of the relative importance of the Uwaysi and suluki strands of his spiritual life, see pp. 188ff.

221 See, for example, Chodkiewicz, *Seal of the Saints*, pp. 140, 146 n. 58. There is a tendency to focus on Khidr as guide in the context of Uwaysi initiation/training, for he is the archetype of direct divine inspiration (see for example Young, 'Ibn 'Arabi', p. 11, which describes him as 'the spiritual guide of all those who attain without the mediation of a teacher'.) However, Khidr is but one of many figures, including prophets and saints, who guide those who are without visible masters among men.

On Ibn 'Arabi's relationship with Khidr (and its significance), see Corbin, *Alone with the Alone*, pp. 53–67. The author describes Khidr as 'the invisible spiritual master, reserved for those who are called to a direct unmediated relationship with the divine world – that is a bond seeking no historical justification in a historical succession of *shaikhs* – for those who owe their investiture to no authority' (see ibid., p. 55; and on Ibn

'Arabi's investiture by Khidr, pp. 63–7). See also 'al-Khadir', EI², IV, pp. 902–5; Stephen Hirtenstein, 'The Mantle of Khidr' (paper presented at Colloque International sur le Soufisme, Damascus, June 2005).

222 Ibn 'Arabi received the mantle of initiation (*khirqa*) from sufi masters on at least four occasions: see Elmore, 'The *Uwaysi* Spirit', p. 47 n. 49. On his early teachers, see Addas, *Quest for the Red Sulphur*, p. 311. He wrote explicitly on suluki sufism and provided instructions to disciples in, for example, *Kitab al-Kunh fi-ma la budd li'l-murid minhu* and *al-Tadbirat al-ilahiyya fi islah al-mamlaka al-insaniyya*. The former is translated as *What the Student Needs* by Tosun Bayrak al-Jerrahi, *JMIAS*, V (1986), pp. 28–55.

223 Young, 'Ibn 'Arabi', p. 11. Cf. the emphasis placed by an associate on the importance of 'imbibing directly from the source', meaning God, in the early transmission of Ibn 'Arabi's works: see Clark, 'Early Best-sellers in the Akbarian Tradition', p. 29.

224 This is understood by some associates in terms of Ibn 'Arabi's argument concerning the continuation of the descent of divine inspiration upon the hearts of the saints after the ending of the prophetic cycle. See, for example, Ibn 'Arabi, *Contemplation of the Holy Mysteries*, trans. Cecilia Twinch and Pablo Beneito (Oxford, 2001), p. 112. The sufi concept of sainthood has always involved a belief in ongoing divine inspiration.

225 Rauf, cited in Feild, *The Last Barrier*, p. 164.

226 See Baldick, *Imaginary Muslims*, pp. 4, 7.

227 See for example van Ess, Sufism and its Opponents, p. 36.

228 See 'A Trip to Turkey', p. 12. Cf. 'Notice to Cooks', where Rauf describes the Mevlevis as 'the sect which aligned itself to ... Rumi'.

There are contrasting evaluations of the extent to which the Mevlevi *tariqa*, as it came to be known, was already formed during Rumi's lifetime. According to 'Mawlawiyya', EI², VI, p. 883: 'Although not called by this name, it appears that such a *tarika* was formed already in [Rumi's] time ... this view is reinforced by the existence of disciples around [him], by his concern for their education, and by his appointment of deputies to carry out this task during his absences'. Cf. Ocak, Religion, p. 200: 'The Mevlevi order was not founded while ... Rumi himself was alive ... the mystical lifestyle he ... developed did not at first have an institutional base'. For a detailed account of the formation of the order, see Lewis, *Rumi: Past and Present*, pp. 432ff.

229 For the debate surrounding whether Ibn 'Arabi consciously 'founded' a *tariqa*, see von Schlegell, *Sufism in the Ottoman Arab World*, pp. 221–30.

230 For the example of his experience of the *khaniqa* in Ayyubid Cairo, see Addas, *Ibn 'Arabi: The Voyage of No Return*, pp. 72–3. The author observes: 'As far as we can tell, Ibn 'Arabi had no time for this kind of organised, communitary mysticism, a mysticism so different from the fluid spiritual universe, so completely devoid of decorum, that he knew in the West'.

231 Cf. with the argument in Shah, *The Way of the Sufi*, pp. 29–30, that sufism is 'action, not institution'. No sufi 'sets up an institution intended to endure. The outer form in which he imparts his ideas is a transient vehicle, designed for local operation. That which is perpetual ... is in another range'.

232 Cf. Carroll, 'Timelessness and Time', p. 79: the author describes a visit to the temple south of Ephesus which housed the oracle of Apollo in Greek and Roman times, itself built on the site of an earlier temple. She suggests that one cannot help but 'experience the magnitude and significance of that place and, at the same time, have a sense that nothing of the spirit which manifested there now remains'.

233 Rauf described one such case in the experience of Mughal Emperor Akbar, who had attempted 'to find a unifying solution for his disparate country in esotericism ... it was the first time ever that esoteric learnings acquired by a sovereign were to be applied to the unification of a motley of people in a state'. Describing his building of 'the utopian Fatehpur' as a new capital, he explains that, here, 'a new spiritual concept was meant to flourish. But it did not. Akbar was not of his time. A new religion is easier to establish where masses are concerned ... The Sufi concept of the all-permeating Unity which is the Absolute Essence, was beyond the reaches of the general levels of his time. In fact, the idea underlying Fatehpur is barely coming into fruition today. In the days of Akbar, anything so informal, so intangible, was incomprehensible to the masses'. Following opposition to Akbar, 'the Sufi way of thought was more or less painfully formalised and was called a new religion: *Dini Ilahi*'. Akbar, however, had not necessarily been 'looking for a new religion. He was simply coaxing all leading religious thinkers of all religions to bring forth and expose the common underlying mystical and esoteric foundations upon which all religions are built, no matter how disparate in practice ... Through the teachings of Salim Chishti, Akbar had personally developed enormously in esoteric thought ... and was ... accepted ... as ... World Teacher of Humanity ... But humanity did not follow him'. See Rauf, *Addresses II*, pp. 99–100, 103–5.

234 Annett, ed., *The Many Ways of Being*, p. 84, writes of associates: 'They think that the various Sufi orders, formed after the death of particular saints, have deteriorated through time, until today they have ... lost contact with the source of their original inspiration'.

235 Rauf reportedly became increasingly reluctant to interact with sufi shaykhs during visits to Turkey, for they would naturally ask who was his shaykh. When he answered that he had no shaykh and never had, they would ask after the source of his knowledge, to which he would reply that he had learned all he knew 'from his mother'.

236 Ryan, Conversion to the Essence, p. 342. Note the attachment of the epithet to Bawa Muhaiyaddeen among Western sufi teachers: see Webb, Tradition and Innovation, pp. 90–1.

Chapter 7

1 Carroll, 'Notes from a Student'.

2 Cf. Hirtenstein, 'Muhyiddin Ibn 'Arabi: The Treasure of Compassion': 'for any sincere seeker after truth, after you read Ibn 'Arabi you read all things differently'. According to Young, 'through Ibn 'Arabi one can understand everything that came before Ibn 'Arabi'.

3 Young addressed this issue in late 2004 in relation to representation of Beshara in the USA, where its activities have proceeded under the rubric of the MIAS (particularly in California, where the Society has a branch office and holds an annual symposium). He commented that it was not entirely desirable or 'as it should be' for Beshara to be presented 'under the cloak of Ibn 'Arabi', and expressed his hope for an effective presence for Beshara in the USA distinct from that of the MIAS.

4 An associate cites the example of parts of the *Futuhat* that address details of sharia.

5 Leaflet publicising short courses, 2004.

6 See 'Courses at Chisholme', p. 27.

7 The translation is drawn from Corbin, *Alone with the Alone*.

8 See Beshara website.

9 See Hirtenstein, *The Unlimited Mercifier*, p. xi.

10 Christopher Ryan, Editorial, *MIAS Newsletter*, 19 (Autumn 2003), p. 1.

11 It should be noted that scholarly interest in Ibn 'Arabi has widely differing points of departure. For example, Ian Almond has recently attempted to compare the mystic with the deconstructionist Jacques Derrida, in relation to the role of 'bewilderment' in their outlooks. See Ian Almond, 'The Honesty of the Perplexed: Derrida and Ibn 'Arabi on "Bewilderment"', *Journal of the American Academy of Religion*, 70: 3 (2002), pp. 517–34.

12 'The Unity of Existence: Ibn 'Arabi and his School', MIAS Symposium Report, May 2003, *MIAS Newsletter*, 19 (Autumn 2003), p. 15. Mohamed Mesbahi is a Moroccan academic.

13 Mohamed Mesbahi, cited in Conference Report, 'Ibn 'Arabi and the World Today', *MIAS Newsletter*, 19 (Autumn 2003), p. 12.

14 Kiliç, '"The Ibn al-'Arabi of the Ottomans"', p. 110. Kiliç is a Turkish academic.

15 Compare with Vincent Cornell, 'Practical Sufism: An Akbarian Foundation for a Liberal Theology of Difference', *JMIAS*, XXXVI (2004), pp. 59–84.

16 For Morris' views in this regard, see for example '"An Essential Translator" – Perceptions and Interpretations: Ibn 'Arabi in the Islamic World Today', Interview with James W. Morris, *MIAS Newsletter*, 18 (Summer 2002), pp. 21–2, and James W. Morris, 'Visit to Indonesia and Malaysia', ibid., p. 16.

17 In this context, we would mention in particular two accessible introductions written specifically for those without prior exposure to the subject: Addas, *Ibn 'Arabi: The Voyage of No Return*, and William C. Chittick, *Ibn 'Arabi: Heir to the Prophets* (Oxford, 2005).

James Winston Morris, *The Reflective Heart: Discovering Spiritual Intelligence in Ibn 'Arabi's Meccan Illuminations* (Louisville, KY, 2005), is an attempt to convey something of Ibn 'Arabi's teaching in the *Futuhat* to those engaged on the spiritual journey, based on a conviction of its direct and universal applicability. This provides explanatory material on the religious–cultural tradition that frames this teaching, and uses contemporary popular imagery (drawn from movies, for example) to illuminate difficult points.

18 Lewis, *Rumi: Past and Present*, p. 1; see pp. 1–4 on the many examples of best-selling translations of his poems and audio-tapes, performances of poetry recitals to live music, etc.

Paradoxically, the International Rumi Committee (UK), formed in 1970 and reorganised as a Society in 1977 with Schimmel as Honorary President, which arranged visits to Konya, organised lectures and sponsored recordings of Mevlevi music, ceased to exist in 1980. See Somers, Whirling and the West, pp. 268–70.

19 A glance in late 2004 at the contents of the shelf on sufism at the Oxford Borders bookstore, as cosmopolitan a setting as any in the UK, revealed no fewer than thirteen different works on/translations of Rumi intended for popular consumption.

There is as yet no 'Pocket Ibn 'Arabi Reader' parallel to *The Pocket Rumi Reader*, ed. Kabir Helminski (Boston and London, 2001). Shambhala has republished fragments in English of the *Tarjuman al-ashwaq* (from Maurice Gloton's translation) accompanied by calligraphic designs, as part of a series: *Perfect Harmony: Sufi Poetry by Ibn 'Arabi*, calligraphy by Hassan Massoudy (Boston and London, 2002). Possibly the only other quasi-popular presentation of Ibn 'Arabi is Michael A. Sells, *Stations of Desire: Love Elegies from Ibn 'Arabi and New Poems* (Jerusalem, 2000). (Note its place of publication, bearing witness to the burgeoning New Age interest in segments of Israeli society referred to earlier. The text is also distributed through Anqa Publishing.) The inside front cover explains that it contains 'the first translations of Ibn 'Arabi's *Turjuman* into modern poetic English'. Sells' original poems in a later section are 'modelled on *The Turjuman* and serve as further commentary to the medieval odes and their extension into the present climate of poetry'.

Translated extracts from Ibn 'Arabi sometimes appear in popular anthologies relating to sufism. These include *The Wisdom of Sufism* (Oxford, 2001), compiled by Leonard Lewisohn, a volume in the inspirational series 'Oneworld of Wisdom', and Andrew Harvey and Eryk Hanut, *Perfume of the Desert: Inspirations from Sufi Wisdom* (Wheaton, Illinois and Chennai, India, 1999).

Hirtenstein, *The Unlimited Mercifier*, discussed below, must finally be mentioned here.

20 See Hermansen, In the Garden of American Sufi Movements, p. 169. In addition to the new renditions into English of Rumi's poems by Barks on audiocassette, she cites the example of the popular Qawwali singer Nusrat Fateh Ali Khan (p. 178 n. 132). See further 'Hybrid Identity Formations', p. 180.

21 Narda Dalgleish (Vastearth Words and Music, Sherborne, Gloucestershire).

22 See Cass, 'Music Review', pp. 6–7.

23 Ibid.

24 Vastearth Words and Music, 2002, produced by Aaron Cass and David Norland, copyrighted jointly to Beshara Publications and Vastearth. For further details, see

Beshara Publications website. By mid-2004, this CD had sold 500 copies and gone into profit. It was also reportedly aired on a prime-time Israeli radio show.

The Vast Earth Orchestra have prepared a second CD under the title *Green Bird*, 'with more music and extracts from Rumi, Niffari, Jili and Ibn 'Arabi. [There is] no mention of Mohammed or Sufism, no obvious religious iconography ... just love and absence, majesty and humility, honey bees and earth ... while composing it we've tried to make no assumptions about the interests of the listener ... We are not trying to represent Beshara or Ibn 'Arabi ... we are not trying to get across a spiritual message ... we are ourselves simply inspired by the material.' (Aaron Cass, correspondence with the author.)

We know of only two examples from the wider music world that draw exclusively and explicitly on Ibn 'Arabi's writings. First is the CD *Do lo humano y lo divino: Poemas de Ibn al-'Arabí adaptados a cante flamenco*, cantaor y adaptacíon Curro Piñana (Madrid, 1998), which applies lyrics from the *Tarjuman* to a traditional flamenco setting. Second is the CD Ibn 'Arabí, *El intérprete de los deseos; Taryumán al-Ashwáq*, by Ensemble Ibn Báya & Cofradía Shushtarí, dir. Omar Metíouí and prod. Eduardo Paníagua, poems selected by Pablo Beneito, presented in Spanish, English and Arabic, trans. by Carlos Varona, Reynold A. Nicholson, Maurice Gloton and Pablo Beneito (Pneuma Coleccíon Al-Andalus).

25 Relevant web material carries the following quotation from the *Futuhat*: 'physical places produce an effect upon subtle hearts'. See Anqa website.

26 According to an 'In the Footsteps of Ibn 'Arabi' flyer: 'This tour is a unique opportunity to travel in the lands that Ibn 'Arabi knew so well in his youth, al-Andalus of the Arabs, and which he describes so vividly in his *Ruh al-quds* (*Sufis of Andalusia*)'. It aims to visit 'all the major sites which he frequented, seeking out the traces of his time and milieu'. The Andalusia tours have been led by Stephen Hirtenstein in his capacity as an Anqa partner and author of *The Unlimited Mercifier*.

The 2004 tour began with a two-day international conference in honour of Ibn 'Arabi in Cordoba, organised by the Fondation Roger Garaudy and supported by the municipal council. For an account of this tour (in Arabic), see Louay 'Abdulilah, "ala khuta Ibn 'Arabi: rihla 'abr al-Andalus', *al-Sharq al-awsat*, 24 December 2004, *safhat* 'Tahqiqat', www.asharqalawsat.com. For an English record, see *MIAS Newsletter*, 21 (Spring 2005), pp. 6–7.

27 See Anqa website. The tour encompassed visits to the major centres of Seljuk power, and explored the influence of Ibn 'Arabi in Ottoman times.

28 Of the twenty-two travellers, twelve had completed Beshara courses, three were from the Sufi Order of the West, two from the *tariqa* Maryamiyya and four of no particular affiliation but with an interest in sufism/Ibn 'Arabi. Travellers were of British, American, Australian, German, Swiss, Bangladeshi and Iraqi nationalities, and their ages ranged from mid-twenties to late sixties.

29 Ibn Yusuf, 'Ibn 'Arabi for Our Generation', p. 35.

30 It will be recalled that the two relatively accessible introductions to Ibn 'Arabi we mentioned earlier (Addas' study of his life, *Ibn 'Arabi: The Voyage of No Return* [English translation] and Chittick's discussion of his thought, *Ibn 'Arabi: Heir to the Prophets*) appeared later, in 2000 and 2005, respectively.

31 Hirtenstein, *The Unlimited Mercifier*, p. x.

32 Ibid.

33 Ibid., e.g. pp. 129, 157–8, 163, 191, 210.

34 Ibid., e.g. pp. 18, 93.

35 Ibid., e.g. pp. 99, 163–5, 194, 232–3, 247–8.

36 Ibid., p. 8.

37 Ibid., p. xi.

38 Cecilia Twinch, 'Education at the Beshara Schools', *Beshara Magazine*, 1, p. 7.

39 See 'Cooking as a Means of Expression: Martin Lam, erstwhile Head Chef of L'Escargot (London), talks about his work', *Beshara Magazine*, 10, pp. 30–2. Rauf's influence on Lam is clear from this.

40 Correspondence with the author (2004): the associate describes this as a notch beneath the National Book Award and the Pulitzer, and possibly more prestigious in literary circles.

41 Jonathan Cape, London, 1998. The author's acknowledgement (p. 480) includes Rauf and his brother Mahmut among those who contributed their 'time and wisdom'. He adds an (unreferenced) epigraph from Ibn 'Arabi at the opening of the book: 'My trace is Yours and my quality is Yours … My inexistence implies your existence, my avarice Your generosity, my muteness Your word, my whisperings Your discourse … Everything in accord with Your gift is made into Your praise'. This is a translation of a rearranged quotation from Ibn 'Arabi, *al-Ittihad al-kawni*, from the French in Ibn 'Arabi, *Le Livre de l'arbre et des quatre oiseaux*, trans. Denis Gril (Paris, 1984). Zabor is a musical journalist and jazz drummer who lives in Brooklyn, New York.

42 Back cover; inside covers. In 1970, the author had joined 'a pseudo-Gurdjieff group' in San Francisco under the direction of an American teacher who later met Feild and Rauf while en route to India. Having decided to remain at Swyre Farm at Rauf's invitation, the teacher had advised the San Francisco group he had left behind to attend Bennett's Academy in Sherborne. Unable to raise the funds for the Academy, Zabor ended up at Swyre Farm in June 1972 and stayed a whole year, leaving by chance just as Feild departed: this period is covered in his *I, Wabenzi*.

As he puts it, he 'passed through' Beshara for a few years thereafter, mainly en route to Turkey, but only 'rejoined' when Rauf invited him to attend a further course at Chisholme in 1983.

43 The following draws on Zabor's Translator's Guide to *The Bear Comes Home* (which encompasses a 'Brief Metaphysical Guide'), and correspondence with this author providing an explanation of it. Thanks are due to Zabor for providing this.

44 See *Kernel of the Kernel*, pp. 9–14.

45 See further www.pbs.org (1998).

46 Hermansen, In the Garden of American Sufi Movements, pp. 169, 167 and 'Hybrid Identity Formations', p. 178. Note that she writes specifically of the USA.

47 Only one work by an associate fits one of the genres projected by Hermansen as more generally associated with universal movements. This is Zabor's personal account of his experience of the early period at Swyre Farm, which can loosely be classified as a quest narrative.

48 No such policy is indeed indicated in the *Rules of the Society*.

49 Its efforts might be compared with those of the Ni'matullahi order, for example. A series of major conferences were organised during the 1990s at the invitation of Javad Nurbakhsh, shaykh of the order. This issued in the series *The Heritage of Sufism*, edited by Lewisohn. The order has also fostered publication through its publishing outfit, Khaniqahi-Nimatullahi Publications (London). On the Ni'matullahis, see Geaves, *The Sufis of Britain*, pp. 138–9. Pir Press (New York), which has close connections with a branch of the Halveti–Jerrahi order, can also be mentioned.

The greatly influential scholarship of sufi Guénonians associated with the Perennialist/ Traditionalist school (more recently works by Schuon and his followers, including Lings and Nasr) on the academic study of religion in the West must also be underlined. See for example Carl W. Ernst, 'Traditionalism, the Perennial Philosophy, and Islamic Studies: Review Article', www.religioperennis.org; Hermansen, In the Garden of American Sufi Movements, p. 167; Sedgwick, *Against the Modern World*, pp. 162ff., 190. As we have noted, Chodkiewicz and Gril, among the best-known scholars of Ibn 'Arabi in France today, are the main disciples of Vâlsan, who was initiated into sufism by Schuon. See below; 'The Rediscovery of the Tradition in the 20ᵗʰ Century', www.religioperennis.org. Note finally Morris' observation that 'the modern international discipline of religious studies is fundamentally grounded – in ways which fortunately only a handful of specialists are aware of – in the writings and teaching of a wide spectrum of European and American Sufis and students of Ibn 'Arabi'. See James Winston Morris, 'Exploring the Universal Dimensions of Islamic Thought: Political Philosophy and Spirituality' (Inaugural Lecture at University of Exeter, 1999), pp. 9–10 and 'Ibn 'Arabi in the "Far West": Visible and Invisible Influences', *JMIAS*, XXIX, pp. 103ff., especially p. 106. For publishers and publications associated with Traditionalism, see Sedgwick, *Against the Modern World*, pp. 167–9.

50 See Stephen Hirtenstein, 'Publications Report', Minutes of the AGM of the MIAS, 11 November 1989, p. 1. The appearance of Hirtenstein and Tiernan, eds, *Muhyiddin Ibn 'Arabi: A Commemorative Volume* a few years later was a significant milestone: this soon became established as an important reference work.

We described the emergence of the MIAS earlier. This was not the first such initiative, for the establishment of an earlier 'Association for the Study of Ibn 'Arabi' in Italy and 'the East' was announced in an issue of the Italian/Arabic periodical *Il Convito/al-Nadi* (1907) published by Enrico Insabato and mentioned earlier. In the preceding issue, 'Illaysh had thanked 'Abd al-Hadi for 'services rendered to civilisation' by 'making Ibn 'Arabi known to people', and urged him to continue his work regardless of what 'those who have not understood the true Islam' might stir up. The programme of this Association, which took the name 'al-Akbariyya', was set out in five points. These form an interesting basis for comparison with the *raison d'être* and work of the MIAS, discussed below, and can be summarised here: (a) To study and disseminate Ibn 'Arabi's teachings 'whether relating to *shari'a* or *haqiqa*', to print his writings and those of his disciples, to comment on these, and to give lectures on him and talks that explain his ideas. (b) To bring together the greatest number possible of those who would 'revive' Ibn 'Arabi, forging a strong bond among them based on brotherhood and intellectual interconnections, from among the elite of the East and the West. (c) To provide material and moral support to any who need this among those who follow the path marked out by Ibn 'Arabi, especially those who spread his call through word or deed. (d) The Association's work should also include study of masters of Eastern sufism like Rumi (but Ibn 'Arabi must remain the focus). (e) The Association will have no link to political matters however they might appear, and 'will not stray beyond research into religion and theosophy'. See Mahmud, *al-Madrasa al-Shadhiliyya al-haditha*, pp. 252–4; Sedgwick, *Against the Modern World*, p. 62; Hatina, 'Where East Meets West', p. 16; Vâlsan, *L'Islam et la function de René Guénon*, pp. 37–8.

51 See *The Rules of the Society* (amended April 1981); emphases added.

52 Chairman's address, Minutes of the AGM of the MIAS, 19 November 1988, p. 2. With respect to the matter of translation, note in a similar vein the implicit claim by 'Abd al-Qadir al-Sufi al-Darqawi concerning the credentials of at-Tarjumana as translator, in *The Seals of Wisdom*: 'Our text has been edited with great care by the translator, and revised many times. The most important aspect of this translation is, however – and we must emphasise this – that its author is herself a living practitioner of the sufic science in the line of Masters that take their doctrine from the Shaykh al-Akbar.' This relates to his claim that the *tariqa* to which the translator belongs (and which he represents) embodies continuity in study of the works of Ibn 'Arabi since the time of al-Andalus.

Some associates take issue with certain scholarly treatments of aspects of Ibn 'Arabi's thought, which they measure by their own understandings. One singles out Chodkiewicz's *Seal of the Saints* as a modern scholarly watershed for 'bringing out the fact that servanthood is the core of Ibn 'Arabi's teaching'. He maintains that this had hitherto been neglected, as modern scholars have tended to be more comfortable with 'the metaphysical aspects' of Ibn 'Arabi's thought. Others are vaguely suspicious of academic approaches in Ibn 'Arabi studies in general. In this, they rehearse Ibn 'Arabi's views concerning the bases of complete understanding, perhaps reflecting also the New Age tendency to oppose the assumption of reason as a vehicle of understanding adequate to all subjects. On the latter, see for example Heelas, *The New Age Movement*, pp. 5, 37. For their part, some academics are disparaging about the writing efforts of some associates: see for example Oliver Leaman's unforgiving review of Coates, *Ibn 'Arabi and Modern Thought*, *JMIAS*, XXXIII (2003), pp.103–5.

53 The interface between movement and Society is illustrated at a superficial level by the duplication of materials between the two. For example, the MIAS web posting Hirtenstein, 'Muhyiddin Ibn 'Arabi: The Treasure of Compassion' is a reprint from *Beshara Magazine*, 12 (Autumn 1990). This interface is also evident in the large contingent of associates attending the annual symposia.

54 A paraphrase based on *Kernel of the Kernel*, p.1, often repeated in associates' writings. See for example Hirtenstein, 'Muhyiddin Ibn 'Arabi: The Treasure of Compassion', and Ch. 5.

55 'Honorary Secretary's Report', Report of the AGM of the MIAS, 26 October 1985, p.4.

56 See 'The Rediscovery of Tradition in the 20th Century', and Sedgwick, *Against the Modern World*, p.135. Gilis has published a number of annotated translations of Ibn 'Arabi's works, including *Le livre des chatons des sagesses*, 1 (Beirut, 1997). He is author of, among others, *Introduction à l'enseignement et au mystère de René Guénon* (Paris, 1986), *René Guénon et l'avènement du troisième Sceau* (Paris, 1991), and *L'Esprit universel de l'Islam* (Algiers, 1989).

57 The same AGM at which the Honorary Secretary's Report cited above was delivered, prior to Gilis' late arrival.

58 Charles-André Gilis, 'An Approach to the Function of Islam in the Teaching of Ibn 'Arabi', Report of the AGM of the MIAS, 26 October 1985, p.8.

59 Ibid. Gilis points to the *Fusus* and the celebrated verses from the *Tarjuman* as encapsulations of this aspect.

60 Ibid., p.9.

61 Ibid; he cited the *Futuhat*, chapter 12, concluding that 'Islamic Law abrogates all other Sacred Laws exactly like the sun, as it appears, absorbs within its light all other stars which then cease to be perceptible.' Cf. Carl A. Keller, Perceptions of Other Religions in Sufism, in Jean Jacques Waardenburg, ed., *Muslim Perceptions of Other Religions: A Historical Survey* (New York, 1999), p.189.

Gilis also demonstrated the coexistence of the two aspects he introduced in Qur'anic and hadith texts.

62 Gilis, 'An Approach to the Function of Islam in the Teaching of Ibn 'Arabi', p.11.

63 Ibid., pp.12–13. Gilis' treatment integrated an observation concerning the status of Islam and its Law in light of the Second Coming of Christ. He pointed out that 'in Ibn 'Arabi's teaching, it shall be precisely one of the tasks of Christ in his Second Coming to restore Muhammadian Law in all its truth and former purity'. This Law had thus become subject to 'a certain occultation'. His emphasis thus rested on a significant detail of the Second Coming omitted from the Beshara projection of this.

64 Ibid., p.13.

65 That is, in their 'purist Islamic' expression associated with his master Vâlsan, on whom see below.

66 'A Note from Mr. Bulent Rauf', p.14. Rauf laboured this point specifically in relation to the issue of membership in the MIAS, having (mis-?) understood from Gilis' comment concerning the way in which it recruits members an implied suggestion that it should do so 'exclusively from among the followers of the Mohammedan Religion'. Thus he reiterated that the Society 'will continue to represent ... a body of people who are devoted to the promulgation and diffusion of knowledge of Ibn 'Arabi and his exposition of the Realities, no matter from what creed or belief the membership of the Society originates'. See ibid., p.15. Cf. Letter by Gilis: 'Correspondence', *MIAS Summer Newsletter*, 1986, p.15.

67 The Gilis affair virtually recapitulated the movement's earlier encounters with the Schuonian Lings and Ralph Austin, at the time associated with Lings, mentioned

earlier. Inter alia, a significant area of disagreement arises in the nature/form of initiatic connections, and the framework for the spiritual life upheld by the two trends. Sufi Guénonians thus have direct initiatic links (typically through living shaykhs) by which they set great store, and function within a *tariqa* matrix under the spiritual authority of a shaykh. The only initiatic connection to speak of in Beshara is of an Uwaysi character.

We referred earlier to the confusion evident in attempts to categorise the Traditionalists/Perennialists in terms of their relation to Islam, an area of particular interest in any attempt to understand mutual perceptions between representatives of this trend and Beshara. Regarding the basis of Guénon's attachment to Islam, for example, Zarcone, 'Rereadings and Transformations of Sufism in the West', pp. 113–14, highlights his 'non-conversion', quoting his own claim to have 'settled' in this tradition (such 'settling' taking place above all for reasons 'of an initiatory nature'). Rawlinson, 'A History of Western Sufism', p. 14, also describes Guénon as 'a Traditionalist first and a Sufi second', an assessment with which Hatina, 'Where East Meets West', p. 30, concurs. Nonetheless, Guénon avoided at least in public any detraction from the importance of the sharia, insisting that sufism cannot be detached from it.

The same question of the relative prioritisation of Traditionalism (or 'Guénonianism') per se and Islam can be posited in relation to the Schuonians: see for example Sedgwick, 'Traditionalist Sufism', pp. 7–8, 11. Note here Schuon's much quoted comment (cited in ibid., p. 7) with regard to his keeping a statue of the Virgin Mary in his room: 'I was always strict in matters of sacred law, yet on the other hand I took my stand above all on the Religio Perennis and never allowed myself to become imprisoned in forms which for myself could have no validity.' Sedgwick, *Against the Modern World*, pp. 123ff., 90, points to evidence that Schuon differed with Guénon in allowing relaxations of the sharia and a 'simplification' of the Islamic ritual obligations, stemming from an emphasis of the importance of esoteric practice (seemingly at the expense of the exoteric framework) and 'adaptation' to life in the West. As we noted earlier, Guénon (and Vâlsan) accused him of shifting from sufi *tariqa*/Islam to some kind of universalism. After Guénon's death Vâlsan's branch of the *tariqa* became increasingly 'Islamic' (openly Muslim and following the sharia), while Schuon's became increasingly universalist. According to ibid., pp. 170ff., for Schuon and a segment of his following this trend intensified particularly from the late 1970s (it had begun to take shape already during the mid-1960s: see pp. 150–1), when the form of universalism adopted involved placing increasing emphasis on Schuon himself (seen by this segment of his followers as 'Master of the Religio Perennis'), and on esotericism as transcending the particularities of all religions, including Islam ('Primordialism'). His non-Muslim following grew in tandem with this shifting emphasis. The post-Schuonian Perennialists repudiate his late 'primordialism' in favour of a strict Islamic approach.

It should be clear by now that, as a follower of Vâlsan, Gilis upholds a strictly Islamic framing of Guénonian Traditionalism.

68 'Correspondence', *MIAS Summer Newsletter*, 1986, p. 15.

69 While non-Beshara Society members have occasionally delivered talks at Chisholme and have thus encountered Beshara in its central institution, there is no evidence of association with the movement resulting from such encounters.

70 As its representatives occupy a growing number of positions within academic institutions, tension may eventually surface over the future development of approaches to the study of sufism. An example of such tension appeared recently in relation to the study of Jewish mysticism, as evidenced by debates during the Fourteenth World Congress of Jewish Studies, held at the Hebrew University of Jerusalem in August 2005: these illustrate the issues at stake. 'A New Age for Mystics', *Ha'aretz*, 4 August 2005, reports that Avraham Elqayam from the Department of Philosophy at Bar-Ilan University provocatively began his lecture on 'Teaching Mysticism in Academia' with guided meditation, and punctuated it with a tape of a flute melody. He called for new, practical, directions in the teaching of kabbalah in universities, a combination of study and knowledge with experience and personal exposure, and the integration of classes in, for example, meditation, music and solitude. Effectively, it was a call for blurring the established dichotomy between the scholar and the kabbalist: just as the philosophy department trains philosophers, he argued, the department for the study of kabbalah should train mystics. Elqayam justified his revolutionary plea in terms of the changing needs of Humanities students in recent years. They are increasingly interested in Jewish spirituality and New Age cultures in general, he pointed out, and they have already experienced different things, used drugs, travelled to India, etc.: 'Mysticism for them is not just a text; it is an experience of the body and the mind.' Academia must rise to the challenge of a student body that wishes not only to study texts that deal with mystical experiences, but also to explore and understand the experience itself, for themselves. Elqayam's proposals sparked considerable opposition among the gathered experts.

For further discussion of the implications of a growing interest in spirituality in the context of education, see David Tacey, *The Spirituality Revolution: The Emergence of Contemporary Spirituality* (Hove, Sussex, 2004), pp. 58ff.

71 We can illustrate associates' approaches, concerns and interests through examples from the 2004 Symposium. During a plenary discussion an associate asked the speakers ('in their capacity as educators who travel widely') whether Ibn 'Arabi 'can be a builder of bridges in healing the extraordinary fissures that are opening up in our world'. She solicited their personal experiences of Ibn 'Arabi 'being alive and well today and helping in this way'. A second associate suggested that 'allowing people to be what they are (based on a recognition of everyone as an expression of the One Being) is a very important thing that Ibn 'Arabi has to bring for today'.

72 Coates, long-standing associate and author of *Ibn 'Arabi and Modern Thought*, is a recently retired professional academic (he was Senior Lecturer in the Department of Psychology at the University of Lincoln, UK).

73 See James Winston Morris, 'Ibn 'Arabi in the "Far West": Visible and Invisible Influences', *JMIAS*, XXIX (2001), p. 113.

74 We borrow this application of the term from Hermansen, In the Garden of American Sufi Movements, p. 168. Applying it in relation to the influence of Perennialist Schuonian scholars Lings and Nasr (who also address a Muslim audience), she argues that 'their impact, and particularly the impact of Nasr on Islamically-inclined youth in Muslim societies such as Turkey, Malaysia and Pakistan represents a sort of "pizza effect" of Muslim thought being re-exported to the East in "new and improved" form after being initially imported to the West'. On the origins of the 'pizza effect' hypothesis, see p. 177 n. 119. Morris' eagerness to see Muslim societies reap the benefits of Ibn 'Arabi's legacy is particularly noteworthy: see, for example, '"An Essential Translator"'.

75 'Honorary Secretary's Report', Report of the AGM of the MIAS, 26 October 1985, p. 4.

76 See ibid.

77 Cf. Chodkiewicz, 'The Diffusion of Ibn 'Arabi's Doctrine', p. 50: 'many indications lead me to believe that the end of the nineteenth century saw the beginning of an "akbarian renaissance" marked both by more numerous links with the *silsila akbariyya*, and by particularly intense intellectual activity with regard to the works of Ibn 'Arabi'. With regard to the latter point, he cites as evidence the many publications appearing in Arabic, in addition to those in Western languages. See also pp. 56–7 n. 51.

78 Editorial, *MIAS Newsletter*, 19 (Autumn 2003), p. 1.

79 See for example 'Ibn 'Arabi in the "Far West"' and '"An Essential Translator"', pp. 20–1.

80 See '"An Essential Translator"', p. 21; cf. Morris, *Orientations*, p. 63. Such statements can create a distorted impression for two reasons. First, one could equally argue that interest in Ibn Taymiyya (Ibn 'Arabi's 'arch opponent') is also 'just about everywhere in the world today', especially given his importance to the expansive salafi sector that all but dominates contemporary Islamic thought. Second, it is impossible to isolate and gauge with any precision the extent of interest in Ibn 'Arabi in the recent past in the Muslim arena: this is the requisite basis for any meaningful comparison. Nonetheless, Morris speaks of a contemporary *resurgence* of interest in Ibn 'Arabi in the Muslim world.

The following observation makes plain Morris' own agenda: '[The] worldwide collective effort to rediscover the profound influences of Ibn 'Arabi and his teachings ... is not just an academic project'. Thus, 'those involved ... are well aware of the contemporary and future significance of Ibn 'Arabi's understanding of the roots of Islamic spirituality and tradition for any lasting effort of renewal and revivification within a global civilisation'. See Morris, Introduction, in Chodkiewicz, ed., *The Meccan Revelations*, 1, p. 26.

    81 Morris, '"... Except His Face"', p. 29.

    82 Lewisohn, Preface, in Lewisohn, ed., *The Heritage of Sufism*, 2, p. xiii.

    83 As Morris puts it, Ibn 'Arabi's ultimate purpose 'was not to demonstrate to his readers a philosophical system or to convey to them some particular limited body of religious, ethical or even spiritual beliefs and teachings. Instead, it is to awaken in each reader, within their own unique situation, their own immediate and effective awareness of the ultimate direction and meaning ... of their life'. See James W. Morris, 'Rediscovering the "Divine Comedy": Eschatology and Spiritual Realisation in Ibn 'Arabi', *MIAS Newsletter*, 19 (Autumn 2003), p. 8; cf. his *Orientations*, p. 86.

    84 Morris, 'Ibn 'Arabi's Rhetoric of Realisation', 1, p. 58; for his further discussion of the notion of spiritual intelligence ('a central theme in Islamic thought'), see ibid., n. 7 and 'Exploring the Universal Dimensions of Islamic Thought', pp. 8–9. For an attempt to define spiritual intelligence, see for example Frances Vaughan, 'What is Spiritual Intelligence?', *Journal of Humanistic Psychology*, 42: 2 (2003), pp. 16–33. Vaughan has written widely on the integration of psychology and spiritual growth, and is a pioneer in the field of transpersonal psychology.

    For a discussion of the methodology of *tahqiq* as spiritual discipline according to Ibn 'Arabi, see William C. Chittick, 'Time, Space, and the Objectivity of Ethical Norms: The Teachings of Ibn al-'Arabi', *Islamic Studies*, 39: 4 (2000), pp. 582–5.

    85 Morris thus writes: 'As readers can quickly verify for themselves, the actual processes of spiritual learning described in [Ibn 'Arabi's] writing ... are indeed universal and immediately accessible all over the world, depending only on the right participants'. See 'Ibn 'Arabi's Rhetoric of Realisation', 1, p. 64 n. 17.

    86 Ibid., p. 86. This assumption underpins Morris' most recent work in this area, *The Reflective Heart*, which ultimately is aimed at a universal readership. Vaughan, 'What is Spiritual Intelligence?', p. 21, concurs with it: 'I believe everyone has the potential for developing spiritual intelligence, just as everyone has a capacity for intuition, thinking, sensing and feeling'. It can be developed 'by a variety of practices for training attention, transforming emotions, and cultivating ethical behavior'; its development depends on 'expanding consciousness to include a widening circle of empathetic identification, sensitivity to subtle realities, and familiarity with various symbolic maps of consciousness'.

    87 Morris indeed suggests that, for a certain type of audience, 'it is pointless ... to distinguish between Muslim and non-Muslim, for what these people are interested in is practical spiritual guidance and clarification, and the particular religious setting is less important. Just as there are a lot of people who are interested in Jewish mysticism, or Buddhist esotericism, without becoming Jews or Buddhists, so there is a large audience interested in Ibn 'Arabi, and it certainly overlaps between Muslims and non-Muslims'. See '"An Essential Translator"', p. 20.

    Cf. Morris, '"... Except His Face"', p. 30: 'The exploration of [Ibn 'Arabi's] writings from [the] perspective of practical spirituality is only in its earliest stages, and ... offers rich prospects for spiritual rediscoveries and the sort of true communication and communion that is based on a shared ground of common spiritual experience'.

The common understanding of Beshara and Morris may appear to break down when Morris suggests that, as with other 'manuals' for spirituality, in reading Ibn 'Arabi in such translations most readers will still find that they need help. Thus, they 'quickly discover that such written instructions are not at all the same as the actual exercises ... that even those exercises, if attempted in isolation, are not really the same as working with an experienced teacher or guide.' See Morris, 'Ibn 'Arabi's Rhetoric of Realisation', 1, p.63. However, he points to 'one of the most encouraging aspects of the apparently global contemporary interest in the *Fusus* ... and other ... translations of Ibn 'Arabi's writings that has developed in recent years'. This is 'the way in which people ... seem to be studying his writings ... in small groups'. He argues that it is in the context of the small, informal group that it becomes possible to advance 'in developing *actual* spiritual intelligence (i.e., beyond the strictly conceptual, mental forms of understanding)', compared with solitary study. 'For each student-participant immediately provides ... insights into the implications of ... the Shaykh's writing. Even more importantly, it is almost impossible, under any conditions, for a solitary person (or for a closed, authoritarian group) to recognise ... their own most characteristic spiritual and mental blind spots and habitually conditioned qualities' (pp.64–5).

Morris' characterisation of a study context that can aid development of spiritual intelligence (a possible viable alternative to the experienced teacher/guide?) is likely to be derived from the case of Beshara, with which he is familiar. On the rise of the 'small group movement' more broadly, see Ch. 8.

88 Morris, 'Ibn 'Arabi's Rhetoric of Realisation', 1, p.63. While much of Morris' analysis focuses on the *Futuhat* specifically, he considers his arguments to apply to all of Ibn 'Arabi's writings.

For an example of Morris' application of Ibn 'Arabi's texts as guide in practical spirituality, see Stuart Kenner, 'Climbing: Ibn 'Arabi on Spirituality in Everyday Life' (Seminar led by Professor James Morris), *MIAS Newsletter*, 15 (Spring 2000), p.2.

89 Comment made by Bernd Radtke, MIAS Symposium, Oxford, May 2004; cf. Homerin, 'Ibn Arabi in the People's Assembly', p.475.

90 See Hirtenstein, *The Unlimited Mercifier*, p.x. Cf. Clark's implicit projection of associates ('Early Best-sellers in the Akbarian Tradition', p.36): 'those of us who read Ibn 'Arabi not as medievalists pursuing an academic study but in search of spiritual help and guidance'.

91 Morris, 'Ibn 'Arabi's Rhetoric of Realisation', 1, p.85. Cf. Coates, 'A Global Magnification of the Essential', *MIAS Newsletter*, 18 (Summer 2002), p.10: 'the study of Ibn 'Arabi is inextricably about the "here and now" and, therefore, about ourselves. For this reason the study of Ibn 'Arabi cannot profitably be construed as a merely ... specialised study of some obscure medieval Arabic metaphysics to which only the classical Arabist has the proper means of access'.

92 Note the extent of Morris' concern with the English-reading audience of Ibn 'Arabi in translation, evident in the lengthy discussion in 'Ibn 'Arabi's Rhetoric of Realisation', 1; for further indication of his views concerning the importance of Western language translation (and the need for a 'judicious' selection of texts for this), see '"An Essential Translator"', p.20.

93 See Chittick, Rumi and *wahdat al-wujud*, p.72.

94 Cf. Ch. 1, and Chodkiewicz, 'The Diffusion of Ibn 'Arabi's Doctrine', p.39. Homerin, 'Ibn Arabi in the People's Assembly', p.465, observes that, in his capacity as Director of Publications, the great Egyptian reformist Muhammad 'Abduh (d.1905) refused to publish the *Futuhat*, arguing that 'works of this sort should not be looked at save by those who are qualified'.

95 In light of such views, the outrage expressed in the following comment by Zarcone, 'Rereadings and Transformations of Sufism in the West', p.117 (which he aims at certain Guénonian strands), is perhaps understandable: 'What then are we to think of the reading of Ibn 'Arabi by Western converts, ignorant of the Arabic language and the Islamic way of life, and, moreover, untrained in the scholarly disciplines of the *madrasa* ...?'

96 See Chittick, Rumi and *wahdat al-wujud*, pp. 71–2. For a translation of the relevant passage from the Introduction to the *Futuhat*, see James Winston Morris, How to Study the *Futuhat*: Ibn 'Arabi's Own Advice, in Hirtenstein and Tiernan, eds, *Muhyiddin Ibn 'Arabi: A Commemorative Volume*, pp. 82–3. The following comment by Austin, *The Bezels of Wisdom*, pp. 19–20, must be read in light of this qualification regarding sufis: 'such works as *The Bezels of Wisdom* were certainly not intended for public consumption, but rather for fellow Sufis, who knew how to deal with the apparent theological dangers implicit in it'.

97 Ibn 'Arabi refers to the *'amma* and the *khassa*.

98 According to Hirtenstein, 'Ibn al-'Arabi' (pre-publication version of article for *Encyclopedia of Religion* [New York, 2005]), his 'all-inclusiveness and flexibility' make Ibn 'Arabi 'one of the most demanding of authors, and one whose subtlety lesser minds have often struggled to comprehend, some falling into rejection and outright opposition. His writing was always considered ... the most elevated exposition of mystical thought in Islam, and therefore unsuitable for the untrained mind'. The training he has in mind is spiritual rather than intellectual, in methods that nurture 'receptivity' by achieving 'an emptying of the place', so that *kashf* can occur.

99 Brass, Foreword, the *White Fusus*, 2; see Ch. 3.

100 The vitality of *kashf* as a source of knowledge among the simplest devotees of Ibn 'Arabi who serve at his shrine complex today is remarkable; for examples, see Taji-Farouki, *At the Resting-place of the Seal of Saints*.

101 Nettler, *Sufi Metaphysics and Qur'anic Prophets*, p. 2.

102 Cf. Young, 'Between the Yea and the Nay', p. 1: 'It is generally accepted that there is an unbridgeable gulf between the way of the mystic and the way of the academic. Indeed, there are foundations for this contention, which can perhaps be summarised by saying that he who follows only an academic approach to Truth can never attain to Truth in all Its fullness'. He continues: 'Yet Truth is single and therefore there must be a relationship between the two different approaches. According to the Qur'an, first God created Adam and subsequently taught him the names. Knowing the names is secondary to being, in the first place, man. Following this order, first one is realised as man and subsequently all the names, including that of "academic", express in their particular ways this same essential Truth'.

103 For Morris, the task is not only to provide texts in the target Western language: it also requires that the translator point to the difficulties and challenges involved in the translation process, to help the reader adopt that meaning which (out of a range of possibilities) best serves their own personal appropriation. His 'Ibn 'Arabi's Rhetoric of Realisation', 1, p. 57, thus examines aspects of the *Futuhat* 'from the perspective of readers limited to English (and other Western languages), especially those characteristics which flow from the ongoing dilemmas of translation and all the accompanying necessities of explanation and contextualisation. Since the spectrum of possibilities facing any translator of Ibn 'Arabi is so vast, it is ... important that non-specialist readers become sufficiently familiar with the ... range of ... basic possibilities that they can begin to actively participate ... in re-translating the approximative English words ... into a more ... nuanced form, especially in relation to their own ... experiences of the spiritual situations ... in question'.

104 Such aims lay directly behind Hirtenstein's *The Unlimited Mercifier*, which we discussed above. Referring to the existence of several excellent Western-language studies of Ibn 'Arabi's life and work, Hirtenstein observes (p. ix) that 'they have mainly been addressed to a specialist and sophisticated audience. Some might argue that this is because Ibn 'Arabi is the most complex thinker and writer in Islamic mysticism ... and that to understand him one needs a wealth of background knowledge in Islam, Quran, Hadith, medieval Arab philosophy, Arabic philology and so on. However, while that may be true from a certain perspective, there can be little doubt that Ibn 'Arabi's writings also possess the remarkable quality of being able to speak to people of all walks of life and beliefs, across the apparent barrier of many centuries and differing cultures. His mystical expressions spring directly from the heart, and it is to that deepest of sentiments that readers respond. With this in mind I agreed [to write a book on him for the general reader] ... simply because I felt there to be an overwhelming need for his teachings to be more accessible.'

105 See Stephen Hirtenstein, 'Publication Report', Minutes of the AGM of the MIAS, 11 November 1989, p. 3.

106 See Ibn Yusuf, 'Ibn 'Arabi for Our Generation', p. 35. The author refers specifically to the appearance of new, widely accessible translations of Rumi's poetry, especially those of Barks. The analogy he draws is with the case of science: here, he suggests, a discovery is credited not to the first person who makes it, 'but to the one who makes it functional in the field of science'.

107 Lewis, Rumi: Past and Present, p. 4. Cf. Schimmel, Mawlana Rumi: Yesterday, Today and Tomorrow, p. 8: 'Especially during the last decades, when love of Rumi became ... fashionable in certain circles ... publications by non-scholars have often emphasized Mawlana's role as the timeless, spaceless ecstatic, the Master of Love'.

108 Lewis, Rumi: Past and Present, p. 10. He adds (p. 11) that 'To understand Rumi, one must obviously understand something of the beliefs and assumptions he held as a Muslim'.

109 Ibid., p. 12. Cf. 'Rumi ... conscientiously upheld the five principal "pillars" of Islam and encouraged others to do so, both in word and deed. However [he] held the spirit behind the observance of these laws of Islam far dearer than the outward performance of any rite'. See also p. 407.

110 On 'Rumi as Sunni', Lewis notes (ibid., pp. 12–14): 'Because the Mevlevi order in later centuries has accepted many Shiite influences, some Shiites ... attempted to claim Rumi as a sympathizer. Though Rumi's heart was generous and his mind quite open when it came to differences of creed, we should not be deceived by his tolerance into imagining that all beliefs were equal to him'. He explains Rumi's attitude towards Shi'is, indicating that he was not a Shi'i himself. On 'Rumi as Hanafi', he explains (pp. 15, 18) that Rumi's thinking would have been strongly shaped by the teachings of the Hanafi jurist–theologian al-Maturidi; he also observes that Rumi was engaged in teaching the religious sciences 'at the professorial rank' at four respected institutions.

111 Ibid., p. 27.

112 Bearing in mind Winkel's warning (Islam and the Living Law, pp. viii–ix): 'Ibn al-'Arabi is misunderstood because his use of language refuses stability and reification. He uses various language formats in order to avoid being constrained. So one quickly learns to avoid pigeon-holing him'. He provides some examples: 'the phrase most associated with Ibn al-'Arabi [wahdat al-wujud] was never used by him; the Sunnis take his insights but denigrate his name; his disciples create a full-blown system out of insights which are themselves defiantly anti-systematic; the Shi'ites base an entire philosophy on that system; modern Sufis think he is dangerous, but the only danger to them is that Ibn al-'Arabi would tell some of them to forget their guru and practice the shariah; orientalists were interested in him because he seemed to be anti-shariah, but reviving his insights would actually serve to invigorate and validate the shariah. In short, everything one thinks about Ibn al-'Arabi must be revised'.

113 Cf. al-Ghorab's characterisation of Ibn 'Arabi as Imam (founder–leader of his own madhhab or school of law), Salafi (i.e. non-innovator), Usuli (following the principles agreed upon by the imams with regard to jurisprudence), and Sufi. See Muhyiddin Ibn al-'Arabi amidst Religions (adyan) and Schools of Thought (madhahib), p. 224.

114 A contemporary Arab author argues that 'Ibn 'Arabi attempted to unite the Islamic sects, and so he took something from each sect and each group, with the result that everyone claimed this man as their own'. See Muhyi al-Din Ibn al-'Arabi, 'Uqlat

al-mustawfiz, ed. and intro. Yusuf Safar Fattum (Damascus, 2002), p. 22. He adds: 'Most Muslims of all different schools venerate Ibn 'Arabi, for every one of the Muslim sects finds something of its teachings in his principles. It is as if he tried to make his own teaching a reference for all the different schools, wishing it to be a microcosm of the Divine Essence, the source of all facts, on which the religions base their claims.' See Muhyi al-Din Ibn al-'Arabi, *Kitab Insha' al-dawa'ir wa'l-jadawil*, ed. and intro. Yusuf Safar Fattum (Damascus, 2001), p. 7.

Refutations of claims that Ibn 'Arabi was a Shi'i of some sort (and particularly a Batini, esotericist or Isma'ili) are common. For example, according to Fattum, *'Uqlat al-mustawfiz*, p. 22: 'Some of the Shi'a mistakenly believe that Ibn 'Arabi was one of their propagandists (*du'at*) based on his theory of mystical unity, or the Oneness of Being. Ibn 'Arabi was clear in his attack on the Batiniyya, however, and cited Abu Hamid al-Ghazali.' The notion that he was an Isma'ili of sorts is often rooted in the opinion that Ibn 'Arabi's approach was very close to that of the Ikhwan al-Safa; cf. Affifi, *The Mystical Philosophy*, p. 185, where the author notes that Ibn 'Arabi often distances himself from the Isma'ilis. On Ibn 'Arabi's views concerning the Shi'a (Imamis) and Batiniyya, see al-Ghorab, Muhyiddin Ibn al-'Arabi amidst Religions (*adyan*) and Schools of Thought (*madhahib*), pp. 202–6, 213–16. Note that many of the ulama who teach the *Fusus* and the *Futuhat* in Iran today claim that Ibn 'Arabi was himself a Shi'i (or had Shi'i sympathies); some claim that these texts have been tampered with. For example, Qom-based Ayat Allah Hasanzadeh Amuli argues that material proving that the author was a Shi'i has been expunged from the *Futuhat*, and a chapter on Fatima has been removed from the *Fusus*. Specific support texts for Shi'i claims arise in the early part of the *Futuhat*; the *'Anqa' mughrib* is also particularly important in this respect. The author thanks Reza Jawzi for this information. On general attitudes towards Ibn 'Arabi in Iranian Twelver Shi'ism historically and today, see De Jong and Radtke, Introduction, pp. 15–16.

Ibn 'Arabi has often been connected with the Zahiri school (linked with the name of Ibn Hazm), and the influence of this school on his thought in matters of law is undeniable. Yet he is more correctly characterised not as a Zahiri (an identification he himself rejected), but as a *mujtahid mutlaq* or someone who is qualified to act autonomously in matters of *ijtihad*. See Chodkiewicz, *An Ocean without Shore*, pp. 54–7; al-Ghorab, Muhyiddin Ibn al-'Arabi amidst Religions (*adyan*) and Schools of Thought (*madhahib*), pp. 199–202; Haddad, *'Aqidat al-'awamm*, pp. 1–2.

With regard to our final characterisation, the term 'Sufi' must be qualified by separating out of it for particular mention the verifiers (*al-muhaqqiqun*) and the people of unveiling and finding (*ahl al-kashf wa'l-wujud*). See al-Ghorab, Muhyiddin Ibn al-'Arabi amidst Religions (*adyan*) and Schools of Thought (*madhahib*), pp. 222–3, and our discussion above concerning Ibn 'Arabi's concept of the elite. Thus as Chittick, 'Time, Space, and the Objectivity of Ethical Norms', pp. 581–2, notes, 'Although Ibn al-'Arabi does on occasion mention the word Sufi in a positive light, he does not use it to refer to himself, nor would he be happy to be called by it without serious qualification ... If we ... want to have a single descriptive label with which he might be happy, the best choice is probably *muhaqqiq*, that is, "verifier" or "realizer".' On this concept, see Chittick, *The Sufi Path of Knowledge*, index ('verification') and *The Self-Disclosure of God*, index ('realization'); above.

115 See for example Addas, *Ibn 'Arabi: The Voyage of No Return*, pp. 120–2. As the author notes, Ibn 'Arabi described the Batiniyya, who claim exemption from observance of the sharia based on an alleged knowledge of its hidden meanings, as 'the most ignorant of men in the field of subtle truths'.

116 Chittick, Ibn 'Arabi and His School, p. 67. Cf. his Ibn 'Arabi, p. 507. For further examples of Ibn 'Arabi's insistence on adherence to the sharia (which he described as 'the path of felicity'), see al-Ghorab, Muhyiddin Ibn al-'Arabi amidst Religions (*adyan*) and Schools of Thought (*madhahib*), pp. 223–4. These include the following (from the *Futuhat*, as translated in ibid., p. 224): 'The path is the obligatory rituals prescribed by the

Real, about the strict application ('azima) of which there can be no relaxation (rukhsa), such relaxations in the application of the law (rukhas) are valid only at the prescribed places.'

Note finally that Ibn 'Arabi alludes often to the distance between what Morris, in Chodkiewicz, ed., *The Meccan Revelations*, 1, p.68 (see also pp.248–9 n.3, 263 n.76), describes as 'the limited, historical conception of the Sharia shared by many of the 'ulama' … and the deeper, more challenging perennial reality of its demands and presuppositions as understood by the awliya', whom Ibn 'Arabi consistently regards as the true "knowers" and "authorities" of the Community'. See further Winkel, *Islam and the Living Law*, and Chodkiewicz, *An Ocean without Shore*.

117 See Leaman, review of Coates, *Ibn 'Arabi and Modern Thought*, p.105.

118 Lewis, *Rumi: Past and Present*, p.2.

119 For an exploration of the resources yielded by Ibn 'Arabi's work as the basis of a potential contribution to 'the present world of ecumenical investigation' from an alternative perspective, see Dom Sylvester Houédard, 'Ibn 'Arabi's Contribution to the Wider Ecumenism', *Muhyiddin Ibn 'Arabi 1165–1240: His Life and Times*, pp.19–29.

120 Ibn 'Arabi, *Tarjuman al-ashwaq* (Beirut, 1966), pp.42–3 (as translated in Corbin, *Alone with the Alone*, p.135): 'O marvel! A garden among the flames … My heart has become capable of all forms. It is a meadow for gazelles and a monastery for Christian monks, A temple for idols and the pilgrim's Ka'aba, The Tables of the Law and the book of the Koran. I profess the religion of Love, and whatever direction Its steed may take, Love is my religion and my faith.' Cited by Young in 'At the Still Point'; Hirtenstein, 'Muhyiddin Ibn 'Arabi: The Treasure of Compassion'; Rauf, *Addresses*, p.71 and *Addresses II*, p.47.

121 Al-Ghorab, Muhyiddin Ibn al-'Arabi amidst Religions (adyan) and Schools of Thought (madhahib), pp.219–22, attributes to their erroneous understanding of these verses the portrayal by some orientalists and non-Muslims of Ibn 'Arabi as (p.220) 'a believer in each and every religion'. He insists on Ibn 'Arabi's distinction between 'the divine self-disclosure in the forms of beliefs' and 'the object of belief'.

Schimmel, *Mystical Dimensions of Islam*, pp.271–2, argues that the seemingly tolerant statement these verses contain 'is not tolerance preached to the rank and file'. Rather, she suggests after Corbin that they contain 'a statement about the author's own lofty spiritual rank'. Chittick, Rumi and the Mawlawiyyah, p.117, describes them as an allusion to 'the nonspecificity or "nonentification" of the heart of the Perfect Man, who experiences continuous theophanies of the Divine Essence, theophanies that "never repeat themselves".'

Keller, Perceptions of Other Religions in Sufism, pp.188–9, concludes from his own analysis that these verses 'are anything but the expression of a genuinely sympathetic perception and appreciation of other religions'. Further: 'As manifestations of Divine Names, all religions have a right to exist and to be practised. But they are included in and overwhelmed by Islam, and so they are in fact abrogated. Their existence is a very precarious one, at once lawful and in contradiction with the true and final Law of God.'

122 Some point to the advice Ibn 'Arabi gave to the Seljuq ruler Kayka'us regarding the treatment of non-Muslims (especially Christians) in his realm. They suggest that, in light of this, constructs of the author (who included his letter to the ruler in the last chapter of the *Futuhat*) as an ecumenist who accepted all religions (and a pacifist) must be questioned. See, for example, al-Ghorab, Muhyiddin Ibn al-'Arabi amidst Religions (adyan) and Schools of Thought (madhahib), p.222, and Keller, Perceptions of Other Religions in Sufism, pp.189–90. See further Giuseppe Scattolin, 'Sufism and Law in Islam: A Text of Ibn 'Arabi (560/1165 – 638/1240) on "Protected People" (Ahl al-Dhimma)', *Islamochristiana*, 24 (1998), pp.37–55. Based on this text, the author characterises Ibn 'Arabi as 'a man of his time, who reflected the limited world-vision of the Medieval age', his openness, tolerance and positive view of other religions notwithstanding. He concludes that Ibn 'Arabi's vision of religions was 'strictly based on and limited by the

traditional data of Islamic law ... as elaborated by Islamic jurisprudence'. See pp. 37, 48–9, 51. Cf. also Addas, *Ibn 'Arabi: The Voyage of No Return*, p. 120.

123 Leaman, review of Coates, *Ibn 'Arabi and Modern Thought*, p. 105. The specific point Leaman makes concerning *wahdat al-wujud* in his judgement of Coates' work might perhaps legitimately be extended to the presentation of Ibn 'Arabi's teachings in general among at least some of those associates who put pen to paper. Their approach can thus suffer from their selective and relatively limited exposure to his corpus.

124 Chittick, Rumi and *wahdat al-wujud*, p. 83. He adds that Chodkiewicz has shown that 'it does not present a balanced statement of Ibn al-'Arabi's teachings'. In sum, it is 'an ecstatic hymn set to the tune of the Persian poetical exclamation, "All is He!"' See also Chittick, The School of Ibn 'Arabi, p. 519.

Zarcone, 'Rereadings and Transformations of Sufism in the West', pp. 117–18, points out that the influence of Ibn 'Arabi's doctrine on the first founders of Western *tariqa*s (the sufi Guénonians) was via this text, which was translated by Aguéli. He argues that it 'exposes the extreme consequences of the mysticism of the Andalusian Sufi and attributes a total unreality to the "created world"'. Zarcone maintains that its influence on Schuon's thought in particular is clear: 'it is his reading of this text, among other things, which authorized him to proclaim the bypassing and even the negation of exoteric forms by esotericism'. The text was published for the first time in France in the periodical *La Gnose* (1911).

125 Cf. Coates, *Ibn 'Arabi and Modern Thought*, p. 33 n. 4: the author confidently asserts that the term *wahdat al-wujud* 'does no injustice whatsoever to Ibn 'Arabi's thought'.

126 Cf. Editorial, *Beshara Magazine*, 8 (1989), p. 3: 'ideas of unity ... are now emerging in many areas of human activity'. Examples are cited from the new science and ecology.

127 See Hirtenstein, 'Ibn al-'Arabi'. Cf. Chittick, 'The Central Point', pp. 31–3: 'It would be much more appropriate – in terms of Ibn 'Arabi's own teachings – to refer to his school of thought as that of human perfection, or as the path to becoming the "perfect human being", *al-insan al-kamil* ... It is obvious in the *Futuhat* that achieving human perfection is the basic issue ... In the same way, there is no special reason to think that the *Fusus al-Hikam* is about *wahdat al-wujud*. Rather, it is also about the stations of human perfection.'

128 Associates concede that, in contrast, his knowledge of the *Futuhat* was considerably limited.

129 See Yiangou, 'Ismail Hakki Bursevi's translation', p. 85; cf. the *White Fusus*, 1, inside cover.

130 For example, Young, 'Ibn 'Arabi: Towards a Universal Point of View', p. 97: 'Ibn 'Arabi was instructed to bring out the *Fusus* to people who will benefit by it. Perhaps there are, and will be, many millions who need to know, and who will benefit by the bringing out of the simple, positive, joyful news of their intrinsic and inseparable unity with their origin, offering freedom from the tyranny of the thoughts of otherness'.

131 The latter is a reference to Ibn 'Arabi's statement in the opening of the Preface: see Ibn 'Arabi, *Fusus al-hikam*, p. 47, and the *White Fusus*, 1, p. 63. *The Bezels of Wisdom*, p. 45, translates this as 'the Station of Eternity'.

132 See Brass, Foreword, the *White Fusus*, 2, p. v.

133 The reference is to Ibn 'Arabi's own account of his meeting with the essential realities of the apostles of God and the prophets from Adam to Muhammad. He reports that this took place at an assembly in Cordoba in AH 586. See *The Bezels of Wisdom*, p. 134.

134 'What is the Difference? A Reaffirmation', p. 30. See also Clark, 'Summer Gathering'.

For the Arabic text in question, see Ibn 'Arabi, *Fusus al-hikam*, p. 110. The following is Austin's translation (*The Bezels of Wisdom*, p. 134) of the few lines beginning with Qur'an 11: 56 ('There is no walking being but He draws it by its forelock. Surely my Lord is on the

Straight Path.'): 'What greater tidings could there be for creation? Indeed, God reminds us of His favour on us in bringing this [verse] to us in the Qur'an. Then Muhammad, who integrates the whole, completes the tidings in transmitting to us the Tradition in which it is said that the Reality is [essentially] the hearing [of the servant, the gnostic], the sight, the hand, the foot and the tongue, indeed, all the senses.'

135 Morris, in Chodkiewicz, ed., *The Meccan Revelations*, 1, p. 13; see also p. 10. As this becomes more widely available through translation, the *Futuhat* will increasingly call into question the stereotypes that dominate such characterisations.

For selected English/French translations of the *Futuhat*, see Chittick, *The Sufi Path of Knowledge* and *The Self-Disclosure of God*; Chodkiewicz *et al.*, trans., *Les Illuminations de la Mecque*; Chodkiewicz, ed., *The Meccan Revelations*, 1, 2 (New York, 2004).

A comment by a Damascus-based sufi author (Haddad, *'Aqidat al-'awamm*, p. 7) provides a recent illustration of the tendency described by Morris: 'Perhaps the most famous misrepresentation of the Shaykh that resulted from the *Fusus* is the attribution to him of the doctrine of "oneness of being" ... in the pantheistic sense'. For the complete quotation, see Ch. 1.

136 See Chodkiewicz, 'The Diffusion of Ibn 'Arabi's Doctrine', pp. 51–2.

137 Interpolation is designated by the term *dass*: interpolations have been variously attributed to Qunawi on the one hand and the Batiniyya on the other. For an assessment of the 'deliberate interpolation' hypothesis, see Chodkiewicz, *The Spiritual Writings of Amir 'Abd al-Kader*, p. 192 n. 51.

138 Contemporary opinions in Damascus provide some illustration.

Haddad, *'Aqidat al-'awamm*; this Damascus-based Lebanese/American Naqshbandi sufi author writes: 'The name of Ibn 'Arabi remains associated with controversy because of those who criticized him severely for the work attributed to him under the title *Fusus al-Hikam* ... The attribution of this work in its present form to Ibn 'Arabi is undoubtedly incorrect as the *Fusus* contradicts some of the most basic tenets of Islam expounded by Ibn 'Arabi himself in his authentic works, such as the finality of Prophethood, the primacy of Prophets over non-Prophets, the abrogation of all religious creeds other than Islam, the everlastingness of the punishment of Hellfire and its dwellers, the abiding therein of anyone that does not accept the Prophet (may the peace and blessing of God be upon him) after his coming, Pharaoh's damnation, etc'. Further, Haddad, 'Ibn 'Arabi', www.sunnah.org: 'Our principle is that anything in the *Fusus* that contradicts Ibn 'Arabi's *'aqida* as set forth in the *Futuhat* (his later work) must be dismissed as spurious unless it can be interpreted to conform to it.'

Muhammad Sa'id Ramadan al-Buti (interview with the author, Oxford, 2001) speaks of 'a historical consensus that the Batiniyya interpolated their own ideas in all widely circulated texts, including those of Ibn 'Arabi'; he cites Ibn al-'Imad, al-Sha'rani and Hajji Khalifa. (On these authors, see Knysh, *Ibn 'Arabi in the Later Islamic Tradition*, index.) Cf. al-Buti, *Hadha walidi*, p. 110 n. 1, where he adds Ibn al-Muqri. He also notes the belief of his late father Mullah Ramadan al-Buti (whose refusal to buy the text we noted earlier) in the possibility that parts of the *Futuhat* may not be correctly attributed to Ibn 'Arabi: see ibid., p. 109. Al-Buti is a (retired) University of Damascus professor and well-known author and broadcaster. On him, see Andreas Christmann, Islamic Scholar and Religious Leader: Shaikh Muhammad Sa'id Ramadan al-Buti, in John Cooper, Ronald Nettler and Mohamed Mahmoud, eds, *Islam and Modernity: Muslim Intellectuals Respond* (London, 2000), pp. 57–81.

139 Interview with the author, Damascus, February 2003. See also Mahmoud al-Ghorab, *Sharh Fusus al-hikam min kalam al-shaykh al-akbar Muhyi al-Din Ibn al-'Arabi* (Damascus, 1985). Al-Ghorab's methodology was to compare the contents of the *Fusus* with Ibn 'Arabi's opinions as set out in his other works which have been 'confirmed' as correctly attributed to him. On this basis, he identified parts of its contents that can be attributed to him, and parts that contradict his opinions, approach and style as established elsewhere. Al-Ghorab deemed those works in Ibn 'Arabi's own hand a more

reliable record of his thought than the oldest extant copy of the *Fusus*, believed to be in Qunawi's hand. Allowing that Qunawi did write it, he argued that this must have been from memory. He also cast doubt on the *sama'* on this copy, and questioned whether it can be assumed that all manuscripts taken from Qunawi's library rightly belonged there: see ibid., pp. 5–16.

Al-Ghorab has authored a substantial series of works on Ibn 'Arabi (all published privately in Damascus). These mostly set out Ibn 'Arabi's position concerning selected themes, based on his writings. They include, for example, *Sharh Kalimat al-sufiyya min kalam al-shaykh al-akbar* (1981); *al-Radd 'ala Ibn Taymiyya min kalam al-shaykh al-akbar* (1981); and *al-Hubb wa'l-mahabba al-ilahiyya min kalam al-shaykh al-akbar* (1992).

140 This article, which he had had translated into English, apparently drew on his *Sharh Fusus al-hikam* (the volume had appeared in a second edition in 1995 and he had attempted there to correct a misperception that he had accused Qunawi *himself* of forging the *Fusus* text). He focused in it on perceived contradictions between the contents of the chapters on Jesus and Elias, and those of Ibn 'Arabi's 'verified' books, particularly the *Futuhat*. Reiterating his earlier arguments, he pointed to the conclusion that (a) Ibn 'Arabi did not produce a work entitled *Fusus al-hikam*. (b) Qunawi did not write the copy of this text that is supposedly from his library. (c) This copy is a forgery wrongly attributed to Ibn 'Arabi and wrongly associated with Qunawi and his library (where it was possibly placed after his death).

141 He raised two issues he claimed al-Ghorab had ignored in his own treatment: (a) The existence of a certificate of audition (*sama'*) on the 'Qunawi' manuscript, indicating that the text had been read out in front of Ibn 'Arabi. (b) The existence of a second certificate of audition, encompassing the names of further known individuals. He added that he personally could see no basis for the argument that the ideas expounded in the *Fusus* are in any way inconsistent with the remainder of Ibn 'Arabi's teachings, and remarked that apparent contradictions can be satisfactorily explained. Al-Ghorab wrote back that more than one text had previously been demonstrated to be falsely attributed to Ibn 'Arabi, and provided evidence for this.

142 See 'A Note from Mr. Bulent Rauf', p. 14. Rauf criticised Gilis' 'show of impatience' and his apparent 'making light' of the *Fusus* (he had reportedly been guilty of this during the question–answer session following his talk at the MIAS AGM described earlier). He accused him of 'insisting almost that there were other works of Ibn 'Arabi that should hold at least equal attention and importance [as the *Fusus*]'. Rauf expressed his surprise at the fact that, in spite of his familiarity with these, Gilis 'should see no difference between all the other works of Ibn 'Arabi, including the *Futuhat*, on the one side and the *Fusus al-Hikam* on the other'.

Rauf's position can be compared with the following assessment by Chittick, *The School of Ibn 'Arabi*, p. 517, citing the critical remarks of al-Tilimsani in his commentary on the *Fusus* (probably the earliest authored by a follower of Ibn 'Arabi): 'Even Ibn 'Arabi's most fervent admirers did not take too seriously his statement that he had received the book from the hand of the Prophet; otherwise, they would not have dared to differ with him.'

143 Martin Notcutt, 'This the Mercy which He has enlarged for You', paper delivered at MIAS Symposium (Oxford, May 2003), cited in *MIAS Newsletter*, 19 (Autumn 2003), p. 15.

144 Chittick, The School of Ibn 'Arabi, pp. 511, 514. This evaluation relates to Qunawi's correspondence with al-Tusi.

145 Ibid., pp. 517–18. For a justification of this 'process of evolution' (which the author suggests reached a mature form with Qaysari, and which consisted in 'an ever more extensive use of philosophical terminology' and 'the development of a special Akbarian technical vocabulary'), see Clark, 'Early Best-sellers in the Akbarian Tradition', pp. 48ff. The author underlines the fact that such evolution of expression came about not as a result of the indulging of personal preferences, but (p. 51) 'as an appropriate response to the cultural environment in which [the early commentators] lived and worked'. Cf. Chodkiewicz's observation, cited by Chittick below.

146 Chittick, The School of Ibn 'Arabi, p. 521.

147 Ibid., p. 511.

148 Ibid., p. 517. Associates would contrast this perception of Qunawi's contribution with Jami's recommendation concerning his importance to a proper understanding of Ibn 'Arabi. This recommendation is cited [from Addas] in Clark, 'Early Best-sellers in the Akbarian Tradition', p. 51, for example: '[Ibn 'Arabi's] intention with regard to the question of *wahdat al-wujud* can only be grasped in a way that harmonises with reason (*'aql*) and with law (*shar'*) through the study of [Qunawi's] works and through understanding them as they should be understood'.

149 Chittick, The School of Ibn 'Arabi, pp. 511, 521 n. 6, characterises Qunawi as the 'most influential and at the same time independently minded of Ibn 'Arabi's immediate disciples'.

150 Cf. Gilis, 'An Approach to the Function of Islam in the Teaching of Ibn 'Arabi', p. 8.

151 Chittick, Ibn 'Arabi and His School, p. 53, remarks that several of Bosnevi's treatises show 'a remarkable spiritual and intellectual affinity with al-Qunawi'. Associates familiar with other *Fusus* commentaries claim that Bosnevi's is 'the closest in spirit to Qunawi's *Fukuk* and to his way of teaching the *Fusus*'. They hint that this is a further aspect of the significance of the *White Fusus*, emanating from Qunawi's closeness to Ibn 'Arabi and his status as transmitter/interpreter of his teachings.

It is noteworthy that, in recent years, an Arabic-reading Beshara study group based in Oxford, UK has read excerpts from Qunawi's commentary.

152 Clark, 'Early Best-sellers in the Akbarian Tradition', p. 53.

Chapter 8

1 While prediction is risky, the importance for academics to engage in 'a serious study of the future' concerning developments in religion is increasingly recognised. See, for example, Linda Woodhead, Paul Heelas and Grace Davie, Introduction, in G. Davie, P. Heelas and L. Woodhead, eds, *Predicting Religion: Christian, Secular and Alternative Futures* (Hampshire, UK, 2003), pp. 11ff.

2 Cf. Parsons, Expanding the Religious Spectrum, pp. 279–80, 285ff., and Chryssides, *Exploring New Religions*, pp. 11ff. For further aspects of the 'newness' of NRMs, see Arweck, New Religious Movements, pp. 276ff.

3 Associates' unease with the term reflects the preference of New Agers and many involved with the sacred today for the term 'spirituality', a theme we have touched on before and to which we will return later. Cf. Hanegraaff, *New Age Religion*, p. 7 n. 25, and 'New Age Movement', pp. 857–8. O'Murchu, *Quantum Theology*, pp. 13–14, 23, furnishes an acute example: the author argues that spirituality, 'the human search for meaning', is a 'fundamental human aspiration' that is both 'cosmic and personal', and 'coterminous with human evolution'. In contrast, religion 'serves a transitory and temporary purpose', and humanity may well be outgrowing its need for it. Acknowledgement of spirituality as an alternative to religion is reflected in growing use of the phrase 'spiritual but not religious'. See, for example, www. spiritualprogressives.org, website of The Network of Spiritual Progressives, a project of the liberal Jewish Tikkun Community (on which see www.tikkun.org) that self-describes as 'an interfaith movement ... welcoming to "spiritual but not religious" secular people as well as religious progressives'. See also Robert Forman, *Grassroots Spirituality: What it is, Why it is here, Where it is going* (Exeter, Devon, 2004), pp. 45ff.

4 Barker, *New Religious Movements: A Practical Introduction*, p. 145, cited in Parsons, Expanding the Religious Spectrum, p. 288. Parsons cites TM and Rajneeshism as examples of movements that explicitly deny that they are religions. Subud can be added to these, for it actively encourages its members to continue in their 'original' religion; see Barrett, *The New Believers*, p. 354.

We noted definitions of religion in contrast to spirituality earlier. To clarify the understanding of religion per se, we can offer two out of many possible definitions. According to Barrett, *The New Believers*, p. 25, a religion is 'a social construct encompassing beliefs and practices which enable people, individually and collectively, to make some sense of the Great Questions of life and death'. Chryssides, *Exploring New Religions*, pp. 14–16, suggests that a group of people constitutes a religious group 'if they offer a means of coping with the key events and the adversities and misfortunes of life, using the key characteristics of religious practice which are identified by scholars such as Smart'. (The reference is to Ninian Smart's six 'dimensions' of religion: experiential, mythic, doctrinal, ethical, ritual and social/institutional.) He adds two further observations concerning the nature of religion: (a) its goal is conceived as the transformation of the entire human race, and (b) it holds that the world's problems cannot be solved by human effort alone, but require supernatural aid.

5 Chryssides, *Exploring New Religions*, pp. 16ff., suggests that there has not been adequate discussion of its application, arguing that the vast majority of new religions have progressed beyond the relatively nebulous 'movement' phase through a process of institutionalisation into a highly structured form of organisation. Yet, as he notes, the term NRM is now so widely used that it would seem perverse to try to amend it. We will return to the issue of structure in light of Beshara's New Age characteristics.

6 As Barrett, *The New Believers*, p. 55, points out, 'Both socially and spiritually, fellowship is an important part of belonging to a movement ... In addition, if you have been a member of a movement, and again especially if you have lived in a community, you will have grown used to doing certain things at certain times. You get up and go to bed, you study and worship, you meditate and recite mantras, you eat, you do manual work, all at set times. In a ... sense, you can become institutionalized.' Young, 'Courses at Chisholme', p. 31, argues that the danger of institutionalisation is 'fairly remote' during a six-month period. Many students do like to return to the School, but 'They do not come back because they have become institutionalised and can't do without their "shot" of institutional food and living, but because to be in the ambience of the awareness of Oneness, and to be amongst those who do like to discuss these things, is a pleasure. It is their life-blood.'

7 The local Beshara study group appears in some ways functionally analogous to the intimate and egalitarian face-to-face support groups that have proliferated in recent decades in Western societies. As Heelas, The Spiritual Revolution: From 'Religion' to 'Spirituality', pp. 367–8, indicates, the massive and socially significant 'small group movement' is 'very much orientated towards ... the life of the soul'. See also Heelas and Woodhead, Homeless Minds Today?, pp. 64–5. Discussion in the Beshara local study group is inclusive, non-judgemental and democratic: it draws on participants' experiences and insights, articulated within the safe and intimate space provided by the group. (In all this it mirrors the ethos of course study sessions, while developing aspects of it further in the absence of supervision.) Comments based on observations by regular participants in the study group in Oxford, UK.

8 This is made explicit in relation to specific others, such as traditional *tariqa*s, other sufi-inspired movements, and parts of the academic community engaged in Ibn 'Arabi studies. Beshara remains open to external participation in *dhikr* meetings held across the UK, and receptive individuals are of course actively encouraged to visit the School.

9 Cf. Feild, *The Last Barrier*, p. xvi.

10 A striking convergence arises in Bennett's understanding (recorded in 1974) of the burgeoning spiritual movements of the 1960s and especially the early 1970s: 'An immense destructive power is at work and it can be combated only upon the invisible planes of understanding and love. There is also unmistakably a creative counter-action that does not originate in the human mind. The influences that enter our ordinary

human experience from these planes of spirituality never cease to flow: they find a home wherever they are willingly admitted and responded to. At the present time, the counter-action is growing more powerful and millions of men and women, especially born after the last great war, are aware of it. All who are touched – even half-consciously – by the realization that a Great Work is in progress, feel drawn to take part in it. This creates the movements of enquiry and search which characterize our time.' See *Witness*, p. iii.

11 It is in this context that insistence on the universality of Beshara must be understood.

12 See 'Courses at Chisholme', p. 26.

13 See for example Clark, 'Summer Gathering'. Cf. 'Rememoration', p. 10: 'To Bulent, Beshara was never confined to Swyre Farm, Sherborne, Chisholme or the schools per se ... For him, Beshara was an essential idea whose purity he hoped to be protected at Chisholme and nurtured by the people who have learnt there.'

14 Young, 'Courses at Chisholme', p. 27, suggests that attending a Beshara course is 'a great help, but it is not absolutely necessary; there is no exclusivity in this matter'. The advantages derive simply from the fact that the School contains 'a source of help which can take effect over a very short period of time'. Cf. Tollemache, 'The Future of the Beshara Trust', p. 40: this describes the School environment as one of 'very special grace', underlining its importance as a source of 'guidance and encouragement'.

15 Rauf had reportedly 'insisted tirelessly' on 'the need for the proper organisation which comes from a body of committed people working together'. See 'Rememoration', p. 11.

16 Clark, 'Summer Gathering'.

17 The reference is to the four basic course disciplines and the five qualities these seek to inculcate: see Ch. 3.

18 In line with this self-understanding, an anonymous article described preparation for/involvement in the movement's expansion during the second half of the 1980s in the following terms: 'It is clear that such expansion is not to do with the makings of organisation ... Rather, as Shakespeare puts it in *The Merchant of Venice*, "The quality of mercy is not strain'd." It is this insistent quality of "not being strain'd" that initiates and promotes expansion. This coincides with Ibn 'Arabi's explanation of the outward breath of the compassionate Ipseity, the *nafas-er-Rahman*'. See 'What is the Difference? A Reaffirmation', p. 30.

19 Cf. Heelas, *The New Age Movement*, pp. 75–6.

20 See Beshara website.

21 Cf. Barker, 'New Religious Movements and Political Orders', pp. 11ff., observing that members of many NRMs believe that the real revolution in society will be achieved by changing the human individual, rather than through structural changes.

22 Young, 'Ibn 'Arabi: Towards a Universal Point of View', p. 95.

23 Clark, 'Summer Gathering'.

24 See 'Courses at Chisholme', p. 27. Cf. Clark, 'Fulfilling Our Potential', p. 42, which maintains that Ibn 'Arabi 'gives us a map to a *lost* land, which is the complete human potential' (our emphasis).

25 Coates, 'Ibn 'Arabi: The Unity of Existence and the Era'.

26 Coates, *Ibn 'Arabi and Modern Thought*, pp. 118–19.

27 'World-accommodating' is used here in terms of Wallis' typology: see Wallis, *The Elementary Forms of the New Religious Life*, pp. 34ff., excerpted in Dawson, ed., *Cults and New Religious Movements*, pp. 54ff. See also Chryssides, *Exploring New Religions*, pp. 26–7. Hermansen, In the Garden of American Sufi Movements, p. 176 n. 93, notes that 'perennialist groups are on the whole more "world-accommodating" of the current social order'.

For a discussion of New Age activities in terms of the spectrum from world-rejecting to world-affirming, see Heelas, *The New Age Movement*, pp. 30ff. and his Prosperity and the New Age Movement: The Efficacy of Spiritual Economics, in Wilson and Cresswell, eds, *New Religious Movements*, pp.52ff. World-rejecting actors reject everything offered by capitalistic modernity, prioritising the best of the inner world and avoiding the contaminating effects of life in the mainstream through detachment. World-affirming actors attach importance to becoming prosperous, and utilising spirituality to the end of experiencing the best of the outer world. Between these two extremes, 'the majority of New Age paths teach that it is possible to experience *the best of both worlds*'. This intermediary position represents 'harmonial religion', and describes all New Age paths that 'attach greater importance to experiences of inner spirituality and the role played by detachment than the world-affirming end of the spectrum, incorporating economic well-being whilst not attaching priority to this goal as do more systematic forms of world-affirmation'. Combining the spiritual with what mainstream society has to offer (and viewing the latter ultimately as the arena of expression of the former), Beshara belongs in this intermediary category. Note that Hanegraaff, *New Age Religion*, pp. 113ff., suggests that otherworldly-thinking and world rejection, at least in its stronger forms, is not typical of New Age thinking. New Agers are thus mostly this-worldly oriented, either completely or somewhat ambivalently.

28 Coates, *Ibn 'Arabi and Modern Thought*, p.8. As Chittick, *Sufism: A Short Introduction*, p.147, describes it, Ibn 'Arabi's understanding of the universe as a whole (which underlies the Beshara projection) is thus 'nothing but an incomprehensibly vast image of God's knowledge, a single infinite veil over the one divine Face'.

29 'Rememoration', p.10.

30 One associate points to the phrase in the Christian Lord's Prayer 'On Earth as it is in Heaven' to illustrate this point, suggesting that it 'correlates' with the Beshara understanding in this respect.

31 Twinch, 'Education at the Beshara Schools', p.7. Cf. Jervis, The Sufi Order, p.231, on Vilayat Khan's position: 'The *pir* encourages his *murids* to implicate themselves in the world; to maintain a sacred atmosphere in the midst of workaday circumstances ... instead of abandoning the world ... in favour of absconding into more rarefied realms. He issues a bodhisattva-like challenge: "Dare you renounce renunciation out of love?"'

32 See *Beshara Magazine*, 1, p.1.

33 Washington, *Madam Blavatsky's Baboon*, pp.352, 360. On his disapproval of gurus and 'guruism', see pp.324–5, 329; of drug use, p.330. The Theosophical Society (and Annie Besant in particular) had appointed Krishnamurti head of the Order of the Star in the East, formed in anticipation of the advent of a 'World Teacher', as which he was proclaimed in 1921. In 1929, he disbanded the Order, rejected authority, and became an itinerant lecturer celebrating personal spiritual freedom and the individual search for Truth: see Krishnamurti, *Total Freedom*, p.9.

34 On the perceived closeness of their approaches, see Hornsby in *Intimations*, p.x; Ch. 2.

35 See Washington, *Madame Blavatsky's Baboon*, p.389. Compare with Bennett's own comment, made after a visit to Turkey towards the end of his life: 'I could ... see ... how much more we have at Sherborne where we have brought together ideas and methods from all parts of the world and so have a repertory of techniques that allows much more rapid progress.'

36 See Hanegraaff, *New Age Religion*, pp.9 n.30, 17 n.49, predicting that the term would 'probably not survive the twentieth century as a generally-used label' for the movement it seeks to denote. Cf. Heelas, *The New Age Movement*, p.112; Hanegraaff, The New Age Movement and the Esoteric Tradition, pp.362–4; James R. Lewis, Approaches to the Study of the New Age Movement, in Lewis and Gordon Melton, eds, *Perspectives on the New Age*, p.2. As an alternative, many prefer to describe their involvement in terms of something vaguer, typically 'spirituality'.

37 Hence, 'holistic spirituality', as in Heelas and Woodhead *et al.*, *The Spiritual Revolution* (on which see further below), and 'contemporary popular spirituality discourse', as in Frisk, 'Is "New Age" A Construction?'. Tacey, *The Spirituality Revolution*, is concerned to educate the New Age 'beyond its crudity'. He critiques (at least some elements of) it on the grounds of its 'infantile and deeply regressed' interests, characterising it as 'a vulgar series of spiritual technologies that exist because there is nothing better on offer'. Yet he is also keen to avoid taking part in using the label New Age (as he believes it has been used since the 1980s) as a 'handy term ... to help us beat spirituality over the head and undermine spiritual stirrings'. See pp. 24–5, 63–4, 68–9.

38 As noted earlier, Hanegraaff, *New Age Religion*, pp. 96–7, posits a distinction between the New Age in a restricted and the New Age in a general sense. The former designates an early idealistic movement of various 'alternative, countercultural communities' that emerged during the 1960s, such as Findhorn in Scotland. Such groups were marked by 'the absolute centrality of the expectation of a New Age of Aquarius', with all activities and speculation circling 'around the central vision of a new and transformed world'. The New Age in a restricted sense has survived as a clearly recognisable subgroup of the New Age in a general sense (in such leading lights as David Spangler and George Trevelyan, for example), while the latter has come to be characterised by several themes: the expectation of a coming new era is thus not necessary in order for a movement/trend to be part of the New Age in the general sense. In the case of Beshara, the expectation of a new age remains an intrinsic and developed element of the worldview, even if this may have receded somewhat over time. This suggests an affinity with the New Age in a restricted sense (which can be characterised as an example of millenarianism), and makes application of the New Age label to Beshara particularly apt. (Note that there is no intention here to imply that Beshara shares with the New Age in a restricted sense its tendency to draw upon the ideas of occultism, in the sense of post-Enlightenment developments of esotericism, especially as found in the Theosophical tradition.) See further ibid., p. 103, and Hanegraaff, The New Age Movement and the Esoteric Tradition, pp. 361–3, 369, 375.

39 See 'New Age Movement', p. 859.

40 See Frisk, 'Is "New Age" A Construction?'

41 Associates indeed evince a lively interest in other spiritual ways, and a few have developed relations with prominent figures within these, including the Panchen Lama.

The movement's perennialist ethos is evident also in its attempt to expose the claimed inclusiveness of its own name. According to an explanatory note in *Beshara Magazine*, 10, p. 1, 'Beshara means "Good News" or "Omen of Joy". In its Arabic form it is found in the Qur'an, in its Aramaic form it is translated as the "Glad Tidings" of the Bible, and it is also found in its Hebrew form in the Torah.' Young, 'Courses at Chisholme', p. 26, expands: 'It is common to three major world traditions; it is firmly entrenched in Hebrew, in the Aramaic language of the Gospels and in the Arabic language, which are the three languages of the Abrahamic tradition ... if there were a word which was also common to the Hindu, Buddhist, Taoist, etc. traditions, then perhaps that would be the word, but there is not such a universal language.'

42 See 'A Question about Freedom' (Notes from the Mead Hall, 17 April 2004), Beshara website. Furthermore: '"I" is no other than the Real and the Real is free ... it is by willingly accepting one's place in the order and stepping into service of the Real that "I" is freed from all that seemed to bind it.' See 'Disengaging from Fixity' (Notes from the Mead Hall, 6 June 2004). Note in this context the projection of concepts of 'obedience' and 'discipline': 'We are talking about free acts of responding (to the invitation to know ourselves), being faithful to our origin.' See 'Obedient to Love' (Notes from the Mead Hall, 17 June 2004). The emphasis on 'freedom from the idea of predetermination' and Self-responsibility can also be mentioned here: 'We ourselves are responsible for our own spiritual freedom ... including all that we do and all that happens to us.' See 'Giving of Ourselves' (Notes from the Mead Hall, 8 February 2004).

43 As noted earlier, Hanegraaff, *New Age Religion*, p. 119 and The New Age Movement and the Esoteric Tradition, p. 371, identifies a rejection of the pervasive dualism of modern Western culture informing the 'holism' of the New Age. The specific focus is on offering alternatives to forms of dualism captured in fundamental distinctions between Creator and creation, man and nature, and spirit and matter. See also Campbell, A New Age Theodicy for A New Age, p. 78.

44 Cf. an associate's comment that the first generation continues to bridge two ways of thinking. One of them remains 'conditioned by religious thought', and displays an understanding of God and spirituality that is 'still theologically based'. The other, in contrast, transcends religious and theological discourses; reflecting a metaphysical discourse, it represents more accurately 'what Beshara is about'.

45 As Heelas, *The New Age Movement*, pp. 37–9, emphasises, the languages and dynamics of traditionalised theism and detraditionalised New Age monism show marked differences. As Groothius, *Unmasking the New Age*, p. 142, puts it, according to the New Age, 'The classic ... spirituality of prayer, faith and obedience to an external God must be replaced by monistic meditation, personal experience and the God within.'

46 Cf. Heelas, *The New Age Movement*, p. 40 n. 15: with regard to the significance of traditional theistic terms in New Age circles, the author cites the example of Bagwan Shree Rajneesh on 'salvation'. Bagwan has declared: 'Nobody is a sinner. I tell you, there is no need for salvation. It is within you.' Groothius, *Unmasking the New Age*, p. 143, elaborates: 'Rajneesh cautions that there is no relationship in or with the divine. A relationship takes at least two people; but *all* is one. He says "The divine has no self so you cannot be related to it ... a devotee ... can never reach the divine because he thinks in terms of relationship: God the Father, God the lover, God the beloved ... he goes on thinking of God as other."' A degree of resonance with a significant facet of Beshara understanding can be upheld.

47 Heelas, *The New Age Movement*, p. 130 n. 9, acknowledges the difficulties encountered in deciding how to count 'those NRMs, such as Hare Krishna, which conjoin elements of Self-spirituality with the dynamics of theistic religiosity'.

48 Clark, 'Summer Gathering'.

49 Carroll, 'Notes from a Student', pp. 1–2.

50 Ibn 'Arabi himself appears to have insisted that neither transcendence nor immanence can be used to refer to God in any exclusive sense: he always kept the embrace of *tashbih* in balance with *tanzih*. See Chittick, Ibn 'Arabi, p. 502.

51 For example, Young, 'Courses at Chisholme', p. 29: 'there was a tremendous interest in spiritual matters at the end of the sixties/beginning of the seventies in this country, with everyone dashing off in different spiritual directions. In London, a nucleus of people formed who were interested in a real spiritual direction, but without wanting to attach themselves to a guru or a teacher. They wanted to get to the heart of the matter, without any intermediary. Also in London at that time was a Turkish man by the name of ... Rauf, who, rejecting the idea of himself as a teacher, pointed in the direction of the work of ... Ibn 'Arabi as being the basis for an approach in this way, without a formal teacher.'

Note that Vilayat Khan also explicitly rejected 'guru worship' and conventional ideas of devotion to the mystic teacher. See Jervis, The Sufi Order, pp. 232–3. Disillusionment with the (specifically 'spiritual') guru institution and its trappings appears to have set in more broadly later in the twentieth century. Having spent many years as a disciple of the Indian Mother Meera, for example, in 1994 Andrew Harvey broke away and repudiated the guru establishment. In quintessential New Age style, he developed his own mystical approach, set out in *The Direct Path: Creating a Journey to the Divine using the World's Mystical Traditions* (London, 2000). Here he underlined the corruption of the 'guru system', and warned that it disempowers the seeker (see pp. 18–20). *The Direct Path* 'represents the culmination of twenty-five years of seeking, inner experience and practice in many of the mystical systems of the world' (inside cover). According to his publicist, Harvey has applied this experience 'to create an illuminating spiritual map that anyone can use to develop a direct path to the divine without relying on churches, gurus, or other intermediaries'. The book offers a collection of personal insights and spiritual exercises that lead directly, it is claimed, to 'the source and spirit of all life'.

52 He was reading a passage from Nicholson's translation of the *Tarjuman al-ashwaq*.

53 Twinch, 'Education at the Beshara Schools'.

54 Personal correspondence with the author, May 2004.

55 See Ch. 5.

56 Hirtenstein, *The Unlimited Mercifier*, p. 165. On 'verification', see Ch. 7.

57 See for example Hanegraaff, The New Age Movement and the Esoteric Tradition, p. 373.

58 As Heelas, *The New Age Movement*, p. 34, points out, there is considerable variation within the New Age with regard to the role accorded to voices of authority coming from sources other than those from within the Self, and the majority do listen to the voices of others. For example, many concede that the ego is so powerful that the individual requires 'outside' help to combat it. Consequently, authority is vested to varying extents in gurus, masters, spiritual agencies, etc.

59 As we have seen, aspects embraced are thus excised from the matrix of authoritative Islamic texts and historical traditions in which they are embedded (as far as the normative–prescriptive import of these texts and traditions is concerned).

60 Heelas, *The New Age Movement*, p. 21.

61 In the sphere of New Age universal sufism, the Golden Sufi Center presents an example of a view antithetical to that of Beshara, for its characteristic insistence on the indispensability and special powers of the teacher. See, for example, Llewellyn Vaughan-Lee, 'The Keeper of the Gates of Grace' and 'Through a Glass Darkly: The Paradoxical Nature of the Relationship with the Teacher', www.goldensufi.org. He describes the guide, teacher or shaykh as 'the one who is the ferryman between the two worlds': he is a figure of authority, and 'an attitude of surrender' is required towards him. Without the grace of the shaykh, he explains, there can be no miracle of transformation. Tweedie's relationship with her teacher, 'unusual in its impersonal nature and lack of intellectual content ... illustrates how the powerful presence of a spiritual guide or guru can tacitly and indirectly influence the student causing radical changes': see 'Irina Tweedie: A Short Biography', www.goldensufi.org. The stated belief that 'ultimately the outer teacher points to the inner teacher, who resides in the depths of the hearts of all men and women' ('Beliefs and Ethics of the Naqshbandi Path', point 16, www.goldensufi.org) illustrates the dialectic between Self- and external teacher-authority in New Age groups.

62 See www.bulentrauf.org, launched June 2005. 'In an age of gurus,' this explains, 'he spurned the title of "teacher", preferring to be a student of Reality, thence to share the wealth of knowledge that he had discovered with his fellow-students.' The irony of the fact that this website draws attention to a man whose explicit preference was to deflect attention away from himself is not lost on some associates.

63 Bruce, *Religion in Modern Britain*, p. 103.

64 Heelas, *The New Age Movement*, p. 38 n. 1.

65 Hanegraaff, *New Age Religion*, p. 14. As examples of the latter category, he cites TM, Hare Krishna and Rajneeshism.

66 Ibid., pp. 15–16, citing arguments from Colin Campbell, 'The Cult, the Cultic Milieu and Secularization', *A Sociological Yearbook of Religion in Britain*, 5 (London, 1972), pp. 119–36, on which see below. Campbell used the notion of seekership especially as developed in John Lofland and Rodney Stark, 'Becoming a World-Saver: A Theory of Conversion to a Deviant Perspective', *American Sociological Review*, 30: 6 (1965), pp. 863–74. For a summary of the thesis of this influential study, see Dawson, Who Joins New Religious Movements and Why, p. 118.

67 Hanegraaff, *New Age Religion*, pp. 16–17.

68 Campbell's contribution to the discussion of the cult–sect dichotomy was to suggest that, given that the cultic milieu is a constant feature of society while the cult is by definition a largely transitory phenomenon, the cultic milieu is a more viable and illuminating focus of sociological concern than the individual cult. See ibid., pp. 15–16. Note that Campbell maintained that the religious culture of the cultic milieu is most prominently characterised by mysticism in the Troeltschean sense, i.e. in the sense of pursuing the goal of ecstatic experience. For further treatment of the concept of the cultic milieu, see Bryan R. Wilson, *The Social Dimensions of Sectarianism: Sects and New Religious Movements in Contemporary Society* (Oxford, 1990).

69 Hanegraaff, *New Age Religion*, p. 18. Note also Bruce, *Religion in Modern Britain*, pp. 118–19.

70 This reservation concerning cults applies especially to the so-called revelatory cults. In the form of 'a group offering a particularized and detailed revealed truth', the cult thus 'represents something of an aberration from the basic principle of tolerance and eclecticism which is prevalent in the [cultic] milieu in general'. See Campbell, 'The Cult, the Cultic Milieu and Secularization', cited in Hanegraaff, *New Age Religion*, p. 18.

The affinity between the looser 'society of seekers' and the 'secondary institutions' posited by Berger *et al.* in *The Homeless Mind* is worthy of note; see Heelas and Woodhead, Homeless Minds Today?, pp. 53ff., and below.

71 See Paul Heelas and Benjamin Seel, An Ageing New Age?, in Davie *et al.*, eds, *Predicting Religion*, p. 244 n. 13. The quotation is from Campbell, 'The Cult, the Cultic Milieu and Secularization', p. 129.

72 See Hanegraaff, *New Age Religion*, p. 15.

73 See Şerif Mardin, Reflections on Said Nursi's Life and Thought, in Ibrahim Abu-Rabi', ed., *Islam at the Crossroads: On the Life and Thought of Bediuzzaman Said Nursi* (Albany, NY, 2003), p. 48.

74 *Varieties of Religion Today*, p. 187, cited in Heelas and Woodhead *et al.*, *The Spiritual Revolution*, p. 77

75 On the contested rational choice theory and religious economies perspective, see for example 'Rational Choice Theory', 'Stark, Rodney' and accompanying bibliographies in William H. Swatos, Jr, ed., *Encyclopaedia of Religion and Society*, hirr.hartsem.edu/ency/; Laurence Iannacone, 'Introduction to the Economics of Religion', *Journal of Economic Literature*, 36: 3 (1997), pp. 1465–95. A basic underlying principle is that, as Rodney Stark, 'Rational Choice Theories of Religion', *Agora*, 2: 1 (1994), p. 2, puts it, 'it makes sense to model religion as the behavior of rational, well-informed actors who choose to "consume" secular commodities'.

76 Linda Woodhead, Studying Religion and Modernity, in Woodhead, ed., *Religions in the Modern World*, p. 12.

77 See also Tacey, *The Spirituality Revolution*. Forman, *Grassroots Spirituality*, documents a 'Grassroots Spirituality Movement' reflecting this shift in North America. The author points out that its size and significance have not been generally grasped.

78 Regular church attendance stood at 7.5% of the UK population in 2000, for example. See Heelas and Woodhead, Homeless Minds Today?, p. 49. An informed prediction from January 2005 envisaged churches in England becoming redundant at the rate of one a week.

79 The suggestive title of McGrath, *In the Twilight of Atheism*, is noteworthy. By way of explanation for this phenomenon, the author cites a move in recent Western thought away from the world of the Enlightenment, based on a realisation of the limits of reason and the failure of the myth of progress. Added to this are demographic changes, a sense of the emptiness of materialism, and an inherent human impulse to search for the spiritual: see pp. 187, 191. See also Forman, *Grassroots Spirituality*, pp. 109ff.

80 For illustrative statistics, see Heelas and Woodhead, Homeless Minds Today?, p. 65; Heelas, The Spiritual Revolution: From 'Religion' to 'Spirituality', pp. 359–61, 365; Colin Campbell, The Easternisation of the West, in Wilson and Cresswell, eds, *New Religious Movements*, p. 36. A sample of the mainstream audio-visual media in Britain over a few weeks during May–June 2005 reflected a growing acknowledgement of these changes, yielding such titles as 'The Return of the Religious'; 'Exploring the World of

New Age Spirituality'; 'Spirituality Shopper'; and television news features on the summer solstice exploring alternative spiritualities.

81 This descriptive arises from the notion, introduced earlier, that in contemporary spirituality (in contrast with religion) life itself, rather than what transcends life, 'becomes God'. See Heelas, The Spiritual Revolution: From 'Religion' to 'Spirituality', pp. 358–9.

82 On this 'broadening out' and the underlying 'cultural turn to life', see ibid., pp. 371ff., and Heelas and Woodhead, Homeless Minds Today?, pp. 49–52, 60. Cf. Taylor, The Ethics of Authenticity, p. 45, referring to 'the continuation in modern culture of a trend that is now centuries old and that places the centre of gravity of the good life not in some higher sphere but in ... "ordinary life", that is, the life of production and the family, of work and love'. Taylor posits 'the affirmation of ordinary life' as a key influence on modern self-identity.

83 See for example Woodhead, Studying Religion and Modernity, pp. 3, 9–10.

84 Taylor, The Ethics of Authenticity, p. 26. See also Heelas and Seel, An Ageing New Age?, p. 239, and Heelas and Woodhead et al., The Spiritual Revolution, p. 2.

85 See Heelas and Woodhead, Homeless Minds Today?, pp. 48–9.

86 In addition to works by Taylor, for elaborations of this argument see works by Eric Hobsbawm (e.g. Age of Extremes [London, 1995]) and Ronald Inglehart (e.g. Modernization and Postmodernization: Cultural, Economic and Political Change in 43 Societies [Princeton, NJ, 1997]), and others cited in Heelas and Woodhead et al., The Spiritual Revolution, p. 5.

87 As described by Linda Woodhead: see Studying Religion and Modernity, p. 9, and Heelas, The Spiritual Revolution: From 'Religion' to 'Spirituality', p. 373.

88 Heelas and Woodhead et al., The Spiritual Revolution, p. 2.

89 Heelas and Seel, An Ageing New Age?, p. 239.

90 Heelas and Woodhead et al., The Spiritual Revolution, pp. 4, 14.

91 Heelas and Woodhead, Homeless Minds Today?, p. 53.

92 Heelas and Woodhead et al., The Spiritual Revolution, pp. 5–6, 77ff. Note that their arguments are tested mainly through evidence from Britain (with additional evidence from the USA). See also Heelas and Seel, An Ageing New Age?, p. 240. There is a broad agreement concerning the characteristic emphases of contemporary spirituality, even if the terminology applied varies widely. For example, Forman, Grassroots Spirituality, pp. 51–2, suggests that the worldwide and trans-traditional spiritual movement he documents involves 'a vaguely panentheistic ultimate that is indwelling, sometimes bodily, as the deepest self and accessed through not-strictly-rational means of self-transformation and group process that becomes the holistic organization for all of life'. See also Roof, Spiritual Marketplace, pp. 33–5.

93 Heelas and Seel, An Ageing New Age?, p. 240. It must be underlined that religion has itself been impacted by the effects of the turn to the self, and there is ample evidence that spiritualities of life (in this case theistic) are a growing force within the sphere of institutionalised, traditional religion, which thus also reflects the transformations that make up the 'spiritual revolution'. Theistic spiritualities of life combine or mix the traditionalised with the detraditionalised, as in the case of 'new paradigm churches'; see Heelas, The Spiritual Revolution: From 'Religion' to 'Spirituality', pp. 366ff., and Heelas and Woodhead, Homeless Minds Today?, pp. 65ff.

Note that Forman, Grassroots Spirituality, argues for cultivation of a 'trans-traditional spirituality' through the organisation of 'trans-traditional processes': his position flows from a perception of tradition as potentially or inherently divisive. See for example p. 173.

94 See Heelas and Woodhead, Homeless Minds Today?, p. 54.

95 Heelas, The Spiritual Revolution: From 'Religion' to 'Spirituality', p. 358. The characteristics of subjective-life spirituality and the attitudes flowing from it present a significant continuum with those of 'Self-spirituality' as the defining motif of the New Age, and Heelas and Woodhead et al. indeed sometimes conflate the two: see, for example, The Spiritual Revolution, pp. 7–8, 54. When pressed, Heelas puts forward two grounds for his shift from the term 'Self-spirituality' to 'subjective-life spirituality'. First, the former term was consistently misunderstood through an overemphasis of individualism (the significance of the capital S often being overlooked). Second, times have changed: the buzz word today is not 'Self' but 'life'. He also suggests that, in contrast with 'inner life spirituality of the 1970s and 80s', which was more dualistic (e.g. anti-ego), 'inner life spirituality of today' is much more holistic. (Correspondence with the author, July 2005.)

96 See Heelas and Seel, An Ageing New Age?, pp. 240–1.

97 Ibid., pp. 235ff. Statistics, commercial indicators, and the broader cultural formations that evince linkages to the NAM point to its reach, and demonstrate that it has diffused into culture especially through consumer-friendly forms; see Heelas, *The New Age Movement*, pp. 106–17, 128–9. Campbell, *The Easternisation of the West*, pp. 40ff., points to the pervasiveness of defining themes of the New Age worldview in the contemporary developed Western world.

98 Heelas and Seel, An Ageing New Age?, pp. 236, 242.

99 Ibid., p. 242.

100 Koszegi, *The Sufi Order in the West*, p. 214, analyses the 'particular brand of sufism' taught by the Sufi Order in terms of 'the general mind-set of the New Age', concluding that the former (which evidently represents a perennialist, detraditionalised expression of monistic sufism) 'seems tailor-made to fit the latter'. While conceding that it is not possible to 'refer to anything so definite as to be neatly defined' when speaking of the New Age mind-set, he posits three characteristic attitudes of 'the young New Agers' to which the Sufi Order's teachings are well-suited: (a) love of exotic, 'secret' teachings, for their novelty; (b) an eclectic, universalist outlook; and (c) utopianism, built on a conviction that the individual can change the world by working on themselves.

Koszegi argues further that the Sufi Order and its teachings 'helped give both form and philosophy to the New Age since its beginnings in the 1960s'. He cites the impact of Samuel Lewis as a teacher and his Universal Dances of Peace, and the Omega Institute (established 1978) as a major forum of the New Age. See ibid., pp. 213–14. In the initial flowering of the New Age in the USA and England, he suggests that the Sufi Order in the West thus 'in many ways assumed a leadership role in the movement', acting as a significant catalyst in its birth and growth: see pp. 213, 220.

101 Evidence from the USA indeed suggests that universal sufis probably form the majority of all sufis there: see Hermansen, In the Garden of American Sufi Movements, p. 169. On a parallel trend in Europe, see Westerlund, Introduction, p. 7 and The Contextualisation of Sufism in Europe, pp. 29, 33.

102 Wilson, The Strange Fate of Sufism, pp. 200, 202; cf. Hermansen, In the Garden of American Sufi Movements, p. 156; Hammer, Sufism for Westerners, p. 143 (which also points to Western women's tendency to associate Islam with rigid patriarchal structures); Westerlund, The Contextualisation of Sufism in Europe, p. 25. See Chittick, *Sufism: A Short Introduction*, pp. 11–12, for an analysis of the relative attractions for Westerners of Islam and sufism.

The demands and discipline of Islamic practice might indeed appear overwhelming compared with spiritual alternatives geared for busy modern life. For example, responding to the fact that young women today feel 'there must be more to life than a great career and relationship' but are 'too busy to fit in organised religion', in March 2004 *Cosmopolitan Magazine* (Britain) appointed a 'Spirituality Editor'. Her task is to advise on possible methods for 'ten to fifteen minutes of daily spiritual nurturing'.

For an introduction to the subject of modern Western perceptions of Islam and Muslims, see the classic works by Edward Said: *Orientalism* (New York, 1978) and *Covering Islam: How the Media and the Experts determine how we see the rest of the World* (New York, 1981).

103 Cf. Hermansen, In the Garden of American Sufi Movements, p. 158 and 'Hybrid Identity Formations', p. 187; Geaves, *The Sufis of Britain*, p. 182.

104 See Kose, *Conversion to Islam*, p. 142. Cf. John Wolffe, Fragmented Universality: Islam and Muslims, in Parsons, ed., *The Growth of Religious Diversity in Britain*, p. 155.

Geaves, *The Sufis of Britain*, pp. 147–50, 153, points out that Nazim al-Haqqani has been particularly successful in promoting the teachings of sufism among non-Muslims. Attracted first by his charisma, many of those who have become followers have later embraced Islam. As the basis of this success, Geaves identifies a liberal approach towards interested non-Muslim parties (without insistence on immediate conversion), and a grasp of the perennialist underpinnings of much of the New Age, the latter informing a tolerance of (and willingness to address) diverse spiritual movements. A follower of al-Haqqani explained to this author that, given the urgency necessitated by the imminent approach of the End Times, the emphasis now is on 'winning the heart': the form can be gradually shaped thereafter.

As far as attraction to a shaykh is concerned, the possible convergence with a high degree of prior involvement in NRMs centring on a charismatic teacher must be noted. In 'Native British Converts to Islam: Who are they? Why do they convert?', *The American Journal of Islamic Social Sciences*, 12: 3 (1995), pp. 349, 359 n. 5 and *Conversion to Islam*, p. 155, Kose indicates the extent to which the converts he interviewed in Britain registered a prior involvement with (especially Eastern) NRMs. He further notes that his sufi converts shared a similar background with those involved in NRMs: see ibid., pp. 148–9.

105 See Webb, Tradition and Innovation, p. 79.

106 In this context, it is possible to posit Beshara as a virtual inversion of the Fellowship. Webb (ibid., pp. 79, 85–6) identifies as a key interpretive theme in Bawa's teachings (and the self-expressions of his followers) 'the "movement" from interior, hidden, unmanifest (*batin*) modes of being to externalized, manifest (*zahir*) modes of being, the latter of which themselves become vehicles of reintegration-realization. This "movement" is seen in the historical development of the community as well as on ontological, cosmological, and individual "levels" of "being".' This theme derives from Bawa's metaphysics of *wahdat al-wujud*, expressed, according to Webb, 'in the traditional … ontological and cosmological framework of an effusion of being from the One to the many'. She explains that, for him, the origination of being is framed in 'an Ibn Sina – Ibn 'Arabi cosmological model of generation of being in which the created orders come into existence with an original act of intellection of God's "wanting to be known"'. From this flows Bawa's teaching on the Perfect Man, who reflects the names and qualities of God, and is the realised person.

As we have indicated, the same ontological–cosmological movement of 'externalisation' is a key theme in Beshara teaching. In light of it, the emergence of Beshara as a tangible phenomenon is itself perceived (in its capacity as a manifestation of the Divine Self-disclosure) to capture a certain 'external' particularism. In contrast with Bawa, however, for whom externalisation ultimately took the form of an explicit and articulated identification with Islam, the *raison d'être* and vision of Beshara point towards the transcendence of this and all other inherently particularist external forms. For Bawa too, of course, the ultimate aim of the *individual* journey is the return to primordial unity: it is specifically concerning the nature of the 'vehicles of reintegration-realization', to use Webb's phrase, that the two movements part company.

107 See Heelas, *The New Age Movement*, pp. 136, 3. Note that he also presents the counter-thesis that, for it to have diffused through the culture as it has, 'it must be in tune with – as well as able to tune in to – some of the central values and assumptions of modernity'. As such, it might be seen as a natural extension of modernity, and as 'a form of religion ideally suited to the modern world'. See Davie, *Religion in Modern Europe*, p. 141.

108 Heelas, The Spiritual Revolution: From 'Religion' to 'Spirituality', p. 359.

109 Heelas, *The New Age Movement*, p. 28 and Prosperity and the New Age Movement, p. 52. See also Campbell, A New Age Theodicy for a New Age, p. 78, and Groothius, *Unmasking the New Age*, p. 29.

110 See Heelas, *The New Age Movement*, p. 139.

111 Coates, 'Ibn 'Arabi: The Unity of Existence and the Era'. Weber believed that rationalisation (the process whereby life has become organised in terms of instrumental considerations) carries in its wake a loss of a sense of magic, mystery, prophecy, and the sacred: see Bruce, *Religion in Modern Britain*, p. 111. Coates elaborates on his comment presented here by suggesting that, for associates, Ibn 'Arabi thus is not only a 'revivifier', but also a 're-enchanter'. For Coates personally, he is 'an antidote to the de-humanising processes of modernity, *without* dismissing modernity'. (Interview with Coates, November 2004.)

112 For a classic discussion of 'the maelstrom of modern life', see Marshall Berman, *All that is Solid Melts into Air: The Experience of Modernity* (London, 1981). For various transformations associated with modernity, see Anthony Giddens, *The Consequences of Modernity* (Oxford, 2000).

113 Pnina Werbner, *Pilgrims of Love: The Anthropology of a Global Sufi Cult* (London, 2003), p. 7, makes the general point: 'Sufism rejects the ideas of individual religious agency, autonomy and rationality which are the bedrock of liberal modernity, stressing instead the embodied charisma, perfection and transcendence of the Sufi master, whose spiritual intimacy with God leads to the magical enchantment of the world'.

114 See, for example, Charles Upton, '"Religious Universalism": A Review of *False Dawn: The United Religions Initiative, Globalism and the Quest for a One-World Religion* by Lee Penn', *Sacred Web*, 15 (2005), pp. 185ff. 'The Traditionalist School', the author reminds us, 'has always taken great care to distinguish itself from the kind of non-traditional universalism preached by Madame Blavatsky, or Aldous Huxley'. Upton projects the ego of the 'anti-traditional religious universalist' (agent of Guénon's 'counter-initiation' in the specific form of a 'spurious religious universalism') as a threat in contemporary times equal to that posed by the ego of the religious fanatic or militant exclusivist. This threat also encompasses the 'false "esoteric" universalist who believes that metaphysics can be a Path in itself, independent of any commitment to a traditional religious way, and whose non-traditional metaphysics (which may have been *abstracted* from the revealed religions, but are no longer effectively connected with any of them) are a great source of pride to him. He sees these generic metaphysics as transcending and superseding the religious traditions themselves'. Beshara would perhaps furnish an example of such a 'false "esoteric" universalism' in Upton's view, constituting a 'counter-initiatic group' that ultimately leads away from true Tradition. Such difficult encounters as we have described in this volume notwithstanding, we would emphasise that, more recently, associates and Traditionalists have met with increasing frequency in cultural and scholarly fora, and some have been willing to collaborate. For a Traditionalist critique of New Age spiritualities more generally, see Charles Upton, *The System of Antichrist: Truth and Falsehood in Postmodernism and the New Age* (Ghent, NY, 2001).

Regarding Traditionalist elitism, Hatina, 'Where East Meets West', p. 26, notes Guénon's perception of the caste system in Hindu tradition, where the highest truth is revealed only to a few: 'For Guénon, the existence of a social hierarchy whose pinnacle consisted of an intellectual elite that drew its authority from a metaphysical source was analogous to harmonic order; disavowing its existence in the name of the modern fiction of egalitarianism only invites social anarchy'.

115 Borella, René Guénon and the Traditionalist School, p. 349.

116 Hermansen, 'Hybrid Identity Formations', p. 188, suggests that this is the case for young American-born Muslims. For a historical overview of Muslims in Britain, see for example Humayun Ansari, *'The Infidel Within': The History of Muslims in Britain* (London, 2004).

117 For the specific example of sufism as stimulus for cross-cultural interaction in the context of the cultural dialogue that emerged towards the end of the Ottoman era between Muslims and Christians in Cairo, Rome and Paris, see Hatina, 'Where East

Meets West'. This partly aimed to further understanding and rapprochement at a time of growing friction between East and West.

More recently, popularised images and practices such as sufi 'whirling' may be serving to create a cultural familiarity in Western arenas with elements associated (if only loosely) with Islam, and hence ultimately to erode fear of the latter. This process takes place in much the same way that recent developments in 'Muslim' Hip Hop in parts of some American cities (like Washington, DC) have brought Islamic phraseology ('through Allah I shine', for example) into the repertoire drawn on by broader local American youth culture.

118 Ernst, *The Shambhala Guide to Sufism*, p. 228. It has been argued that sufism can function as such a bridge because it 'stresses the connections between Islam and other religions': see Westerlund, Introduction, p. 11.

119 These comments are based on informal discussions with members of the Maryamiyya (London, 2004).

120 See Groothius, *Unmasking the New Age*, pp. 17, 153, 155, 163, for example.

121 Nancy Pearcey, *Total Truth: Liberating Christianity from its Cultural Captivity* (Wheaton, IL, 2004), Appendix 2: 'Modern Islam and the New Age Movement', www. ldolphin.org. (For details of the book, see www.gnpcb.org; it has been described as one of the most important Christian books of the last decade.)

122 The NAM is thus 'a more recent expression of a long-standing tendency to import Eastern pantheism into Western culture, which began with Plotinus and neo-Platonism'. See ibid.

123 Ibid.

124 She notes that the early proponents of the Perennial Philosophy (which merged 'Western and Eastern pantheism'), who were all Europeans, 'ended up converting to Islam'. See ibid.

125 The author seems to point the finger at the Muslim world for its role in 'reintroducing to the West' ancient classical writings.

126 Campbell, *The Easternisation of the West*, p. 41.

127 Ibid., p. 45. Campbell sees a significant paradigm shift in the coming to the fore of the 'Eastern paradigm'. He attributes this change to internal indigenous developments relating to the undermining of faith in traditional religion by science, and the subsequent undermining of the optimism which science generated. (The 'Eastern paradigm' is more compatible with modern thought than the 'Western one', and less vulnerable to attack by science.) This shift was assisted (but not caused) by the introduction of Eastern ideas and influences into the West.

128 Ibid.

129 Ibid., p. 47.

130 See Basheer M. Nafi and Suha Taji-Farouki, Introduction, in Taji-Farouki and Nafi, eds, *Islamic Thought in the Twentieth Century*, p. 2. In the Middle East of 1900, for example, less than 10% of the inhabitants were city dwellers; by 1980, 47% were urban, with projections for 2000 at 60%. In 1960, only eleven cities had more than one million inhabitants: by the late 1980s, there were thirty-eight such cities; see Dale F. Eickelman, *The Middle East and Central Asia: An Anthropological Approach* (Upper Saddle River, NJ), p. 85.

131 We allude to the thesis of S. N. Eisenstadt, 'Multiple Modernities', *Daedalus*, 129: 1 (2000), pp. 1–29. See further his 'The Reconstruction of Religious Arenas in the Framework of "Multiple Modernities"', *Millennium: Journal of International Studies*, 29: 3 (2000), pp. 591–611.

132 On the objectification of Islam, see Dale F. Eickelman and James Piscatori, *Muslim Politics* (Princeton, NJ, 1996), pp. 37ff.

133 See, for example, Francis Robinson, Knowledge, Its Transmission and the Making of Muslim Societies, in Francis Robinson, ed., *The Cambridge Illustrated History of the Muslim World* (New York, 1996), pp. 208–49, and his 'Technology and Religious

Change: Islam and the Impact of Print', *Modern Asian Studies*, 27: 1 (1993), pp. 229–51; Dale F. Eickelman, The Art of Memory: Islamic Education and its Social Reproduction, in Juan I. Cole, ed., *Comparing Muslim Societies: Knowledge and the State in a World Civilization* (Ann Arbor, MI, 1992), pp. 97–132. On shifting modes of authority, see Dale F. Eickelman, Islamic Religious Commentary and Lesson Circles: Is there a Copernican Revolution?, in G. W. Most, ed., *Commentaries (Kommentare)* (Gottingen, 1999), pp. 121–46 and 'Inside the Islamic Reformation', *Wilson Quarterly* (Winter 1998), pp. 80–9; Mark Sedgwick, 'Is There a Church in Islam?', *ISIM Review*, 13 (2003), p. 40. In *Islamic Political Identity in Turkey*, pp. 106–8, 130–1, Yavuz illustrates these themes through the Turkish arena.

134 See further Suha Taji-Farouki, Introduction, in Taji-Farouki, ed., *Modern Muslim Intellectuals and the Qur'an* (Oxford, 2004), pp. 12ff.

135 For a discussion of these developments and their impacts, see Dale F. Eickelman and Jon W. Anderson, eds, *New Media in the Muslim World: The Emerging Public Sphere* (Bloomington, IN, 2000).

136 Fazlur Rahman, Approaches to Islam in Religious Studies: A Review Essay, in Richard C. Martin, ed., *Approaches to Islam in Religious Studies* (Oxford, 2001), p. 195.

137 Processes of modernisation (in particular urbanisation, migration, mass education and mass media of communication) pluralise the 'life-worlds' of individuals, leading to an undermining of all taken-for-granted certainties. These processes acquire additional potency under democratic conditions, where the state refrains from trying to impose a monopolistic worldview. When the taken-for-granted status of definitions of reality is lost (especially where social support for them is weak or divided), they become a matter of individual choice. See Berger, Secularization and De-Secularization, p. 296.

138 Khaled Abou El Fadl, 'The Place of Tolerance in Islam', *The Boston Review* (December 2001 – January 2002). For an example of a recent attempt to construct a global Islamic authority (The International Association of Muslim Scholars) led by Yusuf al-Qaradawi, see Bettina Graf, 'In Search of a Global Islamic Authority', *ISIM Review*, 15 (Spring 2005), p. 47.

139 This is a contested term, often projected as a particular phase in the general process of modernity. See Giddens, *The Consequences of Modernity*, pp. 63ff., and Beckford, New Religious Movements and Globalization, p. 254.

140 On the intensive reflexivity characteristic of modernity, see Eisenstadt, 'Multiple Modernities', pp. 3–5, and Giddens, *The Consequences of Modernity*, pp. 36ff.

141 On this concept of globalisation (in contrast with one that emphasises homogenisation), see David Lehmann, Religion and Globalization, in Woodhead, ed., *Religions in the Modern World*, pp. 301–2.

142 While we use the language of 'consumption' in the context of our present discussion with some reservation, it is pertinent that those Muslims we describe here often form the vanguard of a growing consumer culture and the new lifestyles associated with it. For an example of the changing consumer habits of urban Muslim populations more generally, see Mona Abaza, 'Today's Consumption in Egypt', *ISIM Review*, 15 (Spring 2005), pp. 38–9. Note that the phrase 'spiritual marketplace' is taken from Roof, *Spiritual Marketplace: Baby Boomers and the Remaking of American Religion*.

Mark Sedgwick, Establishments and Sects in the Islamic World, in Lucas and Robbins, eds, *New Religious Movements in the 21st Century*, pp. 293–4, suggests that the cultic milieu in the contemporary Muslim world is mainly made up of members of higher socioeconomic classes who have high levels of 'alien' culture contact through the medium of European languages; it thus consists of 'non-Christian Western deviant belief systems'. His observation serves to underline the pertinence of socioeconomic status to engagement with global spiritual resource providers in Muslim arenas, as illustrated below.

143 We intend by this term those *tariqa*s that remain faithful to the basic model of a hierarchical organisation led by a shaykh (as suggested earlier, they may nonetheless incorporate significant changes).

144 For the sufi 'decline' hypothesis and related arguments, see for example Ernest Gellner, *Muslim Society* (Cambridge, 1981) and *Postmodernism, Reason and Religion* (London, 1992); also A. J. Arberry, *Sufism* (London, 1950), and Clifford Geertz, *Islam Observed* (Chicago, 1968).

145 See for example Sirriyeh, *Sufis and Anti-Sufis*, and Ernst, *The Shambhala Guide to Sufism*, pp. 200ff.

146 See for example Alexandre Papas, 'The Sufi and the President in Post-Soviet Uzbekistan', *ISIM Review*, 16 (2005), pp. 38–9.

147 For example, Joseph E. B. Lumbard, ed., *Islam, Fundamentalism, and the Betrayal of Tradition: Essays by Western Muslim Scholars* (Bloomington, IN, 2004), especially chapters 2, 3 and 8. See also Geaves, *Aspects of Islam*, p. 138, and Schmidt, Sufi Charisma on the Internet, pp. 121ff.

148 Ernst, *The Shambhala Guide to Sufism*, p. 220. Through flexibility, openness to change, and effective use of technological and educational resources, 'traditional' *tariqa*s have risen to these challenges with considerable success across the Muslim world. See for example Leif Stenberg, Naqshbandiyya in Damascus: Strategies to establish and strengthen the Order in a Changing Society, in Elisabeth Özdalga, *Naqshbandis in Western and Central Asia: Change and Continuity* (Istanbul, 1999), pp. 101–15.

149 Discussions in Damascus, September 2003.

150 The flourishing of far-flung shaykh-centric transnational *tariqa*s and the vitality of their respective communities must be underlined. Indeed, as Van Bruinessen, 'Sufism and the "Modern"' remarks, 'the "classical" orders had always been transnational in the sense that their networks spread across language and state boundaries'. Contemporary shaykhs take advantage of high-speed international travel to renew channels of personal charismatic contact, while internet resources can function as a medium for attracting new followers (see for example Schmidt, Sufi Charisma on the Internet, p. 117).

151 The global scope of the New Age, originally a movement of modern Western industrialised society (and most influential in North America, Europe, Australia and New Zealand), is now widely recognised. See Heelas, *The New Age Movement*, pp. 120–1; Hanegraaff, New Age Religion, p. 249 and *New Age Religion*, p. 12 n. 35, citing studies from Nigeria, Japan and South Africa. See also Robert T. Carpenter, The Mainstreaming of Alternative Spirituality in Brazil, in Lucas and Robbins, eds, *New Religious Movements in the 21st Century*, pp. 214ff. On Israel, see Ch. 6. In the Muslim arena, Sedgwick, Establishments and Sects in the Islamic World, pp. 305–7, points to the arrival of foreign imports in Cairo: these include the New Acropolis, which has been expanding in the city since the mid-1990s.

152 The process pointed to here illustrates a much broader phenomenon, labelled by some 'glocalization'. This signifies the complex interactions of global and local dynamics in the contemporary world, often involving a synthesis of the global and the local, and underlining their increasing interdependence. See for example Roland Robertson, Glocalization: Time-Space and Homogeneity-Heterogeneity, in Mike Featherstone, Scott Lash and Roland Robertson, eds, *Global Modernities* (London, 1995), pp. 25–44; Rob Wilson and Wimal Dissanayake, eds, *Global/Local: Cultural Production and the Transnational Imaginary* (Durham, NC, 1996); Thomas Friedman, *The Lexus and the Olive Tree* (New York, 2000).

153 There are doubtless many examples from other majority Muslim countries, yet to be documented. One from Cairo illustrates the 'consumption' patterns and syncretism at play, in this case involving an import from the 'East'. Sedgwick, Establishments and Sects in the Islamic World, pp. 306–7, describes the twenty-year rise of the 'Direct Path' under an Egyptian Muslim academic, a follower of the teachings of 'neo-Hindu guru' Krishna Menon. This is centred on a direct path to enlightenment based on Advaita Vedanta, but independent of associated religious practice. The academic delivers Direct Path teaching weekly in Arabic to a Muslim circle (made up mainly of military and civil elites), in the context of reading and interpreting the Qur'an. There is a parallel English group made up of Westerners and highly Westernised Egyptians, to which he conveys the teachings (which he insists contain 'no dogma' and 'no beliefs') unrestrained by the need to render these acceptable via an Islamic idiom. Here, clear warnings against the 'straitjacket' of religion and religious practice are added, using frequent references to Western esoteric writers and Hindu and Buddhist teachings

154 Raphael Voix and Patrick Haenni, 'God by all means ... Eclectic Faith and Sufi Resurgence among the Moroccan Bourgeoisie' (paper delivered at Conference 'Sufism and the "Modern" in Islam', Bogor, Indonesia, September 2003). Thanks are due to Voix and Haenni for providing a copy of this paper, on which these three paragraphs draw.

155 The failure of political ideals in the turn to a reconstituted individual religiosity in Muslim contexts might be explored in comparison with the experiences of Israelis as projected by Beit-Hallahmi, *Despair and Deliverance*: see Ch. 6 for his basic thesis.

156 Voix and Haenni, 'God by all means ...', traces the evolution of the New Age movement in Morocco from the 1960s, when it was focused on the expatriate community, through its gradual rooting among Moroccans during the 1980s and especially from the 1990s. This process was accompanied by explicit processes of re-localisation, achieved by distancing practices from their religious traditions of origin and a search for convergences with sufism. Cf. Sedgwick, *Against the Modern World*, pp. 243–4, suggesting the 'almost total absence of New Age "spiritualist" groups in Morocco'.

157 The Budshishiyya branch of the Qadiriyya *tariqa* in particular has progressed within Moroccan bourgeois circles. See Voix and Haenni, 'God by all means ...', and Sedgwick, *Against the Modern World*, pp. 242–9. Its introduction of the 'Sufi weekend' format to Morocco during the 1990s furnished the opportunity to experiment with *dhikr* in the context of a practical workshop without commitment or paying allegiance to the order's master.

158 Members of the Moroccan bourgeoisie have typically studied in French schools and universities abroad, and have had a minimal religious education, or a 'traditional' one, that has contributed to a later alienation from Islam.

159 This thesis is developed by Haenni in a forthcoming volume, *L'Axe de la vertu: L'Islam de marche ou la nouvelle fascination de l'Amérique*. (Thanks are due to the author for a pre-publication abstract of this.) On the term 'post-Islamism' and the trends denoted by it, see Asef Bayat, 'What is Post-Islamism?', *ISIM Review*, 16 (2005), p. 5.

160 The following draws on a number of articles by Julia Day Howell (thanks are due to her for providing those at the time unpublished): 'Sufism and the Indonesian Islamic Revival', *The Journal of Asian Studies* 60: 3 (2001), pp. 701–26; 'Modernity and the Borderlands of Islamic Spirituality in Indonesia's New Sufi Networks', in Martin van Bruinessen and Julia Day Howell, eds, *Sufism and the 'Modern' in Islam* (London, forthcoming) (this volume, and hence the published version of this text, were unavailable at the time of writing); 'Many Paths to God and Modernity: Of Sufism, Syncretism and Universalism in Cosmopolitan Indonesian Islam', *Social Compass* (forthcoming); 'Muslims, the New Age and Marginal Religions in Indonesia: Changing Meanings of Religious Pluralism', *Social Compass* (forthcoming); 'Seeking Sufism in the Global City: Indonesia's Cosmopolitan Muslims and Depth Spirituality', www.islamsymposium.cityu. edu.hk; 'Indonesia's Urban Sufis: Challenging Stereotypes of Islamic Revival', *ISIM Review*, 6 (2000), p. 17; Julia Day Howell, Subandi and Peter L. Nelson, Indonesian Sufism: Signs of Resurgence, in Clarke, ed., *New Trends and Developments*, pp. 277–91.

For a brief overview of the history and development of sufism in Indonesia, see Knysh, *Islamic Mysticism*, pp. 286–9. For a general web resource, see Bunt, *Virtually Islamic*, pp. 64, 156 n. 66.

161 This is in spite of mid-century predictions of its demise under the combined impacts of educational changes and modernist Muslim reformism.

162 See Howell, 'Indonesia's Urban Sufis' and 'Sufism and the Indonesian Islamic Revival', p. 703.

163 Howell, 'Indonesia's Urban Sufis'.

164 Howell, 'Modernity and the Borderlands of Islamic Spirituality'.

165 Howell, 'Indonesia's Urban Sufis'.

166 The adjective 'practical' here signals a contrast with the stereotype of 'old, other-worldly' sufism, disengaged from everyday social life.

167 Howell, 'Indonesia's Urban Sufis'. On the 'image problems' of the Indonesian *tariqas* and prejudices against them that might deter some secularly-educated middle/upper-class urbanites (projecting them as 'authoritarian and secretive institutions imposing demanding regimes of spiritual practices'), see Howell, 'Sufism and the Indonesian Islamic Revival', pp. 718, 705–6.

168 See Howell, 'Sufism and the Indonesian Islamic Revival', p. 703 and 'Modernity and the Borderlands of Islamic Spirituality'. Throughout, Howell's work provides much evidence of the burgeoning interest in sufism among the urban Muslim middle and upper classes.

169 Howell, 'Sufism and the Indonesian Islamic Revival', pp. 718, 720.

170 Aside from these international cultural forms, it is noteworthy that new sufi activities in urban contexts that appeal to the same clientele but result from the modification of traditional sufi practices and institutions also proceed through 'essentially informal gatherings, loosely networked together, with highly egalitarian relationships among participants'. See ibid., p. 719.

171 In particular, to *tariqas* which have adapted to the expectations of modern urbanites and have urban branches.

172 For details of the sufism short courses, 'linking' strategies with the *tariqas*, and opportunities for continued pursuit of an interest in sufism outside of the *tariqas* developed by short course 'graduates', see Howell, 'Modernity and the Borderlands of Islamic Spirituality', 'Sufism and the Indonesian Islamic Revival', pp. 720–1, and 'Seeking Sufism in the Global City'.

173 See Howell, 'Seeking Sufism in the Global City'.

174 As hosts, course participants meet the travel and hospitality costs of two supervisors from the UK. They also undertake to prepare a private house as course venue (removing furniture, putting down carpets and cushions and making meditation stools, for example), and to oversee provision of food, etc. This represents a significant investment of resources and time. Publicity is by word of mouth exclusively.

175 On this NRM (which has over 3,000 meditation centres in over seventy countries worldwide), see Chryssides, *Exploring New Religions*, pp. 192–202, and www.bkwsu.com. Howell, 'Muslims, the New Age and Marginal Religions', describes the movement in its Indonesian setting, where it appeared in 1982. She points out that it has been careful to accommodate meditation students with ongoing religious commitments, by functioning as a provider of non-denominational 'spirituality'. Hinduism has a strong imprint on cosmology and practice within the movement, which also has a distinctive millennial eschatology: when fully embraced, the latter is not easily reconciled with membership in another religion.

176 The twenty-eight participants during the summer 2005 course included lawyers, engineers, IT professionals, a business consultant, a medical doctor, a senior banker, and the wives of such professionals. The thirty-two participants during courses in summer 2003 included a senior politician, a former army general and a university professor of Islamic philosophy.

177 Details and quotations concerning courses derive from interviews with associates who supervised courses in summer 2003 and 2005. Although the narrative is thus constructed from the Beshara perspective and expressed in associates' words, it does yield insight into participants' attitudes. Given associates' concern for a proper understanding of these attitudes, we can consider their account of these reliable.

178 In both respects, the approach reflects wider trends of inculturation/acculturation, which can lead to adaptations of NRMs in different cultural contexts, and to variations within a movement according to cultural conditions and geographical location.

179 Participants who have attended more than one Jakarta course and wish to proceed further are invited to join an intensive course at Chisholme. The university professor of Islamic philosophy who had attended two Jakarta courses has now completed this course (he is in his early fifties). Such individuals provide an important element of continuity upon which regional representation of Beshara is being built. For example, he has assisted on Jakarta courses since his return.

180 We can further illustrate willingness to perform the *dhikr* with non-Muslim participants through an example from outside Indonesia, among Palestinian citizens of Israel. Nazareth-based Qadiri shaykh 'Abd al-Salam Manasrah (described by his followers as 'the shaykh of the Qadiri *tariqa* in Palestine': his own shaykh was Muhammad Hashim al-Baghdadi) is a founding member of the recently established Tariqa Ibrahimiyya, a Muslim–Jewish mystical group which performs the collective *dhikr*. Manasrah appears to have a few Jewish *murid*s in this context. Jewish founding members of the Tariqa include a reform Rabbi and academics knowledgeable in sufi traditions: they relate themselves to the Jewish sufi tradition inaugurated by the thirteenth-century Rabbi Abraham, son of Maimonides. Avraham Elqayam is active in the group (on him, see Ch. 7 n. 70). See Itzchak Weismann, 'Sufi Brotherhoods in the Syrian Arena: Religious Strategies and Political Implications' (paper read at Conference on 'The Role of Sufism and Sufi Brotherhoods in Contemporary Islam: An Alternative to Political Islam?', Turin, November 2002.)

Note that Manasrah's own (Muslim) group self-describes as *tariqat al-salam* al-Qadiriyya (which they translate as 'The Peace Qaderite Way'). This implies that it is a branch named after Manasrah himself, but also plays on his name ('Abd al-Salam) in light of the contextual pertinence of the notion of peace (*salam*). Manasrah states that his newly inaugurated sufi cultural centre in Nazareth is open to Muslims and non-Muslims. He argues that most Muslims and members of other religions are 'sufi by their innate nature', and that although sufism is thoroughly Islamic, its teachings are not restricted to Muslims. See www.Peace-q-way.org. It is noteworthy that this comprehensive website makes no mention of Manasrah's Ibrahimiyya activities.

181 As Howell, 'Sufism and the Indonesian Islamic Revival', p. 722, observes, through its emphasis on 'felt connection with the Divine as a basis for ethical social prescriptions', 'Practical Sufism' 'strongly reinforces tolerance for religious pluralism'. On the predominantly positive attitude of Indonesian Muslims (and others) to religious pluralism in everyday religious practice, see her 'Muslims, the New Age and Marginal Religions'.

182 See Howell, 'Indonesia's Urban Sufis' and 'Sufism and the Indonesian Islamic Revival', p. 718.

183 Howell, 'Sufism and the Indonesian Islamic Revival', pp. 718–19.

184 On their origins and the evolution of their status vis-à-vis the state Constitution, see ibid., pp. 706–8, 718. On their diversity, see Howell, 'Many Paths to God and Modernity'.

185 For details, see Howell, 'Many Paths to God and Modernity'.

186 Ibid. According to Howell, 'Modernity and the Borderlands of Islamic Spirituality', the international growth movement and New Age ideas began to circulate during the late 1990s.

187 'Modernity and the Borderlands of Islamic Spirituality', p. 14. She identifies a parallel strategy at play in the case of women's magazines that 'psychologise' such practices as Reiki, presenting them as stress reduction methods, for example: 'In that way any competing representations of the spiritual forces energising those techniques can be set aside and the practices adopted without perceived offence to an Islamic faith.'

188 Howell, 'Muslims, the New Age and Marginal Religions' and 'Many Paths to God and Modernity'.

189 'Many Paths to God and Modernity', p. 1.

190 The moving force behind it is Indonesian-born (but long expatriated) and highly cosmopolitan author Bapak Anand. The Anand Ashram adopts a perennialist approach to religion, and offers an experiential programme of spiritual training. See Howell, 'Modernity and the Borderlands of Islamic Spirituality', 'Seeking Sufism in the Global City', and 'Muslims, the New Age and Marginal Religions'.

191 See Howell, 'Many Paths to God and Modernity' and 'Muslims, the New Age and Marginal Religions'.

192 Howell, 'Many Paths to God and Modernity', p. 15.

193 Ibid., p. 13.

194 Ibid., p. 23.

195 Ibid.

196 See M. Hakan Yavuz and John L. Esposito, Introduction, Islam in Turkey: Retreat from the Secular Path?, in M. Hakan Yavuz and John L. Esposito, eds, *Turkish Islam and the Secular State: The Gülen Movement* (Syracuse, NY, 2003), pp. xiii–xiv, xvii. For a concise overview of Islam in contemporary Turkey, see Svante Cornell and Ingvar Svenberg, Turkey, in David Westerlund and Ingvar Svenberg, eds, *Islam Outside the Arab World* (London, 1999), pp. 125–48. A survey of religious beliefs and practice among Turkish citizens during 2000 revealed that 86% regard themselves as 'believers': see M. Hakan Yavuz, 'Is there a Turkish Islam? The Emergence of Convergence and Consensus', *Journal of Muslim Minority Affairs*, 24: 2 (2004), p. 227.

197 Yavuz and Esposito, Introduction, p. xxiii.

198 See Kafadar, The New Visibility of Sufism, pp. 313–15.

199 Yavuz, 'Is there a Turkish Islam?', p. 218.

200 Ibid., p. 219.

201 Kafadar, 'The New Visibility of Sufism', pp. 310–13.

202 For a description of a recent *dhikr* ceremony held in a Halveti–Jerrahi *tekke* and of a Melami meeting, both in Istanbul, see Pablo Beneito, 'Sufi Circles in Istanbul', *Ronda Magazine*, October 2001, pp. 96–8.

203 An example is the case of Ahmet Yivlik (d. 2001), who belonged to a line of Naqshbandi shaykhs. A civil servant, he is described by close disciples as 'a spiritual son of Ibn 'Arabi'. Himself not a scholar, he has rendered at least one sufi work into modern Turkish: Selim Divane, *Miftah-u Muşkilat'il-Arifin Adab-u Raiki'l-Vasilin*, trans. from Ottoman by Ahmed Sadik Yivlik (Istanbul, 1998). Yivlik led a circle of about twenty disciples in Istanbul, including some Westerners and illiterates, reading to them Turkish translations of Ibn 'Arabi's works.

204 Individuals who have attempted to set up private circles to study sufi texts in Istanbul speak of the suspicion they encounter, and the difficulty of convincing potential participants that the intended circle is not an Islamist forum and has no hidden agenda. Interview with Rafik Algan, medical doctor turned sufi writer, and translator into Turkish of *Sufis of Andalusia*, published in Istanbul in 2001.

205 On him, see Henry Bayman, *The Station of No Station: Open Secrets of the Sufis* (Berkeley, 2001). Kayhan translated Sadreddin-i Konevi, *Hadis-i Erbain* (Ankara, 1996). He also published *Ruh ve Beden* (Ankara, 1991), *Irfan Okulunda Oku* (Ankara, 1994), *Adem ve Alem* (n.p., n.d.), and excerpts from the writings of 'Abd al-Qadir al-Jilani. His *silsila* encompasses both al-Jilani and Ahmad Sirhindi, and he can thus be considered at the same time Qadiri and Naqshbandi. He was born in a village near Malatya and recognised for his spiritual status while still a child by a shaykh in a neighbouring village. Following a spell in the army, he worked in the water-works and settled in Ankara. The author thanks his former students for this information, and for providing examples of Kayhan's approach.

206 Shushud succeeded his Melami shaykh Maksud Hulusi (1851–1929); see Massimo Introvigne, 'Niches in the Islamic Religious Market and Fundamentalism: Examples from Turkey and Other Countries', p. 13, www.cesnur.org. For a biography, see *An Excursion into the Depths of Tasavvuf: Discourses by Hasan Shushud*, compiled by Melih Yonsul, trans. Refik Algan, ed. Maura Thornton (private publication for closed distribution, n.p., 2004). His father was Defterdar of Izmir in Istanbul, and the first general manager of the

Agricultural Bank under the Republic. For an example of Shushud's writings, see Hasan Shushud, *Masters of Wisdom of Central Asia*, trans. Muhtar Holland (Coombe Springs, UK, 1983). This sets out the sources on which both Bennett and Shah drew.

207 Kayhan suggested that his students read the Qadiri *wird* for the seven days of the week; he also recommended Naqshbandi *awrad*. It seems individuals did only what they felt able to, and there was no compulsion in this respect. He always had at hand photocopies of various textual excerpts and prayers to give out to visitors.

208 For example, Kayhan's followers recall that some women would come to his house in mini-skirts; gradually, they would adopt a more modest style of dress.

209 *An Excursion into the Depths of Tasavvuf*, p. xii, describes Shushud's approach: 'Not only men, but women, too, in modesty and in awe, joined the Master's sessions ... Certainly, these sessions were not like teachings based upon a particular religion or order. They had not the least to do with the "Good Manners of the Order" (*Tarikat Adabi*). This liberal form of teaching continued until [his] death ... Everyone was free to have his own belief and there was no pressure applied to force anyone to believe in a certain way. After a while, non-Muslims also began attending the sessions'.

For his part, Kayhan (Bayman, *The Station of No Station*, p. 19) 'had no formal organisation to speak of ... there were no dervish convents ... no ceremonies, no special rituals, and no formalities. The convents were disbanded ... but with the Master I learned that there was no need for them. True spirituality could be exercised and conveyed without any formal structure at all – all that is necessary is acceptance on the part of the teacher, and devotion, sincerity, and effort on the part of the student. Having served their purpose, the *takkas* had passed into history as defunct sociological institutions. Instead there were *ad hoc* discussion groups, which came into existence on the spur of the moment and with whomever might be present at that time'.

A further example arises in the case of the illiterate welder-turned-poet profiled in Polymnia Athanassiadi, 'Ismail Emre (1900–1970): A Dervish without an Order', *TURCICA*, 33 (2001), pp. 295–312. The author highlights Emre's categorical denial that he belonged to a dervish order. She describes his informal circle of pupils (including people of 'denominational variety'), and the 'ardent desire to reach union with God' that underpinned his moral philosophy.

The signalling of a self-distancing from the *tariqas* by such teachers is echoed in the case 'of at least one 'Islamic' sufi shaykh in the West, if perhaps for different reasons: Fadhlalla Haeri refers to himself as 'a "post-*tariqa*" shaikh'. See Westerlund, The Contextualisation of Sufism in Europe, p. 22.

210 Cenan was established in 2000 by Sargut and Kenan Gürsoy, the great grandson of Kenan Rifai (d. 1950) and Professor of Philosophy at Galatasaray University, in Rifai's restored house in Fatih, Istanbul. On Kenan Rifai, see below.

211 Sargut grew up in a modern Rifa'i family milieu. Her mother was a student of Kenan Rifai who graduated in English literature. Sargut's teacher, Samiha Ayverdi (d. 1993), was a prolific author and close disciple of Rifai. Sargut herself graduated in chemical engineering and began a career as a high school teacher. When she was twenty-four, Ayverdi instructed her to teach high school students and medical professionals Rumi's *Mathnavi* (Sargut's sister was a medic). She believes that her success in this resulted from Ayverdi 'speaking through her', as she did not herself have the necessary knowledge. Ayverdi later sent her another teacher, who gave her further knowledge of the *Mathnavi* and taught her Qur'anic meanings. She recently retired from her high school career to dedicate herself to her sufi teaching and students, her activities abroad, and her work at the Cenan Foundation and the Women's Association. Sargut is a divorcee.

Sargut's popularity is evident from the large crowds drawn to her talks at Turkish venues. She has a weekly programme on the *Mathnavi*, broadcast on the radio station of the *Nur* movement (on which, see below), and has presented talks on several other radio stations and on television. Internal sources estimate that her students number in the thousands worldwide.

Information on Sargut and her group derives from an interview with her and a number of her students in Istanbul, August 2005. See also www.cemalnur.org.

On Kenan Rifai, an educator, musician and composer born in Salonica and revered as a saint by his followers, see Ch. 4, Samiha Ayverdi, *The Friend*, and 'The Life of Kenan Rifai' (anonymous unpublished paper, 19 pp.). His spiritual education took place under his mother Hatice Cenan and her guide, Edhem of Filibeh, who left a message that Rifai should carry on his spiritual work after his death. Fluent in eight languages, Rifai began to learn English at the age of eighty, believing it to be the future global language. The prominence of women among his followers can be understood in light of his emphasis on the importance of women as the channel through which love, the principal truth of the universe, becomes apparent. Sargut emphasises the role of women in sufism, and has produced a short film on Ayverdi 'to show how a sufi woman should be in this century'.

212 Her concern for what Sargut terms the 'academic' study of sufism explains her interest in inviting Western scholars to speak at religious–cultural events organised at Cenan. For example, an event co-organised by Cenan and the Women's Association to celebrate the birthday of the Prophet (April 2004) featured talks by American and French scholars of sufism Carl Ernst and Paul Ballanfat.

Sargut and Gürsoy aspire to develop the Cenan Foundation into a resource centre on sufism in Turkey and on Kenan Rifai, and an academy where teachers can lecture on sufism.

213 Nonetheless, she emphasises the importance of commitment for the student.

214 These were traditionally composed in the *tariqa*s to accompany ceremonies of collective invocation.

215 Describing the weekly eight-hour Qur'an session, for example, Sargut explains: 'There is discussion and laughter and we eat good things – without indulging too much – and enjoy it all. We take breaks when we are tired, we do the prayer together and then we study some more. It is a "normal" activity, because this is what we choose.' The meaning of each verse is first discussed as understood by sufi authorities such as Rumi, Ibn 'Arabi, Qunawi, Kashani and Bursevi. The group then settles upon a meaning, which is recorded with the ultimate aim of publishing a compilation of Qur'anic meanings 'in a sufi way'. The group usually comprises about twenty-five people, among whom five typically present.

Study of the Kenan Rifai *ilahiyat* proceeds in like fashion, drawing on a range of sufi authorities. Each member of the group offers their understanding of a poem prepared in advance, which is then studied as a group. The ultimate aim is to produce a commentary on the collection.

216 This reflects her increasingly international profile during the past few years (she has spoken at events in Europe and the USA hosted by, among others, various churches). Sargut insists on the importance of openness to other religions, emphasising that all paths lead to God: 'Everyone must believe something', she argues: 'as long as they believe, it's alright'.

217 Turkish critics of the Kenan Rifai line accuse it of an uncompromising insistence on moderateness in matters of religion, issuing in a marked prejudice against the wearing of the headscarf and the sporting of beards (this attitude can be a problem in educational settings, for example); see further below.

While it does not constitute a formal *tariqa*, the self-consciously modern stance of Sargut's group perhaps makes it a contender to fill what Sedgwick, *Against the Modern World*, p. 256, sees as a gap in contemporary Turkey: he thus suggests that 'there is no Turkish order specializing in "modern" Turks in the way that the Budshishiyya specializes in "modern" Moroccans'.

218 One of her students indeed recalls her significant first chance meeting with Sargut, at a hairdresser's salon where she was having her hair dressed.

219 Sargut explains that her teacher Ayverdi 'did not want *tasbih*, as the government did not approve of it'.

220 'We laughed and had a great time', Sargut recalls. Her young students now 'can't wait' for the opportunity to go again. Gürsoy has taken steps to teach the Rifa'i *dhikr* to a few young people in order to keep the tradition alive, but this is 'just as a form': they do not use it.

221 In the case of Kayhan's students, for example, there are among them a few 'elders', to whom they could turn for assistance or guidance during his lifetime. Some continue to do so today, while others prefer not to. It is significant that permission was obtained for building a mosque encompassing a shrine over Kayhan's tomb outside of Ankara, reflecting his good standing with the state.

In the case of the Kenan Rifai line, it will be interesting to track the role of the Cenan Foundation as a possible institutional home, and Sargut's preparation of next-generation teachers.

222 For an introduction to Nursi and the movement he inspired, see Abu-Rabi', ed., *Islam at the Crossroads*.

223 See Fred A. Reed, In the Footsteps of Said Nursi, in ibid., p. 35.

224 See M. Hakan Yavuz, *Nur* Study Circles (*Dershanes*) and the Formation of New Religious Consciousness in Turkey, in Abu-Rabi', ed., *Islam at the Crossroads*, p. 313 n. 7; also his 'Being Modern in the Nurcu Way', *ISIM Review*, 6 (2000), p. 7.

225 Yavuz, 'Is there a Turkish Islam?', p. 220; cf. *Nur* Study Circles, p. 313 n. 7.

226 Conveyed to the author by a Nursi student from Manisa, who believes he heard Şerif Mardin use the expression.

227 Students are careful to point out that Nursi is himself *absent* from the text: the special quality of the latter derives not from his authorship as such, but from the fact that it is in essence 'a reflection of the Qur'an'. This and following references to *Nur* students derive from discussions in Izmir, August 2005. On the present point, see also Metin Karabaşoğlu, Text and Community: An Analysis of the *Risale-i Nur* Movement, in Abu Rabi', ed., *Islam at the Crossroads*, pp. 275–6.

228 For Nursi's views concerning *tariqa* sufism and problems of understanding, practice and attitude he identified in this arena, which he urged his readers to guard against, see for example Bediuzzaman Said Nursi, *Letters, 1928–1932* (From the *Risale-i Nur* Collection, 2) (Istanbul, 2001), pp. 518–35. Nursi's appreciation of the benefits and fruits of the sufi path 'which is on the straight way' is also elaborated there. For phrases cited in our text, see p. 533. See further Bilal Kuşpinar, Nursi's Evaluation of Sufism, in *The Third International Symposium on Bediüzzaman Said Nursi: The Reconstruction of Islamic Thought in the Twentieth Century and Bediüzzaman Said Nursi* (Istanbul, 1997), 2, pp. 72–83. Nursi claimed to be neither sufi shaykh nor sufi, and wished to be known instead as *imam*. He reportedly insisted that it was 'time for *haqiqa* … not *tariqa*': see Küçük, 'Sufi Reactions against the Reforms', p. 9, and Reed, In the Footsteps of Said Nursi, p. 35.

229 Compare with Yavuz, '*Nur* Study Circles', p. 310.

230 Ibid., p. 313 n. 7.

231 The characterisation of the *Nur* movement posited here is further illustrated by one of its offshoots, the Gülen movement. See Zeki Saritoprak, Fethullah Gülen: A Sufi in His Own Way, in Yavuz and Esposito, eds, *Turkish Islam and the Secular State*, pp. 156–69. The author observes that some sufis criticise Gülen (who roots his own understanding in the *Risale-i Nur*) for not having a (sufi) master. Gülen, however, 'believes that having a master is not necessary and that the master does not have to be human. For him, the Qur'an is a superior master and guide. He holds that the way of contemplation is drawn from the Qur'an, and it is not necessary to be confined to a Sufi order'. Moreover, he 'focuses on a path by which one can overcome weaknesses by oneself rather than with a guide'. Saritoprak concludes (p. 169) that, while strictly speaking Gülen is not a sufi, he is 'a Sufi in practice, if not in name'.

232 Numerous works by Hulusi (b. 1945) are currently published by Istanbul 'sufi' publisher Kitsan in several languages, and are widely distributed, often without charge.

His publications are all without copyright. Audio and videotapes by Hulusi are also available. On Hulusi (and for a list of his publications), see www.ahmedhulusi.com and www.kitsan.com. Some of his writings date back to the late 1960s–early 1970s, while others originate in a more recent column on his website. It appears that the Religious Affairs Directorate (Diyanet) has not endorsed his works.

233 Discussion with Kitsan owner, Istanbul, August 2005. 'In our present time of life', Hulusi explains (*Dabaddah: The Universal Mysteries* [Istanbul, 2001], pp. 158–9), 'the affairs of the *tariqa* no more exist, a shaykh (spiritual teacher) and a *dervish* (disciple) relation has ended in [the] true sense; the duality of an educator and educated is gone'. His translator into English elaborates that, as he describes himself as a 'Muhammadan', and insists that nothing should come between the individual and the Prophet, it is natural that Hulusi should not follow a shaykh in the traditional sense. (Ahmed Baki, personal correspondence with the author, October 2005.)

234 His Turkish readers refer to him as *ustad* (teacher/master).

235 As his English translator Ahmad Baki explains, Hulusi has read and drawn on past great sufi authors, and some modern ones (in the latter respect, he explicitly mentions Kenan Rifai). (Personal correspondence with the author, October 2005.)

236 There are references to quantum physics and neuroscience, for example. A single illustration will suffice. Ahmed Hulusi, *Truth of Life* (Istanbul, 2003), p. 51, argues that the function of *dhikr* is to stimulate electrical activity between certain cells in the brain, and its effect is to increase the brain's working capacity. By repeating certain Divine Names, this capacity can be increased in such a way that 'you become equipped with the quality of the actual meanings of those words'.

237 Ahmed Hulusi, *From Friend to Friend: Friends' Handbook of Sufi Words of Wisdom*, as advertised in *Dabaddah*.

238 A few quotations will illustrate this point (we have slightly modified these from the poor English translation). 'You must attain Allah who is in your essence, not a god outside yourself.' (Ahmed Hulusi, *Up to Date Understanding of Islam* [Istanbul, 2001], p. 145.) 'One cannot attain the Universal mysteries within one's essence without getting rid of all the environment-given conditionings …' (*Dabaddah*, p. vii). 'Leave your social conditionings, standards of judgement and emotions aside, allow your True Self within to emerge!' (see www.ahmedbaki.com/english/). 'All that is known as *ibadat* [acts of worship] that you fulfil is for you only! They are never to please a God up in the sky.' (Ahmed Hulusi, *The Voice of Cosmic System*, draft translation, www.esselam.net.)

239 Hulusi is interested in the spirit world and provides advice on contacting spirits. See Ahmed Hulusi, *Spirit, Men, Jinn* (Istanbul, 1972).

240 His earlier writings thus appear to be the fruit of a personal opening in 1966 (the result of his 'releasing himself from the false reality of his ego'). This experience is recorded in Ahmed Hulusi, *Revelations* (Istanbul, 2002/1967), which is his first publication: see p. 9.

241 Ahmed Hulusi, *The Voice of System* (Istanbul, 2000), Introduction.

242 Cf. Yavuz, 'Is there a Turkish Islam?', p. 224. The deregulation of the Turkish religious market began during the 1950s. For an overview, see Introvigne, 'Niches in the Islamic Religious Market', pp. 8ff. More generally, during the 1980s, as Leyla Neyzi, Object or Subject?: The Paradox of 'Youth' in Turkey, in Bryan S. Turner, ed., *Islam: Critical Concepts in Sociology* (London, 2003), IV: *Islam and Social Movements*, p. 370, observes, 'political repression was accompanied by increased freedom of expression on the cultural and personal front. In the 1980s and the 1990s, a variety of … subcultures … entered the public sphere, particularly through the media.'

243 The ubiquitous horoscope in television and news media is one illustration.

244 On this phrase, see Carpenter, The Mainstreaming of Alternative Spirituality in Brazil, p. 217.

245 Istanbul bookstores offer works on UFOs, kabbalah, yoga, the I Ching, zen, buddhism, shinto, dream interpretation, self-help, etc. Translated authors include

Shirley MacLaine, Deepak Chopra and David Spangler, but there are also contributions on subjects listed here by Turkish authors. By way of illustration, Mephisto Bookstore in central Istiklal Caddesi holds well over 500 titles on New Age subjects/spirituality: these are strategically placed at the front of the store, for ease of access by the substantial readership they draw (a pattern repeated in major bookstores across the city). According to the store's manager, readers are typically aged 20–40. Best-sellers at the time of writing included OSHO titles (see below), and *You Can Heal Your Life*, by popular self-help author (and a founder of the self-help movement) Louise Hay. There are several new Turkish publishers dedicated to translating and publishing works on spirituality: for an example, see Ruh ve Madde Yayinlari, www.dharma.com.tr.

The currency of 'occult' ideas is evident from the frequent references to these in recent popular Turkish publications. For refutations of claims concerning reincarnation, for example, see Kemal Osmanbey, *Haqai'q 'an tanasukh al-arwah wa'l-hassa al-sadisa* (Beirut, 2002); Ahmed Hulusi, *Up to Date Understanding of Islam*, pp. 97 ff and *Religious Misunderstandings* (Istanbul, 2002), p. 124. Osmanbey, a medical doctor of Arab extraction who has long been settled in Istanbul and practises acupuncture there, argues that areas encompassed by the Islamic ablution coincide with specific acupuncture points. He has spent many years establishing contact with the spirit world: see, for example, his *Ruh Aleminde bir Seyahat* (Istanbul, 1995). (Interview with Kemal Osmanbey, Istanbul, December 2004.)

Mention must also be made of the debate and media hype surrounding satanism, sparked by the 'ritual' murder of a young woman in an Istanbul cemetery during 1999. See T. Deniz Erkmen, 'Construction of Satanism in Turkish Secularist and Islamist Newspapers', *ISIM Review*, 8 (2001), p. 16. For a further example of the local Turkish 'refraction' of globally disseminated cultural forces, see Pierre Hecker, 'Heavy Metal in a Muslim Context', *ISIM Review*, 16 (August 2005), pp. 8–9.

246 On the number of yoga schools, see for example *Yoga Dergisi*, 2003: 1, pp. 58–9. Meditation opportunities include TM and those offered by OSHO and the Brahma Kumaris (the latter have two centres in Istanbul, but are somewhat closed to outsiders). Neuro-Linguistic Programming is particularly prominent among psychological therapies in Turkey. A kabbalah centre was recently established through a Californian initiative, and the New Acropolis is active in the city via several branches.

247 See the OWO website (www.owo.com.tr). Summer camps held in Antalya at a five-star hotel belonging to the family behind the establishment of OWO include, for example, a 'Gurdjieff Movements Awareness Intensive': see www.gurdjieff-movements.co.uk. Private therapy sessions advertised at OWO include Transformational Breathing and Osho Zen Tarot Counselling.

248 Recommended authors include Paulo Coelho, Gahl Sasson and Eckhart Tolle, for example. Literature distributed free at OWO includes *The Holy Zohar: The Book of Avraham. A Book of Healing and Protection*, published by the Kabbalah Centre Press (Tel Aviv and New York) as part of the Worldwide Zohar Project.

A publishing house is also in the making at OWO. The first publications in progress are a series of renderings into Turkish of works by Hafiz. The first is a translation of Daniel Ladinsky, *I Heard God Laughing: Renderings of Hafiz* (Point Richmond, CA, 2004). It is noteworthy that, thanks to OWO, Hafiz thus comes to a Turkish readership via the work of an American disciple of the Indian teacher Meher Baba. Ladinsky produced his 'renderings' from a literal nineteenth-century English translation of Hafiz. He explains that they 'are not intended to be literal or scholarly or even "accurate"'. See p. xiii.

249 KUN is the OSHO Meditation Centre in Istanbul. OSHO is the name adopted towards the end of his life by the controversial figure Bhagwan Shree Rajneesh (d. 1990), who established centres for his monistic teaching at Pune, India and Oregon, USA, and stressed meditation as the most direct tool for transformation. Rajneesh is often remembered for the various scandals with which he and his movement became associated. For the OSHO movement's official website, see www.osho.com.

KUN describes its location in Istanbul thus: 'five minutes walking distance from where Gurdjieff was teaching his students and also from the Galata Mevlevihane, meeting place for the Mevelvis/Sufis. Surrounded by the funkiest cafes and restaurants and the art scene in Istanbul, it is the buddhafield among the zorba part of town'. See www.oshokun.com/eng. It offers yoga, the full range of OSHO meditation techniques, a range of massage therapies, body awareness in dance, and breath sessions. Summer camps held near Bodrum include Gurdjieff movements combined with meditation and sharing ('to go deep inside and clear away old limitations and beliefs'); family therapy; love and relationship dynamics; and meditation. Together with OWO, KUN offers a week-long 'Path of Love', in which two practitioners oversee a heady range of approaches and therapies designed to support participants 'to passionately focus on their sincere desire or longing to realize their full human and spiritual potential'. It is 'a journey of honest inquiry into our True Nature'.

250 OWO too draws on this celebrated Turkish sufi legacy, naming one of its large halls the 'Mevlana Hall'.

251 For an OSHO discourse on sufism, see for example Osho, *Sufis: The People of the Path* (Pune, India, 2002).

252 The OSHO website describes the 'whirling meditation' thus: 'Sufi whirling is one of the most ancient techniques, one of the most forceful. It is so deep that even a single experience can make you totally different.'

253 For a taste of Zahira's self-perception as sufi teacher, and the clear influence upon this of the OSHO understanding, see the OWO website.

254 Some comment on young people's indiscriminate copying of Western lifestyles, citing the growing drug problem in Turkish cities, for example. In general terms, Turkish openness to the West can be partly explained in terms of an absence of direct colonial experience of it.

255 As suggested by Yavuz and Esposito, Introduction, p. xxi, the aim of the Kemalist reforms had been 'to create a new society and a *Homo kemalicus*, a persona guided by a voluntary positivism and forced amnesia (in other words, no deeper sense of identity)'.

256 This experience was echoed on a practical level by an erstwhile Turkish disciple of OSHO, now in her early fifties, who had been dedicated to Rajneesh and had spent some time in Pune. When she was later introduced to Kayhan, she spontaneously renounced her OSHO discipleship and attached herself to him, for he had instantly made her feel 'important and loved'.

257 John O. Voll, Fethullah Gülen: Transcending Modernity in the New Islamic Discourse, in Yavuz and Esposito, eds, *Turkish Islam and the Secular State*, p. 246. For a collection of essays addressing relevant themes across a broad geographical range, see Johan Meuleman, ed., *Islam in the Era of Globalization: Muslim Attitudes towards Modernity and Identity* (London, 2002).

258 See Heelas and Woodhead *et al.*, *The Spiritual Revolution*, p. 80.

259 Taking as its focus the professional middle and upper-middle classes in Muslim majority arenas, a fruitful line of enquiry might trace the interrelations between wealth creation, the growth of people-centred professions, and education, on the one hand, and the interest in subjective-life and the growth of subjective spiritualities of life, on the other.

260 See Heelas, The Spiritual Revolution: From 'Religion' to 'Spirituality', pp. 373–4, and Heelas and Seel, An Ageing New Age?, pp. 240–1; also Heelas and Woodhead *et al.*, *The Spiritual Revolution*, pp. 61–6 (where the terminology differs). According to Heelas and Woodhead, Homeless Minds Today?, pp. 65–6, 'many primary religious institutions are currently "detraditionalising": downplaying the "hard" authoritative, hierarchical, patriarchal ... nature of traditional religious communities in favour of "softer" characteristics and forms of belonging which allow individuals to find homes, exercise autonomy and resource their lives. The emphasis, in other words, increasingly shifts from without to within, from God to self, from church to community and from

after-life to this life.' Heelas, The Spiritual Revolution: From 'Religion' to 'Spirituality', p. 374, posits Brazil as an example of an arena outside the advanced industrialised West which has growing theistic spiritualities of life.

261 Heelas, The Spiritual Revolution: From 'Religion' to 'Spirituality', pp. 373–4, citing arguments by Ronald Inglehart.

262 Compare with Woodhead *et al.*, Introduction, pp. 11–12.

263 In some respects, our 'intensely modern Muslims' might thus indeed be described as 'post-modern Muslims', or 'modernity-transcending Muslims', in line with an approach sketched by Voll, Fethullah Gülen, pp. 240ff. Voll points out that the frame of modernity (with its distinctive perspective upholding global/local and religious/secular polarities) is not necessarily the one within which contemporary issues and events should be viewed: the frame of a world 'beyond modernity' in which these polarities have broken down might also be applied.

264 Stark, 'Secularization: RIP', p. 263.

Epilogue

1 For example, as we noted earlier, Geaves, *The Sufis of Britain*, pp. 167–8, suggests that Shah's approach in many ways 'epitomised the *Malamati* tradition', for he 'worked in the world and scorned any outer manifestations of Sufi identity'. Thus: 'The descriptions of ... Shah's vision of Sufism clearly indicate his natural empathy for the *Malamati* school of mysticism rather than the organised *tariqa*s that function within mainstream Islam. Although the *Malamati* tradition would not have found much currency in the Muslim world, which emphasised the exoteric obligations of religion ... Shah was able to promote it successfully in the Western world. The appeal of its rejection of exotericism was strong where many people sought spiritual understanding and experience but were unsympathetic towards religious forms.' See also Ch. 4. The Malami motivation for repudiating the outward signs of sufism (and in some cases the exoteric practices of the faith) was ultimately to deflect praise and attract censure. As neither praise nor censure could be expected to result from such repudiation in the context of the modern West, the very thrust of the term and what it denotes is deconstructed. Geaves recently reiterated his argument even more strongly: 'there is no doubt that Idries Shah displayed all the characteristics of the Malamati form of Sufism'. See Geaves, 'Sufism', in Christopher H. Partridge, ed., *Encyclopedia of New Religions: New Religious Movements, Sects, and Alternative Spiritualities* (Oxford, 2004), p. 137. Note that Geaves also finds the Qalandari type helpful to his discussion of universal sufism in contemporary Britain, arguing that 'Both the Malamati and the Qalandar tendencies have influenced the development of universal Sufism in Britain.' See ibid., and his *The Sufis of Britain*, p. 163.

2 See, for example, Arweck and Clarke, eds, *New Religious Movements in Western Europe*, subject list 'Islam'.

3 These are 'The Halveti–Jerrahi Order of Dervishes'; 'The Haqqani Naqshbandis'; the 'Shadhili–Akbari Sufi Order'; 'The Sufi Movement'; 'The Sufi Order of the West'; 'The Bawa Muhaiyaddeen Fellowship'; and 'Subud'. The Nation of Islam, the United Nuwaubian Nation of Moors in the USA and the Baha'i faith complete the list. See Partridge, ed., *Encyclopedia of New Religions*, pp. 127ff. For an accompanying bibliography, see www.lion-publishing.co.uk.

4 The possibility that Israel is subsumed within the West geographically, culturally or politically is of course acknowledged, but it does not invalidate our point.

5 The British arena alone yields ample evidence, whether in the case of Muslim-born British suicide bombers in London and Israel, or the convert 'shoe-bomber'.

6 Geaves, 'Sufism', p. 136, indeed makes this explicit, suggesting that the sufi trends he discusses can all be regarded as 'alternative religions'.

7 J. Gordon Melton, The Fate of NRMs and their Detractors in Twenty-First Century America, in Lucas and Robbins, eds, *New Religious Movements in the 21st Century*, p. 238.

8 Three recent examples of a more integrated approach can be mentioned: (a) Gregory F. Treverton, Heather S. Gregg, Daniel Gibran and Charles W. Yost, *Exploring Religious Conflict* (Santa Monica, CA, 2005), a report published by the RAND Corporation National Security Research Division and funded by the CIA which employs the model of NRMs to examine religiously motivated violence in the Middle East, presenting as case study the Muqtada al-Sadr movement in post-Saddam Iraq. (b) Lucas and Robbins, eds, *New Religious Movements in the 21st Century*, both as a whole, and in several of its individual chapters: see, for example, chapters 1, 5–7 and 9, also 18–19. (c) Articles in *Nova Religio*, 6 (2002) must also be mentioned, including responses to Mark Sedgwick's attempt to apply typologies drawn from Western sociology of religion (denomination, sect, cult) to the Islamic arena, elaborated in his Establishments and Sects in the Islamic World, pp. 283–312.

9 Benjamin Zablocki and J. Anna Looney, Research on New Religious Movements in the Post-9/11 World, in Lucas and Robbins, eds, *New Religious Movements in the 21st Century*, pp. 314, 325.

10 Note for example Sedgwick's reservations concerning the issue of 'newness' in the Islamic arena: see his Establishments and Sects in the Islamic World, p. 288–9.

11 Cf. Davie, *Religion in Modern Europe*, p. 140.

12 Hanegraaff, The New Age Movement and the Esoteric Tradition, p. 377. The frameworks in question were occultist or romanticist in nature. See also Hammer, Sufism for Westerners, pp. 128–9.

13 The expression is borrowed from Charles Kimball, 'Towards a More Hopeful Future: Obstacles and Oppositions in Christian-Muslim Relations', *The Muslim World*, 94: 3 (2004), p. 379.

14 A parallel trend is evident in the case of Indian spirituality: Heelas, *The New Age Movement*, p. 123, describes its export, 'Californianization', and return.

15 As Heelas, *The New Age Movement*, pp. 124–5, argues, the New Age in general has undoubtedly become much more 'mainstream-related', geared to the values, interests and concerns of those who work in the mainstream. Cf. Hanegraaff, The New Age Movement and the Esoteric Tradition, p. 363, which observes that the increasing commercialisation of the NAM from the second half of the 1980s 'has tended to undermine its potential as a countercultural force'. See also Dawson, 'Who Joins New Religious Movements and Why', p. 122.

16 The importance of this was stressed at the Summer Gathering in August 2004.

17 As Heelas and Seel comment in relation to the offspring of the baby-boomer cohort which came of age during the sixties and is involved in New Age spiritualities: 'Having been brought up in terms of the liberal, ontological individualism of their parents, with spiritual (or religious) choices being seen as a private affair, as dependent on the unique experience of the child, it might be expected that ... transmission [of the parents' specific New Age spiritualities] has been weak'. See An Ageing New Age?, p. 232.

18 We are aware of only two who have studied languages of the Muslim world.

19 See Beckford, New Religious Movements and Globalization, pp. 259–60, and Lorne L. Dawson and Jenna Hennebry, New Religions and the Internet: Recruiting in a New Public Space, in Dawson, ed., *Cults and New Religious Movements*, pp. 271ff.

20 See Rodney Stark, Why Religious Movements Succeed or Fail: A Revised General Model, in Dawson, ed., *Cults and New Religious Movements*, pp. 259ff.

21 Ibid., p. 261.

22 Kafadar, The New Visibility of Sufism, p. 313.

23 On the role of baby boomers in transforming the American religious landscape, see Roof, *A Generation of Seekers*, chapter 9, and Brown, Baby Boomers, American Character, and the New Age, pp. 90ff. The European post-war baby boom came to a close soon after the end of the war, but the American one did not end until 1965. (For a succinct introduction to the social and economic environment into which American baby boomers were born, see pp. 91–2.) This generation's influence in shaping aspects of American culture (and economic life) is partly attributable to its numerical strength (it is estimated that baby boomers make up a quarter to a third of the current population). For a satirical look at baby-boomer attitudes ('extraordinarily self-involved', 'self-satisfied', and thinking that they are 'God's gift to mankind'), see Joe Queenan, *Balsamic Dreams: A Short But Self-Important History of the Baby Boomer Generation* (New York, 2001). Inglehart's application of the term 'postmaterialist' to describe this generation is noteworthy: for a summary of its signification, see Roof, *Spiritual Marketplace*, pp. 58–9.

It would be of interest to compare attitudes concerning modes of engagement with the sacred among first-generation Beshara associates today with those of other baby boomers in the UK, elsewhere in Europe, and in the USA (in the latter case, for example, as documented during the 1990s by Roof in *A Generation of Seekers* and *Spiritual Marketplace*). By way of illustration, we can point to recent evidence of fluctuating relations with natal religions among first-generation associates. For example, an associate husband and wife of Jewish provenance have newly begun to observe religious rituals marking out Jewish practice, combining this with a strong commitment to Beshara. And the recent death of another first-generation Jewish associate was marked by a synagogue service, followed by a Beshara commemoration service at Chisholme.

24 Roof, *A Generation of Seekers*, p. 8. The description relates to seekers within the American baby-boomer generation.

25 Roof, *Spiritual Marketplace*, p. 12.

26 Henry Bayman, *The Black Pearl: Spiritual Illumination in Sufism and East Asian Philosophies* (New York, 2005), p. xiv, makes the broader point: 'The juggernaut of modernization has rolled over every delicate flower of the East, until today we are faced with their immediate extinction.'

Appendix 1

Sufism and sufi spirituality in the West: a working typology

Two broad trends can be identified in terms of the Muslim or non-Muslim provenance of individual figures and the founding figures of groups, and their views concerning the relationship between sufism and Islam.

1. 'Islamic' sufism

a. Individuals of non-Muslim, Western provenance encountered sufism in the Muslim world, embraced it within its Islamic framework, converted to Islam and joined established *tariqa*s, facilitating the spread of these to and within Western contexts, and leading to the emergence of new branches there. Their involvement sometimes resulted in the formation of recognisably transformed or new *tariqa*s, which have gradually come to bridge the Muslim world and the West. For them, the spiritual path is conceived in terms of an Islamic frame of reference. Example: René Guénon (d.1949).

b. Individuals of Muslim, non-Western provenance introduced existing *tariqa*s to Western contexts, requiring the embrace of Islam as a condition for participation. In certain cases, concessions were made to the Western cultural context. Examples: Muzaffer Özak (d.1986), Nazim al-Haqqani, Bawa Muhaiyaddeen (d.1986), Javad Nurbakhsh.

2. 'Universal' sufism

a. Individuals of non-Muslim, Western provenance encountered sufism in Muslim contexts, then established new spiritual trends in the West. In this case, sufi resources were divorced from their Islamic framework and used as techniques in human transformation (sometimes in combination with ideas and practices drawn from other mystical traditions, ancient philosophies and sciences). There was no conversion to Islam on the part of the founder or their students. Examples: G. I. Gurdjieff (d.1949), J. G. Bennett (d.1974), Irina Tweedie (d.1999).

b. Finding themselves in the West (or having gone there purposefully), individuals of Muslim, non-Western provenance with sufi affiliations or knowledge were motivated to convey aspects of sufism. In some cases, this issued in profound transformations in sufism from its traditional forms. No requirement to embrace Islam in order to follow a path largely defined in terms of sufi resources was upheld. Examples: Inayat Khan (d.1927), Vilayat Khan (d.2004), Idries Shah (d.1996).

Appendix 2

The life and thought of Ibn 'Arabi: suggested further readings

Different interpretations of Ibn 'Arabi highlight one, more or all of his contributions as metaphysician, theologian, Islamic legal thinker, sufi, Muslim saint and universal spiritual figure. An attempt has been made to strike a balance among these in the readings suggested here, while focusing on the most accessible and recent scholarship. Publication details for works not mentioned in the Bibliography are given here.

Chittick's chapter, 'Ibn 'Arabi and His School', in Nasr, ed., *Islamic Spirituality: Manifestations*, provides a clear introductory treatment (with some translated extracts), as do his two chapters in Nasr and Leaman, eds, *History of Islamic Philosophy* ('Ibn 'Arabi', and 'The School of Ibn 'Arabi'), and his *Ibn 'Arabi: Heir to the Prophets* (Oxford, 2005). Hirtenstein's *The Unlimited Mercifier: The Spiritual Life and Thought of Ibn 'Arabi*, which alternates biographical chapters with discussions of the central elements of Ibn 'Arabi's thought and writings, provides another accessible treatment. Addas' *Ibn 'Arabi: The Voyage of No Return* provides a comprehensive, if brief, overview of the major features of Ibn 'Arabi's life and thought, while her *Quest for the Red Sulphur: The Life of Ibn 'Arabi* offers a much more detailed and dense biography. Chittick's *Imaginal Worlds: Ibn al-'Arabi and the Problem of Religious Diversity* offers a quite detailed yet accessible summary and interpretation of his teachings. No reading list would be complete without Chodkiewicz's discussion of the Qur'anic roots of Ibn 'Arabi's writings and his hermeneutics: *An Ocean without Shore: Ibn 'Arabi, The Book, and The Law*. The same goes for two classic works: Henry Corbin's *Alone with the Alone: Creative Imagination in the Sufism of Ibn 'Arabi*, and Toshihiko Izutsu's comparative study of the mystical thought of Ibn 'Arabi and Lao Tzu, *Sufism and Taoism: A Comparative Study of Key Philosophical Concepts* (Berkeley, 1983).

The most detailed and extensive survey of works by or attributed to Ibn 'Arabi in catalogued manuscripts and printed versions remains Yahia's *Histoire et classification de l'oeuvre d'Ibn 'Arabi*. Among the growing number of translations of such works, those of the two most significant, the *Fusus al-hikam* and the *Futuhat al-Makkiyya*, must be singled out. R.W.J. Austin's *Ibn al-'Arabi: The Bezels of Wisdom* (which includes an informative introduction to Ibn 'Arabi's thought) can be supplemented with Ronald L. Nettler's *Sufi Metaphysics and Qur'anic Prophets: Ibn 'Arabi's Thought and Method in the Fusus al-Hikam*, the latter providing an accessible commentary on ten chapters of the original. *The Meccan Revelations*, edited by Michel Chodkiewicz, presents translations of sections from the *Futuhat* clustering around selected themes, with a helpful introduction to this *opus magnum* and suggestions for further reading by James W. Morris (Volume 1). Morris' *The Reflective Heart: Discovering Spiritual Intelligence in Ibn 'Arabi's Meccan Illuminations* (Louisville, KY, 2005) proceeds from an attitude of personal engagement with the text. Chittick's *The Sufi Path of Knowledge: Ibn al-'Arabi's Metaphysics of Imagination* provides a comprehensive introduction with selected translations relating to specific aspects of Ibn 'Arabi's metaphysics. To these translations, we would add *Sufis of Andalusia: The Ruh al-Quds and al-Durrat al-Fakhira*, a translation of Ibn 'Arabi's biographical sketches relating to sufis of high spiritual attainment in twelfth-century Muslim Spain whom he had met and from whom he had learned. As Martin Lings points out [Foreword, p. 11], this is 'probably easier to read than anything else of his that has come down to us'. Moreover, it serves to correct 'a false impression which many Westerners have of [Ibn 'Arabi], especially those who tend to think of him as a "philosopher" rather than a "mystic"'.

Appendix 3

A Beshara study session: Bosnevi's Commentary on the *Fusus al-hikam*

Text

The text studied in the session we describe is an extract from the chapter entitled 'Of the Wisdom of Beneficence (*al-hikmat al-ihsaniyya*) in the Word of Loqman', from the internal printing **Chapters from the *Fusus al-Hikam*, Part IV** (n.d., 70 pp.), translated by Bulent Rauf from the commentary by Bosnevi (attributed to Bursevi): this chapter arises on pp. 19–38. The fragment studied covers the opening part (pp. 19–23), which is reproduced below:[1]

> It was mentioned before this, as in the Wisdom of Abraham and in several other places, that indeed the totality of immanence (*kawn*) is food (*ghidha'*) and that Man with the determinations is the food of God because God became manifest with the determination of Man's *'ayn*, and the *'ayn-i-thabita* became hidden in that. The Being of the *haqq* which is manifest in the *'ayn-i-thabita* of Man is fed by the determination of the *'ayn-i-thabita*, at the same time *haqq* by Its effulgence of being over Man is its food. When or if for Its own Being the Divine *meshiya* appertained to the Will (*irada*) of nourishment, in other words, by virtue of the degree of Divinity when the Being of the *haqq* which is actualized in the possibilities of the *a'yan* manifested the determinations of the Divine Names which are at the strength of that degree by manifesting in the places of manifestation of the *a'yan* of possibilities and through Its *meshiya* appertained to the Will (*irada*) of being nourished, then the totality of immanence becomes His nourishment and all the Divine determinations which are actualized and manifested through the immanence are also His nourishment simply because *haqq* is manifest in the garments of Qualities and Names through the Divine determinations of immanence, and the immanence is the nourishment of the *haqq*, by virtue of the manifestation (*ta'ayyun*) and the actualization (*muta'ayin*) of the *haqq* in the *a'yan* of the universes and in that which is manifested in the immanences.
>
> By virtue of the fact that the Divine Identity (*huwiyya*) is the same as His Ipseity, He is completely rich beyond need (*ghani*) of the universes and of the totality of the Divine Names. The difference between *meshiya* and *irada* is that His *meshiya* is exactly the same as His Ipseity, and His Will (*irada*) is one of the qualities which necessitate the Name '*murid*'. Sometimes it does happen that the *meshiya* is the same as the *irada* and sometimes it happens that it is different. In certain aspects the *meshiya* is more generalized than the Will (*irada*) and determines that which is appertaining to the *irada*, equally it may appertain to its dissociation (*nafida*) from the *irada* and determine that way, as in the bringing into existence or taking

---

1 The author thanks the Beshara School for permission to reproduce this text. For technical terms, see, for example, Chittick, *The Sufi Path of Knowledge*.

into non-existence (*'adam*). In fact, *meshiya* appertains to bringing into existence as well as to making non-existent, but *irada* is of the realities of the Names thereby necessitating existence as, for instance, in the Koran the word '*irada*' is used for the case where the non-existent is brought into existence, but *irada* appertains to bringing into existence and does not appertain to taking away from existence except where the determination of the *meshiya* is general and determines over the *irada*.

Therefore, *irada* appertains to *meshiya* and when God's *meshiya* appertains to the *irada* concerning our nourishment, our nourishment becomes according to what His *meshiya* demands. That is to say, by bringing into existence our *a'yan* of possibilities, His *meshiya* appertained to the *irada* of making us nourished and He brings us into existence by His own Existence (*wujud*) as His own *meshiya* demands, and consequently since His Identity (*huwiyya*) is hidden in our being (*wujud*), He brings us into manifestation; just as nourishment is hidden in the nourished. Consequently, the Identity (*huwiyya*) of the *haqq* is our food because our being (*wujud*) and shape and appearances are things of actualization, and our being established in reality are by His Being (*wujud*). Therefore, what is actualized (*muta'ayin*) by us is His Being (*wujud*) and our places of manifestation are Him and our nourishment and food result from His effusion of being, just as equally we are His food by the determinations. Equally, our becoming realised and our continuation in subsistence are through His Being, and the subsistence in existence of the determinations of His Names is through our *a'yan*. Under these considerations, if God's *meshiya* appertains to His will for our nourishment, He becomes our nourishment; and according to what our *a'yan* in the *ghayb* demanded and desired from Him, He becomes our nourishment. *Meshiya* appertains both to non-existence and to existence, and Will (*irada*) appertains only to the coming into existence of a non-existent. Consequently, where the *meshiya* and *irada* coincide in the bringing into existence of a thing which is non-existent, they are united, and by virtue of the fact that *meshiya* is the same as Ipseity, and each Name refers to the Ipseity (*dhat*) and is the same as It, then according to this consideration *meshiya* becomes the same as *irada*. According to this, the Shaykh says the *meshiya* of the *haqq* is His *irada*, that is to say, in action and in bringing into being, and in appertaining to and in indicating the Ipseity they are united. Consequently therefore, you must determine and act according to the *meshiya* which necessitates bringing into being and which is the same as the *irada*, since He indeed desired the Will. Hence the *irada* is the aim (*murad*) of the *meshiya*. In other words, in one way the *meshiya* and the *irada* are the same, but in another way they are different. Therefore, you determine by the *meshiya* which appertained to the *irada*, since the *irada* is the aim (*murad*) of the *meshiya*.

In short, the intention of 'Arabi [sic] is that sometimes *meshiya* appertains to the Will and sometimes it appertains to the Will of increase which is Union, sometimes to the Will of decrease which is non-existence. In other words, the *meshiya* of *haqq* aims at increase which is bringing into existence and equally aims at decrease which is bringing into non-existence after bringing into existence. Whereas in any case in either of these parts, the *haqq* has no other *meshiya* than the Absolute *meshiya* which appertains both to the bringing into existence and the taking out of existence. Therefore, the *meshiya* appertains to the general whereas the *irada* appertains to bringing into existence, as has been mentioned. In other words, that which has been mentioned is the difference between *meshiya* and *irada* resulting from the different facets. Therefore be knowledgeable in this, that from one point of view the reality of both these things is no other than the totality of singularity, and in this respect they are both the same *'ayn* and there is no difference between them, and when they appertain to the bringing into being of something they are both the same thing and there is no difference between them. The Shaykh mentioned this problem in this Wisdom because this chapter includes the Wisdom of Nourishment (*rizq*) and without a doubt concerns the arrival of all the nourishment to all the nourished, and this chapter according to its meaning includes the manner of the arrival of the nourishment.

The Wisdom of the knowledge of the reality of things as they are is what God said concerning Loqman: "We gave wisdom to Loqman and when wisdom (*hikma*) is given, great good is established." That is to say: "Indeed We gave Loqman wisdom," and wisdom is the knowledge of the reality of things as they are. Wisdom is a kind of knowledge and that person to whom wisdom has been given, indeed to him is given great goodness and what greater goodness can happen to one than that he is qualified by the knowledge of things as they are with the Divine Knowledge and that he knows and is *'arif* of everything according to what their reality requires and he places them in their proper place. Loqman is the possessor of great goodness by Divine stipulation (*nass*) by virtue of the fact that God has stood witness that Loqman has been given a great deal of goodness (*khayr*).

Sometimes wisdom happens by verbal reference to wisdom which means that that state gives speech in which case speech in its place becomes wisdom. Sometimes however, wisdom is silence when the state gives silence to it, in which case silence also becomes wisdom in its place, just as Loqman stood in silence instead of questioning David as to what he was making. When he saw David working, he wished to ask David what the thing was he was making, but he kept silent until David had finished what he was doing. Then David put it on and said: "Yes, this is war clothing," and Loqman said: "Yes, the creation (*khalq*) is patience," and David said to Loqman: 'Holding one's peace is wisdom and very few act in this way."

An example of the spoken wisdom (*hikma*) is as follows: Loqman said to his son: "If all the works of men were as small as a mustard seed and that mustard seed was in the middle of the desert or in the Heavens or on the earth somewhere, God, who encompasses all from the heights of Heaven to the depths of the earth, takes account of it." The wisdom contained in this is that Loqman referred to God the taking into account of each grain, and God repeated Loqman's words in His Book and did not say that these words were the words of Loqman who had spoken them, which means that these words are the spoken wisdom because if you know that it is impossible that anything can happen outside of the Knowledge of God which encompasses all the Divine knowledges, then it is necessary that you speak according to that.

Then there is the other silent wisdom and that wisdom becomes known by the association of the state which is exemplified by the fact that Loqman refrained from specifying to whom this seed is given. This keeping silent is exactly the same as the wisdom which has not been spoken in that the meaning can be discerned from the state of the person, just as here Loqman mentioned that God was going to reckon by each grain but did not mention specifically the person to whom each grain belonged. What has become understood from this knowledge by inference is that whoever executes a task either good or bad, he will be recompensed according to that action, but the recompense for the good action is necessarily going to happen whereas the recompense for the bad action may not happen at all if God wills. (He did not say to his son that the mustard seed was specific to him but he took the reckoning by the grain in general, and in this way he made the person for whom the grain is reckoned a general being rather than a specific being by not saying 'for you', or 'for other than you'.)

Participants

There are five students present. Four are participating in the intensive course, which is in its final month. A fifth has completed this before, and is spending time at the School. Two supervisors are present: the Principal and the Housekeeper.

Session[2]

All participants are seated around a table in the designated study room in Chisholme House (shoes have been removed and left outside). One supervisor sits at the head of the table, the other at the foot. A copy of Chapters from the *Fusus al-Hikam*, Part IV is set down before each seat. Drinking water and a bottle of cologne are at the centre of the table, where there is also an English dictionary. Two of the five students have brought notebooks and pens with them, which they use to take notes as the session progresses.

The session begins with the passing around of cologne, from which each student pours a little into their hand to wipe the hands and face. A few moments of silent contemplation follow. It is very quiet: everyone in the house is careful not to cause any disturbance, and the only sound is that made by geese on the lawn. The supervisor designated for the session, seated at the head of the table (on this occasion the Principal of the School, referred to hereafter as 'the first supervisor', as he is responsible for the first part of the session) asks who would like to read. A Belgian student (a woman in her fifties) volunteers, and reads the two long opening paragraphs aloud, while everyone follows in the text. There are a few minutes of silent re-reading and contemplation. Another student (a Scottish man in his forties) consults the English dictionary, while the Belgian consults her own English–Dutch one. Directing her question to the first supervisor, she asks about the sentence: **The Being of the *haqq* which is manifest in the *'ayn-i-thabita* of Man is fed by the determination of the *'ayn-i-thabita*, at the same time *haqq* by Its effulgence of being over Man is its food.** The supervisor suggests that she look at *The Twenty-nine Pages* where, he explains, 'it makes exactly this point. God is our food, because it is through Him that we have existence, and we are His food because it is through us that He is endowed with determinations.' The same student resumes her questioning, asking 'When we are His food, how do we see that He is completely rich beyond need?' (a reference to the sentence: **By virtue of the fact that the Divine Identity (*huwiyya*) is the same as His Ipseity, He is completely rich beyond need (*ghani*) of the universes and of the totality of the Divine Names**). The

---

2 The session lasts for two and a quarter hours, including a half-hour break after the first hour. In what follows, direct quotations from the text are presented in bold.

first supervisor explains, 'In terms of His Ipseity, it is so; but in terms of the Names and Qualities, "He loved to be known".[3] Thus, in this aspect, it is like this; in that aspect, it is like that.' He notes the expression **when or if** (para. 1), pointing out that this is 'a subtle way of putting it.' He continues: 'The *meshiya* is equated with the Ipseity. When it appertains to the *irada* of nourishment, *irada* is a quality.' At this point, the same student asks for the precise meaning of 'to appertain', which another student checks in the dictionary: the sense of 'to relate to' is accepted as most appropriate for the context. The supervisor resumes: 'If we were to say that *meshiya* and *irada* were exactly the same and He inclined towards His nourishment, then it would mean that He is not completely rich beyond need.' He points to the end of the second paragraph, which discusses the distinction between *meshiya* and *irada*, noting that the *irada* necessitates existence: 'it is to do with loving to be known; to be clothed in immanence'. He asks if anyone can 'bring this out'. There is no response from the students, and he suggests that they continue reading the text to the end of the treatment of these issues, through the two following paragraphs.

The Scottish student volunteers to read these paragraphs aloud. When he has finished, there is silent re-reading, until the Belgian student asks whether she has understood the thrust of it by describing what she has grasped, focusing on the notion suggested by the statement that **nourishment is hidden in the nourished**. The first supervisor explains that 'The *a'yan* – our *a'yan* – are fed by His being.' She asks for further clarification by suggesting that there are 'two parts', which the first supervisor helps her to identify. These are, first, 'that we are fed by Him', and second, 'that we are His food'. The first supervisor explains that 'this is the same thing happening but from two different sides, and it happens together'. The student asks 'What if we don't have the will to be fed?' To this the first supervisor responds: 'The *a'yan* do demand and ask, though. Our *a'yan* are asking to be brought into existence.' Hence, he continues, 'the second part doesn't need an action from our side'. The student remains somewhat perplexed. A third student, an Englishman in his early twenties, interjects: 'The nourishment is in fact being or existence.' The first supervisor confirms that the discussion 'is purely to do with bringing into being'; thus, he explains, 'it is not to do with aspects of the relative realm'. Clarifying things further, he emphasises that 'the very nature of the *a'yan* is to demand'.

Returning to his earlier question, the first supervisor then asks if anyone can now bring out the relationship between *meshiya* and *irada*. He explains that, 'according to the Qur'an, God says "When We will for a thing to become we say to it 'Be' and it becomes."' (He refers here to the text: **... *irada* is of the realities of the Names thereby necessitating existence as, for instance, in the Koran the word '*irada*' is used for the case where the non-existent is brought into existence ...**) He continues: 'This is the appertainance of the Will (*meshiya*) to the *irada*. "When We will" is when our *meshiya* appertains to our *irada*. It is a coinciding of the Ipseity and the *irada*. This Will (*irada*) refers only to the bringing into existence. Without the "Be", there is non-existence – like turning off

---

3 A reference to the *hadith qudsi* 'I was a Hidden Treasure'.

the light switch. It is the non-appertainance of the *meshiya* to the *irada*.' At this point, the fourth student, a Dutch man in his mid-twenties, interjects: 'the *irada* is not about non-existence.'

The Belgian student resumes her questioning, focusing now on the sentence: **In short, the intention of 'Arabi is that sometimes *meshiya* appertains … to the Will of increase which is Union, sometimes to the Will of decrease which is non-existence.** The first supervisor explains as follows: '"Union" here is a reference to *tawhid*, the end-stage or goal of existence, as it were. It is an allusion to His saying "When one of Our servants is brought to Me."' He proceeds to suggest that the 'Will of increase' can be understood in relation to a baby, for example, which is not yet complete, but on the way. In contrast, the 'Will of decrease' might be thought of in relation to old age, the journey towards death.

The first supervisor then asks if everyone is clearer 'as to how it is – as to when the *meshiya* and *irada* are the same, and when they are different?' There is no answer. He points the students to the sentence: **Hence the *irada* is the aim (*murad*) of the *meshiya*.** The young Dutch student points out that the root of *irada* and *murad* is the same. The first supervisor explains that the '*murad* (aim) of the *meshiya* is that to which the *meshiya* inclines.' He asks one final time if anyone 'does not see it at all?' He then turns to the Dutch student and asks him how he is doing. At this point, the fifth student (an Israeli woman in her late twenties who has already completed the intensive course) returns to the sentence: **In short, the intention of 'Arabi is that sometimes *meshiya* appertains … to the Will of increase which is Union, sometimes to the Will of decrease which is non-existence.** She remarks 'this is challenging: what Union is meant? Is it Union in the Being of the One? Is it the original Union – which exists even if we do not know or see it, and are veiled from it? Or is it the Union towards which we aspire?'

At this point, the session pauses for a half-hour coffee break. When it resumes, the second supervisor (the Housekeeper, a woman in her early thirties) is now at the head of the table, and takes the lead in supervising, while the first supervisor, who continues to participate and explain as needed, sits at its foot. There are a few minutes of silent contemplation. The Dutch student volunteers to read aloud from the text. He reads out the next four paragraphs. When he has finished and the students have spent some minutes silently re-reading the text, the Belgian student asks, 'Who was Loqman?' The first supervisor responds: 'He was at the time of David. He is renowned for his wisdom, and many sayings are attributed to him – he is the epitome of the sage, and seems to have some association to Aesop: are you familiar with Aesop?' Next the Dutch student interjects: 'I really love this line: **Sometimes however, wisdom is silence when the state gives silence to it, in which case silence also becomes wisdom in its place**'. The second supervisor asks 'Can you say what it means to you?' He replies 'The saying **wisdom is silence** is moving – also **the creation … is patience …** to the end of the line. I don't know: it's just really strong.' The first supervisor turns to him and asks (alluding to the text): 'You do note that *sometimes* wisdom is silence? It is to do with the different facets of wisdom.' The second supervisor comments: 'It reminded me of when the letter was delivered to Bilqis and she did not know where it had come from; this was given as a good way to act.'[4] She continues with the question: 'Can anyone say anything about the line **Yes, the creation (*khalq*) is patience?**' The Belgian student responds: 'It gives me the feeling of waiting to see ... and it is something to do with not thinking until you wait for something to be done, otherwise you just speculate in your mind; you can know only when something has been done and you see.' The second supervisor responds: 'What you say ties in for me with the line about holding one's peace being wisdom: **Holding one's peace is wisdom and very few act in this way.** This means refraining from conjecture.' The Belgian student draws the group's attention to the fact that 'Loqman's words were the word of God, as speech is only according to the principle that all knowledge is God's.' Hence, she continues, 'this is how it is for all the prophets, or this is how the prophets all speak'. At this point, the Scottish student notes that 'patience is one of the five things.'[5] He continues with the observation that 'Loqman did not say anything about the war clothing.' The first supervisor explains: 'the matter of the war clothing is from the chapter on David, the wisdom there being that you can only protect from like with like (from iron with iron, and, hence, "I take refuge from You in You").[6] Loqman may have put the question (about the war clothing) to David explicitly or not. David then said: **Yes, this is war clothing**. It's so cool!' The students smile at his appreciative comment. The first supervisor continues: 'This is separating out the wisdom of David (the wisdom of protecting from like with like) and the wisdom of Loqman, which is the wisdom of silence and speech at the appropriate times.'

At this point, the Israeli student comments on the sentence, **Yes, the creation (*khalq*) is patience**: 'the unfolding of the *khalq* requires patience.' The first supervisor agrees: 'it is being done to, undergoing; it is to let Him reveal what He wants to reveal, and to let it come out.' The Dutch student adds 'there is also an element of trust in this patience.' The Israeli student continues: 'Creation in a sense *begins* with the "*kun*" ("Be"), but keeps on going or unfolding, and thus requires patience.' The first supervisor responds: 'But you *are* patience, that is the nature.'

The conversation moves on with the Dutch student's observation that Loqman *did* speak, 'but he did not spell it out. This is a different kind of wisdom.' The Belgian student remarks that 'the mustard seed is a metaphor of the works of man, good and bad.' She emphasises the principle that **the recompense for the good action is necessarily going to happen whereas the recompense for the bad action may not happen at all if God wills**.

The session draws to a close with the supervisor pointing out that it is time to prepare for meditation.

---

4 A reference to the chapter on Solomon in the *Fusus*: see *The Bezels of Wisdom*, pp. 188–9.
5 A reference to the five qualities stressed on the course: patience, veracity, resolution, certainty and trust.
6 See *The Bezels of Wisdom*, p. 205. The students had recently completed study of Bosnevi's treatment of the chapter on David.

Appendix 4

A Beshara *dhikr*

The Mead Hall at Chisholme House has been cleaned and abluted by burning incense and reciting prayers. Once it has been thus prepared, the door to the Hall is kept closed with a chair placed outside and the stairs leading up to it are out of bounds. Just before 9.30 p.m. the door is opened, as people start to arrive. Shoes are removed and left outside. People enter silently and either sit on one of the chairs or sofas around the perimeter of the space, or kneel on the carpet in a circle, facing inwards, greeting others with a smile. They engage in silent contemplation, most clasping their hands on their laps with eyes closed. Incense is brought in a burner and passed around the Hall for a final time. The door is closed. There are nearly forty participants, men and women. All are wearing fresh clothes, for some the finest they have, and are noticeably well groomed for the occasion. Some still have hair wet from showering.

When the clock in the Hall strikes 9.30 p.m., the leader of the *dhikr*, on this occasion in spring 2004 an Israeli man in his forties carrying a rosary, begins with a single *basmala*. Everyone joins in an extended *Hu*. Those who were seated stand up and join those who are kneeling to perform in unison a single extended prostration, facing the centre of the room. They then rise and return to their seats, while those who were kneeling before return to this position on the carpet. The extended *Hu* is then repeated ten times. Everyone then stands in a single large circle, each with their right arm on the shoulder of the person to their right, their left arm around the waist of the person to their left. Two women remain standing behind the circle. They participate verbally in this and all following sections of the *dhikr*, but do not join physically in the circle or the formations that succeed it.[1] The circle moves with one small step to the right, followed by a gentle forward bow. This accompanies the rhythmic repetition of *Hu Allah* for about five minutes. It then slows gradually and comes to a stop, when it breaks up and participants resume their seats or kneeling positions.

Remaining seated or kneeling, all sway gently forward while repeating *Allah* for another five minutes. This slows to a stop, followed by a few moments' silence. Participants then stand up and, holding hands, form another circle. Swaying to the right and then to the left but without stepping, the gathering repeats *Hayy* (The Ever-Living) for five minutes. They speed up at first and then slow down again, before coming to a halt.[2] Seating and kneeling positions are resumed once more, followed by a few minutes of silent contemplation, during which water and cologne are passed around. Participants take a sip or two of water and pass the

---

1 They were at the time menstruating.
2 A variation described by one participant as the more usual pattern in the Beshara *dhikr* is for the gathering to form into a walking spiral, which folds upon itself while reciting *Hu Allah Hayy Allah*.

glass around; they pour a little cologne onto their hands, rubbing this over their hands and faces and, in some cases, their heads, for refreshment.

The gathering stands once more, forming two facing rows along the length of the space, holding hands. They take two substantial strides forward and two backward, while repeating *Dhu'l-Jalal wa'l-Ikram* (The One who possesses Majesty and Generosity) for about five minutes. The movements are executed with some energy, and the formula uttered emphatically. This slows to a halt, and participants resume their seats or kneel on the carpet as before. A few moments of silent contemplation follow. Remaining thus seated or kneeling, the gathering repeats softly and more slowly the formula *Dhu'l-Jamal wa'l-Ihsan* (The One who possesses Beauty and makes Beautiful) for about five minutes. At the end of this and after a few moments of silent contemplation, all repeat the greeting *salam* for about five minutes, remaining seated or kneeling.[3] This is followed by a single *Hu*, much drawn out and sustained continuously. The leader utters the *basmala* once, then recites *surat* al-Inshirah (Qur'an 94). During the latter, all participants hold their hands in the position characteristic of the Muslim *du'a* or supplication, at chest level or higher, palms open or slightly cupped and facing upwards. When the *sura* draws to a close, they all pass their palms over their heads and downwards over their bodies (and some back up again). They remain seated for a few moments of silent contemplation.

The entire gathering then stands in a single large circle around the perimeter of the space, each with their hands crossed over their chests and placed on their shoulders. In this position, a single extended *Hu* is uttered, over the length of seven breaths. Everyone prostrates again, facing inwards. Thereafter, people resume their seated or kneeling positions and remain in silent contemplation for a few moments. This marks the conclusion of the *dhikr*.[4]

The *dhikr* is deemed to be over by 10.10 p.m., and people begin to leave. Others remain while sweets and fruit platters presented with great beauty are passed around and tea is served in fine china to those who wish to stay and socialise.[5]

---

3 One participant pointed out that an alternative form is for participants to walk in an unfolding spiral while greeting each other with the *salam*. In the context of the form adopted on this particular occasion, she explained, the greeting is understood to be 'to Him', rather than between participants.

4 Young explains that 'no fixed order is prescribed for the leader to follow' in concluding the *dhikr*. It is usual practice to sing the *salawat* in unison before the final *Hu*, often accompanied by the *takbir*, but the *dhikr* leader can decide whether to include these formulae, and whether they are sung aloud collectively or recited by them alone inaudibly on the breath. On this particular occasion, the *dhikr* leader's recitation of the *salawat* was inaudible.

5 Note that it was customary in many Turkish *tariqas* for something sweet to be consumed at the end of a *dhikr* gathering, 'in order to complement the sweetness of invoking the divine name with sweetness of the palate'. See Algar, Food in the Life of the Tekke, p. 299.

Appendix 5

Life stories

Journeys to and within Beshara

The line of questioning pursued in the interviews that issued in these life stories was designed to address indicators and salient themes that fall loosely within two areas. The first of these is pre-conversion; the second focuses on first encounters, joining and remaining.

Pre-conversion

The aim here was to explore the religious milieu and socioeconomic status of associates' families, and their own educational backgrounds. We probed pre-conversion psychological states, with particular attention to a possible sense of alienation from the surrounding society and culture, general trauma (due to family problems or deep childhood difficulties, for example), specific trauma (a significant emotional shock, for example), depression, or a sense of mean-inglessness.[1] We also gave attention to the possible use of mind-altering drugs (particularly for interviewees who were part of the sixties counterculture), and involvement with other NRMs or alternative spiritualities en route to Beshara.

First encounters, joining and remaining

In this area we examined watershed experiences during the first encounter with Beshara, exploring how and when a conviction to remain involved became estab-lished. We attempted to evaluate the nature of the developing relationship with the movement in terms of its impact on an associate's links with family and the wider society and on their psychological state, and in terms of their early experi-ences of the movement as community.[2] We gave specific attention to first and continuing encounters with Rauf as the movement's guiding figure.

Selecting and constructing life stories

The texts below were constructed from interviews during which associates talked freely. Occasionally they reflected upon their pasts from a characteristi-cally teleological perspective, and we have retained such asides for what they reveal in the way of their understandings of the journeys described, separating

---

1 The crisis engendered by a specific traumatic event or by general emotional turmoil and personal distress can give rise to cognitive concerns that are then answered by the new worldview embraced: cf. Kose, *Conversion to Islam*, p. 83, and Levine, The Joiners.
2 Psychological benefits of conversion encompass conflict resolution and identity forma-tion, in addition to involvement with a new 'family' that provides companionship and a sense of belonging. Cf. Kose, *Conversion to Islam*, p. 194; Beit-Hallahmi, 'The *Varieties* as an Inspiration'; Levine, The Joiners.

them into square brackets wherever they cut into the narrative. In constructing these texts, we kept editorial intervention to an absolute minimum, in order to retain both the letter and spirit of their authors' narratives. We then returned the texts to them for approval. Some made no changes, but others introduced substantial rephrasing and made certain additions. Such revisions of the spontaneous narrative often resulted from explicit sensitivities concerning privacy, but an element of self-censorship linked to potential peer perceptions was also evident. Consequently, the narratives below represent a synthesis of a spontaneous and free retelling of the journeys in question, and the outcome of a more self-conscious reflection on the narratives thus constructed.

While we do not claim that these life stories are representative of associates in general, we have nonetheless endeavoured to encompass first-generation and younger associates, to reflect widely differing backgrounds and contrasting experiences on encountering the movement, and to include both men and women. Story 4 describes a somewhat critical perspective on aspects of the movement. While its subject positions his own story within (his understanding of) Beshara, based on his views and conduct some associates consider him a maverick or renegade. His story illustrates an internal challenge to coherence and continuity in the movement.

Story 1

I was born in Israel in 1950 to a middle-class family. My father, who worked as a civil servant, was born there too; my mother was born in Turkey. For our family, religion was more a matter of tradition than spiritual endeavour. I studied mechanical engineering in Haifa for four years, and graduated in 1972 when I was twenty-two years old. During my last year at university, I was very much attracted to the 'hippy' culture that had begun to arrive in Israel with the influx of Western Jewish volunteers after the 1967 war. (It was a diluted version of its American–European counterpart.) During these years, I had begun to feel alienated from Israeli culture and social norms, particularly the materialism, to which I could not relate. I also dreaded the prospect of the military service awaiting me, being certain it would kill all aspirations and non-materialistic values.

I joined the military in November 1972. This launched a very significant episode in my life that would last in all for over four years. I was sent to a field unit for my compulsory three years (I had turned down the option of working as an engineer in the army, because that would have meant an initial commitment of five instead of three years). I was commissioned as an officer in August 1973. During the October war, I served at the Egyptian front. This dealt a massive blow to my idealistic hippy notions of unilateral peace, as I saw that self-defence is sometimes necessary ... the whole experience shook me up.

Because of this, at the end of my term I re-enlisted for another eighteen months. I served in the Golan. [In fact, I was stationed only forty kilometres from the tomb of the Shaykh al-Akbar, although there were three Syrian divisions between us. Once, on a clear day, I actually saw Damascus from Mount Hermon.] During the last year of my service, I became increasingly aware that, as a person, I was very unhappy. A certain fear that the 'officer' was taking over from the person troubled me ... I was afraid I was losing myself in the role. Once, during a leave at home, I heard myself speaking to my mother with the voice of the officer, not her son. I also realised that love was missing in my life, and that my failed relationships were a vain attempt to fill this gap.

Towards the end of my service, a lot of pressure was put on me to continue with a promising military career. However, the conviction that there was more to life than a career led me to leave at the end of my term. I travelled to England the very next day in the hope of rekindling a relationship with a woman I had met before my military service. Three days of emotional reunion sufficed to prove this hope imaginary. In order to save face, I decided to stay in England for a while before returning home. I began hitchhiking rather aimlessly.

During my travels, I happened across a person who took me to visit these two 'communes' in Gloucestershire that turned out to be Swyre Farm and Sherborne House. Entering the former, noticing the Arabic inscriptions on the walls caused me both surprise and discomfort, having associated this alphabet with the 'enemy' for many years. My consternation increased further to learn that the people there had Arabic names. I did not manage to form a clear idea of what the place was about, and left with the vague notion that these were a bunch of nice hippies who were trying to become self-sufficient. However, someone whom I met there did invite me to come to stay at Chisholme.

Having made up my mind to visit Chisholme, I made my way northwards very slowly. When I arrived there, the door was opened by a young man, who exclaimed 'Oh, you have come to do the course!', which was a complete surprise to me, since it was the first time I had heard that there were such things as courses at Beshara. However, by the time the introductory course was due to start, I decided to join in, both for the 'experience', and due to the nascent interest evoked by the study and the conversations I had with people there (some of whom were very articulate). I found the meditation odd and the *dhikr* difficult, particularly due to the use of the Arabic names of God. However, I loved *The Twenty-nine Pages*, and I took to it like a fish to water. The study gave me the tools to contemplate questions that had been with me for most of my adult life but which, in the absence of such tools, I had been able to disregard. I had read some types of philosophy and Greek mythology, in relation to these questions, but that did not get me far. The teachings that were presented to me at Chisholme, which sprung from the well of sufism (of which I had never heard before), were of a different level altogether. While my attitude may have been sceptical and even cynical at times, internally I was deeply affected by the course, even though it was only of fourteen days' duration. During this course, we would supplement the diet with rabbits we would snare on the estate. One evening, the person in charge of the kitchen, whom I liked immensely, asked me to go and check the snares, since, to her grave concern, we appeared to be short of a rabbit for dinner. All the snares proved to be empty and, remembering the concern of the cook, I asked for help. And so, as I approached the last snare, my movement disturbed a rabbit, which was hiding in the bracken: it ran straight into the snare. This was the first time I had prayed consciously since childhood.

Towards the end of the course, Bulent arrived unexpectedly at Chisholme. There was much anticipation at seeing him, and I was very curious. He came to tea, which had been set out in the dining room. The moment he walked into the room his presence, which I mistook for personal charisma, was palpable, but in contrast with the types of charisma I had encountered in the military, I found this one to be deeply moving (although I did not see it as clearly at the time).

Bulent also attended the last study session of the course. Everyone went quiet in his presence. But I was determined not to be overawed, so, in response to the last paragraph of *The Twenty-nine Pages* we had just read, I said: 'To accept the Unity of Being as a concept is easy: the difficult matter is to include yourself in it.' For the sake of accuracy, I have to add that I was clueless as to how profound that statement really was. At the end of the session, Bulent indicated that I should approach him, and asked for my name. When I answered, he said: 'Do you know, P, that you are a very urgent case?' I would say that this was an important turning point for me, since I realised that the search for meaning had been central to my life, and that I was now being presented with an opportunity to pursue it. Nonetheless, there was a struggle between my head and my heart, and when I spoke to Bulent about this, he invited me to join the eight-month course at Sherborne House, to find out for myself. I wrote to my father and explained that I had come across a 'spiritual course' that I wanted to attend, and asked for his blessing, which he gave. The course started on 1 September 1977, four months after I had left the Golan.

When I accepted the invitation, I declared to Bulent with remarkable confidence: 'I will come and find the flaw in this teaching.' However, he seemed completely unfazed and just smiled. I believe he was not just amused by the statement, but also pleased to see that my intention was to engage with the study critically. As the course progressed, the more I studied, the more my attitude changed. I began to like the meditation and the *dhikr*, and within about three months my reservations concerning the use of Arabic and the Islamic roots of the teaching fell away. I found many kindred spirits on the course, people who were preoccupied with the same questions (in fact I met my future wife on the first day of it).

Due to my concern for my parents, whose boy had vanished without trace in the wilds of Gloucestershire, I was given permission to visit them after our Turkey trip in December. It was a challenge to communicate the new ideas I had encountered in my native tongue: however, my impression was that they were both pleased for me. I even suspected, for the first time, that my father understood the kind of questioning that had prompted me to attend the course. Later, my mother admitted that she knew I had found my place, even though she would have preferred me to be near her.

I did the second course at Chisholme in 1978, and then went on to supervise on the courses at Sherborne and then Chisholme. In early 1984, Bulent told me it was time I went out into the world: Beshara is not a commune; it is a school. He explained that I had to learn about how God works in the world. I found it difficult, because I did not want to be anywhere else. So I moved to the world, where my connection to the School has continued to provide a strong focal point for the search. Since then, as my professional career progressed from the printing industry to IT, Bulent's injunction has been central to my life, for the true seeker, as he never tired of reminding us, 'is he who is in the world and not of it.'

Story 2

I was born in the south of England in 1948 to a middle-class family of Scottish extraction. My father was an engineer who worked as a regional controller for the Gas Board. I was the youngest of three children in a not very close or communicative family. I was regarded as the black sheep, possibly because I was perceived as outspoken and rebellious compared with my brother and sister, with whom I shared little in common. Religion did not play a large part throughout my upbringing, figuring only in its outer forms, and on the occasions of births, marriages and deaths. I always suspected our home was not an especially happy one in comparison with friends, and my family was rather undemonstrative in terms of emotions. I remember that when I was perhaps eight up until I was about eleven, we lived near a Baptist Church. I would go there by myself, and became quite heavily involved: I was searching for something that was missing from my home and family environment.

I remember coming out of my childhood seeking to find an expression of love, because this had been so lacking in my experience. I did not finish my A levels, but left school at the age of sixteen or seventeen, and moved away more or less immediately. Education had been undervalued in my home, so I found myself doing a secretarial course. I moved to London to work, saving up to try and broaden my horizons by travelling. When I had earned enough, I moved to Montreal, Canada. By this time, I was twenty and happy with this new-found independence. Over the next eighteen months, I met some interesting people there, and it was a time of exploring new ideas and perspectives on life; most of my friends were students and artists. I remember reading a lot, especially Günter Grass, Albert Camus, Jean-Paul Sartre and others. I was attracted to these because they awakened in me a thirst for new ideas, and were a means of trying to reach into a different level of life, new dimensions and new openings, other than those I had so far experienced. I guess I was still searching, and I felt the need to delve deeper into things. It was during this time that I had my first encounter with marijuana, a very new and liberating experience, although part of me was very diffident about it.

After returning to England for three months, I then moved to Paris, where I lived and worked for the next two years. Once again, I was mixing with students and loving the vibrancy and novelty of living in a different culture, seeing and experiencing things that were completely different from what I had been brought up with. I felt the need for something broader. Yet there was always a (perhaps unconscious) searching for something deeper and for more connection with another side of me, which found expression in some of the close relationships I had during this period. From Paris I moved to Germany, where I spent another two years. Without any clear sense of direction I finally returned to England because my father was ill (he later died). I was now twenty-five and beginning to realise that without some kind of further education my horizons would remain limited. I pulled together a portfolio and was offered a place at Art College in North London, completing the foundation course and the first year of a degree course in interior design. Working briefly with a group of architects in London during the summer of 1976, I met X, who introduced me to Beshara. Hearing about Beshara was like finding the key to the door I had had glimpses of, but could never quite reach to the threshold. This drew together the unconnectedness I had for so long been experiencing. It brought clarity and focus to so many unexpressed (yet nonetheless formulated) questions about the meaning of life, especially because of (or since) the death of my father. I had been struck by the futility of a life so conscientiously spent in providing a secure home and nurturing environment for his family, but without engendering any sense of joy or wonderment in doing it.

During this tumultuous period, X and I fell in love with each other. [Looking back, I realise that this was also the awakening of the love affair with the Unity of Existence.] Although I was still reading a lot during these years, especially now the work of Krishnamurti, my search was, as it were, 'on hold', and I had never actively looked for any group to join. I had planned to go to Greece for a holiday for a few weeks, and X gave me a copy of *The Twenty-nine Pages* to take with me to read. I managed to read only the first three pages, but I found something very compelling about it: it was like this was all I ever needed to know, the bare bones as it were, of life itself – and I was completely drawn into it. I knew that I had to do the course X had already arranged to do, and I returned with that intention. I knew I could cover the fees because my father had left me some money. I felt that there was something so compelling in what I had been introduced to through X that there was no question of refusing. We visited Swyre Farm twice during August and September. On the first visit, I found it all very new, especially the idea of being involved with a group. [When I looked back on this later, I was very grateful that I had not had exposure to other groups and had been brought into contact with what I consider to be the 'heart of the matter', although I did not realise it at the time.] The second visit to Swyre Farm was to discuss the possibility of joining the course. I was given an application form to fill out. It was about two weeks before the course was due to begin. I was introduced briefly to Bulent, who was visiting for the weekend, and was interested to see who was joining the course. I was very much in awe at meeting someone, complete with entourage, who clearly had such an aura about him. I was also very shy. I continued to feel overawed in front of him for a long time.

When I was accepted for the course, I told my mother, who was horrified. She was very upset and convinced that I was getting involved in a sect. I told her that, as far as I was concerned, there was no doubt about it because it was a *bona fide* organisation. It was difficult for her because she had recently lost her husband, and there I was adding to her problems. She contacted an old and well-trusted Muslim friend of the family, who had been especially close to my father and had taken it upon himself to look out for us after his untimely death. She asked him to find out what he could about Beshara. He did some searching, and was able to reassure her that it was a *bona fide* thing. There were so many groups around in 1976, many of which had earned a negative press: this gave rise to my mother's concerns. She could not understand why I should want to do something like this, perhaps because she herself had no strong religious faith. She even threatened to disinherit me, although her views eventually softened.

X and I both began the course on 1 October 1976. We had by now become engaged to each other. I found aspects of the course very hard work, especially the study days, and I would look forward to the work days. To this day, I find it very difficult to talk about Ibn 'Arabi and his work in a study situation, but at the same time, I get a huge amount from reading the text. This has a lot to do with the way the study sessions are organised. In the early days, there was so much discussion: the aim was to bring things out, so that there would be clarification. For me, the discussion was distracting attention from the text itself. I had not been to university and this was the first time I was studying anything in depth. I felt I could reach into the text in a way that I could understand it, without a lot of the distraction in what was being said about it. For me, the reading is intensely personal; why voice it? I do realise that some people are very articulate and can add much to a group situation. Bulent, for example, used to pare it down to the most simple. I always held on to the simplicity. I found the rest of it too complicated and confusing. It was not so much through study (especially in those early days) that my heart became involved (although study at the right pitch certainly enhances this), but through the *dhikr*, the meditation and work – 'service'. At times, I found the study off-putting, as I had such difficulties with the text and the study situation. Some days, the text was completely inaccessible to me, probably because of my personal state. Yet, there was never a time when I could have turned my back on it. Initially the whole notion of *dhikr* had taken me by surprise: I found it very strange to begin with, but the meditation was always easier because it was effectively a solitary activity. I also felt more at ease with some people than with others on the course: that year it was a large group of over fifty people. Yet I was aware that we had all been brought together there by our love for what we were involved in.

A dream I had during the fourth month of the course stands out strikingly in my memory. I dreamt of my father who, in the company of a fellow student, said to me: 'You are in union.' I did not really grasp the implications of his words at the time, but they were to continue to reassure me of what I knew within to be true, however confused or doubting my passing states might cause me to be. This eased much of the feelings of difficulty during that first course. (My father appearing in the dream was such a contrast with my mother's continuing perception of Beshara as weird: only towards the end of her life – she died in 1993 – did she concede that it had been a good thing for me.) After that, I became thoroughly immersed in the course. It was such a powerful feeling, and I was so single-mindedly involved, that X became somewhat marginal for me, and by the time the course ended, we had drifted apart. As we neared the end of the course, I knew that I very much wanted to maintain communication with what was going on in Beshara. I was quite apprehensive of how it would be outside of the very protected course environment.

Having heard so much about Chisholme over the preceding six months, within a few weeks I went there to fill the time until the end of the summer, when I was due to resume my art course. Although I rejoined the course, I felt that my interest was now elsewhere, and it no longer held my attention. So I gave it up. In late 1977, I went to Swyre Farm, where I met an American, Y, who had done the first long course at Chisholme and was staying at Swyre Farm for a couple of months. We made an immediate connection and he invited me to visit him in Berkeley, California, where he had recently started up a Beshara centre with others who were also involved. I visited during the summer, and became immersed in the centre, which Y was running full-time (he was also a trained engineer, but had not pursued his career since he became involved in Beshara). The centre ran weekend courses, organised talks, etc. By the time I was due to return to England, we discovered I was pregnant.

Y came to Chisholme to do the first advanced course in the autumn of 1978, and we were married just before his course began. While he was on the Chisholme course, I served as secretary on the Sherborne House course. After the birth of our daughter in spring 1979, we returned to Berkeley to help run the Beshara centre, where we continued to live for a time, and Y did some part-time construction work. Our lives were very busy with our baby, the life of the centre, and trying to earn and save enough money for me to do the second course at Chisholme. In September 1981, we returned to the UK. While Y ran the Nursery there, I did the course. Expecting our second child the following summer, this was not an easy period for me: my hormones were raging and I was constantly having to confront my own inadequacies and shortcomings. At the end of the course, we did not know where to settle: whether to stay in the UK, or return to Berkeley, so we asked Bulent to consult for us regarding where we should go. The outcome was that we should go to Atlanta, where Y's parents lived. At the time, we did not understand why, but we accepted to go anyway, believing the reason would become clear. As it transpired, Y rapidly started losing weight and, in spite of numerous tests, he collapsed and died very suddenly in February 1983, when our second child was just six months old. In a stroke, it became very clear why we had been sent to Atlanta.

I returned to the UK in May and before long to Chisholme, where I spent the next six months or so running the Nursery. This was an intensely sad and dislocated period of my life: I couldn't imagine being anywhere else and yet I felt completely isolated and, once again, lost in terms of my sense of direction and goal. Chisholme always had the ability to cut through to the essentials: leaving one to the depths of oneself, until it became so obvious that the only outcome along that path was a dead-end. The only way was up, so to speak. I decided that it was time to do the course again, as so much had changed for me since I had done it first time round. I felt I needed to go through the material again: I needed not only the reassurance, but to go through it in the knowledge and certainty that there is nothing in existence other than God. In a way, the courses allowed one to act in spite of oneself, because the environment is so all-inclusive and all-embracing. I think that somehow, first time round, doubt had entered into my experience at some level. This time, it was a period of complete certitude and desire to conform to my growing understanding of servanthood. The certitude was that there is nothing other than the wonderful gift of knowledge that we are offered through the teachings of the Shaykh and that it is up to each person as to how he or she chooses to embrace it. The extraordinary mercy of the environment gave me a lot of security in what would otherwise have been a very insecure period. I did the second course straight after the first. The need for me to do these courses was prompted by the fundamental change in my life resulting from Y's death. I could frame his departure in the context of what we studied: I could understand and accept his death as a part of the order. That was when I really grew up.

I left Chisholme in 1985 and made a home for my family in the south of England, but continued to return over the years for reading weeks and other short courses. At the end of 2000, just after I had turned fifty, I became conscious that a very important part of who I am was somehow unfulfilled. My children were close to 'flying the nest' and the future seemed quite bleak, in spite of feeling at ease and happier within myself than I had for years. I began actively searching and asking for another dimension. At about the same time, X had split up from his wife of eighteen years and we established contact again after twenty-five years, with intermittent sightings in the interim. Perhaps this was the answer to an unformed prayer, although I had not known fully for what I had yearned. After many uncertainties, X and I were finally married recently, twenty-eight years after the engagement we never quite managed to break off. I now feel that I have grown up in Beshara, and I am content and at ease in it.

Story 3

I was born in 1980. My father worked as a teacher, and my brothers and I were privileged to attend a private school. Even from before I was born, my parents were involved in Beshara. It was a natural part of my family life. I remember being conscious of the *dhikr* from a very young age: it was very normal for me, because that was what my parents did. I used to sit on the couches at the side during the *dhikr* whenever we visited Chisholme. I also remember my mother saying prayers in Arabic over me while I was going to sleep if I had been distressed by something. That used to comfort me a lot. I thought it was normal to have Arabic calligraphies on the wall: that was what I had seen around me from a very early age. We would visit Chisholme a few times a year as a family. I also visited with friends. I remember when I was ten or eleven, I stopped going to the *dhikr* when I was there: I did not seem to have a strong reason to go.

As a teenager, I went to Chisholme a lot, especially during the summers. It was a cool place to be with friends: there were several teenagers there, the children of people who were living at Chisholme. I did not pay much attention to the Esoteric School side of things. In fact, I was almost completely unaware of it. When I was fourteen, I spent a whole summer there. At that time, the teenagers were building tree houses up by the Monument as a 'secret' place to go and smoke cannabis. It was their way of rebelling, because there is a certain kind of strictness there, in terms of how it is run. It was natural to rebel as teenagers, and there was nowhere else to go. For the five or six teenagers living there, this was a way of escaping and entertaining themselves. Everyone knew about it and they were mostly cool about it. The Principal knew too, and although he disapproved, he let it take its course, and it stopped after a few years as those involved grew out of it.

I remember participating in the first major tree planting (there was an initiative to re-forest the area surrounding Chisholme), which took place for two weeks in 1997 and again in 1998. Many young people were invited to take part. It was an extraordinary experience, not just for me: many felt the power of it. It was at that time, when I was seventeen, that I began to realise the importance of the place distinct from my childhood, and my experience of it as a cool place to hang out with friends (we were still smoking cannabis in the tree houses at that time).

This was also partly because I had begun to talk a lot to the adults there. (I had grown up with many adults around, so I felt very comfortable talking to them.) The tree-planting weeks I spent at Chisholme contributed to my growing up.

I was quite unhappy at school: I felt it was a pressurised environment. I only smoked cannabis on and off there, because I never had the money to buy it. I did only the minimum required in order to achieve the A-level grades I needed for university. I took a gap year and started my first job after a couple of weeks at a hotel with very high standards. It was very demanding. My workmates were all a few years older, and I made a new circle of friends. We would have interesting conversations, meeting up after work to smoke together. I remember one of them introducing me to Ben Harper, an American singer whose work was utterly different from anything I had ever heard: each song had a different taste, but they were all tied together by his voice. The lyrics were also completely expansive. I felt in this new circle of friends that I had leaped at least three years forward, and I would feel the difference when I met with my old school friends. I spent May to August 1999 travelling in the USA. This was the first time I had been on my own, and it opened my eyes, making me grow up even faster.

In the autumn of 1999, I started a degree in Turkish at Manchester. I had decided to study Turkish a long time ago. When I was thirteen, I spent three weeks travelling in Turkey with my father. We had visited Istanbul and I really loved the country and the people. We visited the saints: I remember my first visit to Aziz Mahmud Hüdayi at the time. [Looking back, I think that being there had unlocked something.] From then on, I decided to study Turkish (I had always wanted to study languages). During the first term at university, I had to make two presentations, and on each occasion, I chose to do something about sufism: I was already interested in this and somehow inclined towards it. However, I was unhappy in Manchester. It felt as though I was in the midst of 'teenagers': for them, being at university was all about leaving home and having a good time. I felt I had already done all of that. I had gone there to study something I love, but I felt I did not get it from the Department. I just buried myself in cannabis and tried to forget the situation.

During a conversation with my mother, who was at Chisholme at the time, she suggested I attend two days of a nine-day course that was about to start, over a weekend. I decided to do this. I remember the study during that weekend (and it has been like this every time I have done study). It 'punctured' something. It was (and always is) very enlivening, inducing a sense of 'wow!' It was something very direct (revealing something that otherwise becomes covered up very easily). Each time I have engaged in study, it has been a matter of complete simplicity: what I read contained a perspective that was very clear and without colour – the perspective of the Unity of Existence. Even the physical sheet of paper with the text on it had the feeling of something so simple: there was no agenda, and it was not dressed up in any way. There was no 'cleverness' in it, and yet it was the most intelligent thing I have ever read.

The study was a kind of reminder of what I loved – without me necessarily knowing this – and an implicit comparison with how I was living, as something much better. Consequently, when I returned to Manchester, I was even less happy than before. I decided that I would leave Manchester. I went to Chisholme with my family for the New Year celebrations (it was the Millennium). I told several people at Chisholme about my thoughts of leaving Manchester: most said that I should follow my heart. The whole time was very much one of questioning. I even wrote down a whole series of questions: I was questioning the very fabric of my existence. It was quite basic (for example: 'Why is the sky blue?'), but very important, because I had been brought to a point where I was so unhappy that I was questioning everything. A few days after New Year, I went to the *dhikr* to mark the Night of Power. This was the first time I had been to *dhikr* for several years, and it was my own choice. I also remember that my elder brother was doing the first long course at that time, and I noticed that he had changed and become distant and serious. We were not getting on very well, although we had been very close before he started the course.

I told my parents after New Year that I wanted to leave university, and they suggested I complete the year. I was upset because I believed I should leave straight away, but I went ahead and completed the year. I had made friends with M, who was studying Arabic, and his girlfriend. He was also seeking something, and I felt I had found a kindred spirit in him, which made things a bit better. (He later joined the Naqshbandiyya of Shaykh Nazim.) Although the experience was a little more positive, I found it difficult to motivate myself for the course, which felt dead to me. Towards the end of the academic year, I had begun smoking cannabis again, as did M. At the end of the year, I worked a while and then spent a week in Ireland with friends. During that week, I got the news from my mother that she and my father had separated. It was quite a shock, as I only found out when I called home. Up to that point, I had been planning to return to Manchester, and I had arranged somewhere to live with M and his girlfriend. However, something in the nature of my parents' separation as I experienced it was to do with looking deeper within me. Finding out that their problems were long-standing made things clearer. I looked more deeply at my own situation and decided that I wanted to study in my own way, and that I felt restricted by being in university and being governed by other people's thoughts of how we should study. I realised that the only positive thing for me about being in Manchester was M, and that I wanted to be free, and felt I was being constricted there.

During the week in Ireland, I also fell in love with my best friend's girlfriend. She was the only person who could help me with my family situation, by listening, but I then reacted very badly to seeing her with my best friend. She finally left him and we got together. In September 2000, I went to Chisholme for a week, and stayed for a month helping to construct the retreat building. I worked down south a bit, because my girlfriend was there, and then we split with each other at New Year. I stayed at Chisholme for four or five months doing building work on the retreat building again in early 2001. It was a very difficult and painful time: it is never easy being at Chisholme, because if anything is not right with you it comes out very strongly there. I did not go much to *dhikr* or meditation, but I sat in on study sometimes. I was preoccupied with questions of meaning, God, and the like. I also felt that I was in a black ocean, in the sense that I had come out of a very structured life into the unknown. In fact, the next two years were about dealing with the unknown, and I did not know what I wanted to do. It was a period of wanting and trying to find my place. I moved around a lot:

Edinburgh, Oxford, Chisholme. It was all about finding a place. Each place I was in, I realised that a part of my life was not there (a girlfriend living elsewhere, for example), or that part of me was somehow elsewhere. Consequently, I could never really settle. All the physical relocations were born out of something in me saying, 'Where am I?', and 'Who am I?' I was searching. In December 2001, my father offered to cover the costs for me to go on the Turkey trip. On the first day, we visited Aziz Mahmud Hüdayi (this was the first time I had been back since I was thirteen). I came out in floods of tears. There was a strong sentiment of love, but it manifested in a sense of grief. It was like finding somewhere. It was profoundly moving, but the impact soon passed, and I moved on. In April 2002, I trained as a teacher of English as a foreign language. (I had always been interested in languages, and I thought I might go to Turkey to work there.) The rest of the year I worked.

In January 2003, I went with M and his girlfriend to Turkey. For the first part of the trip, I showed them around Istanbul, Ephesus, etc. Then I went with them to Lefke in Turkish Cyprus, where Shaykh Nazim lives. I wanted to find out about M's experience and why he had chosen the Naqshbandi way, because I thought he was very much of Beshara. It was a difficult ten days, because I was for the first time thrust into something that was a strong contrast with my experience of spirituality in Beshara (which was all I really knew), and something completely different in taste. There was a series of 'tests'. There was *salat*, a sermon every afternoon, and *dhikr* every night. I went to everything at the beginning, but I felt very uncomfortable because everyone was asking me if I was Muslim or going to become Muslim. At the end of the *dhikr* everyone would kiss the shaykh's hand (or foot). One night a man came up to me (I think he was Croatian) and said 'Come and kiss the shaykh's hand.' I explained that I just wanted to remain sitting, but he said that, if I did not kiss the shaykh's hand, I would be his enemy. I was very upset at this, because I felt it was profoundly tactless in the context of their *dhikr*, at which I was a willing guest. I thought to myself that if he had known what he was talking about, he would not have said what he did. I could not help but contrast the whole situation with Chisholme. There was the pressure about whether I was a Muslim, but there was also the general state of the place, which left a lot to be desired. (I appreciated M's argument that the people surrounding the shaykh – there were around twenty living there – were those who needed him most.) I remember slipping on the kitchen floor and being scalded by the water we had boiled to clean it up with, when the pot fell on me. (The kitchen was not in good shape – there was three or four days' washing-up there.) I thought that was highly symbolic. I also felt that the numerous army barracks and boundaries nearby symbolised my own feelings of being hemmed in.

The contrast with Beshara was striking: there was no physical teacher, no shaykh and *murid*. Here, they were hanging on the shaykh's every word. I could understand why they were so reverential, but there did not appear to be any encouragement of the personal search, which hinges on dependence on God. There was a lot of dependence, but it was on the shaykh. There was also little discourse, compared with the focus on study in Beshara. The contrast was so strong that it helped to clarify things for me with regard to Beshara, and very much affirmed that Beshara was for me. It made me aware of things I had not been aware of before concerning Beshara, and why things are how they are there. I had wanted to experience something other than Beshara, and that was why I had gone with M to Lefke.

When I returned to the UK, I worked for a while and then I decided to go to Spain. I was searching for a blank canvas; running away. I still wanted to experience things differently and to be away from everyone I knew, to try and get clarity concerning where I was going. After working for a while I was alone in Barcelona for a few weeks, and felt very uncomfortable: I could barely be with myself. I received an email telling me about the gathering at Chisholme in August 2003, and I immediately knew I wanted to go. My parents helped fund the ticket and I felt reunited with friends, but also with something else. I did the nine-day course in September, and then returned to Spain to bring my things back home. I did not actually decide anything. Rather, at some point, the thought had come that I should do the first long course. I had no control over it. Something from inside me said 'Do the course.' [Later, during the long course, we studied a short piece from Osman Fazli that describes thoughts as 'our messengers from Heaven.' I can understand this experience in light of that. I also believe that something was planted well before, and that I had had a sense for a long time that I would do the long course.] The purpose of the nine-day course is to put you under the order of the long course to a certain degree, because it has a similar rhythm to it. For me, it did not change anything either way: I still felt I had to do the long course. I consulted through the Principal to confirm this, and it came out very strongly as 'yes.'

Although I had read parts of *The Twenty-nine Pages* before while at Chisholme, I did not get it at all, and was very frustrated with the difficult language. On the long course, it completely 'opened up' for me. In fact, the whole course was punctuated for me by moments of clarity (but there were no profound direct intuitions). It was as a whole very open, light and liberating. I always struggled with the meditation, because thoughts kept coming up. We were not given any guidance concerning it (there was no mantra or anything), and I found it difficult throughout, feeling a bit unsure of what to do, but I learned to love it. I loved saying the Names in the *dhikr* and *wazifas*, although a lot of the *dhikr* was quite difficult. I learned to let go of thinking it should be in a certain way.

There were four of us on the course, and we were all very different, which I think was a great blessing. On some occasions, one student would intellectu-alise about what we were studying: on others, they might burst into tears, if they were affected very deeply by something. One student simply felt the blessing of being on the course, without it being a rational thing at all: for them, it was to do with having found an answer. The most important thing we were told about reading, say, the *Fusus*, was that it would be completely locked to us if we did not prepare in the proper way, by having the correct intention, viz., by understanding our dependence, our total servanthood. You are not looking for God on the course; rather you are putting yourself into a position to witness His Self-Revelation. Deflection from allowing the meaning of the text to appear during study (for example, by intellectualising) was a natural thing, because we are all rough-hewn stones, but some days the meaning would be there for all of us, and it was extraordinary. We would feel very light and joyous.

Up until quite close to the end of the course, I thought there might be a great spiritual experience or the unveiling of a great spiritual mystery, something profound and experiential. I gave that up during the *wazifa* course of the last six weeks of the long course, as we began to repeat *Allah* 10,000, 15,000 and 20,000 times. Sometimes it would just flow, with complete ease, like running downhill. At other times, it would be very difficult, and you physically could not do it. On the final night, when we all came together to repeat it 21,000 times, it was very easy, and you felt you could have gone on forever. We were told that that was where you can find the place aimed at by the prescription of the *wazifas*. I remember being completely conscious throughout. Instead of waiting for a great spiritual experience, I now appreciate that is not what it is about. It is in fact about hard slog, and appreciating and understanding what you see.

At the end of the course I think it was like wearing rose-tinted glasses, thinking life would be wonderful. I was on a high about leaving Chisholme, because the course had been difficult. I was happy about the prospect of starting a new life. I first moved to Edinburgh, and even walking down the street was difficult. I practised the three *wazifas* we were given to help us with reintegrating until I felt I did not need them anymore. I still practise the five other *wazifas* that are for general use. Although I need some distance from the School now and my aim is to become established in the world, I intend to do the second course. I met my current girlfriend on the course: she had done it the year before, and was working in the kitchen. Relationships do form on the courses, but the physical aspect is discouraged, because it is distracting. I think our relationship is different from previous ones I have experienced: in previous relationships, if a crisis or difficulty came up, a profound difference of perspective would come out, leading to a break-up. With my current girlfriend, there is a sense of something else. We are on the same 'wavelength'; we have a shared perspective and so we understand each other better.

I had many role models as I was growing up, in the people of Beshara, especially my parents' friends. I remember thinking to myself, 'There must be something good about this study and this place, because these people are extraordinary in their warmth and generosity, they are very interesting, and it is a great ease to be with them and at Chisholme.' (This was in contrast with my friends' parents, for example.) I have worn the *Hizb* (*al-wiqaya*) all my life, and at school people would ask about it, but I usually shrugged it off. I knew it was prayers. Throughout my life as I was growing up there were questions about Beshara and Chisholme, because these were so central to my parents. It was difficult to know what to say in response, but now I understand. As we ended the course, the Principal advised us to respond to questions in accordance with good tact and not to be open if the invitation is not there. Thus, with some people you can be open, while with others you should be a bit careful.

Story 4

I was born in England in 1949. My father was an aeronautical engineer from a middle-class family who had his own company, which folded just before the Second World War. He was from an Anglican background, but never imposed any religious belief on me. My mother was from the Polish gentry and nominally Catholic. Her father, who was immensely rich, had sent her to England in 1939. (Her family members were all killed in the War, their property nationalised by the socialists in its aftermath.) After the War, my father taught himself accountancy, and became a management consultant specialising in colonial government and big colonial businesses. Consequently, we travelled a lot, and I lived abroad from the age of five, being sent back to England to boarding school from the ages of eight to eighteen. This meant that 'home' was a place I passed through, rather than one in which I stayed. I was an only child, as was my father, and effectively my mother, and I still find it difficult to understand the notion of 'family'. I was not lonely as a child; I read a lot, particularly histories and the psychology of heroes and warriors. I was quite shy, and while never fitting into institutions I rarely sought to rebel against them; but having been moved around from place to place, I had learned to accept things as they came to me. I did well at school: I was reasonably bright and sporty, which in the system at the time more or less guaranteed compatibility. My first sense of the transcendent came through the paintings of Paul Klee, to which I was introduced when I was fifteen or sixteen. Up until then, I had been destined to study mathematics or to follow my father into engineering. After I encountered painting and sculpture, I wanted to go to Art School. My father suggested that I do a degree in engineering, and he would then support me through an art degree. I agreed.

After a gap year, I began studying engineering at Cambridge in 1968. I very soon stopped going to lectures, because I found I had minimal interest in the subject. Cambridge had a very radical atmosphere at the time, and there were many people there who subsequently became closely involved with Beshara. For me it was a blast of fresh air. I made the most of what was available, in the arts and socially. I also kept up my sporting interests, particularly in boxing. I scraped through my first year exams, but something had to give. I lost interest in eating and made do on beer and cannabis. My father could see that much had changed in nine months, mostly not to his liking, but he was also concerned that something was amiss. I told him I wanted to switch to architecture, and he agreed.

My second year at university was a creative, if not hedonistic, mix of architecture, anarchism and LSD. At the end of the year, I spent three months with friends in a remote cabin in Donegal, in an unreal world of drugs, as the 'Troubles' were starting. Towards the end of my time there during a walk on the moors, reality interposed in an experience that was very simple and direct, after which I gave up drugs completely. The state induced at that point persisted during my third year: it was sober, clear and light. The neuroses typical of university life were all around, but I felt myself to be in a still centre. I had a steady girlfriend, and applied myself to learning all I could about the art of architecture and the principles of beauty and space. At one point, I attended a talk by Keith Critchlow on what he called 'sacred geometry', which fuelled my fascination further. We subsequently met up from time to time as I explored this new terrain.

I got to know A through a student dance company we were both involved in. Her boyfriend, B, was into everything that was counterculture. I was not particularly interested, and kept my own counsel. I had no interest in groupings, political, spiritual or artistic, and was much more committed to my vocation and my friendships. B kept on talking about Tim (Reshad) Feild, whose groups in London he was attending occasionally. He told me it was something to do with sufism, and suggested that I join. I had read Idries Shah's *The Sufis*, and found it intriguing, but I did not respond to his overtures. He then announced that Reshad was giving a talk in Cambridge and insisted that I attend. I decided to go along.

I could use the metaphor of the blowing of the wind to describe the experience of my 'inner' or spiritual life, specifically at those points where a significant connection is made with the 'outer'. (However, I have always been reluctant to establish a distinction between the inner and the outer; my 'inner' life has always proceeded hand in glove with the outer, and vice versa.) If I use this metaphor, my attending Reshad's talk was the first specific 'Beshara' gust of that wind. [I would now understand this 'wind' as the Breath of the Merciful.] I remember Reshad's striking charisma and the seductive proposition of his talk (though I realised in due course that much of it was mumbo-jumbo). I also saw that there was a quality about the people with him that was 'calling' to others. (People would speak of 'Reshad's raids' at this time: he would take a busload of people to an event, and spread a certain contagion.) After the meeting, a few of us decided to hold our own 'sufi' group in Cambridge. We would meet at a very early deserted church, and engage in various simple spiritual practices. This set in motion a process to which I whole-heartedly committed myself. Paradoxically, I was still disinclined to go anywhere near sects, sufism or the like, but the fact is, the attraction at the heart of it was so strong. You would put aside your disinclination to be involved in certain types of thing because the *invitation* itself was so powerful. This loose grouping and its activities became increasingly important in my life.

In 1971, at the end of my third year at Cambridge, that 'wind' started to blow again, and I felt that I had no option but to go with it. I had no sense of where I was heading, but knew I had to go there. I found out the university's minimum requirement for 'sitting' the exams (I knew I had a first-class degree for my portfolio). I wrote my name and College on each paper, drew a Platonic solid on each with some observation on its universality, stayed for the requisite hour, and then left. My tutor called me in for an interview. He tried to work out what was going on. Was I unhappy? Was this a political gesture? No. What did I want to do? 'I don't know', I replied, and he eventually lost interest. The members of the Architecture Faculty offered me various alternatives, but it was now clear that the time had come to move on. My father was furious at my conduct, and cut me off financially. My mother was quite understanding: she was a bit of a radical herself.

I went to the second Glastonbury Festival in the summer of 1971. I had no idea what to do with my life other than to travel to Iran, something I had wanted to do for a while. I bumped into Keith Critchlow at the Festival, and he suggested I join him at the Architecture Association in London when I got back. My girlfriend and I drove overland to Istanbul with friends, then travelled to and around Iran, staying with people we met along the way. The journey back was strange and difficult: there were moments of danger, and I finally returned home unattached and weakened by illness.

Somehow, I managed to raise the fees and enrolled for a diploma at the Architectural Association in London. This place, it became clear later, was also a nursery for students of Beshara.[3] Keith Critchlow was an inspiring teacher, and became a good friend who was generous with his knowledge and enthusiasm. Keith knew of Reshad's search for a design for the dome (the 'Mihrab') that was to be built within a stone barn at Swyre Farm in Gloucestershire, and was intended as the place of meditation, and a venue for talks and other events. We worked on a scheme and presented it. Our design was accepted, and I went to live there in February 1972 to oversee its building. (It was to be my project for that year of study at the Association.)

I never got involved in the Sufi Order side of things at Swyre Farm: I did not like the taste of it. However, I loved the *dhikr*, and was able to tolerate the meditation. My first reaction on reading *The Twenty-nine Pages* was, 'Do I have to?' But I tried hard at study, because I knew I had to train my mind. My interests were instinctive rather than intellectual, yet it seemed important, so I persevered. I first met Bulent when I arrived to settle in Swyre Farm, as he wanted to hear about the dome project. I was in awe of him: he was held up as a figure to be revered by Reshad and those close to him. He seemed to me to be an embodiment of something which was encompassing, and in comparison with which I felt naïve.

I concentrated on building the dome. I was not close to Reshad or part of his coterie: I think I had lost confidence in him quite early on. I was able to get to know Bulent personally when I stayed with him and Angela at his brother's house in Turkey for a few weeks. (Personal friendships with him were very sweet.) When the first part of the proofs of the *Blue Fusus* arrived and I read it, I was stunned. I thought, 'Ibn 'Arabi is the man!' *The Twenty-nine Pages* did not do this for me, but encountering the *Fusus* was another blast of that 'wind'.

In September 1973, I left Swyre Farm. The Mihrab was in place, and I wanted to get back to the world. I resumed my diploma studies at the Architectural Association, and became busy with the Beshara Design Centre, an enterprise set up with Bulent's encouragement in London's Docklands. (It folded four years later, but its Press and Publications arms survived its demise.) Keith Critchlow was then approached to design a mosque for the Aryamehr (Technical) University in Tehran. He invited me to work with him on the design as my final-year project. In September 1974, we flew to Tehran to present the design to Seyyed Hossein Nasr, then Chancellor of the University; I was then to stay on to prepare production drawings, while Keith would return to England. However, the first design was rejected and I was left with very little on paper to develop into a finished building. With the arrogance of youth (barely questioning what I might be doing: designing a mosque in place of my mentor, in a deeply Islamic country), I got on with the job. I started to develop my own 'geometrical philosophy'. In brief, this rejected the duality inherent in the notions of 'sacred' and 'profane', and led to an estrangement from Keith Critchlow. (However, the duality of 'self' and 'God' was somehow not addressed at this point.) By the spring of 1975, I felt that Tehran was becoming exposed to the winds of Khomeini, and I knew I had to get out fast.

---

3 As Sedgwick, *Against the Modern World*, pp. 215–16, suggests, Critchlow's VITA was later to function as a platform for joining the Maryamiyya, which is well represented among its Faculty.

When I returned to the UK, I found that things had changed a lot around Beshara at Swyre Farm. The decks of the Reshad era had been cleared and a new generation had arrived. The people and the tone were more serious, and study had become more established. I was very impressed with the people who came out of the first long course at Chisholme and was becoming aware, by comparison, of my own spiritual coarseness. I knew I had no choice but to go on the next course, which started in the autumn of 1976 at Sherborne House.

Entering the course in October 1976 was like being swept into a personal hurricane, with the growing realisation that I no longer had control of the pattern of my life. I realised that my vocation as a 'geometer' had led to a fascination with Ibn 'Arabi's metaphysics which had veiled me from his essential message, his 'Beshara' (good news), namely, that of the essential love affair between the Real and Its Image. I learned something of service and humility and the frustrating effects of my own intransigence, but out of all this, I got the message. The paradoxical bonus was that, for the first time in my life, I could think rationally and articulate with some clarity.

Severely chastened, in 1977 I returned to London after the course. The prevalent iconoclasm of the punk era matched my new attitudes, but out of it arose ease, and a licence to take pleasure in life. I enjoyed London, moved to Oxford, made some money designing and building, and looked forward to doing the second course at Chisholme House in 1979.

This course was a delight from beginning to end. It did present some irritations for me, however. For example, there was a tendency to treat 'conversation' as a re-run or catch-up on what had been covered during the first course study. What I wanted, in contrast, was to expand within the immense *joie de vivre* of the matter at hand. Towards the end of the course, this line of thinking crystallised for me into the conviction that Beshara was explicitly about man, and that maybe there was too much God and not enough man in the ethos prevailing at the time at Chisholme. This was a watershed: what came out for me was the beauty of what man is, what is possible for man, and what fascination he holds. If you spend too much time looking for God, you turn Him from being the Absolute Existent into the transcendent divinity, which is a partial god. Thus, you miss the point of Beshara, which is about the Unity of Existence. The result of this partial emphasis is that certain of the Divine Names become dominant: the Names of transcendence associated with fear and obedience, and sanctity and piety, for example, bringing attitudes of self-righteousness and holier-than-thou-ness and a dependence on degrees of religiosity. Self-restraint and unbalance come in, and you forget about the *joie de vivre* (which, for me, is the touchstone of this venture); you lose your sense of humour. My whole sense of self was radically changed as a result of this insight, for I realised that, if you respect man, you love him. Man is the manifest image of God. In dealing with man, you must deal with that something of Him that is manifest there. There is no need to search for God elsewhere and, if you do look for the transcendent divinity, you go far away from man. How all this is made real became the central concern of my life.

I completed the course in 1980 and got married in 1981. I had a child, got a mortgage and pursued my career as an architect. My wife did both the long courses back-to-back during the early 1980s. I visited Chisholme a lot while she was there, and I sensed that something had changed, that the School had become established in its ways. Perhaps this was because Bulent was increasingly in the wings, under the pressure of working on his translation of the *White Fusus*. Or maybe I was changing. Nevertheless, I felt a strong sense of loyalty to Beshara and was happy to engage with study groups, to go to Chisholme and to maintain contact with others.

The next blast of 'wind' blew over all us people of Beshara when Bulent died in the autumn of 1987. After the shock, I felt a profound positive conviction in what was to come. However, in the period following his death, it seemed there was a certain constriction in and around Chisholme, as people responded to the implosion at the centre of things, and certain initiatives that I did not feel comfortable with were being launched there. I began to feel the necessity for Beshara to grow out of the forms it had derived from the Turkish 'line', and to devise a new vernacular (Bulent had used that expression). Based on my insight during the second course, I was focused on the idea that Beshara is explicitly about man and implicitly about God, so I was not interested in anything with any actual or implicit religious content or connotation. I thought it was limiting to see Beshara as definable in a specific way (especially the Ottoman/Turkish/Islamic influence that was prevalent at that time). Developing my understanding of Beshara in terms of my own life, I found myself bifurcating from the mainstream of Beshara. I had less taste for the methods of the School: it was not that it was wrong – it was what it was, but there was also another, complementary, way. I had a sense that, if people saw the School and its ways as the be-all and end-all of Beshara, they were missing the point of 'grown-up' and 'connected' Beshara (i.e., based on the connection being made in the instant between meaning and life). I felt that there was a danger that Beshara would become something exclusive, rather than inclusive.

In 1989, I began to have a stream of powerful intuitions concerning what Sadr al-Din Qunawi refers to as 'total facing'[4] – what does it mean to be a servant to the Absolute Existence? At the time, I was bored with the study groups available. I had introduced C, whom I had recently met, to Ibn 'Arabi: she had been interested in my attitude towards life, and my references to Ibn 'Arabi as 'the man'. C then undertook the first and most of the second course at Chisholme. When she left there in 1990, she and I began a period of intensive conversation that proposed and developed ideas stemming from the meaning of 'Absolute Existence' and the practice of 'total facing'. Others joined in these discussions, and in September 1991, we started a group in the Cotswolds to read the *White Fusus* from beginning to end, as if its meaning were present, rather than something distant to be striven for. We looked for lively and challenging discussion that was not afraid of self-expression or hampered by 'doctrinal correctness'. We wanted to proceed with the understanding that the more open and willing your exposure is to the 'fact' of life, the more immediate and transformative is its effect upon you. (In other words, we wanted to proceed in study and discussion much

---

4 From a comment on *al-Fatiha* by Qunawi, cited by Bosnevi: see the *White Fusus*, 1, p. 15. Cf. Mercer, Introduction, p. 3.

as how I remember Bulent himself used to like it.) About half of the group had done courses at Chisholme. The others, particularly a number from London, were fresh to the *Fusus*: they took to it directly.

I think that at the time I was perceived at the School to be a renegade, perhaps because I had not actually sought its permission to run the group: but, there again, the *Fusus* was available to the wider public in bookstores. It became clear through correspondence that my point of view and that of the Principal of the School were irreconcilable at that time. I felt that there was subservience in Beshara to an order bequeathed by or through Bulent. (I even referred to it in terms of a '*tariqa* Raufiyya', and I was very aware that many aspects of the School operated according to his example.) I felt an overriding necessity to cut through appearances to the kernel.

1992 was a year of radical change for me. I lost my home, which had been a financial guarantee in the Beshara investment scheme: I also lost my parents, all within six months. I inherited some money and bought a new house just outside Oxford. A second group had started in London. I was increasingly convinced that the mainstream of Beshara (as it was at the School) was still clinging to a strand of delicate certainty hanging from the memory of Bulent. C and I were also aware that, within our own groups, strong leading can easily give rise to a receptivity that verges on passivity: this was a problem we had set out to overcome in the first place. Ibn 'Arabi goes straight to the point, and we increasingly understood our response in terms of active participation and the notion of *jihad*. We wanted to explore the taste and meaning of what it means to 'face Him with absolute *tawhid*', in the light of the fact that man is made in His image and no other than Him. This is the very same principle of the Martial Art. Both C and I had a background in boxing, and we devised a practice based on its simple and immediate terms of engagement that would make it possible to develop this exploration. The group finished reading the *Fusus* in the spring of 1994. We then held classes in the 'Noble Art', as it came to be known. Over the years, its processes were tested and refined. However, the 'wind' was beginning to blow. Once more, I did not know where I was going, but knew I had to go there. My marriage ended and the house was sold. Nearly all my ties were severed, and in 2000, I found myself alone in Oxford.

A woman I had been engaged to briefly in the mid-1970s (who I introduced to Beshara at the time, and who is still deeply involved in it) re-established contact. Through our rekindled relationship and marriage in 2004, I also re-established contact with old friends in Beshara. My wife provided me with a place to 'come home'. I appreciated that I had a reputation as something of a maverick, but I had mellowed and the common denominator between myself and the people of Beshara, the Unity of Existence, had never been in question for me. I never considered myself to have 'left' Beshara: I had followed my own inspiration *in* Beshara, and still do. I went with my wife to Chisholme for the gathering of August 2003, and was delighted to hear the Principal of the School pose the question I had spent fourteen years considering: 'Where are we now?' I was more delighted at the following year's gathering to feel that Beshara had come home to itself and was fit for its task of preparing for a continually immanent future. My old concern as to whether my own generation had the passion to bring Beshara into the present was assuaged by a dream I had long ago. In this, the spirit of Beshara came to me in the form of a man, and he said: 'Don't worry about them (the people of Beshara) – I've got their children.'

Story 5

I was born in 1970 in Germany: my father is German and my mother English. The family was middle class: my father worked as a business executive and my mother as a professional. We lived in Germany until I was three, then in Colombia and Mexico until I was six (I could speak three languages by that age.) When I was six, my parents separated. I settled with my mother and brother in England. At this point, I felt something of an outsider in the cultural sense, and this feeling remained with me. Within a few years, my parents had divorced; my father remarried and returned to Germany with his new wife and her son. My brother and I would visit our 'second family' regularly during school vacations. It worked well and there were no difficulties. (In retrospect, I believe the divorce was a significant, even a traumatic, event for me. I also recognise that my parents had very different perspectives, which I think it has been important for me to try to synthesise within my own self somehow.)

When we settled in England, my mother began to attend church. Religion had not been a part of our family at all up to then, but she may have been interested in spirituality for some time, and the immediate choice that presented itself then was church. We went to several churches; I also attended Sunday school and Christian youth groups, and my private day-school held a daily chapel service. While my brother and I were visiting Germany, when I was ten or eleven, my mother attended a weekend course at Sherborne. She liked it very much, and before long took my brother and me there to introduce us to the people she had met. We went several times, but I remember in particular the first time: I was not nervous or apprehensive, but I was interested to find out who these people were. My immediate reaction was that the people were very nice and that I could trust my feelings about them, so I knew it was good. I also knew it was about God, and I knew I liked it. [In terms of my understanding of what Beshara is about, this turned out to be one of the most important moments for me.]

I have a strong memory of one of the first *dhikr*s I attended at Sherborne during my very early teens. It was the first time I had been in what seemed to me a grand room, reached through a long passageway. I remember seeing what looked like hundreds of shoes outside. The carpet and furniture there were old, and although the place was very clean it struck me as being somehow dusty and even tatty. (This sense of the place has stayed with me as a very fond memory of how Beshara was during that earlier time: there was graciousness and whole-someness, in spite of the age and tiredness of the environment.) The atmosphere was very strong: the smell of incense; many people; the large room, and the great sense of occasion. Bulent was there and I remember his presence. He was by then quite old and had health problems, and he always had people around him. I was rather in awe of him. I remember meeting him twice. I was very shy and nervous and could hardly look him in the face, but he was very kindly to me: he was very keen on children and emphasised kindness towards them.

My mother decided to do a first six-month course at Chisholme beginning
in 1982. Consequently, I boarded at school for one term. I visited Chisholme
in the summer for several weeks. I was busy with outdoor activities and had a
great time. I did not attend the *dhikr* and I was not actively interested, but I felt
comfortable with Beshara and was accepting of it. I had a notion that it was about
God; I felt that it was good and maybe more illuminating and explanatory than
other things I had come across. [In retrospect, my interest in Beshara had always
been there, and was gradually becoming more conscious. From the first meeting
with the people at Sherborne I was interested: that interest eventually motivated
me to read and study.] On a visit during my mother's first course, she asked me if
I would like a name. I did not feel strongly about it, but agreed. She asked Bulent,
who consulted, but some days later no name had appeared. When she asked him
again, he explained that he had written the name on a piece of paper and given it
to someone to pass to her. The paper had disappeared, so he consulted again, and
that was how I received my name. [It felt nice to receive it and seemed important
and private, but it did not feel like something I could use as my name until much
later; when it eventually did, that was significant for me.]

I remember how my awareness of Beshara provided me with a new perspective on chapel services at school. I was confirmed at school at the age of fourteen.
I remember thinking I was not sure if I wanted or needed to go through this,
because of Beshara. I did not quite see the point of it, because I knew that there
was another path. I was unsure of the meaning of the confirmation for me: I also
felt I was perhaps doing something a bit hypocritical. Nevertheless, I went ahead,
believing that the fact it meant I would be able to join in communion would
not be a bad thing, and looking forward to the present my father would give
me (confirmation is a significant event in Germany). Yet, I was not particularly
motivated about it, given that part of me thought that there was something else.
My relationship with Christianity was changing, and for a while I did some rather
curious things, which I then grew out of. For example, while kneeling and praying
in chapel, I would repeat a shortened version of the *salawat* I had picked up from
my mother (who was often singing the *salawat*), because it had more meaning
for me than the Christian prayers. I did have a reaction against Christianity: I felt
I had been short-changed by it, because it had not told me about the things I was
discovering elsewhere, and I went away from conventional Christianity. Once I
found an alternative and discovered something in it, I realised that the fact that
Christianity had not seemed right to me was not because I was the problem,
but because nothing in Christianity (as I encountered it) had dealt with spiritual
questions. I may have vaguely thought that I was the problem, but once I had
found something so rich, it had made Christianity seem empty. Once I discovered this mystical tradition in Beshara (which I did not find in Christianity until
later), I suddenly realised what I was missing. (A few years later, I realised that
it is there in Christianity too. I read Maurice Nicoll's *The New Man*, which my
mother had given me: the author uses the Gospels to bring out the spiritual side
of Jesus' teachings. While Nicoll demonstrated that the mystical tradition was
there in Christianity, religious education teachers, priests and the like had totally
missed it out, when for me it was the core of things.) The process was gradual
and not particularly well thought-out: I simply knew that Beshara was good and

that it spoke to me, while I had less of a response to Christianity. Christianity had been a routine part of my life, but it gradually ceased to have importance when I became aware of this other source, in Beshara.

When I was fourteen or fifteen, my mother suggested that I join in a young persons' weekend at Sherborne. It had all the elements of a course: study, meditation, *dhikr*, and work, and we had to prepare a paper at the end. About ten people attended. I remember my first experience of meditation at this time: relatively little guidance was given (as is usual in Beshara), and I sat in silence. This course was an important event for me. [In retrospect, my experience of it was in keeping with my sense of something gradually becoming more conscious and coming out. It was as if there was always an understanding, but without the words to talk about it: these came and developed over the years.] My mother went on to complete the second six-month course at Chisholme, which began in the winter of 1985. I lodged with the family of a friend while she was there and visited Chisholme in the winter.

During the autumn of 1987, I had a bad case of disappointment in love. I was distraught and acutely depressed. I took a few days off school, and it happened to be the time of the Rememoration marking the fortieth day after Bulent's death. [The Rememoration coincided with the night of the great storm. At the time, I did not realise this, but now, as I have become accustomed to notice the correspondences between things, I realise that this was significant.] I went with my mother to Chisholme for the occasion. I remember meeting Dom Sylvester Houédard for the second time at the Rememoration. (A year or two before, I had attended a MIAS Symposium in Oxford with my mother. I had been inspired by something the Dom had said during a plenary session, and had spoken up. My comment had caught his attention because it touched on one of the main themes of his work at the time, and he invited me to have tea with him. In fact, I had tea at the house of an old friend of the Dom's and in the company of the Dom, the Panchen Lama, and a Tibetan monk who was accompanying him too. At the time, I did not realise what was going on, which was probably good or I would have been too nervous.)

In the aftermath of this visit to Chisholme, my mother explained that a nine-day course was a possibility, and suggested this would be a good idea. (She was definitely encouraging me, because she could see the interest.) I agreed. The course was based at Sherborne, and I was the only student (some other people joined in the study). During the nine days of the course, I accompanied my supervisor, who drove Kathleen Raine to Chisholme, where she was due to speak, and then returned to Sherborne to resume the course. I remember studying papers by Bulent from *Addresses*, and fragments from *Whoso Knoweth Himself, Kernel of the Kernel, The Twenty-nine Pages*, the *Tao te Ching* and *Chuang Tsu*. I thought the texts were great, but I realised there was much to learn. I recall two significant events during that course. At home, my brother and I never did the washing-up, and it never crossed my mind that it should be otherwise. I had to be told that certain things (like washing-up) would be expected of me on the course. [This was the kind of education I needed ... as a seventeen-year-old I was not very 'servant-like'.] Once, my supervisor on the course was explaining something to me, and I spoke over him, or jumped the gun. I thought to myself: 'There is likely to be a response to this' ... and during the very next session we studied the paper on 'Humility'.

After completing my A-level examinations at school I attended another nine-day course, at Frilford Grange, in the summer of 1989. There were two students on this course, and it was more conventional and focused when compared with my first nine-day course. It was fantastic: we laughed a lot, and there was a great lightness to it. We studied much more material, and the study was more serious. The contrast with the earlier course was dramatic for me, for I was now essentially an adult.

I had already secured a place to study philosophy and psychology at Oxford, and had planned a gap year. I worked for six months in Germany in the company where my father was working, then travelled for six months to India, Thailand, Australia and the USA. I began my degree in autumn 1990. My mother moved to Scotland to be close to Chisholme, and was to spend six years living near Hawick. This made it easy for me to maintain contact with Beshara, as I would go frequently to Scotland to see her. I remember reading *Kernel of the Kernel*, *Addresses* and other (Beshara) literature while at university, and I remember sometimes talking about it enthusiastically with friends late at night after drinking in the College bar all evening. In the summer of my second year at Oxford, I did another weekend course at Frilford Grange, but I felt that this was not enough anymore: I needed more.

I remember at this time feeling somewhat ambivalent in my feelings concerning Chisholme: I was a little nervous of it, and felt somewhat intimidated, inadequate or unworthy. (These feelings continued and were not properly resolved until I did the second six-month course. I think my unease stemmed partly from the fact that Chisholme is a challenging environment in various ways, and can be quite hard on one. I would at times feel awkward and not quite right in it, without knowing why. This is not to suggest in any way that there was a problem at Chisholme – it was rather to do with me. Perhaps my shyness made it feel a little overwhelming.) This was also a difficult period for Beshara, in the aftermath of Bulent's death, but also because of the financial disaster that had struck some people because of investment in a city scheme that turned out to be a fraud. My own perspective at the time was of a sense of turbulent times for Beshara: Bulent's death had thrown people into difficulties, and there were not many students coming through the School. I even feared it might not still be around when the time would come for me to do a six-month course.

I graduated in 1993 and stayed for six weeks at Chisholme, working on a building job in the Borders. I did not fully engage with life at the School, although I was staying there: I really wanted to celebrate my degree, but I needed to work. I felt a bit deflated and anxious about my future and the possible career options. To me, it seemed very important to find something to do. I had no clarity about the future, but in November, I picked up a book on cognitive behavioural therapy in Brighton, and realised that clinical psychology was after all a job I could do. Through my mother, I arranged work experience in a unit for children with autism in Birmingham. I went back to Scotland as I waited for this to begin, and there I started reading Jung for the first time, whom I found inspirational, and that was what really motivated me to train as a clinical psychologist. (At Oxford one of the first lectures had begun by stating: 'Freud, Jung – that's the last you'll hear of them here!' The course had been very dry and uninspiring.) Jung made psychology come alive for me in terms of spirituality: at that stage he seemed to me the bridge between psychology and spirituality, and this was what inspired me to become a clinical psychologist. (Jung continued to be very important for me for a time, but this importance then receded.)

I proceeded from the work experience placement to the position of an occupational therapy assistant, then became an assistant clinical psychologist, enjoying this very much. I then began applying for jobs and training courses, but it did not go very well. By summer 1995, I had run out of steam: I felt I was lacking in confidence and was losing motivation. I went to Scotland to visit my mother, and she passed on to me a message that the Principal wanted to see me. When I met with him, he asked if I wanted to do the six-month course commencing that winter (he had heard about my situation somehow). Although I immediately replied that I did, I added that I felt it was important for the motivation to be right, and that I was worried I might be running away from other things, given that I was not feeling too positive about my job situation, etc. He replied: 'It's not so important what you are running away from but what you are running *towards*', and I knew straightaway that I would join the course that winter, and confirmed a few days later. [I had always known that I would do the six-month course, but the right moment had not come until then.]

Only a day into the course I could feel that there was a dramatic change, and it was as though much time had passed. This seems to have been brought about by the opening lecture, which set the scene in a very dramatic way and provided a certain meaning and context to the start of the course, a sense of undertaking something very important, which in my case had been long waited for. The first day of the course was marked by a fast, the first ever for me. There were seven students on the course. As time progressed, it became clear that our individual characters and issues would make it difficult for us to develop coherence as a group, and that this presented a task that we as a group would have to undertake. There were certainly tensions, which we struggled with, and managed to some extent. [I understand now that the persons with whom you find yourself on a course form part of the educational process, which is highly personalised. The situation I faced was thus not a random one, but formed part of what I needed to be with at that time.]

I took to the course like a duck to water: I never had a feeling (which some had) of wanting to leave on a daily basis. Although I was thoroughly involved, I see now that it was perhaps in a rather unbalanced way. I seem to have had a pattern of always wanting to succeed and please people, which I was playing out somehow in the context of the course. There was clearly a need to become aware of this, for it to 'come out'. For the first half of the course, I was given the task of 'Boiler man', responsible for keeping the boiler going in the steading (where the students stayed), using available off-cuts of wood to stoke it during every break and rising early to light it every morning. For the first few weeks, there was dry material from the summer, but the new batch was increasingly green and wet, and I could not get it to burn well at all. I would return to the steading to find the fire was out, the steading cold, and no hot water. I tried various tricks like soaking sawdust in diesel and using that, which produced clouds of black smoke. Several people offered to help me, but I did not see how they could; they were very busy on courses too. I declined all help, but about a week later, I found myself in tears and at the end of my tether. I felt I could not go on, and at that point, I turned to those who had offered to help before and asked them to help. At that very moment, a friend (one of the second course correlators) walked past and said 'We like to give the boiler to people who don't like to fail!' He had put his finger on the matter. From that moment, the boiler lit easily.

Things like that happened frequently on the course. Almost daily, I would find myself facing a blockage or an aspect of myself that somehow had to be brought into awareness, and a proper way of dealing with it found. With respect to the boiler, it was about asking for help and depending on God, in contrast with stubborn independence. The lesson became clear to me straightaway. It was a common theme in my experience (and that of other students), because of the centrality of dependence. In such problems as those associated with the boiler, it is invariably a matter of turning to God, asking for help and forgiveness, admitting one's weakness or lack of knowledge, and recognising where the true knowledge, strength and ability are. This is the education in the Oneness of Being. There is only One Being: in hundreds of different ways, we need to be educated in this, and this is what happens on courses, because we are there for that purpose. Moreover, education in the Oneness of Being is equivalent to being educated in self-knowledge and the real Self. Once this has been made the intention, everything that happens is related to that intention and aim. By being on the course, the student has a certain time to concentrate purely on this, although this is equally true elsewhere.

I loved all aspects of the course and really took to it, but my personal tendency was to like the study more than the other elements. I began to have much more of a feeling for the *dhikr* than before; we engaged in it every night. At times, I was not very happy. Things proceeded in waves of a few good days followed by a couple of bad days with black moods. At the time, I did not know what this was about. In retrospect, I realise that it related to the other side of the sense of wanting to please, in the sense of feeling unworthy or inadequate: such feelings would sometimes be triggered by a specific remark or incident. It was psychological stuff, but it also related to the issue of dependency, because it was associated with a limited sense of self, a self that is judged successful, bad, etc. At Chisholme, these sorts of things are dealt with but not in a specific way. The focus of the course brings up and deals with the matter of the limited self through a single-minded concentration on Reality, rather than dealing with the details of the illusion. The emphasis is on the turn to Reality, in whatever way the turn is prompted. The firm course structure is a great help, enabling you to keep focused, giving you something to hold on to in what would otherwise be a difficult place. The difficulty arises out of the recognition that you need to give up the old stuff, but you are not sure what will be there instead. The help the course gives you emanates from the focus on the Real. When you are going through the course, it can feel as though you are experiencing a great difficulty: it can seem to be in opposition to the way you are, which you later realise is not how you really are at all. During the course, my tendency was to get on with things, probably because of my sense of wanting to please, and a feeling that I should be doing whatever it was that was required.

During the last week of the course, I became panicky, and when it ended, I felt in some way that I could not carry on, that I did not know what to do, without it. After I left Chisholme in the summer of 1996, I became quite depressed. I was anxious at going back to the world, where I would have to resume my career and where the pressures on me would recommence. In retrospect, I see that, in a way, my perspective had not really changed. I did in fact feel that, in a way, I was back where I had started. I thought I should feel better than I did. Fortunately, I was helped by a number of factors that smoothed the transition. I quickly moved to live with friends (one of them a Beshara person) in London and was kept busy working on their new house. On the work front, things moved ahead and I eventually got a job as an assistant psychologist (a job that would ultimately prove important for my professional future), and began applying for clinical training courses. However, my boss was a very difficult person and a bully, and, largely because of the pressure at work, by Christmas I was in an emotional state, with panic attacks and insomnia. The situation pushed me to seek psychotherapy and I began sessions with a Jungian analyst. Others were also supportive, so I felt I was being helped through this. I believe now that the first course had shifted things under the surface that were waiting to come out, and this is what was happening. Gradually, things got better: I continued with the Jungian analysis and secured a place on a clinical training course. The job that had caused me such distress was also reaching an end. In the summer of 1997, I went to Turkey and visited all the places we had been to on the Turkey trip: that felt very important to me.

I decided to take the place on the training course in Oxford that had been offered me in autumn 1997, partly because I liked the place and preferred to work somewhere green. However, a major factor in the decision (even if it was at the back of my mind) was the fact that there were many Beshara people in Oxford, so there would be regular *dhikr* and other activities there. I felt I was beginning to grow up in many ways; I was being given what was needed to take on increasing responsibility. I continued with the Jungian analysis, after a while changing to an analyst in Oxford. There were five years between the first course I did and the second one. I think that all that happened in that time was in some way a matter of dealing with things that needed to be dealt with, so that I would be able to go on the second course. At the time, I did not feel I wanted to do the second course, and was a little afraid of it, perhaps because of how the first one had ended for me. I was afraid I might not be able to cope with it. Then I met D, the son of a Beshara person in Oxford, and we instantly connected: this became a very important friendship for me. He did the first course and stayed on at Chisholme. Meanwhile, another Beshara person and I were given a task: to organise a one-day gathering in Oxford which we were to advertise under the title 'The Unity of Existence: what does it mean to me?' This was scheduled for 1999, and we began preparing well in advance. It was very significant for me, because it felt like a huge demand, not like something that we could easily take on. It was a major challenge and we did not feel quite up to it. Yet, it was a real education – like the boiler all over again. The months of preparation had a profound effect on me and refocused me. The event itself went off well. Mainly young people attended. For some of them, it was catalytic: they went on to do courses in the next few years. After the event, I began a study group with another Beshara person in Oxford. We met every week for two years to read the *Blue Fusus* (it was a group of just three for most of this time).

My name was then put forward by the Principal as a possible speaker at an event on meditation organised by the Anthroposophists in Stroud, at which there would also be a Vedanta teacher, a local vicar and other speakers. I agreed to do it, although I felt that I could not do it in the sense that I did not feel qualified. I felt inadequate and a bit of a fraud (because I am not much good at meditation), but knowing I had this task to do focused me, and, again, it was an education. There were preparatory meetings with the group in Stroud. I wrote a paper in which I drew on Bulent, and discussed it with the Principal (I went up to Chisholme for the Millennium celebrations there). I was asking for help and was conscious of my dependency because it seemed like a huge demand. I was reciting continuously 'there is no strength or power save in God' in Arabic. When I delivered it at the event in Stroud, the paper was well received.

This had been another significant event for me, which, in retrospect, I see as part of the preparation I was undergoing for the second course. It became clear to me then that I wanted to do the second course, but I had to spend another year completing my clinical training . When I finished it, I went to Italy for a fortnight on vacation, and over-indulged a bit on excellent food, including a fair amount of pork and alcohol, and felt a bit 'heavy' for it. (Regarding pork, Bulent never ate it, and it is never eaten at Chisholme. When I was preparing for the day event in Oxford, I had decided not to eat pork as a way of self-preparation. I believe that eating pork has a certain effect subtly: this was something I observed in myself. I do eat it sometimes on special occasions and in special dishes when it can be really enjoyed in that context, but I am aware of it and tend to avoid it. Some Beshara people do eat it, and garlic.) Then I went to Chisholme to start the second course in October 2000. I was eager that D should do it at the same time: when I arrived, he was there, and I was delighted to find out that he had decided to do it.

It was a delightful course. There were six students on it. As there was no structure, there was suddenly a need to find a way of being, without the benefit of being told what to do. Apart from the conversation and meals, there was quite a lot of space to work out what to do with, both as individuals and as a group. In the conversation sessions, although there are two correlators there is no assigned text or topic: you have to find that in yourself. There was an amazing sense of lightness and freedom. Three weeks into the course, I was thinking how, in contrast to three years of psychotherapy, there were suddenly huge insights and changes occurring. The matter that had remained unresolved in the first course began to surface in such a way that there was a resolution. I realised it had all been preparation: during the first course, I had not been very self-aware. Since then, there had been three years of psychotherapy, my training as a clinical psychologist, and spiritual preparation (I had been saying the *wird*[5] twice a day for two or three years regularly).

---

5 *Awrad al-usbu'*: see Ch. 6.

I remember that the English translation of the *wird*[6] came out during this course, and we were the first to be able to use it, and it entered into our conversation. Given the lack of set structure, we had to find a way of being, and this gradually unfolded. On Sundays, there was no conversation. The Principal suggested that, instead of conversation, we undertake the task of 'finding what needs doing, and do it.' Our sense of what this meant developed across time. On the first occasion, I walked around saying to myself: 'I will do the first thing I see that needs doing.' With time, however, we realised that it could mean resting, reading something, or having a conversation, as well as work. Gradually, this sense spread to include the whole of life, such that the limited attitude I had had on the first course dissolved: it was to do with facing God or Reality at each moment.

In the conversation, I began to get a sense for what is arising right now, and to distinguish between matters of ego and what is really arising. This is a fruit of conversation, and one of the ways in which conversation educates you – in this discrimination. It is also a matter of neither holding back what wants to come up, nor forcing out what does not. The subject matter of the conversation led to some extraordinary insights for me. A particularly significant moment was when I suddenly became aware of my own pattern of being according to 'should', and realising that all I had done had been coloured by this – even the two courses. (There were two aspects in that respect, in that doing the courses was inherently good, but I had been doing them because I felt I 'should' be.) From that moment, I saw things completely differently. It was some four to six weeks into the course when I realised that 'should' was a kind of motivation that was no good for me anymore. I wanted a real motivation. I knew intellectually that that motivation meant love (i.e., wanting to do something, instead of 'should'), but I did not have it myself. I admitted to myself that I did not know what it meant to *love* God. This upset me to the point of tears.

So, for me, the second course was really about love: this was a big part of it. Several things happened to me during that course, from the very beginning. I experienced strong feelings for a woman at Chisholme who was not at all suitable for me, and possibly not interested in me. I knew there was nothing in it, but I was infatuated. For a long time, she held a fascination in my mind, and I could not shake my feelings for her. Later, I realised that I was being shown that this was a limited love, in accordance with an old pattern (I had had similar feelings for others in the past). Up to the time of the Turkey trip, I had also been noticing someone else, E. I thought I would like to fall in love with *her*: she was very nice, and I could sense that she seemed to like me too. I really wanted to be freed from the infatuation I still had for the other person. Amazingly, within days I began to fall in love with E. It was a delightful love affair, very sweet. This was the first time I had been in love and had been loved back. I was deeply moved and grateful and utterly taken by it. The whole thing was very much in keeping with what the course was about; there was no conflict in me over expressing this love and it was not in any way going against the course. It seemed completely in accordance with the way of things.

---

6 Ibn 'Arabi, *The Seven Days of the Heart*, trans. and presented in English by Beneito and Hirtenstein.

My relationship with E began in mid-December. Three weeks after the New Year, I was in retreat for a week (and involved in preparations for it prior to that). For me, the retreat was the flowering of Divine Love: there was a strong atmosphere of love during the retreat. When I came out of it, I realised I was very much affected by it: it was the culmination of the course for me, although the course went on building afterwards. I had left everything behind on the retreat, including E. But you don't leave Love behind, because that is what there is if nothing else remains. For the retreat period, however, it had not been attached to a particular person. Consequently, it was a little difficult to reconnect with E, but the relationship continued until after the end of the course. I felt buoyant at the end of the course, and felt it was possible simply to continue: something had clearly been established in me.

I set about finding a job, settled in Oxford, and became more actively involved in Beshara in three areas: in each case, I was invited to get involved. During a *dhikr* in Oxford in early 2002, someone who came for the first time requested a study group. Another associate agreed, and he and I set it up and ran it jointly. We used the nine-day course materials first, and then Andrew Harvey's anthology of Rumi, *Light upon Light*, which was just being read at Chisholme.[7] The group consisted of a mixture of associates and outsiders. It has continued to the present, waxing and waning across the years: there are currently three or four regulars. In autumn 2003, I advertised this study group across Oxford (at the Friends Meeting House, the city library and an alternative bookshop, for example). The title of the flyer I used was 'Love and Knowledge: We love what Rumi loved'. It explained: 'We meet for reading and discussion, and we are reading Rumi now'. A number of new people came thanks to the advertising campaign, but only a few stayed. Through the study group, they learned about Beshara. I felt the title of the flyer was very important in establishing the order of the study group: it is about what Rumi loved, not about Rumi. It came from something that Bulent had said in response to the question: 'You go to Konya a lot: you must love Rumi?' Bulent had replied: 'We love what Rumi loved, *and what Rumi loved loves him*.' The second area I became involved in is Beshara Publications: I was invited among others to become partners in this as a way of bringing in fresh blood. Its main aim is to make available and announce the availability of certain books, and there are some new publications in the pipeline too. Finally, I was invited to join the Chisholme Institute as a Director in 2003, again as part of an initiative to bring in younger people. This means I visit Chisholme for the Directors' meetings every three months.

I feel very fortunate that my mother introduced me to Beshara, because I might have been a bit nervous of seeking it out. (I am nervous of funny New Age 'culty' things, and this was probably at the back of my mind when I went to Sherborne for the first time, and realised that the people there were perfectly ordinary. I was aware of this due to the generally suspicious attitude in society at the time concerning cults.) If she had not introduced me to Beshara, I might not have known what to do and may have taken a long time to work it out. Although

---

7 *Light upon Light: Inspirations from Rumi* (New York, 2004).

Beshara had come into my life a long time before it had become a conscious search, it did meet with something in me. There was a gradual process, of the matter becoming established in me.

In my current work as a neuro-psychologist, assessing people with neurological disorders or injuries, what I have learned through Beshara is always present (remembered sometimes more, sometimes less), and sometimes inspires me directly. For example, there may be someone with a specific concern, perhaps about identity or loss of function. I think about this in terms that go beyond the psychological, about who this person really is, and the fact they are not the lost function. Sometimes I convey this to them in terms of ideas, but not as a religious idea or dogma. It is important to maintain a certain vision for someone, and it can come across in subtle ways. On the therapeutic side, I sometimes use meditation with people (this is becoming a mainstream treatment in psychology). During the second course, I came to appreciate the importance of relaxation, because I realised how important it is to be clear and receptive, and this has inspired me to make greater use of relaxation in my practice.

A journey to sufism in Istanbul

The account below is based on an interview conducted in Istanbul in August 2005.

'Yusuf' was born and grew up in Ankara, having spent a few years as a child in the USA, where his father was completing his doctoral studies. His father is an electrical engineer and Dean of Faculty at a Turkish university, his mother an English teacher. The family milieu was shaped by the atheism of his father and paternal relatives. His maternal family retained a belief in God but had little knowledge of Islam and were non-observant, for they saw themselves as 'the children of Ataturk', and considered the overtly religious a potential threat to Turkish laicism. From early on, his father's tastes and intellectual interests influenced Yusuf. He hated classical Turkish music, for example, but loved Western classical music; he cared neither for Ataturkism nor for tradition, but liked philosophy. Under his wing, Yusuf heard about and read Foucault, Said, the writers of the Frankfurt school, and Chomsky. In high school he developed a fascination with Nietzsche and Bakunin. He thought he was a nihilist and was drawn to anarchist ideas and the rebelliousness associated with punk and rock music. Looking back, he reflects that he grew up 'like a Western guy'. He hated the classical Turkish tradition, and became familiar with Western culture and English literature before his own.

Graduating in film studies from the University of Fine Arts, Yusuf worked as an assistant director on projects with Turkish and foreign crews in Istanbul. He became established as a director and set up his own company making television commercials, at the same time teaching university courses in scriptwriting and creativity in advertising. In the aftermath of one of the economic crises that hit Turkey at the time, in 2000 his company collapsed. At the same time, he faced many changes in his personal life relating to his girlfriend and old friends, which produced many contradictions and conflicts. He had a nervous breakdown and was sent to see a psychiatrist who prescribed medication, including antidepressants. He felt the medication made things worse, for he found himself 'like a vegetable', having lost his many interests in life. He reached a point where he thought there was no meaning to life, and might easily have killed himself. Then a friend suggested he go with him to try acupuncture. The practitioner was extremely nice and the treatment helped. He also began to train and play sport, and eventually gave up the medication and began to feel better.

Another friend then suggested he try meditation. 'I had no clue and I did not believe in it', he explains. As 'a very mental guy' ('because of my father'), he rejected the idea as stupid. His friend insisted and showed him the OSHO way of meditation. When he found it helpful, he turned to KUN and began to practise further OSHO styles of meditation. He never felt himself a sannyasin or follower of OSHO, however, for 'I was very happy with my name and my country. It's true I don't like the traditional faith, but I'm open to everything. I'm not against religion, and I don't see religious people as a danger the way my mother does.' The meditation greatly facilitated his recovery, and he began to look beyond KUN to OWO. He found that members of the sixties 'flower power' generation turned 'experts' were now coming from abroad to give sessions at OWO, making money as professionals. He attended Primal, Breath Therapy, 'Discover Yourself' and 'Path of Love' workshops, all of them led by such experts working like psychotherapists, asking questions about childhood traumas, family problems and relationships. He tried to discover his problems through these channels, in the hope of continuing to improve. As he started to understand everything that had happened to him, the experts tried to talk to him about his identity 'in a spiritual way'. He explains that this was his first contact with 'my spirituality, my Big I'. He also attended Gurdjieff movement workshops, and sufi workshops led by Zahira and Videha.

At this time, Yusuf returned to scriptwriting. A main character in one story was a woman wearing the headscarf, who later took it off. He needed to interview such women to find out about their personal lives, but he did not know anyone to talk to. The owner of OWO, his friend, explained that Sargut was going to speak there, and that he could ask her whatever he wanted. He had just read Nigel Watts' *The Way of Love*,[8] and had 'fallen in love' with Shams. He began searching for more materials on Shams, and felt the beginnings of an urge to discover more about sufism. At the beginning of 2004, he attended Sargut's talk at OWO. He went with the intention of asking about the script, and also perhaps raising a few questions about sufism. A prejudice nurtured since childhood towards sufis 'in the old, traditional way', that they 'don't like people like him' and see him as a *kafir* (unbeliever), made him feel he should acquire the information he needed and get away fast. He was struck on seeing Sargut, however, as he had never seen or heard of anyone talking of sufism while being open and uncovered. He 'fell in love' while listening to her during her talk. When it ended he was shy to approach her, but she came to him and asked if he had any questions, which surprised him, and contact was made.

---

8 A popular fictionalised account of the life of Rumi, published in 1999 by HarperCollins.

After meeting Sargut, Yusuf somehow felt 'a very big love' during meditation, and it often moved him to tears. He 'didn't know what to do with this love, which was like a package that came with meditation'. A month after their first meeting, he would find himself crying in public places. He did not want to be seen like that, and asked Sargut what he should do 'with all this love and crying'. She explained that he needed grounding, and suggested the Islamic ritual prayers as a good tool to achieve this. He thought he would give it a try, and started by doing the movements 'like a meditation' as a way to ground himself, but without any of the accompanying formulae and Qur'anic recitations, because he did not know them. 'I tried to get it like a meditation', he explains, 'by following my breathing.'[9] He found it a great help, still feeling great love, but without the tears. He then noticed that, whenever he read the books they were studying (in Sargut's group), his understanding went far beyond his own knowledge: 'it encompassed additional things, like a kind of *kashf*'. Gradually, he 'fell in love' with the ritual prayers, and learned the recitations and formulae to accompany the movements.[10] Then it became 'very meaningful' ('it came together like *tawhid* or unity'), and emerged as 'one of my biggest meditations'. He found himself doing *dhikr* using a *tasbih* or 'counter', without anyone having instructed him to (he recalls how, in like fashion, he had repeated 'Allah' spontaneously while whirling in sufi workshops, without having been thus instructed, and in spite of his utter ignorance of the *sama*'. Then too he had felt 'a big love'). He became immersed in the great sufis of the past, reading the *Mathnavi* and asking Sargut questions, recording and listening over and again to their study sessions. Eventually, he stopped doing other meditations and focused on the ritual prayers, sometimes whirling on his own.

At the same time, Yusuf resumed scriptwriting, to find that his creativity had benefited greatly from his new life. Though he had picked up some freelance work it didn't last, and he had little money. 'But it doesn't matter', he explains: 'I began to learn to surrender to God and accept that everything comes from Him, like my Reality or *haqiqa*'. When he returned to teaching, he discovered that learning scriptwriting is 'more or less the same as *tasawwuf*' (he prefers to use this Arabic/Turkish term, reserving 'sufism' for its 'Western' version, as we shall see). 'You need good people and bad people, and you are the hero of your own life. The journeys are the same'. He describes how Joseph Campbell's writings[11] have influenced him in understanding the mythical structure of scriptwriting: 'all our lives are mythology and we need these stories to understand our *haqiqa*'. His interest in mythology thus 'came together' with his study of *tasawwuf* under Sargut. 'Now I live on this path', he concludes. 'It is very exciting, even amusing. Sometimes you feel a great pain, and you have weaknesses, but it doesn't matter,

---

9 Another Sargut student explains that she first experienced the ritual *salat* as 'a mixture of yoga and meditation' (she had taken up TM after joining Sargut).

10 Sargut students often first learn the *salat* movements, and then the accompanying formulae and Qur'anic material, from friends who have themselves just learned these. Tellingly, one student reports that she had grown up watching her grandmother praying, and so could easily copy the movements.

11 One of the late American writer's best-known works on mythology and comparative religion is *The Hero with a Thousand Faces* (1948).

because you need all these things. If you want to write a good scenario, you need the good and the bad, otherwise it will be very boring'.

Through his journey, Yusuf now discriminates between the offerings of imported sufi workshops and the *tasawwuf* in which he has settled. True to his cosmopolitan tolerance, he refuses to condemn the former outright. Yet he is clear in his projection of its shortcomings, and implicitly distances his own choice both from such deficient 'Western' reconstructions *and* from irrelevant traditional expressions, pointing thereby to the multiplicity of choices that confront even those whose quest has become confined to the sufi arena:

> Western sufi teachers who come to Turkey take some parts of *tasawwuf* and leave out others, but it doesn't work like that and it doesn't provide much. They want to forget the sharia and take the 'good' part, about 'caring' and 'love'. They take *tasawwuf* and try to use it like that. But that's like with chewing gum – when the flavour is gone, you want to throw it away. They use whirling as a meditation tool, to take out energy and stress and to enhance self-awareness. You can go and 'feel the love'. It doesn't matter for them whether you believe in God. If you do, it can be used to make contact more easily with Him, and the love you feel can be called 'God's existence'. Some even say 'I myself am God'. These teachers give Names of God or formulae like *la ilaha illa Allah* like a mantra. Even if they tell you what it means, they leave it up to you what you do with it, because they don't want to be unsympathetic to those participants who are atheists, and they want to be accepted by everyone. But it's just an ecstatic experience that has no relation with real life. Instead of using ecstasy pills, they use mantras to get you high. When you go back to real life these teachers are no longer with you, and you are on your own. It's like hide and seek. People use these workshops to escape from the real world in my opinion, and I have some friends who could not manage with real life after attending these groups. But if you learn *tasawwuf* you live and learn at the same time. Our workshop (with Sargut) is real life. This is where we practise. This is the real workshop: the real world is our scenario and script, because everything comes from Allah, and we don't even exist – it's just like a hologram or matrix. All that happens in life becomes a test for what you learn. You need to take the *shari'a*, *tariqa* and *haqiqa* altogether. In Turkey people need spirituality, but they can't connect with the traditional way ...

Select bibliography

A note on websites and URLs
All websites referenced in the notes were accessed during the period January 2004 – March 2006, and it cannot be guaranteed that they remain current. In some cases, web pages may have been removed from websites; in others, material cited may no longer appear on the same URL. Reflecting this, we generally give only the main website address, and only occasionally provide a specific URL and the date this was accessed.

Internal sources

Beshara

Associates' personal journals
Beshara Magazine, 1–13 (1987–91)
Beshara Newsletter
'Beshara: Swyre Farm' promotional leaflet (n.d.)
Beshara website, www.beshara.org
Bulent Rauf website, www.bulentrauf.org
Carroll, Jane. 'Notes from a Student' (paper presented at MIAS Symposium, Oxford, May 2004)
Chapters from the Fusus al-Hikam, Parts I–IV (unpublished): Part I, 88 pp.; II, 72 pp.; III, 34 pp.; IV, 70 pp. (translation of chapters from the Commentary on the *Fusus al-Hikam* by Abdullah al-Bosnevi, by Bulent Rauf)
Coates, Peter. *Ibn 'Arabi and Modern Thought: The History of Taking Metaphysics Seriously* (Oxford, 2002)
_____ 'Ibn 'Arabi: The Unity of Existence and the Era' (paper presented at MIAS Symposium, Oxford, May 2003)
Culme-Seymour, Angela. *Bolter's Grand-daughter* (Oxford, 2001)
Feild, Reshad. *Going Home: The Journey of a Travelling Man* (Shaftesbury, Dorset, 1996)
_____ *The Invisible Way: A Time to Love – A Time to Die* (Wiltshire, 1979)
_____ *The Last Barrier: A Journey into the Essence of Sufi Teachings* (Great Barrington, MA, 2002/1976)
_____ Lectures delivered at Swyre Farm: 'The Path to Unity' (n.d.); 'The Path of the Mystic' (September 1972); 'The Path of Initiation' (n.d.)
Hirtenstein, Stephen. 'Ibn al-'Arabi', *Encyclopedia of Religion* (New York, 2005), pre-publication version
_____ 'Ibn al-'Arabi', *The Biographical Encyclopaedia of Islamic Philosophy* (London, 2006), 1, 216–26
_____ *The Unlimited Mercifier: The Spiritual Life and Thought of Ibn 'Arabi* (Oxford, and Ashland, OR, 1999)

Ibn 'Arabi, "Whoso Knoweth Himself ...", from the *Treatise on Being (Risale-t-ul-wujudiyyah)*, trans. T. H. Weir (Frilford Grange, Abingdon, Oxfordshire, 1988/1976)

Intimations: Talks with J. G. Bennett at Beshara (Swyre Farm, Aldsworth, 1975)

Ismail Hakki Bursevi's Translation of and Commentary on Fusus al-Hikam by Muhyiddin Ibn 'Arabi, rendered into English by Bulent Rauf with the help of Rosemary Brass and Hugh Tollemache [from the 1832 Bulaq edition of a manuscript written in Turkish and Arabic *c.*1700] (MIAS, Oxford and Istanbul, 1986), 4 vols

al-Jili, 'Abd al-Karim. *Universal Man*: Extracts Translated with Commentary by Titus Burckhardt, trans. into English by Angela Culme-Seymour (Chisholme House, Roxburgh, 1995; Sherborne, Gloucestershire, 1983)

Personal correspondence from Bulent Rauf to close associate (1972–87)

Rauf, Bulent. *Addresses* (Chisholme House, Roxburgh, 1986)

____ *Addresses II* (Chisholme House, Roxburgh, 2001)

____ *The Last Sultans*, ed. Meral Arim and Judy Kearns (Cheltenham, Gloucestershire, 1995)

Ryan, Christopher. Conversion to the Essence, in Turan Koç, ed., *International Symposium on Islamic Thought in Anatolia in the XIIIth and XIVth Centuries and Daud al-Qaysari* (Ankara, 1998), 338–43

A Selection from the Tarjuman al-Ashwaq of Muhyiddin Ibn al-'Arabi, in a literal translation with an abridged version of the author's commentary by Reynold A. Nicholson, with further annotations by Bulent Rauf (n.d., 49 pp.)

'A Trip to Turkey arranged by the Beshara School of Intensive Esoteric Education, Chisholme House', December 1999 and 2003

Turning, written, produced and directed by Diane Cilento, 1975

The Twenty-nine Pages: An Introduction to Ibn 'Arabi's Metaphysics of Unity (Chisholme House, Roxburgh, 1998)

Yiangou, Alison. 'Facing the Unknown: Some Reflections on the Importance of Ibn 'Arabi to Today', *Muhyiddin Ibn 'Arabi A.D. 1165–1240: His Life and Times* (Proceedings of the 7th Annual Symposium of the MIAS, Oxford, March 1999), 30–5

Young, Peter, 'Ibn 'Arabi: Towards a Universal Point of View', *JMIAS*, XXV (1999), 88–97

Zabor, Rafi. *The Bear Comes Home* (London, 1998)

____ *I, Wabenzi: A Souvenir* (New York, 2005)

MIAS/Anqa

Anqa Publishing website, www.ibn-arabi.com

Hirtenstein, Stephen, ed. *Praise* (Oxford, 1997)

____ ed. *Prayer and Contemplation* (Oxford, 1993)

Journal of the Muhyiddin Ibn 'Arabi Society, I–XXXVII (1982–2005)

Mercer, John, ed. *The Journey of the Heart* (Oxford, 1996)

MIAS Newsletter (1981–2005)

MIAS website, www.ibnarabisociety.org

Minutes of the AGM of the MIAS (January 1983 – November 1989)

Minutes of Meetings of the Additional Procedural Committee of the MIAS
(October 1981 – April 1988)
The Rules of the MIAS (amended April 1981)

Other sources

Ibn ʿArabi

Addas, Claude. *Quest for the Red Sulphur: The Life of Ibn ʿArabi*, trans. Peter
Kingsley (Cambridge, 1993)
____ *Ibn ʿArabi: The Voyage of No Return*, trans. David Streight (Cambridge,
2000)
Affifi, A. E. *The Mystical Philosophy of Muhyid Din-Ibnul ʿArabi* (Cambridge,
1939)
Anqa Publishing website, www.ibn-arabi.com
Chittick, William C. 'The Five Divine Presences: From al-Qunawi to al-Qaysari',
The Muslim World, 72 (1982), 107–28
____ Ibn ʿArabi and His School, in Seyyed Hossein Nasr, ed., *Islamic Spirituality*,
2: *Manifestations* (London, 1991), 49–79
____ Ibn ʿArabi; The School of Ibn ʿArabi, in Seyyed Hossein Nasr and Oliver
Leaman, eds, *History of Islamic Philosophy* (London, 2001), 497–509, 510–
23
____ *Imaginal Worlds: Ibn al-ʿArabi and the Problem of Religious Diversity*
(Albany, NY, 1994)
____ *The Self-Disclosure of God: Principles of Ibn al-ʿArabi's Cosmology* (Albany,
NY, 1998)
____ *The Sufi Path of Knowledge: Ibn al-ʿArabi's Metaphysics of Imagination*
(Albany, NY, 1989)
____ 'Time, Space, and The Objectivity of Ethical Norms: The Teachings of Ibn
al-ʿArabi', *Islamic Studies*, 39: 4 (2000), 581–96
Chodkiewicz, Michel. 'The Endless Voyage', in John Mercer, ed., *The Journey of
the Heart* (Oxford, 1996), 71–84
____ Ibn ʿArabi dans l'oeuvre de Henry Corbin, in Mohammad Ali Amir-Moezzi,
Christian Jambet and Pierre Lory, eds, *Henry Corbin: Philosophies et
sagesses des religions du livre* (Turnhout, Belgium, 2005), 81–91
____ *An Ocean without Shore: Ibn ʿArabi, The Book, and the Law*, trans. David
Streight (Albany, NY, 1993)
____ *Seal of the Saints: Prophethood and Sainthood in the Doctrine of Ibn ʿArabi*,
trans. Liadain Sherrard (Cambridge, 1993)
Corbin, Henry. *Alone with the Alone: Creative Imagination in the Sufism of Ibn
ʿArabi* (Princeton, 1997/1969)
Elmore, Gerald T. 'Hamd al-hamd: The Paradox of Praise in Ibn al-ʿArabi's Doctrine
of Oneness', in Stephen Hirtenstein, ed., *Praise* (Oxford, 1997), 59–94
____ *Islamic Sainthood in the Fullness of Time: Ibn al-ʿArabi's Book of the Fabu-
lous Gryphon* (Leiden, 1999)
____ 'The "Millennial" Motif in Ibn al-ʿArabi's Book of the Fabulous Gryphon',
Journal of Religion, 81: 3 (2001), 410–37

al-Ghorab, Mahmoud. Muhyiddin Ibn al-'Arabi amidst Religions (*adyan*) and Schools of Thought (*madhahib*), in Stephen Hirtenstein and Michael Tiernan, eds, *Muhyiddin Ibn 'Arabi: A Commemorative Volume* (Shaftesbury, Dorset, 1993), 200–27

____ *Sharh Fusus al-hikam min kalam al-shaykh al-akbar Muhyi al-Din Ibn al-'Arabi* (Damascus, 1985)

Gril, Denis. Adab and Revelation or One of the Foundations of the Hermeneutics of Ibn 'Arabi, in Stephen Hirtenstein and Michael Tiernan, eds, *Muhyiddin Ibn 'Arabi: A Commemorative Volume* (Shaftesbury, Dorset, 1993), 228–63

Haddad, Gibril Fu'ad. *'Aqidat al-'awamm min ahl al-Islam* (translation with introduction of part of the Introduction to *al-Futuhat al-Makkiyya*: 'Common Doctrine of the Muslims' [Credo of the Masses and People of Submission and *Taqlid*, vol. 1: 162–72]), www.abc.se/~m9783/n/iarabi_e.htm (accessed December 2004)

____ 'Ibn 'Arabi', www.sunnah.org

Hakim, Souad. 'Invocation and Illumination (*al-adhkar wa'l-anwar*) according to Ibn 'Arabi', in Stephen Hirtenstein, ed., *Prayer and Contemplation* (Oxford, 1993), 18–41

____ *al-Mu'jam al-sufi: al-hikma fi hudud al-kalima* (Beirut, 1981)

Hirtenstein, Stephen. 'Ibn al-'Arabi', *Encyclopedia of Religion* (New York, 2005), pre-publication version

____ 'Ibn al-'Arabi', *The Biographical Encyclopaedia of Islamic Philosophy* (London, 2006), 1, 216–26

____ ed. *Praise* (Oxford, 1997)

____ ed. *Prayer and Contemplation* (Oxford, 1993)

____ *The Unlimited Mercifier: The Spiritual Life and Thought of Ibn 'Arabi* (Oxford, and Ashland, OR, 1999)

____ and Michael Tiernan, eds. *Muhyiddin Ibn 'Arabi: A Commemorative Volume* (Shaftesbury, Dorset, 1993)

Homerin, Th. Emil. 'Ibn 'Arabi in the People's Assembly: Religion, Press, and Politics in Sadat's Egypt', *The Middle East Journal*, 40: 3 (Summer 1986), 462–77

Ibn 'Arabi, Muhyi al-Din. *The Bezels of Wisdom*, trans. and intro. R. W. J. Austin (London, 1980)

____ *Contemplation of the Holy Mysteries: Mashahid al-asrar*, trans. Cecilia Twinch and Pablo Beneito (Oxford, 2001)

____ *Divine Sayings: The Mishkat al-Anwar of Ibn 'Arabi*, trans. Stephen Hirtenstein and Martin Notcutt (Oxford, 2004)

____ *Fusus al-hikam*, ed. with notes Abu al-A'la al-'Afifi (Beirut, n.d.)

____ *Les Illuminations de la Mecque/The Meccan Illuminations: textes choisies/selected texts*, trans. Michel Chodkiewicz, Denis Gril and James W. Morris (Paris, 1988)

____ *Journey to the Lord of Power: A Sufi Manual on Retreat*, trans. Rabia Terri Harris (London, 1981)

____ *Kernel of the Kernel*, trans. Ismail Hakki Bursevi, trans. into English by Bulent Rauf (Chisholme House, Roxburgh, 1981)

____ *Kitab Insha' al-dawa'ir wa'l-jadawil*, ed. and intro. Yusuf Safar Fattum (Damascus, 2001)

_____ *Kitab al-Isfar 'an nata'ij al-asfar: Le dévoilement des effets du voyage*. Arabic text edited, translated and presented by Denis Gril (Combas, 1994)

_____ *The Meccan Revelations*, ed. Michel Chodkiewicz, trans. William C. Chittick and James W. Morris (New York, 2002 and 2004), 2 vols

_____ *La Sagesse des prophètes*, trans. with notes Titus Burckhardt (Paris, 1955)

_____ *The Seals of Wisdom*, trans. 'Aisha 'Abd al-Rahman at-Tarjumana (Norwich, 1980)

_____ *The Seven Days of the Heart: Awrad al-usbu' (Wird), Prayers for the Nights and Days of the Week*, trans. and presented in English by Pablo Beneito and Stephen Hirtenstein (Oxford, 2000)

_____ *Sufis of Andalusia: The Ruh al-Quds and al-Durrat al-Fakhira*, trans. and intro. R. W. J. Austin (Sherborne, Gloucestershire, 1988; London, 1971)

_____ *Tarjuman al-ashwaq* (Beirut, 1966)

_____ *The Tarjuman al-Ashwaq: A Collection of Mystical Odes by Muhyiddin Ibn al-'Arabi*, trans. R. Nicholson (London, 1978)

_____ *'Uqlat al-mustawfiz*, ed. and intro. Yusuf Safar Fattum (Damascus, 2002)

Ibn Yusuf, Ya'qub. 'Ibn 'Arabi for Our Generation', *Gnosis*, 7 (1988), 31–5

Ismail Hakki Bursevi's Translation of and Commentary on Fusus al-Hikam by Muhyiddin Ibn 'Arabi, rendered into English by Bulent Rauf with the help of Rosemary Brass and Hugh Tollemache [from the 1832 Bulaq edition of a manuscript written in Turkish and Arabic *c*.1700] (MIAS, Oxford and Istanbul, 1986), 4 vols

Journal of the Muhyiddin Ibn 'Arabi Society, I–XXXVII (1982–2005)

Knysh, Alexander D. *Ibn 'Arabi in the Later Islamic Tradition: The Making of a Polemical Image in Medieval Islam* (Albany, NY, 1999)

Landau, Rom. *The Philosophy of Ibn 'Arabi* (London, 1959)

Mercer, John, ed. *The Journey of the Heart* (Oxford, 1996)

Morris, James W. How to Study the *Futuhat*: Ibn 'Arabi's Own Advice, in Stephen Hirtenstein and Michael Tiernan, eds, *Muhyiddin Ibn 'Arabi: A Commemorative Volume* (Shaftesbury, Dorset, 1993), 73–89

Muhyiddin Ibn 'Arabi, A.D. 1165–1240: His Life and Times (Proceedings of the 7th Annual Symposium of the MIAS, Oxford, March 1999)

Nettler, Ronald L. *Sufi Metaphysics and Qur'anic Prophets: Ibn 'Arabi's Thought and Method in the Fusus al-Hikam* (Cambridge, 2003)

Scattolin, Giuseppe. 'Sufism and Law in Islam: A Text of Ibn 'Arabi (560/1165 – 638/1240) on "Protected People" (*ahl al-dhimma*)', *Islamochristiana*, 24 (1998), 37–55

Sells, Michael A. *Mystical Languages of Unsaying* (Chicago, 1994)

_____ *Stations of Desire: Love Elegies from Ibn 'Arabi and New Poems* (Jerusalem, 2000)

Winkel, Eric. *Islam and the Living Law: The Ibn al-'Arabi Approach* (Oxford, 1997)

Yahia, Osman. *Histoire et classification de l'oeuvre d'Ibn 'Arabi* (Damascus, 1964), 2 vols

Sufism: the twentieth century

Abu-Rabi', Ibrahim M., ed. *Islam at the Crossroads: On the Life and Thought of Bediuzzaman Said Nursi* (Albany, NY, 2003)

www.ahmedhulusi.com

Algar, Hamid. 'The Naqshbandi Order in Republican Turkey', *Islamic World Report*, 1: 3 (1996), 51–67

Ayata, Sencer. Traditional Sufi Orders in the Periphery: Kadiri and Nakşibendi Islam in Konya and Trabzon, in Richard Tapper, ed., *Islam in Modern Turkey: Religion, Politics and Literature in a Secular State* (London), 223–54

Ayverdi, Samiha. *The Friend*, trans. Ismet Tümtürk (Istanbul, 1995)

Bayman, Henry. *The Black Pearl: Spiritual Illumination in Sufism and East Asian Philosophies* (New York, 2005)

____ *The Station of No Stations: Open Secrets of the Sufis* (Berkeley, 2001)

Borella, Jean. René Guénon and the Traditionalist School, in Antoine Faivre and Jacob Needleman, eds, *Modern Esoteric Spirituality* (London, 1993), 330–58

www.cemalnur.org

Doyle, Margaret. 'Translating Ecstasy: Coleman Barks on Rumi with a Side of Curry', www.newtimes.org

Draper, Ian B. From Celts to Kaaba: Sufism in Glastonbury, in David Westerlund, ed., *Sufism in Europe and North America* (London, 2004), 144–56

Ernst, Carl. 'Traditionalism, the Perennial Philosophy, and Islamic Studies', www.religioperennis.org

An Excursion into the Depths of Tasavvuf: Discourses by Hasan Shushud, compiled by Melih Yonsul, trans. Refik Algan, ed. Maura Thornton (n.p., 2004)

Geaves, Ron. *The Sufis of Britain: An Exploration of Muslim Identity* (Cardiff, 2000)

Gilsenan, Michael. *Saint and Sufi in Modern Egypt: An Essay in the Sociology of Religion* (Oxford, 1973)

www.goldensufi.org

Hammer, Olav. Sufism for Westerners, in David Westerlund, ed., *Sufism in Europe and North America* (London, 2004), 127–43

Haeri, Fadhlalla. *The Elements of Sufism* (Shaftesbury, Dorset, 1997)

Hermansen, Marcia. 'Hybrid Identity Formations in Muslim America: The Case of American Sufi Movements', *The Muslim World*, 90 (2000), 158–97

____ In the Garden of American Sufi Movements: Hybrids and Perennials, in Peter B. Clarke, ed., *New Trends and Developments in the World of Islam* (London, 1997), 155–78

____ What's American about American Sufi Movements?, in David Westerlund, ed., *Sufism in Europe and North America* (London, 2004), 36–63

Howell, Julia Day. 'Indonesia's Urban Sufis: Challenging Stereotypes of Islamic Revival', *ISIM Review*, 6 (2001), 17

____ 'Many Paths to God and Modernity: Of Sufism, Syncretism and Universalism in Cosmopolitan Indonesian Islam', *Social Compass* (forthcoming), pre-publication version

____ 'Modernity and the Borderlands of Islamic Spirituality in Indonesia's New Sufi Networks', in Martin van Bruinessen and Julia Day Howell, eds, *Sufism and the 'Modern' in Islam* (London, forthcoming), pre-publication version

____ 'Muslims, the New Age and Marginal Religions in Indonesia: Changing Meanings of Religious Pluralism', *Social Compass* (forthcoming), pre-publication version

____ 'Seeking Sufism in the Global City: Indonesia's Cosmopolitan Muslims and Depth Spirituality', www.islamsymposium.cityu.edu.hk

____ 'Sufism and the Indonesian Islamic Revival', *The Journal of Asian Studies*, 60: 3 (2001), 701–29

Hulusi, Ahmed. *Dabaddah: The Universal Mysteries* (Istanbul, 2001)

____ *Revelations* (Istanbul, 2002/1967)

____ *Truth of Life* (Istanbul, 2003)

____ *Up to Date Understanding of Islam* (Istanbul, 2001)

Iyer, Pico, *Abandon: A Romance* (New York, 2003)

Jervis, James. The Sufi Order in the West and Pir Vilayat 'Inayat Khan: Space-Age Spirituality in Contemporary Euro-America, in Peter B. Clarke, ed., *New Trends and Developments in the World of Islam* (London, 1997), 211–60

Karabaşoğlu, Metin. Text and Community: An Analysis of the *Risale-i Nur* Movement, in Ibrahim M. Abu-Rabi', ed., *Islam at the Crossroads: On the Life and Thought of Bediuzzaman Said Nursi* (Albany, NY, 2003), 263–96

Keller, Carl A. Le Soufisme en Europe occidentale, in Jacques Waardenburg, ed., *Scholarly Approaches to Religion: Interreligious Perceptions and Islam* (Bern, 1994), 359–89

Khan, Pir Vilayat Inayat. *Thinking Like the Universe: The Sufi Path of Awakening*, ed. Pythia Peay (London, 2000)

Koszegi, Michael A. The Sufi Order in the West: Sufism's Encounter with the New Age, in Michael A. Koszegi and J. Gordon Melton, eds, *Islam in North America: A Source Book* (New York, 1992), 211–22

Küçük, Hülya. 'Sufi Reactions against the Reforms after Turkey's National Struggle: How a Nightingale turned into a Crow' (paper read at workshop 'The Triumphs and Travails of Authoritarian Modernisation in Turkey and Iran', Amsterdam, 2003)

____ 'Sufism in the West: Its Brief History and Nature' (paper read at First WOCMES Conference, Mainz, 2002)

Kuşpinar, Bilal. Nursi's Evaluation of Sufism, in *Third International Symposium on Bediüzzaman Said Nursi: The Reconstruction of Islamic Thought in the Twentieth Century and Bediüzzaman Said Nursi* (Istanbul, 1997), 2, 72–83

Ladinsky, Daniel. *I Heard God Laughing: Renderings of Hafiz* (Point Richmond, CA, 2004)

Le Pape, Loïc. Communication Strategies and Public Commitments: The Example of a Sufi Order in Europe, in Stefano Allievi and Jorgen Nielsen, eds, *Muslim Networks and Transnational Communities in and across Europe* (Leiden, 2003), 225–42

Lewin, Leonard, ed. *The Diffusion of Sufi Ideas in the West: An Anthology of New Writings by and about Idries Shah* (Boulder, CO, 1972)

'The Life of Kenan Rifai' (anon. unpublished paper, 19 pp.)

Lumbard, Joseph E. B., ed. *Islam, Fundamentalism, and the Betrayal of Tradition: Essays by Western Muslim Scholars* (Bloomington, IN, 2004)

Mahmud, 'Abd al-Halim. *al-Madrasa al-Shadhiliyya al-haditha* (Cairo, 1968)

Mardin, Şerif. Reflections on Said Nursi's Life and Thought, in Ibrahim M. Abu-Rabi', ed., *Islam at the Crossroads: On the Life and Thought of Bediuzzaman Said Nursi* (Albany, NY, 2003), 45–50

Moore, James. 'Neo-Sufism: The Case of Idries Shah', *Religion Today*, III: 3 (1987), 4–6

Nasr, Seyyed Hossein. Biography of Frithjof Schuon, in Seyyed Hossein Nasr and William Stoddardt, eds, *Religion of the Heart: Essays presented to Frithjof Schuon on his eightieth birthday* (Washington, DC, 1991), 1–6.

Nurbakhsh, Javad. *Jesus in the Eyes of the Sufis* (London, 1983)

Nursi, Bediuzzaman Said. *Letters, 1928–1932* [From the *Risale-i Nur* Collection, 2] (Istanbul, 2001)

www.oshokun.com

www.owo.com.tr

Özkardeş, Mehmet Ali. *The Essence of the Qur'an* (Istanbul, 1978)

____ *What is the Meaning of the Word Laic which can be Suitable to Divine Knowledge?* (Istanbul, 1973)

www.Peace-q-way.org

Rawlinson, Andrew. 'A History of Western Sufism', *Diskus*, 1: 1, 45–83

'The Rediscovery of the Tradition in the 20th Century', www.religioperennis.org

Reed, Fred A. In the Footsteps of Said Nursi, in Ibrahim M. Abu-Rabi', ed., *Islam at the Crossroads: On the Life and Thought of Bediuzzaman Said Nursi* (Albany, NY, 2003), 33–44

Saritoprak, Zeki. Fethullah Gülen: A Sufi in His Own Way, in M. Hakan Yavuz and John L. Esposito, eds, *Turkish Islam and the Secular State: The Gülen Movement* (Syracuse, NY, 2003), 156–69

Schmidt, Garbi. Sufi Charisma on the Internet, in David Westerlund, ed., *Sufism in Europe and North America* (London, 2004), 109–26

Schuon, Frithjof. *Esoterism as Principle and as Way*, trans. William Stoddardt (Middlesex, 1981)

Sedgwick, Mark. *Against the Modern World: Traditionalism and the Secret Intellectual History of the Twentieth Century* (Oxford, 2004)

____ 'Traditionalist Sufism', *ARIES*, 22 (1999)

Shah, Idries. *The Sufis* (London, 1977/1964)

____ *The Way of the Sufi* (London, 1968)

Sirriyeh, Elizabeth. Sufi Thought and its Reconstruction, in Suha Taji-Farouki and Basheer M. Nafi, eds, *Islamic Thought in the Twentieth Century* (London, 2004), 104–27

Smith, Jane I. Seyyed Hossein Nasr: Defender of the Sacred and Islamic Traditionalism, in Yvonne Y. Haddad, ed., *Muslims of America* (New York, 1993), 80–95

Somers, Jeffrey. Whirling and the West: The Mevlevi Dervishes in the West, in Peter B. Clarke, ed., *New Trends and Developments in the World of Islam* (London, 1997), 261–76

'The Soul of Rumi: A Conversation with Coleman Barks', www.gracecathedral.org

Stoddardt, William, ed. *The Essential Titus Burckhardt: Reflections on Sacred Art, Faiths and Civilizations* (Bloomington, IN, 2003)

_____ Titus Burckhardt: An Outline of his Life and Works, in Titus Burckhardt, *Mirror of the Intellect: Essays on Traditional Science and Sacred Art*, trans. and ed. William Stoddardt (Cambridge, 1987)

www.sufiorder.org

Sviri, Sara. *Daughter of Fire* by Irina Tweedie: Documentation and Experiences of a Modern Naqshbandi Sufi, in Peter B. Clarke and Elizabeth Puttick, eds, *Women as Teachers and Disciples in Traditional and New Religions* (Lewiston, KY, 1993), 77–90

The Times, Mysticism Supplement, 26 October 2002

www.traditionalists.org

Vâlsan, Michel. *L'Islam et la fonction de René Guénon* (Paris, 1984)

Voix, Raphael, and Patrick Haenni. 'God by all means ... Eclectic Faith and Sufi Resurgence among the Moroccan Bourgeoisie' (paper read at Conference 'Sufism and the "Modern" in Islam', Bogor, Indonesia, 2003)

Voll, John O. Fethullah Gülen: Transcending Modernity in the New Islamic Discourse, in M. Hakan Yavuz and John L. Esposito, eds, *Turkish Islam and the Secular State: The Gülen Movement* (Syracuse, NY, 2003), 238–47

Waterfield, Robin. *René Guénon and the Future of the West: The Life and Writings of a Twentieth Century Metaphysician* (Wellingborough, Northamptonshire, 1987)

Webb, Gisela. Tradition and Innovation in Contemporary American Islamic Spirituality: The Bawa Muhaiyaddeen Fellowship, in Yvonne Y. Haddad and Jane I. Smith, eds, *Muslim Communities in North America* (Albany, NY, 1994), 75–108

Werbner, Pnina. *Pilgrims of Love: The Anthropology of a Global Sufi Cult* (London, 2003)

Westerlund, David, ed. *Sufism in Europe and North America* (London, 2004)

_____ The Contextualisation of Sufism in Europe, in David Westerlund, ed., *Sufism in Europe and North America* (London, 2004), 13–35

Wilson, Peter. The Strange Fate of Sufism in the New Age, in Peter B. Clarke, ed., *New Trends and Developments in the World of Islam* (London, 1997), 179–210

Yavuz, M. Hakan. The Matrix of Modern Turkish Islamic Movements: The Naqshbandi Sufi Order, in Elisabeth Özdalga, ed., *Naqshbandis in Western and Central Asia: Change and Continuity* (Istanbul, 1999), 129–46

_____ *Nur* Study Circles (*Dershanes*) and the Formation of New Religious Consciousness in Turkey, in Ibrahim M. Abu-Rabi', ed., *Islam at the Crossroads: On the Life and Thought of Bediuzzaman Said Nursi* (Albany, NY, 2003), 297–316

Zarcone, Thierry. 'Rereadings and Transformations in Sufism in the West', *Diogenes*, 47/3 no. 187 (1999), 110–21

_____ La Turquie républicaine (1923–1993), in Alexandre Popovic and Gilles Veinstein, eds, *Les Vois d'Allah: Les ordres mystiques dans le monde musulman des origines à aujourd'hui* (Paris, 1996), 372–9

Cultural change, religion and spirituality: twentieth-century West and globally

Aldgate, Anthony, James Chapman and Arthur Marwick, eds. *Windows on the Sixties: Exploring Key Texts of Media and Culture* (London, 2000)

Annett, Stephen, ed. *The Many Ways of Being: A Guide to Spiritual Groups and Growth Centres in Britain* (London, 1976)

Arweck, Elisabeth. New Religious Movements, in Linda Woodhead, ed., *Religions in the Modern World: Traditions and Transformations* (London, 2002), 264–88

_____ and Peter Clarke, eds. *New Religious Movements in Western Europe: An Annotated Bibliography* (Westport, CT, 1997)

Barker, Eileen. 'New Religious Movements', Farmington Papers, Modern Theology, 12 (The Farmington Institute for Christian Studies, Oxford) (1999)

_____ *New Religious Movements: A Practical Introduction* (London, 2000/1989)

_____ 'New Religious Movements and Political Orders', Centre for the Study of Religions and Society, Pamphlet Library no. 15 (1987)

_____ New Religious Movements: Their Incidence and Significance, in B. R. Wilson and J. Cresswell, eds, *New Religious Movements: Challenge and Response* (London, 1999), 15–31

_____ The Scientific Study of Religion? You must be Joking!, in Lorne L. Dawson, ed., *Cults and New Religious Movements: A Reader* (Oxford, 2003), 7–25

Barrett, David V. *The New Believers: A Survey of Sects, Cults and Alternative Religions* (London, 2001)

Beckford, James A. New Religious Movements and Globalization, in Phillip Charles Lucas and Thomas Robbins, eds, *New Religious Movements in the 21st Century: Legal, Political, and Social Challenges in Global Perspective* (New York, 2004), 253–64

Beit-Hallahmi, Benjamin. *Despair and Deliverance: Private Salvation in Contemporary Israel* (Albany, NY, 1992)

Bennett, John G. *Gurdjieff Today* (Sherborne, Gloucestershire, 1974)

_____ *How We Do Things* (Sherborne, Gloucestershire, 1974)

_____ *The Masters of Wisdom* (London, 1977)

_____ *Witness: The Autobiography of John Bennett* (London, 1975)

Berger, Peter L. Secularization and De-Secularization, in Linda Woodhead, ed., *Religions in the Modern World: Traditions and Transformations* (London, 2002), 291–6

_____ Brigitte Berger and Hansfried Kellner, *The Homeless Mind: Modernization and Consciousness* (New York, 1973)

Beynon, John, and David Dunkerly, eds. *Globalization: A Reader* (London, 2000)

Bloom, William, ed. *The New Age: An Anthology of Essential Writings* (London, 1991)

Brown, Susan Love. Baby Boomers, American Character, and the New Age: A Synthesis, in James R. Lewis and J. Gordon Melton, eds, *Perspectives on the New Age* (Albany, NY, 1992), 87–96

Bruce, Steve. *Religion in Modern Britain* (Oxford, 1995)

Campbell, Colin. 'The Cult, The Cultic Milieu and Secularization', *A Sociological Yearbook of Religion in Britain*, 5 (London, 1972), 119–36

____ The Easternisation of the West, in B. R. Wilson and J. Cresswell, eds, *New Religious Movements: Challenge and Response* (London, 1999), 35–48

____ A New Age Theodicy for a New Age, in Linda Woodhead with Paul Heelas and David Martin, eds, *Peter Berger and The Study of Religion* (London, 2001), 73–84

Carpenter, Robert T. The Mainstreaming of Alternative Spirituality in Brazil, in Phillip Charles Lucas and Thomas Robbins, eds, *New Religious Movements in the 21st Century: Legal, Political, and Social Challenges in Global Perspective* (New York, 2004), 213–28

Chryssides, George D. *Exploring New Religions* (London, 1999)

Clarke, Peter B. Introduction: Change and Variety in New Religious Movements in Western Europe, c. 1960 to the Present, in Elisabeth Arweck and Peter B. Clarke, eds, *New Religious Movements in Western Europe: An Annotated Bibliography* (Westport, CT, 1997)

Cohen, Robin, and Paul Kennedy, *Global Sociology* (Basingstoke, 2000)

Coleman, John. Editorial, in John Coleman and Gregory Brown, eds, *New Religious Movements* (Concilium: Religion in the Eighties) (Edinburgh, 1983)

Cox, Harvey. *Turning East: The Promise and Peril of the New Orientalism* (London, 1979/1977)

Davie, Grace. 'Believing without Belonging: Is this the Future of Religion in Britain?', *Social Compass*, 37 (1990), 455–69

____ *Religion in Britain since 1945: Believing without Belonging* (Oxford, 1994)

____ *Religion in Modern Europe: A Memory Mutates* (Oxford, 2000)

____ Paul Heelas and Linda Woodhead, eds. *Predicting Religion: Christian, Secular and Alternative Futures* (Hampshire, UK, 2003)

Davies, Paul. 'The End of the World according to William Blake and J. G. Bennett', *Sacred Web*, 8 (2001), 105–20

Dawson, Lorne, L., ed. *Cults and New Religious Movements: A Reader* (Oxford, 2003)

____ Who Joins New Religious Movements and Why: Twenty Years of Research and What have we Learned?, in Lorne L. Dawson, ed., *Cults and New Religious Movements: A Reader* (Oxford, 2003), 116–30

____ and Jenna Hennebry, New Religions and the Internet: Recruiting in a New Public Space, in Lorne L. Dawson, ed., *Cults and New Religious Movements: A Reader* (Oxford, 2003), 271–91

Eisenstadt, S. N. 'Multiple Modernities', *Daedalus*, 129: 1 (2000), 1–29

Ellwood, Robert. Asian Religions in North America, in John Coleman and Gregory Brown, eds, *New Religious Movements* (Concilium: Religion in the Eighties) (Edinburgh, 1983), 17–22

The Encyclopaedia of Religion, ed. in chief, Mircea Eliade (New York, 1987)

Ferguson, Marilyn. *The Aquarian Conspiracy: Personal and Social Transformation in the 1980s* (Los Angeles, 1980)

Forman, Robert. *Grassroots Spirituality: What it is, Why it is Here, Where it is Going* (Exeter, Devon, 2004)

Frisk, Lisolette. 'Is "New Age" A Construction? Searching a New Paradigm of Contemporary Religion', www.cesnur.org

Garb, Jonathan. 'The Image of the Saint in Twentieth Century Jewish Mysticism' (lecture delivered at Hebrew University of Jerusalem, 4 August 2004)

Giddens, Anthony. *The Consequences of Modernity* (Oxford, 2000)

Gordon Melton, J. The Fate of NRMs and their Detractors in Twenty-First Century America, in Phillip Charles Lucas and Thomas Robbins, eds, *New Religious Movements in the 21st Century: Legal, Political, and Social Challenges in Global Perspective* (New York, 2004), 229–40

Groothius, Douglas R. *Unmasking the New Age: Is there a New Religious Movement trying to transform Society?* (Dowers Grove, IL, 1991/1986)

Hanegraaff, Wouter J. New Age Religion, in Linda Woodhead, ed., *Religions in the Modern World: Traditions and Transformations* (London, 2002), 249–63

____ The New Age Movement and the Esoteric Tradition, in Roelof van den Broek and Wouter J. Hanegraaff, eds, *Gnosis and Hermeticism From Antiquity to Modern Times* (Albany, NY, 1998), 360–82

____ *New Age Religion and Western Culture: Esotericism in the Mirror of the Secular* (Leiden, 1996)

____ with Antoine Faivre, Roelof van den Broek and Jean-Pierre Brach, eds. *Dictionary of Gnosis & Western Esotericism* (Leiden, 2005), 1–2

Harvey, Andrew. *The Direct Path: Creating a Journey to The Divine using the World's Mystical Traditions* (London, 2000)

Heelas, Paul, *The New Age Movement: The Celebration of the Self and the Sacralization of Modernity* (Oxford, 1996)

____ Prosperity and the New Age Movement: The Efficacy of Spiritual Economics, in B. R. Wilson and J. Cresswell, eds, *New Religious Movements: Challenge and Response* (London, 1999), 49–77

____ The Spiritual Revolution: From 'Religion' to 'Spirituality', in Linda Woodhead, ed., *Religions in the Modern World: Traditions and Transformations* (London, 2002), 357–77

____ and Benjamin Seel, An Ageing New Age?, in Grace Davie, Paul Heelas and Linda Woodhead, eds, *Predicting Religion: Christian, Secular and Alternative Futures* (Hampshire, UK, 2003), 229–47

____ and Linda Woodhead, Homeless Minds Today?, in Linda Woodhead with Paul Heelas and David Martin, eds, *Peter Berger and The Study of Religion* (London, 2001), 44–72

____ and Linda Woodhead with Benjamin Seel, Bronislaw Szerszynski and Karin Tusting, *The Spiritual Revolution: Why Religion is Giving Way to Spirituality* (Oxford, 2004)

Hervieu-Legér, Danièle. The Twofold Limit of the Notion of Secularization, in Linda Woodhead with Paul Heelas and David Martin, eds, *Peter Berger and The Study of Religion* (London, 2001), 112–26

Kose, Ali. Conversion to Islam: A Study of Native British Converts (London, 1996)

____ 'Native British Converts to Islam: Who are They? Why do they Convert?', *The American Journal of Islamic Social Sciences*, 12: 3 (1995), 347–59

Koszegi, Michael A. and J. Gordon Melton, eds. *Islam in North America: A Sourcebook* (New York, 1992)

Krishnamurti, J. *Total Freedom: The Essential Krishnamurti* (New York, 1996)

Lehmann, David. Religion and Globalization, in Linda Woodhead, ed., *Religions in the Modern World: Traditions and Transformations* (London, 2002), 299–315

Lenoir, Frederic. 'The Adaptation of Buddhism to the West', *Diogenes*, 47/3 no. 187 (1999), 100–10

Levine, Saul. The Joiners, in Lorne L. Dawson, ed., *Cults and New Religious Movements: A Reader* (Oxford, 2003), 131–42

Lewis, James R. Approaches to the Study of the New Age Movement, in James R. Lewis and J. Gordon Melton, eds, *Perspectives on the New Age* (Albany, NY, 1992), 1–12

____ and J. Gordon Melton, eds. *Perspectives on the New Age* (Albany, NY, 1992)

Marwick, Arthur. *Britain in Our Century: Images and Controversies* (London, 1984)

____ *Culture in Britain since 1945* (Oxford, 1991)

____ Introduction: Locating Key Texts amid the Distinctive Landscape of the Sixties, in Anthony Aldgate, James Chapman and Arthur Marwick, eds, *Windows on the Sixties: Exploring Key Texts of Media and Culture* (London, 2000), xi–xxi

____ *The Sixties: Cultural Revolution in Britain, France, Italy and the United States, c. 1958–1974* (Oxford, 1998)

Matrisciana, Caryl. *Gods of the New Age* (Basingstoke, Hampshire, 1986)

McGrath, Alister. *The Twilight of Atheism: The Rise and Fall of Disbelief in the Modern World* (New York, 2004)

Musgrove, Frank. *Ecstasy and Holiness: Culture and the Open Society* (London, 1974)

Needleman, Jacob. G. I. Gurdjieff and his School, in Antoine Faivre and Jacob Needleman, eds, *Modern Esoteric Spirituality* (London, 1993), 359–80

O'Murchu, Diarmuid. *Quantum Theology: Spiritual Implications of the New Physics*, rev. and updated edn (New York, 2004)

Parsons, Gerald. Expanding the Religious Spectrum: New Religious Movements in Modern Britain, in Gerald Parsons, ed., *The Growth of Religious Diversity: Britain from 1945*, 1: *Traditions* (London, 1993), 275–304

Partridge, Christopher H., ed. *Encyclopedia of New Religions: New Religious Movements, Sects, and Alternative Spiritualities* (Oxford, 2004)

Pearcey, Nancy. *Total Truth: Liberating Christianity from its Cultural Captivity* (Wheaton, IL, 2004)

Roof, Wade Clark. *A Generation of Seekers: The Spiritual Lives of the Baby Boom Generation* (San Francisco, 1993)

____ *Spiritual Marketplace: Baby Boomers and the Remaking of American Religion* (Princeton, 1999)

Roszak, Theodore. *The Making of a Counter Culture: Reflections on the Technocratic Society and its Youthful Opposition* (Berkeley, 1995/1969)

Stark, Rodney. 'Becoming a World-Saver: A Theory of Conversion to a Deviant Perspective', *American Sociological Review*, 30: 6 (1965), 863–74

____ 'Secularization: RIP', *Sociology of Religion*, 60: 3 (1999), 249–73

____ Why Religious Movements Succeed or Fail: A Revised General Model, in Lorne L. Dawson, ed., *Cults and New Religious Movements: A Reader* (Oxford, 2003), 259–70

Swatos Jr., William H., ed. *Encyclopaedia of Religion and Society*, hirr.hartsem. edu/ency/

Tacey, David. *The Spirituality Revolution: the Emergence of Contemporary Spirituality* (Hove, Sussex, 2004)

Taylor, Charles. *The Ethics of Authenticity* (Cambridge, MA, 1991)

Tipton, Steven M. *Getting Saved from the Sixties: Moral Meaning in Conversion and Cultural Change* (Berkeley, 1982)

Vaughan, Frances. 'What is Spiritual Intelligence?', *Journal of Humanistic Psychology*, 42: 2 (2003), 16–33

Wallis, Roy. *The Elementary Forms of the New Religious Life* (London, 1984)

Washington, Peter. *Madame Blavatsky's Baboon: Theosophy and the Emergence of the Western Guru* (London, 1993)

Wilson, Bryan R. *Contemporary Transformations of Religion* (New York, 1976)

____ Introduction, in B. R. Wilson and J. Cresswell, eds, *New Religious Movements: Challenge and Response* (London, 1999), 1-12

____ and J. Cresswell, eds. *New Religious Movements: Challenge and Response* (London, 1999)

____ Secularization: Religion in the Modern World, in S. Sutherland and P. B. Clarke, eds, *The Study of Religion: Traditional and New Religions* (London, 1991), 195–208

Woodhead, Linda. Studying Religion and Modernity, in Linda Woodhead, ed., *Religions in the Modern World: Traditions and Transformations* (London, 2002), 1–13

____ with Paul Heelas and David Martin, eds. *Peter Berger and the Study of Religion* (London, 2001)

Wuthnow, Robert. The New Spiritual Freedom, in Lorne L. Dawson, ed., *Cults and New Religious Movements: A Reader* (Oxford, 2003), 89–112

Zablocki, Benjamin, and J. Anna Looney, Research on New Religious Movements in the Post-9/11 World, in Phillip Charles Lucas and Thomas Robbins, eds, *New Religious Movements in the 21st Century: Legal, Political, and Social Challenges in Global Perspective* (New York, 2004), 313–28

Sufism: historical and general

Algar, Ayla. Food in the Life of the Tekke, in Raymond Lifchez, ed., *The Dervish Lodge: Architecture, Art and Sufism in Ottoman Turkey* (Berkeley, 1992), 296–303

Algar, Hamid. Devotional Practices of the Khalidi-Naqshbandis of Ottoman Turkey, in Raymond Lifchez, ed., *The Dervish Lodge: Architecture, Art and Sufism in Ottoman Turkey* (Berkeley, 1992), 209–27

Ashraf, Syed Ali. The Inner Meaning of the Islamic Rites: Prayer, Pilgrimage, Fasting, Jihad, in Seyyed Hossein Nasr, ed., *Islamic Spirituality: Foundations* (London, 1987), 111–30

Baldick, Julian. *Imaginary Muslims: The Uwaysi Sufis of Central Asia* (London, 1993)

Barnes, John Robert. The Dervish Orders in the Ottoman Empire, in Raymond Lifchez, ed., *The Dervish Lodge: Architecture, Art and Sufism in Ottoman Turkey* (Berkeley, 1992), 33–48

Brown, John P. *The Darvishes or Oriental Spiritualism*, ed. H. A. Rose (Oxford, 1927)

Buehler, Arthur F. *Sufi Heirs of the Prophet: The Indian Naqshbandiyya and the Rise of the Mediating Sufi Shaykh* (Columbia, SC, 1998)

Chittick, William C. Rumi and the Mawlawiyyah, in Seyyed Hossein Nasr, ed., *Islamic Spirituality: Foundations* (London, 1987), 105–26

____ Rumi and *wahdat al-wujud*, in Amin Banani, Richard Houannisian and Georges Sabagh, eds, *Poetry and Mysticism in Islam: The Heritage of Rumi* (Cambridge, 1994), 70–111

____ *The Sufi Path of Love: The Spiritual Teachings of Rumi* (Albany, NY, 1983)

____ *Sufism: A Short Introduction* (Oxford, 2000)

Chodkiewicz, Michel. *The Spiritual Writings of Amir 'Abd al-Kader*, trans. J. Chrestensen, T. Manning, *et al.* (Albany, NY, 1995)

Denny, Frederick M. 'God's Friends': The Sanctity of Persons in Islam, in Richard Kieckhefer and George D. Bond, eds, *Sainthood: Its Manifestations in World Religions* (Berkeley, 1988), 69–97

Ernst, Carl. *The Shambhala Guide to Sufism* (Boston, 1997)

____ trans. and selected, *Teachings of Sufism* (Boston, 1999)

van Ess, Josef. Sufism and its Opponents: Reflections on Topoi, Tribulations and Transformations, in Frederick de Jong and Bernd Radtke, eds, *Islamic Mysticism Contested: Thirteen Centuries of Controversies and Polemics* (Leiden, 1999), 22–44

Feldman, Walter. Musical Genres and Zikir of the Sunni Tarikats of Istanbul, in Raymond Lifchez, ed., *The Dervish Lodge: Architecture, Art and Sufism in Ottoman Turkey* (Berkeley, 1992), 187–202

Friedlander, Ira (Shams). A Note on the Khalwatiyyah–Jerrahiyyah Order, in Seyyed Hossein Nasr, ed., *Islamic Spirituality: Manifestations* (London, 1991), 233–8

____ *The Whirling Dervishes (Being an Account of the Sufi Order known as the Mevlevis and its founder the poet and mystic Mevlana Jalalu'ddin Rumi)* (Albany, NY, 1992; New York, 1975)

Galip, Şeyh. *Beauty and Love*, trans. Victoria Rowe Holbrook (New York, 2005)

Godlas, Alan. *Sufism's Many Paths*, www.uga.edu

Holbrook, Victoria Rowe. *The Unreadable Shores of Love: Turkish Modernity and Mystic Romance* (Austin, TX, 1994)

al-Jilani, Hadrat 'Abd al-Qadir. *The Secret Of Secrets*, interpreted by Tosun Bayrak al-Jerrahi al-Halveti (Cambridge, 1992) de Jong, Frederick, and Bernd Radtke, Introduction, in Frederick de Jong and Bernd Radtke, eds, *Islamic Mysticism Contested: Thirteen Centuries of Controversies and Polemics* (Leiden, 1999), 1–21

Kafadar, Cemal. The New Visibility of Sufism in Turkish Studies and Cultural Life, in Raymond Lifchez, ed., *The Dervish Lodge: Architecture, Art and Sufism in Ottoman Turkey* (Berkeley, 1992), 307–22

Karamustafa, Ahmet T. *God's Unruly Friends: Dervish Groups in the Islamic Later Middle Period, 1200–1500* (Salt Lake City, 1994)

____ Early Sufism in Eastern Anatolia, in Leonard Lewisohn, ed., *The Heritage of Persian Sufism, 1: Classical Persian Sufism from its Origins to Rumi (700–1300)* (Oxford, 1999), 175–98

Keller, Carl A. Perceptions of Other Religions in Sufism, in Jean Jacques Waardenburg, ed., *Muslim Perceptions of Other Religions: A Historical Survey* (New York, 1999), 181–94

Knysh, Alexander. *Islamic Mysticism: A Short History* (Leiden, 2000)

Lapidus, Ira M. Sufism and Ottoman Islamic Society, in Raymond Lifchez, ed., *The Dervish Lodge: Architecture, Art and Sufism in Ottoman Turkey* (Berkeley, 1992), 15–32

Lewis, Franklin D. *Rumi: Past and Present, East and West. The Life, Teachings and Poetry of Jalal al-Din Rumi* (Oxford, 2000)

Lewisohn, Leonard, ed. *The Heritage of Persian Sufism, 1: Classical Persian Sufism from its Origins to Rumi (700–1300)* (Oxford, 1999); 2: *The Legacy of Medieval Persian Sufism (1150–1500)* (Oxford, 1999)

Lings, Martin. *What is Sufism?* (Cambridge, 1995)

Michon, Jean-Louis. The Spiritual Practices of Sufism, in Seyyed Hossein Nasr, ed., *Islamic Spirituality: Foundations* (London, 1987), 265–93

Mystical Poems of Rumi 2 (Second Selection, Poems 201–400), trans. A. J. Arberry, ed. E. Yarshetar (Chicago, 1991)

Nafi, Basheer M. 'Tasawwuf and Reform in Pre-Modern Islamic Culture: In Search of Ibrahim al-Kurani', *Die Welt des Islams*, 42: 3 (2002), 307–55

Nasr, Seyyed Hossein, ed. *Islamic Spirituality: Foundations* (London, 1987)

____ ed. *Islamic Spirituality: Manifestations* (London, 1991)

____ The Qur'an as the Foundation of Islamic Spirituality, in Seyyed Hossein Nasr, ed., *Islamic Spirituality: Foundations* (London, 1987), 3–10

Nizami, Khaliq Ahmad. The Qadiriyyah Order, in Seyyed Hossein Nasr, ed., *Islamic Spirituality: Manifestations* (London, 1991), 6–25

Ocak, Ahmet Yaşar. 'Les réactions socio-religieuses contre l'idéologie officielle ottomane et la question de *Zendeqa ve Ilhad* (hérésie et athéisme) au XVIe siècle', *TURCICA*, 23 (1991), 71–82

____ Religion, in Ekmeleddin Ihsanoğlu, ed., *History of the Ottoman State, Society and Civilisation* (Istanbul, 2002), 2, 177–232

Özdalga, Elizabeth, ed. *Naqshbandis in Western and Central Asia: Change and Continuity* (Istanbul, 1999)

Öztürk, Yaşar Nuri. *The Eye of the Heart: An Introduction to Sufism and the Tariqats of Anatolia and the Balkans*, trans. Richard Blakney (Istanbul, 1995)

Popovic, Alexandre, and Gilles Veinstein, eds. *Les Voies d'Allah: les ordres mystiques dans le monde musulman des origines à aujourd'hui* (Paris, 1996)

al-Qashani, 'Abd al-Razzaq. *A Glossary of Sufi Technical Terms*, trans. Nabil Safwat, rev. edn, David Pendelbury (London, 1991)

Qasimi, Ja'far. The Life of the Prophet, in Seyyed Hossein Nasr, ed., *Islamic Spirituality: Foundations* (London, 1987), 65–96

Radtke, Bernd. The Concept of *Wilaya* in Early Sufism, in Leonard Lewisohn, ed., *The Heritage of Persian Sufism*, 1: *Classical Persian Sufism from its Origins to Rumi (700–1300)* (Oxford, 1999), 483–97

Said Richards, Gabriel. 'The Sufi Approach to Food: A Case Study of Adab', *The Muslim World*, 90 (2000), 198–217

Schimmel, Annemarie. Mawlana Rumi: Yesterday, Today and Tomorrow, in A. Banani, R. Houannisian and G. Sabagh, eds, *Poetry and Mysticism in Islam: The Heritage of Rumi* (Cambridge, 1994), 5–27

____ *Mystical Dimensions of Islam* (Chapel Hill, NC, 1975)

____ *Sufism and Spiritual Life in Turkey*, in Seyyed Hossein Nasr, ed., *Islamic Spirituality: Manifestations* (London, 1987), 223–32

____ *The Triumphal Sun: A Study of the Works of Jalaloddin Rumi* (London, 1978)

von Schlegell, Barbara Rosenow. *Sufism in the Ottoman Arab World: Shaykh 'Abd al-Ghani al-Nabulusi (d. 1143/1731)*, D. Phil thesis, University of California, Berkeley, 1997

Şenocak, Kemaleddin. *Kutbu'l-arifin Seyyid Aziz Mahmud Hüdayi* (Istanbul, 1970)

Shah-Kazemi, Reza. The Metaphysics of Interfaith Dialogue: Sufi Perspectives on the Universality of the Qur'anic Message, in James Cutsinger, ed., *Paths to the Heart: Sufism and the Christian East* (Bloomington, IN, 2002), 140–90

____ 'The Notion and Significance of *Ma'rifa* in Sufism', *Journal of Islamic Studies*, 13: 2 (2002), 155–81

____ *The Other in the Light of the One: The Universality of the Qur'an and Interfaith Dialogue* (Cambridge, 2006), pre-publication version

Sirriyeh, Elizabeth. *Sufis and Anti-Sufis: The Defence, Rethinking and Rejection of Sufism in the Modern World* (London, 1998)

Tanman, M. Baha. Settings for the Veneration of Saints, in Raymond Lifchez, ed., *The Dervish Lodge: Architecture, Art and Sufism in Ottoman Turkey* (Berkeley, 1992), 130–71

Trimingham, J. Spencer. *The Sufi Orders in Islam* (Oxford, 1971)

Üftade, Hazret-i Pir-i. *Le Divan*, trans. Paul Ballanfat (Paris, 2001). *The Nightingale in the Garden of Love*, trans. A. Culme-Seymour (Oxford, 2005)

Veinstein, Gilles, and Nathalie Clayer, L'Empire ottoman, in Alexandre Popovic and Gilles Veinstein, eds, *Les Voies d'Allah: Les ordres mystiques dans le monde musulman des origines à aujourd'hui* (Paris, 1996), 322–41

Yilmaz, H. Kamil. *Aziz Mahmud Hüdayi: Hayati, Eserleri, Tarikati* (Istanbul, 1999)

Islam: general

Abou El Fadl, Khaled. 'The Place of Tolerance in Islam', *The Boston Review*, December 2001–January 2002

'Ata' ur-Rahim, Muhammad, and Ahmad Thomson. *Jesus, Prophet of Islam* (London, 1997)

Brown, Daniel. *Rethinking Tradition in Modern Islamic Thought* (Cambridge, 1999)

Bunt, Gary. *Virtually Islamic: Computer-mediated Communication and Cyber Islamic Environments* (Cardiff, 2000)

al-Buti, Muhammad Sa'id Ramadan. *Hadha walidi* (Damascus, 1998/1995)

Cragg, Kenneth. *Jesus and the Muslim: An Exploration* (London, 1985)

Eickelman, Dale F. and James Piscatori. *Muslim Politics* (Princeton, 1996)

Encyclopaedia of Islam, 2nd edn, ed. C.E. Bosworth *et al.* (Leiden, 1954–)

Geaves, Ron. *Aspects of Islam* (London, 2005)

al-Ghazali, *The Ninety-Nine Beautiful Names of God: al-Maqsad al-asna fi sharh asma' Allah al-husna*, trans. with notes by David B. Burrell and Nazih Daher (Cambridge, 1992)

Guillaume, Alfred. *The Life of Muhammad: A Translation of Ibn Ishaq's Sirat Rasul Allah* (Oxford, 1998)

Haddad, Yvonne Y., and Jane I. Smith, eds. *Muslim Communities in North America* (Albany, NY, 1994)

Hasluck, F. W. *Christianity and Islam under the Sultans* (Oxford, 1929)

Hodgson, Marshall G. S. *The Venture of Islam*, 2: *The Expansion of Islam in the Middle Periods* (Chicago, 1977)

Hourani, Albert. *Arabic Thought in the Liberal Age, 1798–1939* (Cambridge, 1989)

Inalcik, Halil. *The Ottoman Empire: The Classical Age, 1300–1600*, trans. Norman Itzowitz and Colin Imber (London, 1973)

Introvigne, Massimo. 'Niches in the Islamic Religious Market and Fundamentalism: Examples from Turkey and other Countries', www.cesnur.org

Lawrence, Bruce. *Defenders of God: The Fundamentalist Revolt against the Modern Age* (London, 1990)

Morris, James W. *Orientations: Islamic Thought in a World Civilization* (Sarajevo, 2001)

Nafi, Basheer M., and Suha Taji-Farouki, Introduction, in Suha Taji-Farouki and Basheer M. Nafi, eds, *Islamic Thought in the Twentieth Century* (London, 2004)

The Oxford Encyclopaedia of the Modern Islamic World, ed. in chief, John L. Esposito (New York, 1994)

Padwick, Constance E. *Muslim Devotions: A Study of Prayer-Manuals in Common Use* (Oxford, 1996/1961)

Rahman, Fazlur. Approaches to Islam in Religious Studies: A Review Essay, in Richard C. Martin, ed., *Approaches to Islam in Religious Studies* (Oxford, 2001)

al-Rumi, 'Abd al-'Aziz b. Zayd, *et al. Mu'allafat al-Shaykh al-Imam Muhammad Ibn 'Abd al-Wahhab* (Riyadh, Saudi Arabia, n.d.)

Sadri, Mahmoud, and Ahmad Sadri, trans. and eds. *Reason, Freedom and Democracy in Islam: Essential Writings of 'Abdolkarim Soroush* (Oxford, 2000)

Sardar, Ziauddin. *Desperately Seeking Paradise: Journeys of a Sceptical Muslim* (London, 2004)

Schimmel, Annemarie. *And Muhammad is His Messenger: The Veneration of The Prophet in Islamic Piety* (Chapel Hill, NC, 1985)

Sedgwick, Mark. Establishments and Sects in the Islamic World, in Phillip Charles Lucas and Thomas Robbins, eds, *New Religious Movements in the 21st Century: Legal, Political, and Social Challenges in Global Perspective* (New York, 2004), 283–312

Shankland, David. *Islam and Society in Turkey* (Huntingdon, Cambridgeshire, 1999)

Taji-Farouki, Suha. Introduction, in Suha Taji-Farouki, ed., *Modern Muslim Intellectuals and the Qur'an* (Oxford, 2004), 1–36

Tapper, Richard, ed. *Islam in Modern Turkey: Religion, Politics and Literature in a Secular State* (London, 1991)

Translation of the Meanings of Sahih al-Bukhari, trans. Muhammad Muhsin Khan (Lahore, 1979)

Yavuz, M. Hakan. *Islamic Political Identity in Turkey* (Oxford, 2003)

____ 'Is there a Turkish Islam? The Emergence of Convergence and Consensus', *Journal of Muslim Minority Affairs*, 24: 2 (2004), 213–32

____ 'The Return of Islam? New Dynamics in State-Society Relations and the Role of Islam in Turkish Politics', *Islamic World Report*, 1: 3 (1996), 77–86

____ and John L. Esposito, eds. *Turkish Islam and the Secular State: The Gülen Movement* (Syracuse, NY, 2003)

Index